英汉双解财会词典

AN ENGLI$H-CHINE$E DICTIONAR¥ OF ACCOUNTING

（新版）

外语教学与研究出版社
FOREIGN LANGUAGE TEACHING AND RESEARCH PRESS
北京 BEIJING

京权图字：01－2004－5467

图书在版编目(CIP)数据

英汉双解财会词典：新版／(英）科林（Collin，S. M. H.）著；唐运冠译．—2版．—北京：外语教学与研究出版社，2009.9
书名原文：An English-Chinese Dictionary of Accounting
ISBN 978－7－5600－8976－8

Ⅰ．英… Ⅱ．①科… ②唐… Ⅲ．财务会计—双解词典—英、汉
Ⅳ．F234.4－61

中国版本图书馆 CIP 数据核字（2009）第 163303 号

出 版 人：于春迟
责任编辑：申 葳
封面设计：覃一彪
出版发行：外语教学与研究出版社
社　　址：北京市西三环北路 19 号（100089）
网　　址：http://www.fltrp.com
印　　刷：北京双青印刷厂
开　　本：850×1168　1/32
印　　张：16.00
版　　次：2009 年 10 月第 1 版　2010 年 8 月第 2 次印刷
书　　号：ISBN 978－7－5600－8976－8
定　　价：31.90 元
*　*　*
购书咨询：(010)88819929　电子邮箱：club@fltrp.com
如有印刷、装订质量问题，请与出版社联系
联系电话：(010)61207896　电子邮箱：zhijian@fltrp.com

物料号：189760001

出 版 说 明

由外语教学与研究出版社引进翻译的《英汉双解财会词典》自2002年出版以来，受到了财会专业学生及从业人员的普遍认可。随着时代的发展，该领域近几年涌现了大量新词新义，为了紧跟时代，更好地满足读者的需要，现推出《英汉双解财会词典》(新版)。

新版在增补新词新义的同时秉承并发扬了上一版的特色：

收词全面，各科兼顾：本词典将会计学、金融学和财务学的词汇及知识融为一体，涵盖面很广，适用读者群也较广。

解释详尽，深入浅出：本词典并非仅仅译出词条的对应词，而是用浅显易懂的语言对每个词条作了解释，即便是非专业人士也不会遇到理解障碍。

例证引文，原汁原味：本词典不但例证丰富，而且还从多种著名英文报刊中摘取了近900条引文，帮助读者在报刊鲜活地道的语言中理解词条含义。

标注音标，贴心周到：本词典为所有词条标注了国际音标，即便是较长的复合词也进行了标注，杜绝哑巴英语，这在同类词典中并不多见。

注释丰富，附录实用：词典中各种注释随处可见，内容涉及语法、英美差别、专业知识等方面。同义词、反义词等信息也标注详尽。书末附有各种财务报表的参考范本，非常实用。

综合上述特色，相信本词典一定会成为财会专业学生及从业人员的良伴。在本词典的翻译及编校过程中，我们竭尽全力使译文准确、规范，在各个环节力求完美。但由于词典编辑工作繁复琐碎，疏漏之处在所难免，敬请读者批评指正。

外语教学与研究出版社
学术与辞书出版分社

《英汉双解财会词典》(新版)工作人员名单

翻　　译:唐运冠

责任编辑:申　蒇

前期统筹:夏　天

编校人员:吴　硕　徐传斌　杨书旗　周子平

Preface

This dictionary provides a basic vocabulary of terms used in accounting, from personal finance and investments to company accounts, balance sheets and stock valuations. It is ideal for students of accounting and for anyone who needs to check the meaning of an accountancy term, from people working in businesses who may not be professional accountants to translators or those for whom English is an additional language.

Each headword is explained in clear, straightforward English and examples are given to show how the word may be used in context. There are also quotations from newspapers and specialist magazines. Sample documents and financial statements are also provided.

Thanks are due to Jeremy Kourdi for his help and advice during the production of this new edition.

前　言

本财会词典是一本会计术语词典，它涵盖了从个人金融与投资到公司账目、资产负债表及股票估值等领域的基础专业词汇。本词非常适合会计专业学生、非专业会计师的商界人士、翻译工作者及母语为非英语者查询会计词汇时使用。

本词典对每个中心词都进行简单明了的解释，并举例说明它们在具体语境下的使用方法。书中还摘引了一些报纸和专业杂志中的相关语句，书末附有一些文件和财务报表的参考样本。

在编写这一新版词典的过程中，Jeremy Kourdi 先生给予我们许多帮助和建议，谨此向他表示诚挚的感谢！

Symbols 符号

■	before a new part of speech 表示另一词性
○	before examples 用于例证前
□	before a phrase or collocation 用于短语或搭配前
◇	before an idiom 用于习语前
➪	a definition of the word will be found at the place indicated 表示可在所示地方找到该词的定义
➧	extra information will be found at the place indicated 表示可在所示地方找到更多信息

Pronunciation 发音

The following symbols have been used to show the pronunciation of the main words in the dictionary.

Stress has been indicated by a main stress mark (ˈ) and a secondary stress mark (ˌ). Note that these are only guides, as the stress of the word changes according to its position in the sentence.

下列符号用以表示字典中主要词汇的发音。

重音以主重音符号(ˈ)及次重音符号(ˌ)表示。注意，这些标记仅供参考，因为单词的重音会因其在句子中的不同位置而变化。

Vowels 元音		*Consonants* 辅音	
æ	back	b	buck
ɑː	harm	d	dead
ɒ	stop	ð	other
aɪ	type	dʒ	jump
aʊ	how	f	fare
aɪə	hire	g	gold
aʊə	hour	h	head
ɔː	course	j	yellow
ɔɪ	annoy	k	cab
e	head	l	leave
eə	fair	m	mix
eɪ	make	n	nil
əʊ	go	ŋ	sing
ɜː	word	p	print
iː	keep	r	rest
i	happy	s	save
ə	about	ʃ	shop
ɪ	fit	t	take
ɪə	near	tʃ	change
u	actual	θ	theft
uː	pool	v	value
ʊ	book	w	work
ʊə	tour	ʒ	measure
ʌ	shut	z	zone

A

AAA *abbr* American Accounting Association 美国会计协会

AARF *abbr* Australian Accounting Research Foundation 澳大利亚会计研究基金会

AAT *abbr* Association of Accounting Technicians 助理会计协会

abacus /ˈæbəkəs/ *noun* a counting device consisting of parallel rods strung with beads, still widely used for business and accounting in China and Japan 算盘

abandonment /əˈbændənmənt/ *noun* an act of giving up voluntarily something that you own, such as an option or the right to a property（对期权、财产等的）放弃 □ **abandonment of a claim** giving up a claim in a civil action（民事诉讼中的）放弃要求

abatement /əˈbeɪtmənt/ *noun* **1.** an act of reducing 降低，打折扣 **2.** a reduction in a payment, e. g., if a company's or individual's total assets are insufficient to cover their debts or legacies（因公司或个人的总资产不足以偿还全部债务或遗产等造成的）付款减少

ABB *abbr* activity-based budgeting 作业基础预算

abbreviated accounts /əˌbriːvieɪtɪd əˈkaʊnts/ *noun* a shortened version of a company's annual accounts that a small or medium sized company can file with the Registrar of Companies, instead of a full version 简式账目：一种简约化的公司年度账目，中小型企业可以用来替代完整账目提交给公司注册处

ab initio /ˌæb ɪˈnɪʃiəʊ/ *Latin phrase meaning* 'from the beginning'（拉丁语）从头开始

abnormal /æbˈnɔːm(ə)l/ *adjective* not normal, atypical 异常的，反常的

abnormal gain /æbˌnɔːm(ə)l ˈɡeɪn/ *noun* any reduction in the volume of process loss below that set by the normal loss allowance. Abnormal gains are generally costed as though they were completed products 非常收益：因流程损失低于正常损失容限产生的收益，通常按成品进行成本核算

abnormal loss /æbˌnɔːm(ə)l ˈlɒs/ *noun* any losses which exceed the normal loss allowance. Abnormal losses are generally costed as though they were completed products 非常损失：超出正常损失容限的任何损失，通常按成品进行成本核算

above par /əˌbʌv ˈpɑː/ *adjective* referring to a share with a market price higher than its par value 溢价的：指股票的市价高于其面值

above the line /əˌbʌv ðə ˈlaɪn/ *adjective*, *adverb* **1.** used to describe entries in a company's profit and loss accounts that appear above the line separating entries showing the origin of the funds that have contributed to the profit or loss from those that relate to its distribution. Exceptional and extraordinary items appear above the line 线上项目的(地):用来划分公司损益账中的记项,把涉及盈亏的资金和与其分配有关的资金区别开来。特殊及异常项目均是线上项目 ○ *Exceptional items are noted above the line in company accounts*. 特殊项目被列在公司账户的线上项目中。**2.** relating to revenue items in a government budget (政府预算中关于收入项目)经常性项目的(地) **3.** relating to advertising for which payment is made (such as an ad in a magazine or a stand at a trade fair) and for which a commission is paid to an advertising agency (付费广告)经常性项目的(地) Compare 比较 **below the line**

abridged accounts /əˌbrɪdʒd əˈkaʊnts/ *noun* financial statements produced by a company that fall outside the requirements stipulated in the Companies Act 经删节的账目

absorb /əbˈzɔːb/ *verb* **1.** to take in a small item so that it forms part of a larger one 兼并 ▫ **a business which has been absorbed by a competitor** a small business which has been made part of a larger one 被竞争对手兼并的企业 **2.** to assign an overhead to a particular cost centre in a company's production accounts so that its identity becomes lost 吸收;归纳;分摊 ◊ 参阅 **absorption costing**

absorbed overhead /əbˌzɔːbd ˈəʊvəhed/ *noun* an overhead attached to products or services by means of **overhead absorption rates** 已分摊间接费用:按间接费用分摊率分摊到产品或服务中的间接费用

absorption /əbˈzɔːpʃən/ *noun* the process of making a smaller business part of a larger one, so that the smaller company in effect no longer exists 合并,兼并

absorption costing /əbˈzɔːpʃən ˌkɒstɪŋ/ *noun* **1.** a form of costing for a product that includes both the direct costs of production and the indirect overhead costs as well 全部成本法:一种同时包括生产的直接成本和间接成本的产品成本核算方法 **2.** an accounting practice in which fixed and variable costs of production are absorbed by different cost centres. Providing all the products or services can be sold at a price that covers the allocated costs, this method ensures that both fixed and variable costs are recovered in full 吸收成本法;分摊成本法:一种生产的固定及可变成本均被分摊到不同成本中心的会计方法。若全部产品或服务均可售出,而且售价能涵盖所分摊的成本,则该方法可保证全部收回固定及可变成本 ◊ 参阅 **marginal costing**

absorption rate /əbˈzɔːpʃən ˌreɪt/ *noun* a rate at which overhead costs are absorbed into each unit of production 吸收率;分摊率

abstract /ˈæbstrækt/ *noun* a short form of a report or document 摘要,概括 ○ *to make an abstract of the company accounts* 做一份公司账目摘要

Academy of Accounting Historians /əˌkædəmi əv əˈkaʊntɪŋ hɪˌstɔːriənz/ *noun* a US organisation, founded in 1973, that promotes the study of the history of accounting 美国会计

史学会:成立于 1973 年,旨在促进会计史研究的美国机构

ACAUS /ˈeɪkæs/ *abbr* Association of Chartered Accountants in the United States 美国特许会计师协会

ACCA *abbr* Association of Chartered Certified Accountants 特许注册会计师协会

accelerate /əkˈseləreɪt/ *verb* to reduce the amount of time before a maturity date 加速;使提前到期

acceleration /əkˌseləˈreɪʃ(ə)n/ *noun* the speeding up of debt repayment 加速还款;债务提前偿还

acceleration clause /əkˌseləˈreɪʃ(ə)n ˌklɔːz/ *noun US* a clause in a contract providing for immediate payment of the total balance if there is a breach of contract (美)加速条款,提前偿付条款:合同中规定发生违约事件时立即偿还全部债务余额的条款

accept /əkˈsept/ *verb* **1.** to take something which is being offered 接受 **2.** to say 'yes' or to agree to something 认可;同意 ○ *She accepted the offer of a job in Australia.* 她接受了一份在澳大利亚的工作。○ *He accepted £2,000 in lieu of notice.* 他接受了2,000英镑作为遣解聘的结算工资。

acceptance /əkˈseptəns/ *noun* **1.** the act of signing a bill of exchange to show that you agree to pay it 承兑,认付 □ **to present a bill for acceptance** to present a bill for payment by the person who has accepted it 出示承兑汇票 **2.** a bill which has been accepted 已承兑的票据 **3.** the act of accepting an offer of new shares for which you have applied (新股的)认购

acceptance credit /əkˈseptəns ˌkredɪt/ *noun* an arrangement of credit from a bank, where the bank accepts bills of exchange drawn on the bank by the debtor: the bank then discounts the bills and is responsible for paying them when they mature. The debtor owes the bank for the bills but these are covered by letters of credit 承兑信用证:银行的一种信用安排,银行承兑借方开出的以银行为付款人的汇票,然后对它进行贴现并到期付款。借方欠付银行汇票款项,但该款项由信用证作担保

acceptance sampling /əkˈseptəns ˌsɑːmplɪŋ/ *noun* the process of testing a small sample of a batch to see if the whole batch is good enough to be accepted 抽样验收

accepting house /əkˈseptɪŋ ˈhaʊs/, **acceptance house** /əkˈseptəns ˈhaʊs/ *noun* a firm, usually a merchant bank, which accepts bills of exchange at a discount, in return for immediate payment to the issuer, in this case the Bank of England 承兑银行

Accepting Houses Committee /əkˌseptɪŋ ˌhaʊzɪz kəˈmɪti/ *noun* the main London merchant banks, which organise the lending of money with the Bank of England. They receive slightly better discount rates from the Bank 承兑银行委员会

acceptor /əkˈseptə/ *noun* a person who accepts a bill of exchange by signing it, thus making a commitment to pay it by a specified date 承兑人

accident insurance /ˌæksɪd(ə)nt ɪnˈʃʊərəns/ *noun* insurance which will pay the insured person when an accident takes place 意外(事故)保险

accommodation /əˌkɒməˈdeɪʃ(ə)n/

noun money lent for a short time 融通,短期贷款

accommodation address /əˌkɒməˈdeɪʃ(ə)n əˌdres/ *noun* an address used for receiving messages, but which is not the real address of the company 权宜通信地址:公司收取信件的地址,但并非公司的实际地址

accommodation bill /əˌkɒməˈdeɪʃ(ə)n ˌbɪl/ *noun* a bill of exchange where the person signing (the 'drawee') is helping another company (the 'drawer') to raise a loan 通融票据

account /əˈkaʊnt/ *noun* **1.** a record of financial transactions over a period of time, such as money paid, received, borrowed or owed 账,账目,账户 ○ *Please send me your account* or *a detailed* or *an itemised account*. 请把你的账目(或明细账)递给我。**2.** (*in a shop*) an arrangement which a customer has to buy goods and pay for them at a later date, usually the end of the month(顾客在店铺的)赊购账 ○ *to have an account* or *a charge account* or *a credit account with Harrods* 在哈罗兹商店赊账 ○ *Put it on my account* or *charge it to my account*. 把这费用记到我的账上。**3.** a customer who does a large amount of business with a firm and has an account with it 客户,户头 ○ *Smith Brothers is one of our largest accounts*. 史密斯兄弟公司是我们最大的客户之一。○ *Our sales people call on their best accounts twice a month*. 我们的销售人员每月拜访他们最好的客户两次。**4.** a period during which shares are traded for credit, and at the end of which the shares bought must be paid for 赊购期:赊购股票的时期,在赊购期末必须付清所购股票票款(NOTE: On the London Stock Exchange, there are twenty-four accounts during the year, each running usually for ten working days 在伦敦证券交易所,一年有 24 个赊购期,每个赊购期通常为 10 个工作日)**5.** a structured record of financial transactions that may be maintained as a list or in a more formal structured credit and debit basis 分类账

accountability /əˌkaʊntəˈbɪlɪti/ *noun* the fact of being responsible to someone for something, e.g. the accountability of directors to the shareholders 负责(如董事对股东负责)

accountable /əˈkaʊntəb(ə)l/ *adjective* referring to a person who has to explain what has taken place or who is responsible for something 有责任的,有义务加以说明的(NOTE: you are accountable **to** someone **for** something)

accountancy /əˈkaʊntənsi/ *noun* the work of an accountant 会计工作 ○ *They are studying accountancy* or *They are accountancy students*. 他们正在学习会计学(或他们是会计专业的学生)。(NOTE: The US term is **accounting** in this meaning 该义的美国用语为 **accounting**)

accountancy bodies /əˈkaʊntənsi ˌbɒdiːz/ *noun* professional institutions and associations for accountants 会计组织

accountancy profession /əˌkaʊntənsi prəˈfeʃ(ə)n/ *noun* the professional bodies that establish entry standards, organise professional examinations, and draw up ethical and technical guidelines for accountants 专业会计管理机构

accountant /əˈkaʊntənt/ *noun* a person who keeps a company's accounts or deals with an individual person's tax affairs 会计师：负责为公司记录账目，或处理个人税务事项的人员 ○ *the chief accountant of a manufacturing group* 制造集团总会计师 ○ *The accountant has shown that there is a sharp variance in our labour costs.* 会计师指出我们的劳动成本发生了明显变化。

Accountants' International Study Group /əˌkaʊntənts ˌɪntənæʃ(ə)nəl ˈstʌdi ˌgruːp/ *noun* a body of professional accounting bodies from the United States, Canada, and the United Kingdom that was established in 1966 to research accounting practices in the three member countries. After publishing 20 reports, it was disbanded in 1977 with the foundation of the International Federation of Accountants 会计师国际研究组：由美国、加拿大及英国的多家专业会计机构于1966年共同组建的会计专业团体，以研究上述3个会员国的会计实务为宗旨，先后发布了20份研究报告。该研究组于1977年国际会计师联合会成立后解散

accountant's opinion /əˌkaʊntənts əˈpɪnjən/ *noun* a report of the audit of a company's books, carried out by a certified public accountant 审计意见，审计报告（NOTE：The US term is **audit opinion** 美国用语为 **audit opinion**）

accountants' report /əˌkaʊntənts rɪˈpɔːt/ *noun* in the United Kingdom, a report written by accountants that is required by the London Stock Exchange to be included in the prospectus of a company seeking a listing on the Exchange 会计师报告：英国伦敦证券交易所要求申请上市公司列入招股说明书的书面会计报告

account code /əˈkaʊnt kəʊd/ *noun* a number assigned to a particular account in a numerical accounting system, e.g., a chart of accounts 账户编码：按数字顺序为每一个账户进行编号，如账户分类表

account end /əˌkaʊnt ˈend/ *noun* the end of an accounting period 账户截止：会计核算期的截止

account executive /əˈkaʊnt ɪgˌzekjʊtɪv/ *noun* 客户账目经理，业务员 **1.** an employee who looks after customers or who is the link between customers and the company [为客户服务或代表公司负责与客户联系的员工] **2.** an employee of an organisation such as a bank, public relations firm or advertising agency who is responsible for looking after particular clients and handling their business with the organization [银行、公关公司或广告公司内负责代理特定客户业务的员工]

account form /əˈkaʊnt fɔːm/ *noun* a balance sheet laid out in horizontal form. It is the opposite of 'report' or 'vertical' form 账户格式，账项：以水平格式呈现的资产负债表，与"报告"或"垂直"格式相反

accounting /əˈkaʊntɪŋ/ *noun* **1.** the work of recording money paid, received, borrowed or owed 会计，会计核算 ○ *accounting methods* 会计核算方法 ○ *accounting procedures* 会计程序 ○ *an accounting machine* 会计机器 **2.** accountancy, the work of an accountant as a course of study 会计学

'...applicants will be professionally qualified and have a degree in Commerce or Accounting'

"申请人应具备专业资格，并持有商科或会

计学的学位”[*Australian Financial Review*《澳大利亚金融评论报》]

Accounting and Finance Association of Australia and New Zealand /əˌkaʊntɪŋ ən ˌfaɪnæns əˌsəʊsiˌeɪʃ(ə)n əv ɒsˈtreɪliə ən ˌnjuːˈziːlənd/ *noun* an organisation for accounting and finance academics, researchers, and professionals working in Australia and New Zealand 澳大利亚和新西兰会计与财务协会 Abbreviation 缩写 **AFAANZ**

accounting bases /əˌkaʊntɪŋ ˈbeɪsiːz/ *plural noun* the possible ways in which accounting concepts may be applied to financial transactions, e. g. the methods used to depreciate assets, how intangible assets or work in progress are dealt with 会计基础:将会计概念应用于金融交易的方式,包括资产折旧方法、无形资产或在制品价值核算等

accounting concept /əˈkaʊntɪŋ ˌkɒnsept/ *noun* a general assumption on which accounts are prepared. The main concepts are: that the business is a going concern, that revenue and costs are noted when they are incurred and not when cash is received or paid, that the present accounts are drawn up following the same principles as the previous accounts, that the revenue or costs are only recorded if it is certain that they will be incurred 会计概念:建账的基本假设,主要概念有:对经营的业务进行持续监控;对收入和花费的登记以发生时间为准,而非按照现金的取得或支付时间为依据;做账原则应保持一贯性;只对确定会发生的收入和花费进行记录

accounting conventions /əˈkaʊntɪŋ kənˌvenʃ(ə)nz/ *noun* the fundamental assumptions that govern the practice of accounting, e.g., consistency and prudence 会计惯例,会计常规:指导会计业务的基本假设 Also called 亦称作 **accounting concepts** ⇨参阅 **conceptual framework**

accounting date /əˈkaʊntɪŋ ˌdeɪt/ *noun* the date on which an accounting period ends, usually 31st December for annual accounts but it can in fact be any date 会计日:会计核算期截止的日期,年度账目的会计日通常为 12 月 31 日,但实际上可以是任何日期

accounting entity /əˈkaʊntɪŋ ˌentəti/ *noun* the unit for which financial statements and accounting records are prepared, e.g., a limited company or a partnership 会计主体:编制财务报表和会计账册的单位,包括有限公司、合伙企业等 ⇨参阅 **reporting entity**

accounting equation /əˌkaʊntɪŋ ɪˈkweɪʒ(ə)n/ *noun* the basic formula that underpins double-entry bookkeeping. It can be expressed most simply as ‘assets + expenses = liabilities + capital + revenue’ where the debit amounts to the left of the equals sign must be equivalent to the credit amounts to the right 会计等式,会计恒等式:复式簿记的基本公式,可以用一个最简单的等式“资产 + 开支 = 负债 + 资本 + 收益”来表示,公式中等号左边的借方金额必须等于右边的贷方金额 Also called 亦称作 **balance sheet equation**

accounting event /əˌkaʊntɪŋ ɪˈvent/ *noun* a transaction recorded in a business’s books of account 会计事项,会计业务:业务账簿中记录的交易项目

accounting fees /əˈkaʊntɪŋ ˌfiːz/ *plural noun* fees paid to an accountant for preparing accounts, which are deductible against tax 会计费用：付给会计人员编制账目的酬金，可在纳税时扣除

accounting manual /əˌkaʊntɪŋ ˈmænjuəl/ *noun* a handbook or set of instructions that set out all procedures and responsibilities of those engaged in an entity's accounting systems 会计手册，会计规则：列示出实体会计系统中所包涵的所有程序和责任的手册或一套指导规范

accounting period /əˈkaʊntɪŋ ˌpɪərɪəd/ *noun* a period of time at the end of which the firm's accounts are made up 会计期，会计年度：指一段时间，在这段时间的末尾需对企业的账目进行结算

accounting policies /əˈkaʊntɪŋ ˌpɒlɪsiz/ *noun* the accounting bases used by a company when preparing its financial statements 会计政策：公司编制财务报表的会计基础

Accounting Principles Board /əˌkaʊntɪŋ ˈprɪnsɪp(ə)lz ˌbɔːd/ *noun* the US body which issued Opinions that formed much of US Generally Accepted Accounting Principles up to 1973 when the Financial Accounting Standards Board (FASB) took over that role 会计原则委员会：为制定美国公认会计准则提供大量意见的机构，1973年被美国财务会计准则委员会(FASB)取代 Abbreviation 缩写 **APB**

accounting procedure /əˈkaʊntɪŋ prəˌsiːdʒə/ *noun* an accounting method developed by an individual or organisation to deal with routine accounting tasks 会计程序：个人或机构用来完成日常会计事务的一套会计方法

accounting rate of return /əˌkaʊntɪŋ reɪt əv rɪˈtɜːn/ *noun* a method of valuing shares in a company where the company's estimated future profits are divided by the rate of return required by investors 会计收益率，会计回报率：一种公司股票估值方法，以公司估算的未来利润除以投资者要求的回报率 Abbreviation 缩写 **ARR**

accounting reference date /əˌkaʊntɪŋ ˈref(ə)rəns ˌdeɪt/ *noun* the last day of a company's accounting reference period 会计参照日：公司会计参照期的最后一日

accounting reference period /əˌkaʊntɪŋ ˈref(ə)rəns ˌpɪəriəd/ *noun* 会计参照期 **1.** the period for which a company makes up its accounts. In most, but not all, cases, the period is 12 months. [公司建账期，大多为12个月] **2.** the period for which corporation tax is calculated [公司税计算期]

accounting software /əˌkaʊntɪŋ ˈsɒftweə/ *noun* programs used to enter and process accounts information on an office computer 会计软件

accounting standard /əˌkaʊntɪŋ ˈstændəd/ *noun* an authoritative statement of how particular types of transaction and other events should be reflected in financial statements. Compliance with accounting standards will normally be necessary for financial statements to give a true and fair view 会计标准：关于如何在财务报表中反映特定交易类别和其他事件的权威说明。财务报表通常必须符合会计准则，以确保其真实公正

accounting standards /əˌkaʊntɪŋ ˈstændədz/ *plural noun* rules of accounting practice recommended by the Accounting Standards Board (or FASB in the USA) 会计准则：会计业务的实践规范，具体准则在英国由会计准则委员会建议，在美国由财务会计准则委员会(FASB)建议

Accounting Standards Board /əˌkaʊntɪŋ ˈstændədz bɔːd/ *noun* a committee set up by British accounting institutions to monitor methods used in accounting 会计准则委员会：由英国会计机构设立的对会计方法进行管理的委员会 Abbreviation 缩写 **ASB**

Accounting Standards Committee /əˌkaʊntɪŋ ˈstændədz kəˌmɪti/ *noun* a UK accounting standards issuing body whose functions were taken over by the ASB in 1990 会计准则理事会：英国的会计准则发布机构，其职能于 1990 年被 ASB 接管 Abbreviation 缩写 **ASC**

accounting technician /əˌkaʊntɪŋ tekˈnɪʃ(ə)n/ *noun* a person who assists in the preparation of accounts but who is not a fully qualified accountant 助理会计：协助账目编制、但本身并不完全具备会计资格的人员

account payee /əˌkaʊnt peɪˈiː/ *noun* the words printed on most UK cheques indicating that the cheque can only be paid into the account of the person or business to whom the cheque is written, or be cashed for a fee at an agency offering a cheque cashing service 账户收款人：印于多数英国支票上，表示该支票只能转入支票指定的收款人或收款企业账户，或者只能在提供支票兑现服务的代办机构付手续费兑取现金

accounts department /əˈkaʊnts dɪˌpɑːtmənt/ *noun* a department in a company which deals with money paid, received, borrowed or owed 会计部门，财务科，会计处

accounts manager /əˈkaʊnts ˌmænɪdʒə/ *noun* the manager of an accounts department 会计经理

accounts payable /əˌkaʊnts ˈpeɪəb(ə)l/ *noun* money owed by a company 应付账款

accounts receivable /əˌkaʊnts rɪˈsiːvəb(ə)l/ *noun* money owed to a company 应收账款 Abbreviation 缩写 **AR**

accrete /əˈkriːt/ *verb* to have something added to it, especially of a fund to have interest added to it 增值，增加，增长(尤指资金随利息的增加而增长)

accretion /əˈkriːʃ(ə)n/ *noun* the process of adding interest to a fund over a period of time 增值，(资金随利息的)增加，增长

accrual /əˈkruːəl/ *noun* **1.** the act of noting financial transactions when they take place, and not when payment is made 应计会计：在财务交易发生时记账，而不是在完成支付后记账 **2.** a gradual increase by addition 积累，增长

accruals concept /əˈkruːəlz ˌkɒnsept/ *noun* the concept that accounts are prepared with financial transactions accrued. Revenue and costs are both reported during the accounting period to which they refer 应付应收概念，应计概念：指账目应随财务交易的发生而建立的概念。在此概念下，收入和费用均应作为其所属会计期间的收入和费用入账

accrue /ə'kruː/ *verb* **1.** to record a financial transaction in accounts when it takes place, and not when payment is made or received 应计:对每笔交易的记录入账以发生时间为准,而非以款项的收支为准 **2.** to increase and be due for payment at a later date 累积增长 ○ *Interest accrues from the beginning of the month*. 利息从月初开始累计。

accrued dividend /əˌkruːd ˌdɪvɪ'dend/ *noun* a dividend earned since the last dividend was paid 应计股利,累积股息

accrued expense /əˌkruːd ɪk'spens/ *noun* an expense that has been incurred within a given accounting period but not yet paid 应计开支:发生在指定会计期间的尚未支付的开支

accrued income /əˌkruːd 'ɪnkʌm/ *noun* revenue entered in accounts, although payment has not yet been received 应计收入:已经入账的收入,尽管该款项尚未收到

accrued interest /əˌkruːd 'ɪntrəst/ *noun* interest which has been earned by an interest-bearing investment 应计利息,应计未付利息 ○ *Accrued interest is added quarterly*. 应计利息按季累计。

accrued liabilities /əˌkruːd ˌlaɪə'bɪlɪtiz/ *noun* liabilities which are recorded in an accounting period, although payment has not yet been made. This refers to liabilities such as rent, electricity, etc. 应计负债:已经记录在会计期内的债务,尽管该开支尚未支付,如租金、电费等

accumulate /ə'kjuːmjʊleɪt/ *verb* to grow in quantity by being added to, or to get more of something over a period of time 积累,累积,累计 ○ *We allow dividends to accumulate in the fund*. 我们允许股利累积到资金中。

accumulated depreciation /əˌkjuːmjʊleɪtɪd dɪˌpriːʃi'eɪʃ(ə)n/ *noun* the total amount by which an asset has been depreciated since it was purchased 累计折旧:一项资产从购买日起的总计折旧额

accumulated earnings tax /əˌkjuːmjʊˌleɪtɪd 'ɜːnɪŋz tæks/, **accumulated profits tax** /əˌkjuːmjʊˌleɪtɪd 'prɒfɪts tæks/ *noun US* a tax on earnings above a specified limit which are unjustifiably retained in a business to avoid paying higher personal income tax (美)累计收益税:对超过指定限额的无特定用途的企业留存盈余征收的一项税种,以防止企业为私人逃避高额个人所得税

accumulated profit /əˌkjuːmjʊleɪtɪd 'prɒfɪt/ *noun* a profit which is not paid as dividend but is taken over into the accounts of the following year 累计利润,累计盈利:不作为股利发放而是留存转入次年账目的利润

accumulated reserves /əˌkjuːmjʊleɪtɪd rɪ'zɜːvz/ *plural noun* reserves which a company has put aside over a period of years 累计储备,公积金

accumulation /əˌkjuːmjʊ'leɪʃ(ə)n/ *noun* the process of growing larger by being added to, or of getting more and more of something 累积,积累,积蓄

ACH /ˌeɪ siː 'eɪtʃ/ *abbr US* Automated Clearing House(美)自动票据交换所

acid test /ˌæsɪd 'test/ *noun* an accounting ratio used to measure an organisation's liquidity. It is calculated by taking the business's current assets, minus its stocks, divided by its current liabilities. The higher the ratio, the better: a low ratio is usually a sign that a company is overstretched 酸性测试:用以衡量组织流动性的会计比率,计算方法为将企业的流动资产减去存货再除以流动负债。比率越高越好,因为低比率通常表示公司资金紧张

acid test ratio /ˌæsɪd ˌtest ˈreɪʃiəʊ/ *noun* same as 同 **liquidity ratio**

acquire /əˈkwaɪə/ *verb* to buy 买,收购,取得 ○ *to acquire a company* 收购一家公司 ○ *We have acquired a new office building in the centre of town.* 我们在市中心购买了一幢新写字楼。

acquirer /əˈkwaɪərə/ *noun* a person or company which buys something 买家

acquisition /ˌækwɪˈzɪʃ(ə)n/ *noun* **1.** something bought 购置物 ○ *The chocolate factory is our latest acquisition.* 这个巧克力工厂是我们最近的一笔收购。**2.** the takeover of a company. The results and cash flows of the acquired company are brought into the group accounts only from the date of acquisition: the figures for the previous period for the reporting entity should not be adjusted. The difference between the fair value of the net identifiable assets acquired and the fair value of the purchase consideration is goodwill 收购(被收购公司的业绩及现金流量自收购日起并入集团账户,报告主体之前的数字不作调整。被并公司可识别资产净值的公允价值与收购代价的公允价值之差构成商誉) **3.** the act of getting or buying something 获得(或购买)行为

acquisition accounting /ˌækwɪˈzɪʃ(ə)n əˌkaʊntɪŋ/ *noun* a full consolidation, where the assets of a subsidiary company which has been purchased are included in the parent company's balance sheet, and the premium paid for the goodwill is written off against the year's earnings 盘购会计:指企业编制合并报表的一种会计方法,所购买的子公司资产被纳入母公司资产负债表,为商誉所支付的溢价与年度盈利相抵消

across-the-board /əˌkrɒsðəˈbɔːd/ *adjective* applying to everything or everyone 全面的,包括一切的 ○ *an across-the-board price increase* or *wage increase* 全面提价(或提薪)

act /ækt/ *noun* a law passed by parliament which must be obeyed by the people (议会通过的强制性)条例,法令,法案

ACT *abbr* Advance Corporation Tax 预付公司税

active /ˈæktɪv/ *adjective* involving many transactions or activities 活跃的,繁忙的 ○ *an active demand for oil shares* 对石油股票的热切需求 ○ *an active day on the Stock Exchange* 证券交易所繁忙的一天 ○ *Computer shares are very active.* 电脑类股票交易活跃。

active account /ˌæktɪv əˈkaʊnt/ *noun* an account, such as a bank account or investment account, which is used to deposit and withdraw money frequently 活动账户(指收支频繁的账户,如银行账户或投资账户)

active partner /ˌæktɪv ˈpɑːtnə/ *noun* a partner who works in a company that is a partnership 任职合伙人:供职于合伙公司的合伙人

activity-based budgeting /ækˌtɪvɪtiˌbeɪst ˈbʌdʒɪtɪŋ/ *noun* the allocation of resources to individual activities. Activity-based budgeting involves determining which activities incur costs within an organisation, establishing the relationships between them, and then deciding how much of the total budget should be allocated to each activity 作业基础预算法：把资源分配到个别作业的预算方法。它先确定组织的哪些作业会产生成本，再确立这些作业之间的关系，然后决定应给各项作业分配多少预算 Abbreviation 缩写 **ABB**

activity-based management /æk₍tɪvɪti ₍beɪst ˈmænɪdʒmənt/ *noun* a system of management that uses activity-based cost information for a variety of purposes including cost reduction, cost modelling, and customer profitability analysis 作业基础管理法：根据作业成本信息来实现成本削减、成本模型及客户盈利能力分析等一系列目标的管理制度 Abbreviation 缩写 **ABM**

activity chart /ækˈtɪvɪti tʃɑːt/ *noun* a plan showing work which has been done, made so that it can be compared to a previous plan showing how much work should be done 业务进展图：显示已完成工作量的进度表，此表可用来同显示应完成工作量的进度表进行对比

activity cost pool /æk₍tɪvɪti ˈkɒst ₍puːl/ *noun* a grouping of all cost elements associated with an activity 作业成本集：与某项作业有关的全部成本要素的集合

activity driver analysis /æk₍tɪvɪti ₍draɪvə əˈnæləsɪs/ *noun* the identification and evaluation of the activity drivers used to trace the cost of activities to cost objects. It may also involve selecting activity drivers with potential to contribute to the cost management function with particular reference to cost reduction 作业动因分析：分辨及评估作业动因，以确定实际作业成本有无达到成本目标。此分析也可能包含选择有助于削减成本的作业动因

act of God /₍ækt əv ˈɡɒd/ *noun* something you do not expect to happen and which cannot be avoided, e.g. a storm or a flood（暴风雨或洪水之类的）自然灾害，不可抗力（NOTE：Acts of God are not usually covered by insurance policies 天灾一般不在保险范围之内）

actual /ˈæktʃuəl/ *adjective* real or correct 实际的；真实的 ○ *What is the actual cost of one unit?* 实际单位成本是多少？○ *The actual figures for directors' expenses are not shown to the shareholders.* 没有把董事开支的实际数字告知股东。

actual cash value /₍æktʃuəl kæʃ ˈvæljuː/ *noun* the amount of money, less depreciation, that it would cost to replace something damaged beyond repair with a comparable item 实际现金价值：替换被损物品所需的成本减去折旧后所得的金额

actual price /₍æktʃuəl ˈpraɪs/ *noun* a price for a commodity which is for immediate delivery 实际价格，现货价格

actuals /ˈæktʃuəlz/ *plural noun* real figures 实际数字 ○ *These figures are the actuals for last year.* 这些是去年的实际数字。

actuarial /₍æktʃuˈeəriəl/ *adjective* calculated by an actuary 精算的 ○ *The premiums are worked out according to actuarial calculations.* 保险费是依据保险统计计算得出来的。

actuarial tables /ˌæktʃueəriəl ˈteɪb(ə)lz/ *noun* lists showing how long people are likely to live, used to calculate life assurance premiums and annuities 保险公司精算项目表

actuary /ˈæktʃuəri/ *noun* a person employed by an insurance company or other organisation to calculate the risk involved in an insurance, and therefore the premiums payable by people taking out insurance 精算员，精算师：由保险公司或其他机构雇佣的人员，负责对保险中所含的风险进行计算，以确定承保人员应支付的保险费用

ACU *abbr* Asian Currency Unit 亚洲货币单位

add /æd/ *verb* to put figures together to make a total 加（数字）○ *If you add the interest to the capital you will get quite a large sum*. 把利息加到本金中会是一大笔钱。○ *Interest is added monthly*. 按月加息。

added value /ˌædɪd ˈvæljuː/ *noun* an amount added to the value of a product or service, equal to the difference between its cost and the amount received when it is sold. Wages, taxes, etc. are deducted from the added value to give the profit 增值，附加价值

addend /ˈædend/ *noun* a number added to the augend in an addition 加数

addition /əˈdɪʃ(ə)n/ *noun* **1.** a thing or person added 附加的人（或物）○ *The management has stopped all additions to the staff*. 公司已不再增加任何员工。○ *We are exhibiting several additions to our product line*. 我们正在展示几种新投产的产品。○ *The marketing director is the latest addition to the board*. 营销主任是董事会的最新成员。**2.** an arithmetical operation consisting of adding together two or more numbers to make a sum 加法 ○ *You don't need a calculator to do simple addition*. 简单的加法不需要使用计算器。

additional /əˈdɪʃ(ə)nəl/ *adjective* extra which is added 附加的，追加的，额外的 ○ *additional costs* 额外费用 ○ *They sent us a list of additional charges*. 他们给我们发了一张附加费清单。○ *Some additional clauses were added to the contract*. 合同增加了一些附加条款。○ *Additional duty will have to be paid*. 必须支付附加关税。

additional personal allowance /əˌdɪʃ(ə)nəl ˌpɜːs(ə)n(ə)l əˈlauəns/ *noun* a tax allowance which can be claimed by a single person who has a child of school age living with them, formerly called the ‘single-parent allowance’ 额外人口宽免：单身者抚养学龄儿童时可以申请的收入免税额，旧称“单亲宽免”

additional premium /əˌdɪʃ(ə)nəl ˈpriːmɪəm/ *noun* a payment made to cover extra items in an existing insurance 追加保费：对保单中增加的保险项目支付的费用

additional voluntary contributions /əˌdɪʃ(ə)n(ə)l ˌvɒlənt(ə)ri ˌkɒntrɪˈbjuːʃ(ə)nz/ *plural noun* extra payments made voluntarily by an employee to a pension scheme on top of the normal contributions, up to a maximum of 15% of gross earnings 自愿追加的养老金：员工在退休金计划的正常供款之外自愿追加的供款额，最高可达总收入的 15% Abbreviation 缩写 **AVCs**

address /əˈdres/ *verb* to write the

details of an address on an envelope or package 写通讯地址于 ○ *a letter addressed to the managing director* 一封写给总经理的信 ○ *an incorrectly addressed package* 一个写错地址的包裹 ○ *Please address your enquiries to the manager*. 如有疑问可向经理咨询。

addressee /ædre'siː/ *noun* a person to whom a letter or package is addressed 收件人

address list /ə'dres lɪst/ *noun* a list of names and addresses of people and companies 地址目录,通讯录

add up /ˌæd 'ʌp/ *verb* to put several figures together to make a total 总计,合计 ○ *He made a mistake in adding up the column of figures*. 他在合计这列数字时出了错。

add up to /ˌæd 'ʌp tʊ/ *verb* to make a total of 合计 ○ *The total expenditure adds up to more than £1,000*. 总支出合计超过 1,000 英镑。

adequacy /'ædɪkwəsi/ *noun* the fact of being large enough or good enough for something 适当,足够

adjudicate /ə'dʒuːdɪkeɪt/ *verb* to give a judgement between two parties in law or to decide a legal problem (法律)判决,裁定 ○ *to adjudicate a claim* 裁决一起索赔案 ○ *to adjudicate in a dispute* 裁定一项纠纷

adjudication /əˌdʒuːdɪ'keɪʃ(ə)n/ *noun* the act of giving a judgement or of deciding a legal problem 判决,裁定

adjudication of bankruptcy /əˌdʒuːdɪkeɪʃ(ə)n əv 'bæŋkrʌptsi/ *noun* a legal order making someone bankrupt (宣告)破产裁定

adjudication tribunal /əˌdʒuːdɪ'keɪʃ(ə)n traɪˌbjuːn(ə)l/ *noun* a group which adjudicates in industrial disputes 劳资纠纷裁决法庭

adjudicator /ə'dʒuːdɪkeɪtə/ *noun* a person who gives a decision on a problem 判决者,裁定者 ○ *an adjudicator in an industrial dispute* 劳资纠纷的裁决者

adjust /ə'dʒʌst/ *verb* to change something to fit new conditions 调节,调整 ○ *Prices are adjusted for inflation*. 依通胀调整价格。

'...inflation-adjusted GNP moved up at a 1.3% annual rate'
"经通胀调整后的 GNP 年增长率为 1.3%" [*Fortune*《财富》]

'Saudi Arabia will no longer adjust its production to match short-term supply with demand'
"沙特阿拉伯将不再为平衡短期供需关系而调整其产量" [*Economist*《经济学家》]

'...on a seasonally-adjusted basis, output of trucks, electric power, steel and paper decreased'
"根据季节性调整,卡车、电力、钢铁及造纸业的产量下降" [*Business Week*《商业周刊》]

adjustable rate mortgage /əˌdʒʌstəb(ə)l reɪt 'mɒːgɪdʒ/ *noun* a mortgage where the interest rate changes according to the current market rates 可调息抵押贷款,可调息按揭 Abbreviation 缩写 **ARM**

adjustable rate preferred stock /əˌdʒʌstəb(ə)l reɪt prɪˌfɜːd 'stɒk/ *noun* a preference shares on which dividends are paid in line with the interest rate on Treasury bills 可调息优先股(其股利支付率与短期国库券利率相一致) Abbreviation 缩写 **ARPS**

adjusted gross income /əˌdʒʌstɪd grəʊs 'ɪnkʌm/ *noun US* a person's total annual income less expenses, pension contributions, capital losses, etc., used as a basis to calculate federal income tax（美）调整后总收益，调整后总所得：扣除开支、退休金供款、资本损失等之后的年度总收益，用以计算联邦所得税 Abbreviation 缩写 **AGI**

adjuster /əˈdʒʌstə/ *noun* a person who calculates losses for an insurance company（保险公司的）理算员，理算师

adjusting entry /əˌdʒʌstɪŋ ˈentri/ *noun* an entry in accounts which is made to correct a mistake in the accounts（对误列账目进行更正的）调整分录

adjustment /əˈdʒʌstmənt/ *noun* **1.** the act of adjusting 调节，调整 ○ *to make an adjustment to salaries* 进行工资调整 ○ *an adjustment of prices to take account of rising costs* 考虑到成本上升而进行的价格调整 **2.** a slight change 微调 ○ *Details of tax adjustments are set out in the enclosed document.* 附件中列出了税务调整的详情。**3.** an entry in accounts which does not represent a receipt or payment, but which is made to make the accounts correct（为准确反映财务状况所作的账目）调整 **4.** a change in the exchange rates, made to correct a balance of payment deficit 变更：为了更正国际收支赤字而对汇率进行的变更

administer /ədˈmɪnɪstə/ *verb* to organise, manage or direct the whole of an organisation or part of one 组织，管理 ○ *She administers a large pension fund.* 她掌管着一大笔养老基金。○ *It will be the HR manager's job to administer the induction programme.* 入职培训由人力资源经理负责。

administered price /ədˈmɪnɪstəd praɪs/ *noun US* a price fixed by a manufacturer which cannot be varied by a retailer（美）管制价格，受控价格，限价：由制造商确定的零售商不能变更的价格（NOTE: The UK term is **resale price maintenance** 英国用语为 **resale price maintenance**）

administration /ədˌmɪnɪˈstreɪʃ(ə)n/ *noun* **1.** the action of organising, controlling or managing a company（对某个公司的）组织，管理，经营 **2.** an appointment by a court of a person to manage the affairs of a company（为处理某一公司事务的法院）委派

administration costs /ədˌmɪnɪˈstreɪʃ(ə)n ˌkɒsts/, **administration expenses** /ədˌmɪnɪˈstreɪʃ(ə)n ɪkˌspensɪz/ *plural noun* the costs of management, not including production, marketing or distribution costs 管理费用，行政开支（不包括生产、销售或配销成本）

administrative /ədˈmɪnɪstrətɪv/ *adjective* referring to administration 管理的，行政的 ○ *administrative details* 管理细则 ○ *administrative expenses* 管理费用

administrative expenses /ədˌmɪnɪstrətɪv ɪkˈspensɪz/ *plural noun* costs of administration 管理费用，行政开支

administrative receiver /ədˌmɪnɪstrətɪv rɪˈsiːvə/ *noun* a person appointed by a court to administer the affairs of a company（受法院委派管理公司事务的）行政接管人

administrative receivership /ədˌmɪnɪstrətɪv rɪˈsiːvəʃɪp/ *noun* the appointment of an administrative receiver by a debenture holder（由债券持有

人委派行政接管人的)行政接管

administrator /əd'mɪnɪstreɪtə/ *noun* **1.** a person who directs the work of other employees in a business 管理者,行政管理人员 ○ *After several years as a college teacher, she hopes to become an administrator.* 在担任大学教师数年后,她希望成为一名行政管理人员。**2.** a person appointed by a court to manage the affairs of someone who dies without leaving a will 遗产管理人

ADR *abbr* American Depositary Receipt 美国存券收据,美国保管收据

ad valorem /ˌæd və'lɔːrəm/ *adjective* used to describe a tax or commission, e.g., Value Added Tax, that is calculated on the value of the goods or services provided, rather than on their number or size 从价的:用以说明依据所提供产品或服务的价值而不是按数量或大小计算的税项或佣金(如增值税)○ *ad valorem duty* 从价关税 ○ *ad valorem tax* 从价税

ad valorem duty /ˌæd və'lɔːrem ˌdjuːti/ *noun* the duty calculated on the sales value of the goods 从价关税

ad valorem tax /ˌæd və'lɔːrem tæks/ *noun* a tax calculated according to the value of the goods taxed 从价税

advance /əd'vɑːns/ *noun* money paid as a loan or as a part of a payment to be made later 贷款;预付款 ○ *She asked if she could have a cash advance.* 她询问能否给她预付一些现金。○ *We paid her an advance on account.* 我们给她预付了部分账款。○ *Can I have an advance of £100 against next month's salary?* 我能不能从下月工资中预支出 100 英镑? ■ *adjective* early, or taking place before something else happens 预先的,事前的 ○ *advance payment* 预付款项 ○ *Advance holiday bookings are up on last year.* 休假预订率比去年有所上升。○ *You must give seven days' advance notice of withdrawals from the account.* 若从账户取款,必须提前七天通知。■ *verb* **1.** to pay an amount of money to someone as a loan or as a part of a payment to be made later 预付,借给 ○ *The bank advanced him £100,000 against the security of his house.* 银行以他的房子为抵押贷给他 10 万英镑。**2.** to make something happen earlier 提前 ○ *The date of the AGM has been advanced to May 10th.* 年度股东大会的时间提早至 5 月 10 日。○ *The meeting with the German distributors has been advanced from 11.00 to 09.30.* 与德国经销商的会晤从 11:00 提前到 09:30。

Advance Corporation Tax /ədˌvɑːns ˌkɔːpə'reɪʃ(ə)n tæks/ *noun* a tax which was abolished in 1999, paid by a company in advance of its main corporation tax payments. It was paid when dividends were paid to shareholders and was deducted from the main tax payment when that fell due. It appeared on the tax voucher attached to a dividend warrant 预付公司税:公司交纳主要的公司税之前,在分派股东股利时所交的税,它从到期的公司税中扣除,表现为股利支付书上附贴的一张纳税凭证。该税于 1999 年被废除 Abbreviation 缩写 **ACT**

advance payment guarantee /ədˌvɑːns ˌpeɪmənt ˌɡærən'tiː/, **advance payment bond** /ədˌvɑːns 'peɪmənt bɒnd/ *noun* a guarantee that enables a buyer to recover an advance payment made under a contract or order if the supplier fails to fulfil its contractual obligations 预付款担保：保证在供应商未能履行其合约责任时，买方能够收回其预付款项的担保

adverse /ˈædvɜːs/ *adjective* unfavourable 不利的，坏的，无益的

adverse balance /ˌædvɜːs ˈbæləns/ *noun* the deficit on an account, especially a nation's balance of payments account 收支赤字，逆差（尤指一国的收支账户）

adverse opinion /ˌædvɜːs əˈpɪnjən/ *noun US* an auditor's report that a company's financial statement is not a fair representation of the company's actual financial position （美）（审计报告中关于公司财务报表同实际财务状况不符的）反面意见，反对意见

adverse variance /ˌædvɜːs ˈveəriəns/ *noun* variance which shows that the actual result is worse than expected 不利差异：实际业绩低于预期值的差异

advice /ədˈvaɪs/ *noun* a notification telling someone what has happened 通知

adviser /ədˈvaɪzə/, **advisor** *noun* a person who suggests what should be done 顾问 ○ *He is consulting the company's legal adviser*. 他正在向公司的法律顾问咨询。

advisory /ədˈvaɪz(ə)ri/ *adjective* as an adviser 顾问的，咨询的 ○ *She is acting in an advisory capacity*. 她在以一个顾问的身份行事。

advisory board /ədˈvaɪz(ə)ri ˌbɔːd/ *noun* a group of advisors 顾问委员会，咨询委员会

advisory funds /ədˈvaɪz(ə)ri ˌfʌndz/ *plural noun* funds placed with a financial institution to invest on behalf of a client, the institution investing them at its own discretion 咨询基金，委托投资资金：客户存放在金融机构委托其代为投资的资金

AFBD *abbr* Association of Futures Brokers and Dealers 期权经纪人和交易人协会

affiliated /əˈfɪlieɪtɪd/ *adjective* connected with or owned by another company 联营的，附属的 ○ *Smiths Ltd is one of our affiliated companies*. 史密斯股份有限公司是我们的一家附属公司。

affiliated enterprise /əˌfɪlieɪtɪd ˈentəpraɪz/, **affiliated company** /əˌfɪlieɪtɪd ˈkʌmp(ə)ni/ *noun* company which is partly owned by another (though less than 50%), and where the share-owning company exerts some management control or has a close trading relationship with the associate 附属公司，联号，联营公司：一家公司部分归另一公司所有（尽管股权少于50%），后者对其附属公司行使一定的管理控制权或者与其有紧密的商业联系 ○ *one of our affiliated companies* 我们的附属公司之一

aftermarket /ˈɑːftəˌmɑːkɪt/ *noun* a market in new shares, which starts immediately after trading in the shares begins（在新股上市交易之后开始的）新股交易市场，售后市场，二级市场

after tax /ˌɑːftə ˈtæks/ *adverb* after tax has been paid 已税，税后

after-tax profit /ˌɑːftəˈtæks ˌprɒfɪt/ *noun* a profit after tax has been deducted 税后利润

age analysis of debtors /eɪdʒ əˌnæləsɪs əv ˈdetəs/ *noun* the amount owed by debtors, classified by age of debt 债务人账龄分析

aged debtors analysis /ˌeɪdʒd

ˌdetəz əˈnæləsɪs/, **ageing schedule** /ˌeɪdʒɪŋ ˈʃedjuːl/ *noun* a list which analyses a company's debtors, showing the number of days their payments are outstanding 账龄分析;逾期账款分析:用于分析公司债务人情况的列表,它显示债款过期的天数

agency /ˈeɪdʒənsi/ *noun* **1.** an office or job of representing another company in an area (在某一地区的)代理处,代理 ○ *They signed an agency agreement* or *an agency contract*. 他们签署了一份代理协议(或一份代理合同)。**2.** an office or business which arranges things for other companies (代理事务的)代理机构

agency bank /ˈeɪdʒənsi bæŋk/ *noun* a bank which does not accept deposits, but acts as an agent for another, usually foreign, bank 代理银行:该银行不吸收存款,只作为另一家银行(通常是外国银行)的代理

agency bill /ˈeɪdʒənsi bɪl/ *noun* a bill of exchange drawn on the local branch of a foreign bank 代理期票:向外国银行的本地分支机构开出的汇票

agency broker /ˈeɪdʒənsi ˌbrəʊkə/ *noun* a dealer who acts as the agent for an investor, buying and selling for a commission (为投资人代理买卖证券的)代理经纪人

agency worker /ˌeɪdʒənsi ˈwɜːkə/ *noun* a person who is employed by an agency to work for another company. He or she is taxed as an employee of the agency, not of the company where he or she actually works (代理机构雇用的为别的公司工作的)代理人,代理员工

agenda /əˈdʒendə/ *noun* a list of things to be discussed at a meeting 议事日程,会议议程 ○ *The conference agenda* or *the agenda of conference* 会议的议事日程 ○ *After two hours we were still discussing the first item on the agenda*. 两个小时过去了,我们还在讨论议事日程的第一项。○ *We usually put finance at the top of the agenda*. 我们通常把财务事宜放在议事日程之首。○ *The chair wants two items removed from* or *taken off the agenda*. 主席想去掉会议议程中的两项。

agent /ˈeɪdʒənt/ *noun* **1.** a person who represents a company or another person in an area 代理人 ○ *to be the agent for BMW cars* 作为宝马汽车的代理人 ○ *to be the agent for IBM* 作为 IBM 的代理人 **2.** a person in charge of an agency 代理机构的主管 ○ *an advertising agent* 广告代理商 ○ *The estate agent sent me a list of properties for sale*. 地产代理发给我一份待售房产的清单。○ *Our trip was organised through our local travel agent*. 我们的行程由本地的旅行社负责安排。

agent bank /ˈeɪdʒənt bæŋk/ *noun* a bank which uses the credit card system set up by another bank 代理银行:该银行使用由其他银行建立的信用卡系统

agent's commission /ˌeɪdʒənts kəˈmɪʃ(ə)n/ *noun* money, often a percentage of sales, paid to an agent 代理佣金,代理手续费

age-related /ˈeɪdʒrɪˌleɪtɪd/ *adjective* connected with a person's age 与年龄相关的;与年龄挂钩的

age-related allowance /eɪdʒrɪˌleɪtɪd əˈlaʊəns/ *noun* an extra tax allowance which a person over 65 may be entitled to 老龄税务优惠:65 岁以上的老人可享受的额外税务优惠

aggregate /ˈægrɪgət/ *adjective* total, with everything added together 总的,总计的,累积的 ○ *aggregate output* 总产出

aggregate demand /ˌægrɪgət dɪˈmɑːnd/ *noun* the total demand for goods and services from all sectors of the economy including individuals, companies and the government 总需求 ○ *Economists are studying the recent fall in aggregate demand*. 经济学家正在研究最近总需求下滑的情况。○ *As incomes have risen, so has aggregate demand*. 收入增长拉动总需求增加。

aggregate risk /ˌægrɪgət ˈrɪsk/ *noun* the risk which a bank runs in lending to a customer 合计风险:银行向客户贷款时所面临的风险

aggregate supply /ˌægrɪgət səˈplaɪ/ *noun* all goods and services on the market 总供给 ○ *Is aggregate supply meeting aggregate demand*? 总供给能否满足总需求?

AGI *abbr US* adjusted gross income (美)调整后总收益,调整后总所得

agio /ˈædʒɪəʊ/ *noun* **1.** a charge made for changing money of one currency into another, or for changing banknotes into cash 手续费:将一种货币兑换成另一种货币或将银行本票兑换成现金所收取的手续费 **2.** the difference between two values, such as between the interest charged on loans made by a bank and the interest paid by the bank on deposits, or the difference between the values of two currencies 差价,贴水(如银行贷款利息与银行存款利息的差价或两种货币价值的差价)

AGM /ˌeɪ dʒiː ˈem/ *abbr* Annual General Meeting 年度股东大会

agreed /əˈgriːd/ *adjective* having been accepted by everyone 同意的;议定的,协定的 ○ *We pay an agreed amount each month*. 我们每月支付议定的金额。○ *The agreed terms of employment are laid down in the contract*. 合同列明了协定的聘用条款。

agreed price /əˌgriːd ˈpraɪs/ *noun* a price which has been accepted by both the buyer and seller 议定价格,商定价格

agree with /əˈgriː wɪð/ *verb* **1.** to say that your opinions are the same as someone else's 同意,赞同(某人的意见) ○ *I agree with the chairman that the figures are lower than normal*. 我同意主席关于数字低于正常水平的看法。**2.** to be the same as 与…一致,与…相符 ○ *The auditors' figures do not agree with those of the accounts department*. 审计师的数字与会计部门的数字不一致。

AICPA *abbr* American Institute of Certified Public Accountants 美国注册会计师学会

airmail transfer /ˈeəmeɪl ˌtrænsfɜː/ *noun* an act of sending money from one bank to another by airmail 航空信汇:通过航空邮件在银行间汇款

alien corporation /ˌeɪliən ˌkɔːpəˈreɪʃ(ə)n/ *noun US* a company which is incorporated in a foreign country (美)外国公司

A list /ˈeɪ lɪst/ *noun* a list of members of a company at the time it is wound up who may be liable for the company's unpaid debts 公司清盘时负责承担公司未偿还债务的股东名单

all-in price /ˌɔːlɪn ˈpraɪs/ *noun* a price which covers all items in a purchase such as goods, delivery, tax or insurance (货款、运费、税费等)各费在

内的价格

all-in rate /ˌɔːlɪn ˈreɪt/ *noun* **1.** a price which covers all the costs connected with a purchase, such as delivery, tax and insurance, as well as the cost of the goods themselves 包括一切(如送货、税费、保险以及产品成本等)的价格 **2.** a wage which includes all extra payments such as bonuses and merit pay (包括红利和绩效工资等各种额外报酬在内的)全部工资

allocate /ˈæləkeɪt/ *verb* to divide something in various ways and share it out 分配,分摊,调拨,划归 ○ *How are we going to allocate the available office space?* 我们将如何分配可用的办公室空间? ■ *noun* to assign a whole item of cost, or of revenue, to a single cost unit, centre, account, or time period (成本或收益的)分配,分摊

allocated costs /ˈæləˌkeɪtɪd kɒsts/ *plural noun* overhead costs which have been allocated to a specific cost centre 分配的成本

allocation /ˌæləˈkeɪʃ(ə)n/ *noun* the process of providing sums of money for particular purposes, or a sum provided for a purpose 分配,分摊,拨款 ○ *the allocation of funds to a project* 给某个项目的拨款

allot /əˈlɒt/ *verb* to share out 分配,分发,配给

allotment /əˈlɒtmənt/ *noun* **1.** the process of sharing out something, especially money between various departments, projects or people(尤指各部门、项目或人员之间的资金)分配,拨款 ○ *The allotment of funds to each project is the responsibility of the finance director.* 财务主任负责给各个项目拨款。**2.** the act of giving shares in a new company to people who have applied for them (将公司新股向申购者的)分配 ○ *share allotment* 股票分配 ○ *payment in full on allotment* 全额付款认购

allow /əˈlaʊ/ *verb* **1.** to say that someone can do something 允许,准许 ○ *Junior members of staff are not allowed to use the chairman's lift.* 低级职员不允许使用董事长的电梯。○ *The company allows all members of staff to take six days' holiday at Christmas.* 公司允许全体职工圣诞节放假六天。**2.** to give 给予 ○ *to allow 5% discount to members of staff* 给职工5%的折扣 **3.** to agree to or accept legally (法律上)同意,接受 ○ *to allow a claim* or *an appeal* 同意某项要求(或请求)

allowable /əˈlaʊəb(ə)l/ *adjective* legally accepted (法律上)允许的 Opposite 反义 **disallowable**

allowable deductions /əˌlaʊəb(ə)l dɪˈdʌkʃ(ə)ns/ *plural noun* deductions from income which are allowed by the Inland Revenue, and which reduce the tax payable 准予减免额:(英国)国内税务局允许从收入中扣除以减少应付税的金额

allowable expenses /əˌlaʊəb(ə)l ɪkˈspensɪz/ *plural noun* business expenses which can be claimed against tax 可以抵税的费用

allowable losses /əˌlaʊəb(ə)l ˈlɒsɪz/ *plural noun* losses, e.g. on the sale of assets, which are allowed to be set off against gains 可以冲抵的损失(如出售资产时)

allowance /əˈlaʊəns/ *noun* **1.** money which is given for a special reason 津贴,补贴 ○ *a travel allowance* or *a travelling allowance* 差旅津贴 **2.** a part of an income which is not taxed (税收)减免(额) ○ *allowances against tax* or *tax allowances* 税收减免额 ○ *personal allowances* 个人收入税款减免 **3.** money removed in the form of a discount 折扣,折让 ○ *an allowance for depreciation* 折旧备抵 ○ *an allowance for exchange loss* 汇兑损失备抵

'... the compensation plan includes base, incentive and car allowance totalling $50,000+'
"补偿计划包括总计 50,000 美元以上的基本津贴、绩效奖金和汽车补贴"[*Globe and Mail* (*Toronto*)《环球邮报》(多伦多)]

allowance for bad debt /əˌlaʊəns fə bæd ˈdet/ *noun* a provision made in a company's accounts for debts which may never be paid 坏账备抵,呆账备抵

allowances against tax /əˌlaʊənss əˈgenst tæks/ *plural noun* part of someone's income which is not taxed (收入)税款减免部分

allow for /əˈlaʊ fɔː/ *verb* to give a discount for something, or to add an extra sum to cover something 因…而打折扣;增加款项以涵盖… ○ *to allow for money paid in advance* 扣除预付款项 ○ *Add on an extra 10% to allow for postage and packing*. 再增加 10%以涵盖邮递和包装费。

all-risks policy /ˌɔːlˈrɪsks ˌpɒlɪsi/ *noun* an insurance policy which covers risks of any kind, with no exclusions 一切险保单

amalgamate /əˈmælgəmeɪt/ *verb* to join together with another group 合并 ○ *The amalgamated group includes six companies*. 合并后的集团包括六家公司。

amalgamation /əˌmælgəˈmeɪʃ(ə)n/ *noun* the joining together of several trade unions to increase their strength 合并

American Accounting Association /əˌmerɪkən əˈkaʊntɪŋ əˌsəʊsieɪʃ(ə)n/ *noun* a US voluntary organisation for those with an interest in accounting research and best practice, which aims to promote excellence in the creation, dissemination and application of accounting knowledge and skills 美国会计协会:美国致力于会计研究和最佳实践的志愿组织,其宗旨是促进会计知识与技能的发展、传播和应用 Abbreviation 缩写 **AAA**

American Depositary Receipt /əˈmerɪkən dɪˈpɒzɪtri rɪˈsiːt/ *noun* a document issued by an American bank to US citizens, making them unregistered shareholders of companies in foreign countries. The document allows them to receive dividends from their investments, and ADRs can themselves be bought or sold 美国存券收据,美国保管收据:美国银行向美国公民发行的单据,准予持有者成为外国公司的不记名股东,并凭此单据获得其投资股利,此收据可以自行买卖 Abbreviation 缩写 **ADR**

American Institute of Certified Public Accountants /əˌmerɪkən ˌɪnstɪtjuːt əv ˌsɜːtɪfaɪd ˌpʌblɪk əˈkaʊntənts/ *noun* the national association for certified public accountants in the United States 美国注册公共会计师学会 Abbreviation 缩写 **AICPA**

amortisable /ˌæmɔːˈtaɪzəb(ə)l/ *adjective* being possible to amortise 可摊销的,可分期偿还的 ○ *The capital cost is amortisable over a period of ten* *years*. 这笔资本支出可在10年内分期偿还。

amortisation /əˌmɔːtaɪˈzeɪʃ(ə)n/, **amortising** *noun* an act of amortising 摊销，分期偿还 ○ *amortisation of a debt* 分期偿还一笔债务

amortisation period /əˌmɔːtaɪˈzeɪʃ(ə)n ˌpɪəriəd/ *noun* the length of a lease, used when depreciating the value of the asset leased (用于折旧计算租赁资产价值的)分期偿还期，摊还期

amortise /əˈmɔːtaɪz/, **amortize** *verb* **1.** to repay a loan by regular payments, most of which pay off the interest on the loan at first, and then reduce the principal as the repayment period progresses 分期偿还(债务)：大多数情况下均是先偿还贷款利息，然后再逐期偿还本金 ○ *The capital cost is amortised over five years*. 这笔资本支出将在五年内分期偿还。**2.** to depreciate or to write down the capital value of an asset over a period of time in a company's accounts 折旧，摊提(资产)：折旧或减少公司一段时间内账面资产的价值

amount /əˈmaʊnt/ *noun* a quantity of money 金额，数额 ○ *A small amount has been deducted to cover our costs*. 已扣除少额款项以补偿我们的成本。○ *A large amount is still owing*. 仍欠付一大笔款项。○ *What is the amount to be written off*? 将注销的金额是多少？

amount paid up /əˌmaʊnt peɪd ˈʌp/ *noun* an amount paid for a new issue of shares, either the total payment or the first instalment, if the shares are offered with instalment payments 已付清金额，付讫金额：已支付的新股发行金额，可以是全部付清，也可以是按分期付款发售股票时付清首期付款

analyse /ˈænəlaɪz/, **analyze** *verb* to examine someone or something in detail 分析；详细检查 ○ *to analyse a statement of account* 分析会计报表 ○ *to analyse the market potential* 分析市场潜力

analysis /əˈnæləsɪs/ *noun* a detailed examination and report 分析 ○ *a job analysis* 工作分析 ○ *market analysis* 市场分析 ○ *Her job is to produce a regular sales analysis*. 她的工作是定期提供销售分析。(NOTE: The plural is **analyses** 复数为 **analyses**)

analyst /ˈænəlɪst/ *noun* a person who analyses 分析员 ○ *a market analyst* 市场分析员 ○ *a systems analyst* 系统分析员

annual /ˈænjuəl/ *adjective* for one year 每年的，年度的 ○ *an annual statement of income* 年度损益表 ○ *They have six weeks' annual leave*. 他们有六个星期的年假。○ *The company has an annual growth of 5%*. 公司的年增长率为5%。○ *We get an annual bonus*. 我们获得一笔年终奖。

'...real wages have risen at an annual rate of only 1% in the last two years'
"实际工资在过去两年的年增长率仅为1%"
[*Sunday Times*《星期日泰晤士报》]

'...the remuneration package will include an attractive salary, profit sharing and a company car together with four weeks' annual holiday'
"工作待遇包括优厚的薪酬、利润提成和公司提供的汽车，还可以享受四周的年假"
[*Times*《泰晤士报》]

annual accounts /ˌænjuəl əˈkaʊnts/ *plural noun* the accounts prepared at the end of a financial year 年度账户，年度财务报表 ○ *The annual accounts have been sent to the shareholders.* 年度财务报表已递交给股东。

annual depreciation /ˌænjuəl dɪˌpriːʃiˈeɪʃ(ə)n/ *noun* a reduction in the book value of an asset at a particular rate per year 年度折旧 ◊ 参阅 **straight line depreciation**

annual depreciation provision /ˌænjuəl dɪˌpriːʃiˈeɪʃ(ə)n prəˌvɪʒ(ə)n/ *noun* an allocation of the cost of an asset to a single year of the asset's expected year 年度折旧备抵：即年度累积折旧，在资产的存续期分配到一年的折旧额

annual exemptions /ˌænjuəl ɪgˈzempʃns/ *plural noun* amount of income which is exempt from tax. For example, the first £7,900 in capital gains in any one year is exempt from tax 年度税款豁免（如一年中前7,900英镑的资本增益可以免税）

Annual General Meeting /ˌænjuəl ˌdʒen(ə)rəl ˈmiːtɪŋ/ *noun* an annual meeting of all shareholders of a company, when the company's financial situation is presented by and discussed with the directors, when the accounts for the past year are approved and when dividends are declared and audited 年度股东大会：每年举行一次的由所有股东参加的会议，在会上呈报公司的财务状况并与董事进行讨论，同时批准上年的财务报表，并宣布和审计股利 Abbreviation 缩写 **AGM**（NOTE：The US term is **annual meeting** or **annual stockholders' meeting** 美国用语为 **annual meeting** 或 **annual stockholders' meeting**）

annual income /ˌænjuəl ˈɪnkʌm/ *noun* money received during a calendar year 年收入，年薪

annualised /ˈænjuəlaɪzd/, **annualized** *adjective* shown on an annual basis 按年度的，按年率计算的

'... he believes this may have caused the economy to grow at an annualized rate of almost 5 per cent in the final quarter of last year'
"他相信，这可能使得经济在去年最后一季取得近五个百分点的年率增长"［*Investors Chronicle*《投资者纪事》］

annualised percentage rate /ˌænjuəlaɪzd pəˈsentɪdʒ reɪt/ *noun* a yearly percentage rate, calculated by multiplying the monthly rate by twelve 年百分率：按年计算的利率，该比率用12乘以月比率计算得出 Abbreviation 缩写 **APR**（NOTE：The annualised percentage rate is not as accurate as the Annual Percentage Rate (APR), which includes fees and other charges 年百分率不如年利率（APR）精确，后者包括各种费用）

annually /ˈænjuəli/ *adverb* each year 每年地 ○ *The figures are updated annually.* 这些数字每年都在更新。

annual return /ˌænjuəl rɪˈtɜːn/ *noun* an official report which a registered company has to make each year to the Registrar of Companies 年度纳税申报表：注册公司每年必须向公司注册处提交的正式报告

annuitant /əˈnjuːɪtənt/ *noun* a person who receives an annuity 领年金者，年金受益人：领取养老金的人

annuity /əˈnjuːɪti/ *noun* money paid each year to a retired person, usually in return for a lump-sum payment. The value of the annuity depends on how long the person lives, as it usually cannot be passed on to another person. Annuities are fixed payments, and lose their value with inflation, whereas a pension can be index-linked 年金,年金保险:指对退休者每年发放的钱款(多用于代替一次性付清的钱款)。年金的价值取决于年金受益人的寿命,因为它不能让渡给他人。年金的支付额是固定的,因而会随通胀而贬值,退休金则可以与物价指数相挂钩 ○ *to buy* or *to take out an annuity* 购买(或申请)年金 ○ *She has a government annuity* or *an annuity from the government*. 她享有政府年金。

annuity certain /əˌnjuːɪti ˈsɜːtən/ *noun* an annuity that provides payments for a specific number of years, regardless of life or death of the annuitant 固定年金:按固定年数支付的年金,不论年金受益人是否在世

annuity contract /əˌnjuːɪti kənˈtrækt/ *noun* a contract under which a person is paid a fixed sum regularly for life 年金合同

antedate /ˌæntɪˈdeɪt/ *verb* to put an earlier date on a document 倒填日期,填早日期 ○ *The invoice was antedated to January 1st*. 发票日期被倒填为1月1日。

anti /ænti/ *prefix* against 表示"反、抗、阻、防、对、排斥"的意义

anti-inflationary /ˌæntiɪnˈfleɪʃ(ə)n(ə)ri/ *adjective* restricting or trying to restrict inflation 反通货膨胀的 ○ *anti-inflationary measures* 反通货膨胀措施

anti-trust /ˌæntɪˈtrʌst/ *adjective* attacking monopolies and encouraging competition 反托拉斯的,反垄断而鼓励竞争的 ○ *anti-trust measures* 反垄断措施

anti-trust laws /ˌæntɪˈtrʌst lɔːz/, **antitrust legislation** /æntɪˌtrʌst ˌledʒɪˈsleɪʃ(ə)n/ *plural noun* laws in the US which prevent the formation of monopolies 反托拉斯法,反垄断法

APB *abbr* **1.** Accounting Principles Board 会计原则委员会 **2.** Auditing Practices Board 审计实务委员会

applicant /ˈæplɪkənt/ *noun* a person who applies for something 申请人;求购者 ○ *an applicant for a job* or *a job applicant* 求职者 ○ *an applicant to an industrial tribunal* 劳动仲裁申请人 ○ *There were thousands of applicants for shares in the new company*. 这家新公司收到数千份股票认购。

application /ˌæplɪˈkeɪʃ(ə)n/ *noun* **1.** the act of asking for something, usually in writing, or a document in which someone asks for something, e.g. a job 申请,正式要求(通常以书面形式呈现);申请信,(表达请求的)文件 ○ *shares payable on application* 申请即付股票 ○ *She sent off six applications for job* or *six job applications*. 她寄出六份求职书。**2.** effort or diligence 努力;勤奋 ○ *She has shown great application in her work on the project*. 她在这个项目的工作中非常努力。

application form /ˌæplɪˈkeɪʃ(ə)n ˌfɔːm/ *noun* a form to be filled in when applying for a new issue of shares or for a job 申请表

application of funds /ˌæplɪˈkeɪʃ(ə)n əv fʌndz/ *noun* details of the way in which funds have been spent during an accounting period (会计期内)资金(的详细)用途

appointment /əˈpɔɪntmənt/ *noun* **1.** an arrangement to meet 约见,约会 ○ *to make* or *to fix an appointment* *with someone for two o'clock* 与某人相约在两点会面 ○ *He was late for his appointment.* 他约会迟到了。○ *She had to cancel her appointment.* 她不得不取消约会。**2.** the act of being appointed to a job, or of appointing someone to a job 被任命,被指定;委任 □ **on his appointment as manager** when he was made manager 他被任命为经理时

apportion /ə'pɔːʃ(ə)n/ *verb* to share out something, e. g. costs, funds or blame 分摊(成本、资金或责任等) ○ *Costs are apportioned according to projected revenue.* 按照预计收入分摊成本。

apportionment /ə'pɔːʃ(ə)nmənt/ *noun* the sharing out of costs 分摊,分配,分派

appraisal /ə'preɪz(ə)l/ *noun* a calculation of the value of someone or something 估价,评估

'...we are now reaching a stage in industry and commerce where appraisals are becoming part of the management culture. Most managers now take it for granted that they will appraise and be appraised'
"在现今的工商界,评价机制已成为管理文化的一部分。在大多数经理人眼中,评价和被评价都是很自然的"[*Personnel Management*《人事管理》]

appraise /ə'preɪz/ *verb* to assess or to calculate the value of something or someone 估价,评价;鉴定

appreciate /ə'priːʃieɪt/ *verb* **1.** to notice how good something is 鉴赏 **2.** (*of currency, shares, etc.*) to increase in value (货币、股票等)升值

appreciation /əˌpriːʃi'eɪʃ(ə)n/ *noun* **1.** an increase in value 增值 Also called 亦称作 **capital appreciation 2.** the act of valuing something highly 高评价,赏识 ○ *She was given a pay rise in appreciation of her excellent work.* 由于工作出色她得到了加薪。

appropriate /ə'prəʊprieɪt/ *verb* to put a sum of money aside for a special purpose 拨款 ○ *to appropriate a sum of money for a capital project* 为资本项目拨款

appropriation /əˌprəʊpri'eɪʃ(ə)n/ *noun* the act of putting money aside for a special purpose 拨款 ○ *appropriation of funds to the reserve* 向储备金的拨款

appropriation account /əˌprəʊpri'eɪʃ(ə)n əˌkaʊnt/ *noun* the part of a profit and loss account which shows how the profit has been dealt with, e.g., how much has been given to the shareholders as dividends and how much is being put into the reserves 拨款账户,分拨账:损益账中表明利润分配的部分,如多少用于向股东发放股利和多少留作储备

approval /ə'pruːv(ə)l/ *noun* the act of saying or thinking that something is good 核准,认可,同意 ○ *to submit a budget for approval* 将预算提交批准

approve /ə'pruːv/ *verb* **1.** □ **to approve of something** to think something is good 赞成,对…表示满意 ○ *The chairman approves of the new company letter heading.* 董事长对新的公司信头表示满意。○ *The sales staff do not approve of interference from the accounts division.* 销售人员对会计部门的干预不满。**2.** to agree to something officially 批准,核定 ○ *to approve the terms of a contract* 批准合同条款 ○ *The proposal was approved by the* *board*. 这项提案得到了董事会批准。

approved accounts /əˌpruːvd əˈkaʊnts/ *noun* accounts that have been formally accepted by a company's board of directors 批准账目：经公司董事会正式接受的账目

approved scheme /əˌpruːvd ˈskiːm/ *noun* a pension scheme or share purchase scheme which has been approved by the Inland Revenue 批准计划：经国内税务局批准的退休金计划或购股计划

approved securities /əˌpruːvd sɪˈkjʊərɪtiz/ *plural noun* state bonds which can be held by banks to form part of their reserves 核定证券：银行持有的可以作为其部分储备金的国家债券（NOTE：The list of these bonds is the 'approved list' 该债券的清单称为 approved list(批准清单)）

approximate /əˈprɒksɪmət/ *adjective* not exact，but almost correct 近似的，大约的 ○ *The sales division has made an approximate forecast of expenditure*. 销售部门对费用作了一个大概的预算。

approximately /əˈprɒksɪmətli/ *adverb* not quite exactly，but close to the figure shown 近似地，大概地 ○ *Expenditure on marketing is approximately 10% down on the previous quarter*. 营销支出比上一季度大约下降了10%。

approximation /əˌprɒksɪˈmeɪʃ(ə)n/ *noun* a rough calculation 近似值，粗略估计 ○ *Each department has been asked to provide an approximation of expenditure for next year*. 每个部门都被要求提供来年的支出估算。○ *The final figure is only an approximation*. 最终的数字只是一个粗略的估值。

APR *abbr* annualised percentage rate 年百分率

APRA *abbr* Australian Prudential Regulation Authority 澳大利亚审慎金融监管局

AR *abbr* accounts receivable 应收账款

arbitrage /ˈɑːbɪˌtrɑːʒ/ *noun* the business of making a profit from the difference in value of various assets，e.g. by selling foreign currencies or commodities on one market and buying on another at almost the same time to profit from different exchange rates，or by buying currencies forward and selling them forward at a later date，to benefit from a difference in prices 套汇，套利，套购：从各种资产的差价中赚取利润，例如由一个市场上买进外汇或商品，而几乎在同一时间内在另一市场上卖出，从而赚取汇率差价；或买进远期外汇过后再卖出，从而赚取差价

arbitrage syndicate /ˈɑːbɪtrɑːʒ ˌsɪndɪkət/ *noun* a group of people who together raise the capital to invest in arbitrage deals 套利辛迪加：专门聚集资金用于套利交易的集团

arbitration /ˌɑːbɪˈtreɪʃ(ə)n/ *noun* the settling of a dispute by an outside party agreed on by both sides 仲裁，公断，调解 ○ *to take a dispute to arbitration* or *to go to arbitration* 将争议提交仲裁(或进行仲裁) ○ *arbitration in an industrial dispute* 劳动纠纷仲裁 ○ *The two sides decided to submit the dispute to arbitration* or *to refer the question to arbitration*. 双方决定将争议(或将问题)提交仲裁。

arbitrator /ˈɑːbɪtreɪtə/ *noun* a person not concerned with a dispute who is chosen by both sides to try to settle it 仲裁员，公断人 ○ *an industrial arbitrator* 劳资仲裁员 ○ *They refused to accept* or *they rejected the arbitrator's ruling*. 他们拒绝接受仲裁员的裁决。

area manager /ˌeəriə ˈmænɪdʒə/ *noun* a manager who is responsible for a company's work in a specific part of the country 地区经理

arithmetic mean /ˌærɪθmetɪk ˈmiːn/ *noun* a simple average calculated by dividing the sum of two or more items by the number of items 算术平均值，算术中间值

around /əˈraʊnd/ *preposition* **1.** approximately 大概，大约 ○ *The office costs around £2,000 a year to heat*. 办公室取暖费一年大约 2,000 英镑。○ *Her salary is around $85,000*. 她的工资是 8.5 万美元左右。**2.** with a premium or discount 表示升水（或贴水）的幅度

ARPS *abbr* adjustable rate preferred stock 可调息优先股

ARR *abbr* accounting rate of return 会计收益率，会计回报率

arrangement fee /əˈreɪndʒmənt fiː/ *noun* a charge made by a bank to a client for arranging credit facilities 安排费：银行就安排信贷融通向客户收取的费用

arrears /əˈrɪəz/ *plural noun* money which is owed, but which has not been paid at the right time 应付欠款，（过期未付的）欠款 ○ *a salary with arrears effective from January 1st* 始于 1 月 1 日的工资拖欠 ○ *We are pressing the company to pay arrears of interest*. 我们敦促公司支付欠付的利息。○ *You must not allow the mortgage payments to fall into arrears*. 你不能拖欠按揭还款。

article /ˈɑːtɪk(ə)l/ *noun* a section of a legal agreement such as a contract or treaty（合同或条约之类的合法协议的）条款 ○ *See article 8 of the contract*. 见合同第八款。

articles of association /ˌɑːtɪk(ə)lz əv əˌsəʊsiˈeɪʃ(ə)n/ *plural noun* a document which lays down the rules for a company regarding such matters as the issue of shares, the conduct of meetings and the appointment of directors 组织章程：规定公司关于发行股票、召开股东大会、董事任命方面的规则性文件 ○ *This procedure is not allowed under the articles of association of the company*. 按公司章程这个程序是不允许的。

articles of incorporation /ˌɑːtɪk(ə)lz əv ɪnˌkɔːpəˈreɪʃ(ə)n/ *plural noun US* a document which sets up a company and lays down the relationship between the shareholders and the company （美）公司章程：公司成立并规定股东与公司关系的文件（NOTE: The UK term is **Memorandum of Association** 英国用语为 **Memorandum of Association**）

ASB *abbr* Accounting Standards Board 会计准则委员会

ASC *abbr* Accounting Standards Committee 会计准则理事会

A shares /ˈeɪ ˌʃeəz/ *plural noun* ordinary shares with limited voting rights or no voting rights at all A 股，甲种普通股：享有有限投票权或没有投票权的普通股

asked price /ˌɑːskd ˈpraɪs/ *noun* a price at which a commodity or stock is offered for sale by a seller, also called ‘offer price’ in the UK 卖方要价，报

价(英国亦称作 offer price)

asking price /ˈɑːskɪŋ ˌpraɪs/ *noun* a price which the seller is hoping will be paid for the item being sold 卖方要价 ○ *the asking price is £24,000* 卖方要价 2.4 万英镑

as per /ˌæz ˈpɜː/ ➧参阅 **per**

assess /əˈses/ *verb* to calculate the value of something or someone 确定,评定,估价 ○ *to assess damages at £1,000* 估计损失为1,000英镑 ○ *to assess a property for the purposes of insurance* 对资产进行投保估价

assessment /əˈsesmənt/ *noun* a calculation of value 估价 ○ *a property assessment* 资产评估 ○ *a tax assessment* 税款估定 ○ *They made a complete assessment of each employee's contribution to the organisation.* 他们就每个员工对组织的贡献作了一次全面评估。

asset /ˈæset/ *noun* something which belongs to a company or person, and which has a value 资产,财产 ○ *He has an excess of assets over liabilities.* 他的资产多过负债。○ *Her assets are only £640 as against liabilities of £24,000.* 她的资产仅有 640 英镑,负债却达 2.4 万英镑之多。

'...many companies are discovering that a well-recognised brand name can be a priceless asset that lessens the risk of introducing a new product'
"许多公司都逐渐认识到,一个知名品牌是一笔无价资产,它能够降低推出新产品的风险"[*Duns Business Month*《邓氏商业月刊》]

asset-backed securities /ˌæsetbækt sɪˈkjʊərɪtiz/ *plural noun* shares which are backed by the security of assets 资产担保证券

asset backing /ˈæset ˌbækɪŋ/ *noun* a support for a share price provided by the value of the company's assets 资产担保:以公司的资产价值支撑股价

asset-rich company /ˌæsetrɪtʃ ˈkʌmp(ə)ni/ *noun* company with valuable tangible assets, such as property, which provide firm backing for its shares 拥有高价值有形资产(如物业)的公司(这些资产为公司股价提供坚强的后盾)

assets /ˈæsets/ *plural noun* liabilities plus owners' equity 资产

asset stripper /ˈæset ˌstrɪpə/ *noun* a person who buys a company to sell its assets 资产倒卖者:购买一家公司然后出售其资产的人

asset stripping /ˈæset ˌstrɪpɪŋ/ *noun* the practice of buying a company at a lower price than its asset value, and then selling its assets 资产剥夺,资产拆卖:以低于其资产价值的价格购买公司,然后将其资产出售

asset turnover ratio /ˌæset ˈtɜːnəʊvə ˌreɪʃiəʊ/ *noun* the number of times assets are turned over by sales during the year, calculated as turnover divided by total assets less current liabilities 资产周转比率:一年内资产通过销售周转的次数,以销售额除以减去流动负债的总资产计算

asset value /ˌæset ˈvæljuː/ *noun* the value of a company calculated by adding together all its assets 资产价值:将公司全部资产相加所得的公司总价值

assign /əˈsaɪn/ *verb* **1.** to give something to someone by means of an official legal transfer 过户,转让 ○ *to assign a right to someone* 将权利转让

给某人 ○ *to assign shares to someone* 将股票过户给某人 **2.** to give someone a job of work to do and make him or her responsible for doing it 指派,分派 ○ *She was assigned the task of checking the sales figures.* 她被派去核对销售额。

assignation /ˌæsɪɡˈneɪʃ(ə)n/ *noun* a legal transfer 转让,过户 ○ *the assignation of shares to someone* 把股份转让给某人 ○ *the assignation of a patent* 专利权转让

assignee /ˌæsaɪˈniː/ *noun* a person who receives something which has been assigned to him or her 受托人,受让人

assignment /əˈsaɪnmənt/ *noun* the legal transfer of a property or right (法律上的)财产转让,权利转让 ○ *the assignment of a patent* or *of a copyright* 专利权(或版权)的转让 ○ *to sign a deed of assignment* 签署转让契据

assignor /ˌæsaɪˈnɔː/ *noun* a person who assigns something to someone (财产、权利等的)转让人

associate /əˈsəʊsiət/ *adjective* linked 有联系的 ■ *noun* **1.** a person who works in the same business as someone 合伙人,伙伴,同事 ○ *She is a business associate of mine.* 她是我的生意伙伴。**2.** a person or company linked to another in a takeover bid 联系人:在兼并中关联的个人或公司

associate company /əˌsaʊsiət ˈkʌmp(ə)ni/ *noun* a company which is partly owned by another company 联营公司,联号:被其他公司部分拥有的公司

associated company /əˌsəʊsieɪtɪd ˈkʌmp(ə)ni/ *noun* a company which is partly owned by another company (though less than 50%), which exerts some management control over it or has a close trading relationship with it 联营公司:被其他公司部分拥有的公司(股权少于 50%),持股公司对联营公司行使一定的管理控制权或者与其保有紧密的业务联系 ○ *Smith Ltd and its associated company, Jones Brothers* 史密斯有限公司和它的联营公司琼斯兄弟公司

associate director /əˌsəʊsiət daɪˈrektə/ *noun* a director who attends board meetings, but has not been elected by the shareholders 联席董事:参加董事会会议但尚未由股东选举选出的董事

Association of Accounting Technicians /əˌsəʊsieɪʃ(ə)n əv əˈkaʊntɪŋ ˌteknɪʃ(ə)nz/ *noun* an organisation which groups accounting technicians and grants membership to people who have passed its examinations 专业会计员协会:专业会计员的组织机构,并为通过其资格考试的人提供会员资格 Abbreviation 缩写 **AAT**

Association of Authorized Public Accountants /əˌsəʊsieɪʃ(ə)n əv ˌɔːθəraɪzd ˌpʌblɪk əˈkaʊntənts/ *noun* an organisation which groups accountants who have been authorised by the government to work as auditors 特许公共会计师协会:经政府批准可从事审计职业的会计师组织

Association of Chartered Accountants in the United States /əˌsəʊsieɪʃ(ə)n əv ˌtʃɑːtəd əˌkaʊntənts ɪn ði juːˌnaɪtɪd ˈsteɪts/ *noun* an organisation representing Chartered Accountants from Australia, Canada, England and Wales, Ireland, New Zealand, Scotland and South Africa who are based in the United States 美国特许会计师协会：澳大利亚、加拿大、英格兰和威尔士、爱尔兰、新西兰、苏格兰和南非的特许会计师的代表组织，总部设在美国 Abbreviation 缩写 **ACAUS**

Association of Chartered Certified Accountants /əˌsəʊsieɪʃ(ə)n əv ˌtʃɑːtəd ˌsɜːtɪfaɪd əˈkaʊntənts/ *noun* an organisation whose members are certified accountants 特许注册会计师协会 Abbreviation 缩写 **ACCA**

Association of Corporate Treasurers /əˌsəʊsieɪʃ(ə)n əv ˌkɔːp(ə)rət ˈtreʒərəz/ *noun* an organisation which groups company treasurers and awards membership to those who have passed its examinations 公司财务经理协会：公司财务经理的组织，为通过其资格考试的人提供会员资格

Association of Financial Advisers /əˌsəʊsieɪʃ(ə)n əv faɪˌnænʃ(ə)l ədˈvaɪzəz/ *noun* a trade association that represents the interests of independent financial advisers 财务顾问协会

Association of Futures Brokers and Dealers /əˌsəʊsieɪʃ(ə)n əv ˈfjuːtʃəz ˌbrəʊkəz ən ˌdiːləz/ *noun* a self-regulating organisation which oversees the activities of dealers in futures and options 期货经纪人及交易商协会：规范期货、期权交易的自律组织 Abbreviation 缩写 **AFBD**

assumable mortgage /əˌsjuːməb(ə)l ˈmɔːɡɪdʒ/ *noun US* a mortgage which can be passed to another person （美）可转让抵押，可承让按揭

assumption /əˈsʌmpʃən/ *noun* a general belief 假设，假定 ○ *We are working on the assumption that the exchange rate will stay the same.* 我们开展工作的基础是假设汇率保持不变。

assurance /əˈʃʊərəns/ *noun* a type of insurance which pays compensation for an event that is certain to happen at some time, especially for the death of the insured person 保险（尤指人寿保险） Also called 亦称作 **life assurance, life insurance**

assure /əˈʃʊə/ *verb* to insure someone, or someone's life, so that the insurance company will pay compensation when that person dies 给…保险，给…投人寿保险 ○ *He has paid the premiums to have his wife's life assured.* 他为他的妻子交了人寿保险费。(NOTE: **Assure, assurer** and **assurance** are used in Britain for insurance policies relating to something which will certainly happen (such as death); for other types of policy (i. e. those against something which may or may not happen, such as an accident) use the terms **insure, insurer** and **insurance** 在英国，**assure**、**assurer** 和 **assurance** 用于与必定会发生的事情（如死亡）有关的保单，其他类型的保单（即针对可能发生也可能不发生的事情的保单，如意外事故）则使用 **insure**、**insurer** 和 **insurance**)

assurer /əˈʃʊərə/, **assuror** *noun* an insurer or a company which insures 保险公司，承保人

AST *abbr* Automated Screen Trading 自动对盘交易系统

at best /ˌæt ˈbest/ *adverb* □ **sell at best** an instruction to a stockbroker to sell shares at the best price possible 以最获利的价格售出：对股票经纪人下达的以尽可能最获利的价格出售股票的指令

at call /ˌæt ˈkɔːl/ *adverb* immediately available （银行）按通知偿付，即期

付款

ATM /ˌeɪ tiː ˈem/ *abbr* automated teller machine 自动提款机

'Swiss banks are issuing new cards which will allow cash withdrawals from ATMs in Belgium, Denmark, Spain, France, the Netherlands, Portugal and Germany'
"瑞士的银行正在发行新型信用卡，持卡人可以在比利时、丹麦、西班牙、法国、荷兰、葡萄牙和德国的自动提款机上提现"[*Banking Technology*《银行业技术》]

'... the major supermarket operator is planning a new type of bank that would earn 90% of its revenue from fees on automated teller machine transactions. With the bank setting up ATMs at 7,000 group outlets nationwide, it would have a branch network at least 20 times larger than any of the major banks'
"主要的超市运营商正在规划一种新型银行，这种银行90%的收入都来自自动提款机的交易费。如果此类银行能在遍布全国的7,000家超市店面布放自动提款机，那么它的分支网络规模将是任何一家大银行的至少20倍"[*Nikkei Weekly*《日经周报》]

at par /ˌæt ˈpɑː/ *phrase* equal to the face value 按面值，平价

at sight /ˌæt ˈsaɪt/ *adverb* immediately, when it is presented 即期，见票即付 ○ *a bill of exchange payable at sight* 见票即付的汇票

attach /əˈtætʃ/ *verb* to fasten or to link 贴；附属 ○ *I am attaching a copy of my previous letter.* 我将附上我上封信的副本。○ *Please find attached a copy of my letter of June 24th.* 请查看随附的本人6月24日信函的副本。○ *The company attaches great importance to good timekeeping.* 公司极重视守时的行为。

attachment /əˈtætʃmənt/ *noun* the act of holding a debtor's property to prevent it being sold until debts are paid 扣押财产，查封

attachment of earnings /əˌtætʃmənt əv ˈɜːnɪŋz/ *noun* legal power to take money from a person's salary to pay money, which is owed, to the court 扣押收入：依法强行从某人的工资中扣除一部分来偿还对法院的欠款

attachment of earnings order /əˌtætʃmənt əv ˈɜːnɪŋz ˌɔːdə/ *noun* a court order to make an employer pay part of an employee's salary to the court to pay off debts 扣押收入令：要求雇主将员工的部分工资支付给法院以偿还债务的法庭命令

attachment order /əˈtætʃmənt ˌɔːdə/ *noun* an order from a court to hold a debtor's property to prevent it being sold until debts are paid 查封令，扣押令：法院作出的查封债务人的财产以防止其变卖，直到债务偿清为止的命令

attest /əˈtest/ *noun* a formal statement, e.g. a statement by an auditor that a company's financial position is correctly stated in the company's accounts 认证，证明(例如审计师关于公司账目如实地反映了公司财务状况的声明)

attributable profit /əˌtrɪbjʊtəb(ə)l ˈprɒfɪt/ *noun* a profit which can be shown to come from a particular area of the company's operations 有归属的利润，可归属利润：可证明为来自公司特定运营领域的利润

auction /ˈɔːkʃən/ *noun* **1.** a method of selling goods where people want to buy compete with each other by saying how much they will offer for it, and the item is sold to the person who makes the highest offer 拍卖 ○ *Their furniture will be sold in the auction rooms next week*. 他们的家具将于下周在拍卖厅拍卖。○ *They announced a sale by auction of the fire-damaged stock*. 他们宣布对因火灾受损的存货进行拍卖。○ *The equipment was sold by auction* or *at auction*. 该设备通过拍卖售出。□ **to put an item up for auction** to offer an item for sale at an auction 把某物进行拍卖 **2.** a method of selling government stock, where all stock on issue will be sold, and the highest price offered will be accepted, as opposed to tendering 出售政府证券的一种方式,所有要发行的证券均售给报价最高者(与投标方式不同) ■ *verb* to sell something at an auction 拍卖 ○ *The factory was closed and the machinery was auctioned off*. 这家工厂倒闭了,其机器被拍卖。

auctioneer /ˌɔːkʃəˈnɪə/ *noun* the person who conducts an auction 拍卖人,拍卖商

auction system /ˈɔːkʃən ˌsɪstəm/ *noun* a system where prices are agreed as the result of marketmakers offering stock for sale on the trading floor (as opposed to a quote system, where prices are quoted on a computerised screen) 拍卖系统:由庄家在交易地点提供待售物品并议定价格的系统(不同于报价系统,后者是在电脑屏幕上提供报价)

audit /ˈɔːdɪt/ *noun* the examination of the books and accounts of a company 审计,查账 ○ *to carry out the annual audit* 进行年审 ■ *verb* to examine the books and accounts of a company 审计,查(账) ○ *Messrs Smith have been asked to audit the accounts*. 请史密斯公司来查账。○ *The books have not yet been audited*. 这些账簿尚未经审计。□ **to audit the stock** to carry out a stock control, in front of witnesses, so as to establish the exact quantities and value of stock 审核存货:在证人面前进行存货控制,以确定存货的确切数量和价值

Audit Commission /ˌɔːdɪt kəˈmɪʃ(ə)n/ *noun* British government agency whose duty is to audit the accounts of ministries and other government departments 审计署 (NOTE: The US term is **General Accounting Office** 美国用语为 **General Accounting Office**)

audited accounts /ˌɔːdɪtɪd əˈkaʊnts/ *noun* a set of accounts that have been thoroughly scrutinised, checked, and approved by a team of auditors 经审核账目,已稽查账目,核定总账,审定决算

audit fee /ˈɔːdɪt fiː/ *noun* a fee charged by an auditor for auditing a company's accounts 审计费,查账费

auditing /ˈɔːdɪtɪŋ/ *noun* the work of examining the books and accounts of a company 审计,查账,审核

Auditing Practices Board /ˌɔːdɪtɪŋ ˈpræktɪsɪz ˌbɔːd/ *noun* a body responsible for developing and issuing professional auditing standards in the United Kingdom and the Republic of Ireland. The APB was created in 1991 following an agreement between the six members of the Consultative Committee of Accountancy Bodies 审计实务委员会:英国及爱尔兰共和国负责制定和颁布专业审计准则的机构,1991年由会计团体咨询委员会的六个成员协定创立 Abbreviation 缩写 **APB**

audit opinion /ˌɔːdɪt əˈpɪnjən/ *noun US* a report of the audit of a company's books, carried out by a certified public accountant（美）审计意见，审计报告（NOTE：The UK term is **accountant's opinion** 英国用语为 **accountant's opinion**）

auditor /ˈɔːdɪtə/ *noun* a person who audits 审计师，审计员，稽核员

auditors' fees /ˈɔːdɪtəz fiːz/ *plural noun* fees paid to a company's auditors，which are approved by the shareholders at an AGM 审计费：支付给公司审计师的费用，金额由股东在年度股东大会上批准

auditors' qualification /ˌɔːdɪtəz ˌkwɒlɪfɪˈkeɪʃ(ə)n/ *noun* a form of words in a report from the auditors of a company's accounts，stating that in their opinion the accounts are not a true reflection of the company's financial position 审计师的保留意见：公司审计师报告中的一种措辞，表明他们认为账目并未真实地反映公司的财务状况 Also called 亦称作 **qualification of accounts**

auditors' report /ˌɔːdɪtəz rɪˈpɔːt/ *noun* a report written by a company's auditors after they have examined the accounts of the company 审计报告（NOTE：If the auditors are satisfied，the report certifies that，in their opinion，the accounts give a 'true and fair' view of the company's financial position 如果对情况表示满意，审计师将在报告中表明他们认为账目真实而公正地反映了公司的财务状况）

audit programme /ˌɔːdɪt ˈprəʊɡræm/ *noun* a listing of all the steps to be taken when auditing a company's accounts 审计程序，审计计划

audit regulation /ˈɔːdɪt ˌreɡjʊleɪʃ(ə)n/ *noun* the regulating of auditors by government（政府的）审计监管

audit report /ˌɔːdɪt rɪˈpɔːt/ *noun* same as 同 **auditors' report**

audit risk /ˈɔːdɪt rɪsk/ *noun* the risk that auditors may give an inappropriate audit opinion on financial statements 审计风险：审计师可能对财务报表提供不恰当的审计意见的风险

audit trail /ˈɔːdɪt treɪl/ *noun* the records that show all the stages of a transaction，e.g. a purchase，a sale or a customer complaint，in the order in which they happened 审计线索，审计脉络：对一项交易的各个阶段（如购买、销售或客户投诉）进行的有序记录（NOTE：An audit trail can be a useful tool for problem-solving and，in financial markets，may be used to ensure that the dealers have been fair and accurate in their proceedings 审计线索是解决问题的有用工具，在金融市场上，它可以用来确保交易员办事公正和准确）

augend /ˈɔːɡend/ *noun* the number to which another number（the addend）is added to produce the sum 被加数：与另外一数（加数）相加来求和的数

Australian Prudential Regulation Authority /ɒˌstreɪliən prʊˌdenʃ(ə)l ˌreɡjʊˈleɪʃ(ə)n ɔːˌθɒrəti/ *noun* a federal government body responsible for ensuring that financial institutions are able to meet their commitments 澳大利亚审慎金融监管局 Abbreviation 缩写 **APRA**

AUT *abbr* authorised unit trust 认可单位信托

authenticate /ɔːˈθentɪkeɪt/ *verb* to say that something is true or genuine 证实，鉴定

authorise /ˈɔːθəraɪz/，**authorize** *verb* **1.** to give permission for something to be done 批准,准许 ○ *to authorise payment of £10,000* 准予支付10,000英镑 **2.** to give someone the authority to do something 委任,授权 ○ *to authorise someone to act on the company's behalf* 授权某人代表公司行事

authorised /ˈɔːθəraɪzd/, **authorized** *adjective* permitted 批准的,准许的

authorised capital /ˌɔːθəˌraɪzd ˈkæpɪt(ə)l/ *noun* an amount of capital which a company is allowed to have, as stated in the memorandum of association 核定资本,法定资本:公司章程中列明的准予公司拥有的资本数额

authorised stock /ˌɔːθəraɪzd ˈstɒk/ *noun* same as 同 **authorised capital**

authorised unit trust /ˌɔːθəraɪzd ˈjuːnɪt trʌst/ *noun* the official name for a unit trust which has to be managed according to EU directives 认可单位信托:须依照欧盟指令管理的单位信托的正式名称 Abbreviation 缩写 **AUT**

automated /ˈɔːtəmeɪtɪd/ *adjective* worked automatically by machines 自动的,自动化的 ○ *a fully automated car assembly plant* 全自动汽车组装厂

Automated Clearing House /ˌɔːtəmeɪtɪd ˈklɪərɪŋ haʊs/ *noun US* an organisation set up by the federal authorities to settle transactions carried out by computer, such as automatic mortgage payments and trade payments between businesses (美)自动化票据交换所:联邦政府建立的、用计算机进行交易结算(如在企业间进行自动按揭付款和交易付款)的组织 Abbreviation 缩写 **ACH**

Automated Screen Trading /ˌɔːtəmeɪtɪd ˈskriːn ˌtreɪdɪŋ/ *noun* a system where securities are bought, sold and matched automatically by computer 自动对盘交易系统:用计算机自动进行证券买卖及对盘的系统 Abbreviation 缩写 **AST**

automated teller machine /ˌɔːtəmeɪtɪd ˈtelə məˌʃiːn/ *noun* a machine which gives out money when a special card is inserted and special instructions given 自动提款机:插入一种特殊的卡片并给予特殊指令后即可提取现金的机器 Abbreviation 缩写 **ATM**

automation /ˌɔːtəˈmeɪʃ(ə)n/ *noun* the use of machines to do work with very little supervision by people 自动,自动化,自动操作

availability /əˌveɪləˈbɪlɪti/ *noun* the fact of being easy to obtain 可得性,可用性

available capital /əˌveɪləb(ə)l ˈkæpɪt(ə)l/ *noun* capital which is ready to be used 可用资金

average /ˈæv(ə)rɪdʒ/ *noun* **1.** a number calculated by adding several figures together and dividing by the number of figures added 平均数 ○ *the average for the last three months* or *the last three months' average* 最近三个月的平均数 ○ *sales average* or *average of sales* 平均销售额 **2.** the sharing of the cost of damage or loss of a ship between the insurers and the owners (海损的)公平分担:由货主和保险商分担海上损坏或丢失的费用 ■ *adjective* equal to the average of a set of figures 平均的 ○ *the average increase in salaries* 工资的平均增长额 ○ *The average cost per unit is too high.* 单位平均成本过高。 ○ *The average sales per* *representative are rising*. 销售代表的平均销售额不断增加。■ *verb* to work out an average figure for something 平均数为…

'...a share with an average rating might yield 5 per cent and have a PER of about 10'
"一支普通评级的股票的收益率可能达到5%,市盈率约为10"[*Investors Chronicle*《投资者纪事》]

'...the average price per kilogram for this season to the end of April has been 300 cents'
"截止4月底本季的每千克平均价格为300分"[*Australian Financial Review*《澳大利亚金融评论报》]

average adjuster /ˌæv(ə)rɪdʒ əˈdʒʌstə/ *noun* a person who calculates how much of a maritime insurance is to be paid by the insurer against a claim 海损理算人

average adjustment /ˌæv(ə)rɪdʒ əˈdʒʌstmənt/ *noun* a calculation of the share of the cost of damage or loss of a ship that an insurer has to pay 海损理算

average due date /ˌæv(ə)rɪdʒ djuː ˈdeɪt/ *noun* the average date when several different payments fall due 平均到期日:几种不同支付日的平均日期

average income per capita /ˌæv(ə)rɪdʒ ˈɪnkʌm pə ˈkæpɪtə/ *noun* same as 同 **per capita income**

average out /ˌæv(ə)rɪdʒ ˈaʊt/ *verb* to come to a figure as an average 平均值为… ○ *It averages out at 10% per annum*. 每年平均达到10%。○ *Sales increases have averaged out at 15%*. 销售增长率平均为15%。

averager /ˈævərɪdʒə/ *noun* a person who buys the same share at various times and at various prices to get an average value 盈亏相抵者:在不同时间以不同价格购买同一股票而取得其平均价格的人

average-sized /ˌævərɪdʒˈsaɪzd/ *adjective* of a similar size to most others, not very large or very small 中等尺寸的,普通尺码的 ○ *They are an average-sized company*. 这是一家中等规模的公司。○ *She has an average-sized office*. 她有一间普通大小的办公室。

averaging /ˈævərɪdʒɪŋ/ *noun* the buying or selling of shares at different times and at different prices to establish an average price 平均法,盈亏相抵:在不同时间以不同价格买入或卖出某一股票以达到平均价格

avoidance /əˈvɔɪd(ə)ns/ *noun* the act of trying not to do something or not to pay something 避免,逃避 ○ *tax avoidance* 避税

award /əˈwɔːd/ *noun* something given by a court, tribunal or other official body, especially when settling a dispute or claim 裁决,裁定 ○ *an award by an industrial tribunal* 由劳资法庭作出的一项裁定 ○ *The arbitrator's award was set aside on appeal*. 经上诉,仲裁决议被驳回。○ *The latest pay award has been announced*. 最新的支付裁决已经宣布。

B

BAA /ˌbiː eɪ ˈeɪ/ *abbr* British Accounting Association 英国会计学会

baby bonds /ˈbeɪbi bɒndz/ *plural noun US* bonds in small denominations which the small investor can afford to buy（美）小额债券：小投资者买得起的小面值债券

back /bæk/ *adjective* referring to the past 过期的，拖欠的 ○ *a back payment* 一笔拖欠款 ■ *verb* to help someone, especially financially 帮助，（尤指）资助 ○ *The bank is backing us to the tune of £10,000.* 银行给我们的贷款多达10,000英镑。○ *She is looking for someone to back her project.* 她正在找人为她的计划提供资助。□ **to back someone** to help someone financially 资助某人 ○ *The bank is backing him to the tune of £100,000.* 银行向他提供总额达100,000英镑的贷款。

'... the businesses we back range from start-up ventures to established companies in need of further capital for expansion'
"不论是正在创业的公司或者是需要资本实现进一步扩张的成熟的公司，都是我们资助的对象"［*Times*《泰晤士报》］

backdate /bækˈdeɪt/ *verb* to put an earlier date on a document such as a cheque or an invoice 倒填日期：在支票、发票等上写上比实际为早的日期 ○ *Backdate your invoice to April 1st.* 将你的发票日期倒填为4月1日。

back duty /ˈbæk ˌdjuːti/ *noun* a duty or tax which is due but has not yet been paid 未缴税款，拖欠税款

back-end loaded /ˌbækend ˈləʊdɪd/ *adjective* referring to an insurance or investment scheme where commission is charged when the investor withdraws his or her money from the scheme（指保险或投资计划）佣金于期末收取的：当投资者从保险或投资计划中抽回资金时收取佣金 Compare 比较 **front-end loaded**

backer /ˈbækə/ *noun* **1.** a person or company that backs someone 赞助人，支持者 ○ *One of the company's backers has withdrawn.* 公司的一个赞助商退出了。**2.** □ **the backer of a bill** the person who backs a bill 票据背书人

backing /ˈbækɪŋ/ *noun* support, especially financial support 支持，（尤指）资金支持 ○ *She has the backing of an Australian bank.* 她得到一家澳大利亚银行的资助。○ *The company will succeed only if it has sufficient backing.* 该公司只有得到足够的资助才能成功。○ *She gave her backing to the proposal.* 她支持这项提议。

'...the company has received the backing of a number of oil companies who are willing to pay for the results of the survey'
"公司得到许多石油公司的资助，他们都愿

意花钱购买勘测结果”[*Lloyd's List*《劳氏日报》]

back interest /ˌbæk ˈɪntrəst/ *noun* interest which has not yet been paid 未付利息

backlog /ˈbæklɒg/ *noun* an amount of work, or of items such as orders or letters, which should have been dealt with earlier but is still waiting to be done 积压的工作；积压的订单；未回复的信件 ○ *The warehouse is trying to cope with a backlog of orders.* 仓库正在尽力处理积压的订单。○ *We're finding it hard to cope with the backlog of paperwork.* 我们发现积压的文书工作难以应付。

backlog depreciation /ˈbæklɒg dɪˌpriːʃieɪʃ(ə)n/ *noun* depreciation which has not been provided in previous accounts because of an increase in the value of the asset during the current year due to inflation 欠提折旧：由于当年资产因通货膨胀升值而未在以前账户中计入的那部分折旧

back office /ˌbæk ˈɒfɪs/ *noun US* the part of a broking firm where the paperwork involved in buying and selling shares is processed（美）结算室：经纪公司进行股票买卖等文书工作的地方

back out /ˌbæk ˈaʊt/ *verb* to stop being part of a deal or an agreement 退出，不履行 ○ *The bank backed out of the contract.* 银行不履行合约。○ *We had to cancel the project when our German partners backed out.* 德国合伙人退出了，我们只好取消了该项目。

back payment /ˈbæk ˌpeɪmənt/ *noun* **1.** a payment which is due but has not yet been paid 拖欠款 **2.** the act of paying money which is owed 补缴拖欠款

back rent /ˈbæk rent/ *noun* a rent due but not paid 欠租，滞纳租金 ○ *The company owes £100,000 in back rent.* 该公司欠租 100,000 英镑。

back tax /ˈbæk tæks/ *noun* tax which is owed 欠税

back-to-back loan /ˌbæktəˌbæk ˈləʊn/ *noun* a loan from one company to another in one currency arranged against a loan from the second company to the first in another currency 背对背贷款，对销贷款：一家公司以一种货币给予另一家公司贷款，同时后一家公司又以另一种货币给予前一家公司相同的贷款 Also called 亦称作 **parallel loan**（NOTE：Back-to-back loans are（used by international companies to get round exchange controls 跨国公司使用背对背贷款来规避外汇管制）

backup /ˈbækʌp/ *adjective* supporting or helping 支持性的，有帮助的 ○ *We offer a free backup service to customers.* 我们向客户提供免费支持服务。○ *After a series of sales tours by representatives, the sales director sends backup letters to all the contacts.* 在销售代表的一系列外出推销之后，销售经理给所有客户寄去了补充信函。

backup copy /ˈbækʌp ˌkɒpi/ *noun* a copy of a computer disk to be kept in case the original disk is damaged（计算机）备份磁盘

backup withholding /ˈbækʌp wɪθˌhəʊldɪŋ/ *noun US* a tax retained from investment income so that the IRS is sure of getting the tax due（美）保证预扣税：从投资收入中保留的税款，以保证国内税务局收到应付税款

backwardation /ˌbækwəˈdeɪʃ(ə)n/

noun **1.** a penalty paid by the seller when postponing delivery of shares to the buyer 交割延期费：卖方因推迟向买方交割股票而交纳的罚金 **2.** a situation where the spot price of a commodity or currency is higher than the futures price 现货溢价：商品或货币的现货价格高于期货价格

backward integration /ˌbækwəd ɪntɪˈɡreɪʃ(ə)n/ *noun* a process of expansion in which a business which deals with the later stages in the production and sale of a product acquires a business that deals with an earlier stage in the same process, usually a supplier 后向整合，后向一体化：产品生产及销售链条的下游企业收购上游企业（通常是供应商），从而实现扩张的过程 ○ *Buying up rubber plantations is part of the tyre company's backward integration policy.* 买进全部橡胶种植园是该轮胎公司后向整合政策的一部分。○ *Backward integration will ensure cheap supplies but forward integration would bring us nearer to the market.* 后向整合可以保证廉价供应，前向整合则让我们更贴近市场。Also called 亦称作 **vertical integration**（NOTE：The opposite is 反义为 **forward integration**）

backwards spreading /ˌbækwədz ˈspredɪŋ/ *noun* spacing income over a period of a number of previous years 后向分散，后向分摊：把收入分摊到若干个先前年度的做法

BACS /bæks/ *noun* a company set up to organise the payment of direct debits, standing orders, salary cheques and other payments generated by computers. It operates for all the British clearing banks and several building societies; it forms part of APACS 银行自动结算服务：对直接扣账、长期自动转账委托、工资支票等费用支付及其他电脑生成的付款进行组织管理的公司。它向所有英国清算银行及若干住屋互助协会提供服务，是英国支付清算协会（APACS）的一部分 Compare 比较 **CHAPS**. Full form 全称为 **Bankers' Automated Clearing Services**

bad bargain /ˌbæd ˈbɑːɡɪn/ *noun* an item which is not worth the price asked 蚀本生意

bad buy /ˌbæd ˈbaɪ/ *noun* a thing bought which was not worth the money paid for it 买得不合算的东西

bad cheque /ˌbæd ˈtʃek/ *noun* a cheque which is returned to the drawer for any reason 退票，空头支票：因某种原因遭退回的支票

bad debt /bæd ˈdet/ *noun* a debt which will not be paid, usually because the debtor has gone out of business, and which has to be written off in the accounts 坏账，呆账：无法收回的应收款项（通常由于债务人破产），企业必须将坏账从资产账目中注销 ○ *The company has written off £30,000 in bad debts.* 该公司注销了三万英镑的坏账。

bad debt provision /bæd ˈdet prəˌvɪʒ(ə)n/ *noun* money put aside in accounts to cover potential bad debts 坏账备抵，坏账准备：用于弥补坏账损失的资金

bad debts recovered /ˌbæd dets rɪˈkʌvəd/ *noun* money formerly classified as bad debts and therefore written off that has since been recovered either wholly or in part 收回呆账，收回已冲销的呆账：全部或部分收回先前已归入呆账并已注销的款项

badges of trade /ˌbædʒɪz əv ˈtreɪd/ *noun* a collection of principles established by case law to determine whether or not a person is trading. If so, he or she is taxed under different rules from non-traders 经营标志：依据判例法判断一个人是否参与经营的原则。经营者和非经营者适用于不同的税收法律

bailment /ˈbeɪlmənt/ *noun* a transfer of goods by someone (the 'bailor') to someone (the 'bailee') who then holds them until they have to be returned to the bailor（财物的）寄托，委托（NOTE: Putting jewels in a bank's safe deposit box is an example of bailment 把珠宝存放在银行的保险箱内就属于寄托）

bail out /ˌbeɪl ˈaʊt/ *verb* to rescue a company which is in financial difficulties 帮助公司摆脱财务困境

'...the government has decided to bail out the bank which has suffered losses to the extent that its capital has been wiped out' "对于因蒙受损失而出现资本赤字的银行，政府决定帮助它们摆脱财务困境"[*South China Morning Post*《南华早报》]

balance /ˈbæləns/ *noun* **1.** the amount which has to be put in one of the columns of an account to make the total debits and credits equal 余额：为使借方总额等于贷方总额而加到账户某一方的数额 □ **balance brought down *or* forward** the closing balance of the previous period used as the opening balance of the current period 结转余额，余额承前：上期期末的余额作为本期期初余额 □ **balance carried down *or* forward** the closing balance of the current period 结转余额，余额转后：本期期末余额 **2.** the rest of an amount owed 欠款差额，尾数 ○ *You can pay £100 deposit and the balance within 60 days.* 你可以先付100英镑定金，其余款项在60天内付清。■ *verb* **1.** to be equal, i.e. the assets owned must always equal the total liabilities plus capital 平衡（即资产 = 负债 + 所有者权益）**2.** to calculate the amount needed to make the two sides of an account equal 结算（使账户两边平衡）○ *I have finished balancing the accounts for March.* 我已将3月份的账目轧平。**3.** to plan a budget so that expenditure and income are equal 作预算（使收入与支出平衡）○ *The president is planning for a balanced budget.* 总裁力求预算平衡。

balanced budget /ˌbælənst ˈbʌdʒɪt/ *noun* a budget where expenditure and income are equal 平衡预算：收支相等的预算

balance off /ˌbæləns ˈɒf/ *verb* to add up and enter the totals for both sides of an account at the end of an accounting period in order to determine the balance 结帐，使平衡：于会计期末对账目两边各项进行总账合计，从而确定余额

balance of payments /ˌbæləns əv ˈpeɪmənts/ *noun* a comparison between total receipts and payments arising from a country's international trade in goods, services and financial transactions 国际收支差额，国际收支平衡表：一个国家在国际贸易中，有关商品、劳务以及资金往来的总收入与总支出的对比 Abbreviation 缩写 **BOP** □ **balance of payments current account** record of imports and exports of goods and services and the flows of money between countries arising from investments 国际收支平衡表中的经常账户：关于进出口商品、劳务以及由于国家间

投资引起的资金流动的记录 □ **long-term balance of payments** record of movements of capital relating to overseas investments and the purchase of companies overseas 长期国际收支：与海外投资和购买海外公司有关的资本流动的记录

balance of payments deficit /ˌbæləns əv ˈpeɪməntz ˌdefɪsɪt/ *noun* a situation when a country imports more than it exports 国际收支逆差：一国进口大于出口

balance of payments surplus /ˌbæləns əv ˈpeɪmənts ˌsɜːpləs/ *noun* a situation where a country sells more to other countries than it buys from them 国际收支顺差：一国进口小于出口

balance sheet /ˈbæləns ʃiːt/ *noun* a statement of the financial position of a company at a particular time, such as the end of the financial year or the end of a quarter, showing the company's assets and liabilities 资产负债表：反映公司某特定时期(例如在会计年度末或季度末)财务状况的报表，表明公司的资产和负债情况 ○ *Our accountant has prepared the balance sheet for the first half-year.* 我们的会计编制好了上半年的资产负债表。○ *The company balance sheet for the last financial year shows a worse position than for the previous year.* 上个财年的资产负债表显示公司的状况比前年还要糟糕。○ *The company balance sheet for 1984 shows a substantial loss.* 公司1984年的资产负债表显示出公司有重大亏损。□ **balance sheet asset value** value of a company calculated by adding together all its assets (资产负债表中的)资产总额 □ **balance sheet date** the date (usually the end of a financial or accounting year) when a balance sheet is drawn up 结算日，资产负债表日：编制资产负债表的日期(通常在财政或会计年度末)

balance sheet audit /ˌbæləns ʃiːt ˈɔːdɪt/ *noun* a limited audit of the items on a company's balance sheet in order to confirm that it complies with the relevant standards and requirements 资产负债表审计：对公司资产负债表上的项目进行的有限审计，以确认其符合相关的标准和要求

balance sheet total /ˌbæləns ʃiːt ˈtəʊt(ə)l/ *noun* in the United Kingdom, the total of assets shown at the bottom of a balance sheet and used to classify a company according to size 资产负债表总额：(英)在资产负债表底端显示的资产总和，用以反映企业规模

balancing item /ˈbælənsɪŋ ˌaɪtəm/, **balancing figure** /ˈbælənsɪŋ ˌfɪɡə/ *noun* an item introduced into a balance sheet to make the two sides balance 平衡项目，平衡数字：在资产负债表中加入以实现两边平衡的项目

balloon /bəˈluːn/ *noun* a loan where the last repayment is larger than the others 气球贷款，大额尾付贷款：其中最后一笔还款数额最大

balloon mortgage /bəˌluːn ˈmɔːɡɪdʒ/ *noun US* a mortgage where the final payment (called a 'balloon payment') is larger than the others 气球式抵押，大额尾付抵押贷款：(美)最后一笔还款额(称为"期末大笔偿还额")比其他还款额大的抵押贷款

BALO *noun* a French government publication that includes financial statements of public companies 法律义务公告栏：法国政府出版物，内容包括上市公司的财务报表 Full form 全称为 **Bulletin des Annonces Légales**

Obligatoires

bank /bæŋk/ *noun* a business which holds money for its clients, lends money at interest, and trades generally in money 银行 ○ *the First National Bank* 第一国家银行 ○ *the Royal Bank of Scotland* 苏格兰皇家银行 ○ *She put all her earnings into the bank.* 她把所有的收入都存进银行。○ *I have had a letter from my bank telling me my account is overdrawn.* 我收到银行通知单，说我的账户已经透支了。■ *verb* to deposit money into a bank or to have an account with a bank 把钱存入银行；在银行开户 ○ *He banked the cheque as soon as he received it.* 他一收到支票就把它存入了银行。

bankable /ˈbæŋkəb(ə)l/ *adjective* acceptable by a bank as security for a loan 银行可承兑的，银行肯担保的

bankable paper /ˌbæŋkəb(ə)l ˈpeɪpə/ *noun* a document which a bank will accept as security for a loan 银行可承兑票据

bank account /ˈbæŋk əˌkaʊnt/ *noun* an account which a customer has with a bank, where the customer can deposit and withdraw money 银行往来账户，银行账户 ○ *to open a bank account* 开立银行账户 ○ *to close a bank account* 结清银行账户 ○ *How much money do you have in your bank account?* 你银行账户里有多少钱？○ *If you let the balance in your bank account fall below £100, you have to pay bank charges.* 如果你的银行账户余额少于100英镑，你就必须付银行手续费。（NOTE: The US term is **banking account** 美国用语为 **banking account**）

bank advance /ˈbæŋk ədˌvɑːns/ *noun* same as 同 **bank loan** ○ *She asked for a bank advance to start her business.* 她申请了一笔银行贷款作为生意的启动资金。

bank balance /ˈbæŋk ˌbæləns/ *noun* the state of a bank account at any particular time 银行账户状态，银行存款余额 ○ *Our bank balance went into the red last month.* 我们的银行存款账户上月出现了赤字。

bank base rate /ˌbæŋk ˈbeɪs ˌreɪt/ *noun* a basic rate of interest, on which the actual rate a bank charges on loans to its customers is calculated 银行基本利率

bank bill /ˈbæŋk bɪl/ *noun* **1.** a bill of exchange by one bank telling another bank, usually in another country, to pay money to someone 银行汇票：一家银行开出的通知另一家银行（通常在异国）付款给某人的汇票 **2.** *US* same as（美）同 **banknote**

bank book /ˈbæŋk bʊk/ *noun* a book given by a bank or building society which shows money which you deposit or withdraw from your savings account or building society account 银行储蓄存折，银行存折 Also called 亦称作 **passbook**

bank borrowing /ˌbæŋk ˈbɒrəʊɪŋ/ *noun* money borrowed from a bank（一家）银行贷款 ○ *The new factory was financed by bank borrowing.* 新工厂通过银行贷款进行融资。

bank borrowings /ˈbæŋk ˌbɒrəʊɪŋz/ *noun* money borrowed from banks（多家）银行贷款

bank card /ˈbæŋk kɑːd/ *noun* a credit card or debit card issued to a customer by a bank for use instead of cash when buying goods or services 银

行卡：银行向客户发放的信用卡或借记卡，在购买产品或服务时代替现金使用（NOTE：There are internationally recognised rules that govern the authorisation of the use of bank cards and the clearing and settlement of transactions in which they are used 在银行卡使用授权及使用银行卡进行交易的结算方面，有国际公认监管规则）

bank certificate /ˈbæŋk səˌtɪfɪkət/ *noun* a document, often requested during an audit, that is signed by a bank official and confirms the balances due or from a company on a specific date 银行证明书：通常在审计时要求提供的经银行官员签署的文件，写明公司在某个特定日期的到期余额或所剩余额

bank charges /ˈbæŋk ˌtʃɑːdʒɪz/ *plural noun* charges which a bank makes for carrying out work for a customer 银行手续费（NOTE：The US term is **service charge** 美国用语为 **service charge**）

bank confirmation /bæŋk ˌkɒnfəˈmeɪʃ(ə)n/ *noun* verification of a company's balances requested by an auditor from a bank 银行确认书：银行按照审计师的要求提供的公司存款余额证明

bank credit /ˈbæŋk ˌkredɪt/ *noun* loans or overdrafts from a bank to a customer 银行信贷

bank deposits /bæŋk dɪˈpɒzɪts/ *plural noun* all money placed in banks by private or corporate customers 银行存款

bank draft /ˈbæŋk drɑːft/ *noun* an order by one bank telling another bank, usually in another country, to pay money to someone 银行汇票

banker /ˈbæŋkə/ *noun* **1.** a person who is in an important position in a bank 银行家 **2.** a bank 银行 ○ *The company's banker is Barclays*. 公司的开户行是巴克莱银行。

banker's acceptance /ˌbæŋkəz əkˈseptəns/ *noun* a bill of exchange guaranteed by a bank 银行承兑汇票

Bankers' Automated Clearing Services /ˌbæŋkəz ˌɔːtəmeɪtɪd ˈklɪərɪŋ ˌsɜːvɪsɪz/ *plural noun* 银行自动结算服务 Full form of **BACS** 为 **BACS** 的全称

banker's credit card /ˌbæŋkəz ˈkredɪt ˌkɑːd/ *noun* a credit card issued by a bank, as opposed to cards issued by stores. Typical such cards are Visa, Access, MasterCard, etc. 银行信用卡：银行签发的信用卡，与商店签发的相对。最常用的信用卡有 Visa 卡、Access 卡、MasterCard 卡等

banker's draft /ˌbæŋkəz ˈdrɑːft/ *noun* a draft payable by a bank in cash on presentation 银行汇票 Abbreviation 缩写 **B/D**

banker's lien /ˌbæŋkəz ˈliːn/ *noun* the right of a bank to hold some property of a customer as security against payment of a debt 银行留置权：银行持有客户的部分财产作为还债抵押的权利

banker's order /ˈbæŋkəz ˌɔːdə/ *noun* an order written by a customer asking a bank to make a regular payment 银行定期付款委托书，本票：客户要求银行代为定期付款的书面委托书 ○ *He pays his subscription by banker's order*. 他用银行本票支付其申购金。

banker's reference /ˌbæŋkəz ˈref(ə)rəns/ *noun* a written report issued by a bank regarding a particular customer's creditworthiness 银行资信证明:银行签发的关于某客户信誉状况的书面报告

bank giro /ˈbæŋk ˌdʒaɪrəʊ/ *noun* a method used by clearing banks to transfer money rapidly from one account to another 银行直接转账制:清算银行使用的账户之间迅速转账的方法

bank holiday /ˌbæŋk ˈhɒlɪdeɪ/ *noun* a weekday which is a public holiday when the banks are closed 银行公休日,法定假日 ○ *New Year's Day is a bank holiday*. 元旦是银行休假日。○ *Are we paid for bank holidays in this job?* 这项工作在银行公休日时付薪吗?

bank identification number /ˌbæŋk ˌaɪdentɪfɪˈkeɪʃ(ə)n ˌnʌmbə/ *noun* an internationally organised six-digit number which identifies a bank for charge card purposes 银行识别代码:一种6位数的国际通用代码,在使用信用卡付费时用来识别发卡银行 Abbreviation 缩写 **BIN**

banking /ˈbæŋkɪŋ/ *noun* the business of banks 银行业;银行业务 ○ *He is studying banking*. 他正在学习银行业务。○ *She has gone into banking*. 她进入了银行业。

banking account /ˈbæŋkɪŋ əˌkaʊnt/ *noun US* an account which a customer has with a bank (美)银行账户

Banking Ombudsman /ˌbæŋkɪŋ ˈɒmbʊdzmən/ *noun* an official whose duty is to investigate complaints by members of the public against banks 银行申诉专员:专门调查公众对银行投诉的官员

banking products /ˌbæŋkɪŋ ˈprɒdʌkts/ *plural noun* goods and services produced by banks for customers, e.g. statements, direct debits 银行产品:银行提供的产品或服务(如对账单、直接借记等)

bank loan /ˈbæŋk ləʊn/ *noun* a loan made by a bank to a customer, usually against the security of a property or asset 银行贷款 ○ *She asked for a bank loan to start her business*. 为了创业,她申请了一笔银行贷款。Also called 亦称作 **bank advance**

bank manager /ˈbæŋk ˌmænɪdʒə/ *noun* the person in charge of a branch of a bank 银行(分行)经理 ○ *They asked their bank manager for a loan*. 他们向银行分部经理申请贷款。

bank mandate /ˈbæŋk ˌmændeɪt/ *noun* a written order to a bank, asking it to open an account and allow someone to sign cheques on behalf of the account holder, and giving specimen signatures and relevant information 银行开户授权书:给银行的书面指令,要求银行开户及允许某人代表账户持有人签署支票,并提供签名样本和相关资料

banknote /ˈbæŋknəʊt/ *noun* **1.** a piece of printed paper money 钞票,纸币 ○ *a counterfeit £20 bantnote* 一张20英镑的假币○ *He pulled out a pile of used bantnotes*. 他掏出一叠旧钞票。(NOTE: The US term is **bill** 美国用语为 **bill**) **2.** *US* a non-interest bearing note, issued by a Federal Reserve Bank, which can be used as cash (美)银行券:联邦储备银行发行的无息票据,可充当现金使用

bank reconciliation /bæŋk ˌrekənsɪlɪˈeɪʃ(ə)n/ *noun* the act of making sure that the bank statements agree with the company's ledgers 银行往来对账:确保银行结单与公司的分类账相符

bank reserves /ˌbæŋk rɪˈzɜːvz/ *noun* cash and securities held by a bank to cover deposits 银行准备金,银行储备:银行持有的作为存款保障的现金和证券

bank return /ˈbæŋk rɪˌtɜːn/ *noun* a regular report from a bank on its financial position 银行营业报告,银行报表

bankrupt /ˈbæŋkrʌpt/ *noun*, *adjective* (a person) who has been declared by a court not to be capable of paying his or her debts and whose affairs are put into the hands of a receiver 破产的;破产者:法院宣布无力偿债同时其业务被接管的(人) ○ *a bankrupt property developer* 一位破产的房地产开发商 ○ *She was adjudicated* or *declared bankrupt*. 她被宣布破产。○ *He went bankrupt after two years in business*. 他经营两年之后破产了。■ *verb* to make someone become bankrupt 使某人破产 ○ *The recession bankrupted my father*. 经济衰退使我父亲破产了。

bankruptcy /ˈbæŋkrʌptsi/ *noun* the state of being bankrupt 破产 ○ *The recession has caused thousands of bankruptcies*. 经济衰退导致数千家企业破产。(NOTE: The plural is **bankruptcies** 复数为 **bankruptcies**)

bankruptcy order /ˈbæŋkrʌptsi ˌɔːdə/ *noun* same as 同 **declaration of bankruptcy**

bankruptcy petition /ˌbæŋkrʌptsi pəˈtɪʃ(ə)n/ *noun* an application to a court asking for an order making someone bankrupt (向法院提交的要求宣布某人破产的)破产申请书

bankruptcy proceedings /ˌbæŋkrʌptsi prəˈsiːdɪŋz/ *plural noun* court case to make someone bankrupt 破产诉讼程序

bank statement /ˈbæŋk ˌsteɪtmənt/ *noun* a written statement from a bank showing the balance of an account at a specific date 银行结单,银行对账单:银行开出的表明在特定日期账户所剩余额的账单

bank syndicate /ˈbæŋk ˌsɪndɪkət/ *noun* a group of major international banks which group together to underwrite a massive loan 银行辛迪加,银团:为共同提供巨额贷款而组成的国际银行集团

bank transfer /ˈbæŋk ˌtrænsfɜː/ *noun* an act of moving money from a bank account to another account 银行转账,银行汇款

bargain /ˈbɑːɡɪn/ *noun* **1.** an agreement on the price of something (关于价格的)协议,合同 ○ *to strike a bargain* or *to make a bargain* 订立合同,成交 **2.** something which is cheaper than usual 廉价商品,便宜货 ○ *That car is a (real) bargain at £500*. 这车才500英镑,真便宜。**3.** a sale and purchase of one lot of shares on the Stock Exchange (证交所的)交易:在证券交易所内进行的股票买卖 ■ *verb* to try to reach agreement about something, especially a price, usually with each person or group involved putting forward suggestions or offers which are discussed until a compromise is arrived at 讨价还价 ○ *You will have to bargain with the dealer if you want a discount*. 你若想打折的话,必须与卖方讨价还价。○ *They spent two hours* *bargaining about* or *over the price*. 他们花了两个小时讨价还价。(NOTE: You bargain **with** someone **over** or **about** or **for** something.)

bargain hunting /ˈbɑːɡɪn ˌhʌntɪŋ/ *noun* looking for cheap goods or shares, which no one has noticed 淘便宜货(或低价股票)

bargaining /ˈbɑːɡɪnɪŋ/ *noun* the act of trying to reach agreement about something, e.g. a price or a wage increase for workers 讨价还价;工资谈判

bargaining position /ˈbɑːɡɪnɪŋ pəˌzɪʃ(ə)n/ *noun* the offers or demands made by one group during negotiations 谈判地位

bargain price /ˌbɑːɡɪn ˈpraɪs/ *noun* a cheap price 廉价 ○ *These carpets are for sale at a bargain price*. 这些地毯廉价出售。

bargain sale /ˌbɑːɡɪn ˈseɪl/ *noun* the sale of all goods in a store at cheap prices 大甩卖,大减价

barter /ˈbɑːtə/ *noun* a system in which goods are exchanged for other goods and not sold for money 易货贸易

'...under the barter agreements, Nigeria will export 175,000 barrels a day of crude oil in exchange for trucks, food, planes and chemicals'
"根据易货贸易协议,尼日利亚将每天出口175,000桶原油,以换取卡车、食品、飞机和化学制品"[*Wall Street Journal*《华尔街日报》]

bartering /ˈbɑːtərɪŋ/ *noun* the act of exchanging goods for other goods and not for money 易货贸易

base /beɪs/ *noun* **1.** the lowest or first position 基础;基数;基期;底价 ○ *Turnover increased by 200%, but started from a low base*. 营业额增长了200%,但基数很低。**2.** a place where a company has its main office or factory, or a place where a businessperson's office is located 基地,大本营,总部 ○ *The company has its base in London and branches in all the European countries*. 该公司总部在伦敦,分支机构遍布欧洲各国。○ *She has an office in Madrid which he uses as a base while travelling in Southern Europe*. 当她在南欧旅行时,她以在马德里的办事处作为基地。■ *verb* □ **to base something on something** to calculate something using something as your starting point or basic material for the calculation 以…为基础(或起点),依据 ○ *We based our calculations on the forecast turnover*. 我们的计算以预计营业额为依据。□ **based on** calculating from 以…为依据,建立在…基础上,从…开始计算 ○ *based on last year's figures* 在去年数字的基础上 ○ *based on population forecasts* 以人口预测为基础

'...the base lending rate, or prime rate, is the rate at which banks lend to their top corporate borrowers'
"基础利率(亦称为优惠利率),是银行向其重要公司客户放贷的利率"[*Wall Street Journal*《华尔街日报》]

'...other investments include a large stake in the Chicago-based insurance company'
"其他投资包括持有这家总部设在芝加哥的保险公司的大量股份"[*Lloyd's List*《劳氏日报》]

base currency /ˈbeɪs ˌkʌrənsi/ *noun* a currency against which exchange rates of other currencies are quoted 基准货币:作为计算其他货币

汇率基准的货币

base period /ˈbeɪs ˌpɪəriəd/ *noun* *US* (美)基准期,基期 **1.** a period against which comparisons are made 作为比较参照对象的期间 **2.** the time that an employee must work before becoming eligible for state unemployment insurance benefits 员工在符合国家失业保险福利的条件之前必须工作的时间期限 ○ *Because she had not worked for the base period, she had to rely on the support of her family when she lost her job.* 由于她工作未满基础期,因此失业时就只能依靠家人的帮助了。○ *The new government shortened the base period, in order to increase social service spending.* 新政府缩短了基础期,以增加社会服务开支。

base-weighted index /ˌbeɪs-ˌweɪtɪd ˈɪndeks/ *noun* an index which is weighted according to the base year 基期加权指数:根据基年进行加权计算的指数

base year /ˈbeɪs jɪə/ *noun* the first year of an index, against which changes occurring in later years are measured 基准年度,基年:指数的第一年,作为衡量其后年度变动的参照

basic /ˈbeɪsɪk/ *adjective* **1.** normal 正常的 **2.** simple, or from which everything starts 简单的,基本的 ○ *She has a basic knowledge of the market.* 她对市场有初步的了解。○ *To work at the cash desk, you need a basic qualification in maths.* 在收银台工作,你要有数学底子。

basic balance /ˌbeɪsɪk ˈbæləns/ *noun* the balance of current account and long-term capital accounts in a country's balance of payments 基本差额:一国(国际)收支差额中的经常项目和长期资本的余额

basic commodities /ˌbeɪsɪk kəˈmɒdɪtiz/ *plural noun* ordinary farm produce, produced in large quantities, e.g. corn, rice or sugar 大宗农产品(例如玉米、大米、蔗糖等)

basic discount /ˌbeɪsɪk ˈdɪskaʊnt/ *noun* a normal discount without extra percentages 基准折扣率,基准折价:没有其他扣除比率的折扣 ○ *Our basic discount is 20%, but we offer 5% extra for rapid settlement.* 我们的基准折扣是 20%,但对快速结算的交易我们再加 5%的额外折扣。

basic pay /ˌbeɪsɪk ˈpeɪ/ *noun* a normal salary without extra payments 基本工资

basic product /ˌbeɪsɪk ˈprɒdʌkt/ *noun* the main product made from a raw material 基本产品:由原材料生产出的主要产品

basic rate /ˌbeɪsɪk ˈreɪt/ *noun* the minimum rate for a job 最低工资

basic rate tax /ˈbeɪsɪk reɪt ˌtæks/ *noun* the lowest rate of income tax 最低所得税率

basic salary /ˌbeɪsɪk ˈsæləri/ *noun* same as 同 **basic pay**

basic wage /ˌbeɪsɪk ˈweɪdʒ/ *noun* same as 同 **basic pay** ○ *The basic wage is £110 a week, but you can expect to earn more than that with overtime.* 基本工资是每周 110 英镑,但如果你加班的话可以挣得更多。

basis /ˈbeɪsɪs/ *noun* **1.** a point or number from which calculations are made 计算基数 ○ *We forecast the turnover on the basis of a 6% price increase.* 我们以价格上涨 6%为基础来预测营业额。(NOTE: The plural is **bases** 复数为 **bases**) **2.** the general terms of agreement or general principles on which something is decided or done（作决定或采取措施的）原则，依据 ○ *This document should form the basis for an agreement*. 该文件应成为协议的基础。○ *We have three people working on a freelance basis*. 我们有三个人是自由职业者。（NOTE：The plural is **bases** 复数为 **bases**）□ **on a short-term, long-term basis** for a short or long period 短期（或长期）○ *He has been appointed on a short-term basis*. 他被短期任用。

basis of apportionment /ˌbeɪsɪs əv əˈpɔːʃ(ə)nmənt/ *noun* a way in which common overhead costs are shared among various cost centres 分配标准，分摊标准：将共同间接费用分配于不同成本中心的方法

basis of assessment /ˌbeɪsɪs əv əˈsesmənt/ *noun* a method of deciding in which year financial transactions should be assessed for taxation 课税标准：确定在哪一年对金融业务进行征税的方法

basis period /ˌbeɪsɪs ˈpɪəriəd/ *noun* the period during which transactions occur, used for the purpose of deciding in which they should be assessed for taxation 基期：交易发生的期间，用于确定征税项目

basis point /ˈbeɪsɪs pɔɪnt/ *noun* an one hundredth of a percentage point (0.01%), the basic unit used in measuring market movements or interest rates 基点：万分之一(0.01%)，用于衡量市场变动或利率的基本单位

basis swap /ˈbeɪsɪs swɒp/ *noun* the exchange of two financial instruments, each with a variable interest calculated on a different rate 基准掉期：以不同的利率为计算基础、具有变动利息的两种金融工具的互换

basket of currencies /ˌbɑːskɪt əv ˈkʌrənsiz/ *noun* same as 同 **currency basket**

batch /bætʃ/ *noun* **1.** a group of items which are made at one time（产品的）一批 ○ *This batch of shoes has the serial number 25-02*. 这批鞋的序列号为 25-02。**2.** a group of documents which are processed at the same time（文件处理的）一批 ○ *Today's batch of invoices is ready to be mailed*. 今天的这批发票可以寄出了。○ *The factory is working on yesterday's batch of orders*. 这家工厂正在生产昨天的那批订单。○ *The accountant signed a batch of cheques*. 会计签发了一批支票。○ *We deal with the orders in batches of fifty at a time*. 我们以 50 份为一批来处理这些订单。■ *verb* to put items together in groups 将…分批 ○ *to batch invoices* or *cheques* 将发票（或支票）分批

batch costing /ˌbætʃ ˈkɒstɪŋ/ *noun* a method of calculating the price of one item as part of a batch of items made at the same time 分批成本计算法：计算同一批产品单位价格的方法

batch number /ˈbætʃ ˌnʌmbə/ *noun* a number attached to a batch 批号 ○ *When making a complaint always quote the batch number on the packet*. 投诉时务请提供包装袋上的批号。

batch processing /ˈbætʃ ˌprəusesɪŋ/ *noun* a system of data processing where information is collected into batches before being loaded into the computer 批处理：先把数据分批，然后再载入计算机的数据处理系统

batch production /ˈbætʃ prəˌdʌkʃən/ *noun* production in batches 批量生产

b/d *abbr* brought down 转下页，过下页

B/D *abbr* banker's draft 银行汇票

bear /beə/ *noun* a person who sells shares, commodities or currency because he or she thinks their price will fall and it will be possible to buy them again more cheaply later 做空头者，卖空的人：预计价格会下跌而卖出股票、商品或货币，并期望以后再廉价买进的人 Opposite 反义 **bull** ■ *verb* **1.** to give interest 附息，生息 ○ *government bonds which bear 5% interest* 利率为5%的政府债券 **2.** to have something, especially to have something written on it 具有，写有 ○ *an envelope which bears a London postmark* 盖有伦敦邮戳的信封 ○ *a letter bearing yesterday's date* 日期为昨天的信 ○ *The cheque bears the signature of the company secretary.* 支票上有公司秘书的签名。○ *The share certificate bears his name.* 股权证上有他的名字。**3.** to pay costs 负担，支付（费用）○ *The costs of the exhibition will be borne by the company.* 展览费由公司负担。○ *The company bore the legal costs of both parties.* 该公司承担双方的诉讼费用。（NOTE: **bearing – bore – borne**）

bear covering /ˈbeə ˌkʌvərɪŋ/ *noun* a point in a market where dealers who sold stock short, now buy back at lower prices to cover their positions 补空：交易者卖空股票之后，再以低价购回以弥补空头的时点

bearer /ˈbeərə/ *noun* a person who holds a cheque or certificate 持票人

bearer bond /ˈbeərə ˌbɒnd/, **bearer security** /ˈbeərə sɪˌkjʊərɪti/ *noun* a bond which is payable to the bearer and does not have a name written on it 不记名债券：向持有者支付的债券，债券上没有所有者的名字

bearing /ˈbeərɪŋ/ *adjective* producing 出产的；计息的 ○ *certificates bearing interest at 5%* 按5%生息的凭证 ○ *interest-bearing deposits* 有息存款

bear market /ˈbeə ˌmɑːkɪt/ *noun* a period when share prices fall because shareholders are selling since they believe the market will fall further 熊市，跌市：因股东看跌市场而卖出股票所导致的股价下跌的时期 Opposite 反义 **bull market**

bear position /ˈbeə pəˌzɪʃ(ə)n/ *noun* a short position, that is, selling shares which you do not own with the intention of buying them back later at a lower price, so as to be able to settle 空头地位：即卖出并不持有的股票，并期望日后以低价买进以便交割

bear raid /ˈbeə reɪd/ *noun* the act of selling large numbers of shares to try to bring down prices 空头打压：大量卖出股票来打压市场的行为

behavioural accounting /bɪˌheɪvjərəl əˈkaʊntɪŋ/ *noun* an approach to the study of accounting that emphasises the psychological and social aspects of the profession in addition to the more technical areas 行为会计：一种会计学研究方法，它不仅强调会计专业里技术性较强的领域，而且还强调会计专业的心理和社会层面

bellwether /ˈbelweðə/ *noun* a leading share which is thought of as an indicator of market trends as a whole, e.g. Lloyds in the UK 领导股，龙头股，领先股：被看作是整体市场走势

风向标的主要股票，如英国的劳埃德银行

below par /bɪˌləʊ ˈpɑː/ *adjective* referring to a share with a market price lower than its par value（股票）市价低于面值

below the line /bɪˌləʊ ðə ˈlaɪn/ *adjective, adverb* used to describe entries in a company's profit and loss account that show how the profit is distributed, or where the funds to finance the loss originate 线下项目的（地）：用于描述公司损益表中的项目，该表显示利润分配方式或弥补亏损所用资金的来源

below-the-line expenditure /bɪˌləʊðəˌlaɪn ɪkˈspendɪtʃə/ *noun* **1.** payments which do not arise from a company's usual activities, e.g. redundancy payments 线下项目支出，例外支出：不属于公司日常经营活动的支出（例如遣散费） **2.** extraordinary items which are shown in the profit and loss account below net profit after taxation, as opposed to exceptional items which are included in the figure for profit before taxation 线下项目：损益表中在税后净利下列示的非常项目（与包括在税前利润中的特殊项目相对）

benchmark /ˈbentʃmɑːk/ *noun* a point or level which is important, and can be used as a reference when making evaluations or assessments 基准：在进行评估或估价时可用作参照的重要点数或级别

benchmark accounting policy /ˌbentʃmɑːk əˈkaʊntɪŋ ˌpɒlɪsi/ *noun* one of a choice of two possible policies within an International Accounting Standard. The other policy is marked as an 'allowed alternative', although there is no indication of preference 基准会计政策：《国际会计准则》中的两种备选政策之一，另一种政策标记为"备选"（实则两种选择无优劣之分）

beneficial interest /ˌbenɪfɪʃ(ə)l ˈɪntrəst/ *noun* a situation where someone is allowed to occupy or receive rent from a house without owning it 受益权：允许某人占有某房产或收取房产的租金，但并不拥有该房产

beneficial occupier /ˌbenɪfɪʃ(ə)l ˈɒkjʊpaɪə/ *noun* a person who occupies a property but does not own it fully 受益占有人：占有但不完全拥有该资产的人

beneficiary /ˌbenɪˈfɪʃəri/ *noun* a person who gains money from something 受益人，受款人 ○ *the beneficiaries of a will* 遗嘱受益人

benefit /ˈbenɪfɪt/ *verb* **1.** to make better or to improve 改善，有益于 ○ *A fall in inflation benefits the exchange rate.* 通货膨胀的下降对汇率有利。 **2.** □ **to benefit from** *or* **by something** to be improved by something, to gain more money because of something 受益于，得益于 ○ *Exports have benefited from the fall in the exchange rate.* 出口因汇率下调而受益。○ *The employees have benefited from the profit-sharing scheme.* 雇员从分红计划中受益。

'...the retail sector will also benefit from the expected influx of tourists'
"预期旅游者的涌入也会使零售业受益"
[*Australian Financial Review*《澳大利亚金融评论报》]

'...what benefits does the executive derive from his directorship? Compensation has increased sharply in recent years and fringe benefits for directors have proliferated'

"管理人员从其职位中得到了哪些好处？薪酬近几年大幅度增加，董事的附加福利也在激增"［*Duns Business Month*《邓氏商业月刊》］

'...salary is negotiable to £30,000, plus car and a benefits package appropriate to this senior post'

"工资面议，最高30,000英镑，外加轿车和与此高级职位配套的福利待遇。"［*Financial Times*《金融时报》］

'California is the latest state to enact a program forcing welfare recipients to work for their benefits'

"加利福尼亚是最新一个通过法案要求领救济者必须工作才能领取救济金的州。"［*Fortune*《财富》］

'...salary range is $54,957 - $81,189, with a competitive benefits package'

"工资介于54,957美元和81,189美元之间，外加优厚的福利待遇"［*Washington Post*《华盛顿邮报》］

benefit in kind /ˌbenɪfɪt ɪn ˈkaɪnd/ *noun* a benefit other than money received by an employee as part of his or her total compensation package, e.g. a company car or private health insurance. Such benefits are usually subject to tax 实物福利：员工获得的作为其总体待遇一部分的非金钱利益，如公司汽车或私人医疗保险，这些利益通常须纳税

Benford's Law /ˈbenfədz lɔː/ *noun* a law discovered by Dr Benford in 1938, which shows that in sets of random numbers, it is more likely that the set will begin with the number 1 than with any other number 本福德法则：本福德博士于1938年发现的法则，它揭示在多组随机数字中，以数字1开头的几率要高于其他数字

BEP *abbr* breakeven point 盈亏平衡点

bequeath /bɪˈkwiːð/ *verb* to leave property, money, etc. (but not freehold land) to someone in a will 遗赠（动产，即不包括完全保有的地产）

bequest /bɪˈkwest/ *noun* something such as property or money (but not freehold land), given to someone in a will 遗赠物，遗产（不包括完全保有的地产）○ *He made several bequests to his staff*. 他给他的职员留下了好几笔遗赠。

beta /ˈbiːtə/ *noun* a measurement of the return on investment in a stock compared against a one percentage point return on the stock market in general: it shows the volatility in the price of the share compared to the FTSE All-Share Index 贝塔：将某支股票的投资回报与总体股市一个百分点回报进行比较的衡量方法，它揭示股价相对于富时全类股指数的波动性

b/f *abbr* brought forward 承前页

BFH *noun* in Germany, the supreme court for issues concerning taxation 德国联邦财务法院：德国处理税务事务的最高法院 Full form 全称为 **Bundesfinanzhof**

bid /bɪd/ *noun* **1.** an offer to buy something at a specific price 递价，出价要约 ⇨ 参阅 **takeover bid** □ **to make a bid for something** to offer to buy something 出价收购 ○ *We made a bid for the house*. 我们报出这房子的买价。○ *The company made a bid for its rival*. 该公司出价收购其竞争对手。□ **to make a cash bid** to offer to pay cash for something 报出现金价 □ **to put in** *or* **enter a bid for something** to offer to buy something, usually in writing 出价买某物（通常是书面的）**2.** an offer to sell something or do a piece of work at a specific price 要价，

开价 ○ *She made the lowest bid for the job*. 她对这份工作开出了最低价。■ *verb* to offer to buy 出价购买 □ **to bid for something** (*at an auction*) to offer to buy something (拍卖中)出价购买 □ **he bid £1,000 for the jewels** he offered to pay £1,000 for the jewels 他出价1,000英镑买这些珠宝

bidder /ˈbɪdə/ *noun* a person who makes a bid, usually at an auction 出价人,投标人 ○ *Several bidders made offers for the house*. 几个投标商报价买这所房子。

bidding /ˈbɪdɪŋ/ *noun* the act of making offers to buy, usually at an auction 喊价,出价;投标 □ **the bidding started at £1,000** the first and lowest bid was £1,000 投标起价是1,000英镑 □ **the bidding stopped at £250,000** the last bid, i. e. the successful bid, was for £250,000 最后成交价是25万英镑 □ **the auctioneer started the bidding at £100** the auctioneer suggested that the first bid should be £100 拍卖师报出100英镑的起价

bid market /ˈbɪd ˌmɑːkɪt/ *noun* a market where there are more bids to buy than offers to sell 买方市场:买盘大于卖盘的市场

bid rate /ˈbɪd reɪt/ *noun* a rate of interest offered on deposits 出价:对存款报出的利率

big business /ˌbɪg ˈbɪznɪs/ *noun* very large commercial firms 大企业

Big Four /ˌbɪg ˈfɔː/ *noun* **1.** the four large British commercial banks: Barclays, Lloyds TSB, HSB and Natwest, now joined by several former building societies that have become banks 英国四大商业银行:指巴克莱、劳埃德、恒生和国民威斯敏斯特(如今几家前身为住房互助协会的银行也加入了其中) **2.** the four largest Japanese securities houses: Daiwa, Nikko, Nomura and Yamaichi 日本四大证券行:大和、日兴、野村、山一

bilateral /baɪˈlæt(ə)rəl/ *adjective* between two parties or countries 双边的 ○ *The minister signed a bilateral trade agreement*. 部长签署了一项双边贸易协定。

bilateral clearing /baɪˌlæt(ə)rəl ˈklɪərɪŋ/ *noun* the system of annual settlements of accounts between some countries, where accounts are settled by the central banks 双边清算:在国家之间进行的年度双边清算的系统,它通过中央银行之间的账户进行清算

bilateral credit /baɪˌlæt(ə)rəl ˈkredɪt/ *noun* credit allowed by banks to other banks in a clearing system, to cover the period while cheques are being cleared 双边信用:清算体系中的银行间信用(适用于结清支票这段期间)

bill /bɪl/ *noun* **1.** a written list of charges to be paid 账单 ○ *The sales assistant wrote out the bill*. 销售助理开出了账单。○ *Does the bill include VAT?* 账单包括增值税吗?○ *The bill is made out to Smith Ltd*. 账单是开给史密斯有限公司的。○ *The builder sent in his bill*. 建筑商送来了他的账单。○ *She left the country without paying her bills*. 她未付清账单就离开了该国。**2.** a list of charges in a restaurant (餐馆里的)账单 ○ *Can I have the bill please?* 请给我结账好吗?○ *The bill comes to £20 including service*. 算上服务费,账单共计20英镑。○ *Does the bill include service?* 账单里包括服务费吗?○ *The waiter has added 10% to the bill for service*. 服务员在账单里加了10%的服务费。**3.** a written paper promising to pay money 汇票 □ **bills payable** (**B** ***or*** **P**) bills, especially bills of exchange, which a company will have to pay to its creditors 应付票据(尤指商业汇票) □ **bills receivable** (**B** ***or*** **R**) bills, especially bills of exchange, which are due to be paid by a company's debtors 应收票据(尤指商业汇票) **4.** *US* same as (美)同 **banknote** ○ *a $5 bill* 一张五美元的钞票 (NOTE: The UK term is **note** or **banknote** 英国用语为 **note** 或 **banknote**) **5.** a draft of a new law which will be discussed in Parliament 议案,法案 ■ *verb* to present a bill to someone so that it can be paid 开账单 ○ *The plumbers billed us for the repairs.* 水管工人给我们开了维修账单。

bill broker /ˈbɪl ˌbrəʊkə/ *noun* a discount house, a firm which buys and sells bills of exchange for a fee 票据经纪公司:通过买卖汇票获取收入的贴现公司

billing /ˈbɪlɪŋ/ *noun* the work of writing invoices or bills 开发票,开账单

billion /ˈbɪljən/ *noun* one thousand million 10 亿 (NOTE: In the USA, it has always meant one thousand million, but in UK English it formerly meant one million million, and it is still sometimes used with this meaning. With figures it is usually written **bn**: **$5bn** say 'five billion dollars' 该词在美国专指 10 亿,但在英国它最初指 10,000 亿,现在有时仍用该义。连带数字的时候它通常写为 **bn**: **$5bn**,即"50 亿美元")

'...gross wool receipts for the selling season to end June 30 appear likely to top $2 billion'
"截至到 6 月 30 日销售季节结束,羊毛销售毛收入可能要超过 20 亿美元" [*Australian Financial Review*《澳大利亚金融评论报》]

'...at its last traded price the bank was capitalized at around $1.05 billion'
"根据最近的交易价格,该银行的核定资本大约为 10.5 亿美元" [*South China Morning Post*《南华早报》]

bill of exchange /ˌbɪl əv ɪksˈtʃeɪndʒ/ *noun* a document, signed by the person authorising it, which tells another person or a financial institution to pay money unconditionally to a named person on a specific date 汇票:由出票人签发的委托付款人在特定日期无条件付款给指定收款人的票据 (NOTE: Bills of exchange are usually used for payments in foreign currency 汇票通常用于外汇支付)

bill of lading /ˌbɪl əv ˈleɪdɪŋ/ *noun* a list of goods being shipped, which the transporter gives to the person sending the goods to show that the goods have been loaded 提单:所运货物的清单,它由承运人交给托运人以示货物已装载

bill of sale /ˌbɪl əv ˈseɪl/ *noun* a document which the seller gives to the buyer to show that the sale has taken place 出货单,销售证:卖方提供给买方以证明销售已发生的单据

bill payable /ˌbɪl ˈpeɪəb(ə)l/ *noun* a promissory note or bill of exchange payable 应付汇票

bill receivable /ˌbɪl rɪˈsiːvəb(ə)l/ *noun* a promissory note or bill of exchange receivable 应收汇票

BIN *abbr* bank identification number 银行识别代码

bin card /ˈbɪn kɑːd/ *noun* a stock record card in a warehouse 存料卡:记录仓库里存货的卡片

bind /baɪnd/ *verb* to tie or to attach 束缚，限制（NOTE：**binding – bound**）

binder /ˈbaɪndə/ *noun US* a temporary agreement for insurance sent before the insurance policy is issued（美）暂保单，临时保险单：在正式保险单签发之前的临时保险协议（NOTE：The UK term is **cover note** 英国用语为 **cover note**）

binding /ˈbaɪndɪŋ/ *adjective* being a legal requirement that someone does something 有（法律）约束的，有束缚力的 ○ *a binding contract* 有约束力的合同 ○ *This document is not legally binding.* 这个文件没有法律约束力。

BiRiLiG *noun* the 1985 German accounting directives law 1985 年德国会计指令法 Full form 全称为 **Bilanzrichtliniengesetz**

black economy /blæk ɪˈkɒnəmi/ *noun* goods and services which are paid for in cash, and therefore not declared for tax 黑色经济，隐蔽经济：通过现金结算商品和劳务交易，因而未申报纳税的经济活动 Also called 亦称作 **hidden economy, parallel economy, shadow economy**

black market /ˌblæk ˈmɑːkɪt/ *noun* the buying and selling of goods or currency in a way which is not allowed by law 黑市：非法进行商品或货币买卖的市场 ○ *There is a flourishing black market in spare parts for cars.* 汽车配件的黑市交易很猖獗。

blank /blæŋk/ *adjective* with nothing written on it 空白的

blank cheque /ˌblæŋk ˈtʃek/ *noun* a cheque with the amount of money and the payee left blank, but signed by the drawer 空白支票：经出票人签字但不写明金额或受票人的支票

blanket lien /ˌblæŋkɪt ˈliːn/ *noun US* a lien on a person's property, including personal effects（美）全部留置权，全部扣押权：对某人财产（包括私人财物）的留置权

blind trust /ˈblaɪnd trʌst/ *noun* a trust set up to run a person's affairs without the details of any transaction being known to the person concerned 保密委托，隐蔽信托：指对当事人有关事务进行运作，而不透露有关当事人任何交易详情的一种委托形式（NOTE：Blind trusts are set up by politicians to avoid potential conflicts of interest 政界人士通过保密委托来避免潜在的利益冲突）

block /blɒk/ *noun* a series of items grouped together 一批，一组 ○ *I bought a block of 6,000 shares.* 我买了 6,000 股的大宗股票。■ *verb* to stop something taking place 阻止 ○ *He used his casting vote to block the motion.* 他行使了决定性否决权以阻止这项动议。○ *The planning committee blocked the redevelopment plan.* 计划委员会否决了这一再开发计划。

block booking /ˌblɒk ˈbʊkɪŋ/ *noun* an act of booking of several seats or rooms at the same time（座位或房间的）成批预订 ○ *The company has a block booking for twenty seats on the plane* or *for ten rooms at the hotel.* 该公司在飞机上团订了 20 个座位（或在酒店预订了 10 个房间）。

blocked account /ˌblɒkt əˈkaʊnt/ *noun* a bank account which cannot be used, usually because a government has forbidden its use 冻结账户，封存账户：通常为政府禁止动用的账户

blocked currency /ˌblɒkt ˈkʌrənsi/ *noun* a currency which cannot be taken out of a country because of government exchange controls 冻结货币：因为政府外汇管制而不能带出国的货币 ○ *The company has a large account in blocked roubles*. 该公司有大量卢布冻结在账户上。

blocked funds /ˌblɒkt ˈfʌndz/ *noun* money that cannot be transferred from one place to another, usually because of exchange controls imposed by the government of the country in which the funds are held 冻结资金：因为政府的外汇管制而被禁止转移的资金

block trading /ˌblɒk ˈtreɪdɪŋ/ *noun* trading in very large numbers of shares 大宗股票交易

blowout /ˈbləʊaʊt/ *noun US* a rapid sale of the whole of a new stock issue (*informal*)（美，非正式）所有新发行股票的迅速售出

Blue Book /ˌbluː ˈbʊk/ *noun* an annual publication of national statistics of personal incomes and spending patterns 蓝皮书：国民收入和消费的年度统计报告

blue chip /ˈbluː tʃɪp/ *noun* a very safe investment, a risk-free share in a good company 蓝筹股，绩优股：业绩优良的公司的无风险股票，是一种极为安全的投资

Blue list /ˈbluː lɪst/ *noun US* a daily list of municipal bonds and their ratings, issued by Standard & Poors（美）蓝色清单：标准普尔公司发布的美国市政公债及其信用等级的每日一览表

blue sky laws /ˌbluː ˈskaɪ ˌlɔːz/ *plural noun US* state laws to protect investors against fraudulent traders in securities（美）《蓝天法》：美国各州为防止证券交易中的欺诈行为而制定的保护投资者的法律

board /bɔːd/ *noun* **1.** ➧ 参阅 **board of directors** ○ *He sits on the board as a representative of the bank*. 他作为银行代表参加董事会。○ *Two directors were removed from the board at the AGM*. 在年度股东大会上罢免了两名董事。**2.** a group of people who run an organisation, trust or society 委员会：管理企业、信托公司或社团的一组人员 **3.** □ **on board** on a ship, plane or train 在船（或飞机、火车）上 ■ *verb* to go on to a ship, plane or train 登上（船、飞机或火车）○ *Customs officials boarded the ship in the harbour*. 海关官员登上了停在港口的那条船。

'CEOs, with their wealth of practical experience, are in great demand and can pick and choose the boards they want to serve on'

"由于执行总裁具有丰富的实践经验，所以市场需求很大，他们可以自由选择愿意效力的董事会"［*Duns Business Month*《邓氏商业月刊》］

board meeting /ˈbɔːd ˌmiːtɪŋ/ *noun* a meeting of the directors of a company 董事会会议

Board of Customs and Excise /bɔːd əv ˌkʌstəmz ən ɪkˈsaɪz/ *noun* the ruling body of the Customs and Excise 关税与消费税局

board of directors /ˌbɔːd əv daɪˈrektəz/ *noun* 董事会 **1.** a group of directors elected by the shareholders to run a company［由股东选出的负责管理公司的一批董事］○ *The bank has two representatives on the board of directors*. 董事会里有两位银行代表。**2.** *US* a group of people elected by the shareholders to draw up company policy and to appoint the president and other executive officers who are responsible for managing the company（美）[由公司股东选出的制定公司政策、任命总裁及其他管理人员的团体]

'...a proxy is the written authorization an investor sends to a stockholder meeting conveying his vote on a corporate resolution or the election of a company's board of directors'
"委托书是投资者送交股东大会、内附其对公司决议或董事会选举的投票的书面授权书"[*Barrons*《巴伦》]

Board of Inland Revenue /bɔːd əv ˌɪnlənd ˈrevənjuː/ *noun* the ruling body of the Inland Revenue, appointed by the Treasury 国内税务局：财政部指定的国内税收管理机构

bona fide /ˌbəʊnə ˈfaɪdi/ *adjective* trustworthy, which can be trusted 真诚的，诚信的

bond /bɒnd/ *noun* **1.** a contract document promising to repay money borrowed by a company or by the government on a specific date, and paying interest at regular intervals 债券，付款保证书：公司或政府承诺在某特定日期偿还所借款项，并定期支付利息的契约性文件 **2.** □ **goods (held) in bond** goods held by customs until duty has been paid 保税货物：未缴纳关税前先存入海关保税仓库，直至完税后才能提走的货物 □ **entry of goods under bond** bringing goods into a country in bond 保税货物进关 □ **to take goods out of bond** to pay duty on goods so that they can be released by customs（完税后）从保税仓库中提走货物 **3.** a form of insurance fund which is linked to a unit trust, but where there is no yield because the income is automatically added to the fund 保险基金的一种形式，它与单位投资信托相挂钩，但因收入会自动加入基金而不会产生收益

bond discount /ˌbɒnd dɪsˈkaʊnt/ *noun* the difference between the face value of a bond and the lower price at which it is issued 债券折价：债券面值与其发行时的较低价之差

bonded /ˈbɒndɪd/ *adjective* held in bond 保税的

bonded warehouse /ˌbɒndɪd ˈweəhaʊs/ *noun* a warehouse where goods are stored until excise duty has been paid 保税仓库

bondholder /ˈbɒndhəʊldə/ *noun* a person who holds government bonds 债券持有人

bondised /ˈbɒndaɪzd/, **bondized** *adjective* referring to an insurance fund linked to a unit trust（保险基金）与单位投资信托相挂钩的

bond market /ˈbɒnd ˌmɑːkɪt/ *noun* a market in which government or municipal bonds are traded 债券市场

bond premium /ˌbɒnd ˈpriːmiəm/ *noun* the difference between the face value of a bond and a higher price at which it is issued 债券溢价：债券面值与其发行时的较高价之差

bond-washing /ˈbɒndˌwɒʃɪŋ/ *noun* the act of selling securities cum dividend and buying them back later ex dividend, or selling US Treasury bonds with the interest coupon, and buying them back ex-coupon, so as to reduce tax 债券清洗：卖出带息证券并待支付股利后再买进，或卖出带息的美国国库券并待支付利息后再低价买进，从而减少税务支出

bond yield /ˈbɒnd jiːld/ *noun* income produced by a bond, shown as a percentage of its purchase price 债券收益:债券带来的收入,用购买价的百分比表示

bonus /ˈbəʊnəs/ *noun* an extra payment in addition to a normal payment 红利,奖金,津贴

bonus issue /ˌbəʊnəs ˈɪʃuː/ *noun* a scrip issue or capitalisation issue, where a company transfers money from reserves to share capital and issues free extra shares to the shareholders. The value of the company remains the same, and the total market value of shareholders' shares remains the same, the market price being adjusted to account for the new shares 红股派送:作为红利发放的股票。公司把留存收益账户的资金转到股本账户,因而相当于发行了一些新股。公司价值在发行前后没变,股东持有股票的市值总额也没变,只是股票的市场价格会因新股的流通而作调整 Also called 亦称作 **share split** (NOTE: The US term is **stock dividend** or **stock split** 美国用语为 **stock dividend** 或 **stock split**)

bonus share /ˈbəʊnəs ʃeə/ *noun* an extra share given to an existing shareholder 红利股:给现有股东的额外股票

book /bʊk/ *noun* **1.** a set of sheets of paper attached together 册,簿;账本,账簿 ▫ **a company's books** the financial records of a company 公司账簿 **2.** a statement of a dealer's exposure to the market, i.e. the amount which he or she is due to pay or has borrowed 交易商的市场敞口报告(即他的应付款项或已借款的数额) ▫ **to make a book** to have a list of shares which he or she is prepared to buy or sell on behalf of clients 列出股票清单:列出准备代客户买卖的股票一览表

bookkeeper /ˈbʊkkiːpə/ *noun* a person who keeps the financial records of a company or an organization 簿记员,记账员

bookkeeping /ˈbʊkkiːpɪŋ/ *noun* the work of keeping the financial records of a company or an organization 簿记

bookkeeping barter /ˌbʊkkiːpɪŋ ˈbɑːtə/ *noun* the direct exchange of goods between two parties without the use of money as a medium, but using monetary measures to record the transaction 簿记易货贸易:交易双方不使用货币而直接交易商品,但使用货币手段来记录交易

bookkeeping transaction /ˈbʊkkiːpɪŋ trænˌzækʃən/ *noun* a transaction which involves changes to a company's books of accounts, but does not alter the value of the company in any way, e.g. the issue of bonus shares 簿记交易:只影响公司账面记录而不以任何方式改变公司资产价值的交易,例如派送红股

book of account /ˌbʊk əv əˈkaʊnt/ *noun* an account book, a book which records financial transactions 账簿,账册

book of prime entry /ˌbʊk əv ˌpraɪm ˈentri/ *noun* a chronological record of a business's transactions arranged according to type, e.g., cash or sales. The books are then used to generate entries in a double-entry bookkeeping system 原始账簿:按时间顺序分类(如现金或销售)呈列业务交易的记录,这些账簿随后用于生成复式簿记系统中的分录 Also called 亦称作 **book of original entry**

book sales /ˈbʊk seɪlz/ *plural noun* sales as recorded in the sales book 账

面销售额

books of prime entry /ˌbʊks əv ˌpraɪm ˈentri/ *plural noun* books of account recording a company's financial transactions 原始账簿

book value /ˈbʊk væljuː/ *noun* the value of an asset as recorded in the company's balance sheet 账面价值

boom /buːm/ *noun* a time when sales, production or business activity are increasing 高涨，景气，繁荣 ○ *a period of economic boom* 经济繁荣期 ○ *the boom of the 1990s* 20 世纪 90 年代的繁荣

boom industry /ˈbuːm ˌɪndəstri/ *noun* an industry which is expanding rapidly 迅速增长的行业

booming /ˈbuːmɪŋ/ *adjective* expanding or becoming prosperous 发展的，繁荣的 ○ *a booming industry* or *company* 迅速发展的行业（或公司）○ *Technology is a booming sector of the economy*. 科技业是一个迅速发展的经济板块。

boost /buːst/ *noun* help given to increase something 提高，推动 ○ *This publicity will give sales a boost*. 这次宣传对销售有推动作用。○ *The government hopes to give a boost to industrial development*. 政府希望推动工业的发展。■ *verb* to make something increase 使增加，提高 ○ *We expect our publicity campaign to boost sales by 25%*. 我们预期这次宣传活动能使销售额增加 25%。○ *The company hopes to boost its market share*. 公司希望扩大其市场份额。○ *Incentive schemes are boosting production*. 奖励机制推动着产量的提高。

'...the company expects to boost turnover this year to FFr 16bn from FFr 13.6bn last year'
"今年该公司预期把销售额从去年的 136 亿法国法郎增加到 160 亿法国法郎"［*Financial Times*《金融时报》］

BOP *abbr* balance of payments 国际收支差额

border /ˈbɔːdə/ *noun* a frontier between two countries 边境，国境

border tax adjustment /ˈbɔːdə tæks əˌdʒʌstmənt/ *noun* a deduction of indirect tax paid on goods being exported or imposition of local indirect tax on goods being imported 边境税调整：出口商品退税，即退还已征的间接税，或按国内间接税对进口商品征税

borrow /ˈbɒrəʊ/ *verb* **1.** to take money from someone for a time, possibly paying interest for it, and repaying it at the end of the period 借（款），借贷 ○ *She borrowed £1,000 from the bank*. 她从银行借了 1,000 英镑。○ *The company had to borrow heavily to repay its debts*. 公司不得不大量贷款来偿还债务。○ *They borrowed £25,000 against the security of the factory*. 他们以工厂作抵押借了 2.5 万英镑。**2.** to buy at spot prices and sell forward at the same time 以现货价买进同时以期货方式转手出售

borrower /ˈbɒrəʊə/ *noun* a person who borrows 借款人 ○ *Borrowers from the bank pay 12% interest*. 银行的借款人需支付 12%的利息。

borrowing /ˈbɒrəʊɪŋ/ *noun* the action of borrowing money 借款（行为）○ *The new factory was financed by bank borrowing*. 这家新工厂通过银行贷款融资。

'...we tend to think of building societies as

having the best borrowing rates and indeed many do offer excellent terms'
"我们通常认为住房互助协会提供最优惠的借款利率,事实上他们中有许多的确提供十分优惠的条款"[*Financial Times*《金融时报》]

borrowing costs /ˈbɒrəʊɪŋ kɒsts/ *plural noun* the interest and other charges paid on money borrowed 借贷成本:指贷款利息和其他费用

borrowing power /ˈbɒrəʊɪŋ ˌpaʊə/ *noun* the amount of money which a company can borrow 借款能力:一个公司的借款限额

borrowings /ˈbɒrəʊɪŋz/ *plural noun* money borrowed 借款 ○ *The company's borrowings have doubled*. 该公司的欠债翻了一倍。

bottom /ˈbɒtəm/ *verb* to reach the lowest point 触底 □ **the market has bottomed out** the market has reached the lowest point and does not seem likely to fall further 市场已触底

bottom line /ˌbɒtəm ˈlaɪn/ *noun* **1.** the last line on a balance sheet indicating profit or loss 账本底线,盈亏一览结算线:列于资产负债表的最后一行,显示利润或亏损 □ **the boss is interested only in the bottom line** he is only interested in the final profit 老板只对最终的利润感兴趣 **2.** the final decision on a matter 最终结果 ○ *The bottom line was that the work had to completed within budget*. 最终结果是工作必须在预算范围内完成。

bottom-up budgeting /ˌbɒtəm-ˈʌp ˌbʌdʒɪtɪŋ/ *noun* same as 同 **participative budgeting**

bought day book /bɔːt deɪ bʊk/ *noun* a book used to record purchases made on credit 赊购货物日记账

bought ledger /ˈbɔːt ˌledʒə/ *noun* a book in which purchases are recorded 进货总账;进货分类账

bought ledger clerk /ˌbɔːt ˈledʒə ˌklɑːk/ *noun* an office employee who deals with the bought ledger or the sales ledger 登记进货或销售分类账的职员

bounce /baʊns/ *verb* to be returned by the bank to the person who has tried to cash it, because there is not enough money in the payer's account to pay it 拒付支票:因付款人账户金额不足,支票被银行拒付并退回给试图兑现者 ○ *She paid for the car with a cheque that bounced*. 她用一张拒付支票支付购车款。

bracket /ˈbrækɪt/ *noun* a group of items or people taken together 一组,一批 □ **she is in the top tax bracket** she pays the highest level of tax 她按最高税率标准纳税

branch accounts /ˌbrɑːntʃ əˈkaʊnts/ *plural noun* accounts showing transactions belonging to the branches of a large organisation, i.e., between a branch and other branches or its head office, or other companies outside the organization 分支机构账户:列示大机构的分支机构交易的账户,即分支机构与其他分支机构或其总公司之间,或与集团外部的公司之间的交易

branch manager /ˌbrɑːntʃ ˈmænɪdʒə/ *noun* a person in charge of a branch of a company 分公司经理

'...a leading manufacturer of business, industrial and commercial products requires a branch manager to head up its mid-western Canada operations based in Winnipeg'
"一家工商业产品的主要制造商需要一名分公司经理去领导其在加拿大中西部以温尼

伯为基地的经营业务”[*Globe and Mail* (*Toronto*)《环球邮报》(多伦多)]

branch office /ˌbrɑːntʃ ˈɒfɪs/ *noun* a less important office, usually in a different town or country from the main office 分支机构,分公司,分行

brand /brænd/ *noun* a make of product, which can be recognised by a name or by a design 商标,品牌,牌子 ○ *the top-selling brands of toothpaste* 最畅销的牙膏品牌○ *The company is launching a new brand of soap*. 该公司正推出一个新的肥皂品牌。

'...the multiple brought the price down to £2.49 in some stores. We had not agreed to this deal and they sold out very rapidly. When they reordered we would not give it to them. This kind of activity is bad for the brand and we cannot afford it'
“这家连锁店在一些店面把价格降到了2.49英镑。虽然产品很快就销售一空,但我们并不赞同这种做法。当他们再次订货时,我们已不再接受他们的订单了。因为他们的这种行为会对品牌造成负面影响,这是我们无法接受的”[*The Grocer*《食品商》]

'...you have to look much further down the sales league to find a brand which has not been around for what seems like ages'
“新生品牌在销售排行上总是靠后站”[*Marketing*《市场》]

'...major companies are supporting their best existing brands with increased investment'
“大公司纷纷增加投资支持他们现有的最佳品牌”[*Marketing Week*《市场周刊》]

brand name /ˈbrænd neɪm/ *noun* a name of a particular make of product 品牌名称

breach /briːtʃ/ *noun* a failure to carry out the terms of an agreement 违反;破坏;不履行

breach of contract /ˌbriːtʃ əv ˈkɒntrækt/ *noun* the failure to do something which has been agreed in a contract 违约

breach of trust /ˌbriːtʃ əv ˈtrʌst/ *noun* a situation where a person does not act correctly or honestly when people expect him or her to 失职,背信

break /breɪk/ *noun* **1.** a pause between periods of work 中止,暂停 ○ *She keyboarded for two hours without a break*. 她连续不停地敲了两个小时键盘。○ *She typed for two hours without a break*. 她连续打了两个小时的字。**2.** a sharp fall in share prices 股价暴跌 ■ *verb* **1.** to fail to carry out the duties of a contract 违反,违背 ○ *The company has broken the contract* or *the agreement by selling at a lower price*. 该公司违约低价出售商品。**2.** to cancel a contract 取消,中止(合同) ○ *The company is hoping to be able to break the contract*. 公司希望能够取消合同。(NOTE: [all verb senses] **breaking – broke – broken**)

breakages /ˈbreɪkɪdʒɪz/ *plural noun* breaking of items (物品的)破损,破碎 ○ *Customers are expected to pay for breakages*. 顾客损坏物品须赔偿。

break down /ˌbreɪk ˈdaʊn/ *verb* **1.** to stop working because of mechanical failure 出故障 ○ *The fax machine has broken down*. 传真机坏了。**2.** to stop 停止 ○ *Negotiations broke down after six hours*. 六小时后谈判破裂了。**3.** to show all the items in a total list of costs or expenditure 将(成本或开支)分项列出,按细目分类 ○ *We broke the expenditure down into fixed and variable costs*. 我们将费用分列为固定成本和可变成本。

breakdown /ˈbreɪkdaʊn/ *noun* **1.** an act of stopping working because of mechanical failure 故障，损坏 ○ *We cannot communicate with our Nigerian office because of the breakdown of the telephone lines.* 因为电话线路故障，我们无法与尼日利亚办事处取得联系。**2.** an act of stopping talking 谈话中止；谈判中止 ○ *a breakdown in wage negotiations* 工资谈判破裂 **3.** an act of showing details item by item 细目，分门别类 ○ *Give me a breakdown of investment costs.* 给我一份投资成本分类细账。

breakeven /ˌbreɪkˈiːv(ə)n/ *verb* to balance costs and receipts, so as to make neither a profit nor a loss 收支相抵，损益平衡 ○ *last year the company only just broke even* 去年公司仅仅不赔不赚 ○ *we broke even in our first two months of trading* 我们在头两个月的营业中收支相抵 ■ *noun* a situation where there is neither a profit nor a loss 收支相抵，无盈亏

breakeven analysis /breɪkˈiːv(ə)n əˌnæləsɪs/ *noun* **1.** the analysis of fixed and variable costs and sales that determines at what level of production the breakeven point will be reached 保本分析：关于固定与可变成本及销售额的分析，以确定在什么生产水平线上，能够达到保本 ○ *The breakeven analysis showed that the company will only break even if it sells at least 1,000 bicycles a month.* 保本分析表明，每月必须售出最少1,000辆自行车，公司才能保本。**2.** a method of showing the point at which a company's income from sales will be equal to its production costs so that it neither makes a profit nor makes a loss 损益两平分析：表明在什么情况下公司的销售收入将等于其生产成本、令其既无盈利亦无亏损的分析方法（NOTE：Breakeven analysis is usually shown in the form of a chart and can be used to help companies make decisions, set prices for their products and work out the effects of changes in production or sales volume on their costs and profits 保本分析通常用图表来表示，可用来帮助公司作出决策、设定产品价格及确定产量或销量变动对成本和利润的影响）

breakeven point /breɪkˈiːv(ə)n pɔɪnt/ *noun* the point or level of financial activity at which expenditure equals income, or the value of an investment equals its cost so that the result is neither a profit nor a loss 盈亏平衡点，保本点：支出等于收入或投资价值等于成本、既无盈利亦无亏损的金融活动点或水平 Abbreviation 缩写 **BEP**

break-out /ˈbreɪkaʊt/ *noun* a movement of a share price above or below its previous trading level 突破：股价较以前交易水平上升或下降

break up /ˌbreɪk ˈʌp/ *verb* to split something large into small sections 分列，拆散 ○ *The company was broken up and separate divisions sold off.* 公司已经解散，各部门也被拆卖。

break-up value /ˈbreɪkʌp ˌvæljuː/ *noun* **1.** the value of the material of a fixed asset 残值：固定资产的材料价值 ○ *What would the break-up value of our old machinery be?* 我们的旧机器的残值是多少？○ *Scrap merchants were asked to estimate the tractors' break-up value.* 废品收购商被请来对这台拖拉机的残值进行估价。**2.** the value of various parts of a company taken separately 拆卖价值：公司各个部分分别出售所得的价值

bribe /braɪb/ *noun* money given secretly and usually illegally to someone in authority to get them to help 贿赂 ○ *The minister was dismissed for taking a bribe*. 部长因受贿而被免职。

bricks-and-mortar /ˌbrɪksən-ˈmɔːtə/ *adjective* referring to the fixed assets of a company, especially its buildings 公司固定资产的(尤指建筑物),实体的

bridge finance /ˈbrɪdʒ ˌfaɪnæns/ *noun* loans to cover short-term needs 过渡性融资,临时筹资:满足短期需要的贷款

bridging loan /ˈbrɪdʒɪŋ ləʊn/ *noun* a short-term loan to help someone buy a new house when the old one has not yet been sold 临时贷款,过渡性贷款:在某人尚未售出旧房子时,用于帮助其购买新房子的短期贷款(NOTE: The US term is **bridge loan** 美国用语为 **bridge loan**)

bring down /ˌbrɪŋ ˈdaʊn/ *verb* to reduce 降低,减少 ○ *Petrol companies have brought down the price of oil*. 石油公司降低了油价。

bring forward /ˌbrɪŋ ˈfɔːwəd/ *verb* **1.** to make something take place earlier 使提前 ○ *to bring forward the date of repayment* 将还款日期提前 ○ *The date of the next meeting has been brought forward to March*. 下次会议的时间被提前到了 3 月份。**2.** to take an account balance from the end of the previous period as the starting point for the current period 承前页,结转:将上期期末账目余额作为当期账目起点 ○ *Balance brought forward: £365.15*. 结转余额:365.15 英镑。

bring in /ˌbrɪŋ ˈɪn/ *verb* to earn an amount of interest 获取(利息) ○ *The shares bring in a small amount*. 这些股票赚了点小钱。

British Accounting Association /ˌbrɪtɪʃ əˈkaʊntɪŋ əˌsəʊsieɪʃ(ə)n/ an organisation whose aim is to promote accounting education and research in the United Kingdom 英国会计学会 Abbreviation 缩写 **BAA**

broker /ˈbrəʊkə/ *noun* a dealer who acts as a middleman between a buyer and a seller 经纪人

brokerage /ˈbrəʊkərɪdʒ/, **broker's commission** /ˌbrəʊkəz kəˈmɪʃ(ə)n/ *noun* **1.** payment to a broker for a deal carried out 经纪人佣金 **2.** same as 同 **broking**

brokerage firm /ˈbrəʊkərɪdʒ fɜːm/, **brokerage house** /ˈbraʊkərɪdʒ haʊs/ *noun* a firm which buys and sells shares for clients (股票)经纪人公司

broker-dealer /ˌbrəʊkəˈdiːlə/ *noun* a dealer who buys shares and holds them for resale, and also deals on behalf of investor clients 自营经纪人:进行个人股票买卖同时也代客户买卖股票的交易商

broker's commission /ˌbrəʊkəz kəˈmɪʃ(ə)n/ *noun* the payment to a broker for a deal which he or she has carried out 经纪人佣金:经纪人进行一次交易所收取的费用(NOTE: Formerly, the commission charged by brokers on the London Stock Exchange was fixed, but since 1986, commissions have been variable 以前伦敦证券交易所经纪人佣金是固定的,但自 1986 年以后改为可变佣金)

broking /ˈbrəʊkɪŋ/ *noun* the business of dealing in stocks and shares (从事股票和证券交易的)经纪业

brought down /ˌbrɔːt ˈdaʊn/,

brought forward /ˌbrɔːt ˈfɔːwəd/ *noun* balance in an account from the previous period taken as the starting point for the current period 承前，结转：将上期期末账目余额作为当期账目起点 ○ *Balance brought down or forward: £365.15.* 结转余额：365.15 英镑。Abbreviation 缩写 **b/d, b/f**

B/S *abbr* balance sheet 资产负债表

B shares /ˈbiː ˌʃeəz/ *plural noun* ordinary shares with special voting rights, often owned by the founder of a company and his or her family B股：附带特殊投票权的普通股，通常由公司创始人及其家族成员拥有

buck /bʌk/ *noun US* a dollar (*informal*)（美，非正式）（一）美元

bucket shop /ˈbʌkɪt ʃɒp/ *noun* a firm that sells cheap airline or other travel tickets (*informal*)（非正式）销售廉价机票（或其他车船票）的公司

'... at last something is being done about the thousands of bucket shops across the nation that sell investment scams by phone'
"终于对全国数以千计通过电话实施投资诈骗的投机公司采取了措施"[*Forbes Magazine*《福布斯杂志》]

budget /ˈbʌdʒɪt/ *noun* **1.** a plan of expected spending and income for a period of time 预算：一定时期内的预期收入与支出的计划 ○ *to draw up a budget for salaries for the coming year* 制订来年的工资预算 ○ *We have agreed the budgets for next year.* 我们同意了下一年度的预算。**2.** □ **the Budget** the annual plan of taxes and government spending proposed by a finance minister. In the UK, the budget is drawn up by the Chancellor of the Exchequer 财政预算：由财政部长提出的年度国家税收收入和政府支出的财政计划；在英国，财政预算由财政大臣制定 ○ *The minister put forward a budget aimed at boosting the economy.* 财政部长提出了旨在促进经济增长的财政预算。■ *verb* to plan probable income and expenditure 编制预算 ○ *We are budgeting for £10,000 of sales next year.* 我们计划明年的销售额会达到一万英镑。

'... he budgeted for further growth of 150,000 jobs (or 2.5 per cent) in the current financial year'
"他计划在本财政年度内再增加 15 万个（或 2.5%）就业岗位"[*Sydney Morning Herald*《悉尼先驱晨报》]

'... the Federal government's budget targets for employment and growth are within reach according to the latest figures'
"根据最新数字，联邦政府能够实现就业和经济增长方面的预算"[*Australian Financial Review*《澳大利亚金融评论报》]

budget account /ˈbʌdʒɪt əˌkaʊnt/ *noun* a bank account where you plan income and expenditure to allow for periods when expenditure is high, by paying a set amount each month 预算账户：允许客户对收支进行计划的银行账户，在开支较多时允许每月支付固定金额

budgetary /ˈbʌdʒɪt(ə)rɪ/ *adjective* referring to a budget 预算的

budgetary control /ˌbʌdʒɪt(ə)ri kənˈtrəʊl/ *noun* controlled spending according to a planned budget 预算控制

budgetary policy /ˌbʌdʒɪt(ə)ri ˈpɒlɪsi/ *noun* the policy of planning income and expenditure 预算政策

budgetary requirements /ˌbʌdʒɪt(ə)ri rɪˈkwaɪəməntz/ *plural noun* the rate of spending or income required to meet the budget forecasts 预算需要，所需预算经费

budget committee /ˌbʌdʒɪt kəˈmɪti/ *noun* the group within an organisation responsible for drawing up budgets that meet departmental requirements, ensuring they comply with policy, and then submitting them to the board of directors 预算委员会：组织内部设立的团队，负责根据有关政策和部门需要编制预算，并提交董事会

Budget Day /ˈbʌdʒɪt deɪ/ *noun* the day when the Chancellor of the Exchequer presents the budget to Parliament. This is usually in March, but with an advance budget statement in November 预算日：财政大臣向议会提交预算的日期，预算日通常是在每年 3 月份，但需先在上年 11 月份提交预告预算书

budget deficit /ˈbʌdʒɪt ˌdefɪsɪt/ *noun* 预算赤字 **1.** a deficit in a country's planned budget, where income from taxation will not be sufficient to pay for the government's expenditure [在国家财政预算中，税收收入不足以支付政府开支的赤字情况] **2.** a deficit in personal finances where a household will borrow to finance large purchases which cannot be made out of income alone [在个人家庭理财中，需要借贷来完成单靠收入不足以支付的大额购买的赤字情况]

budget department /ˈbʌdʒɪt dɪˌpɑːtmənt/ *noun* a department in a large store which sells cheaper goods (大型商店中的)廉价商品部

budget director /ˌbʌdʒɪt daɪˈrektə/ *noun* the person in an organisation who is responsible for running the budget system 预算主任：机构中预算系统的负责人

budgeted capacity /ˌbʌdʒɪtɪd kəˈpæsɪti/ *noun* an organisation's available output level for a budget period according to the budget. It may be expressed in different ways, e.g., in machine hours or standard hours 预算产能：根据预算，机构在预算期间的可用产能。它可通过不同的方式来表述，如机器运转时间或标准时数

budgeted revenue /ˌbʌdʒɪtɪd ˈrevənjuː/ *noun* the income that an organisation expects to receive in a budget period according to the budget 预算收入

budgeting /ˈbʌdʒɪtɪŋ/ *noun* the preparation of budgets to help plan expenditure and income 预算编制

budget lapsing /ˈbʌdʒɪt ˌlæpsɪŋ/ *noun* withdrawal of unspent budget allowance due to the expiry of the budget period 预算失效，预算终止：因预算期届满而撤销未支出的预算准备款项

budget manual /ˌbʌdʒɪt ˈmænjuəl/ *noun* a handbook or set of documents that detail budgetary procedure for a company or organization 预算指南，预算手册

budget period /ˌbʌdʒɪt ˈpɪəriəd/ *noun* a period of time covered by a budget 预算期

budget variance /ˌbʌdʒɪt ˈveəriəns/ *noun* the difference between the cost as estimated for a budget and the actual cost 预算差异：预算估计成本与实际成本之差

buffer stocks /ˈbʌfə ˈstɒks/ *plural noun* stocks of a commodity bought by an international body when prices are low and held for resale at a time when prices have risen, with the intention of reducing sharp fluctuations in world prices of the commodity 缓冲存货,调节存量:国际组织在低价时购入、准备在价格上升时再售出的存货,以缓和国际市场上商品价格的剧烈波动

building and loan association /ˌbɪldɪŋ ən ˈləʊn əˌsəʊsieɪʃ(ə)n/ *noun US* same as (美)同 **savings and loan**

building society /ˈbɪldɪŋ səˌsaɪəti/ *noun* a financial institution which accepts and pays interest on deposits, and lends money to people who are buying property against the security of the property which is being bought 建房贷款互助会,住房互助协会:提供购房抵押贷款的金融机构。它专门接受存款并支付利息,同时以所购房产为抵押向购房者提供贷款 ○ *We put our savings into a building society* or *into a building society account*. 我们将节余存入住房互助协会(账户)。○ *I have an account with the Nationwide Building Society*. 我在全国住房互助协会开立了一个账户。○ *I saw the building society manager to ask for a mortgage*. 我找了住房互助协会的经理,要求获得抵押贷款。

build into /ˈbɪld ˌɪntuː/ *verb* to include something in something which is being set up 使成为…的一部分 ○ *You must build all the forecasts into the budget*. 你必须把所有预测情况都编入预算。

build up /ˌbɪld ˈʌp/ *verb* **1.** to create something by adding pieces together 建立,建成,组合 ○ *She bought several shoe shops and gradually built up a chain*. 她买下几家鞋店,并逐渐把它们组建成了一个连锁店。**2.** to expand something gradually 逐渐扩张,逐渐建立 ○ *to build up a profitable business* 逐步扩展盈利业务 ○ *to build up a team of sales representatives* 逐渐扩大销售代表队伍

buildup /ˈbɪldʌp/ *noun* a gradual increase 增进,逐渐增加 ○ *a buildup in sales* or *a sales buildup* 销售额的逐渐增加 ○ *There will be a big publicity buildup before the launch of the new model*. 新型号推出之前,将会有一场大规模的广告宣传。○ *There has been a buildup of complaints about customer service*. 关于客服的投诉逐渐增多。

built-in obsolescence /ˈbɪltɪn ɒbsəˌles(ə)ns/ *noun* a method of ensuring continuing sales of a product by making it in such a way that it will soon become obsolete 产品的内在报废,商品内在陈旧性:在设计产品时有意令其很快过时,以确保新产品持续销售的手段

bulk buying /ˌbʌlk ˈbaɪɪŋ/ *noun* the act of buying large quantities of goods at low prices (低价)大批购买,大量采购

bull /bʊl/ *noun* a person who believes the market will rise, and therefore buys shares, commodities or currency to sell at a higher price later 买空者,做多头者:因相信市场行情会上升而购买股票、商品或货币以便在将来价格较高时售出的人 Opposite 反义 **bear**

'...lower interest rates are always a bull factor for the stock market'
"较低的利率对股市来说总是一个利好消息"[*Financial Times*《金融时报》]

bullet bond /ˈbʊlɪt bɒnd/ *noun US* a eurobond which is only redeemed when it is mature (美)一次性偿还债券:只有到期才可赎回的欧元债券 (NOTE: Bullet bonds are used in payments between central banks and also act as currency backing 它用于中央银行之间的支付以及作为货币储备）

bullet loan /ˈbʊlɪt ləʊn/ *noun US* a loan which is repaid in a single payment（美）一次性偿还贷款：到期一次还本付息的贷款

bullion /ˈbʊliən/ *noun* a gold or silver bars 金条；银条；金块；银块 ○ *A shipment of gold bullion was stolen from the security van.* 一批金条被从押运车上盗走了。○ *The price of bullion is fixed daily.* 金价是每日确定的。

bull market /ˈbʊl ˌmɑːkɪt/ *noun* a period when share prices rise because people are optimistic and buy shares 牛市，上涨行情 Opposite 反义 **bear market**

bull position /ˈbʊl pəˌzɪʃ(ə)n/ *noun* a strategy of buying shares in the hope that they will rise 多头地位：期望股票会上涨而买进股票

bumping /ˈbʌmpɪŋ/ *noun US* a lay-off procedure that allows an employee with greater seniority to displace a more junior employee（美）（职位的）排挤 ○ *The economic recession led to extensive bumping in companies where only the most qualified were retained for some jobs.* 经济衰退导致各公司职位广遭排挤，只有一些最胜任的人被留下。○ *The trade unions strongly objected to bumping practices since they considered that many employees were being laid off unfairly.* 工会对职位排挤表示强烈反对，因为他们认为许多员工被裁毫无道理。

business /ˈbɪznɪs/ *noun* **1.** work in buying, selling or doing other things to make a profit 生意，商业；业务 ○ *We do a lot of business with Japan.* 我们同日本有许多商业往来。○ *Business is expanding.* 业务正在扩展。○ *Business is slow.* 商业不景气。○ *Repairing cars is 90% of our business.* 汽车修理占我们业务的 90%。○ *We did more business in the week before Christmas than we usually do in a month.* 圣诞节前的一周，我们的业务量比平时一个月还要多。○ *Strikes are very bad for business.* 罢工使商业遭受很大损失。○ *What's your line of business?* 你做什么生意？**2.** a commercial company 公司，商行 ○ *He owns a small car repair business.* 他拥有一个小的修车铺。○ *She runs a business from her home.* 她在家经营一个小公司 ○ *I set up in business as an insurance broker.* 我开办了一家保险经纪公司。**3.** the affairs discussed 讨论的事项 ○ *The main business of the meeting was finished by 3 p.m.* 会议主要议程到下午 3 点结束了。

Business Accounting Deliberation Council /ˌbɪznɪs əˌkaʊntɪŋ dɪˌlɪbəˈreɪʃ(ə)n ˌkaʊns(ə)l/ *noun* in Japan, a committee controlled by the Ministry of Finance that is responsible for drawing up regulations regarding the consolidated financial statements of listed companies（日本）企业会计审议委员会：日本财务省的下属委员会，负责制定上市公司综合财务报表的规则

business address /ˈbɪznɪs əˌdres/ *noun* the details of number, street and town where a company is located（公司）营业地址

business call /ˈbɪznɪs kɔːl/ *noun* a visit to talk to someone about business 商务拜访：拜访某人以洽谈生意

business card /ˈbɪznɪs kɑːd/ *noun*

a card showing a businessperson's name and the name and address of the company he or she works for 商务名片

business centre /ˈbɪznɪs ˌsentə/ *noun* the part of a town where the main banks, shops and offices are located 商业中心

business combination /ˌbɪznɪs ˌkɒmbɪˈneɪʃ(ə)n/ *noun* an action when one or more businesses become subsidiaries of another business 商业合并:一家公司或多家公司被另一家公司兼并成为子公司的行为

business computer /ˈbɪznɪs kəmˌpjuːtə/ *noun* a powerful small computer programmed for special business uses 商用计算机

business correspondence /ˈbɪznɪs kɒrɪˌspɒndəns/ *noun* letters concerned with a business 商业信函

business cycle /ˈbɪznɪs ˌsaɪk(ə)l/ *noun* the period during which trade expands, slows down and then expands again 商业周期:贸易从扩展到放缓到再扩展的周期 Also called 亦称作 **trade cycle**

business day /ˈbɪznɪs deɪ/ *noun* a weekday when banks and stock exchanges are open for business (银行和证券交易所的)营业日

business expenses /ˈbɪznɪs ɪkˌspensɪz/ *plural noun* money spent on running a business, not on stock or assets 营业费用:用于经营(而非用于购买股票和资产)的费用

business hours /ˈbɪznɪs ˌaʊəz/ *plural noun* the time when a business is open, usually 9.00 a.m. to 5.30 p.m. 营业时间(一般是上午 9 点到下午 5 点半)

businessman /ˈbɪznɪsmæn/ *noun* a man engaged in business 商人;实业家

business name /ˈbɪznɪs neɪm/ *noun* a name used by a company for trading purposes 商号名称

business plan /ˈbɪznɪs plæn/ *noun* a document drawn up to show how a business is planned to work, with cash flow forecasts, sales forecasts, etc., often used when trying to raise a loan, or when setting up a new business 企业计划:关于企业怎样运作以及现金流量预测、销售预测等事项的文件,通常用于申请贷款或设立新企业

business property relief /ˌbɪznɪs ˌprɒpəti rɪˈliːf/ *noun* in the United Kingdom, a reduction in the amount liable to inheritance tax on certain types of business property 企业财产减免:英国对某类企业财产给予的继承税减免

business ratepayer /ˌbɪznɪs ˈreɪtpeɪə/ *noun* a business which pays local taxes on a shop, office, factory, etc. 商业纳税人:为名下所属的商店、办事处、工厂等支付地方税的企业

business rates /ˈbɪznɪs reɪts/ *noun* in the United Kingdom, a tax on businesses calculated on the value of the property occupied. Although the rate of tax is set by central government, the tax is collected the local authority 商业地方税:在英国按所占用财产价值计算的商业税。税率由中央政府设定,税款则由地方机构收取

business review /ˌbɪznɪs rɪˈvjuː/ *noun* a report on business carried out over the past year. It forms part of the directors' report 经营回顾报告:关于在过去一年中开展业务的报告,它构成董事会报告的一部分

business segment /ˌbɪznɪs seg'ment/ *noun* a section of a company which can be distinguished from the rest of the company by its own revenue and expenditure 业务部门:有自己的收入和支出,可以和公司其他部门相区别的部门

business transaction /'bɪznɪs trænˌzækʃən/ *noun* an act of buying or selling 商业交易

business travel /ˌbɪznɪs 'træv(ə)l/ *noun* travel costs incurred in the course of work, as opposed to private travel or daily travel to your usual place of work 商务旅行,出差

businesswoman /'bɪznɪswʊmən/ *noun* a woman engaged in business 女商人;女企业家

buy /baɪ/ *verb* to get something by paying money 买,购进 ○ *to buy wholesale and sell retail* 批发买进,零售卖出 ○ *to buy for cash* 现金购买 ○ *She bought 10,000 shares*. 她买了一万股股票。○ *The company has been bought by its leading supplier*. 该公司被其主要供应商收购了。(NOTE: **buying – bought**) □ **to buy at best** to buy securities at the best price available, even if it is high 以最佳价格买进:以最有利的价格(即使是高价格)买进证券

buy back /ˌbaɪ 'bæk/ *verb* to buy something which you sold earlier 回购:买回自己先前售出的某物 ○ *She sold the shop last year and is now trying to buy it back*. 她去年卖掉了这家店铺,现在正试图买回来。

buyback /'baɪbæk/ *noun* **1.** a type of loan agreement to repurchase bonds or securities at a later date for the same price as they are being sold 债券回购:在以后某个日期按原来的售价购回债券的贷款协议 **2.** an international trading agreement where a company builds a factory in a foreign country and agrees to buy all its production 回购协议:国际贸易协议的一种,即公司在外国设立工厂,并承诺将购买该工厂的全部产品

'... the corporate sector also continued to return cash to shareholders in the form of buy-backs, while raising little money in the form of new or rights issues'
"企业还在以回购的方式继续向股东返还现金,但通过发行新股或权利股筹集到的资金却很少"[*Financial Times*《金融时报》]

buyer /'baɪə/ *noun* **1.** a person who buys 买方 **2.** a person who buys stock on behalf of a trading organisation for resale or for use in production 进货代表:代表商业机构购买存货以便再出售或在生产中使用的人

buyer's market /'baɪəz ˌmɑːkɪt/ *noun* a market where products are sold cheaply because there are few people who want to buy them 买方市场 Opposite 反义 **seller's market**

buy in /ˌbaɪ 'ɪn/ *verb* **1.** (*of a seller at an auction*) to buy the thing which you are trying to sell because no one will pay the price you want (拍卖中卖方)买回:因为无人肯出卖方预期的价格,卖方买回自己想卖出的东西 **2.** to buy stock to cover a position 补进(股票):买进股票以抵补头寸 **3.** (*of a company*) to buy its own shares (公司)买进自己的股票

buying /'baɪɪŋ/ *noun* the act of getting something for money 购买

buying department /'baɪɪŋ dɪˌpɑːtmənt/ *noun* the department in a company which buys raw materials or goods for use in the company（公司）采购部门

buying power /ˈbaɪɪŋ ˌpaʊə/ *noun* the ability to buy 购买力 ○ *The buying power of the pound has fallen over the last five years.* 英镑的购买力在过去五年里持续下降。

buyout /ˈbaɪaʊt/ *noun* the purchase of a controlling interest in a company 垄断性收购:购买一家公司的控股权益

'...we also invest in companies whose growth and profitability could be improved by a management buyout'
"我们也投资于那些可以通过管理层收购来促进增长和提高盈利的公司"［*Times*《泰晤士报》］

'...in a normal leveraged buyout, the acquirer raises money by borrowing against the assets or cash flow of the target company'
"在一般的举债收购中,购买者用目标公司的资产或现金流量作为抵押来筹集资金"［*Fortune*《财富》］

bylaws /ˈbaɪlɔːz/ *noun* a rule made by a local authority or organisation, and not by central government 地方法规;公司规章:由地方机构或组织(而非中央政府)制定的规则

by-product /ˈbaɪˌprɒdʌkt/ *noun* a product made as a result of manufacturing a main product 副产品

C

c/a *abbr* capital account 资本账户

C/A *abbr* current account 往来账户；活期存款账户

cage /keɪdʒ/ *noun US*（美）**1.** the part of a broking firm where the paperwork involved in buying and selling shares is processed 文书室：经纪公司分理股票买卖中所涉文书工作的部门（NOTE：The UK term is **back office** 英国用语为 **back office**）**2.** a section of a bank where a teller works, surrounded by glass windows 出纳室：有玻璃栅窗的银行出纳员工作间

calculate /ˈkælkjʊleɪt/ *verb* **1.** to find the answer to a problem using numbers 计算，核算 ○ *The bank clerk calculated the rate of exchange for the dollar*. 银行职员计算了兑换美元的汇率。**2.** to estimate 估计，推测 ○ *I calculate that we have six months' stock left*. 我估计我们还剩下六个月的存货。

calculation /ˌkælkjʊˈleɪʃ(ə)n/ *noun* the answer to a problem in mathematics 计算结果 ○ *According to my calculations, we have six months' stock left*. 根据我的计算，我们还剩下六个月的存货。□ **we are £20,000 out in our calculations** we have made a mistake in our calculations and arrived at a figure which is £20,000 too much or too little 我们的计算结果有两万英镑对不上

calendar variance /ˌkælɪndə ˈveəriəns/ *noun* variance which occurs if a company uses calendar months for the financial accounts but uses the number of actual working days to calculate overhead expenses in the cost accounts 日历差异：公司在会计报表中使用日历月份，而在成本账中使用实际工作天数来计算间接费用时所发生的差异

calendar year /ˌkælɪndə ˈjɪə/ *noun* a year from the 1st January to 31st December 日历年，自然年

call /kɔːl/ *noun* **1.** a demand for repayment of a loan by a lender 还贷要求，催偿通知 **2.** a demand to pay for new shares which then become paid up 股款催缴 ■ *verb* to ask for a loan to be repaid immediately 催缴欠款

callable bond /ˌkɔːləb(ə)l ˈbɒnd/ *noun* a bond which can be redeemed before it matures 可赎回债券

callable capital /ˌkɔːləb(ə)l ˈkæpɪt(ə)l/ *noun* the part of a company's capital which has not been called up 通知即缴的股本

call account /ˈkɔːl əˌkaʊnt/ *noun* a type of current account where money can be withdrawn without notice 活期存款账户

call-back pay /ˈkɔːlbæk ˌpeɪ/ *noun* pay given to an employee who has been called back to work after their usual working hours 加班工资,加班费

called up capital /ˌkɔːld ʌp ˈkæpɪt(ə)l/ *noun* a share capital in a company which has been called up but not yet paid for 已催缴股本

'... a circular to shareholders highlights that the company's net assets as at August 1, amounted to £47.9 million — less than half the company's called-up share capital of £96.8 million. Accordingly, an EGM has been called for October 7'
"致股东的通函强调,公司 8 月 1 日的净资产为 4,790 万英镑——不到公司已催缴股本 9,680 万英镑的一半。因此,公司决定在 10 月 7 日召开特别股东大会"[*Times*《泰晤士报》]

call in /ˌkɔːl ˈɪn/ *verb* **1.** to visit 来访,拜访 ○ *Their sales representative called in twice last week.* 他们的销售代表上周来了两次。**2.** to ask for a debt to be paid 要求还清欠债

call-in pay /ˈkɔːlɪn ˌpeɪ/ *noun* payment guaranteed to employees who report for work even if there is no work for them to do 报到工资:付给没有工作做时仍然报到上班的员工的报酬 ○ *Call-in pay is often necessary to ensure the attendance of employees where there is at least the possibility of work needing to be done.* 为保证在至少有工作需要完成时员工能够出勤,支付报到工资常常是必要的。

call money /ˈkɔːl ˌmʌni/ *noun* money loaned for which repayment can be demanded without notice 活期贷款:毋须通知即可要求偿还的贷款 Also called 亦称作 **money at call**, **money on call**

call option /ˈkɔːl ˌɒpʃən/ *noun* an option to buy shares at a future date and at a specific price 购股选择权:在将来某日按某一特定价格购买股票的选择权

call-over price /ˌkɔːlˈəʊvə praɪs/ *noun* a price which is applied when selling is conducted by a chairman, and not by open outcry 公开作价价格:由董事长制定的交易价格,不对外喊价

call price /ˈkɔːl praɪs/ *noun* a price to be paid on redemption of a US bond(债券)赎回价

call purchase /ˈkɔːl ˌpɜːtʃɪs/, **call sale** /ˈkɔːl seɪl/ *noun* a transaction where the seller or purchaser can fix the price for future delivery 期货交易:买卖双方可以确定将来交割价格的交易

calls in arrear /ˌkɔːls ɪn əˈrɪə/ *plural noun* money called up for shares, but not paid at the correct time and a special calls in arrear account is set up to debit the sums owing 欠付已催缴股款:已催缴但未如期支付的股款,为此特别设立一个欠付已催缴股款账户来将所欠款额记入该账户的借方

call up /ˌkɔːl ˈʌp/ *verb* to ask for share capital to be paid 催缴股本

Canadian Institute of Chartered Accountants /kəˌneɪdiən ˌɪnstɪtjuːt əv ˌtʃɑːtəd əˈkaʊntənts/ *noun* in Canada, the principal professional accountancy body that is responsible for setting accounting standards 加拿大特许会计师协会 Abbreviation 缩写 **CICA**

cancel /ˈkænsəl/ *verb* to stop something which has been agreed or planned 停止,取消 ○ *to cancel an appointment* or *a meeting* 取消约会(或

会议) ○ *The government has cancelled the order for a fleet of buses.* 政府取消了一批公共汽车的订单。○ *The manager is still ill, so the interviews planned for this week have been cancelled.* 经理的病还没好,所以原计划这周的采访取消了。(NOTE: **cancelling – cancelled**)

cancellation /ˌkænsəˈleɪʃ(ə)n/ *noun* the act of stopping something which has been agreed or planned 停止,取消 ○ *the cancellation of an appointment* 约会的取消 ○ *the cancellation of an agreement* 协议的撤销

cancel out /ˌkænsəl ˈaʊt/ *verb* (*of two things*) to balance each other or act against each other so that there is no change in the existing situation (两事物)抵消 ○ *The two clauses cancel each other out.* 这两个条款互相抵消。○ *Higher costs have cancelled out the increased sales revenue.* 成本增加抵消了销售收入的增长。

cap /kæp/ *noun* an upper limit placed on something, such as an interest rate (对利率等规定的)上限 Opposite 反义 **floor** ■ *verb* to place an upper limit on something 规定…的上限 ○ *to cap a local authority's budget* 规定地方政府的预算上限 ○ *to cap a department's budget* 限制部门的预算 (NOTE: **capping – capped**)

CAPA *noun* a large association of accountancy bodies that operate in Asia and the Pacific Rim countries 亚太地区会计师联合会 Full form 全称为 **Confederation of Asian and Pacific Accountants**

capacity /kəˈpæsɪti/ *noun* **1.** the amount which can be produced, or the amount of work which can be done 生产能力;生产量 ○ *industrial* or *manufacturing* or *production capacity* 工业(或制造、生产)能力 **2.** the amount of space 库容量,贮藏量 □ **to use up spare or excess capacity** to make use of time or space which is not fully used 充分利用空闲时间(或闲置空间) **3.** ability 能力 ○ *She has a particular capacity for detailed business deals with overseas companies.* 她具备与海外公司洽谈具体商业交易的特殊才能。

'... analysts are increasingly convinced that the industry simply has too much capacity'
"分析人士日益相信该行业产能过剩"
[*Fortune*《财富》]

capacity usage variance /kəˌpæsɪti ˌjuːsɪdʒ ˈveəriəns/ *noun* the difference in gain or loss in a given period compared to budgeted expectations, caused because the hours worked were longer or shorter than planned 产能利用差异:特定阶段的盈亏与预期值之间存在的差异,由实际工作时数长于或短于计划时数导致

capacity variance /kəˌpæsɪti ˈveəriəns/ *noun* variance caused by the difference between planned and actual hours worked 生产能力差异:计划工作时数和实际工作时数不同引起的差异

Caparo case /kəˈpɑːrəʊ ˌkeɪs/ *noun* in England, a court decision taken by the House of Lords in 1990 that auditors owe a duty of care to present (not prospective) shareholders as a body but not as individuals 卡帕罗判例:英国国会上议院于1990年作出的法庭裁决,判定审计师对现有股东(而非未来股东)整体(而非个人)负有谨慎审计的

责任

CAPEX *abbr* capital expenditure 资本支出

capital /ˈkæpɪt(ə)l/ *noun* **1.** the money, property and assets used in a business 资本，资金 ○ *a company with £10,000 capital* or *with a capital of £10,000* 有一万英镑资本的公司 **2.** money owned by individuals or companies, which they use for investment 投资资本

'...issued and fully paid capital is $100 million, comprising 2,340 shares of $100 each and 997,660 ordinary shares of $100 each'
"已发行并已缴清的股本是一亿美元，包括每股100美元的股份2,340股和每股100美元的普通股997,660股"[*Hong Kong Standard*《香港虎报》]

capital account /ˈkæpɪt(ə)l əˌkaʊnt/ *noun* **1.** an account of dealings such as money, invested in or taken out of the company by the owners of a company 资本账户：记录公司拥有人将资金投入或从公司取出等交易的账户 **2.** items in a country's balance of payments which do not refer to the buying and selling merchandise, but refer to investments 资本项目：一国国际收支中商品的资本投资项目，不包括商品买卖项目 **3.** the total equity in a business 权益总额

capital adequacy /ˌkæpɪt(ə)l ˈædɪkwəsi/, **capital adequacy ratio** /ˌkæpɪt(ə)l ˈædɪkwəsi ˌreɪʃiəʊ/ *noun* the amount of money which a bank has to have in the form of shareholders' capital, shown as a percentage of its assets 资本充足比率：银行必须以股本形式拥有的资金占资产的百分比 Also called 亦称作 **capital-to-asset ratio** (NOTE: The amount is internationally agreed at 8% 国际上的通行比率为8%)

capital allowances /ˌkæpɪt(ə)l əˈlaʊənsɪz/ *plural noun* the allowances based on the value of fixed assets which may be deducted from a company's profits and so reduce its tax liability 资本减免额：根据固定资产价值确定的减免额度，从公司利润中扣除，可使纳税额减少

capital asset pricing model /ˌkæpɪt(ə)l ˌæset ˈpraɪsɪŋ ˌmɒd(ə)l/ *noun* a method of calculating the expected return on a share, by showing what percentage of future return is dependent on the movements of the stock market taken as a whole 资本资产定价模型：一种计算股票预期回报的方法，呈现资本的未来回报与证券市场整体波动之间的百分比关系 Abbreviation 缩写 **CAPM**

capital base /ˌkæpɪt(ə)l ˈbeɪs/ *noun* the capital structure of a company (shareholders' capital plus loans and retained profits) used as a way of assessing the company's worth 资本基础：即公司的资本结构（股本资本、负债和留存盈余之和），可用于评估公司价值

capital bonus /ˌkæpɪt(ə)l ˈbəʊnəs/ *noun* an extra payment by an insurance company which is produced by a capital gain 资本红利：保险公司从资本收益中支付的红利

capital budget /ˌkæpɪt(ə)l ˈbʌdʒɪt/ *noun* a budget for planned purchases of fixed assets during the next budget period 资本预算：用于下一个预算期的固定资产购置

capital commitments /ˌkæpɪt(ə)l kəˈmɪtmənts/ *plural noun* expenditure on assets which has been authorised by directors, but not yet spent at the end of a financial period 资本承付：经董事授权可用于购买资产、但在财务期间临近结束时仍未动用的开支费用

capital consumption /ˌkæpɪt(ə)l kənˈsʌmpʃ(ə)n/ *noun* in a given period, the total depreciation of a national economy's fixed assets based on replacement costs 资本消耗：在指定时期内，根据重置成本计算的某国民经济体的固定资产总折旧

capital costs /ˌkæpɪt(ə)l ˈkɒsts/ *noun* expenses on the purchase of fixed assets 资本成本，资本费用：用于购置固定资产的费用

capital employed /ˌkæpɪt(ə)l ɪmˈplɔɪd/ *noun* an amount of capital consisting of shareholders' funds plus the long-term debts of a business 已动用资本：企业包括股东资金以及长期债务在内的资本

capital equipment /ˌkæpɪt(ə)l ɪˈkwɪpmənt/ *noun* equipment which a factory or office uses to work 固定设备，资本设备：工厂或办事处用于生产办公的设备

capital expenditure /ˌkæpɪt(ə)l ɪkˈspendɪtʃə/ *noun* money spent on fixed assets such as property, machines and furniture 资本支出，固定资产开支 Also called 亦称作 **capital investment**, **capital outlay**. Abbreviation 缩写 **CAPEX**

capital expenditure budget /ˌkæpɪt(ə)l ɪkˌspendɪtʃə ˈbʌdʒɪt/ *noun* a budget for planned purchases of fixed assets during the budget period 资本支出预算

capital flight /ˌkæpɪt(ə)l ˈflaɪt/ *noun* the transfer of large sums of money between countries to seek higher rates of return or to escape a political or economic disturbance 资本外逃，资本外流，资金抽离：不同国家间大笔资金的转移，旨在寻求更高回报或规避政治、经济动荡的影响 Also called 亦称作 **flight of capital**

capital gain /ˌkæpɪt(ə)l ˈgeɪn/ *noun* an amount of money made by selling a fixed asset 资本收益：出售固定资产所得收益 Opposite 反义 **capital loss**

capital gains /ˌkæpɪt(ə)l ˈgeɪnz/ *plural noun* money made by selling a fixed asset or by selling shares 资本利得，资本收益：出售固定资产或股份所得收益（NOTE：If the asset is sold for less than its purchase price, the result is a capital loss 若资产售价低于买价，则为资本损失）

capital gains expenses /ˌkæpɪt(ə)l geɪns ɪkˈspensɪz/ *plural noun* expenses incurred in buying or selling assets, which can be deducted when calculating a capital gain or loss 资本利得支出，资本收益支出：因买卖资产发生的支出，在计算资本利得或损失时可扣除

capital gains tax /ˌkæpɪt(ə)l ˈgeɪnz tæks/ *noun* a tax on the difference between the gross acquisition cost and the net proceeds when an asset is sold. In the United Kingdom, this tax also applies when assets are given or exchanged, although each individual has an annual capital gains tax allowance that exempts gains within that tax year below a stated level. In addition, certain assets may be exempt, e.g., a person's principal private residence and transfers of assets between spouses 资本利得税：对资产总成本和出售净收入的差额征收的税款。在英国，给予或交换资产时亦征税，但每个人都享有年度资本利得税宽免，即该税务年度内低于规定水平的收益可以免税。此外，有些资产也可享受豁免，例如私人住所及配偶间的资产转让 Abbreviation 缩写 **CGT**

capital goods /ˈkæpɪt(ə)l gʊdz/ *plural noun* machinery, buildings and raw materials which are used to make other goods 资本货物，生产资料：即机器、厂房、原材料等，用于生产其他商品

capital-intensive industry /ˌkæpɪt(ə)lɪnˈtensɪv ˌɪndəstri/ *noun* an industry which needs a large amount of capital investment in plant to make it work 资本密集型行业：需要大量资本投入才能运转的行业

capital investment appraisal /ˌkæpɪt(ə)l ɪnˌvestmənt əˈpreɪz(ə)l/ *noun* an analysis of the future profitability of capital purchases as an aid to good management 资本投资评价：对资本购置未来盈利能力的分析，用于完善经营管理

capitalisation of costs /ˌkæpɪt(ə)laɪzeɪʃ(ə)n əv ˈkɒsts/ *noun* the act of including costs usually charged to the profit and loss account in the balance sheet. The effect is that profits are higher than if such costs are matched with revenues in the same accounting period 成本资本化：把通常应列入损益表的成本列入资产负债表的行为。此类成本如果在同一会计期内与收入配比，利润就会被高估

capitalise /ˈkæpɪt(ə)laɪz/, **capitalize** *verb* **1.** to invest money in a working company 投资于（运营公司）□ **the company is capitalised at £10,000** the company has a working capital of £10,000 该公司的营运资金为一万英镑 **2.** to convert reserves or assets into capital 使资本化：将准备金或资产转化为资本

'...at its last traded price the bank was capitalized at around $1.05 billion with 60 per cent in the hands of the family'
"按最后交易价格，银行的现有资金约为10.5亿美元，其中60%为个人存款"［*South China Morning Post*《南华早报》］

capitalise on /ˈkæpɪt(ə)laɪz ɒn/ *verb* to make a profit from 利用；从…获利 ○ *We are seeking to capitalise on our market position.* 我们正寻求利用我们的市场地位。

capitalism /ˈkæpɪt(ə)lɪz(ə)m/ *noun* the economic system in which each person has the right to invest money, to work in business and to buy and sell, with no restrictions from the state 资本主义

capitalist /ˈkæpɪt(ə)lɪst/ *adjective* working according to the principles of capitalism 资本主义的 ○ *the capitalist system* 资本主义制度 ○ *the capitalist countries* or *world* 资本主义国家（或世界）

capitalist economy /ˌkæpɪt(ə)lɪst ɪˈkɒnəmi/ *noun* an economy in which each person has the right to invest money, to work in business and to buy and sell, with no restrictions from the state 资本主义经济

capital levy /ˌkæpɪt(ə)l ˈlevi/ *noun* a tax on the value of a person's property and possessions 财产税，资本税

capital loss /ˌkæpɪt(ə)l ˈlɒs/ *noun* a loss made by selling assets 资本损失：

出售资产造成的损失 Opposite 反义 **capital gain**

capital maintenance concept /ˌkæpɪt(ə)l ˈmeɪntənəns ˌkɒnsept/ *noun* a concept used to determine the definition of profit, that provides the basis for different systems of inflation accounting 资本保持概念,资本维护概念:用于确定利润定义的概念,是不同通货膨胀会计制度的基础

capital market /ˌkæpɪt(ə)l ˈmɑːkɪt/ *noun* an international market where money can be raised for investment in a business 资本市场:可以筹集企业投资资金的国际市场

capital outlay /ˌkæpɪt(ə)l ˈaʊtleɪ/ *noun* same as 同 **capital expenditure**

capital profit /ˌkæpɪt(ə)l ˈprɒfɪt/ *noun* a profit made by selling an asset 资本利润:出售资产所得利润

capital reconstruction /ˌkæpɪt(ə)l ˌriːkənˈstrʌkʃən/ *noun* the act of putting a company into voluntary liquidation and then selling its assets to another company with the same name and same shareholders, but with a larger capital base 资产重组:使某公司进行自愿清偿,然后将其资产出售给名称及股东均相同但资本基础更大的另一家公司的行为

capital redemption reserve /ˌkæpɪt(ə)l rɪˈdempʃən rɪˌsɜːv/ *noun* an account required to prevent a reduction in capital, where a company purchases or redeems its own shares out of distributable profits 资本赎回储备,资本偿还准备金:防止资本缩减的资金账户,公司通过该账户使用可分配利润购入或赎回自身股份

capital reorganisation /ˌkæpɪt(ə)l riːˌɔːgənaɪˈzeɪʃ(ə)n/ *noun* the process changing the capital structure of a company by amalgamating or dividing existing shares to form shares of a higher or lower nominal value 资本重组:为改变公司的资本结构,将现有股票合并或分割为面值更大或更小股票的过程

capital reserves /ˌkæpɪt(ə)l rɪˈzɜːvz/ *plural noun* **1.** money from profits, which forms part of the capital of a company and can be used for distribution to shareholders only when a company is wound up 资本准备金:构成公司资本的利润,只有在公司清盘时才能分派给股东 Also called 亦称作 **undistributable reserves 2.** the share capital of a company which comes from selling assets and not from their usual trading 资本储备:来自资产出售而非正常业务的公司股本

capital shares /ˌkæpɪt(ə)l ˈʃeəz/ *plural noun* (*on the Stock Exchange*) shares in a unit trust which rise in value as the capital value of the units rises, but do not receive any income (证券交易所的)资本股票:单位信托公司的股票,当单位资本价值上升,该股票价值也上升,但不会有任何收益(NOTE: The other form of shares in a split-level investment trust are income shares, which receive income from the investments, but do not rise in value 另外一种可分割投资信托中的股票是收益股票,该种股票会有投资收益,但价值不会上升)

capital structure /ˌkæpɪt(ə)l ˈstrʌktʃə/ *noun* the relative proportions of equity capital and debt capital within a company's balance sheet 资本结构:公司资产负债表内股本权益与债务资本的相对比例

capital tax /ˈkæpɪt(ə)l tæks/ *noun* a

tax levied on the capital owned by a company, rather than on its spending 资本税：对公司拥有的资本（而非其开支）征收的税项 ➪ 参阅 **capital gains tax**

capital to asset ratio /ˌkæpɪt(ə)l tə ˈæset ˌreɪʃiəʊ/, **capital/asset ratio** *noun* same as 同 **capital adequacy**

capital transactions /ˌkæpɪt(ə)l trænˈzækʃ(ə)nz/ *noun* transactions affecting non-current items such as fixed assets, long-term debt, or share capital, rather than revenue transactions 资本交易：影响固定资产、长期债务或股本等非流动项目的交易，而非收入交易

capital transfer tax /ˌkæpɪt(ə)l ˈtrænsfɜː ˌtæks/ *noun* in the United Kingdom, a tax on the transfer of assets that was replaced in 1986 by inheritance tax 资本转让税：英国税种，1986 年被遗产税取代

capital turnover ratio /ˌkæpɪt(ə)l ˌtɜːnəʊvə ˈreɪʃiəʊ/ *noun* turnover divided by average capital during the year 资本周转率：一年内的营业额除以平均资本

CAPM *abbr* capital asset pricing model 资本资产定价模型

capped floating rate note /ˌkæpt ˈfləʊtɪŋ reɪt ˌnəʊt/ *noun* a floating rate note which has an agreed maximum rate 封顶浮息票据

captive market /ˌkæptɪv ˈmɑːkɪt/ *noun* a market where one supplier has a monopoly and the buyer has no choice over the product which he or she must purchase 卖方市场：供应商处于垄断地位、买方对产品没有选择而必须购买的市场

carriage /ˈkærɪdʒ/ *noun* the transporting of goods from one place to another 运输 ○ *to pay for carriage* 支付运费

carriage forward /ˌkærɪdʒ ˈfɔːwəd/ *noun* a deal where the customer pays for transporting the goods 运费到付

carriage free /ˌkærɪdʒ ˈfriː/ *adverb* the customer does not pay for the shipping 运费免付

carriage inwards /ˌkærɪdʒ ˈɪnwədz/ *noun* delivery expenses incurred through the purchase of goods 购货运费：购买商品时产生的运费

carriage outwards /ˌkærɪdʒ ˈaʊtwədz/ *noun* delivery expenses incurred through the sale of goods 销货运费：销售商品时产生的运费

carriage paid /ˌkærɪdʒ ˈpeɪd/ *noun* a deal where the seller has paid for the shipping 运费已付

carry /ˈkæri/ *noun* the cost of borrowing to finance a deal（为一笔交易筹资而产生的）负债成本（NOTE：**carries – carrying – carried**）

carry back /ˌkæri ˈbæk/ *verb* to take back to an earlier accounting period 抵前

carry down /ˌkæri ˈdaʊn/, **carry forward** /ˌkæri ˈfɔːwəd/ *verb* to take an account balance at the end of the current period as the starting point for the next period 结转：将账户本期期末余额转入下期期初

carry forward /ˌkæri ˈfɔːwəd/ *verb* to take an account balance at the end of the current period or page as the starting point for the next period or page 结转，转次页：将账户本期期末或本页页末余额转入下期期初或下页页首

carrying cost /ˈkæriɪŋ kɒst/ *noun* any expense associated with holding stock for a given period, e.g., from the time of delivery to the time of dispatch. Carrying costs will include storage and insurance 囤积成本,置存成本:在特定时期(如从交货到发运这段时间)持有存货产生的相关费用,包括存储费用和保险费

carry-over /ˈkæriˌəʊvə/ *noun* the stock of a commodity held at the beginning of a new financial year 遗留物,结转货:在新的会计年度初期持有的商品存货

cartel /kɑːˈtel/ *noun* a group of companies which try to fix the price or to regulate the supply of a product so that they can make more profit 卡特尔,企业联合:试图固定价格和控制某种产品的供应来获取更多利润的企业联合体

cash /kæʃ/ *noun* **1.** money in the form of coins or notes 现金 **2.** the using of money in coins or notes 现款使用

cashable /ˈkæʃəb(ə)l/ *adjective* able to be cashed 可提现的 ○ *A crossed cheque is not cashable at any bank*. 划线支票在任何银行都不能提现。

cash account /ˈkæʃ əˌkaʊnt/ *noun* an account which records the money which is received and spent 现金账户:记录现金收支的账户

cash accounting /ˌkæʃ əˈkaʊntɪŋ/ *noun* 现金收付制会计,现金记账 **1.** an accounting method in which receipts and expenses are recorded in the accounting books in the period when they actually occur [在实际发生期间记录收支账目的会计方法] **2.** in the United Kingdom, a system for Value Added Tax that enables the tax payer to account for tax paid and received during a given period, thus allowing automatic relief for bad debts [英国的一种增值税制度,纳税人可以记录于指定期间支付及收取的税款,从而自动获得坏账宽免]

cash advance /ˌkæʃ ədˈvɑːns/ *noun* a loan in cash against a future payment 预付现金

cash and carry /ˌkæʃ ən ˈkæri/ *noun* **1.** a large store selling goods at low prices, where the customer pays cash and takes the goods away immediately 付现自运商场,现购自运商场:在低价售货的大商场,顾客用现金支付并立即带走货物 ○ *We get our supplies every morning from the cash and carry*. 我们每天早上从现购自运商场采购日用品。**2.** the activity of buying a commodity for cash and selling the same commodity on the futures market 用现金买进某种商品,再在期货市场上将其出售

'... the small independent retailer who stocks up using cash and carries could be hit hard by the loss of footfall associated with any increase in smuggled goods'
"如果走私品泛滥,通过现购自运囤积货物的小型独立零售商可能会因客流量减少而遭受重创" [*The Grocer*《食品商》]

cash at bank /ˌkæʃ ət ˈbæŋk/ *noun* the total amount of money held at the bank by an individual or company 银行往来账户存款

cashback /ˈkæʃbæk/ *noun* a discount system where a purchaser receives a cash discount on the completion of the purchase 返现:一种折扣方

法，买方可在采购后获得现金折扣

cash balance /ˈkæʃ ˌbæləns/ *noun* a balance in cash, as opposed to amounts owed 现金余额

cash basis /ˈkæʃ ˌbeɪsɪs/ *noun* a method of preparing the accounts of a business, where receipts and payments are shown at the time when they are made, as opposed to showing debts or credits which are outstanding at the end of the accounting period 现收现付制：一种公司账目编制方法，收支账目按发生的时间呈列，而不是呈列为会计期末的债务或贷方余额 Also called 亦称作 **receipts and payments basis**

cash budget /ˈkæʃ ˌbʌdʒɪt/ *noun* a plan of cash income and expenditure 现金预算：现金收支的计划

cash card /ˈkæʃ kɑːd/ *noun* a plastic card used to obtain money from a cash dispenser 现金卡：从取款机上提现的一种塑料卡片

cash cow /ˈkæʃ kaʊ/ *noun* a product or subsidiary company that consistently generates good profits but does not provide growth 现金牛，摇钱树：在产量不变的条件下仍能不断提供可观利润的产品或分公司

cash crop /ˈkæʃ krɒp/ *noun* an agricultural crop grown for sale to other buyers or to other countries, rather than for domestic consumption 经济作物：为向他人或国外销售而种植的农作物，而非用于家庭或国内消费

cash deal /ˌkæʃ ˈdiːl/ *noun* a sale done for cash 现金交易

cash desk /ˈkæʃ desk/ *noun* the place in a store where you pay for the goods bought（商场的）收银台

cash discount /ˌkæʃ ˈdɪskaʊnt/ *noun* a discount given for payment in cash 付现折扣 Also called 亦称作 **discount for cash**

cash dispenser /ˈkæʃ dɪˌspensə/ *noun* a machine which gives out money when a special card is inserted and instructions given 自动取款机

cash dividend /ˌkæʃ ˈdɪvɪdend/ *noun* a dividend paid in cash, as opposed to a dividend in the form of bonus shares 现金股息（与之相反的是股票股息）

cash economy /ˌkæʃ ɪˈkɒnəmi/ *noun* a black economy, where goods and services are paid for in cash, and therefore not declared for tax 现金经济：一种地下经济活动，指用现金支付货物和劳务以逃税

cash equivalent /ˌkæʃ ɪˈkwɪvələnt/ *noun* the equivalent in cash terms of an asset which is enjoyed 现金等值：用现金计算的与资产等同的价值

cash equivalents /ˌkæʃ ɪˈkwɪvələnts/ *noun* short-term investments that can be converted into cash immediately and that are subject to only a limited risk. There is usually a limit on their duration, e.g., three months 现金等价物：可即时换成现金且风险有限的短期投资。现金等价物的有效期通常很短（如三个月）

cash float /ˈkæʃ fləʊt/ *noun* cash put into the cash box at the beginning of the day or week to allow change to be given to customers 流动金，备用金：一周或一天开始时放进钱箱以备找零用的现金

cash flow /ˈkæʃ fləʊ/ *noun* cash which comes into a company from sales (cash inflow) or the money which goes out in purchases or overhead expenditure (cash outflow) 现金

流量:通过销售流入公司的现金(现金流入),或因采购或间接费用开支而流出的现金(现金流出)

cash-flow accounting /ˌkæʃfləʊ əˈkaʊntɪŋ/ *noun* the practice of measuring the financial activities of a company in terms of cash receipts and payments, without recording accruals, prepayments, debtors, creditors and stocks 现金流量会计:用现金收支来衡量企业财务活动的做法,它不记录应计款项、预付款、应收账款、应付账款和存货

cash flow budget /ˈkæʃ fləʊ ˌbʌdʒɪt/ *noun* a cash budget, a plan of cash income and expenditure 现金流量预算

cash flow forecast /ˈkæʃ fləʊ ˌfɔːkɑːst/ *noun* a forecast of when cash will be received or paid out 现金流量预测

cash-flow risk /ˈkæʃfləʊ ˌrɪsk/ *noun* the risk that a company's available cash will not be sufficient to meet its financial obligations 现金流量风险:公司的可用现金不能满足其财务需要

cash flow statement /ˈkæʃ fləʊ ˌsteɪtmənt/ *noun* a record of a company's cash inflows and cash outflows over a specific period of time, typically a year 现金流量表:公司在指定期间内(通常是一年)的现金流入及现金流出记录

cash fraction /ˌkæʃ ˈfrækʃən/ *noun* a small amount of cash paid to a shareholder to make up the full amount of part of a share which has been allocated in a share split 现金零头:在因拆股而分配给股东零碎股份时,向股东支付以补足其金额的小额现金

cash-generating unit /ˌkæʃ-ˌdʒenəreɪtɪŋ ˈjuːnɪt/ *noun* the smallest identifiable group of assets that generates cash inflows and outflows that can be measured 现金产生单位:产生可以衡量的现金流入及流出最小可识别资产单位

cashier /kæˈʃɪə/ *noun* **1.** a person who takes money from customers in a shop or who deals with the money that has been paid (商店)出纳员,收银员 **2.** a person who deals with customers in a bank and takes or gives cash at the counter 银行出纳员,柜台职员

cashier's check /kæˌʃɪəz ˈtʃek/ *noun US* a bank's own cheque, drawn on itself and signed by a cashier or other bank official (美)银行本票:由银行出纳员或其他银行官员签发的由银行付款的票据

cash in /ˌkæʃ ˈɪn/ *verb* to sell shares or other property for cash 兑现:卖出股票或其他财产以换取现金

cash inflow /ˌkæʃ ˈɪnfləʊ/ *noun* receipts of cash or cheques 现金流入:现金或支票收款

cash in on /ˌkæʃ ˈɪn ɒn/ *verb* to profit from 从…获利 ○ *The company is cashing in on the interest in computer games.* 该公司利用人们对计算机游戏的兴趣从中获利。

cash items /ˈkæʃ ˌaɪtəmz/ *plural noun* goods sold for cash 现金科目,现金账项:出售以换取现金的物品

cashless society /ˌkæʃləs səˈsaɪəti/ *noun* a society where no one uses cash, all purchases being made by credit cards, charge cards, cheques or direct transfer from one account to another 无现金社会:所有的购买都通

过信用卡、赊账卡、支票或直接转账进行

cash limit /kæʃ ˈlɪmɪt/ *noun* **1.** a fixed amount of money which can be spent during some period 现金限额：在某一时期所能支出现金的限额 **2.** a maximum amount someone can withdraw from an ATM using a cash card（自动提款机）提款限额

cash offer /ˈkæʃ ˌɒfə/ *noun* an offer to pay in cash, especially an offer to pay cash when buying shares in a takeover bid 现金报价：用现金支付的要约，特别用于在兼并出价中用现金购买股票

cash outflow /ˌkæʃ ˈaʊtfləʊ/ *noun* expenditure in cash or cheques 现金流出：现金或支票的支出

cash payment /ˈkæʃ ˌpeɪmənt/ *noun* payment in cash 现金支付

cash payments journal /kæʃ ˌpeɪmənts ˈdʒɜːn(ə)l/ *noun* a chronological record of all the payments that have been made from a company's bank account 现金支出日记账：按照时间顺序记录公司所有现金支出

cash position /ˈkæʃ pəˌzɪʃ(ə)n/ *noun* a state of the cash which a company currently has available 现金头寸：公司目前拥有的可用现金

cash price /ˈkæʃ praɪs/ *noun* a lower price or better terms which apply if the customer pays cash 现金售价：客户付现时可享受的较低价格或优惠

cash purchase /ˈkæʃ ˌpɜːtʃɪs/ *noun* a purchase made for cash 现金购买

cash receipts journal /kæʃ rɪˌsiːts ˈdʒɜːn(ə)l/ *noun* a chronological record of all the receipts that have been paid into a company's bank account 现金收入日记账：按照时间顺序记录公司所有现金收入

cash register /ˈkæʃ ˌredʒɪstə/ *noun* a machine which shows and adds the prices of items bought, with a drawer for keeping the cash received 现金出纳机

cash reserves /ˈkæʃ rɪˌzɜːvz/ *plural noun* a company's reserves in cash deposits or bills kept in case of urgent need 现金准备，准备金：公司的现金存款或票据，以备紧急需要 ○ *The company was forced to fall back on its cash reserves.* 公司不得不动用准备金。

cash sale /ˈkæʃ seɪl/ *noun* a transaction paid for in cash 现金销售

cash terms /ˈkæʃ tɜːmz/ *plural noun* lower terms which apply if the customer pays cash 付现条件：客户付现时享受的优惠

cash transaction /ˈkæʃ trænˌzækʃən/ *noun* a transaction paid for in cash 现金交易

cash up /ˌkæʃ ˈʌp/ *verb* to add up the cash in a shop at the end of the day 清款，结账：一天营业结束后，合计商店里的现金

cash voucher /ˈkæʃ ˌvaʊtʃə/ *noun* a piece of paper which can be exchanged for cash 现金券：可兑换现金的一种纸券 ○ *With every £20 of purchases, the customer gets a cash voucher to the value of £2.* 顾客每购买20英镑的货物，就可以获得价值两英镑的现金券。

casting vote /ˌkɑːstɪŋ ˈvəʊt/ *noun* a vote used by the chairman in the case where the votes for and against a proposal are equal 决定权，决定票：当议案赞成及反对票数相等时，（会议）主席的投票 ○ *The chairman has the casting vote.* 主席拥有决定权。○ *She used* *her casting vote to block the motion*. 她使用她的决定票来阻止这项提议。

casual /ˈkæʒuəl/ *adjective* informal or not serious 随意的，非正式的，不严肃的

casual labour /ˌkæʒuəl ˈleɪbə/ *noun* workers who are hired for a short period 临时工

casual work /ˈkæʒuəl wɜːk/ *noun* work where the employees are hired only for a short period 临时工作，暂时工作

casual worker /ˌkæʒuəl ˈwɜːkə/ *noun* an employee who can be hired for a short period 临时工

CCA *abbr* current cost accounting 现时成本会计

CD /siː ˈdiː/ *abbr* certificate of deposit 定期存款证明

ceiling /ˈsiːlɪŋ/ *noun* the highest point that something can reach, e. g. the highest rate of a pay increase 最高限额，上限（如最高加薪率）○ *to fix a ceiling for a budget* 为预算规定一个最高限额 ○ *There is a ceiling of $ 100,000 on deposits*. 存款额的上限为 10 万美元。○ *Output reached its ceiling in June and has since fallen back*. 产量于 6 月达到最高点，然后回落。○ *What ceiling has the government put on wage increases this year*? 政府规定今年的提薪上限是多少？

central /ˈsentrəl/ *adjective* organised from one main point 中央的，中心的

central bank discount rate /ˌsentrəl bæŋk ˈdɪskaʊnt reɪt/ *noun* the rate at which a central bank discounts bills such as treasury bills 中央银行贴现率：中央银行对票据（如国库券）贴现所用的利率

central bank intervention /ˌsentrəl bæŋk ˌɪntəˈvenʃ(ə)n/ *noun* an action by a central bank to change base interest rates, to impose exchange controls or to buy or sell the country's own currency in an attempt to influence international money markets 中央银行干预：中央银行为影响国际货币市场而采取的改变基准利率、实行外汇管制、买卖本国货币等措施

central government /ˌsentrəl ˈɡʌv(ə)nmənt/ *noun* the main government of a country as opposed to municipal, local, provincial or state governments 中央政府（与之相对的是市政府、地方政府、省政府或州政府）

centralise /ˈsentrəlaɪz/, **centralize** *verb* to organise from a central point 集中 ○ *All purchasing has been centralised in our main office*. 我们的总部集中进行采购。○ *The group benefits from a highly centralised organisational structure*. 这个集团得益于一个高度集中的组织架构。○ *The company has become very centralised, and far more staff work at headquarters*. 该公司现已高度集中，在总部工作的员工多了许多。

central purchasing /ˌsentrəl ˈpɜːtʃɪsɪŋ/ *noun* purchasing organised by a central office for all branches of a company 集中采购，统一购买：由公司中心机构组织的为各分支机构统一采购

centre /ˈsentə/ *noun* 中心 **1.** an important town ［重要的城镇］○ *Sheffield is a major industrial centre*. 谢菲尔德是一个大型工业中心。○ *Nottingham is the centre for the shoe industry*. 诺丁汉是制鞋业的中心。**2.** a department, area, or function to which costs and/or revenues are charged [(独立核算成本及/或收入的)部门、地区或职能] (NOTE: [all senses] The US spelling is **center** [以上所有义项]美国拼法为 **center**)

certain annuity /ˌsɜːt(ə)n əˈnjuːɪti/ *noun* an annuity which will be paid for a specific number of years only 固定年金:按特定年限支付的年金

certificate /səˈtɪfɪkət/ *noun* an official document carrying an official declaration by someone, and signed by that person 证书;证明

certificated bankrupt /səˌtɪfɪkeɪtɪd ˈbæŋkrʌpt/ *noun* a bankrupt who has been discharged from bankruptcy with a certificate to show that he or she was not at fault 持书破产者:证明破产不是由于其过错的证明持有人

certificate of approval /səˌtɪfɪkət əv əˈpruːv(ə)l/ *noun* a document showing that an item has been approved officially 许可证

certificate of deposit /səˌtɪfɪkət əv dɪˈpɒzɪt/ *noun* a document from a bank showing that money has been deposited at a guaranteed interest rate for a certain period of time 定期存款证明,存单 Abbreviation 缩写 **CD**

'...interest rates on certificates of deposit may have little room to decline in August as demand for funds from major city banks is likely to remain strong. After delaying for months, banks are now expected to issue a large volume of CDs. If banks issue more CDs on the assumption that the official discount rate reduction will be delayed, it is very likely that CD rates will be pegged for a longer period than expected'
"8月份,存单利率下调空间不大,因为大城市里的银行对资金的需求可能依然会保持强劲。在数月的推迟之后,银行现在可望发放大量的存单。如果银行此类存单的大量发放是建立在政府会推迟贴现率下调的假设上,那么存单利率保持钉住的期限极可能超过预期" [*Nikkei Weekly*《日经周报》]

certificate of incorporation /səˌtɪfɪkət əv ɪnˌkɔːpəˈreɪʃ(ə)n/ *noun* a document issued by Companies House to show that a company has been legally set up and officially registered 公司注册证,公司执照

certificate of origin /səˌtɪfɪkət əv ˈɒrɪdʒɪn/ *noun* a document showing where imported goods come from or were made 原产地证明书

certificate of quality /səˌtɪfɪkət əv ˈkwɒlɪti/ *noun* a certificate showing the grade of a soft commodity 质量证书

certificate of registration /səˌtɪfɪkət əv ˌredʒɪˈstreɪʃ(ə)n/ *noun* a document showing that an item has been registered 注册执照

certificate to commence business /səˌtɪfɪkət tə kəˌmens ˈbɪznɪs/ *noun* a document issued by the Registrar of Companies which allows a registered company to trade 经营许可证

certified accountant /ˌsɜːtɪfaɪd əˈkaʊntənt/ *noun* an accountant who has passed the professional examinations and is a member of the Chartered Association of Certified Accountants 注册会计师:通过了专业考试、成为注册会计师协会会员的会计师

Certified Accounting Technician /ˌsɜːtɪfaɪd əˌkaʊntɪŋ tekˈnɪʃ(ə)n/ *noun* a person who has passed the first stage course of the Association of Chartered Certified Accountants (ACCA) 注册助理会计:通过了注册会计

师协会(ACCA)第一阶段课程考试的人 Abbreviation 缩写 **CAT**

certified cheque /ˌsɜːtɪfaɪd ˈtʃek/, **certified check** *noun* a cheque which a bank says is good and will be paid out of money put aside from the payer's bank account 保付支票:银行承认有效的、将从付款人账户中支付的支票

certified public accountant /ˌsɜːtɪfaɪd ˌpʌblɪk əˈkaʊntənt/ *noun US* an accountant who has passed the examinations of the AICPA and been given a certificate by a state, allowing him or her to practise in that state (美)注册会计师:通过了美国注册会计师协会考试、并获得州政府颁发的证书允许其在该州执业的会计师 Abbreviation 缩写 **CPA**

certify /ˈsɜːtɪfaɪ/ *verb* to make an official declaration in writing 证明:书面正式声明 ○ *I certify that this is a true copy*. 我声明这份副本是真的。○ *The document is certified as a true copy*. 该文件被证实是真的。(NOTE: **certifies – certifying – certified**)

cessation /seˈseɪʃ(ə)n/ *noun* the stopping of an activity or work 停止

cession /ˈseʃ(ə)n/ *noun* the act of giving up property to someone, especially a creditor 让予,财产转让(尤指转让财产权益给债权人)

CGT *abbr* capital gains tax 资本利得税

CH *abbr* Companies House 公司登记注册办事处

chairman /ˈtʃeəmən/ *noun* **1.** a person who is in charge of a meeting (会议)主席 ○ *Mr Howard was chairman* or *acted as chairman* 霍华德先生是(会议)主席 **2.** a person who presides over the board meetings of a company 董事长 ○ *the chairman of the board* or *the company chairman* 董事长 □ **the chairman's report, the chairman's statement** an annual report from the chairman of a company to the shareholders 董事长报告:公司董事长向股东提交的年度报告

'... the corporation's entrepreneurial chairman seeks a dedicated but part-time president. The new president will work a three-day week'
"作为企业的创始人,董事长正在寻求一个有事业心的兼职总裁。新总裁一周要工作三天"[*Globe and Mail* (*Toronto*)《环球邮报》(多伦多)]

Chamber of Commerce /ˌtʃeɪmbər əv ˈkɒmɜːs/ *noun* a group of local business people who meet to discuss problems which they have in common and to promote commerce in their town 商会:地方商人的组织,他们在一起讨论共同面临的问题,以及如何推动所在城镇商业的发展

Chancellor of the Exchequer /ˌtʃɑːnsələr əv ðiː ɪksˈtʃekə/ *noun* the chief finance minister in a government 财政大臣(NOTE: The US term is **Secretary of the Treasury** 美国用语为 **Secretary of the Treasury**)

change /tʃeɪndʒ/ *noun* **1.** money in coins or small notes 零钱 □ **to give someone change for £10** to give someone coins or notes in exchange for a ten pound note 给某人换10英镑的零钱 **2.** money given back by the seller, when the buyer can pay only with a larger note or coin than the amount asked 找头 ○ *She gave me the wrong change*. 她给我找错钱了。○ *You paid the £5.75 bill with a £10 note, so* *you should have £4.25 change*. 你用10英镑的纸币付5.75英镑的账单，应找你4.25英镑。**3.** an alteration of the way something is done or of the way work is carried out 改变，变换 □ **change in accounting principles** using a method to state a company's accounts which is different from the method used in the previous accounts. This will have to be agreed with the auditors, and possibly with the Inland Revenue 会计准则变动：使用与先前不同的方法呈列公司账目。该变动必须经审计师同意，甚至可能需经国内税务局同意 ■ *verb* **1.** □ **to change a £20 note** to give someone smaller notes or coins in place of a £20 note 将20英镑换成零钱 **2.** to give one type of currency for another 兑换货币 ○ *to change £1,000 into dollars* 将1,000英镑兑换成美元 ○ *We want to change some traveller's cheques*. 我们想换些旅行支票。

change machine /ˈtʃeɪndʒ məˌʃiːn/ *noun* a machine which gives small change for a note or larger coin 找零机：将纸币或大额硬币换成零钱的机器

channel /ˈtʃæn(ə)l/ *noun* a means by which information or goods pass from one place to another（传输信息或商品的）渠道，途径 ■ *verb* to send in some direction 把（资金等）导向 ○ *They are channelling their research funds into developing European communication systems*. 他们将研究基金投入到欧洲通讯系统开发中。（NOTE：**channelling – channelled**）

CHAPS *noun* a computerised system for clearing cheques organised by the banks 票据交换所自动支付系统 Compare 比较 **BACS**. Full form 全称为 **Clearing House Automated Payments System**

Chapter 7 /ˌtʃæptə ˈsevən/ *noun* a section of the US Bankruptcy Reform Act 1978, which sets out the rules for the liquidation of an incorporated company 第7款：美国1978年《破产改革法》中的一款，其中列出了股份有限公司清算规则

Chapter 11 /ˌtʃæptə ɪˈlevən/ *noun* a section of the US Bankruptcy Reform Act 1978, which allows a corporation to be protected from demands made by its creditors for a period of time, while it is reorganised with a view to paying its debts. The officers of the corporation will negotiate with its creditors as to the best way of reorganising the business 第11款：美国1978年《破产改革法》中的一款，当公司在一定期限内为偿清债务而进行重组时，此条款为公司提供保护，允许公司在此期间毋须满足债权人的偿债要求，公司高层管理人员将与其债权人一起讨论重组企业的最佳途径

Chapter 13 /ˌtʃæptə θɜːˈtiːn/ *noun* a section of the Bankruptcy Reform Act 1978, which allows a business to continue trading and to pay off its creditors by regular monthly payments over a period of time 第13款：美国1978年《破产改革法》中的一款，它允许企业在一定期限内继续营业并按月定额偿清其债务

character set /ˈkærɪktə set/ *noun* a list of all the characters which can be printed or displayed 字符集：可打印或显示的所有符号一览表

charge /tʃɑːdʒ/ *noun* **1.** money which must be paid, or the price of a service 应付款项；服务费 ○ *to make no charge for delivery* 免费送货 ○ *to* *make a small charge for rental* 廉价租赁 ○ *There is no charge for this service* or *No charge is made for this service*. 该服务免费。**2.** a guarantee of security for a loan, for which assets are pledged 抵押:用资产作质押的贷款担保 ■ *verb* **1.** to ask someone to pay for services later 叫某人稍晚再付服务费 **2.** to ask for money to be paid 叫某人付款 ○ *to charge £5 for delivery* 运输费 5 英镑 ○ *How much does he charge*? 他收费多少? □ **he charges £16 an hour** he asks to be paid £16 for an hour's work 他一小时收费 16 英镑 **3.** to take something as guarantee for a loan 以某物作为贷款抵押

chargeable /ˈtʃɑːdʒəb(ə)l/ *adjective* able to be charged 应收费的 ○ *repairs chargeable to the occupier* 占用者应付的维修费

chargeable asset /ˌtʃɑːdʒəb(ə)l ˈæset/ *noun* an asset which will produce a capital gain when sold. Assets which are not chargeable include your family home, cars, and some types of investments such as government stocks 应税资产:在出售时有资本利得的资产,毋须课税的资产包括房产、汽车、政府定息债券等投资

chargeable business asset /ˌtʃɑːdʒəb(ə)l ˌbɪznɪs ˈæset/ *noun* an asset which is owned by a business and is liable to capital gains if sold 应税商业资产:企业拥有且出售时应付资本利得税的资产

chargeable gains /ˌtʃɑːdʒəb(ə)l ˈgeɪnz/ *plural noun* gains made by selling an asset such as shares, on which capital gains will be charged 应税收益:出售股票等资产获得的收益,这些收益应缴纳资本利得税

chargeable transfer /ˌtʃɑːdʒəb(ə)l ˈtrænsfɜː/ *noun* in the United Kingdom, gifts that are liable to inheritance tax. Under UK legislation, individuals may gift assets to a certain value during their lifetime without incurring any liability to inheritance tax. These are regular transfers out of income that do not affect the donor's standard of living. Additionally, individuals may transfer up to £3,000 a year out of capital 应税转让:在英国,馈赠需缴纳遗产税。根据英国法律,一生中个人可以进行一定价值的免遗产税的资产馈赠。这些馈赠是出自收入且不影响捐赠人生活标准的定期转让。此外,个人每年还可进行最多 3,000 英镑的资本转让

charge account /ˈtʃɑːdʒ əˌkaʊnt/ *noun* an arrangement which a customer has with a store to buy goods and to pay for them at a later date, usually when the invoice is sent at the end of the month 赊账;赊购账户:客户和商店之间订立的一种协议,客户向商店赊账购货,通常在月底商店开出发票时客户才结账(NOTE: The customer will make regular monthly payments into the account and is allowed credit of a multiple of those payments 顾客每月往账户里定额存款,而后即可按这些金额的一定倍数赊账购货)

charge and discharge accounting /ˌtʃɑːdʒ ən ˈdɪstʃɑːdʒ əˌkaʊntɪŋ/ *noun* formerly, a bookkeeping system in which a person charges himself or herself with receipts and credits himself or herself with payments. This system was used extensively in medieval times before the advent of double-entry bookkeeping 收支会计:以前由某人自行记入收款和扣除付款的一种

簿记制度。该制度曾在中世纪被广泛采用,直到出现复式簿记

charge by way of legal mortgage /ˌtʃɑːdʒ baɪ weɪ əv ˌliːɡ(ə)l ˈmɔːɡɪdʒ/ *noun* a way of borrowing money on the security of a property, where the mortgagor signs a deed which gives the mortgagee an interest in the property 以财产为抵押的借款方式:在这种借款方式中,抵押人签署契约,受押人(贷方)对抵押资产享有权益

charge card /ˈtʃɑːdʒ kɑːd/ *noun* a type of credit card for which a fee is payable, but which does not allow the user to take out a loan, e.g. American Express. The total sum must be charged at the end of each month 赊账卡:一种付费卡,但不允许使用该卡贷款,如美国运通卡。使用者每月底必须付清所有费用

chargee /tʃɑːˈdʒiː/ *noun* a person who has the right to force a debtor to pay 债权人

charges forward /ˌtʃɑːdʒɪz ˈfɔːwəd/ *noun* charges which will be paid by the customer 买方付费

charitable /ˈtʃærɪtəb(ə)l/ *adjective* benefiting the general public as a charity 慈善的,公众受益的

charitable deductions /ˌtʃærɪtəb(ə)l dɪˈdʌkʃ(ə)nz/ *plural noun* deductions from taxable income for contributions to charity 慈善性支出扣除:将慈善捐款从应课税收入中扣除

charitable purposes /ˌtʃærɪtəb(ə)l ˈpɜːpəsɪz/ *plural noun* the aims of a charity 慈善目的

charitable trust /ˌtʃærɪtəb(ə)l trʌst/, **charitable corporation** /ˌtʃærɪtəb(ə)l ˌkɔːpəˈreɪʃ(ə)n/ *noun* a trust which benefits the public as a whole, which promotes education or religion, which helps the poor or which does other useful work 慈善信托:一种以受益公众为目的的信托机构,如促进教育或宗教、帮助穷人或做其他有益的工作

charity /ˈtʃærɪti/ *noun* an organization which offers free help or services to those in need 慈善机构 ○ *Because the organisation is a charity it does not have to pay taxes*. 该组织是慈善机构,所以不用纳税。○ *The charity owes its success to clever marketing strategies in its fund-raising*. 慈善机构成功的关键在于其巧妙的筹资宣传策略。

charity accounts /ˌtʃærɪti əˈkaʊnts/ *noun* the accounting records of a charitable institution, that include a statement of financial activities rather than a profit and loss account. In the United Kingdom, the accounts should conform to the requirements stipulated in the Charities Act (1993) 慈善机构账目:慈善机构的会计记录,它包括一份财务活动报表(而不是损益表)。在英国,这些账目应符合 1993 年慈善法的要求

Charity Commissioners /ˈtʃærɪti kəˌmɪʃ(ə)nəz/ *plural noun* UK body which governs charities and sees that they follow the law and use their funds for the purposes intended 慈善机构管理部门:英国对慈善机构是否遵守法律和专款专用进行管理的机构

chart /tʃɑːt/ *noun* a diagram displaying information as a series of lines, blocks, etc. 图表

charter /ˈtʃɑːtə/ *noun* a document giving special legal rights to a group 特许状,执照,许可证 ○ *a shoppers' char-*

ter or *a customers' charter* 顾客特许状 ■ *verb* to hire for a special purpose (为特殊目的)租赁 ○ *to charter a plane* or *a boat* or *a bus* 租一架飞机(或一艘船或一辆公共汽车)

chartered /ˈtʃɑːtəd/ *adjective* referring to a company which has been set up by charter, and not registered under the Companies Act 特许的:公司根据特许经营执照成立而非按公司法注册 ○ *a chartered bank* 特许银行

chartered accountant /ˌtʃɑːtəd əˈkaʊntənt/ *noun* an accountant who has passed the professional examinations and is a member of the Institute of Chartered Accountants 特许会计师:通过了专业考试并成为特许会计师协会成员的会计师 Abbreviation 缩写 **CA**

Chartered Association of Certified Accountants /ˌtʃɑːtəd əˌsəʊsieɪʃ(ə)n əv ˌsɜːtɪfaɪd əˈkaʊntənts/ *noun* the former name of the Association of Chartered Certified Accountants 特许公认会计师协会:特许注册会计师协会的前称

chartered bank /ˌtʃɑːtəd ˈbæŋk/ *noun* a bank which has been set up by government charter, formerly used in England, but now only done in the USA and Canada 特许银行:政府批准发给特许执照的银行,这种做法英格兰曾用过,目前只有美国和加拿大还在使用

chartered company /ˌtʃɑːtəd ˈkʌmp(ə)ni/ *noun* a company which has been set up by royal charter, and Full form of not registered under the Companies Act 特许公司:经皇家特许而非按公司法成立的公司

Chartered Institute of Public Finance and Accountancy /ˌtʃɑːtəd ˌɪnstɪtjuːt əv ˌpʌblɪk ˌfaɪnæns ən əˈkaʊntənsi/ Full form of **CIPFA** 为 **CIPFA** 的全称

Chartered Institute of Taxation /ˌtʃɑːtəd ˌɪnstɪtjuːt əv tækˈseɪʃ(ə)n/ *noun* in the United Kingdom, an organisation for professionals in the field of taxation, formerly the Institute of Taxation 特许税务师协会:英国的税务专业组织,从前叫税务师协会

charting /ˈtʃɑːtɪŋ/ *noun* the work of using charts to analyse stock market trends and forecast future rises or falls 图表分析:通过图表分析股市趋势并预测未来价格涨跌的方法

chartist /ˈtʃɑːtɪst/ *noun* a person who studies stock market trends and forecasts future rises or falls (股市)图表分析人

chart of accounts /ˈtʃɑːt əv əˈkaʊnts/ *noun* a detailed and ordered list of an organisation's numbered or named accounts. Originally devised in Germany, it provides a standard list of account codes for assets, liabilities, capital, revenue, and expenses. It is still used in Germany on a voluntary basis and was adopted as part of the French general accounting plan after the second world war 会计科目表,账户一览表:有关某组织账目编号或名称的详细系统的一览表。它最初由德国创制,提供资产、负债、资本、收益和开支账目代码的标准清单。现仍在德国自愿使用,二战后曾被采纳作为法国总会计计划的一部分

chattel mortgage /ˈtʃæt(ə)l ˌmɔːɡɪdʒ/ *noun* money lent against the security of an item purchased, but not against real estate 动产抵押:以所购物

品而非不动产作为抵押的借贷

chattels real /ˌtʃæt(ə)lz ˈrɪəl/ *noun* leaseholds 准不动产；定期租赁地产

cheap labour/ˌtʃiːp ˈleɪbə/ *noun* workers who do not earn much money 廉价劳动力

cheap money/ˌtʃiːp ˈmʌni/ *noun* money which can be borrowed at a low rate of interest 低息贷款，低息资金

cheat/tʃiːt/ *verb* to trick someone so that he or she loses money 欺骗 ○ *He cheated the Inland Revenue out of thousands of pounds.* 他从国内税务局骗税数千英镑。○ *She was accused of cheating clients who came to ask her for advice.* 她被指控欺骗前来咨询的客户。

check/tʃek/ *noun* **1.** a sudden stop 突然停止 **2.** investigation or examination 检查，调查 ○ *a routine check of the fire equipment* 对消防设备进行常规检查 ○ *The auditors carried out checks on the petty cash book.* 审计师检查了小额现金账簿。**3.** *US* (*in a restaurant*) a bill (美)(餐厅)账单 **4.** *US* a mark on paper to show that something is correct (美)(记在纸上表明正确的)符号 ○ *Make a check in the box marked 'R'.* 勾选标有 R 的方框。(NOTE: The UK term is **tick** 英国用语为 **tick**) ■ *verb* **1.** to stop or delay something 停止；拖延 ○ *to check the entry of contraband into the country* 阻止走私货进入国境 ○ *to check the flow of money out of a country* 阻止资金流出某国 **2.** to examine or to investigate something 检查，调查 ○ *to check that an invoice is correct* 确保发票正确 ○ *to check and sign for goods* 检查并签发货物 □ **she checked the computer printout against the invoices** she examined the printout and the invoices to see if the figures were the same 她将计算机的打印件与发票相对照，看数字是否一致 **3.** *US* to mark something with a sign to show that it is correct (美)在纸上画上表示正确的符号 ○ *check the box marked 'R'* 勾选标有 R 的方框 (NOTE: The UK term is **tick** 英国用语为 **tick**)

checkable /ˈtʃekəb(ə)l/ *adjective* *US* referring to a deposit account on which checks can be drawn (美)(存款账户)可开出支票的

checkbook/ˈtʃekbʊk/ *noun* US spelling of **cheque book** 为 **cheque book** 的美国拼法

check routing symbol/tʃek ˈruːtɪŋ ˌsɪmbəl/ *noun* *US* a number shown on an American cheque which identifies the Federal Reserve district through which the cheque will be cleared, similar to the British 'bank sort code' (美)支票结算号码：支票上用于识别结算支票的联邦储备区号码，类似于英国的"银行分类代码"

check sample /ˈtʃek ˌsɑːmp(ə)l/ *noun* a sample to be used to see if a consignment is acceptable 验货样品

cheque/tʃek/ *noun* a note to a bank asking them to pay money from your account to the account of the person whose name is written on the note 支票 ○ *a cheque for £10* or *a £10 cheque* 10英镑的支票 (NOTE: The US spelling is **check** 美国拼法为 **check**)

cheque account/ˈtʃek əˌkaʊnt/ *noun* same as 同 **current account**

cheque book/ˈtʃek bʊk/ *noun* a booklet with new blank cheques 支票簿 (NOTE: The usual US term is

checkbook 美国常用 **checkbook**）

cheque card/ˈtʃek kɑːd/, **cheque guarantee card** /ˌtʃek ɡærənˈtiː kɑːd/ *noun* a plastic card from a bank which guarantees payment of a cheque up to some amount, even if the user has no money in his account 支票卡，支票保付卡：即使用户账户中没有钱，银行仍保证对支票支付一定款项的塑料卡凭证

cheque requisition/ˈtʃek ˌrekwɪzɪʃ(ə)n/ *noun* an official note from a department to the company accounts staff asking for a cheque to be written 支票申请单

cheque stub/ˈtʃek stʌb/ *noun* a piece of paper left in a cheque book after a cheque has been written and taken out 支票存根

cheque to bearer/ˌtʃek tə ˈbeərə/ *noun* a cheque with no name written on it, so that the person who holds it can cash it 来人支票，无记名支票：上面未写姓名、任何持有者均可兑现的支票

chief/tʃiːf/ *adjective* most important 最重要的，主要的 ○ *He is the chief accountant of an industrial group*. 他是一个工业集团的总会计师。○ *She is the chief buyer for a department store*. 她是一家百货公司的采购主管。

chief executive/tʃiːf ɪɡˈzekjʊtɪv/, **chief executive officer** /tʃiːf ɪɡˈzekjʊtɪv ˌɒfɪsə/ *noun US* the most important director in charge of a company （美）首席执行官 Abbreviation 缩写 **CEO**

Chief Secretary to the Treasury/ˌtʃiːf ˌsekrətri tə ðə ˈtreʒ(ə)ri/ *noun* a government minister responsible to the Chancellor of the Exchequer for the control of public expenditure 财政部首席大臣：就公共支出的管理向财政大臣负责的政府部长（NOTE：In the USA, this is the responsibility of the **Director of the Budget** 在美国，负责该职责的是预算主任 **Director of the Budget**）

Chinese walls/ˌtʃaɪniːz ˈwɔːlz/ *plural noun* imaginary barriers between departments in the same organisation, set up to avoid insider dealing or conflict of interest. For example, if a merchant bank is advising on a planned takeover bid, its investment department should not know that the bid is taking place, or they would advise their clients to invest in the company being taken over 难以逾越的壁垒，严重障碍：同一组织内部不同部门之间的假想障碍，设置这种障碍是为了避免内幕交易或利益冲突。例如，假设一家商业银行正在为一项兼并要约提供咨询，那么该银行的投资部门就不应获知此事，否则它会劝它的客户投资于这家将被兼并的企业

chop/tʃɒp/ *noun* a mark made on a document to show that it has been agreed, acknowledged, paid, or that payment has been received 图章；官印：表明协议已获同意、文件已收到、欠款已支付或已收到的印记

chose/tʃəʊz/ *French word meaning* 'item' or 'thing'（法语）项目，物品，所有物 □ **chose in possession** physical thing which can be owned (such as a piece of furniture) 实际占有的动产（如一件家具）

chose in action/ˌtʃəʊz ɪn ˈækʃən/ *noun* the legal term for a personal right which can be enforced or claimed as if it were property, e.g. a patent, copyright or debt 权利财产，未实际占有的动产：法律上指可经诉讼

取得的财产权(例如专利权、版权或债权)

Christmas bonus/ˌkrɪsməs ˈbəʊnəs/ *noun* an extra payment made to staff at Christmas 圣诞节奖金:在圣诞节发给员工的奖金

chronological order/ˌkrɒnəlɒdʒɪk(ə)l ˈɔːdə/ *noun* the arrangement of records such as files and invoices in order of their dates(文件、发票的)按时间顺序(排列)

churning/tʃɜːnɪŋ/ *noun* **1.** a practice employed by stockbrokers, where they buy and sell on a client's discretionary account in order to earn their commission. The deals are frequently of no advantage to the client 过度买卖,挤油交易:股票经纪人使用客户的全权委托账户进行买卖以赚取佣金的做法。这种交易往往对客户不利 **2.** a practice employed by insurance salesmen where the salesman suggests that a client should change his or her insurance policy solely in order to earn the salesman a commission 煽动交易,揩油交易:保险销售员为赚取佣金而建议客户更改其保险单的做法

'... more small investors lose money through churning than almost any other abuse, yet most people have never heard of it. Churning involves brokers generating income simply by buying and selling investments on behalf of their clients. Constant and needless churning earns them hefty commissions which bites into the investment portfolio'
"小投资者因为遭受过度买卖而蒙受损失的情形要多于其他欺骗行为,但大多数人都从未听说过过度买卖这个说法。在过度买卖中,经纪人纯粹为了赚取收入而代表客户买卖投资。频繁的不必要的过度买卖令经纪人从投资组合中鲸吞了巨额佣金"[*Guardian*《卫报》]

CICA *abbr* Canadian Institute of Chartered Accountants 加拿大特许会计师协会

CIPFA *noun* a leading professional accountancy body in the UK, specialising in the public services 特许公共财务与会计协会:英国主要的专业会计机构,专门从事公共服务 Full form 全称为 **Chartered Institute of Public Finance and Accountancy**

circularisation of debtors /ˌsɜːkjʊləraɪzeɪʃ(ə)n əv ˈdetəz/ *noun* the sending of letters by a company's auditors to debtors in order to verify the existence and extent of the company's assets 债权人询证函:公司审计师致债权人的信函,以函证公司资产的存在和规模

circularise/ˈsɜːkjʊləraɪz/, **circularize** *verb* to send a circular to 将通知发送给 ○ *The committee has agreed to circularise the members of the society.* 委员会同意发送通知给社团成员。○ *They circularised all their customers with a new list of prices.* 他们向所有客户发送新的价格表。

circular letter/ˌsɜːkjʊlə ˈletə/ *noun* a letter sent to many people 通函

circular letter of credit /ˌsɜːkjʊlə ˌletər əv ˈkredɪt/ *noun* a letter of credit sent to all branches of the bank which issues it 巡回信用证,旅行信用证:发送给签发行所有支行的信用证

circulate /ˈsɜːkjʊleɪt/ *verb* **1.** to send or to give out without restrictions (不受限制地)寄送,分发 **2.** to send information to 传播,散布(信息)○ *They circulated a new list of prices to* *all their customers*. 他们向所有客户发送了新的价格目录。○ *They circulated information about job vacancies to all colleges in the area*. 他们向该地区所有大专院校发送了招聘信息。

circulating capital /ˌsɜːkjʊleɪtɪŋ ˈkæpɪt(ə)l/ *noun* capital in the form of cash or debtors, raw materials, finished products and work in progress which a company requires to carry on its business 流动资金，流动资本

circulation /ˌsɜːkjʊˈleɪʃ(ə)n/ *noun* **1.** the act of sending information（信息的）传送，传播 ○ *The company is trying to improve the circulation of information between departments*. 公司正努力改善各部门之间的信息传递。**2.** movement 流通

circulation of capital /ˌsɜːkjʊleɪʃ(ə)n əv ˈkæpɪt(ə)l/ *noun* a movement of capital from one investment to another 资本周转

civil action /ˌsɪv(ə)l ˈækʃən/ *noun* a court case brought by a person or a company against someone who has done them wrong 民事诉讼

claim /kleɪm/ *noun* an act of asking for something that you feel you have a right to 索取，要求；主张 ■ *verb* **1.** to ask for money, especially from an insurance company 要求赔偿，（尤其是向保险公司）索赔 ○ *He claimed £100,000 damages against the cleaning firm*. 他要求保洁公司赔偿100,000英镑。○ *She claimed for repairs to the car against her insurance policy*. 她要求依照她的保险单赔偿修车费。**2.** to say that you have a right to something or that something is your property 声言对…拥有权利（或所有权）○ *She is claiming possession of the house*. 她声称拥有这幢房子。○ *No one claimed the umbrella found in my office*. 没有人来认领我办公室那把雨伞。**3.** to state that something is a fact 声称，主张 ○ *He claims he never received the goods*. 他声称他从未收到过这些物品。○ *She claims that the shares are her property*. 她声称这些股票是她的财产。

claimant /ˈkleɪmənt/ *noun* a person who makes a claim against someone in the civil courts 索赔人，原告（NOTE: This term has now replaced **plaintiff**. The other side in a case is the **defendant** 该用语现已改为 **plaintiff**。诉讼的另一方为 **defendant**）

claimer /ˈkleɪmə/ *noun* same as 同 **claimant**

claim form /ˈkleɪm fɔːm/ *noun* a form which has to be filled in when making an insurance claim 索赔申请书

claims department /ˈkleɪmz dɪˌpɑːtmənt/ *noun* a department of an insurance company which deals with claims（保险公司）理赔部

claims manager /ˈkleɪmz ˌmænɪdʒə/ *noun* the manager of a claims department 理赔部经理

classical system of corporation tax /ˌklæsɪk(ə)l ˌsɪstəm əv ˌkɔːpəˈreɪʃ(ə)n ˌtæks/ *noun* a system in which companies and their owners are liable for corporation tax as separate entities. A company's taxed income is therefore paid out to shareholders who are in turn taxed again. This system operates in the United States and the Netherlands. It was replaced in the United Kingdom in 1973 by an imputation system 传统公司税制度：公司及其所有人作为分开的实体缴交公司税

的制度。根据该制度，公司的税后收入作为股利分配给股东，然后股东也要相应地再次纳税。目前美国及荷兰使用该体制。在英国，1973 年被归属制取代

classify /ˈklæsɪfaɪ/ *verb* to put into classes or categories according to specific characteristics 将…分类 (NOTE: **classifies – classifying – classified**)

class of assets /ˌklɑːs əv ˈæsets/ *noun* the grouping of similar assets into categories. This is done because under International Accounting Standards Committee rules, tangible assets and intangible assets cannot be revalued on an individual basis, only for a class of assets 资产分类：将同类资产归为一类。这样做是因为国际会计准则委员会规定，有形资产和无形资产不能个别估值，而只能对一个资产类别进行估值

clause /klɔːz/ *noun* a section of a contract （合同）条款 ○ *There are ten clauses in the contract of employment.* 该雇用合同有 10 项条款。○ *There is a clause in this contract concerning the employer's right to dismiss an employee.* 该合同中有一条关于雇主有权解雇员工的条款。■ *verb* to list details of the relevant parties to a bill of exchange 在汇票上详细列明相关各方

claw back /ˌklɔː ˈbæk/ *verb* to take back money which has been allocated 回补：将已分配的资金收回 ○ *Income tax claws back 25% of pensions paid out by the government.* 政府通过税收收回已发放养老金的 25%。○ *Of the £1m allocated to the project, the government clawed back £100,000 in taxes.* 在政府对项目投资的 100 万英镑中，通过税收收回了 10 万英镑。

clawback /ˈklɔːbæk/ *noun* **1.** money taken back, especially money taken back by the government from grants or tax concessions which had previously been made 资金收回（尤指政府从先前给予的宽免或税务优惠中收回资金） **2.** the allocation of new shares to existing shareholders, so as to maintain the value of their holdings 将新股分配给现有股东，以保持其股权价值不变

clean bill of lading /ˌkliːn bɪl əv ˈleɪdɪŋ/ *noun* a bill of lading with no note to say the shipment is faulty or damaged 清洁提单：并未注明货物有残损的提单

clean float /ˈkliːn fləʊt/ *noun* an act of floating a currency freely on the international markets, without any interference from the government 清洁浮动：政府对国际市场上的货币流通不进行干预

clean opinion /kliːn əˈpɪnjən/, **clean report** /kliːn rɪˈpɔːt/ *noun* an auditor's report that is not qualified （审计师报告的）无保留意见

clean surplus concept /kliːn ˌsɜːpləs ˈkɒnsept/ *noun* the idea that a company's income statement should show the totality of gains and losses, without any of them being taken directly to equity 净盈余观念，净盈余原理：公司的损益表中应列明全部盈亏，而不将任何盈亏直接转到股本的观念

clearance certificate /ˈklɪərəns səˌtɪfɪkət/ *noun* a document showing that goods have been passed by customs 结关证书：海关允许货物放行的文件

clearance sale /ˈklɪərəns seɪl/ *noun* a sale of items at low prices to get rid of stock 清仓大减价销售

clearing /ˈklɪərɪŋ/ *noun* **1.** □ **clearing of goods through customs** passing of goods through customs 货物结关放行 **2.** □ **clearing of a debt** paying all of a debt 债务结算:付清所有的债务 **3.** an act of passing of a cheque through the banking system, transferring money from one account to another 票据交换,结算:通过银行系统内的支票划转进行转账的行为

clearing agency /ˌklɪərɪŋ ˈeɪdʒənsi/ *noun US* central office where stock exchange or commodity exchange transactions are settled (美)票据交换所:进行股票交易或商品交易的中心场所(NOTE: The UK term is **clearing house** 英国用语为 **clearing house**)

clearing bank /ˈklɪərɪŋ bæŋk/ *noun* a bank which clears cheques, especially one of the major British High Street banks, specialising in usual banking business for ordinary customers such as loans, cheques, overdrafts and interest-bearing deposits 清算银行,票据交换银行:进行票据结算的银行,尤指英国高街银行之一,它专门为一般客户提供普通银行业务服务,如贷款、支票、透支、有息存款等

clearing house /ˈklɪərɪŋ haʊs/ *noun* a central office where clearing banks exchange cheques, or where stock exchange or commodity exchange transactions are settled 票据交换所:清算银行进行支票交换、股票交易或商品交易的中心场所

Clearing House Automated Payments System /ˌklɪərɪŋ haʊs ˌɔːtəmeɪtɪd ˈpeɪmənts ˌsɪstəm/ *noun* Full form of **CHAPS** 为 **CHAPS** 的全称

clear profit /ˌklɪə ˈprɒfɪt/ *noun* a profit after all expenses have been paid 净利,纯利:支付所有开支后的利润 ○ *We made $6,000 clear profit on the deal.* 这笔交易我们净赚了6,000美元。

clerical error /ˌklerɪk(ə)l ˈerə/ *noun* a mistake made by someone doing office work 记录错误:文书工作时发生的错误

client /ˈklaɪənt/ *noun* a person with whom business is done or who pays for a service 客户,顾客 ○ *One of our major clients has defaulted on her payments.* 我们的一个大客户没有按规定付款。

client account /ˌklaɪənt əˈkaʊnt/ *noun* a bank account opened by a solicitor or estate agent to hold money on behalf of a client 客户账户,委托人账户:律师或房地产代理商代表客户所开的银行账户

clientele /ˌkliːɒnˈtel/ *noun* all the clients of a business or all the customers of a shop 客户,顾客:公司或商店的所有客户或顾客

close /kləʊz/ *verb* **1.** □ **to close the accounts** to come to the end of an accounting period and make up the profit and loss account 结账:在会计期末编制损益表 **2.** to bring something to an end 结束 □ **she closed her building society account** she took all the money out and stopped using the account 她从住房互助协会的账户中取出所有的钱,然后注销了这个账户 **3.** to stop doing business for the day 打烊,停止营业 ○ *The office closes at 5.30.* 办事处五点半关门。○ *We close early on Saturdays.* 星期六我们关门较早。

close company /ˌkləʊs ˈkʌmp(ə)ni/ *noun* a privately owned company controlled by a few shareholders (in the UK, fewer than five) where the public may own a small number of the shares 不公开招股公司,封闭式公司:由少数几个股东(在英国为五个以下)控制的私人公司,公众可能只拥有少量股份 (NOTE: The US term is **close corporation** or **closed corporation** 美国用语为**close corporation** 或 **closed corporation**)

closed economy /ˌkləʊzd ɪˈkɒnəmi/ *noun* a type of economy where trade and financial dealings are tightly controlled by the government 封闭型经济,闭关自守的经济:贸易和金融都由政府紧密控制的一种经济类型

closed-end credit /ˌkləʊzdend ˈkredɪt/ *noun* FINANCE, BANKING, AND ACCOUNTING, GENERAL MANAGEMENT a loan, plus any interest and finance charges, that is to be repaid in full by a specified future date. Loans that have property or motor vehicles as collateral are usually closed-end (金融、银行、会计和综合管理)固定期限信贷:须在指定的日期前连同利息和融资费用一起偿清的贷款。以地产或机动车辆作为连带抵押的贷款通常都属于固定期限信贷 ➪ 参阅 **revolving credit** (NOTE: Most loans for the purchase of property or motor vehicles are closed-end credits 用于购买地产或机动车辆的贷款大都属于固定期限信贷)

closed-end fund /ˌkləʊzdend ˈfʌnd/ *noun* an investment company with a fixed capital which investments can only be made by buying shares in the company 闭端式基金:具有固定资本额的投资公司,投资只能通过购买公司股票来完成

closed fund /ˌkləʊzd ˈfʌnd/ *noun* a fund, such as an investment trust, where the investor buys shares in the trust and receives dividends. This is as opposed to an open-ended trust, such as a unit trust, where the investor buys units, and the investment is used to purchase further securities for the trust 封闭式基金:一种基金,例如投资信托,投资者在信托公司购买股票并收取股利。与之相反的是开放型信托或公开投资信托,例如单位信托,投资者购买单位信托,其投资又被信托公司用于购买其他证券

closed market /ˌkləʊzd ˈmɑːkɪt/ *noun* a market where a supplier deals only with one agent or distributor and does not supply any others direct 封闭式市场:一个供应商只与一个代理商或批发商交易,不向其他顾客直接供货的市场 ○ *They signed a closed-market agreement with an Egyptian company.* 他们与一家埃及公司签订了一项封闭式市场协议。

close-ended /ˌkləʊsˈendɪd/, **closed-end** /ˈkləʊzdend/ *adjective* referring to an investment which has a fixed capital, such as an investment trust 资本额固定的,限额的

closely held /ˌkləʊsli ˈheld/ *adjective* referring to shares in a company which are controlled by only a few shareholders 股东有限的:一个公司的股份只由少数几个股东控制的

close off /ˌkləʊz ˈɒf/ *verb* to come to the end of an accounting period and make up the profit and loss account 结账:在会计期末编制损益表

closing /ˈkləʊzɪŋ/ *adjective* **1.** final or coming at the end 结束的,最后的 **2.** at the end of an accounting period 会计期末的 ○ *At the end of the quarter the bookkeeper has to calculate the* *closing balance*. 簿记员在季度末须计算季末余额。■ *noun* **1.** the shutting of a shop or being shut 停业 **2.** □ **the closing of an account** the act of stopping supply to a customer on credit 结账：停止向某客户赊销

closing balance /ˌkləʊzɪŋ ˈbæləns/ *noun* the balance at the end of an accounting period 期末余额

closing bid /ˈkləʊzɪŋ bɪd/ *noun* the last bid at an auction, the bid which is successful 收盘出价：拍卖中的最后一次出价，即胜出的价格

closing date /ˈkləʊzɪŋ deɪt/ *noun* the last date 结账日，截止日 ○ *The closing date for tenders to be received is May 1st*. 投标的截止日期是5月1日。

closing-down sale /ˌkləʊzɪŋˈdaʊn ˌseɪl/ *noun* the sale of goods when a shop is closing for ever 清盘销售，停业销售：商店永久停业前的清仓销售

closing entries /ˌkləʊzɪŋ ˈentriz/ *noun* in a double-entry bookkeeping system, entries made at the very end of an accounting period to balance the expense and revenue ledgers 结账分录：在复式簿记系统中，于会计期末作出的记录，以结算开支及收益分类账

closing entry /ˌkləʊzɪŋ ˈentri/ *noun* an entry which closes an account 结账分录

closing out /ˌkləʊzɪŋ ˈaʊt/ *noun US* the act of selling goods cheaply to try to get rid of them (美)廉价清仓

closing price /ˈkləʊzɪŋ praɪs/ *noun* the price of a share at the end of a day's trading 收盘价，收市价：股票于交易日结束时的价格

closing rate /ˈkləʊzɪŋ reɪt/ *noun* the exchange rate of two or more currencies at the close of business of a balance sheet date, e.g. at the end of the financial year 期末汇率，收盘汇率：结算日(如会计年末)停止营业时两种或两种以上货币的汇率

closing-rate method /ˈkləʊzɪŋreɪt ˌmeθəd/ *noun* a technique for translating the figures from a set of financial statements into a different currency using the closing rate. This method is often used for the accounts of a foreign subsidiary of a parent company 期末汇率法：使用期末汇率将一组财务报表的数字转换成以另一种货币表述的一种方法，该方法通常用于母公司下属外国分公司的账目

closing stock /ˌkləʊzɪŋ ˈstɒk/ *noun* a business's remaining stock at the end of an accounting period. It includes finished products, raw materials, or work in progress and is deducted from the period's costs in the balance sheets 期末存货：企业于会计期末的剩余存货，它包括成品、原材料和正在生产中的产品，并在资产负债表内从该期间的成本中扣除 ○ *At the end of the month the closing stock was 10% higher than at the end of the previous month*. 这个月末的存货比上个月末多出了10%。

closing time /ˈkləʊzɪŋ taɪm/ *noun* the time when a shop or office stops work 关门时间，下班时间

closure /ˈkləʊʒə/ *noun* the act of closing 关闭

C/N *abbr* credit note 贷记通知单

CNCC *abbr* Compagnie Nationale des Commissaires aux Comptes 法国注册审计师协会

co- /kəʊ/ *prefix* working or acting together 一起工作(或行动)

CoCoA *abbr* continuously contemporary accounting 持续适应环境会计

co-creditor /ˌkəʊˈkredɪtə/ *noun* a person who is a creditor of the same company as you are 共同债权人

code /kəʊd/ *noun* **1.** a system of signs, numbers or letters which mean something 代码 **2.** a set of rules 法规，法典

code of practice /ˌkəʊd əv ˈpræktɪs/ *noun* **1.** rules drawn up by an association which the members must follow when doing business 业务守则；业务条例 **2.** the formally established ways in which members of a profession agree to work 专业守则，行业规范 ○ *Advertisers have agreed to abide by the code of practice set out by the advertising council.* 广告商们同意遵守广告委员会制定的行业规范。

codicil /ˈkəʊdɪsɪl/ *noun* a document executed in the same way as a will, making additions or changes to an existing will 遗嘱附录：对已有遗嘱修改或增加、与遗嘱具有同样效力的文件

coding /ˈkəʊdɪŋ/ *noun* the act of putting a code on something 编码 ○ *the coding of invoices* 发票的编码

co-director /ˈkəʊdaɪˌrektə/ *noun* a person who is a director of the same company as you 联席董事：同为某公司董事的人

co-financing /ˌkəʊˈfaɪnænsɪŋ/ *noun* the act of arranging finance for a project from a series of sources 共同筹资，共同资助：从多个来源安排项目融资

co-insurance /ˌkəʊɪnˈʃʊərəns/ *noun* an insurance policy where the risk is shared among several insurers 共同保险，共保：由多个保险人共担风险的保险单

cold call /ˌkəʊld ˈkɔːl/ *noun* a telephone call or sales visit where the salesperson has no appointment and the client is not an established customer 贸然访问：销售人员在没有预约的情况下，突然对潜在客户进行的电话（或上门）推销 ■ *verb* to make a cold call 贸然访问

cold start /ˌkəʊld ˈstɑːt/ *noun* the act of beginning a new business or opening a new shop with no previous turnover to base it on 冷启动：在没有可借鉴经验的情况下开展新业务或开设新工厂

collateral /kəˈlæt(ə)rəl/ *noun* a security, such as negotiable instruments, shares or goods, used to provide a guarantee for a loan 担保品，抵押品

'... examiners have come to inspect the collateral that thrifts may use in borrowing from the Fed'
"检查官对储蓄机构向联邦储备借款时可能用到的担保品进行检查"［*Wall Street Journal*《华尔街日报》］

collateralisation /kəˌlæt(ə)rəlaɪˈzeɪʃ(ə)n/ *noun* the act of securing a debt by selling long-term receivables to another company which secures them on the debts 出售长期应收款给另一家公司作为债务的担保

collateralise /kəˈlæt(ə)rəlaɪz/, **collateralize** *verb* to secure a debt by means of a collateral 抵押担保

collect /kəˈlekt/ *verb* **1.** to get money which is owed to you by making the person who owes it pay 收款，收账 **2.** to take things away from a place 拿走，领取 ○ *We have to collect the stock from the warehouse.* 我们不得不将存货从仓库里搬出来。■ *adverb, adjective* referring to a phone call which the person receiving the call agrees to pay for (电话)受话人付费(的)

collectables /kəˈlektɪb(ə)lz/ *plural noun* items which people collect, e. g. stamps, playing cards or matchboxes 收集品,收藏品

collectibility /kəˌlektɪˈbɪlɪti/ *noun* ability of cash owed to be collected 欠款收回的能力

collecting agency /kəˈlektɪŋ ˌeɪdʒənsi/ *noun* an agency which collects money owed to other companies for a commission 收款代理商,收账公司

collecting bank /kəˈlektɪŋ bæŋk/ *noun* a bank into which a person has deposited a cheque, and which has the duty to collect the money from the account of the writer of the cheque 托收银行:收取客户支票,并负责向开票账户收款的银行

collection /kəˈlekʃən/ *noun* **1.** the act of getting money together, or of making someone pay money which is owed 集资;收账 ○ *tax collection* or *collection of tax* 税款的收取 **2.** the fetching of goods 取货 ○ *The stock is in the warehouse awaiting collection.* 仓库中的存货待取。

collection ratio /kəˌlekʃən ˈreɪʃiəʊ/ *noun* the average number of days it takes a firm to convert its accounts receivable into cash 应收账项比率:公司收回其应收账款所需的平均天数 Also known as 亦称作 **days' sales outstanding**

collections /kəˈlekʃənz/ *plural noun* money which has been collected 收回的款项

collector /kəˈlektə/ *noun* a person who makes people pay money which is owed 收款人 ○ *He works as a debt collector.* 他是一名收债人。

column /ˈkɒləm/ *noun* a series of numbers arranged one underneath the other 栏,列 ○ *to add up a column of figures* 将一栏数字相加 ○ *Put the total at the bottom of the column.* 将总数填在这栏数字的最底下。

combined financial statement /kəmˌbaɪnd faɪˌnænʃəl ˈsteɪtmənt/ *noun* a written record covering the assets, liabilities, net worth, and operating statement of two or more related or affiliated companies 合并财务报表:包括两个或两个以上关联或联属公司的资产、负债、净值及经营报表的书面记录

commerce /ˈkɒmɜːs/ *noun* the buying and selling of goods and services 商业

commercial /kəˈmɜːʃ(ə)l/ *adjective* **1.** referring to business 商业的 **2.** profitable 盈利的

commercial aircraft /kəˌmɜːʃ(ə)l ˈeəkrɑːft/ *noun* an aircraft used to carry cargo or passengers for payment 商用飞机

commercial bank /kəˈmɜːʃ(ə)l bæŋk/ *noun* a bank which offers banking services to the public, as opposed to a merchant bank 商业银行(与商人银行相对)

commercial bill /kəˌmɜːʃ(ə)l ˈbɪl/ *noun* a bill of exchange issued by a company (a trade bill) or accepted by a bank (a bank bill) (as opposed to Treasury bills which are issued by the government) 商业汇票:公司签发的汇票(商业承兑汇票)或银行承兑的汇票(银行承兑汇票)(与政府发行的国库券

相对）

commercial directory /kəˈmɜːʃ(ə)l daɪˌrekt(ə)ri/ *noun* a book which lists all the businesses and business people in a town 工商企业索引，商业通讯录

commercial failure /kəˌmɜːʃ(ə)l ˈfeɪljə/ *noun* a financial collapse or bankruptcy 商业破产

commercial law /kəˌmɜːʃ(ə)l ˈlɔː/ *noun* the laws regarding business 商法

commercial lawyer /kəˌmɜːʃ(ə)l ˈlɔːjə/ *noun* a person who specialises in company law or who advises companies on legal problems 商业律师

commercial loan /kəˌmɜːʃ(ə)l ˈləʊn/ *noun* a short-term renewable loan or line of credit used to finance the seasonal or cyclical working capital needs of a company 商业贷款：为公司提供季节或周期运作资金的短期循环贷款或信贷额度

commercially /kəˈmɜːʃ(ə)li/ *adverb* in a business way 商业地

commercial paper /kəˌmɜːʃ(ə)l ˈpeɪpə/ *noun* an IOU issued by a company to raise a short-term loan 商业票据 Abbreviation 缩写 **CP**

commercial port /kəˌmɜːʃ(ə)l ˈpɔːt/ *noun* a port which has only goods traffic and no passengers 商务港：只从事货物运输的港口

commercial property /kəˌmɜːʃ(ə)l ˈprɒpəti/ *noun* a building, or buildings, used as offices or shops 商用建筑：用作写字楼或商场的建筑物

commercial report /kəˌmɜːʃ(ə)l rɪˈpɔːt/ *noun* an investigative report made by an organisation such as a credit bureau that specialises in obtaining information regarding a person or organisation applying for something such as credit or employment 商业调查报告：由专门获取（贷款或工作）申请人（组织）信息的机构（如信贷机构）提供的调查报告

commercial substance /kəˌmɜːʃ(ə)l ˈsʌbstəns/ *noun* the economic reality that underlies a transaction or arrangement, regardless of its legal or technical denomination. For example, a company may sell an office block and then immediately lease it back: the commercial substance may be that it has not been sold 商业实质：一项交易或安排背后的经济事实（而不论其法律或文字层面）。例如，一家公司可能会出售一幢写字楼，然后又马上将它租回，这项交易的商业实质可能是写字楼未售出

commercial year /kəˌmɜːʃ(ə)l ˈjɪə/ *noun* an artificial year treated as having 12 months of 30 days each, used for calculating such things as monthly sales data and inventory levels 商业财政年度：每年 12 个月、每月 30 天的人为界定的年度，用于计算每月销售数据和存货水平

commission /kəˈmɪʃ(ə)n/ *noun* **1.** money paid to a salesperson or agent, usually a percentage of the sales made 佣金；回扣 ○ *She gets 10% commission on everything she sells.* 她从她所售商品中收取 10%的佣金。○ *He is paid on a commission basis.* 他的报酬是佣金制的。**2.** a group of people officially appointed to examine some problem 委员会；调查团：被正式委派检查某些问题的一组人 ○ *He is the chairman of the government commission on export subsidies.* 他是政府出口补贴委员会的主席。

commission agent /kəˈmɪʃ(ə)n

ˌeɪdʒənt/ *noun* an agent who is paid a percentage of sales 佣金代理商

commission broker /kəˈmɪʃ(ə)n ˌbrəʊkə/ *noun* a stockbroker who works for a commission 证券经纪人

commissioner /kəˈmɪʃ(ə)nə/ *noun* an ombudsman 特派员，专员

Commissioner of Inland Revenue /kəˌmɪʃ(ə)nə əv ˌɪnlənd ˈrevənjuː/ *noun* a person appointed officially to supervise the collection of taxes, including income tax, capital gains tax and corporation tax, but not VAT 国内税务专员：官方指定的监督征税的人，所征税种包括所得税、资本利得税和公司税，但不包括增值税

Commissioners of the Inland Revenue /kəˌmɪʃ(ə)nəz əv ðiː ˌɪnlənd ˈrevənjuː/ *noun* in the United Kingdom, officials responsible for hearing appeals by taxpayers against their tax assessment 国内税务专员：英国负责听证纳税人对其税收估值上诉的官员

commission house /kəˈmɪʃ(ə)n haʊs/ *noun* a firm which buys or sells for clients, and charges a commission for this service 委托交易商行，代办行：代客户买卖商品并收取佣金的公司

commission rep /kəˈmɪʃ(ə)n rep/ *noun* a representative who is not paid a salary but receives a commission on sales 佣金代理人：无工资，靠抽取销售佣金获利的代理人

commit /kəˈmɪt/ *verb* □ **to commit yourself to** to guarantee something, especially a loan issue, or to guarantee to do something 保证，担保（尤指贷款）

commitment /kəˈmɪtmənt/ *noun* something which you have agreed to do 承诺，保证 ○ *to make a commitment* or *to enter into a commitment to do something* 作出承诺 ○ *The company has a commitment to provide a cheap service*. 该公司承诺提供廉价服务。

commitment document /kəˌmɪtmənt ˈdɒkjʊmənt/ *noun* a contract, change order, purchase order, or letter of intent pertaining to the supply of goods and services that commits an organisation to legal, financial, and other obligations 承诺文件：使某组织对所提供的产品和服务负有法律、财务及其他责任的合同、交换订单、购买订单或意向书

commitment fee /kəˈmɪtmənt fiː/ *noun* a fee paid to a bank which has arranged a line of credit which has not been fully used 承诺费：因未按承诺完全使用银行给予的贷款额度而支付给银行的费用

commitments basis /kəˌmɪtmənts ˈbeɪsɪs/ *noun* the method of recording the expenditure of a public sector organisation at the time when it commits itself to it rather than when it actually pays for it 承诺基准：在某一公共组织承诺支付时（而不是在它实际支付时）记录开支的做法

commitments for capital expenditure /kəˌmɪtmənts fə ˌkæpɪt(ə)l ɪkˈspendɪtʃə/ *noun* the amount a company has committed to spend on fixed assets in the future. In the United Kingdom, companies are legally obliged to disclose this amount, and any additional commitments, in their annual report 已承付资本支出：公司承诺的未来固定资产开支金额。在英国，公司须依法在年度报告中披露该金额及任何其他承诺

Committee on Accounting Procedure /kəˌmɪti ɒn əˈkaʊntɪŋ prəˌsiːdʒə/ *noun* in the United States, a committee of the American Institute of Certified Public Accountants that was responsible between 1939 and 1959 for issuing accounting principles, some of which are still part of the Generally Accepted Accounting Principles 会计程序委员会：美国注册会计师协会的一个下属委员会，它于 1939 年至 1959 年期间负责颁布会计准则，其中有些准则现仍被公认会计准则所采纳

commodity /kəˈmɒdɪti/ *noun* something sold in very large quantities, especially a raw material such as a metal or a food such as wheat 商品：特指金属、小麦之类大量出售的原材料及食品

commodity exchange /kəˈmɒdɪti ɪksˌtʃeɪndʒ/ *noun* a place where commodities are bought and sold 商品交易所

commodity futures /kəˌmɒdɪti ˈfjuːtʃəz/ *plural noun* commodities traded for delivery at a later date 商品期货 ○ *Silver rose 5% on the commodity futures market yesterday.* 昨天的商品期货市场银价上涨了 5%。

commodity market /kəˈmɒdɪti ˌmɑːkɪt/ *noun* a place where people buy and sell commodities 商品市场

commodity trader /kəˈmɒdɪti ˌtreɪdə/ *noun* a person whose business is buying and selling commodities 商品交易商(者)

common cost /ˌkɒmən ˈkɒst/ *noun* a cost which is apportioned to two or more cost centres 共同成本：分摊到两个或更多成本中心的成本

Common Market /ˈkɒmən ˈmɑːkɪt/ *noun* □ **the European Common Market** formerly the name for the European Community, an organization which links several European countries for the purposes of trade 欧洲共同市场：欧洲共同体的前称，它是欧洲部分国家成立的贸易组织

common ownership /ˌkɒmən ˈəʊnəʃɪp/ *noun* a situation where a business is owned by the employees who work in it 共有所有权

common pricing /ˌkɒmən ˈpraɪsɪŋ/ *noun* the illegal fixing of prices by several businesses so that they all charge the same price 共同定价：几个企业私下制定的相同价格，以避免价格战

common stock /ˌkɒmən ˈstɒk/ *noun US* ordinary shares in a company, giving shareholders a right to vote at meetings and to receive dividends (美)普通股：公司的普通股票，它给予股票持有者在股东大会上的投票权和收取股利的权利

Compagnie Nationale des Commissaires aux Comptes *noun* in France, an organisation that regulates external audit 法国注册审计师协会：主管外部审计的机构 Abbreviation 缩写 **CNCC**

Companies Registration Office /ˌkʌmp(ə)niz ˌredʒɪˈstreɪʃ(ə)n ˌɒfɪs/ *noun* an office of the Registrar of Companies, the official organisation where the records of companies must be deposited, so that they can be inspected by the public 公司注册办事处：存放公司记录以便公众查阅的官方机构 Abbreviation 缩写 **CRO**. Also called 亦称作 **Companies House**

company /ˈkʌmp(ə)ni/ *noun* a business organisation, a group of people organised to buy, sell or provide a service, usually for profit 公司

company auditor /ˌkʌmp(ə)ni ˈɔːdɪtə/ *noun* the individual or firm of accountants a company appoints to audit its annual accounts 公司审计师

company car /ˌkʌmp(ə)ni ˈkɑː/ *noun* a car which belongs to a company and is lent to an employee to use for business or other purposes 公车,公司用车:属于公司但为商业或其他目的借给雇员使用的车

company director /ˌkʌmp(ə)ni daɪˈrektə/ *noun* a person appointed by the shareholders to help run a company 公司董事:由股东委派经营公司业务的人

company flat /ˌkʌmp(ə)ni ˈflæt/ *noun* a flat owned by a company and used by members of staff from time to time 公司公寓,公司住房:公司所属并提供给员工使用的住房(NOTE: The US term is **company apartment** 美国用语为 **company apartment**)

company law /ˌkʌmp(ə)ni ˈlɔː/ *noun* laws which refer to the way companies work 公司法

company pension scheme /ˌkʌmp(ə)ni ˈpenʃən skiːm/ *noun* same as 同 **occupational pension scheme** ○ *She decided to join the company's pension scheme.* 她决定加入职业退休金计划。

company promoter /ˌkʌmp(ə)ni prəˈməʊtə/ *noun* a person who organises the setting up of a new company 公司发起人

company registrar /ˌkʌmp(ə)ni ˈredʒɪstrɑː/ *noun* the person who keeps the share register of a company 公司注册主管:保管公司股份登记册的人

company secretary /ˌkʌmp(ə)ni ˈsekrɪt(ə)ri/ *noun* a person who is responsible for a company's legal and financial affairs 公司秘书:负责公司法律和财务事务的人

comparability /ˌkɒmp(ə)rəˈbɪlɪti/ *noun* a feature in the financial statements of two or more companies that enables an analyst to make a faithful comparison between them (多家公司财务报表之间的)可比性,相似性

comparable /ˈkɒmp(ə)rəb(ə)l/ *adjective* possible to compare 可比较的,比得上的,类似的 ○ *The two sets of figures are not comparable.* 这两组数字没有可比性。

comparative balance sheet /kəmˌpærətɪv ˈbæləns ʃiːt/ *noun* one of two or more financial statements prepared on different dates that lend themselves to a comparative analysis of the financial condition of an organization 比较资产负债表:于不同日期编制的财务报表,作为对某组织财务状况进行比较分析的参照

compare with /kəmˈpeə wɪð/ *verb* to examine two things to see where they are the same and where they differ 比较 ○ *How do the sales this year compare with last year's?* 今年的销售额与去年相比如何? ○ *Compared with the previous month, last month was terrific.* 与以前的月份相比,上月的情况好极了。

compensate /ˈkɒmpənseɪt/ *verb* to give someone money to make up for a loss or injury 赔偿(损失或伤害) ○ *In this case we will compensate a manager for loss of commission.* 在这种情况下,我们将赔偿经理的佣金损失。 ○ *The company will compensate the* *employee for the burns suffered in the accident*. 公司将对员工的事故烧伤提供赔偿。(NOTE: You compensate someone **for** something.)

compensating balance /ˌkɒmpənseɪtɪŋ ˈbæləns/ *noun* the amount of money which a customer has to keep in a bank account in order to get free services from the bank 补偿性存款:客户须在银行账户中保有以获得银行免费服务的金额

compensating errors /ˌkɒmpənseɪtɪŋ ˈerəz/ *plural noun* two or more errors which are set against each other so that the accounts still balance 抵消性错误:借方和贷方的两个或更多错误互相抵消,使账户仍然平衡

compensation /ˌkɒmpənˈseɪʃ(ə)n/ *noun* **1.** □ **compensation for damage** payment for damage done 损坏赔偿 □ **compensation for loss of office** payment to a director who is asked to leave a company before their contract ends 解职费,离职补偿:对未到合同期即被解除职务的董事的补偿 □ **compensation for loss of earnings** payment to someone who has stopped earning money or who is not able to earn money (失业或退休)救济金:对没有收入或没有收入能力的人的补偿费 **2.** *US* a salary (美)报酬,工资

'...compensation can also be via the magistrates courts for relatively minor injuries'
"对于相对较轻的伤害,也可以通过治安法院获得赔偿"[*Personnel Management*《人事管理》]

compensation deal /ˌkɒmpənˈseɪʃ(ə)n diːl/ *noun* a deal where an exporter is paid (at least in part) in goods from the country to which he or she is exporting 补偿贸易:进口方用产品(至少是部分)偿付出口商的一种贸易方式

compensation fund /ˌkɒmpənˈseɪʃ(ə)n fʌnd/ *noun* a fund operated by the Stock Exchange to compensate investors for losses suffered when members of the Stock Exchange default 补偿基金:证券交易所经营的基金,用于补偿由证券交易所职员失职给投资者带来的损失

compensation package /ˌkɒmpənˈseɪʃ(ə)n ˌpækɪdʒ/ *noun* the salary, pension and other benefits offered with a job 一揽子报酬:某项工作提供的工资、退休金和其他福利待遇

'...golden parachutes are liberal compensation packages given to executives leaving a company'
"金降落伞是给予离职经理丰厚的一揽子报酬"[*Publishers Weekly*《出版者周刊》]

compete /kəmˈpiːt/ *verb* □ **to compete with someone** *or* **with a company** to try to do better than another person or another company 与某人或某公司竞争 ○ *We have to compete with cheap imports from the Far East*. 我们必须与远东进口的便宜货竞争。○ *They were competing unsuccessfully with local companies on their home territory*. 他们竞争不过该国的本土公司。□ **the two companies are competing for a market share** *or* **for a contract** each company is trying to win a larger part of the market, trying to win the contract 这两家公司为占有更大的市场份额或获得一份合同而竞争

competition /ˌkɒmpəˈtɪʃ(ə)n/ *noun* a situation where companies or individuals are trying to do better than others, e.g. trying to win a larger share of the market, or to produce a better or cheaper product or to control the use of resources 竞争

'... profit margins in the industries most exposed to foreign competition are worse than usual'
"对于最易受国外竞争的行业,其利润率比平常更糟" [*Sunday Times*《星期日泰晤士报》]

'... competition is steadily increasing and could affect profit margins as the company tries to retain its market share'
"竞争日趋激烈,公司为保持市场份额,其利润率可能会受到影响" [*Citizen* (*Ottawa*)《公民》(渥太华)]

competitive /kəmˈpetɪtɪv/ *adjective* involving competition 有竞争性的,有竞争力的

'... the company blamed fiercely competitive market conditions in Europe for a £14m operating loss last year'
"公司把去年1,400万英镑的经营亏损归咎于欧洲市场的竞争太过激烈" [*Financial Times*《金融时报》]

competitive devaluation /kəmˌpetɪtɪv ˌdiːvæljuˈeɪʃ(ə)n/ *noun* a devaluation of a currency to make a country's goods more competitive on the international markets (货币)竞争性贬值:为使本国产品在国际市场上更具竞争力而使本国货币贬值

competitive pricing /kəmˌpetɪtɪv ˈpraɪsɪŋ/ *noun* the practice of putting low prices on goods so as to compete with other products 竞争性价格:推出低价以获得竞争优势

competitive products /kəmˌpetɪtɪv ˈprɒdʌkts/ *plural noun* products made to compete with existing products 竞争性产品:为与现有产品竞争而推出的产品

competitor /kəmˈpetɪtə/ *noun* a person or company that is competing with another 竞争者 ○ *Two German firms are our main competitors.* 两家德国公司是我们的主要竞争对手。

'... sterling labour costs continue to rise between 3% and 5% a year faster than in most of our competitor countries'
"英国的人工成本以每年3%～5%的速度持续上涨,这个速度比我们大多数竞争对手的国家都快" [*Sunday Times*《星期日泰晤士报》]

complete /kəmˈpliːt/ *verb* to sign a contract for the sale of a property and to exchange it with the other party, so making it legal 履行,实践:双方签署并交换销售合同,使其具有法律效力

completed contract method /kəmˌpliːtɪd ˈkɒntrækt ˌmeθəd/ *noun* a way of accounting for a particular contractual obligation, e.g., a long-term construction project, whereby the profit is not recorded until the final completion of the project, even if there has been some revenue while the project was still in progress 完成合同法,全部完工法:特定合约责任(如长期建筑项目)的一种会计方法,使用该方法时,利润直到项目竣工后才进行记录,即便在项目进行期间已获得部分收入

completion /kəmˈpliːʃ(ə)n/ *noun* the act of finishing something 完成

completion date /kəmˈpliːʃ(ə)n deɪt/ *noun* a date when something will be finished 完成日期

compliance /kəmˈplaɪəns/ *noun*

agreement to do what is ordered 遵从，依从

compliance costs /kəmˈplaɪəns kɒsts/ *noun* expenses incurred as a result of meeting legal requirements, e.g., for safety requirements or to comply with company law 遵规成本，守法费用：依照法律要求，如履行安全法或公司法，而支付的费用

compliance department /kəmˈplaɪəns dɪˌpɑːtmənt/ *noun* a department in a stockbroking firm which makes sure that the Stock Exchange rules are followed and that confidentiality is maintained in cases where the same firm represents rival clients 守纪部，监察部：证券经纪公司的一个部门，其职能是监管证券交易规则的执行，并确保在公司代表两个互为竞争者的客户时坚持保密原则

compliance officer /kəmˈplaɪəns ˌɒfɪsə/ *noun* an employee of a financial organisation whose job is to make sure that the organisation complies with the regulations governing its business 守纪部职员，监察部职员：金融机构中负责确保组织遵守相关业务法规的雇员

composition /ˌkɒmpəˈzɪʃ(ə)n/ *noun* an agreement between a debtor and creditors, where the debtor settles a debt by repaying only part of it 债务和解协议：债权人和债务人之间达成的协议，债务人只需偿还部分债务即算结清负债

compound /kəmˈpaʊnd/ *verb* **1.** to agree with creditors to settle a debt by paying part of what is owed （互让）解决债务，和解债务：债权人同意债务人只偿还部分债务即算结清负债 **2.** to add to 使增加，使复合 ○ *The interest is compounded daily.* 利息每天复合计算。

compound discount /ˌkɒmpaʊnd ˈdɪskaʊnt/ *noun* the difference between the nominal amount of a particular sum in the future and its present discounted value. So, if £150 in a year's time is worth £142 now, the compound discount is £8 复利贴现：特定金额的未来面额与其当前贴现值之差。假设一年后价值为 150 英镑面额的现值是 142 英镑，则复利贴现为 8 英镑

compound interest /ˌkɒmpaʊnd ˈɪntrəst/ *noun* interest which is added to the capital and then earns interest itself 复利：利息加上本金后再计算利息

compound journal entry /ˌkɒmpaʊnd ˌdʒɜːn(ə)l ˈentri/ *noun* an entry in a journal that comprises more than individual equally matched debit and credit items 复合日记账分录，混合日记账分录：不只包含个别相等的借项及贷项的分录

comprehensive income /ˌkɒmprɪhensɪv ˈɪnkʌm/ *noun* a company's total income for a given accounting period, taking into account all gains and losses, not only those included in a normal income statement. In the United States, comprehensive income must be declared whereas in the United Kingdom it appears in the statement of total recognised gains and losses 综合所得：公司于指定会计期间内包括所有盈亏（而不仅仅是普通损益表中的盈亏）的总收入。美国规定公司必须公布综合所得，英国则规定将综合所得呈列在经确认的总盈亏表中

comprehensive insurance /ˌkɒmprɪhensɪv ɪnˈʃʊərəns/, **comprehensive policy** /ˌkɒmprɪhensɪv ˈpɒlɪsi/ *noun* an insurance policy which covers you against all risks which are likely to happen 综合保险：涵盖所有可能风险的一种险别

comprehensive tax allocation /ˌkɒmprɪhensɪv ˈtæks ˌæləkeɪʃ(ə)n/ *noun* the setting aside of money to cover deferred tax 综合所得税分摊：拨出递延税项准备金

compromise /ˈkɒmprəmaɪz/ *noun* an agreement between two sides, where each side gives way a little 妥协，折中，和解 ○ *Management offered £5 an hour, the union asked for £9, and a compromise of £7.50 was reached.* 管理层给的工资为一小时5英镑，工会要求的是一小时9英镑，最后达成了一小时7.5英镑的折中方案。■ *verb* to reach an agreement by giving way a little 妥协，让步 ○ *She asked £15 for it, I offered £7 and we compromised on £10.* 她要价15英镑，我还价7英镑，最后以10英镑成交。

comptroller /kənˈtrəʊlə/ *noun* a financial controller 主管会计

Comptroller and Auditor General /kənˌtrəʊlə ən ˌɔːdɪtə ˈdʒen(ə)rəl/ *noun* in the United Kingdom, the head of the National Audit Office who reports back to Parliament on the audit of government departments 主审计长：英国国家审计局官员，负责向议会报告政府部门的审计事宜

compulsory annuity /kəmˌpʌlsəri əˈnjuːɪti/ *noun* in the United Kingdom, the legal requirement that at least 75% of the funds built-up in a personal pension plan have to be used to purchase an annuity by the age of 75 强制性年金：英国法律规定，在75岁之前必须将个人退休金计划中至少75%的资金拿来购买年金

compulsory liquidation /kəmˌpʌlsəri ˌlɪkwɪˈdeɪʃ(ə)n/ *noun* liquidation which is ordered by a court 强制清算

compulsory winding up /kəmˌpʌlsəri ˌwaɪndɪŋ ˈʌp/ *noun* liquidation which is ordered by a court 强制清盘

computable /kəmˈpjuːtəb(ə)l/ *adjective* possible to calculate 可计算的

computation /ˌkɒmpjʊˈteɪʃ(ə)n/ *noun* a calculation 计算

computational error /ˌkɒmpjʊteɪʃ(ə)nəl ˈerə/ *noun* a mistake made in calculating 计算错误

compute /kəmˈpjuːt/ *verb* to calculate, to do calculations 计算，估算

computer /kəmˈpjuːtə/ *noun* an electronic machine which calculates or stores information and processes it automatically 计算机

computer department /kəmˈpjuːtə dɪˌpɑːtmənt/ *noun* a department in a company which manages the company's computers 电脑部

computer file /kəmˈpjuːtə faɪl/ *noun* a section of information on a computer, e.g. the payroll, list of addresses or list of customer accounts 计算机储存文件，电脑档案：如计算机中所储存的工资表、地址、客户账户表等信息

computerise /kəmˈpjuːtəraɪz/, **computerize** *verb* to change something from a manual system to one using computers 计算机化 ○ *We have computerised all our records.* 我们所有的记录都已经电脑化。○ *Stock control is now completely computerised.* 库存管理现已完全电脑化。

computerised /kəmˈpjuːtəraɪzd/, **computerized** *adjective* carried out by computers 计算机化的，由计算机执行的 ○ *a computerised invoicing or filing system* 电脑化的开发票（或归档）系统

computer listing /kəmˌpjuːtə ˈlɪstɪŋ/ *noun* a printout of a list of items taken from data stored in a computer 计算机清单

computer manager /kəmˈpjuːtə ˌmænɪdʒə/ *noun* a person in charge of a computer department 计算机部主管

computer network /kəmˌpjuːtə ˈnetwɜːk/ *noun* a computer system where several PCs are linked so that they all draw on the same database 计算机网络

computer operator /kəmˈpjuːtər ˌɒpəreɪtə/ *noun* a person who operates a computer 计算机操作员

computer program /kəmˈpjuːtə ˌprəʊɡræm/ *noun* instructions to a computer telling it to do a particular piece of work 计算机程序 ○ *to buy a graphics program* 购买一套制图程序 ○ *The accounts department is running a new payroll program.* 会计部正在运行一套新的工资表程序。

computer programmer /kəmˌpjuːtə ˈprəʊɡræmə/ *noun* a person who writes computer programs 计算机编程员

computer programming /kəmˌpjuːtə ˈprəʊɡræmɪŋ/ *noun* the work of writing programs for computers 计算机编程

computer-readable /kəmˌpjuːtəˈriːdəb(ə)l/ *adjective* able to be read and understood by a computer 可机读的 ○ *computer-readable codes* 计算机可读代码

computer services /kəmˌpjuːtə ˈsɜːvɪsɪz/ *plural noun* work using a computer, done by a computer bureau 计算机服务

computer system /kəmˈpjuːtə ˌsɪstəm/ *noun* a set of programs, commands, etc., which run a computer 计算机系统

computing /kəmˈpjuːtɪŋ/ *noun* the operating of computers 计算机操作

computing speed /kəmˈpjuːtɪŋ spiːd/ *noun* the speed at which a computer calculates 计算速度

concealment of assets /kənˌsiːlmənt əv ˈæsets/ *noun* the act of hiding assets so that creditors do not know they exist 隐匿资产：将资产藏起来不让债权人知道

concept /ˈkɒnsept/ *noun* an idea 概念，观念，思想 □ **concept of capital maintenance** idea that profit is only recorded if the capital of the company, measured in terms of its net assets, increases during an accounting period (assets can be measured at historical cost or in units of constant purchasing power) 资本保全观念：只有在以净资产计量的资本在一个会计期间内增加的情况下才应确认的利润（资产可按历史成本计价或按不变购买力单位计价） □ **concept of maintenance of operating capacity** concept of capital maintenance measured in terms of the changes in the current values of fixed assets, stock and working capital (profit can only be taken if the total value of these assets, called the 'net operating assets', including adjustments for changes in prices affecting these assets, increases during an accounting period) 经营能力保全观念：以固定资

产、存货和营运资本的现行价值变化来计量的资本保全原则(只有当这些被称为"净经营资产"的总值(包括对这些资产造成影响的价格变化所作的调整)在会计期间内增加时,利润才应被确认)

conceptual framework /kənˌseptʃʊəl ˈfreɪmwɜːk/ *noun* a set of theoretical principles that underlies the practice and regulation of financial accounting. In the United States, this is expressed in the Statements of Financial Accounting Concepts issued by the Financial Accounting Standards Board. In the United Kingdom, it is expressed in the Statement of Principles issued by the Accounting Standards Board 观念性构架:财务会计实务及监管的基础理论原则。美国财务会计的观念性构架是财务会计准则委员会颁布的财务会计概念公告,在英国是会计准则委员会颁布的原则公告

concern /kənˈsɜːn/ *noun* a business or company 企业,公司

concession /kənˈseʃ(ə)n/ *noun* **1.** the right to use someone else's property for business purposes 特许权:为商业目的而使用他人财产的权利 **2.** the right to be the only seller of a product in a place 独家销售权 ○ *She runs a jewellery concession in a department store.* 她在一家百货商场经营着一个获特许销售权的珠宝店。**3.** an allowance, e.g. a reduction of tax or price 折让(如减税或减价)

concessionaire /kənˌseʃəˈneə/ *noun* a person or business that has the right to be the only seller of a product in a place 独家销售权享有人

concessionary fare /kənˌseʃ(ə)nəri ˈfeə/ *noun* a reduced fare for some types of passenger such as pensioners, students or employees of a transport company 优惠交通费:对某类乘客(如领取退休金者、学生或运输公司的雇员)收取的较低费用

conciliation /kənˌsɪliˈeɪʃ(ə)n/ *noun* the practice of bringing together the parties in a dispute with an independent third party, so that the dispute can be settled through a series of negotiations 调停,调解

condition /kənˈdɪʃ(ə)n/ *noun* **1.** something which has to be carried out as part of a contract or which has to be agreed before a contract becomes valid (合同)条款,条件 **2.** a general state or the general way of life in a place 状况,生活条件 ○ *item sold in good condition* 商品销售情况良好 ○ *The union has complained of the bad working conditions in the factory.* 工会抱怨该工厂恶劣的工作环境。○ *What was the condition of the car when it was sold?* 这辆汽车出售时车况怎么样? ○ *Adverse trading conditions affected our profits.* 不利的贸易条件影响了我们的利润。

conditional /kənˈdɪʃ(ə)n(ə)l/ *adjective* provided that specific conditions are taken into account 有条件的,视…而定

conditionality /kənˌdɪʃ(ə)ˈnælɪti/ *noun* the fact of having conditions attached 条件性,条件限制

conditional sale /kənˌdɪʃ(ə)nəl ˈseɪl/ *noun* a sale which is subject to conditions, such as a hirepurchase agreement 有条件销售(如分期付款赊购协议)

conditions of employment /kənˌdɪʃ(ə)nz əv ɪmˈplɔɪmənt/ *plural noun* the terms of a contract of employment 雇用条件

conditions of sale /kənˌdɪʃ(ə)nz əv ˈseɪl/ *plural noun* agreed ways in which a sale takes place, e. g. discounts or credit terms 销售条件(例如折扣或信用条件)

Confederation of Asian and Pacific Accountants /kənˌfedəˌreɪʃ(ə)n əv ˌeɪʒ(ə)n ən pəˌsɪfɪk əˈkaʊntənts/ *noun* Full form of **CAPA** 为 **CAPA** 的全称

conference proceedings /ˈkɒnf(ə)rəns prəˌsiːdɪŋz/ *plural noun* a written report of what has taken place at a conference 会议记录

confidential report /ˌkɒnfɪdenʃəl rɪˈpɔːt/ *noun* a secret document which must not be shown to other people 机密报告

confirm /kənˈfɜːm/ *verb* to say again that something agreed before is correct 确认,证实 ○ *to confirm a hotel reservation* or *a ticket* or *an agreement* or *a booking* 确认酒店预订(或门票、协议、预约)

confirmation /ˌkɒnfəˈmeɪʃ(ə)n/ *noun* the act of making certain 确认,证实

conflict of interest /ˌkɒnflɪkt əv ˈɪntrəst/ *noun* a situation where a person or firm may profit personally from decisions taken in an official capacity 假公济私

conglomerate /kənˈglɒmərət/ *noun* a group of subsidiary companies linked together and forming a group, each making very different types of products 联合大企业,集团公司:各子公司联合形成的集团,每个子公司负责制造各种不同的商品

connected persons /kəˌnektɪd ˈpɜːs(ə)nz/ *noun* for purposes of disclosure under the UK Companies Act, certain people who are related to or connected with members of the board of directors,, including his or her spouse and children 关联人士:就英国公司法规定的披露事项而言,关联人士指与董事会成员有联系或相关联的人,包括董事的配偶及子女

Conseil National de la Comptabilité *noun* in France, a committee appointed by the government that is responsible for drawing up the Plan Comptable Général (General Accounting Plan) 法国国家会计委员会

consensus ad idem /kənˌsensəs æd ˈaɪdem/ *Latin phrase* meaning 'agreement to this same thing': real agreement to a contract by both parties (拉丁语)一致同意

conservative /kənˈsɜːvətɪv/ *adjective* careful, not overestimating 小心的,稳健的,保守的 ○ *His forecast of expenditure was very conservative* or *He made a conservative forecast of expenditure*. 他对费用的预测相当保守。

'... we are calculating our next budget income at an oil price of $15 per barrel. We know it is a conservative projection, but we do not want to come in for a shock should prices dive at any time during the year'
"我们按每桶15美元的油价计算下期预算收入。我们知道这是一个保守的预测,只是不想在年内任何时间油价骤跌时惊慌失措"
[*Lloyd's List*《劳氏日报》]

conservatively /kənˈsɜːvətɪvli/ *adverb* not overestimating 保守地,不高估地 ○ *The total sales are conservatively estimated at £2.3m*. 总销售额保守估计为230万英镑。

consider /kən'sɪdə/ *verb* to think seriously about something 考虑

consideration /kənˌsɪdə'reɪʃ(ə)n/ *noun* **1.** serious thought 考虑 ○ *We are giving consideration to moving the head office to Scotland*. 我们正在考虑将总部迁至苏格兰。**2.** something valuable exchanged as part of a contract 补偿,对价:按合同规定相互交换的有价值物品

consignation /ˌkɒnsaɪ'neɪʃ(ə)n/ *noun* the act of consigning 发货,委托,寄售

consignee /ˌkɒnsaɪ'niː/ *noun* a person who receives goods from someone for their own use or to sell for the sender 收货人,受托人,承销人

consignment /kən'saɪnmənt/ *noun* **1.** the sending of goods to someone who will sell them for you 寄售 **2.** a group of goods sent for sale 寄售品 ○ *A consignment of goods has arrived*. 寄售货物已到达。○ *We are expecting a consignment of cars from Japan*. 我们正等待来自日本的一批寄售轿车。

'...some of the most prominent stores are gradually moving away from the traditional consignment system, under which manufacturers agree to repurchase any unsold goods, and in return dictate prices and sales strategies and even dispatch staff to sell the products'
"一些最主要的百货商店正逐步摆脱传统的寄售制度。根据传统寄售制度,制造商同意购回任何未售出的商品,但条件是由他们指定商品销售价格和销售策略,甚至委派员工去销售产品"[*Nikkei Weekly*《日经周报》]

consignment accounts /kənˌsaɪnmənt ə'kaʊnts/ *plural noun* accounts kept by both consignee and consignor, showing quantities, dates of shipment, and payments for stocks held 委托销售账目:受托人、委托人分别持有的记有货物数量、发货日期和付款情况的账目

consignment note /kən'saɪnmənt nəʊt/ *noun* a note saying that goods have been sent 寄售通知书

consignor /kən'saɪnə/ *noun* a person who consigns goods to someone 寄售委托人

consistency /kən'sɪstənsi/ *noun* one of the basic accounting concepts, that items in the accounts should be treated in the same way from year to year 一贯性:会计的基本概念之一,要求会计账户中各科目的处理方法应常年一致

consolidate /kən'sɒlɪdeɪt/ *verb* **1.** to include the accounts of several subsidiary companies as well as the holding company in a single set of accounts 合并:把母公司和子公司的账户都纳入一个账户内 **2.** to group goods together for shipping 聚集货物以便运输

consolidated accounts /kənˌsɒlɪdeɪtɪd ə'kaʊnts/ *plural noun* accounts where the financial position of several different companies, i. e. a holding company and its subsidiaries, are recorded together 合并报表,合并账户:同时记录几个公司(即控股公司及其子公司)财务状况的报表

consolidated balance sheet /kənˌsɒlɪdeɪtɪd 'bæləns ʃiːt/ *noun* a balance sheets of subsidiary companies grouped together into the balance sheet of the parent company 合并资产负债表:将子公司合并到母公司资产负债表后形成的资产负债表

consolidated cash flow statement /kənˌsɒlɪdeɪtɪd kæʃ fləʊ 'steɪtmənt/ *noun* a cash flow statement for a group of enterprises and its parent company as a whole 合并现金流量表：将企业集团及其母公司视为一个整体来反映的现金流量表

consolidated fund /kənˌsɒlɪdeɪtɪd ˈfʌnd/ *noun* money in the Exchequer which comes from tax revenues and is used to pay for government expenditure 统一基金：英国财政部的资金，来源于税收、并用于支付政府的开支

consolidated income statement /kənˌsɒlɪdeɪtɪd ˈɪnkʌm ˌsteɪtmənt/ *noun* an income statement for a group of enterprises and its parent company as a whole 合并收益表：将一个企业集团及其母公司作为一个整体来反映的收益表

consolidated profit and loss account /kənˌsɒlɪdeɪtɪd ˌprɒfɪt ən ˈlɒs əˌkaʊnt/ *noun* profit and loss accounts of the holding company and its subsidiary companies, grouped together into a single profit and loss account 合并损益表：由控股公司及其子公司的损益表合并而成的损益表（NOTE：The US term is **profit and loss statement** or **income statement** 美国用语为 **profit and loss statement** 或 **income statement**）

consolidated shipment /kənˌsɒlɪdeɪtɪd ˈʃɪpmənt/ *noun* goods from different companies grouped together into a single shipment 混合装载运输：将不同公司的货物同一批装运

consolidation /kənˌsɒlɪˈdeɪʃ(ə)n/ *noun* **1.** the grouping together of goods for shipping 聚集货物以便运输 **2.** the act of taking profits from speculative investments and investing them safely in blue-chip companies 将投机性投资中所获利润投资于安全的蓝筹股

consolidation adjustments /kənˌsɒlɪˈdeɪʃ(ə)n əˌdʒʌstmənts/ *noun* necessary changes and deletions made to financial records when consolidating the accounts of a group of enterprises 合并调整：在合并一个企业集团的账目时对财务记录进行的必要修改和删除

consolidation difference /kənˌsɒlɪˈdeɪʃ(ə)n ˌdɪf(ə)rəns/ *noun* the difference between the price paid for a subsidiary and the value of the assets and liabilities obtained in the purchase 合并差异：购买子公司的价格与所获得的资产和负债价值之差

consols /ˈkɒnsɒlz/ *plural noun* government bonds which pay interest but do not have a maturity date 英国统一公债：支付利息但无偿还日的政府债券

consortium /kənˈsɔːtiəm/ *noun* a group of companies which work together 联营企业 ○ *A consortium of Canadian companies* or *A Canadian consortium has tendered for the job.* 一家加拿大联营公司参加了该项目的投标。（NOTE：The plural is **consortia** 复数为 **consortia**）

'...the consortium was one of only four bidders for the £2 billion contract to run the lines, seen as potentially the most difficult contract because of the need for huge investment'
"该企业集团是这项价值 20 亿英镑生产线运行合同仅有的四个投标商之一，这份合同因需巨额投资而被视为最难完成的合同"
[*Times*《泰晤士报》]

constant /ˈkɒnstənt/ *adjective* unchanging 一贯的,不变的 ○ *The calculations are in constant dollars.* 该计算假设美元汇率不变。

constant purchasing power /ˌkɒnstənt ˈpɜːtʃɪsɪŋ ˌpaʊə/ *noun* same as 同 **current purchasing power**

consult /kənˈsʌlt/ *verb* to ask an expert for advice 咨询 ○ *We consulted our accountant about our tax.* 我们向会计师咨询税务问题。

consultancy /kənˈsʌltənsi/ *noun* the act of giving specialist advice 咨询业务 ○ *a consultancy firm* 一家咨询公司 ○ *She offers a consultancy service.* 她提供咨询服务。

Consultative Committee of Accountancy Bodies /kənˌsʌltətɪv kəˌmɪti əv əˈkaʊntənsi ˌbɒdiz/ *noun* an organisation established in 1974 that represents and encourages coordination between the six professional accountancy bodes in the United Kingdom and Ireland 会计团体咨询委员会:成立于1974年,代表英国和爱尔兰六家专业会计团体,并促进它们之间的合作

consulting /kənˈsʌltɪŋ/ *adjective* giving specialist advice 顾问的,咨询的 ○ *a consulting engineer* 顾问工程师,工程顾问

consulting actuary /kənˌsʌltɪŋ ˈæktjuəri/ *noun* an independent actuary who advises large pension funds 精算顾问:对大额退休金基金提供咨询建议的独立精算师

consumable goods /kənˌsjuːməb(ə)l ˈgʊdz/, **consumables** /kənˈsjuːməb(ə)lz/ *plural noun* goods which are bought by members of the public and not by companies 消耗品,消费品 Also called 亦称作 **consumer goods**

consumer /kənˈsjuːmə/ *noun* a person or company that buys and uses goods and services 消费者 ○ *Gas consumers are protesting at the increase in prices.* 煤气消费者抗议煤气涨价。○ *The factory is a heavy consumer of water.* 这家工厂是用水大户。

'...forecasting consumer response is one problem which will never be finally solved'
"消费者的反应难以预测"[*Marketing Week*《市场周刊》]

'...consumer tastes in the UK are becoming much more varied'
"英国消费者的品位日益多样化"[*Marketing*《市场》]

'...the marketing director's brief will be to develop the holiday villages as a consumer brand, aimed at the upper end of the tourist market'
"营销主任的大意是要把这个度假村开发成一个高端旅游市场的消费品牌"[*Marketing Week*《市场周刊》]

consumer council /kənˌsjuːmə ˈkaʊns(ə)l/ *noun* a group representing the interests of consumers 消费者协会

consumer credit /kənˌsjuːmə ˈkredɪt/ *noun* the credit given by shops, banks and other financial institutions to consumers so that they can buy goods 消费信贷:由银行、商场和其他金融机构向消费者提供的信贷,以购买商品(NOTE: Lenders have to be licensed under the Consumer Credit Act, 1974. The US term is **installment credit** 信贷提供方须按1974年消费信贷法获得许可证。美国用语为 **installment credit**)

Consumer Credit Act, 1974 /kənˌsjuːmə ˈkredɪt ækt/ *noun* an Act of Parliament which licenses lenders, and requires them to state clearly the full terms of loans which they make, including the APR 1974 年消费信贷法:关于向信贷提供方发放执照、责令其明确指出全部贷款条件(包括年利率)的议会法案

consumer goods /kənˌsjuːmə ˈɡʊdz/ *plural noun* same as 同 **consumable goods**

consumer panel /kənˈsjuːmə ˌpæn(ə)l/ *noun* a group of consumers who report on products they have used so that the manufacturers can improve them or use what the panel says about them in advertising (有代表性的)消费者群体:对所用产品提供意见的消费者群体,制造商可根据他们的意见改进产品或作广告

Consumer Price Index /kənˌsjuːmə ˈpraɪs ˌɪndeks/ *noun* an American index showing how prices of consumer goods have risen over a period of time, used as a way of measuring inflation and the cost of living 消费物价指数:美国表示消费品价格在一段时间内上升情况的指数,用以衡量通胀及生活成本 Abbreviation 缩写 **CPI** (NOTE: The UK term is **retail prices index** 英国用法为 **retail prices index**)

'... analysis of the consumer price index for the first half of the year shows that the rate of inflation went down by about 12.9 per cent'
"上半年的消费物价指数分析表明,通货膨胀率下降了约 12.9%" [*Business Times (Lagos)*《商业时报》(拉各斯)]

consumer protection /kənˌsjuːmə prəˈtekʃən/ *noun* the activity of protecting consumers against unfair or illegal traders 消费者保护:保护消费者权益免受不法商户的侵害

consumer research /kənˌsjuːmə rɪˈsɜːtʃ/ *noun* research into why consumers buy goods and what goods they may want to buy 消费者需求调查

consumer spending /kənˌsjuːmə ˈspendɪŋ/ *noun* spending by private house-holds on goods and services 消费支出

'... companies selling in the UK market are worried about reduced consumer spending as a consequence of higher interest rates and inflation'
"英国市场上的经销商担心,高利率和高通胀会减少消费支出" [*Business*《商业》]

consumption tax /kənˈsʌmpʃ(ə)n tæks/ *noun* a tax used to encourage people to buy less of a particular good or service by increasing its price. This type of tax is often levied in times of national hardship 消费税:通过提价抑制人们购买某种商品或劳务的税收。这种税通常是在国家遇到困难时征收

Contact Committee /ˌkɒntækt kəˈmɪti/ *noun* an advisory body, established by the European Union, that oversees the application of European accounting directives and makes recommendations to the European Commission about changes to those directives 联系委员会:欧盟成立的一个咨询团体,它监督欧洲会计指令的应用并就如何修改这些指令向欧洲委员会提供建议

contango /kənˈtæŋɡəʊ/ *noun* **1.** the payment of interest by a stockbroker for permission to carry payment for shares from one account to the next 交易延期费;延期交割费:经同意,股票经纪人将股票价款支付日期推后一个结

算日而支付的利息(NOTE: Contango is no longer applied on the London Stock Exchange because of the rolling account system, but it is still applied on some other exchanges 由于实行滚动会计制度,伦敦证券交易所已不再收取交易延期费,但其他一些交易所仍收取该费用) **2.** a cash price which is lower than the forward price 期货溢价:期货价格高于现货价格

contango day /kən'tæŋgəʊ deɪ/ *noun* formerly, the day when the rate of contango payments was fixed 交易延期费结算日

contested takeover /kənˌtestɪd 'teɪkəʊvə/ *noun* a takeover bid where the board of the target company does not recommend it to the shareholders and tries to fight it 有争议的收购:目标公司的董事会没有把收购投标提交给股东,同时试图反对该收购 Also called 亦称作 **hostile bid**

contingency /kən'tɪndʒənsi/ *noun* a possible state of emergency when decisions will have to be taken quickly (需迅速决策的)紧急情况,意外事故

contingency fund /kən'tɪndʒənsi fʌnd/ *noun* money set aside in case it is needed urgently 意外开支准备金,应急基金

contingent expenses /kənˌtɪndʒənt ɪk'spensɪz/ *plural noun* expenses which will be incurred only if something happens 意外费用

contingent gain /kənˌtɪndʒənt 'geɪn/ *noun* a gain which is incurred only if something happens 或有收益:仅在发生某事时才会产生的收益

contingent liability /kənˌtɪndʒənt laɪə'bɪlɪti/ *noun* a liability which may or may not occur, but for which provision is made in a company's accounts, as opposed to 'provisions', where money is set aside for an anticipated expenditure 或有负债:可能发生也可能不发生的负债,但应在公司账户中预留准备金,这有别于为可预见支出而预留的准备金

contingent loss /kənˌtɪndʒənt 'lɒs/ *noun* a possible loss that is conditional on the occurrence of a certain event in the future 或有损失:仅在发生某事时才会带来的损失

contingent policy /kənˌtɪndʒənt 'pɒlɪsi/ *noun* an insurance policy which pays out only if something happens, such as if a person named in the policy dies before the person due to benefit 或有保险单:仅在发生某事时(例如保险单受益人在其未受益之前死亡)才会支付赔偿金的保险单

continuous /kən'tɪnjʊəs/ *adjective* with no end or with no breaks 持续的,连续不断的 ○ *a continuous production line* 一条连续的生产线

continuous disclosure /kənˌtɪnjʊəs dɪs'kləʊʒə/ *noun* in Canada, the practice of ensuring that complete, timely, accurate, and balanced information about a public company is made available to shareholders 持续披露:在加拿大用来确保完整、及时、准确和公允地向股东提供有关上市公司信息的做法

continuously contemporary accounting /kənˌtɪnjʊəsli kənˌtemp(ə)rəri ə'kaʊntɪŋ/ *noun* an accounting system that measures assets and liabilities at their current cash price. Profit and loss can therefore be viewed in terms of changes in the value as all items are measured in the same way 持

续适应环境会计：按当前现金价格衡量资产和负债的一种会计制度。由于所有科目都按同一方法衡量，因此可以根据价值的变化看待盈亏 Abbreviation 缩写 **CoCoA**

contra /ˈkɒntrə/ *noun* an accounting term used when debits are matched with related credits in an account or set of accounts 抵消：一个账户或一组账户中的借方与有关贷方相匹配时使用的会计术语

contra account /ˈkɒntrə əˌkaʊnt/ *noun* an account which offsets another account, e.g. where a company's supplier is not only a creditor in that company's books but also a debtor because it has purchased goods on credit 抵消账户，对消账户：抵消另一个账户的账户。例如某公司的供应商在该公司的账簿中既是贷方，又因其赊购公司商品而成为借方时，便形成抵消账户

contract *noun* /ˈkɒntrækt/ **1.** a legal agreement between two parties 合同，契约 ○ *to draw up a contract* 草拟一份合同 ○ *to draft a contract* 起草一份合同 ○ *to sign a contract* 签署一份合同 □ **the contract is binding on both parties** both parties signing the contract must do what is agreed 合同对签约双方均具有约束力 □ **under contract** bound by the terms of a contract 受合同条款约束 ○ *The firm is under contract to deliver the goods by November.* 合同要求该公司在11月份之前发货。□ **to void a contract** to make a contract invalid 使合同无效 **2.** □ **by private contract** by private legal agreement 秘密合同（协议）**3.** an agreement for the supply of a service or goods 供应协议：提供商品或劳务的协议 ○ *to enter into a contract to supply spare parts* 签署配件供应合同 ○ *to sign a contract for £10,000 worth of spare parts* 签署一份价值一万英镑的配件供应合同 **4.** (*Stock Exchange*) a deal to buy or sell shares, or an agreement to purchase options or futures（股票交易）买卖股票的交易；购买期权（或期货）的协议 ■ *verb* /kənˈtrækt/ to agree to do some work on the basis of a legally binding contract 订合同 ○ *to contract to supply spare parts* or *to contract for the supply of spare parts* 签订配件供应的合同

contract costing /ˌkɒntrækt ˈkɒstɪŋ/ *noun* a method of costing large projects, where the contracted work will run over several accounting periods 合同成本计算：需数个会计期才能完成的大型工程成本计算方法

contracting party /kənˌtræktɪŋ ˈpɑːti/ *noun* a person or company that signs a contract 缔约方，合同当事人

contract note /ˈkɒntrækt nəʊt/ *noun* a note showing that shares have been bought or sold but not yet paid for, also including the commission（股票）买卖单据，买卖契约：列明经纪人代客户买卖但尚未付款的股票价格和数量（包括佣金在内）的清单

contract of employment /ˌkɒntrækt əv ɪmˈplɔɪmənt/ *noun* a contract between an employer and an employee stating all the conditions of work 雇用合同 Also called 亦称作 **employment contract**

contract of service /ˌkɒntrækt əv ˈsɜːvɪs/ *noun* a legal agreement between an employer and an employee whereby the employee will work for the employer and be directed by them, in return for payment 劳务合同

contractor /kənˈtræktə/ *noun* a

person or company that does work according to a written agreement 承包商

contractual /kən'træktʃʊəl/ *adjective* according to a contract 根据合同的，合同规定的 ○ *contractual conditions* 合同条件 □ **to fulfil your contractual obligations** to do what you have agreed to do in a contract 履行合同规定的义务

contractual liability /kənˌtræktʃʊəl ˌlaɪə'bɪlɪti/ *noun* a legal responsibility for something as stated in a contract 合同义务：合同中规定的责任

contractually /kən'træktjʊəli/ *adverb* according to a contract 根据合同 ○ *The company is contractually bound to pay our expenses.* 根据合同，该公司须支付我们的费用。

contractual obligation /kənˌtræktʃʊəl ˌɒblɪ'geɪʃ(ə)n/ *noun* something that a person is legally forced to do through having signed a contract to do 合同义务 □ **to fulfil your contractual obligations** to do what you have agreed to do in a contract 履行合同规定的义务

contract work /'kɒntrækt wɜːk/ *noun* work done according to a written agreement 包工：根据协议所做的工作

contra entry /'kɒntrə ˌentri/ *noun* an entry made in the opposite side of an account to make an earlier entry worthless, i.e. a debit against a credit 抵消分录，对消分录：在会计账目上相反登录的账目，用于冲销先前账目（即借方与贷方相互抵消）

contribute /kən'trɪbjuːt/ *verb* to give money or add to money 捐款，供款 ○ *We agreed to contribute 10% of the profits.* 我们同意捐出利润的10%。○ *They had contributed to the pension fund for 10 years.* 他们向养老金基金缴费已经10年了。

contribution /ˌkɒntrɪ'bjuːʃ(ə)n/ *noun* **1.** money paid to add to a sum 供款，缴款，捐款 **2.** the difference between sales value and the variable costs of a unit sold. This goes to cover fixed costs and provide the profit 贡献毛利：商品销售价格与商品单位可变成本之间的差额，用于弥补固定成本和提供利润

contribution income statement /ˌkɒntrɪbjuːʃ(ə)n 'ɪnkʌm ˌsteɪtmənt/ *noun* a way of presenting an income statement in which fixed costs are shown as a deduction from the total contribution. This format is often used as part of management accounting 贡献收益表：将固定成本从总贡献中扣除的损益表呈列方法，通常用于管理会计

contribution margin /ˌkɒntrɪ'bjuːʃ(ə)n mɑːdʒɪn/ *noun* a way of showing how much individual products or services contribute to net profit 贡献利润，贡献毛利：表明单个产品或服务对净利的贡献额度的一种方法

contribution of capital /kɒntrɪˌbjuːʃ(ə)n əv 'kæpɪt(ə)l/ *noun* money paid to a company as additional capital 增加资本：作为追加资本而支付给公司的资金

contributor of capital /kənˌtrɪbjʊtər əv 'kæpɪt(ə)l/ *noun* a person who contributes capital 股本认购者

contributory /kən'trɪbjʊt(ə)ri/ *adjective* causing or helping to cause 有贡献的，起作用的，有助于…的 ○ *Falling exchange rates have been a contributory factor in the company's loss of profits.* 汇率下调是造成公司亏损的一

个原因。

contributory pension scheme /kənˌtrɪbjʊt(ə)ri ˈpenʃən skiːm/ *noun* a scheme where the employee pays a proportion of his or her salary into the pension fund 分担养老金计划：雇员将一定比例的工资缴入养老基金的计划

control account /kənˌtrəʊl əˈkaʊnt/ *noun* an account used to record the total amounts entered in a number of different ledger accounts. It also acts as a means of checking the accuracy of the ledger accounts 统制账户：用来记录所有分类账的登记总额，同时也是检查分类账准确性的一种手段

controllable variance /kənˌtrəʊləb(ə)l ˈveəriəns/ *noun* a difference between actual and budgeted amounts that is considered as being within the control of the budget centre manager 可控制差异：被认为处在预算中心经理可控制范围内的实际与预算金额之间的差异

controlled /kənˈtrəʊld/ *adjective* ruled or kept in check 受控制的

controlled company /kənˌtrəʊld ˈkʌmp(ə)ni/ *noun* company where more than 50% (or in the USA, 25%) of the shares belong to one owner 受控公司，分公司：个人拥有超过半数(美国为25%)股权的公司

controlled economy /kənˌtrəʊld ɪˈkɒnəmi/ *noun* an economy where most business activity is directed by orders from the government 受控经济：大多数商业活动直接受政府法令控制的经济

controller /kənˈtrəʊlə/ *noun* **1.** a person who controls something, especially the finances of a company (尤指公司财务)控制者 **2.** *US* the chief accountant in a company (美)总会计师，主审计长

control period /kənˌtrəʊl ˈpɪəriəd/ *noun* the fraction of the financial year, e.g., a month, for which separate totals are given in a budget 控制时期：财年的一部分(如一个月)，在预算中编制此部分的总额

conversion /kənˈvɜːʃ(ə)n/ *noun* **1.** a change 改变，转换 **2.** the action of changing convertible loan stock into ordinary shares 将可转换债券转成普通股

conversion costs /kənˈvɜːʃ(ə)n kɒsts/ *plural noun* cost of changing raw materials into finished or semi-finished products, including wages, other direct production costs and the production overhead 转换成本：将原材料转化为成品或半成品的成本，包括工资、其他直接生产成本和生产管理费用

conversion of funds /kənˌvɜːʃ(ə)n əv ˈfʌndz/ *noun* the act of using money which does not belong to you for a purpose for which it is not supposed to be used 资金挪用：把不属于自己的资金挪作他用

conversion period /kənˈvɜːʃ(ə)n ˌpɪəriəd/ *noun* a time during which convertible loan stock may be changed into ordinary shares 证券转换期：可兑换债券转换为普通股的时限

conversion price /kənˈvɜːʃ(ə)n praɪs/, **conversion rate** /kənˈvɜːʃ(ə)n reɪt/ *noun* **1.** a price at which preference shares are converted into ordinary shares 兑换价：优先股转换成普通股的价格 **2.** a rate at which a currency is changed into a foreign currency 转换率：一种货币兑换另一种货币的汇率

conversion value /kən'vɜːʃ(ə)n ˌvæljuː/ *noun* a value of convertible stock, including the extra value of the ordinary shares into which they may be converted 兑换价值：可兑换证券的价值，包括其可转换为普通股的额外价值

convert /kən'vɜːt/ *verb* **1.** to change money of one country for money of another 兑换 ○ *We converted our pounds into Swiss francs.* 我们将英镑兑换成瑞士法郎。**2.** □ **to convert funds to your own use** to use someone else's money for yourself 挪用他人资金

convertibility /kənˌvɜːtə'bɪləti/ *noun* the ability of a currency to be exchanged for another easily 可兑换性

convertible currency /kənˌvɜːtəb(ə)l 'kʌrənsi/ *noun* a currency which can easily be exchanged for another 可自由兑换的货币

convertible debenture /kənˌvɜːtəb(ə)l dɪ'bentʃə/ *noun* a debenture or loan stock which can be exchanged for ordinary shares at a later date 可转换公司信用债券：可在以后转换成普通股的信用债券或债务证券

convertible loan stock /kənˌvɜːtəb(ə)l 'ləʊn stɒk/ *noun* money lent to a company which can be converted into shares at a later date 可转换公司债券：可在以后转换为股票的对某公司的贷款

convertibles /kən'vɜːtəb(ə)lz/ *plural noun* corporate bonds or preference shares which can be converted into ordinary shares at a set price on set dates 可转换证券：可于指定日期按指定价格转换为普通股的公司债券或优先股

conveyance /kən'veɪəns/ *noun* a legal document which transfers a property from the seller to the buyer 产权转让证书

conveyancer /kən'veɪənsə/ *noun* a person who draws up a conveyance 承办产权转让的律师

conveyancing /kən'veɪənsɪŋ/ *noun* the work of legally transferring a property from a seller to a buyer 产权转让

cooling-off period /ˌkuːlɪŋ'ɒf ˌpɪəriəd/ *noun* **1.** (*during an industrial dispute*) a period when negotiations have to be carried on and no action can be taken by either side (劳资纠纷中的)冷却期，缓和期：谈判期间，劳资双方都不得采取任何行动的时期 **2.** a period during which someone who is about to enter into an agreement may reflect on all aspects of the arrangement and change his or her mind if necessary 思考期：给予协议签署方的考虑期限，在此期间可改变主意 ○ *New York has a three day cooling-off period for telephone sales.* 在纽约，电话购物有三天的思考期。

cooperative /kəʊ'ɒp(ə)rətɪv/ *adjective* willing to work together 合作的，协作的 ○ *The workforce has not been cooperative over the management's productivity plan.* 工人对管理层的增产计划一直不予合作。

cooperative society /kəʊ'ɒp(ə)rətɪv səˌsaɪəti/ *noun* an organisation where customers and employees are partners and share the profits 合作社：客户和员工成为合作伙伴并分享利润的组织

cooperative store /kəʊ'ɒp(ə)rətɪv stɔː/ *noun* a store owned by those who shop there as well as by its workers 合

作商店：由购物者和员工共同拥有的商店

coproperty /kəʊˈprɒpəti/ *noun* ownership of property by two or more people together 共有财产

coproprietor /ˌkəʊprəˈpraɪətə/ *noun* a person who owns a property with another person or several other people 财产共有人

copying machine /ˈkɒpiɪŋ məˌʃiːn/ *noun* a machine which makes copies of documents 复印机

copyright /ˈkɒpiraɪt/ *noun* an author's legal right to publish his or her own work and not to have it copied, lasting seventy years after the author's death 版权，著作权：作者拥有的出版作品、不允许被复制的权利，其有效期可延续至作者去世后 70 年

Copyright Act /ˈkɒpiˌraɪt ækt/ *noun* an Act of Parliament making copyright legal, and controlling the copying of copyright material 版权法案：使版权合法化，并对享有版权作品的翻印进行管理的议会法案

copyright deposit /ˌkɒpiraɪt dɪˈpɒzɪt/ *noun* the act of depositing a copy of a published work in a copyright library, which is part of the formal copyrighting of copyright material 版权寄存，著作权缴存：将已出版的作品副本存放在版权图书馆，这是出版物正式获得版权的一部分

copyright holder /ˌkɒpiraɪt ˈhəʊldə/ *noun* a person who owns a copyright and who can expect to receive royalties from it 版权拥有者：拥有版权并可收取版权费的人

copyright law /ˈkɒpiraɪt lɔː/ *noun* laws concerning the protection of copyright 版权法

copyright notice /ˌkɒpiraɪt ˈnəʊtɪs/ *noun* a note in a book showing who owns the copyright and the date of ownership 版权证书，版权标志：书中关于谁拥有版权以及从什么时候开始拥有版权的声明

corporate /ˈkɔːp(ə)rət/ *adjective* referring to corporations or companies, or to a particular company as a whole 法人的，公司的

'... the prime rate is the rate at which banks lend to their top corporate borrowers'
"基准利率是银行向信用评级最高的公司借款人贷款时的利率"［*Wall Street Journal*《华尔街日报》］

'... if corporate forecasts are met, sales will exceed $ 50 million next year'
"如果公司预测准确，那么明年销售额将超过 5,000 万美元"［*Citizen* （*Ottawa*）《公民》（渥太华）］

corporate bond /ˈkɔːp(ə)rət bɒnd/ *noun* a loan stock officially issued by a company to raise capital, usually against the security of some of its assets 公司债券：公司为筹资而正式发行的信用债券，它通常以公司的部分资产作为抵押（NOTE：The company promises to pay an amount of interest on a set date every year until the redemption date，when it repays the loan 公司承诺每年定期支付一定的利息，直到还完贷款为止）

corporate finance /ˌkɔːp(ə)rət ˈfaɪnæns/ *noun* the financial affairs of companies 公司财务

corporate governance /ˌkɔːp(ə)rət ˈɡʌv(ə)nəns/ *noun* a theory of the way companies should be run 公司管理：关于公司运作方式的一套理论

corporate loan /ˌkɔːp(ə)rət ˈləʊn/ *noun* a loan issued by a corporation 公司贷款

corporate name /ˌkɔːp(ə)rət ˈneɪm/ *noun* the name of a large corporation 公司名称

corporate plan /ˌkɔːp(ə)rət ˈplæn/ *noun* a plan for the future work of a whole company 公司计划

corporate planning /ˌkɔːp(ə)rət ˈplænɪŋ/ *noun* 公司规划 **1.** the process of planning the future work of a whole company [规划整个公司未来运作的过程] **2.** planning the future financial state of a group of companies [关于集团公司未来财务状况的规划]

corporate profits /ˌkɔːp(ə)rət ˈprɒfɪts/ *plural noun* the profits of a corporation 公司利润

'...corporate profits for the first quarter showed a 4 per cent drop from last year'
"第一季度公司的利润比去年下降了四个百分点"[*Financial Times*《金融时报》]

corporate raider /ˌkɔːp(ə)rət ˈreɪdə/ *noun* a person or company which buys a stake in another company before making a hostile takeover bid 公司掠夺者，企业狙击手：为恶意收购而购买该公司股本的个人或公司

corporation /ˌkɔːpəˈreɪʃ(ə)n/ *noun* **1.** a large company 法人，公司 **2.** *US* a company which is incorporated in the United States (美)(在美国成立的)公司 **3.** a municipal authority 市政当局

corporation income tax /ˌkɔːpəreɪʃ(ə)n ˈɪnkʌm tæks/ *noun* a tax on profits made by incorporated companies 公司所得税：向股份公司征收的利润所得税

corporation loan /ˌkɔːpəˈreɪʃ(ə)n ləʊn/ *noun* a loan issued by a local authority 地方贷款：地方当局发行的债券

corporation tax /ˌkɔːpəˈreɪʃ(ə)n tæks/ *noun* a tax on profits and capital gains made by companies, calculated before dividends are paid 公司税：对公司利润和资本利得在分红前所征的税 Abbreviation 缩写 **CT**

correcting entry /kəˌrektɪŋ ˈentri/ *noun* an entry made in accounts to make something right which was previously wrong 更正分录，校正分录：为改正账户中的错误而作出的分录

correction /kəˈrekʃən/ *noun* an act of making something correct 纠正，改正 ○ *She made some corrections to the text of the speech*. 她对发言稿作了一些修正。

'...there were fears in October that shares were overvalued and bears were ready to enter the market. This only proved to be a small correction'
"10月份，有人担心股价虚高，熊市即将到来。事实证明那只是股市的一次小回档"[*Investors Chronicle*《投资者纪事》]

COSA *abbr* cost of sales adjustment 销售成本调整

cost /kɒst/ *noun* the amount of money which has to be paid for something 价格，价钱 ○ *What is the cost of a first class ticket to New York*? 到纽约的头等舱机票多少钱？○ *Computer costs are falling each year*. 电脑价格每年都在下降。○ *We cannot afford the cost of two cars*. 我们付不起两辆车的费用。

cost accountant /ˈkɒst əˌkaʊntənt/ *noun* an accountant who gives managers information about their business costs 成本会计师

cost accounting /ˈkɒst əˌkaʊntɪŋ/ *noun* the process of preparing special accounts of manufacturing and sales costs 成本会计：为制造和销售成本编制特定账目的过程

cost allocation /kɒst ˌæləˈkeɪʃ(ə)n/ *noun* a way in which overhead expenses are related to various cost centres 成本分摊：将间接费用与各个成本中心挂钩的方法

cost analysis /ˈkɒst əˌnæləsɪs/ *noun* the process of calculating in advance what a new product will cost 成本分析：预先计算新产品成本的过程

cost apportionment /kɒst əˈpɔːʃ(ə)nmənt/ *noun* the sharing out of common overhead costs among various cost centres 成本分配：在各个成本中心之间分配共同的间接费用

cost-benefit analysis /kɒstˈbenɪfɪt əˌnæləsɪs/ *noun* the process of comparing the costs and benefits of various possible ways of using available resources 成本收益分析：比较可用资源不同使用方法的成本和收益的过程 Also called 亦称作 **benefit-cost analysis**

cost centre /ˈkɒst ˌsentə/ *noun* 成本中心 **1.** a person or group whose costs can be itemised and to which costs can be allocated in accounts [成本可逐条列出，并在账目中可以分摊成本的个人或团体] **2.** a unit, a process, or an individual that provides a service needed by another part of an organisation and whose cost is therefore accepted as an overhead of the business [向另一个组织部门提供所需服务的单位、流程或个人，因此其成本被确认为企业的间接费用]

cost (at cost) concept /ˌkɒst (ət ˈkɒst) ˌkɒnsept/ *noun* the practice of valuing assets with reference to their acquisition cost 成本(按成本)概念：参照购买成本为资产估值的做法

cost-cutting /ˈkɒstˌkʌtɪŋ/ *adjective* intended to reduce costs 削减成本的 ○ *We have taken out the second telephone line as a cost-cutting exercise.* 为了削减成本，我们取消了第二条电话线。■ *noun* the process of reducing costs 削减成本 ○ *As a result of cost-cutting, we have had to make three secretaries redundant.* 为了削减成本，我们裁掉了三个秘书。

cost-effective /ˌkɒstɪˈfektɪv/ *adjective* giving good value when compared with the original cost 成本低廉的，经济的 ○ *We find advertising in the Sunday newspapers very cost-effective.* 我们发现在星期天的报纸上作广告相当合算。

cost-effectiveness /ˌkɒstɪˈfektɪvnəs/, **cost efficiency** /ˌkɒst ɪˈfɪʃ(ə)nsi/ *noun* the quality of being cost-effective 成本效益 ○ *Can we calculate the cost-effectiveness of air freight against shipping by sea?* 我们能计算出空运与海运相比而言的成本效益吗？

cost factor /ˈkɒst ˌfæktə/ *noun* the problem of cost 成本因素

costing /ˈkɒstɪŋ/ *noun* a calculation of the manufacturing costs, and so the selling price, of a product 成本核算：通过计算生产费用来确定产品的售价 ○ *The costings give us a retail price of $2.95.* 通过成本计算，我们将零售价定为 2.95 美元。○ *We cannot do the costing until we have details of all the* *production expenditure*. 我们必须先获得所有生产支出的详细资料,然后才能进行成本核算。

costly /ˈkɒstli/ *adjective* costing a lot of money, or costing too much money 花钱多的,昂贵的 ○ *Defending the court case was a costly process*. 诉讼抗辩花费巨大。○ *The mistakes were time-consuming and costly*. 这些错误耗费了大量时间和金钱。

cost management /kɒst ˈmænɪdʒmənt/ *noun* the application of management accounting concepts, methods of data collection, analysis, and presentation, in order to provide the information required to enable costs to be planned, monitored, and controlled 成本管理:应用管理会计概念以及数据收集、分析和呈列方法,以提供规划、监督和控制成本所需的信息

cost of borrowing /kɒst əv ˈbɒrəʊɪŋ/ *noun* an interest rate paid on borrowed money 借贷成本:借款支付的利息

cost of capital /ˌkɒst əv ˈkæpɪt(ə)l/ *noun* interest paid on the capital used in operating a business 资本成本:对企业经营资本支付的利息

cost of goods sold /ˌkɒst əv ˌɡʊdz ˈsəʊld/ *noun* same as 同 **cost of sales**

cost of living /ˌkɒst əv ˈlɪvɪŋ/ *noun* money which has to be paid for basic items such as food, heating or rent 生活费用:满足生活基本需求的费用,如饮食、取暖或租赁: ○ *to allow for the cost of living in the salary adjustments* 在工资调整中考虑到生活费用

cost-of-living allowance /ˌkɒstəvˈlɪvɪŋ əˌlaʊəns/ *noun* an addition to normal salary to cover increases in the cost of living 生活费用津贴:在工资中加入用以弥补生活费用上涨的补助费(NOTE: The US term is **COLA** 美国用语为 **COLA**)

cost-of-living bonus /ˌkɒstəvˈlɪvɪŋ ˌbəʊnəs/ *noun* money paid to meet an increase in the cost of living 生活费用补贴:为弥补生活费上涨而支付的额外资金

cost-of-living increase /ˌkɒstəvˈlɪvɪŋ ˌɪnkriːs/ *noun* an increase in salary to allow it to keep up with the increased cost of living 生活费用补助:随着生活费的上涨而提薪

cost-of-living index /ˌkɒstəvˈlɪvɪŋ ˌɪndeks/ *noun* a way of measuring the cost of living which is shown as a percentage increase on the figure for the previous year. It is similar to the consumer price index, but includes other items such as the interest on mortgages 生活费用指数:生活费相对于前一年增加的百分比。该指数与消费物价指数类似,但包括了按揭利息等其他项目

cost of sales /ˌkɒst əv ˈseɪlz/ *noun* all the costs of a product sold, including manufacturing costs and the staff costs of the production department, before general overheads are calculated 销售成本:所售产品的所有成本,包括在计算总间接成本之前的制造成本和制造车间人工成本 Also called 亦称作 **cost of goods sold**

cost of sales adjustment /ˌkɒst əv ˈseɪlz əˌdʒʌstmənt/ *noun* an adjustment made in current cost accounting to a company's historical cost profit figure to take into account the effect of inflation on the value of materials used in production during the accounting period. If prices are rising, the COSA will reduce historical cost profit 销售成本调整：在现行成本会计中，考虑到剔除通货膨胀对会计期间内所使用原材料价值的影响，而对公司按历史成本计算的利润进行调整。如物价上涨，销售成本调整将减少按历史成本计算的利润 Abbreviation 缩写 **COSA**

cost plus /ˌkɒst ˈplʌs/ *noun* a system of calculating a price, by taking the cost of production of goods or services and adding a percentage to cover the supplier's overheads and margin 成本加成：一种计算价格的制度，它在商品或劳务生产成本的基础上追加一定百分比，以弥补供应商的间接费用及利润 ○ *We are charging for the work on a cost plus basis.* 我们用成本加成法收取这项工作的费用。

cost price /ˈkɒst praɪs/ *noun* a selling price which is the same as the price, either the manufacturing price or the wholesale price, which the seller paid for the item 成本价：卖价与卖方为其支付的成本（制造成本或批发价格）相等时的价格

costs /kɒsts/ *plural noun* the expenses involved in a court case 诉讼费 ○ *The judge awarded costs to the defendant.* 法官判决由被告承担诉讼费用。○ *Costs of the case will be borne by the prosecution.* 本案的诉讼费用将由原告承担。

cost-volume-profit analysis /ˌkɒstˌvɒljuːmˈprɒfɪt əˌnæləsɪs/ *noun* an analysis of the relationship between gross profit and costs of production at different selling prices and output volumes 成本—销量—利润分析：关于在不同售价和产量情况下毛利与生产成本之间关系的分析 Also called 亦称作 **CVP analysis**

council tax /ˈkaʊnsəl tæks/ *noun* a tax paid by individuals or companies to a local authority. Introduced in April 1993 as a replacement for the much maligned community charge, or 'poll tax', council tax depends on the value of the residential or commercial property occupied 家庭税：个人或公司向地方税务局缴纳的税项。该税于 1993 年 4 月引入，以取代备受争议的人头税。家庭税额依所占用的住宅或商用物业的价值而定

count /kaʊnt/ *verb* **1.** to add figures together to make a total 加总，算出总额 ○ *She counted up the sales for the six months to December.* 她对到 12 月为止的六个月销售额进行了加总。**2.** to include something 包括 ○ *Did you count my trip to New York as part of my sales expenses?* 你把我去纽约的旅行费用包括在销售费用里了吗？

counter- /kaʊntə/ *prefix* against 表示"反"、"逆"、"对应"

counterbid /ˈkaʊntəbɪd/ *noun* a higher bid in reply to a previous bid （买方）竞价：针对前一报价报出更高的价 ○ *When I bid £20 she put in a counterbid of £25.* 我出价 20 英镑，她竞价出 25 英镑。

counter-claim /ˈkaʊntəˌkleɪm/ *noun* a claim for damages made in reply to a previous claim 反索赔：针对前一索赔提出的反索赔 ○ *Jones claimed £25,000 in damages against Smith, and Smith entered a counter-claim of £50,000 for loss of office.* 琼斯向史密斯提出 2.5 万英镑的损害赔偿，而史密斯因失去职位反索赔 5 万英镑。

counterfeit /ˈkaʊntəfɪt/ *adjective* referring to false or imitation money （货币）伪造的，假的 ○ *Shops in the ar-*

ea have been asked to look out for counterfeit £20 notes. 该地区的商店被告知提防20英镑的假币。■ *verb* to make imitation money 伪造(货币)

counterfoil /ˈkaʊntəfɔɪl/ *noun* a slip of paper kept after writing a cheque, an invoice or a receipt, as a record of the deal which has taken place (支票、发票或收据的)存根,票根

countermand /ˌkaʊntəˈmɑːnd/ *verb* to say that an order must not be carried out 取消(订单等) ○ *to countermand an order* 取消订单 □ **to countermand an order** to say that an order must not be carried out 取消一份订单

counter-offer /ˈkaʊntərˌɒfə/ *noun* a higher or lower offer made in reply to another offer 还盘:针对另一报价报出更高或更低的价 ○ *Smith Ltd made an offer of £1m for the property, and Blacks replied with a counter-offer of £1.4m.* 史密斯有限公司对这项房产发盘100万英镑,布莱克公司还盘140万英镑。

'...the company set about paring costs and improving the design of its product. It came up with a price cut of 14%, but its counter-offer — for an order that was to have provided 8% of its workload next year — was too late and too expensive'
"该公司开始削减成本和改进产品设计。并提出将价格下调14%;但对于一份占其来年生产量8%的订单来说,它的还盘价太高而且也报得太迟了" [*Wall Street Journal*《华尔街日报》]

counterparty /ˈkaʊntəpɑːti/ *noun* the other party in a deal (交易中的)另一方,对方

counterpurchase /ˈkaʊntəpɜːtʃɪs/ *noun* an international trading deal, where a company agrees to use money received on a sale to purchase goods in the country where the sale was made 反向购买,互购:在国际贸易中,销售方同意将收到的销售款项用于在销售发生国购买商品

countersign /ˈkaʊntəsaɪn/ *verb* to sign a document which has already been signed by someone else 会签,连署,副签:在别人已签署过的文件上签字 ○ *All our cheques have to be countersigned by the finance director.* 所有支票都必须由财务经理会签。○ *The sales director countersigns all my orders.* 销售主任副签了我所有的订单。

countertrade /ˈkaʊntətreɪd/ *noun* a trade which does not involve payment of money, but something such as a barter or a buy-back deal instead 对销贸易,返销贸易:不涉及货币支付,而采用易货或回购等形式的交易

countervailing duty /ˈkaʊntəveɪlɪŋ ˌdjuːti/ *noun* a duty imposed by a country on imported goods, where the price of the goods includes a subsidy from the government in the country of origin 反补贴税,反倾销税:对原产国政府给予补贴的进口商品征收的关税 Also called 亦称作 **antidumping duty**

counting house /ˈkaʊntɪŋ haʊs/ *noun* a department dealing with cash (*dated*) (过时用法)会计室,账房,存账室

country risk /ˈkʌntri rɪsk/ *noun* the risk associated with undertaking transactions with, or holding assets in, a particular country. Sources of risk might be political, economic, or regulatory instability affecting overseas taxation, repatriation of profits, nationalisation, currency instability, etc. 国别风险:在特定国家进行交易或持有资产所涉及的风险,包括政治、经济或政策波动对海外税收、利润回汇、国有化、货币波动等的影响

coupon /ˈkuːpɒn/ *noun* **1.** a piece of paper used in place of money 代金券 **2.** a slip of paper attached to a government bond certificate which can be cashed to provide the annual interest 息票:附在政府债券上可兑现年利息的纸条

coupon rate /ˈkuːpɒn reɪt/ *noun* percentage fixed interest rate on a government bond or a debenture 息票率:政府债券或信用债券上固定的利率

coupon security /ˈkuːpɒn sɪˌkjʊərɪti/ *noun* a government security which carries a coupon and pays interest, as opposed to one which pays no interest but is sold at a discount to its face value 附息证券:附有息票并支付利息的政府债券,与之相对的是折价发行的零息债券

covenant /ˈkʌvənənt/ *noun* a legal contract (合法)合同,契约 ■ *verb* to agree to pay annually a specified sum of money to a person or organisation by contract. When payments are made under covenant to a charity, the charity can reclaim the tax paid by the donee 订立契约:订立契约同意每年定额支付给某人或组织。当根据契约付款给慈善机构时,慈善机构可领回受捐人缴纳的税款 ○ *to covenant to pay £10 per annum* 立约每年支付10英镑

cover /ˈkʌvə/ *noun* an amount of money large enough to guarantee that something can be paid for 保证金:足以保证支付某款项的金额 ○ *Do you have sufficient cover for this loan?* 你有足以担保这笔贷款的保证金吗? ■ *verb* **1.** to provide protection by insurance against something 为…保险 ○ *The insurance covers fire, theft and loss of work.* 该保险为火灾、失窃和失业提供保险。□ **to cover a risk** to be protected by insurance against a risk 抵补风险:通过保险得到某类风险的保护 **2.** to have, earn or provide enough money to pay for something 弥补,抵偿 *We do not make enough sales to cover the expense of running the shop.* 我们的销售额不足以抵偿经营商店的开支。○ *Breakeven point is reached when sales cover all costs.* 当销售额正好清偿所有成本时,就是达到了收支平衡点。**3.** to ask for security against a loan which you are making 提供贷款抵押

'... three export credit agencies have agreed to provide cover for large projects in Nigeria'
"有三家出口信贷机构已同意为尼日利亚的大型工程项目提供担保"[*Business Times* (*Lagos*)《商业时报》(拉各斯)]

coverage /ˈkʌv(ə)rɪdʒ/ *noun US* protection guaranteed by insurance (美)保险总额,保险范围,投保险别 ○ *Do you have coverage against fire damage?* 你有没有投保火灾险?

'...from a PR point of view it is easier to get press coverage when you are selling an industry and not a brand'
"从公关的角度看,推销一个行业要比推销一个品牌更容易吸引媒体的注意"[*PR Week*《公关周刊》]

covered bear /ˌkʌvəd ˈbeə/ *noun* a bear who holds the stock which he or she is selling 抛补空头:持有所售股票

的空头方

cover note /ˈkʌvə ˌnəʊt/ *noun* a letter from an insurance company giving details of an insurance policy and confirming that the policy exists 保险证明，暂保单，承保单：保险公司开出的关于保险单详细内容并确认保险单已经存在的信函

cover price /ˈkʌvə praɪs/ *noun* the price of a newspaper or magazine which is printed on the cover and paid by the final purchaser 封面价格：报纸或杂志印在封面上的购买者应付的价格

CP *abbr* commercial paper 商业票据

CPA *abbr* certified public accountant 注册会计师

CPI *abbr* Consumer Price Index 消费物价指数

creative accountancy /kriˌeɪtɪv əˈkaʊntənsi/, **creative accounting** /kriˌeɪtɪv əˈkaʊntɪŋ/ *noun* an adaptation of a company's figures to present a better picture than is correct, usually intended to make a company more attractive to a potential buyer, or done for some other reason which may not be strictly legal 创造性会计：为使公司对潜在购买者更有吸引力或出于某种严格意义上并不合法的原因，改变公司账表上的数字以粉饰美化公司

credit /ˈkredɪt/ *noun* **1.** a period of time allowed before a customer has to pay a debt incurred for goods or services 信用期，赊账期：允许顾客延缓支付商品或劳务费用的期限 ○ *to give someone six months' credit* 给予某人六个月的信用期 ○ *to sell on good credit terms* 以优惠的信贷条件销售 **2.** an amount entered in accounts to show a decrease in assets or expenses or an increase in liabilities, revenue or capital. In accounts, credits are entered in the right-hand column 贷方：记入表示资产或费用减少，或负债、收入、资本增加的金额。贷方通常记在账户的右边一栏 ○ *to enter £100 to someone's credit* 将100英镑记入某人账户的贷方 ○ *to pay in £100 to the credit of Mr Smith* 将100英镑记入史密斯先生的贷方 Compare 比较 **debit** ■ *verb* to put money into someone's account, or to note money received in an account 贷记：将资金记入某人账户或将收到的款项记入账户 ○ *to credit an account with £100* or *to credit £100 to an account* 在某账户贷方记入100英镑（或在账户中贷记100英镑）

credit account /ˈkredɪt əˌkaʊnt/ *noun* an account which a customer has with a shop which allows him or her to buy goods and pay for them later 赊购账户：商店允许客户进行赊购的账户

credit balance /ˈkredɪt ˌbæləns/ *noun* a balance in an account showing that more money has been received than is owed 贷方余额：账户中表明已收款多于欠款的余额 ○ *The account has a credit balance of £100.* 该账户贷方余额为100英镑。

credit bank /ˈkredɪt bæŋk/ *noun* a bank which lends money 信贷银行：发放贷款的银行

credit card /ˈkredɪt kɑːd/ *noun* a plastic card which allows you to borrow money and to buy goods without paying for them immediately. You must pay the balance to the credit card company at a later date 信用卡

credit card holder /ˈkredɪt kɑːd ˌhəʊldə/ *noun* **1.** a person who has a credit card 信用卡持卡人 **2.** a plastic wallet for keeping credit cards 信用卡卡夹

credit card sale /ˈkredɪt kɑːd ˌseɪl/ *noun* the act of selling where the buyer uses a credit card to pay 信用卡销售:买方使用信用卡结账的销售

credit column /ˈkredɪt ˌkɒləm/ *noun* the right-hand column in accounts showing money received 贷方栏:呈列已收款项的账户右边一栏

credit control /ˈkredɪt kənˌtrəʊl/ *noun* a check that customers pay on time and do not owe more than their credit limit 信用管理,信贷控制:检查顾客是否及时还款、贷款数目是否超过他们的信贷限额

credit controller /ˈkredɪt kənˌtrəʊlə/ *noun* a member of staff whose job is to try to get payment of overdue invoices 收账员:负责收回逾期账款的职员

credit entry /ˈkredɪt ˌentri/ *noun* an entry on the credit side of an account 贷方分录:记入账户贷方的分录

credit facilities /ˈkredɪt fəˌsɪlɪtiz/ *plural noun* an arrangement with a bank or supplier to have credit so as to buy goods 信贷便利,信贷服务:银行或供应商提供的用于购货的信贷服务

credit freeze /ˈkredɪt friːz/ *noun* a period when lending by banks is restricted by the government 信用紧缩:政府限制银行贷款的时期

credit limit /ˈkredɪt ˌlɪmɪt/ *noun* the largest amount of money which a customer can borrow 信用限额:顾客可借贷的最高金额

credit line /ˈkredɪt laɪn/ *noun* an overdraft, the amount by which a person can draw money from an account with no funds, with the agreement of the bank 透支额:银行允许客户在其账户没有资金时提款的最高限额

credit note /ˈkredɪt nəʊt/ *noun* a note showing that money is owed to a customer 贷记通知单:列明卖方所欠客户款项的通知 ○ *The company sent the wrong order and so had to issue a credit note.* 该公司送错了一笔订单,所以必须发出一张贷记通知单。Abbreviation 缩写 **C/N**

creditor /ˈkredɪtə/ *noun* a person or company that is owed money, i. e. a company's creditors are its liabilities 债权人

creditor days /ˈkredɪtə deɪz/ *noun* the number of days on average that a company requires to pay its creditors 应付账款天数:偿还应付账款所需的平均天数 ◊ 参阅 **debtor days**

creditors /ˈkredɪtəz/ *noun* a list of all liabilities in a set of accounts, including overdrafts, amounts owing to other companies in the group, trade creditors, payments received on account for goods not yet supplied, etc. 应付账款:列出所有的负债(包括银行透支、对集团内其他子公司的欠款、赊销方、对未发货物的预收款等)的一组账目

creditors' meeting /ˈkredɪtəz ˌmiːtɪŋ/ *noun* a meeting of all the people to whom an insolvent company owes money, to decide how to obtain the money owed 债权人会议:所有债权人参加并决定如何收回破产公司债务的会议

credit rating /ˈkredɪt ˌreɪtɪŋ/ *noun* an amount which a credit agency feels a customer will be able to repay 信用评级,信用额度:资信调查机构所评定的客户借款额

credit reference /ˌkredɪt ˈref(ə)rəns/ *noun* a credit rating or other indication of the creditworthiness of a company or individual 信用资料：公司或个人的信用评级或其他信誉资料

credit report /ˌkredɪt rɪˈpɔːt/ *noun* information about an individual or entity relevant to a decision to grant credit 信用报告：某人或实体的信用信息，与决定是否给予信贷相关

credit risk /ˈkredɪt rɪsk/ *noun* a risk that a borrower may not be able to repay a loan 信用风险：贷款不能收回的风险

credit side /ˈkredɪt saɪd/ *noun* the righthand column of accounts showing money received 贷方：呈列已收款项的账户右边一栏

credit squeeze /ˈkredɪt skwiːz/ *noun* a period when lending by the banks is restricted by the government 信用紧缩：政府限制银行贷款的时期

credit union /ˈkredɪt ˌjuːnjən/ *noun* a group of people who pay in regular deposits or subscriptions which earn interest and are used to make loans to other members of the group 信用合作社，信贷协会，存款互助协会：其成员定期以存款或会费形式支付款项而获得利息的协会，这些款项被用于向协会成员贷款

creditworthiness /ˈkredɪtˌwɜːðinəs/ *noun* the ability of a customer to pay for goods bought on credit 信誉，信用可靠性

creditworthy /ˈkredɪtwɜːði/ *adjective* having enough money to be able to buy goods on credit 有信用的，资信可靠的 ○ *We will do some checks on her to see if she is creditworthy.* 我们将对她进行一些审查，看看她的资信是否可靠。

crisis /ˈkraɪsɪs/ *noun* a serious economic situation where decisions have to be taken rapidly （经济）危机 ○ *a banking crisis* 银行业危机 ○ *The government stepped in to try to resolve the international crisis.* 政府介入试图解决这次国际危机。○ *Withdrawals from the bank have reached crisis level.* 挤提已经非常严重了。

crisis management /ˈkraɪsɪs ˌmænɪdʒmənt/ *noun* 危机管理 **1.** management of a business or a country's economy during a period of crisis [在危机时期对企业或国家经济的管理] **2.** actions taken by an organisation to protect itself when unexpected events or situations occur that could threaten its success or continued operation [在发生意外事件时，组织为保护自身免受威胁而采取的措施]（NOTE: Crisis situations may result from external factors such as the development of a new product by a competitor or changes in legislation, or from internal factors such as a product failure or faulty decision-making, and often involve the need to make quick decisions on the basis of uncertain or incomplete information 危机局势可能源自外部，例如竞争对手开发新产品；或来自内部，例如产品失败或决策失误。在危机局势下，通常需要根据不确定或不完整的信息迅速作出决策）

critical-path method /ˌkrɪtɪk(ə)l-ˈpɑːθ ˌmeθəd/ *noun* a technique used in project management to identify the activities within a project that are critical to its success, usually by showing on a diagram or flow chart the order in which activities must be carried out so that the project can be completed in the shortest time and at the least cost

关键路径法：项目管理中使用的一种技术，它往往考虑必须采取哪些措施才能在最短的时间内以最低的成本完成项目，并在图表或流程图上列出这些措施及其顺序，从而确定可令项目取得成功的关键措施

CRO *abbr* Companies Registration Office 公司注册办事处

cross-border /ˌkrɒsˈbɔːdə/ *adjective* from one country to another, covering several countries 穿越两国边境的，跨国的

cross-border services /krɒsˌbɔːdə ˈsɜːvɪsɪz/ *plural noun* accountancy services provided by an accountancy firm in one country for a client in another country （会计师事务所的）跨国服务

crossed cheque /ˌkrɒst ˈtʃek/ *noun* a cheque with two lines across it showing that it can only be deposited at a bank and not exchanged for cash 划线支票：上面划有两条线，表明只能存入银行而不能兑现的支票

cross holding /ˈkrɒs ˌhəʊldɪŋ/ *noun* a situation where two companies own shares in each other in order to stop either from being taken over 交叉持股：两个公司互相持有对方股票，以防止被对方收购的情况 ○ *The two companies have protected themselves from takeover by a system of cross holdings.* 这两家公司通过交叉持股来防止被收购。

cross out /ˌkrɒs ˈaʊt/ *verb* to put a line through something which has been written 划去，注销 ○ *She crossed out £250 and put in £500.* 她划掉了250英镑，同时记入了500英镑。

cross rate /ˈkrɒs reɪt/ *noun* an exchange rate between two currencies expressed in a third currency 套汇汇率，交叉汇率：以第三方货币表示的两种货币间汇率

cross-selling /ˌkrɒsˈselɪŋ/ *noun* the act of selling two products which go with each other, by placing them side by side in a store 交叉出售：将两件产品捆绑出售

crown jewels /ˌkraʊn ˈdʒuːəlz/ *plural noun* the most valuable assets of a company, the reason why other companies may want to make takeover bids 公司最有价值的资产（其他公司想收购该公司的原因）

crude petroleum /ˌkruːd pəˈtrəʊliəm/ *noun* raw petroleum which has not been processed 原油

crystallise /ˈkrɪstəlaɪz/, **crystallize** *verb* to become chargeable on an asset 具体化：将资产变为可征收的款项 ○ *A deferred gain is crystallised when you realise the gain by selling the asset.* 递延收益在通过出售资产变现收益时具体化。

CT *abbr* corporation tax 公司税

cum /kʌm/ *preposition* with 附有，带有

cum all /ˌkʌm ˈɔːl/ *adverb* including all entitlements 附有一切权利

cum coupon /kʌm ˈkuːpɒn/ *adverb* with a coupon attached or before interest due on a security is paid 附息地，支付证券利息前

cum rights /ˌkʌm ˈraɪts/ *adverb* sold with the right to purchase new shares in a rights issue 附权地：出售时附带权证发行中的新股认购权

cumulative /ˈkjuːmjʊlətɪv/ *adjective* added to regularly over a period of time 累积的

cumulative interest /ˌkjuːmjʊlətɪv ˈɪntrəst/ *noun* the interest which is added to the capital each year 累计利息：每年加入本金的利息

cumulative preference share /ˌkjuːmjʊlətɪv ˈpref(ə)rəns ʃeə/, **cumulative preferred stock** /ˌkjuːmjʊlətɪv prɪˌfɜːd ˈstɒk/ *noun* a preference share which will have the dividend paid at a later date even if the company is not able to pay a dividend in the current year 累积分派的优先股：尽管当年不支付股利，但其股利将会延至以后年度支付的优先股

cumulative weighted average cost /ˌkjuːmjʊlətɪv ˌweɪtɪd ˈæv(ə)rɪdʒ kɒst/, **cumulative weighted average price**/ˌkjuːmjʊlətɪv ˌweɪtɪd ˈæv(ə)rɪdʒ praɪs/ *noun* the average price per unit of stock delivered in a period calculated each time a new delivery is received (as opposed 'periodic weighted average') 累积加权平均成本（或价格）：在一段时间内，每次收到新进货物时计算出的单位存货平均价格（与"期间加权平均成本（或价格）"相对）

currency /ˈkʌrənsi/ *noun* **1.** money in coins and notes which is used in a particular country 货币 **2.** a foreign currency, the currency of another country 外国货币（NOTE：**Currency** has no plural when it refers to the money of one country **currency** 指一国货币时没有复数形式，例如：*He was arrested trying to take currency out of the country*）

'... today's wide daily variations in exchange rates show the instability of a system based on a single currency, namely the dollar'

"今天汇率大幅度波动，表明了建立在单一货币（即美元）基础之上汇率机制的不稳定性"［*Economist*《经济学家》］

'... the level of currency in circulation increased to N4.9 billion in the month of August'

"8月份流通中的货币量增加到49亿尼日利亚奈拉"［*Business Times*（*Lagos*）《商业时报》（拉各斯）］

currency backing /ˈkʌrənsi ˌbækɪŋ/ *noun* gold or government securities which maintain the strength of a currency 货币支持：用于支持某种货币国际实力的黄金或政府有价证券

currency band /ˈkʌrənsi bænd/ *noun* the exchange rate levels between which a currency is allowed to move without full devaluation 汇率波动范围：允许某种货币汇率波动而不完全贬值的范围

currency basket /ˈkʌrənsi ˌbɑːskɪt/ *noun* a group of currencies, each of which is weighted, calculated together as a single unit against which another currency can be measured 一揽子货币，一组货币：按其中每种货币价值加权平均计算出的一个可以衡量其他货币的单位

currency clause /ˈkʌrənsi clɔːz/ *noun* a clause in a contract which avoids problems of payment caused by changes in exchange rates, by fixing the exchange rate for the various transactions covered by the contract 货币条款：固定合同中各项交易的汇率，以避免汇率波动导致支付问题的合同条款

currency futures /ˈkʌrənsi ˌfjuːtʃəz/ *plural noun* purchases of foreign currency for delivery at a future date 货币期货：购买在未来某日交割的外币

currency hedging /ˈkʌrənsi

ˌhedʒɪŋ/ *noun* a method of reducing exchange rate risk by diversifying currency holdings and adjusting them according to changes in exchange rates 货币对冲，套期保值：通过分散货币持仓和依汇率波动调整持仓来降低汇率风险的方法

currency mismatching /ˈkʌrənsi ˌmɪsmætʃɪŋ/ *noun* the activity of borrowing money in the currency of a country where interest rates are low and depositing it in the currency of a country with higher interest rates. The potential profit from the interest rate margin may be offset by changes in the exchange rates which increase the value of the loan in the company's balance sheet 货币不配比：以利率较低国家的货币借贷，再以利率较高国家的货币存入的行为。利率差产生的潜在利润可能被汇率波动所抵消，从而增加贷款在公司资产负债表中的价值

currency movements /ˈkʌrənsi ˌmuːvmənts/ *plural noun* changes in exchange rates between countries 汇率波动

currency note /ˈkʌrənsi nəʊt/ *noun* a bank note 流通券

currency reserves /ˈkʌrənsi rɪˌzɜːvz/ *noun* foreign money held by a government to support its own currency and to pay its debts 货币储备：政府为支持本国货币及偿还债务而持有的外币

currency swap /ˈkʌrənsi swɒp/ *noun* **1.** an agreement to use a certain currency for payments under a contract in exchange for another currency (the two companies involved can each buy one of the currencies at a more favourable rate than the other) 货币互兑：根据合同用某种货币支付以换取其他货币的协议（双方都可以按优于另一方的汇率购买一种外汇） **2.** the buying or selling of a fixed amount of a foreign currency on the spot market, and the selling or buying of the same amount of the same currency on the forward market 货币调期：在现货市场上买进或卖出一定量的外币，同时在远期市场上卖出或买进同量的同种货币

current account /ˈkʌrənt əˌkaʊnt/ *noun* **1.** an account in an bank from which the customer can withdraw money when he or she wants. Current accounts do not always pay interest 活期存款账户：可根据需要随时提现的银行账户。活期存款账户不一定支付利息 ○ *to pay money into a current account* 把资金存入活期存款账户 Also called 亦称作 **cheque account** (NOTE: The US term is **checking account** 美国用语为 **checking account**) **2.** an account of the balance of payments of a country relating to the sale or purchase of raw materials, goods and invisibles 往来账户：记录一国与原材料、商品和无形资产买卖有关的付款余额的账户

'...a surplus in the current account is of such vital importance to economists and currency traders because the more Japanese goods that are exported, the more dollars overseas customers have to pay for these products. That pushes up the value of the yen'
"往来账户盈余对于经济学家和货币交易商非常重要，因为出口的日本商品越多，海外客户为这些产品所支付的美元就越多。这可以促使日元升值" [*Nikkei Weekly*《日经周报》]

'...customers' current deposit and current

accounts also rose to $655.31 million at the end of December'
"客户的活期存款和活期存款账户在12月末也上升到了6.5531亿美元"[*Hong Kong Standard*《香港虎报》]

current assets /ˌkʌrənt ˈæsets/ *plural noun* the assets used by a company in its ordinary work, e.g. materials, finished goods, cash and monies due, and which are held for a short time only 流动资产:公司用于日常事务短期持有的资产,如原材料、成品、现金和应收账款

current cost /ˌkʌrənt ˈkɒst/ *noun* the amount it would cost to replace an asset at current prices 现时成本:按现行价格置换某项资产的成本

current cost accounting /ˌkʌrənt ˈkɒst əˌkaʊntɪŋ/ *noun* a method of accounting which notes the cost of replacing assets at current prices, rather than valuing assets at their original cost 现时成本会计:一种会计方法,它记录现时重置资产的成本价值,而不是按原始成本估算资产价值 Abbreviation 缩写 **CCA**

current liabilities /ˌkʌrənt laɪəˈbɪlɪtiz/ *plural noun* the debts which a company has to pay within the next accounting period. In a company's annual accounts, these would be debts which must be paid within the year and are usually payments for goods or services received 流动负债:公司将在下一个会计期内偿还的债务。在公司的年度报表中,流动负债是将在一年内支付购买商品和劳务的费用

current purchasing power /ˌkʌrənt ˈpɜːtʃɪsɪŋ ˌpaʊə/ *noun* a method of accounting which takes inflation into account by using constant monetary units (actual amounts multiplied by a general price index) 现时购买力:用不变货币单位(实际数量乘以一般物价指数)来计量通胀影响的一种会计方法 Also called 亦称作 **constant purchasing power**

current rate of exchange /ˌkʌrənt reɪt əv ɪksˈtʃeɪndʒ/ *noun* today's rate of exchange 现行汇率:当天的汇率

current ratio /ˌkʌrənt ˈreɪʃiəʊ/ *noun* a ratio of current assets to current liabilities showing if a company may not be able to meet its immediate debts 流动比率:公司流动资产与流动负债的比率,它表明公司能否偿清其到期债务

current year /ˌkʌrənt ˈjɪə/ *noun* the year in which an accounting period falls 本年度,当前年度:会计期所在的年度 ○ *Under self-assessment, income is taxed on a current year basis – i.e. it is taxed in the year in which it is received.* 在自我评税中,收入按当前年度基准课税,亦即在实际取得收入的年度课税。

current yield /ˌkʌrənt ˈjiːld/ *noun* a dividend calculated as a percentage of the current price of a share on the stock market 现时收益率:在股票市场上用股票现时价格百分比计算的股利

curve /kɜːv/ *noun* a line which is not straight, e.g. a line on a graph 曲线 ○ *The graph shows an upward curve.* 该图显示了一条上升的曲线。

cushion /ˈkʊʃ(ə)n/ *noun* money which allows a company to pay interest on its borrowings or to survive a loss 安全余量,缓冲资金:公司用以支付借款利息或承受损失的资金 ○ *We have sums on deposit which are a useful cushion when cash flow is tight.* 我们有大量的银行存款可以在现金流转

紧张时以作缓冲。

custodian /kʌˈstəʊdiən/ *noun* a bank whose principal function is to maintain and grow the assets contained in a trust 保管行,托管行:主要职能是保管信托资产并令其增值的银行

custom /ˈkʌstəm/ *noun* the use of a shop by regular shoppers 惠顾,经常的光顾

customer /ˈkʌstəmə/ *noun* a person or company that buys goods 顾客 ○ *The shop was full of customers.* 这家商店挤满了顾客。○ *Can you serve this customer first please?* 能不能先为这位顾客服务? ○ *She's a regular customer of ours.* 她是我们的常客。(NOTE: The customer may not be the consumer or end user of the product 顾客不一定是产品的消费者或最终用户)

'... unless advertising and promotion is done in the context of an overall customer orientation, it cannot seriously be thought of as marketing'
"广告宣传若不是建立在以顾客为本的框架内,就不能被看作是真正的营销"[*Quarterly Review of Marketing*《市场评论季刊》]

customer service department /ˌkʌstəmə ˈsɜːvɪs dɪˌpɑːtmənt/ *noun* a department which deals with customers and their complaints and orders 顾客服务部:同顾客打交道,处理其投诉和订单

customise /ˈkʌstəmaɪz/, **customize** *verb* to change something to fit the special needs of a customer 定制,定做 ○ *We use customised computer terminals.* 我们使用的是特制的计算机终端。

customs barrier /ˈkʌstəmz ˌbæriə/ *noun* customs duty intended to make trade more difficult 关税壁垒:旨在遏制贸易的关税

customs broker /ˈkʌstəmz ˌbrəʊkə/ *noun* a person or company that takes goods through customs for a shipping company 报关经纪人;报关行:代为船舶公司报关的个人或公司

customs clearance /ˈkʌstəmz ˌklɪərəns/ *noun* **1.** the act of passing goods through customs so that they can enter or leave the country 结关,海关放行:货物通过海关以便进出某国 **2.** a document given by customs to a shipper to show that customs duty has been paid and the goods can be shipped 结关证:海关签发给承运人的文件,证明货物关税已支付,可以装运 ○ *to wait for customs clearance* 等候结关

customs declaration /ˈkʌstəmz dekləˌreɪʃ(ə)n/ *noun* a statement showing goods being imported on which duty will have to be paid 报关单:列有进口货物及应缴关税的单证 ○ *to fill in a customs declaration form* 填写报关单

customs duty /ˈkʌstəmz ˌdjuːti/ *noun* a tax on goods imported into a country 关税:对进口货物征收的税项

customs entry point /ˌkʌstəmz ˈentri pɔɪnt/ *noun* a place at a border between two countries where goods are declared to customs 报关处:货物报关的两国边界处

customs examination /ˈkʌstəmz ɪɡˌzæmɪneɪʃ(ə)n/ *noun* an inspection of goods or baggage by customs officials 验关:海关官员对货物或行李进行的检查

customs formalities /ˈkʌstəmz fɔːˌmælɪtiz/ *plural noun* a declaration of goods by the shipper and examination of them by customs 海关手续:货物报关及海关检查

customs officer /ˈkʌstəmz ˌɒfɪsə/ *noun* a person working for the Customs and Excise Department 海关官员,海关关员

customs official /ˈkʌstəmz əˌfɪʃ(ə)l/ *noun* a person working for the Customs and Excise Department 海关官员,海关关员

customs seal /ˈkʌstəmz siːl/ *noun* a seal attached by a customs officer to a box, to show that the contents have not passed through customs 海关封条:海关官员在箱子上贴的封条,表明里面的物品未通过海关检查

customs tariff /ˈkʌstəmz ˌtærɪf/ *noun* a list of taxes to be paid on imported goods 关税税则:对进口货物征收的税目

customs union /ˈkʌstəmz ˌjuːnjən/ *noun* an agreement between several countries that goods can travel between them, without paying duty, while goods from other countries have to pay special duties 关税同盟:几个国家之间互免关税、而对其他国家进入这些国家的货物则征收特别关税的协议

cut /kʌt/ *noun* **1.** the sudden lowering of a price, salary or the number of jobs (价格、工资或职位数目)突降,削减 ○ *price cuts* or *cuts in prices* 减价 □ **he took a cut in salary, he took a salary cut** he accepted a lower salary 他被减了薪 **2.** a share in a payment (支付的)份额 ○ *She introduces new customers and gets a cut of the sales rep's commission.* 她为公司介绍了新客户,因此得到一份销售代理佣金。■ *verb* **1.** to lower something suddenly (突然)下调,降低 ○ *We are cutting prices on all our models.* 我们对所有款式都进行了减价。○ *We have taken out the second telephone line in order to try to cut costs.* 为了降低成本,我们取消了第二条电话线。**2.** to reduce the number of something 减少(数量)

'... state-owned banks cut their prime rates a percentage point to 11%'
"国有银行将其基准利率削减了1个百分点至11%"[*Wall Street Journal*《华尔街日报》]

'... the US bank announced a cut in its prime from 10½ per cent to 10 per cent'
"美国银行宣布将基准利率从10.5%削减至10%"[*Financial Times*《金融时报》]

'Opec has on average cut production by one third since 1979'
"自1979年以来,欧佩克的产量平均削减了三分之一"[*Economist*《经济学家》]

cutback /ˈkʌtbæk/ *noun* a reduction 减少,削减 ○ *cutbacks in government spending* 政府开支的削减

cut down (on) /ˌkʌt ˈdaʊn (ɒn)/ *verb* to reduce suddenly the amount of something used 突降,削减(使用数量) ○ *The government is cutting down on welfare expenditure.* 政府正着手削减福利开支。○ *The office is trying to cut down on electricity consumption.* 办公室正试图渐少电力消耗。○ *We have installed networked computers to cut down on paperwork.* 我们安装了联网计算机,以减少文书工作量。

cut-off /ˈkʌtɒf/ *noun* a date and procedure for isolating the flow of cash and goods, stocktaking and the related documentation, to ensure that all aspects of a transaction are dealt with in the same financial period 截止:用日期和程序对现金与商品流动、

存货盘点及有关文件记录进行划分，以确保交易的所有方面都在同一会计期间内处理

CVP analysis *noun* same as 同 **cost-volume-profit analysis**

cycle /ˈsaɪk(ə)l/ *noun* a set of events which happen in a regularly repeated sequence 循环，周期

cyclical factors /ˌsɪklɪk(ə)l ˈfæktəz/ *plural noun* the way in which a trade cycle affects businesses 周期性因素：贸易周期影响商业的方式

D

D / A *abbr* deposit account 存款账户

Daimyo bond /ˈdaɪmjəʊ bɒnd/ *noun* a Japanese bearer bond which can be cleared through European clearing houses 大名债券:日本的一种无记名债券,它可以在欧洲票据交换所交割

damages /ˈdæmɪdʒɪz/ *plural noun* money claimed as compensation for harm done 损害赔偿金 ○ *to claim £1000 in damages* 要求 1,000 英镑的损害赔偿 ○ *to be liable for damages* 负担损害赔偿 ○ *to pay £25,000 in damages* 支付 2.5 万英镑的损害赔偿金

D & B *abbr* Dun and Bradstreet 邓白氏公司

danger money /ˈdeɪndʒə ˌmʌni/ *noun* extra money paid to employees in dangerous jobs 危险工作津贴:对危险性工作的额外支付 ○ *The workforce has stopped work and asked for danger money.* 工人已停工,要求发放危险工作津贴。○ *He decided to go to work on an oil rig because of the danger money offered as an incentive.* 由于有危险工作津贴作为激励,他决定去石油钻塔工作。

data bank /ˈdeɪtə bæŋk/ *noun* a store of information in a computer 数据库:计算机中储存数据的地方

data capture /ˈdeɪtə ˌkæptʃə/, **data entry** /ˌdeɪtə ˈentri/ *noun* the act of putting information onto a computer by keyboarding or by scanning 信息取得,数据收集:用键盘或通过扫描将信息输入数据库

data processing /ˌdeɪtə ˈprəʊsesɪŋ/ *noun* the act of selecting and examining data in a computer to produce information in a special form 数据处理:选择及审查计算机中的数据以生成特定格式的信息

Datastream /ˈdeɪtəstriːm/ *noun* a data system available online, giving information about securities, prices, stock exchange transactions, etc. 在线数据系统:可以提供关于证券、价格、股票交易等信息的在线数据系统

dated /ˈdeɪtɪd/ *adjective* with a date written on it 注有日期的 ○ *Thank you for your letter dated June 15th.* 谢谢你 6 月 15 日的来信。

date of bill /ˌdeɪt əv ˈbɪl/ *noun* a date when a bill will mature 票据到期日

date of record /ˌdeɪt əv ˈrekɔːd/ *noun* the date when a shareholder must be registered to qualify for a dividend 记录日期:股东为了取得分红资格而注册登记的日期

date stamp /ˈdeɪt stæmp/ *noun* a stamp with rubber figures which can be moved, used for marking the date on documents 日戳

dawn raid /dɔːn ˈreɪd/ *noun* a sudden planned purchase of a large number of a company's shares at the beginning of a day's trading 开盘抢购：在交易日开始时有计划地大量突击购入某公司的股票（NOTE：Up to 15% of a company's shares may be bought in this way，and the purchaser must wait for seven days before purchasing any more shares．Sometimes a dawn raid is the first step towards a takeover of the target company 用这种方式最多可购得公司 15%的股票，买方如想购得该公司更多股票需至少在七天之后。这种购买有时是兼并目标公司的第一步）

day book /ˈdeɪ bʊk/ *noun* a book with an account of sales and purchases made each day 日记账：每天的购销账

day order /ˈdeɪ ˌɔːdə/ *noun* an order to a stockbroker to buy or sell on a specific day 当日指令：委托证券经纪人在某一特定日期买进或卖出的指令

day shift /ˈdeɪ ʃɪft/ *noun* a shift worked during the daylight hours 白班，日班

day trader /ˈdeɪ ˌtreɪdə/ *noun* a person who buys shares and sells them within the same day 当日交易者：在同一天买卖同种股票的交易者

DCF *abbr* discounted cash flow 贴现的现金流量

DD *abbr* direct debit 直接借记，直接扣账

dead account /ˌded əˈkaʊnt/ *noun* an account which is no longer used 呆账，坏账，死账

dead loss /ˌded ˈlɒs/ *noun* a total loss 纯损失，总损失 ○ *The car was written off as a dead loss*．这辆车被当作净损失注销了。

dead money /ˌded ˈmʌni/ *noun* money which is not invested to make a profit 呆滞资金，闲置钱：没有用于投资获利的资金

dead season /ˈded ˌsiːz(ə)n/ *noun* the time of year when there are few tourists about 淡季：一年中游客很少的季节

deal /diːl/ *noun* a business agreement，affair or contract 业务协议，交易，合同 ○ *The sales director set up a deal with a Russian bank*．销售经理与一家俄罗斯银行达成一笔交易。○ *The deal will be signed tomorrow*．这份协议将在明天签署。○ *They did a deal with an American airline*．他们与一家美国航空公司做了一笔生意。■ *verb* to buy and sell 交易，买卖 □ **to deal in leather *or* options** to buy and sell leather or options 做皮革（或期权）生意

dealer /ˈdiːlə/ *noun* **1．** a person who buys and sells 商人 ○ *a used-car dealer* 二手车经销商 **2．** a person or firm that buys or sells on their own account，not on behalf of clients 交易商：不是代表客户，而是为了自身利益进行买卖的人或公司

dealing /ˈdiːlɪŋ/ *noun* **1．** the business of buying and selling on the Stock Exchange，commodity markets or currency markets 交易：在股票、商品或货币市场上进行的买卖 □ **dealing for *or* within the account** buying shares and selling the same shares during an account，which means that the dealer has only to pay the difference between the price of the shares bought and the price obtained for them when they are sold 账面交易：在一个账户中买卖同一种股票，这意味着交易商只需支付买价和卖价的差额部分 **2．** the business of buying and selling goods 买卖商品

dear /dɪə/ *adjective* expensive, costing a lot of money 昂贵的,高价的 ○ *Property is very dear in this area*. 这个地区的房地产很贵。

dear money /ˈdɪə ˌmʌni/ *noun* money which has to be borrowed at a high interest rate, and so restricts expenditure by companies 高息借款:只能以高利率筹得从而限制了公司支出的贷款 Also called 亦称作 **tight money**

death /deθ/ *noun* the act of dying 死亡

death benefit /ˈdeθ ˌbenɪfɪt/ *noun* insurance benefit paid to the family of someone who dies in an accident at work 死亡抚恤金:向因公死亡者的家属发放的抚恤金

death in service /ˌdeθ ɪn ˈsɜːvɪs/ *noun* an insurance benefit or pension paid when someone dies while employed by a company (公司给已故职工发放的)抚恤金

debenture /dɪˈbentʃə/ *noun* agreement to repay a debt with fixed interest using the company's assets as security 债券:以公司资产作担保来偿还债务及固定利息的协议 ○ *The bank holds a debenture on the company*. 银行持有该公司的债券。

debenture bond /dɪˈbentʃə bɒnd/ *noun US* (美) **1.** a certificate showing that a debenture has been issued 公司债券:已发行债券的证明 **2.** an unsecured loan 信用债券:无担保的债券

debenture capital /dɪˈbentʃə ˌkæpɪt(ə)l/ *noun* a capital borrowed by a company, using its fixed assets as security 借入资本,债券资本:公司以固定资产作担保而借入的资本

debenture holder /dɪˈbentʃə ˌhəʊldə/ *noun* a person who holds a debenture for money lent 债券持有人

debenture stock /dɪˈbentʃə stɒk/ *noun* a capital borrowed by a company, using its fixed assets as security 债券股,公司债券:公司以固定资产作担保而借入的资本

debit /ˈdebɪt/ *noun* an amount entered in accounts which shows an increase in assets or expenses or a decrease in liabilities, revenue or capital. In accounts, debits are entered in the left-hand column 借方:表明资产、费用增加或负债、收入、资本减少的账户分录。在账户中,借方在左边一栏输入 Compare 比较 **credit**

debitable /ˈdebɪtəb(ə)l/ *adjective* able to be debited 可记入借方的

debit balance /ˈdebɪt ˌbæləns/ *noun* a balance in an account showing that more money is owed than has been received 借方余额:表明欠款大于已收款的账户余额 ○ *Because of large payments to suppliers, the account has a debit balance of £1,000*. 由于支付给供应商巨额款项,账户出现了1,000英镑的借方余额。

debit card /ˈdebɪt kɑːd/ *noun* a plastic card, similar to a credit card, but which debits the holder's account immediately through an EPOS system 借记卡:与信用卡类似的塑料硬卡,通过电子售点系统将款项借记入持有人账户

debit column /ˈdebɪt ˌkɒləm/ *noun* the left-hand column in accounts showing the money paid or owed to others 借方栏:列示已付或应付他人款项的账户左边一栏

debit entry /ˈdebɪt ˌentri/ *noun* an

entry on the debit side of an account 借方分录

debit note /ˈdebɪt nəʊt/ *noun* a note showing that a customer owes money 借项通知单：表明客户欠款的凭证 ○ *We undercharged Mr Smith and had to send him a debit note for the extra amount.* 我们少收了史密斯先生的钱，不得不就剩余金额开出一张借项通知单。

debits and credits /ˌdebɪts ən ˈkredɪts/ *plural noun* money which a company owes and money it receives, or figures which are entered in the accounts to record increases or decreases in assets, expenses, liabilities, revenue or capital 借贷：公司应付或收到的金额，或记入账户表示资产、费用、负债、收入或资本增减的数字

debit side /ˈdebɪt saɪd/ *noun* a left-hand column of accounts showing money owed or paid to others 借方：列示已付或应付他人款项的账户左边一栏

debt /det/ *noun* money owed for goods or services 欠款，债务 ○ *The company stopped trading with debts of over £1 million.* 由于债务超过100万英镑，公司停止运营。□ **he is in debt to the tune of £250,000** he owes £250,000 他欠债25万英镑

debt collecting /ˈdet kəˌlektɪŋ/ *noun* collecting money which is owed 讨债

debt collection /ˈdet kəˌlekʃən/ *noun* the act of collecting money which is owed 讨债

debt collection agency /ˈdet kəˌlekʃən ˌeɪdʒənsi/ *noun* a company which collects debts for other companies for a commission 收账公司，讨债公司：帮助其他公司收回欠款并收取佣金的公司

debt collector /ˈdet kəˌlektə/ *noun* a person who collects debts 收债人

debt counselling /ˈdet ˌkaʊnsəlɪŋ/ *noun* the work of advising people who are in debt of the best ways to arrange their finances so as to pay off their debts 债务咨询：建议债务人如何合理安排财务以便还债

debt factoring /ˈdet ˌfæktərɪŋ/ *noun* the business of buying debts at a discount. A factor collects a company's debts when due, and pays the creditor in advance part of the sum to be collected, so 'buying' the debt 债务代理：折价购买债务的业务。代理商买进一公司的到期债务，并提前还给债权人部分债务，即"购买"债务

debtor /ˈdetə/ *noun* a person who owes money 债务人

debtor days /ˈdetə deɪs/ *noun* the number of days on average that it takes a company to receive payment for what it sells 应收账款天数：公司收回应收账款所需的平均天数 ⇨ 参阅 **creditor days**

debtors /ˈdetəz/ *noun* all money owed to a company as shown in the accounts 应收账款

debtors control account /ˌdetəz kənˈtrəʊl əˌkaʊnt/ *noun* an account used to summarise the balances on the individual sales ledger accounts 应收账款控制账户：用于汇总各销售分类账上应收账款余额的账户

debtor side /ˈdetə saɪd/ *noun* the debit side of an account 借方

debtors ledger /ˌdetəz ˈledʒə/ *noun* sales ledger 销售分类账，应收账款分类账

debtors turnover ratio /ˌdetəz ˈtɜːnəʊvə ˌreɪʃiəʊ/ *noun* the average time which debtors take to pay 应收账款周转率:支付应收账款所需的平均时间

debt ratio /ˈdet ˌreɪʃiəʊ/ *noun* the debts of a company shown as a percentage of its equity plus loan capital 负债比率:公司债务占其股本加贷款资本的百分比

debt rescheduling /ˈdet riːˈʃedjuːlɪŋ/ *noun* FINANCE, BANKING, AND ACCOUNTING, GENERAL MANAGEMENT the process of reorganising the way in which debts are repaid. Debt rescheduling may be necessary if a company is unable to pay its debts and may involve postponing debt payments, postponing payment of interest, or negotiating a new loan(金融、银行、会计、综合管理)重新安排还债日期,重新安排债务:重新安排还债方式的过程。公司无法偿还债务时即需重新安排债务,它可能涉及延期偿还债务、延期支付利息或协商新贷款

decile /ˈdesaɪl/ *noun* one of a series of nine figures below which one tenth or several tenths of the total fall 十分位数

decimalisation /ˌdesɪm(ə)laɪˈzeɪʃ(ə)n/, **decimalization** *noun* the process of changing to a decimal system 十进制转换

decimalise /ˈdesɪm(ə)laɪz/, **decimalize** *verb* to change something to a decimal system 转换成十进制

decimal point /ˌdesɪm(ə)l ˈpɔɪnt/ *noun* a dot which indicates the division between the whole unit and its smaller parts, e.g. 4.75 小数点

decimal system /ˈdesɪm(ə)l ˌsɪstəm/ *noun* a system of mathematics based on the number 10 十进制

decision support system /dɪˌsɪʒ(ə)n səˈpɔːt ˌsɪstəm/ *noun* a computer-based system which presents auditor judgements in a structured way and can be used to create audit programmes or document the assessment of business risk 决策支持系统:有组织地呈列审计师的判断的计算机系统,它可以用来创建审计程序或记录业务风险评估

decision tree /dɪˈsɪʒ(ə)n triː/ *noun* a model for decision-making, showing the possible outcomes of different decisions 树形决策图:列示不同决策可能产生不同结果的一种决策模型 ○ *This computer programme incorporates a decision tree.* 这个计算机程序包括一个树形决策图。

declaration /ˌdekləˈreɪʃ(ə)n/ *noun* an official statement 宣告

declaration date /ˌdekləˈreɪʃ(ə)n deɪt/ *noun US* the date on which a board of directors declares the dividend to be paid (美)宣告日期:董事会宣布股利支付的日期

declaration of bankruptcy /ˌdekləreɪʃ(ə)n əv ˈbæŋkrʌptsi/ *noun* an official statement that someone is bankrupt 宣告破产

declaration of solvency /ˌdekləˌreɪʃ(ə)n əv ˈsɒlv(ə)nsi/ *noun* a document, lodged with the Registrar of Companies, that lists the assets and liabilities of a company seeking voluntary liquidation to show that the company is capable of repaying its debts within 12 months 有偿债能力声明:寄存在公司注册处的一份文件,它列明寻求自动清盘公司的资产与负债,以证明

公司有能力在12个月内偿还债务

declare /dɪˈkleə/ *verb* to make an official statement of something, or announce something to the public 宣布,宣告 ○ *to declare someone bankrupt* 宣告某人破产 ○ *The company declared an interim dividend of 10p per share*. 该公司宣布期中股利为每股10便士。

declared /dɪˈkleəd/ *adjective* having been made public or officially stated 已宣告的

declared value /dɪˌkleəd ˈvæljuː/ *noun* the value of goods entered on a customs declaration 申报价值,设定价值

decline /dɪˈklaɪn/ *verb* to fall slowly or decrease 缓慢下降,减少 ○ *Shares declined in a weak market*. 市场疲弱,股价下跌。○ *New job applications have declined over the last year*. 去年新求职者的人数下降了。○ *The economy declined during the last government*. 上一届政府执政期间经济下滑了。○ *The purchasing power of the pound declined over the decade*. 十年来,英镑的购买力持续下降。

'Saudi oil production has declined by three quarters to around 2.5m barrels a day'
"沙特的石油产量下降了四分之三,现已降到每天250万桶左右"[*Economist*《经济学家》]

'...this gives an average monthly decline of 2.15 per cent during the period'
"这使得期内平均每月下降了2.15%"[*Business Times* (*Lagos*)《商业时报》(拉各斯)]

'...share prices disclosed a weak tendency right from the onset of business and declined further, showing losses over a broad front'
"公司股价从一开始就显现出疲弱态势,其后进一步下跌,呈现全面亏损"[*The Hindu*《印度教徒报》]

declining balance method /dɪˌklaɪnɪŋ ˈbæləns ˌmeθəd/ *noun US* same as (美)同 **reducing balance method**

decrease /dɪˈkriːs/ *verb* to fall or to become less 下降,减少 ○ *Imports are decreasing*. 进口额持续下降。○ *The value of the pound has decreased by 5%*. 英镑已贬值5%。

deduct /dɪˈdʌkt/ *verb* to take money away from a total 减去,扣除 ○ *to deduct £3 from the price* 从价格中扣除三英镑 ○ *to deduct a sum for expenses* 扣除一笔开支金额 ○ *After deducting costs the gross margin is only 23%*. 扣除成本之后,毛利仅为23%。○ *Expenses are still to be deducted*. 尚需扣除费用。

deductible /dɪˈdʌktɪb(ə)l/ *adjective* possible to deduct 可扣除的

deduction /dɪˈdʌkʃən/ *noun* the removing of money from a total, or the amount of money removed from a total 扣减;扣款 ○ *Net salary is salary after deduction of tax and social security*. 纯工资是扣除了税款和社会保险之后的工资。○ *The deduction from her wages represented the cost of repairing the damage she had caused to the machinery*. 从她的工资中扣除了她造成的机械损坏维修成本。□ **deductions from salary** *or* **salary deductions** *or* **deductions at source** money which a company removes from salaries to give to the government as tax, national insurance contributions, etc. 工资扣除;从源扣税:公司从工资中扣除的款项,用以支付政府税项、国民保险供款等

deed /diːd/ *noun* a legal document or

written agreement 契约,契据文书

deed of arrangement /ˌdiːd əv əˈreɪndʒmənt/ *noun* agreement made between a debtor and creditors whereby the creditors accept an agreed sum in settlement of their claim rather than make the debtor bankrupt 调解契约:债权人及债务人双方达成的协议,债权人接受议定金额来结清其债务,而不选择让债务人破产

deed of assignment /ˌdiːd əv əˈsaɪnmənt/ *noun* a document which legally transfers a property from a debtor to a creditor 转让契约:将某财产合法地从债务人转让给债权人的契约

deed of covenant /ˌdiːd əv ˈkʌvənənt/ *noun* a legal document in which a person or organisation promises to pay a third party a sum of money on an annual basis. In certain countries this arrangement may have tax advantages. For example, in the United Kingdom, it is often used for making regular payments to a charity 捐款契据:某人或某组织承诺按年向第三方付款的法律文件。在某些国家,这种协议可以减少纳税。例如在英国,它通常被用来定期向慈善机构捐款

deed of partnership /ˌdiːd əv ˈpɑːtnəʃɪp/ *noun* agreement which sets up a partnership 合伙协议,合伙契约

deed of transfer /ˌdiːd əv ˈtrænsfɜː/ *noun* a document which transfers the ownership of shares (股份所有权的)转让契约

deep discount /ˌdiːp ˈdɪskaʊnt/ *noun* a very large discount 大幅度折扣

'... when it needed to make its financial results look good, it shipped a lot of inventory. It did this by offering deep discounts to distributors'

"为了使财务状况显得好看些,它发运了大量的存货。而为了做到这一点,它给经销商们提供了大幅度的折扣" [*Forbes*《福布斯杂志》]

deep discounted bonds /diːp ˌdɪskaʊntɪd ˈbɒndz/ *plural noun* Eurobonds which are issued at a very large discount but which do not produce any interest 大幅度折价债券:以大幅度折价的方式发行但不产生任何利息的欧元债券

deep pocket /ˌdiːp ˈpɒkɪt/ *noun* company which provides finance for another 深口袋:向另一家公司提供融资的公司

defalcation /ˌdiːfælˈkeɪʃ(ə)n/ *noun* an illegal use of money by someone who is not the owner but who has been trusted to look after it 挪用,侵吞:信托受信人盗用受托的他人资金

default /dɪˈfɔːlt/ *noun* a failure to carry out the terms of a contract, especially failure to pay back a debt 违约:没有履行合同条款,尤指到期不能还债 ■ *verb* to fail to carry out the terms of a contract, especially to fail to pay back a debt 违约 ○ *There was a major financial crisis when the bank defaulted.* 银行违约导致重大财务危机。

defaulter /dɪˈfɔːltə/ *noun* a person who defaults 缺席者;拖欠者;违约者

default notice /dɪˌfɔːlt ˈnəʊtɪs/ *noun* a formal document issued by a lender to a borrower who is in default 违约通知:贷款人向拖欠债务的借款人发出的正式文件(NOTE: The US term is **notice of default** 美国用语为 **notice of default**)

defence counsel /dɪˈfens ˌkaʊnsəl/ *noun* a lawyer who represents the defendant in a lawsuit 辩护律师

defer /dɪˈfɜː/ *verb* to put back to a later date, to postpone 递延，推迟 ○ *We will have to defer payment until January*. 我们不得不推迟到 1 月份再付款。○ *The decision has been deferred until the next meeting*. 决策已被推迟到下次会议再行讨论。（NOTE: **deferring – deferred**）

deferment /dɪˈfɜːmənt/ *noun* the act of leaving until a later date 推迟，延期 ○ *deferment of payment* 延期付款 ○ *deferment of a decision* 决定的推迟

deferred /dɪˈfɜːd/ *adjective* put back to a later date 递延的，延期的

deferred consideration /dɪˌfɜːd kənˌsɪdəˈreɪʃ(ə)n/ *noun* instalment payments for the acquisition of new subsidiaries usually made in the form of cash and shares, where the balance due after the initial deposit depends on the performance of the business acquired 递延补偿：收购新的子公司时通常以现金加股票的形式分期付款，在支付首期定金后，结欠款取决于被兼并企业的业绩

deferred creditor /dɪˌfɜːd ˈkredɪtə/ *noun* a person who is owed money by a bankrupt but who is paid only after all other creditors 延期偿付债权人：在其他债权人之后才能得到破产者偿付的债权人

deferred expenditure /dɪˌfɜːd ɪkˈspendɪtʃə/ *noun* expenditure incurred now but reflected in the accounts of future years 递延支出：当期发生但反映在未来账户上的支出

deferred payment /dɪˌfɜːd ˈpeɪmənt/ *noun* 递延付款 **1.** money paid later than the agreed date [在议定日之后支付的款项] **2.** payment for goods by instalments over along period [在较长时期内分期支付购货款]

deferred payments /dɪˌfɜːd ˈpeɪmənts/ *noun* money paid later than the agreed date 递延付款：在议定日之后支付的款项 ○ *The company agreed to defer payments for three months*. 该公司同意推迟付款三个月。

deferred revenue /dɪˌfɜːd ˈrevənjuː/ *noun* revenue carried forward to future accounting periods 递延收入：转入未来会计期的收入

deferred tax /dɪˌfɜːd ˈtæks/ *noun* a tax which may become payable at some later date 递延税款：应于某个未来日期支付的税款

deficiency /dɪˈfɪʃ(ə)nsi/ *noun* a lack of something, or the amount by which something, e.g. a sum of money, is less than it should be 缺乏，亏数，不足 ○ *There is a £10 deficiency in the petty cash*. 零用现金少了 10 英镑。

deficit /ˈdefɪsɪt/ *noun* the amount by which spending is higher than income 亏损，赤字，逆差

deficit financing /ˈdefɪsɪt ˌfaɪnænsɪŋ/ *noun* a type of financial planning by a government in which it borrows money to cover the difference between its tax income and its expenditure 赤字筹资：政府的一种财务规划，它通过借款来弥补其税收与开支之差

deflation /diːˈfleɪʃ(ə)n/ *noun* a general reduction in economic activity as a result of a reduced supply of money and credit, leading to lower prices 经济紧缩，通货紧缩：因货币及信贷供应量减少而导致的总体经济活动下降，造成物价降低 ○ *The oil crisis resulted in* *worldwide deflation*. 石油危机导致全球性的经济紧缩。Opposite 反义 **inflation**

'... the reluctance of people to spend is one of the main reasons behind 26 consecutive months of price deflation, a key economic ill that has led to price wars, depressed the profit margins of state enterprises and hit incomes among the rural population'
"人们不愿消费是连续 26 个月价格紧缩的主要原因之一,这一经济上的弊病引发了价格战,压缩了国有企业的边际利润,同时也影响了农村居民的收入"[*Financial Times*《金融时报》]

deflationary /diːˈfleɪʃ(ə)n(ə)ri/ *adjective* causing deflation (引起)减缩的,通货紧缩的 ○ *The government has introduced some deflationary measures in the budget*. 政府在预算中采用了一些通货紧缩措施。

'... the strong dollar's deflationary impact on European economies as national governments push up interest rates'
"在各国政府提高利率的情况下,美元坚挺对欧洲经济产生的紧缩影响"[*Duns Business Month*《邓氏商业月刊》]

deflator /diːˈfleɪtə/ *noun* the amount by which a country's GNP is reduced to take inflation into account 减缩指数:考虑通货膨胀因素后,国民生产总值减少的量

degearing /diːˈgɪərɪŋ/ *noun* a reduction in gearing, reducing a company's loan capital in relation to the value of its ordinary shares 啮合比率降低:公司的贷款资本与其普通股价值的比率下降

degressive tax /dɪˌgresɪv ˈtæks/ *noun* a tax whose payments depend on an individual's salary. Those on smaller salaries pay a lower percentage their income than those with larger salaries 累减税,累退税,累减比例税:依个人工资而定的税项。低工资者的纳税额占其收入的百分比要低于高工资者

del credere /ˌdel ˈkreɪdəri/ *noun* an amount added to a charge to cover the possibility of not being paid 货价保护,买方资力保证费:为避免货款不能支付而额外收取的费用

del credere agent /del ˈkreɪdəri ˌeɪdʒənt/ *noun* an agent who receives a high commission because he or she guarantees payment by customers 担保付款代理人,买方资力担保代理商:因为担保代收货款而收取卖方高额佣金的代理商

delinquency /dɪˈlɪŋkwənsi/ *noun* *US* the fact of being overdue in payment of an account, an interest payment, etc. (美)拖欠债务,逾期不付款

delinquent /dɪˈlɪŋkwənt/ *adjective* *US* referring to an account or payment of tax which is overdue (美)(欠款或税款支付)逾期的,拖欠的

deliver /dɪˈlɪvə/ *verb* to transport goods to a customer 交货,递送 □ **goods delivered free** *or* **free delivered goods** goods transported to the customer's address at a price which includes transport costs 目的地交付货物:将货物送到客户指定地点,价格中已包含了运输费 □ **goods delivered on board** goods transported free to the ship or plane but not to the customer's warehouse 船上或飞机上交付货物:价格中只包括将货物送上船或飞机的运费,而不包括将其送至顾客仓库的运费

delivered price /dɪˈlɪvəd praɪs/ *noun* a price which includes packing and transport 到货价：包括包装费和运输费的价格

delivery /dɪˈlɪv(ə)ri/ *noun* **1.** a consignment of goods being delivered 交付的一批货物 ○ *We take in three deliveries a day*. 我们每天收取三批货。○ *There were four items missing in the last delivery*. 上批货物中少了四件。**2.** the transport of a commodity to a purchaser 交付：将商品运送给买方 **3.** the transfer of a bill of exchange or other negotiable instrument to the bank which is due to make payment 交割：将汇票或其他议付票据转给付款行

delivery month /dɪˈlɪv(ə)ri mʌnθ/ *noun* a month in a futures contract when actual delivery will take place 交货月份：期货合约中发生实际交货的月份

delivery note /dɪˈlɪv(ə)ri nəʊt/ *noun* a list of goods being delivered, given to the customer with the goods 交货清单：与货物一起交给顾客的列示所交货物的清单

delivery of goods /dɪˌlɪv(ə)ri əv ˈɡʊdz/ *noun* the transport of goods to a customer's address 供货，交货：运送货物至客户处

delivery order /dɪˈlɪv(ə)ri ˌɔːdə/ *noun* the instructions given by the customer to the person holding her goods, to tell her where and when to deliver them 提货单：客户向持货人发出的关于交货地点和时间的指令

delivery time /dɪˈlɪv(ə)ri taɪm/ *noun* the number of days before something will be delivered 交货期，交货时间：从订货到发货的时间间隔

delivery van /dɪˈlɪv(ə)ri væn/ *noun* a van for delivering goods to customers 送货车

demand /dɪˈmɑːnd/ *noun* **1.** an act of asking for payment 付款要求 **2.** an act of asking for something and insisting on getting it（坚持得到某物的）要求 ○ *the union's list of demands* 工会的要求清单 ○ *The management refused to give in to union demands for a meeting*. 管理层拒绝了工会进行会谈的要求。**3.** the need that customers have for a product or their eagerness to buy it 需求 ○ *There was an active demand for oil shares on the stock market*. 石油股在股市上很抢手。○ *The factory had to cut production when demand slackened*. 由于需求下降，工厂不得不减产。○ *The office cleaning company cannot keep up with the demand for its services*. 这家办公保洁公司的服务供不应求。□ **this book is in great demand** *or* **there is a great demand for this book** many people want to buy it 这本书很畅销 □ **to meet** *or* **fill a demand** to supply what is needed 满足需求 ○ *The factory had to increase production to meet the extra demand*. 该工厂不得不增加产量以满足额外的需求。■ *verb* to ask for something and expect to get it 要求（并期望得到某物）○ *She demanded a refund*. 她要求退款。○ *The suppliers are demanding immediate payment of their outstanding invoices*. 供货商要求他们立刻付清未付货款。○ *The shop stewards demanded an urgent meeting with the managing director*. 商店管理员要求紧急会见总经理。

'...spot prices are now relatively stable in the run-up to the winter's peak demand'
"在冬季需求高峰到来之前，现货价格相对

稳定”[*Economist*《经济学家》]

‘... the demand for the company's products remained strong throughout the first six months of the year with production and sales showing significant increases’
“在本年度前六个月内，该公司的产品始终保持着旺盛的需求，产销量均有大幅增长”[*Business Times* (*Lagos*)《商业时报》(拉各斯)]

‘... growth in demand is still coming from the private rather than the public sector’
“需求的增长仍来自于私营而非国营部门”[*Lloyd's List*《劳氏日报》]

demand bill /dɪˈmɑːnd bɪl/ *noun* a bill of exchange which must be paid when payment is asked for 即期汇票：见票即付的汇票

demand price /dɪˈmɑːnd praɪs/ *noun* the price at which a quantity of goods will be bought 需求价格：购买一定数量商品所愿意支付的价格

demerge /diːˈmɜːdʒ/ *verb* to separate a company into several separate parts 将(某公司)分成独立公司

demerger /diːˈmɜːdʒə/ *noun* the separation of a company into several separate parts, especially used of companies which have grown by acquisition 分离：将公司(尤指已通过收购实现合并的企业)分成几个独立部分

demise /dɪˈmaɪz/ *noun* **1.** a death 死亡 ○ *On his demise the estate passed to his daughter*. 他去世后，遗产由女儿继承。**2.** the act of granting a property on a lease (租赁中财产的)转让

demonetisation /diːˌmʌnɪtaɪˈzeɪʃ(ə)n/, **demonetization** *noun* the act of stopping a coin or note being used as money 非货币化，废止流通，使失去通货资格

demonetise /diːˈmʌnɪtaɪz/, **demonetize** *verb* to stop a coin or note being used as money 废止流通，使失去通货资格

demurrage /dɪˈmʌrɪdʒ/ *noun* money paid to a customer when a shipment is delayed at a port or by customs 滞留费：由于货物在海关或港口耽搁而向买方支付的款项

demutualisation /diːˌmjuːtjuəlaɪˈzeɪʃ(ə)n/, **demutualization** *noun* the process by which a mutual society, such as a building society, becomes a publicly owned corporation 非互助化，解除互助化：互助协会(如住房互助协会)变为公有企业的过程

demutualise /diːˈmjuːtjuəlaɪz/, **demutualize** *verb* to stop having mutual status, by becoming a Plc and selling shares to the general public on the stock market 非互助化，解除互助化：通过转制为公众股份有限公司并上市，而不再具有互助身份

denomination /dɪˌnɒmɪˈneɪʃ(ə)n/ *noun* a unit of money on a coin, banknote or stamp (货币或邮票)面额，货币单位 ○ *We collect coins of all denominations for charity*. 我们为慈善机构募集所有面额的硬币。○ *Small denomination notes are not often counterfeited*. 很少有人伪造小面额的钞票。

departmental /ˌdiːpɑːtˈment(ə)l/ *adjective* referring to a department 部门的

departmental accounts /ˌdiːpɑːtment(ə)l əˈkaʊnts/ *plural noun* accounts which analyse the sales of different departments or products of a company 分部账户：分析各部门销售或公司产品的账户

Department of Trade and

Industry /dɪˌpɑːtmənt əv ˌtreɪd ənd ˈɪndəstri/ *noun* a British government department which deals with areas such as commerce, international trade and the stock exchange 贸易和工业部:英国政府处理商业、国际贸易和股票交易等事务的部门 Abbreviation 缩写 **DTI**

deposit /dɪˈpɒzɪt/ *noun* **1.** money placed in a bank for safe keeping or to earn interest (银行)存款 **2.** money given in advance so that the thing which you want to buy will not be sold to someone else 押金,保证金,订金 ○ *to pay a deposit on a watch* 支付购买手表的订金 ○ *to leave £10 as deposit* 留下10英镑作为押金 ■ *verb* **1.** to put documents somewhere for safe keeping 存放(文件) ○ *to deposit shares with a bank* 将股票存放在银行 ○ *We have deposited the deeds of the house with the bank.* 我们将房契放到银行保管。○ *He deposited his will with his solicitor.* 他将遗嘱存放在律师处。**2.** to put money into a bank account 存款:将资金存入银行账户 ○ *to deposit £100 in a current account* 将100英镑存入活期账户

deposit account /dɪˈpɒzɪt əˌkaʊnt/ *noun* a bank account which pays interest but on which notice has to be given to withdraw money 定期存款,存款账户 Abbreviation 缩写 **D/A**

depositary /dɪˈpɒzɪtəri/ *noun US* a person or corporation which can place money or documents for safekeeping with a depository (美)受托人,保管人,存储所 ⇨ 参阅 **American Depositary Receipt** (NOTE: Do not confuse with **depository** 不要与 **depository** 混淆)

depositor /dɪˈpɒzɪtə/ *noun* a person who deposits money in a bank, building society, etc. 储户

depository /dɪˈpɒzɪt(ə)ri/ *noun* a person or company with whom money or documents can be deposited 受托人;受托公司 (NOTE: Do not confuse with **depositary** 不要与 **depositary** 混淆)

deposit slip /dɪˈpɒzɪt slɪp/ *noun* a piece of paper stamped by the cashier to prove that you have paid money into your account 存款单

deposit-taking institution /dɪˌpɒzɪtˌteɪkɪŋ ˌɪnstɪˈtjuːʃ(ə)n/, **depository institution** /dɪˌpɒzɪt(ə)ri ˌɪnstɪˈtjuːʃ(ə)n/ *noun* an institution which is licensed to receive money on deposit from private individuals and to pay interest on it, e.g. a building society, bank or friendly society 存款吸收机构:吸收私人存款并支付利息的资质机构,例如住房互助协会、银行或友好协会

depreciable /dɪˈpriːʃiəb(ə)l/ *adjective* possible to depreciate 应提折旧的,可提折旧的

depreciable asset /dɪˌpriːʃiəb(ə)l ˈæset/ *noun* an asset which will be used over more than one accounting period, but which has a limited life and so can be depreciated 应提折旧资产:使用时间将超过一个会计期间,但寿命期有限而应计提折旧的资产

depreciate /dɪˈpriːʃieɪt/ *verb* **1.** to reduce the value of assets in accounts 折旧 ○ *We depreciate our company cars over three years.* 我们公司汽车的折旧期为三年。**2.** to lose value 贬值 ○ *a share which has depreciated by 10% over the year* 一年内贬值了10%

的股票 ○ *The pound has depreciated by 5% against the dollar.* 英镑对美元贬值了5%。

'... this involved reinvesting funds on items which could be depreciated against income for three years'
"这涉及到可能在三年内计提折旧抵减收入的项目的再投资"[*Australian Financial Review*《澳大利亚金融评论报》]

'... buildings are depreciated at two per cent per annum on the estimated cost of construction'
"建筑物按所估建造成本的2%提取每年的折旧"[*Hong Kong Standard*《香港虎报》]

'... the euro's downward drift sparked alarmed reactions from the European Central Bank which has seen the new currency depreciate by almost 15% since its launch'
"欧元自发行以来已经贬值近15%,这不断下滑的趋势给欧洲中央银行拉响了警报"[*Times*《泰晤士报》]

depreciation /dɪˌpriːʃɪˈeɪʃ(ə)n/ *noun* **1.** a reduction in value of an asset 折旧 **2.** a loss of value 贬值 ○ *a share which has shown a depreciation of 10% over the year* 一年内贬值了10%的股票 ○ *the depreciation of the pound against the dollar* 英镑对美元的贬值

depreciation rate /dɪˌpriːʃɪˈeɪʃ(ə)n reɪt/ *noun* the rate at which an asset is depreciated each year in the company accounts 折旧率:每年在公司账户中对资产提取折旧的比率

depress /dɪˈpres/ *verb* to reduce something 降低 ○ *Reducing the money supply has the effect of depressing demand for consumer goods.* 减少货币供应会导致消费品需求渐少。

depressed market /dɪˌprest ˈmɑːkɪt/ *noun* a market where there are more goods than customers 萧条市场

deregulate /diːˈregjʊleɪt/ *verb* to remove government controls from an industry 解除控制,放开:政府撤销对某行业的干预 ○ *The US government deregulated the banking sector in the 1980s.* 20世纪80年代,美国政府取消了对银行业的控制。

deregulation /diːˌregjʊˈleɪʃ(ə)n/ *noun* the reduction of government control over an industry 撤销管制:减少政府对某行业的干预 ○ *the deregulation of the airlines* 航空公司管理放开

'... after the slump in receipts last year that followed liner shipping deregulation in the US, carriers are probably still losing money on their transatlantic services. But with a possible contraction in capacity and healthy trade growth, this year has begun in a much more promising fashion than last'
"去年美国对班轮运输管理放开之后,承运人收入暴跌,他们跨大西洋的运输业务很可能现在仍在亏损,但随着运输中可能存在的对承载量的限制和行业的健康发展,今年年初的形势已比去年乐观了许多"[*Lloyd's List*《劳氏日报》]

derivative instruments /dɪˌrɪvətɪv ˈɪnstrʊmənts/, **derivatives** /dɪˈrɪvətɪvz/ *plural noun* any forms of traded security such as option contracts, which are derived from ordinary bonds and shares, exchange rates or stock market indices 派生单据:从普通债券和股票、汇率或股市指数派生出来的任何形式的交易证券,例如期权合约

designated account /ˌdezɪgneɪtɪd əˈkaʊnt/ *noun* an account opened and held in one person's name, but which also features another person's name for extra identification purposes 指定账户：以某人的名字开立和持有的账户，但它也记有另一人的名字，以备鉴定之需

devaluation /ˌdiːvæljuˈeɪʃ(ə)n/ *noun* a reduction in the value of a currency against other currencies（货币）贬值 ○ *the devaluation of the rand* 兰特贬值

devalue /diːˈvæljuː/ *verb* to reduce the value of a currency against other currencies 贬值 ○ *The pound has been devalued by 7%.* 英镑贬值了7%。

development costs /dɪˈveləpmənt kɒsts/ *plural noun* costs of developing new or improved products 开发成本：开发新产品或改进旧产品的成本

devise /dɪˈvaɪz/ *noun* the act of giving freehold land to someone in a will（不动产的）遗赠：在遗嘱中将土地完全保有权赠与某人 ■ *verb* to give freehold property to someone in a will 遗赠（不动产）

devisee /dɪvaɪˈziː/ *noun* a person who receives freehold property in a will（不动产）受赠人

differential /ˌdɪfəˈrenʃəl/ *adjective* showing a difference 有差异的

differential tariffs /ˌdɪfərenʃəl ˈtærɪfs/ *plural noun* different tariffs for different classes of goods as, e.g., when imports from some countries are taxed more heavily than similar imports from other countries 差别税则，差别关税：对不同类别货物征收不同关税，例如对从某国进口货物征收的关税高于对从其他国家进口类似货物的关税

digit /ˈdɪdʒɪt/ *noun* a single number 数字，位数 ○ *a seven-digit phone number* 七位数的电话号码

digital analysis /ˌdɪdʒɪt(ə)l əˈnæləsɪs/ *noun* auditing techniques that investigate the digits in accounting numbers to reveal fraud and error 数字分析法：通过审查会计数字的位数来发现舞弊和错误的审计技术

digital computer /ˌdɪdʒɪt(ə)l kəmˈpjuːtə/ *noun* a computer which calculates on the basis of numbers 数字计算机

dilution of shareholding /daɪˌluːʃ(ə)n əv ˈʃeəhəʊldɪŋ/ *noun* a situation where the ordinary share capital of a company has been increased, but without an increase in the assets so that each share is worth less than before 权益稀释：当公司普通股本增加而资产并未同步增加时，每股的价值低于以前每股价值的情况（NOTE：The US term is **stockholding** 美国用语为 **stockholding**）

dime /daɪm/ *noun US* ten cent coin (*informal*)（美）10美分硬币（非正式）

diminish /dɪˈmɪnɪʃ/ *verb* to become smaller 减少 ○ *Our share of the market has diminished over the last few years.* 在过去几年中，我们的市场份额减少了。

direct cost /daɪˌrekt ˈkɒst/ *noun* a cost which can be directly related to the making of a product, i.e. its production cost 直接成本：可与制造产品直接联系的成本，即产品生产成本

direct cost variance /daɪˌrekt kɒst ˈveəriəns/ *noun* the difference between the planned direct costs for a product and the actual direct costs 直接成本差异：某产品的计划直接成本与实际直接成本之间的差异

direct debit /daɪˌrekt ˈdebɪt/ *noun* a system where a customer allows a company to charge costs to his or her bank account automatically and where the amount charged can be increased or decreased with the agreement of the customer 直接借记，直接扣账：客户允许公司直接从其银行账户中付款，扣除的金额额度需征得客户同意 ○ *I pay my electricity bill by direct debit.* 我通过直接扣账支付电费。Abbreviation 缩写 **DD**

direct expenses /daɪˌrekt ɪkˈspensɪz/ *plural noun* expenses excluding materials, labour or purchase of stock for resale which are incurred in making a product 直接费用：不包括制造产品过程中发生的材料、劳动或购买转售存货的费用

directional testing /daɪˌrekʃən(ə)l ˈtestɪŋ/ *noun* an auditing technique by which work is reduced by testing debits only for overstatement and credits only for understatement 方向测试：通过检查借方是否存在多报现象、贷方是否存在少报现象来减少工作量的一种审计技术

directive /daɪˈrektɪv/ *noun* an order or command to someone to do something, especially an order from the Council of Ministers or Commission of the European Union referring to a particular problem 命令，指示 ○ *The Commission issued a directive on food prices.* 委员会发出了一道关于食品价格的指令。

direct labour costs /daɪˌrekt ˈleɪbə ˌkɒsts/ *noun* the cost of the employees employed which can be allocated to a product, not including materials or overheads 直接人工成本：雇用员工制造产品的成本，这些成本可分摊到产品中（不包括原材料或间接费用）

direct mail /daɪˌrekt ˈmeɪl/ *noun* the practice of selling a product by sending publicity material to possible buyers through the post 直接邮售：通过向潜在客户邮寄宣传资料来销售产品的做法 ○ *These calculators are only sold by direct mail.* 这种计算器只通过直接邮售方式出售。○ *The company runs a successful direct-mail operation.* 该公司的直接邮售业务很成功。

‘...all of those who had used direct marketing techniques had used direct mail, 79% had used some kind of telephone technique and 63% had tried off-the-page selling’
“在所有采用直接营销技术的企业中，100%全都采用了直接邮售，79%采用了电话销售，63%采用了报刊加页广告销售”［*Precision Marketing*《精准营销》］

direct-mail advertising /daɪˌrekt-meɪl ˈædvətaɪzɪŋ/ *noun* advertising by sending leaflets to people through the post 直接邮寄广告

direct materials cost /daɪˌrekt məˈtɪəriəls kɒst/ *noun* the cost of the materials which are used in making a product and for which costs can be directly related to that product 直接材料成本：制造产品所用材料的成本，且这些成本能与该产品直接联系

directorate /daɪˈrekt(ə)rət/ *noun* a group of directors 理事会，董事会

director's fees /daɪˈrektəz fiːz/ *plural noun* money paid to a director for attendance at board meetings 董事费：因董事出席董事会会议而向其支付的费用

directorship /daɪˈrektəʃɪp/ *noun* the post of director 董事职位 ○ *She was offered a directorship with Smith*

Ltd. 史密斯有限公司给她提供了一个董事职位。

'...what benefits does the executive derive from his directorship? In the first place compensation has increased sharply in recent years'
"高层管理人员从其职位得到哪些待遇？首先是近几年报酬的大幅增加" [*Duns Business Month*《邓氏商业月刊》]

directors' report /daɪˌrektəz rɪˈpɔːt/ *noun* the annual report from the board of directors to the shareholders 董事会报告：由董事会向股东提交的年度报告

direct product profitability /daɪˌrekt ˌprɒdʌkt ˌprɒfɪtəˈbɪlɪti/ *noun* used primarily within the retail sector, DPP involves the attribution of costs other than the purchase price (e.g., distribution, warehousing, retailing) to each product line. Thus a net profit, as opposed to a gross profit, can be identified for each product 直接产品盈利性：主要针对零售业，它包括除购买价格以外各个产品系列的成本（如经销、存储、零售）分配，从而计算出各个产品的净利润（而非毛利）

direct selling /daɪˌrekt ˈselɪŋ/ *noun* the work of selling a product direct to the customer without going through a shop 直销：向顾客直接销售产品而不通过商店的销售方式

direct share ownership /daɪˌrekt ˈʃeə ˌəʊnəʃɪp/ *noun* the ownership of shares by private individuals, buying or selling through brokers, and not via holdings in unit trusts 直接股票所有权：私人个体通过经纪人买卖股票获得的股票所有权，而不是通过单位信托获得

direct tax /daɪˌrekt ˈtæks/ *noun* a tax paid directly to the government, e.g. income tax 直接税：直接向政府缴纳的税项，如所得税

direct taxation /daɪˌrekt tækˈseɪʃ(ə)n/ *noun* a tax which is paid direct to the government, e.g. income tax 直接赋税：直接向政府缴纳的税项，如所得税 ○ *The government raises more money by direct taxation than by indirect*. 政府通过直接税收筹集的资金要比间接税多。

dirty float /ˈdɜːti fləʊt/ *noun* a process of floating a currency, where the government intervenes to regulate the exchange rate 肮脏浮动，管理浮动：汇率受政府干预控制的浮动汇率体制

disallow /ˌdɪsəˈlaʊ/ *verb* not to accept a claim for insurance 否决，拒绝（保险索赔）○ *She claimed £2,000 for fire damage, but the claim was disallowed*. 她要求获得2,000英镑的火灾损失赔偿，但被保险公司拒绝了。

disallowable /ˌdɪsəˈlaʊəb(ə)l/ *adjective* not able to be allowed for tax relief（税务优惠）应剔除的 ○ *The use of a car for private travel is a disallowable expense*. 将汽车用于私人旅行的开支不应享受税务宽免。Opposite 反义 **allowable**

disburse /disˈbɜːs/ *verb* to pay money 付款，支付

disbursement /dɪsˈbɜːsmənt/ *noun* the payment of money 付款

discharge *noun* /ˈdɪstʃɑːdʒ/ **1.** a payment of debt 还债 □ **in full discharge of a debt** as full payment of a debt 完全清偿债务 **2.** □ **in discharge of her duties as director** while carrying out her duties as director 履行其作为董事

的职责 ■ *verb* /dɪs'tʃɑːdʒ/ **1.** □ **to discharge a bankrupt** to release someone from bankruptcy because they have has paid their debts 解除破产：还清债务后被免于破产 **2.** □ **to discharge a debt, to discharge your liabilities** to pay a debt or your liabilities in full 偿清债务 **3.** to dismiss an employee 辞退，解雇 ○ *to discharge an employee for negligence* 以失职为由辞退一名员工

discharged bankrupt /dɪsˌtʃɑːdʒd 'bæŋkrʌpt/ *noun* a person who has been released from being bankrupt because his or her debts have been paid 已清偿债务的破产人：某人于偿清债务后被免于破产

disclaimer /dɪs'kleɪmə/ *noun* a legal refusal to accept responsibility 弃权或不申述条款，否认条款，免责声明：合法地拒绝承担责任

disclose /dɪs'kləʊz/ *verb* to tell something that was previously unknown to other people or secret 揭发，披露 ○ *The bank has no right to disclose details of my account to the tax office.* 银行无权将我的账户详情披露给税务局。

disclosure /dɪs'kləʊʒə/ *noun* the act of telling something that was previously unknown to other people or secret 揭发，披露 ○ *The disclosure of the takeover bid raised the price of the shares.* 兼并要约的公开使股票价格上涨。

disclosure of shareholding /dɪsˌkləʊʒər əv 'ʃeəhəʊldɪŋ/ *noun* the act of making public the fact that someone owns shares in a company 持股披露：向公众披露某人在某公司持有股票

discount *noun* /'dɪskaʊnt/ **1.** the percentage by which the seller reduces the full price for the buyer 折扣（百分比）○ *to give a discount on bulk purchases* 对团购给予折扣 □ **to sell goods at a discount** *or* **at a discount price** to sell goods below the normal price 打折销售 □ **10% discount for cash** *or* **10% cash discount** you pay 10% less if you pay in cash 10%的现金折扣 **2.** the amount by which something is sold for less than its value 贴水：某物售价低于其价值的金额 ■ *verb* /dɪs'kaʊnt/ **1.** to reduce prices to increase sales 打折扣 **2.** □ **to discount bank bills, to re-discount bankbills** to buy bills, issued by banks, at less than their face value (the Central Bank buys the bills and in this way is able to provide the banks with cash) 再贴现票据：以低于面值的价格购买银行发行的票据（中央银行购买这种票据，藉以向银行提供资金）**3.** to react to something which may happen in the future, such as a possible takeover bid or currency devaluation 对将来可能发生的某事作出反应（例如可能的兼并要约或货币贬值）

'...pressure on the Federal Reserve Board to ease monetary policy and possibly cut its discount rate mounted yesterday'
"昨天，要求联邦储备委员放宽货币政策和下调贴现率的施压进一步加大"［*Financial Times*《金融时报》］

'...banks refrained from quoting forward US/Hong Kong dollar exchange rates as premiums of 100 points replaced the previous day's discounts of up to 50 points'
"银行不再提供美元对港币的远期汇率报价，因为100点的升水取代了前一天50点的贴水"［*South China Morning Post*《南华早报》］

discountable /'dɪskaʊntəb(ə)l/ *ad-*

jective possible to discount 可贴现的，可享受折扣的 ○ *These bills are not discountable*. 这些票据不能贴现。

discount broker /ˈdɪskaʊnt ˌbrəʊkə/ *noun* a broker who charges a lower commission than other brokers 贴现票据经纪人：收取较低佣金的经纪人

discounted cash flow /ˌdɪskaʊntɪd ˈkæʃ fləʊ/ *noun* the calculation of the forecast return on capital investment by discounting future cash flows from the investment, usually at a rate equivalent to the company's minimum required rate of return 贴现的现金流量：通过贴现投资的未来现金流量来预测资本投资项目收益的方法，贴现率通常等于公司要求的最低收益率 Abbreviation 缩写 **DCF**

discounted value /ˌdɪskaʊntɪd ˈvæljuː/ *noun* the difference between the face value of a share and its lower market price 贴现价值：股票面值与其较低市价之间的差额

discounter /ˈdɪskaʊntə/ *noun* a person or company that discounts bills or invoices, or sells goods at a discount 票据贴现人（或公司）；折扣店店主；折扣店：贴现票据或出售廉价商品的个人或公司

'... invoice discounting is an instant finance raiser. Cash is advanced by a factor or discounter against the value of invoices sent out by the client company. Debt collection is still in the hands of the client company, which also continues to run its own bought ledger'
"发票贴现是一种快速筹资手段。代理人或贴现人按客户公司发出的发票价值垫付现金，客户公司仍持有讨债权，并继续管理其自己的购买分类账"［*Times*《泰晤士报》］

'... a 100,000 square-foot warehouse generates ten times the volume of a discount retailer; it can turn its inventory over 18 times a year, more than triple a big discounter's turnover'
"一个10万平方尺的仓库可以容纳一个折扣商十倍的营业量，这可以使存货一年周转18次，相当于一个大型折扣商周转次数的三倍还要多"［*Duns Business Month*《邓氏商业月刊》］

discount house /ˈdɪskaʊnt haʊs/ *noun* **1.** a financial company which specialises in discounting bills 贴现公司：专门贴现票据的财务公司 **2.** a shop which specializes in selling cheap goods bought at a high discount 折扣商店：专门廉价出售其用高折扣价格买进的商品的商店

discount price /ˈdɪskaʊnt praɪs/ *noun* the full price less a discount 折扣价：全价减去折扣

discount rate /ˈdɪskaʊnt reɪt/ *noun* the rate charged by a central bank on any loans it makes to other banks 贴现率：中央银行给其他银行贷款时的利率

discount store /ˈdɪskaʊnt stɔː/ *noun* a shop which specialises in cheap goods bought at a high discount 折扣商场：廉价出售用高折扣价格买进商品的商场

discrepancy /dɪˈskrepənsi/ *noun* a situation where figures are not correct 不符，差异，错误

discretion /dɪˈskreʃ(ə)n/ *noun* the ability to decide what should be done 判断力，决定能力

discretionary /dɪˈskreʃ(ə)n(ə)ri/ *adjective* possible if someone wants 随意的，自行决定的

discretionary account /dɪˌskreʃ(ə)n(ə)ri əˈkaʊnt/ *noun* a client's account with a stockbroker, where the broker invests and sells at his or her own discretion without the client needing to give him specific instructions 全权管理户头,委托账户:客户在证券经纪商处开设的投资户头,而证券经纪商可以自行决定该户头的投资或买卖

discretionary client /dɪˌskreʃ(ə)n(ə)ri ˈklaɪənt/ *noun* a client whose funds are managed on a discretionary basis 全权委托客户:委托他人全权管理其资金的客户

discretionary funds /dɪˌskreʃ(ə)n(ə)ri ˈfʌndz/ *plural noun* funds managed on a discretionary basis 可全权处理的资金,自主资金:按全权委托方式管理的资金

discretionary trust /dɪˌskreʃ(ə)n(ə)ri ˈtrʌst/ *noun* a trust where the trustees decide how to invest the income and when and how much income should be paid to the beneficiaries 全权信托:由受托人决定如何投资和何时分配收入以及分配多少的信托

diseconomies of scale /dɪsɪˌkɒnəmiz əv ˈskeɪl/ *plural noun* a situation where increased production leads to a higher production cost per unit or average production cost 规模不经济:产量的增加反而促使单位成本或平均生产成本上升的情况

disequilibrium /ˌdɪsiːkwɪˈlɪbriəm/ *noun* an imbalance in the economy when supply does not equal demand (供需)不平衡

dishonoured cheque /dɪsˌɒnəd ˈtʃek/ *noun* a cheque which the bank will not pay because there is not enough money in the account to pay it 拒付支票:因付款账户中没有足够的资金支付而被银行拒付的支票

disinvest /ˌdɪsɪnˈvest/ *verb* to reduce investment by not replacing capital assets when they wear out 负投资,减少投资:当资本资产损耗时不进行更新而导致的投资减少

disinvestment /ˌdɪsɪnˈvestmənt/ *noun* a reduction in capital assets by not replacing them when they wear out 负投资,减少投资:资本资产耗尽时不进行更新而导致的资本资产减少

disk drive /ˈdɪsk draɪv/ *noun* a part of a computer which makes a disk spin round in order to read it or store information on it 磁盘驱动器:计算机中驱动硬盘运转以存储及读取信息的部分

dispatch /dɪˈspætʃ/ *verb* to send goods to customers 发送,发运 ○ *The goods were dispatched last Friday.* 货物已于上周五发出。

dispatch note /dɪˈspætʃ nəʊt/ *noun* a note saying that goods have been sent 发货通知单

dispensation /ˌdɪspenˈseɪʃ(ə)n/ *noun* arrangement between an employer and the Inland Revenue by which business expenses paid to an employee are not declared for tax 免除,豁免:雇主与国内税务局达成的约定,即给予员工的业务开支不必报税

disposable personal income /dɪˌspəʊzəb(ə)l ˌpɜːs(ə)nəl ˈɪnkʌm/ *noun* the income left after tax and national insurance have been deducted 可支配个人收入:扣除税收和社会保险之后的收入 Also called 亦称作 **take-home pay**

disposal /dɪˈspəʊz(ə)l/ *noun* a sale 出售 ○ *a disposal of securities* 证券的出售 ○ *The company has started a systematic disposal of its property portfolio.* 该公司开始有计划地出售其物业投资组合。□ **lease *or* business for dis-**

posal a lease or business for sale 待转让的租约(或待售的企业)

disqualification /dɪsˌkwɒlɪfɪˈkeɪʃ(ə)n/ *noun* **1.** the act of making someone disqualified to do something 资格的取消 **2.** a court order which forbids a person from being a director of a company. A variety of offences, even those termed as 'administrative', can result in some being disqualified for up to five years (董事)资格的取消:禁止某人担任公司董事的法庭命令。有多种违规行为(甚至如"行政"方面的过失)可导致长达五年的董事资格剥夺

'Even 'administrative offences' can result in disqualification. A person may be disqualified for up to five years following persistent breach of company legislation in terms of failing to file returns, accounts and other documents with the Registrar'
"甚至'行政记过'也可以导致被取消董事资格。如果一个人总是违反公司法规,如未在公司注册处备案申税单、财务报表和其他文件,他就会在其后五年内被剥夺做该项工作的资格"[*Accountancy*《会计学》]

disqualify /dɪsˈkwɒlɪfaɪ/ *verb* to make a person unqualified to do something, such as to be a director of a company 取消…的资格(如担任公司董事)

dissolution /ˌdɪsəˈluːʃ(ə)n/ *noun* the ending of a partnership (合作关系的)解除,终止;(合伙企业的)解散

dissolve /dɪˈzɒlv/ *verb* to bring to an end 结束,终止,解散 ○ *to dissolve a partnership* 散伙,解散合伙企业

distrain /dɪˈstreɪn/ *verb* to seize goods to pay for debts 扣押:扣押财物以抵偿债务

distress /dɪˈstres/ *noun* the act of taking someone's goods to pay for debts 扣押:扣押某人的财物以抵偿债务的行为

distress merchandise /dɪˈstres ˌmɜːtʃəndaɪs/ *noun US* goods sold cheaply to pay a company's debts (美)削价出售的商品:便宜出售以偿债的商品

distress sale /dɪˈstres seɪl/ *noun* a sale of goods at low prices to pay a company's debts 扣押物拍卖,廉价出售:为抵偿公司债务而低价出售商品

distributable /dɪsˈtrɪbjʊtəb(ə)l/ *adjective* possible to distribute 可分配的

distributable profits /dɪsˌtrɪbjʊtəb(ə)l ˈprɒfɪts/ *plural noun* profits which can be distributed to shareholders as dividends if the directors decide to do so 可分配利润:经董事同意,可作为股利分配给股东的利润

distribute /dɪˈstrɪbjuːt/ *verb* **1.** to share out dividends 分配(股利) ○ *Profits were distributed among the shareholders*. 把利润分配给股东。**2.** to send out goods from a manufacturer's warehouse to retail shops 分发,发送(货物) ○ *Smith Ltd distributes for several smaller companies*. 史密斯有限公司为几家小公司送货。○ *All orders are distributed from our warehouse near Oxford*. 所有订单都从我们在牛津附近的仓库发货。

distributed profits /dɪˌstrɪbjʊtɪd ˈprɒfɪts/ *plural noun* profits passed to shareholders in the form of dividends 已分配利润:以股利形式分配给股东的利润

distribution /ˌdɪstrɪˈbjuːʃ(ə)n/ *noun* the act of sending goods from the manufacturer to the wholesaler and then to retailers 分发，发送，分销 ○ *Stock is held in a distribution centre which deals with all order processing.* 货物存放在负责处理所有订单的分销中心处。○ *Distribution costs have risen sharply over the last 18 months.* 过去18个月分销成本猛增。○ *She has several years' experience as distribution manager.* 她有几年担任分销经理的经验。

'British distribution companies are poised to capture a major share of the European market'
"英国分销公司正准备占据欧洲市场的主要份额"[*Management News*《管理新闻》]

distribution cost /ˌdɪstrɪˈbjuːʃ(ə)n kɒst/, **distribution expense** /ˌdɪstrɪˌbjuːʃ(ə)n ɪkˈspens/, **distribution overhead** /ˌdɪstrɪˌbjuːʃ(ə)n ˈəʊvəhed/ *noun* expenditure involved in warehousing, packing and sending stocks for sale 分销成本：仓储、包装及发送待售存货涉及的开支

distribution network /ˌdɪstrɪˈbjuːʃ(ə)n ˌnetwɜːk/ *noun* a series of points or small warehouses from which goods are sent all over a country 分销网，推销网：把货物发送到全国各地的一系列网点或小型仓库

distribution of income /ˌdɪstrɪbjuːʃ(ə)n əv ˈɪnkʌm/ *noun* payment of dividends to shareholders 收入分配：向股东支付股利

distribution slip /ˌdɪstrɪˈbjuːʃ(ə)n slɪp/ *noun* a paper attached to a document or to a magazine, showing all the people in an office who should read it 文件传阅名单：贴在文件或杂志上的纸条，列明办公室中需阅读该文件或杂志的人员名单

distributor /dɪˈstrɪbjʊtə/ *noun* a company which sells goods for another company which makes them 经销商

distributorship /dɪˈstrɪbjʊtəʃɪp/ *noun* the position of being a distributor for a company 经销商身份

District Bank /ˌdɪstrɪkt ˈbæŋk/ *noun* one of the 12 US banks that make up the Federal Reserve System. Each District Bank is responsible for all banking activity in its area 地方银行，地区银行：组成美国联邦储备系统的12家银行之一。每个地区银行负责其所在地区的所有银行业务

diversification /daɪˌvɜːsɪfɪˈkeɪʃ(ə)n/ *noun* the process of adding another quite different type of business to a firm's existing trade 多样化经营，多种经营

diversify /daɪˈvɜːsɪfaɪ/ *verb* **1.** to add new types of business to existing ones（在现有业务基础上）使多样化，多种经营 ○ *The company is planning to diversify into new products.* 该公司计划增加新产品。**2.** to invest in different types of shares or savings so as to spread the risk of loss 多样化（投资），分散（投资）：投资不同类型的证券以便分散投资风险

divestiture /daɪˈvestɪtʃə/ *noun* a sale of an asset 放弃，弃除（资产）：出售资产

dividend /ˈdɪvɪdend/ *noun* a percentage of profits paid to shareholders 股息，股利：支付给股东的利润百分比 □ **to raise *or* increase the dividend** to pay out a higher dividend than in the previous year 提高股利：支付比去年更高的股利 □ **to omit *or* pass the dividend** to pay no dividend 不支付股利

dividend cover /ˈdɪvɪdend ˌkʌvə/

noun the ratio of profits to dividends paid to shareholders 股利保证倍数：利润与股利的比率

dividend forecast /ˈdɪvɪdend ˌfɔːkɑːst/ *noun* a forecast of the amount of an expected dividend 股利预测

dividend mandate /ˌdɪvɪdend mænˈdeɪt/ *noun* an authorisation by a shareholder to the company, to pay his or her dividends directly into a bank account 股利指令：股东授权公司将其应得股利直接存入某银行账户

dividend per share /ˌdɪvɪdend pə ˈʃeə/ *noun* an amount of money paid as dividend for each share held 每股股利

dividend warrant /ˌdɪvɪdend ˈwɒrənt/ *noun* a cheque which makes payment of a dividend 股利单：用以支付股利的支票（NOTE：The US term is **dividend check** 美国用语为 **dividend check**）

dividend yield /ˈdɪvɪdend jiːld/ *noun* a dividend expressed as a percentage of the current market price of a share 股利收益率：每股股利占目前每股市价的百分比

dividend yield basis /ˌdɪvɪdend jiːld ˈbeɪsɪs/ *noun* a method of valuing shares in a company, calculated as the dividend per share divided by the expected dividend yield 股利收益率法：以每股股利除以预计股利收益来计算公司股票价值的方法

divisional headquarters /dɪˌvɪʒ(ə)nəl ˌhedˈkwɔːtəz/ *plural noun* the main office of a division of a company 分公司总部

divisor /dɪˈvaɪzə/ *noun* an operand used to divide a dividend in a division operation 除数，约数

document /ˈdɒkjʊmənt/ *noun* a paper, especially an official paper, with written information on it 文件，公文 ○ *He left a file of documents in the taxi*. 他把一个文件夹落在出租车上了。○ *She asked to see the documents relating to the case*. 她要求查看与该案件有关的文件。

documentary /ˌdɒkjʊˈment(ə)ri/ *adjective* in the form of documents 公文的，文件的 ○ *documentary evidence* 书面证明

documentary credit /ˌdɒkjʊment(ə)ri ˈkredɪt/ *noun* a credit document used in export trade, when a bank issues a letter of credit against shipping documents 跟单信用证：出口贸易中使用的一种信用证单据，银行在客户提交发运单据后开具信用证

documentary proof /ˌdɒkjʊment(ə)ri ˈpruːf/ *noun* a proof in the form of a document 证明文件，书面证明

documentation /ˌdɒkjʊmenˈteɪʃ(ə)n/ *noun* all the documents referring to something 文件集：关于某事项的所有文件 ○ *Please send me the complete documentation concerning the sale*. 请将所有有关销售的文件给我。

dole queue /ˈdəʊl kjuː/ *noun* a line of people waiting to collect their unemployment money 排队领取失业救济金的一群人（NOTE：The US term is **dole line** 美国用语为 **dole line**）

dollar /ˈdɒlə/ *noun* a unit of currency used in the US and other countries, regions such as Australia, Bahamas, Barbados, Bermuda, Brunei, Canada, Fiji, Jamaica, New Zealand, Singapore and Zimbabwe 元；美元：美国和其他一些国家（如澳大利亚、巴哈马、巴巴多斯、百慕大群岛、文莱、加拿大、斐济、牙买加、新西兰、新加坡和津巴布

韦)使用的货币单位 ○ *The US dollar rose 2%.* 美元升值 2%。○ *They sent a cheque for fifty Canadian dollars.* 他们发出一张 50 加拿大元的支票。○ *It costs six Australian dollars.* 它值六澳大利亚元。

dollar area /ˈdɒlər ˌeəriə/ *noun* an area of the world where the US dollar is the main trading currency 美元区:世界上将美元作为主要贸易通货的地区

dollar balances /ˈdɒlə ˌbælənsɪz/ *noun* a country's trade balances expressed in US dollars 美元余额:用美元表示的国际贸易余额

dollar crisis /ˈdɒlə ˌkraɪsɪs/ *noun* a fall in the exchange rate for the US dollar 美元危机:美元汇率下跌

dollar gap /ˌdɒlə ˈgæp/ *noun* a situation where the supply of US dollars is not enough to satisfy the demand for them from overseas buyers 美元短缺:供应的美元不足以满足海外买方的需求

dollar millionaire /ˌdɒlə ˌmɪljəˈneə/ *noun* a person who has more than one million dollars 百万富翁

dollar stocks /ˈdɒlə stɒks/ *plural noun* shares in US companies 美国公司的股票

domestic production /dəˌmestɪk prəˈdʌkʃən/ *noun* the production of goods for use in the home country 国内生产:满足国内需要的商品生产

domicile /ˈdɒmɪsaɪl/ *noun* the country where someone lives or where a company's office is registered 永久居住国;公司注册处:某人居住的国家或公司注册的地址 ■ *verb* □ **she is domiciled in Denmark** she lives in Denmark officially 她正式在丹麦定居

donation /dəʊˈneɪʃ(ə)n/ *noun* a gift, especially to a charity 捐赠品,捐款(尤指对慈善机构的捐赠)

donee /ˌdəʊˈniː/ *noun* a person who receives a gift from a donor 受赠人

donor /ˈdəʊnə/ *noun* a person who gives, especially someone who gives money 捐赠人,捐款人

dormant /ˈdɔːmənt/ *adjective* no longer active or no longer operating 不活跃的,闲置的

dormant account /ˌdɔːmənt əˈkaʊnt/ *noun* **1.** a bank account which is no longer used 不活动账户:不再使用的银行账户 **2.** a past customer who is no longer buying 不活动客户:不再购买的客户 ○ *Let's re-establish contact with some of our dormant accounts.* 我们与一些不活动的客户恢复联系吧。○ *All the old reports on dormant accounts have been filed away.* 关于不活动账户的所有旧报告均已归档。

dormant company /ˌdɔːmənt ˈkʌmp(ə)ni/ *noun* company which has not made any transactions during an accounting period 休眠公司,不活跃公司:在一个会计期间内未进行任何交易的公司

double-entry bookkeeping /ˌdʌb(ə)lˌentri ˈbʊkkiːpɪŋ/ *noun* the most commonly used system of bookkeeping, based on the principle that every financial transaction involves the simultaneous receiving and giving of value, and is therefore recorded twice 复式簿记:最常用的一种簿记制度,它的基本原则是每笔财务交易都同时涉及价值的获得和付出,因此要记录两次

double taxation /ˌdʌb(ə)l tækˈseɪʃ(ə)n/ *noun* the act of taxing the same income twice 双重征税:对一笔收入重复征税的行为

double taxation agreement /ˌdʌb(ə)l tækˈseɪʃ(ə)n əˌgriːmənt/, **double taxation treaty** /ˌdʌb(ə)l tækˈseɪʃ(ə)n ˌtriːti/ *noun* an agreement between two countries that a person living in one country shall not be taxed in both countries on the income earned in the other country 双重征税协议:两国之间关于一国居民不应就来自另一国的收入纳两次税而达成的避免双重征税的协议

double taxation relief /ˌdʌb(ə)l tækˈseɪʃ(ə)n rɪˌliːf/ *noun* a reduction of tax payable in one country by the amount of tax on income, profits or capital gains already paid in another country 双重课税减免:因为已在其他国家缴纳收入、利润和资本利得的税款,因此在本国应交的税款中作相应减免

doubtful debt /ˌdaʊtf(ə)l ˈdet/ *noun* a debt which may never be paid 可疑债务:可能永远得不到偿还的债务

doubtful loan /ˌdaʊtf(ə)l ˈləʊn/ *noun* a loan which may never be repaid 可疑贷款:可能永远得不到偿还的贷款

down /daʊn/ *adverb*, *preposition* in a lower position or to a lower position 降低,向下 ○ *The inflation rate is gradually coming down.* 通货膨胀率在逐渐下降。○ *Shares are slightly down on the day.* 今日股价小幅度下跌。○ *The price of petrol has gone down.* 油价已经下降。

downgrade /ˈdaʊngreɪd/ *verb* **1.** to reduce the importance of someone or of a job 降低(某人或某个职位的重要性) ○ *The post was downgraded in the company reorganisation.* 公司重组后,该职位被降级了。**2.** to reduce the forecast for a share 降低(某股票的预期价)

down payment /ˌdaʊn ˈpeɪmənt/ *noun* a part of a total payment made in advance 定金 ○ *We made a down payment of $100.* 我们付了100美元的定金。

downside factor /ˈdaʊnsaɪd ˌfæktə/, **downside potential** /ˌdaʊnsaɪd pəˈtenʃ(ə)l/ *noun* the possibility of making a loss in an investment (投资)亏损的可能性

downside risk /ˈdaʊnsaɪd rɪsk/ *noun* a risk that an investment will fall in value (投资价值)下降的风险 Opposite 反义 **upside potential**

down time /ˈdaʊn taɪm/ *noun* the time when a machine is not working or not available because it is broken or being mended 停工时间:因机器出现故障或正在维修而造成的停机时间

downturn /ˈdaʊntɜːn/ *noun* the movement towards lower prices, sales or profits (价格、销售额或利润)下降,下滑 ○ *a downturn in the market price* 市价下跌 ○ *The last quarter saw a downturn in the economy.* 上季度经济出现下滑了。

draft /drɑːft/ *noun* **1.** an order for money to be paid by a bank 汇票 ○ *We asked for payment by banker's draft.* 我们要求使用银行汇票支付。**2.** a first rough plan or document which has not been finished 草案 ○ *The finance department has passed the final draft of the accounts.* 财务部通过了报表的最后一稿。○ *A draft of the contract* or *The draft contract is* *waiting for the MD's comments*. 合同草案正等待总经理批示。○ *He drew up the draft agreement on the back of an envelope*. 他在信封背面草拟协议。■ *verb* to make a first rough plan of a document 草拟，起草 ○ *to draft a letter* 草拟一封信 ○ *to draft a contract* 草拟一份合同 ○ *The contract is still being drafted* or *is still in the drafting stage*. 合同仍在起草之中。

drafting /ˈdrɑːftɪŋ/ *noun* an act of preparing the draft of a document（文件的）起草 ○ *The drafting of the contract took six weeks*. 起草合同花了六个星期。

drain /dreɪn/ *noun* a gradual loss of money flowing away（资金）逐渐流失，外流，枯竭，耗尽 ○ *The costs of the London office are a continual drain on our resources*. 伦敦办事处的开支不断消耗我们的财力。■ *verb* to remove something gradually 使耗尽，使逐渐枯竭 ○ *The expansion plan has drained all our profits*. 这项扩张计划耗尽了我们所有的利润。○ *The company's capital resources have drained away*. 该公司的资本来源已逐渐枯竭。

draw /drɔː/ *verb* **1.** to take money away 取款，提款 ○ *to draw money out of an account* 从账户中取款 **2.** to write a cheque 开出支票 ○ *She paid the invoice with a cheque drawn on an Egyptian bank*. 她用一家埃及银行开出的支票支付了发票款。(NOTE: **drawing – drew – drawn**)

drawback /ˈdrɔːbæk/ *noun* **1.** something which is not convenient or which is likely to cause problems 不利因素，缺点 ○ *One of the main drawbacks of the scheme is that it will take six years to complete*. 该计划的主要缺点之一就是需要耗时六年才能完成。**2.** a rebate on customs duty for imported goods when these are then used in producing exports 退税，出口退税：用进口材料制造出口商品时，将进口材料已缴纳的关税退回

drawdown /ˈdrɔːdaʊn/ *noun* the act of drawing money which is available under a credit agreement 提款（指信贷协议下的借款）

drawee /drɔːˈiː/ *noun* the person or bank asked to make a payment by a drawer 付款人，受票人

drawer /ˈdrɔːə/ *noun* the person who writes a cheque or a bill asking a drawee to pay money to a payee 出票人：签发支票或汇票要求受票人支付票面金额的人

drawing account /ˈdrɔːɪŋ əˌkaʊnt/ *noun* a current account, or any account from which the customer may take money when he or she wants 提款账户：银行活期账户，客户需要资金时可随时从该账户提取

drawings /ˈdrɔːɪŋz/ *plural noun* money or trading stock taken by a partner from a partnership, or by a sole trader from his or her business 提款，提存：合伙人从合伙企业（或独资人从其企业）提走款项或经营物资

drawings account /ˌdrɔːɪŋz əˈkaʊnt/ *noun* an account showing amounts drawn by partners in a partnership 提款账目：列明合伙人从合伙企业提取款项的账目

draw up /ˌdrɔː ˈʌp/ *verb* to write a legal document 起草（正式文件）○ *to draw up a contract* or *an agreement* 起草合同（或协议）○ *to draw up a company's articles of association* 起草公司章程

drop /drɒp/ *noun* a fall 下降 ○ *a*

drop in sales 销售下降 ○ *Sales show a drop of 10%.* 销售额下降10%。○ *The drop in prices resulted in no significant increase in sales.* 降价并未带来销售额的显著提升。■ *verb* to fall 下降 ○ *Sales have dropped by 10% or have dropped 10%.* 销售额下降了10%。○ *The pound dropped three points against the dollar.* 英镑对美元下降了三个点。

'... while unemployment dropped by 1.6 per cent in the rural areas, it rose by 1.9 per cent in urban areas during the period under review'
"在观察期内，农村地区失业率下降了1.6%，但同期城市的失业率却上升了1.9%"［*Business Times*（*Lagos*）《商业时报》（拉各斯）］

'... corporate profits for the first quarter showed a 4 per cent drop from last year's final three months'
"公司今年一季度利润环比下降4%"［*Financial Times*《金融时报》］

'... since last summer American interest rates have dropped by between three and four percentage points'
"自从去年夏天开始，美国的利率下降了三四个百分点"［*Sunday Times*《星期日泰晤士报》］

droplock bond /ˈdrɒplɒk bɒnd/ *noun* a floating rate bond which will convert to a fixed rate of interest if interest rates fall to some level 固定下限式浮动利率债券：当利率下降至某一水平时就会转化为固定利率的浮动利率债券

dry goods /ˌdraɪ ˈgʊdz/ *plural noun* cloth, clothes and household goods 干货：布匹、服装及家用物品

DTI *abbr* Department of Trade and Industry 贸易和工业部

dual /ˈdjuːəl/ *adjective* referring to two things at the same time（同时）两个的，双重的，二元的

dual currency bond /ˌdjuːəl ˈkʌrənsi bɒnd/ *noun* a bond which is paid for in one currency but which is repayable in another on redemption 双重货币债券：以一种货币购买而以另一种货币赎回的债券

dual listing /ˌdjuːəl ˈlɪstɪŋ/ *noun* the listing of a share on two stock exchanges 双重挂牌：一种股票在两个证券交易所上市挂牌交易

dual pricing /ˌdjuːəl ˈpraɪsɪŋ/ *noun* the fact of giving different prices to the same product depending on the market in which it is sold 双重定价：根据不同销售市场对同种产品的不同定价

dual resident /ˌdjuːəl ˈrezɪd(ə)nt/ *noun* a person who is legally resident in two countries 双重居民：同时为两个国家合法居民的人

dud /dʌd/ *noun, adjective* referring to a coin or banknote which is false or not good, or something which does not do what it is supposed to do (*informal*)（非正式）假币；无用的东西；（硬币或钞票）假的，无效的；（某物）未起到应有作用的 ○ *The £50 note was a dud.* 这张50英镑的钞票是假的。

dud cheque /ˌdʌd ˈtʃek/ *noun* a cheque which cannot be cashed because the person writing it has not enough money in the account to pay it 作废支票：因为签发人的账户中没有足够资金而无法兑现的支票

due /djuː/ *adjective* owed 欠款的，应付的 ○ *a sum due from a debtor* 债务人应付的款项 □ **to fall** *or* **become due** to be ready for payment 到期的，可以

支付的

'...many expect the US economic indicators for April, due out this Thursday, to show faster economic growth'
"对于将在本周四公布的美国 4 月份经济指标,很多人都希望能看到经济的较快增长"[*Australian Financial Review*《澳大利亚金融评论报》]

due diligence /ˌdjuː ˈdɪlɪdʒəns/ *noun* the examination of a company's accounts prior to a potential takeover by another organisation. This assessment is often undertaken by an independent third party 尽职调查,适当查证:在准备收购某公司前对其账目进行的审查。这项评估通常由独立的第三方进行

dues /djuːz/ *plural noun* orders taken but not supplied until new stock arrives (货物)预订单

dumping /ˈdʌmpɪŋ/ *noun* the act of getting rid of excess goods cheaply in an overseas market 倾销:在海外市场上廉价清理过剩商品 ○ *The government has passed anti-dumping legislation.* 政府通过了反倾销法案。○ *Dumping of goods on the European market is banned.* 欧洲市场禁止商品倾销。

Dun and Bradstreet /ˌdʌn ən ˈbrædstriːt/ *noun* an international organisation that sources credit information from companies and their creditors which it then makes available to subscribers 邓白氏公司:从各个公司及其债权人处获得信用资料、再提供给订购人的一家国际组织 Abbreviation 缩写 **D & B**

duplicate /ˈdjuːplɪkət/ *noun* a copy 副本 ○ *He sent me the duplicate of the contract.* 他给我寄来了合同副本。

duplicating machine /ˈdjuːplɪkeɪtɪŋ məˌʃiːn/ *noun* a machine which makes copies of documents 复印机

duplication /ˌdjuːplɪˈkeɪʃ(ə)n/ *noun* the act of doing something that is already being done in the same way by somebody else, copying 重复(他人的行为);复制

Dutch auction /ˌdʌtʃ ˈɔːkʃən/ *noun* an auction in which the auctioneer offers an item for sale at a high price and then gradually reduces the price until someone makes a bid 荷兰式拍卖,降价拍卖:拍卖人报出高价,然后逐渐降价直到有人投标为止的拍卖

duty /ˈdjuːti/ *noun* a tax which has to be paid 税,关税 ○ *Traders are asking the government to take the duty off alcohol* or *to put a duty on cigarettes.* 交易商们要求政府取消酒类的关税(或对香烟征收关税)。

'Canadian and European negotiators agreed to a deal under which Canada could lower its import duties on $150 million worth of European goods'
"加拿大和欧洲经过谈判达成协议,根据该协议,加拿大应对价值 1.5 亿美元的欧洲商品降低进口关税"[*Globe and Mail* (*Toronto*)《环球邮报》(多伦多)]

'...the Department of Customs and Excise collected a total of N79m under the new advance duty payment scheme'
"关税和消费税部门根据新的预付税计划,一共征收到 7,900 万尼日利亚奈拉的税款"[*Business Times* (*Lagos*)《商业时报》(拉各斯)]

duty-free /ˌdjuːtiˈfriː/ *adjective, adverb* sold with no duty to be paid 免税的(地) ○ *She bought duty-free perfume at the airport.* 她在机场买了一瓶免税香水。○ *He bought the watch* *duty-free*. 他买了一块免税手表。

duty-free shop /ˌdjuːtiˈfriː ʃɒp/ *noun* a shop at an airport or on a ship where goods can be bought without paying duty 免税商店

duty-paid goods /ˌdjuːtiˈpeɪd gʊdz/ *plural noun* goods where the duty has been paid 已付关税的商品

E

e /iː/ *prefix* referring to electronics or the Internet 电子的；互联网的

EAA *abbr* European Accounting Association 欧洲会计学会

e. & o.e. *abbr* errors and omissions excepted 如有错漏，有权更正

early withdrawal /ˌɜːli wɪðˈdrɔːəl/ *noun* the act of withdrawing money from a deposit account before the due date 提前取款 ○ *Early withdrawal usually incurs a penalty.* 提前取款一般需支付罚金。

earmark /ˈɪəmɑːk/ *verb* to reserve for a special purpose 指定…作特定用途 ○ *to earmark funds for a project* 给这一项目拨款 ○ *The grant is earmarked for computer systems development.* 这笔拨款专用于计算机系统开发。

earn /ɜːn/ *verb* **1.** to be paid money for working 挣（钱）○ *to earn £100 a week* 一周挣 100 英镑 ○ *Our agent in Paris certainly does not earn his commission.* 我们的巴黎代理商肯定挣不到佣金。○ *Her new job is more of a transfer than a promotion, since she doesn't earn any more.* 她的新职位与其说是升职不如说是调动，因为她的工资没有任何增加。○ *How much do you earn in your new job?* 你的新工作挣多少钱？ **2.** to produce interest or dividends 生（利）（指利息或股利）○ *a building society account which earns interest at 10%* 一个利率为 10%的住房互助协会账户 ○ *What level of dividend do these shares earn?* 这些股票获利如何？

earned income /ɜːnd ˈɪnkʌm/ *noun* income from wages, salaries, pensions, fees, rental income, etc., as opposed to 'unearned' income from investments 劳动所得：来自于工资、薪金、养老金等的收入（与投资产生的"非劳动"所得相对）

earnest /ˈɜːnɪst/ *noun* money paid as an initial payment by a buyer to a seller, to show commitment to the contract of sale 定金，保证金

earning capacity /ˈɜːnɪŋ kəˌpæsɪti/ *noun* the amount of money someone should be able to earn 赚钱能力，收益能力

earning potential /ˈɜːnɪŋ pəˌtenʃəl/ *noun* 获利潜力 **1.** the amount of money a person should be able to earn in his or her professional capacity [一个人凭借其专业能力可以挣到的钱数] **2.** the amount of dividend which a share is capable of earning [股票所能带来的股利金额]

earning power /ˈɜːnɪŋ ˌpaʊə/ *noun* the amount of money someone should be able to earn 收益能力 ○ *She is such a fine designer that her earning power* *is very large*. 她是一位非常出色的设计师，所以很能赚钱。

earnings /ˈɜːnɪŋz/ *plural noun* **1.** salary, wages, dividends or interest received 收入：所得的工资、薪水、股利和利息的总称 ○ *High earnings in top management reflect the heavy responsibilities involved*. 高级管理人员收入高，是因为他们承担了重大的责任。○ *The calculation is based on average earnings over three years*. 这是根据三年的平均收入算出的。**2.** the profit made by a company（公司的）利润，收益

'... the US now accounts for more than half of our world-wide sales. It has made a huge contribution to our earnings turnaround'
"美国现在占我们全球销售额的一半以上，对我们的盈利贡献很大"［*Duns Business Month*《邓氏商业月刊》］

'... last fiscal year the chain reported a 116% jump in earnings, to $6.4 million or $1.10 a share'
"该连锁店宣布，其上一财政年度的盈利猛增116%，达到640万美元，每股收益合1.1美元"［*Barrons*《巴伦》］

earnings before interest, taxes, depreciation and amortisation /ˌɜːnɪŋz bɪˌfɔː ˌɪntrəst ˌtæksɪz dɪˌpriːʃieɪʃ(ə)n ənd əˌmɔːtaɪˈzeɪʃ(ə)n/ *plural noun* the earnings generated by a business's fundamental operating performance, frequently used in accounting ratios for comparison with other companies. Interest on borrowings, tax payable on those profits, depreciation, and amortisation are excluded on the basis that they can distort the underlying performance 扣除利息、税款、折旧及摊销前的盈利：企业的日常经营运作产生的盈利，经常用于会计比率以便同其他公司进行比较。如果借款利息、所得税、折旧及摊销会干扰企业的运作表现，则需先扣除这些项目再作比较 Abbreviation 缩写 **EBIT, EBITDA**

earnings before interest and tax /ˌɜːnɪŋz bɪˌfɔː ˈɪntrəst ən tæks/ *noun* the amount earned by a business before deductions are made for tax and interest payments 未扣利息及税金收益

earnings cap /ˈɜːnɪŋz kæp/ *noun* the upper limit on the amount of salary that can be taken into account when calculating pensions 收入上限：计算养老金时可供参考的工资额上限

earnings performance /ˈɜːnɪŋz pəˌfɔːməns/ *noun* a way in which shares earn dividends 盈利表现：股票产生股利的一种方式

earnings per share /ˌɜːnɪŋz pə ˈʃeə/ *plural noun* the money earned in dividends per share, shown as a percentage of the market price of one share 每股收益：每股股利金额，表示为每股市价的百分比 Abbreviation 缩写 **EPS**

earnings-related contributions /ˌɜːnɪŋzrɪˌleɪtɪd ˌkɒntrɪˈbjuːʃ(ə)nz/ *plural noun* contributions to social security which rise as the employee's earnings rise 与收入相关的社会保险供款（供款额度随收入一起提高）

earnings-related pension /ˌɜːnɪŋzrɪˌleɪtɪd ˈpenʃən/ *noun* a pension which is linked to the size of a person's salary 与收入相关的退休金

earnings yield /ˈɜːnɪŋz jiːld/ *noun* the money earned in dividends per share as a percentage of the current market price of the share 收益率：以

股票当前市价百分比表示的每股股利

ease /iːz/ *verb* to fall a little 微跌 ○ *The share index eased slightly today.* 今天股指小幅下挫。

easy market /ˌiːzi ˈmɑːkɪt/ *noun* a market where few people are buying, so prices are lower than they were before 疲软市场：买方很少导致价格较低的市场 ○ *The Stock Exchange was easy yesterday.* 昨天股市疲软。

easy money /ˌiːzi ˈmʌni/ *noun* **1.** money which can be earned with no difficulty 易赚的钱 **2.** a loan available on easy repayment terms 低息贷款

easy money policy /ˌiːzi ˈmʌni pɒləsi/ *noun* a government policy of expanding the economy by making money more easily available, e. g. through lower interest rates and easy access to credit 放松银根政策：政府为促进经济增长而采取鼓励贷款的政策，如调低利率及降低信贷门槛

easy terms /ˌiːzi ˈtɜːmz/ *plural noun* financial terms which are not difficult to accept（贸易中的）优惠条件，易接受的财务条件 ○ *The shop is let on very easy terms.* 该店铺以非常优惠的条件出租。

EBITDA, EBIT *abbr* earnings before interest, taxes, depreciation and amortization 扣除利息、税款、折旧及摊销前的盈利

EBRD *abbr* European Bank for Reconstruction and Development 欧洲复兴开发银行

e-business /ˈiː ˌbɪznəs/ *noun* a general term that refers to any type of business activity on the Internet, including marketing, branding and research 电子商务，电子化企业运营 ○ *E-business is a rising part of the economy.* 电子商务是经济领域中新兴的角色。

'...the enormous potential of e-business is that it can automate the link between suppliers and customers'
"电子商务的巨大潜力在于，它能自动实现供应商与客户的联系"[*Investors Chronicle*《投资者纪事》]

ECB *abbr* European Central Bank 欧洲中央银行

ECGD *abbr* Export Credit Guarantee Department 出口信贷担保局

e-commerce /ˈiːˌkɒmɜːs/ *noun* a general term that is usually used to refer to the process of buying and selling goods over the Internet 电子商务

'...the problem is that if e-commerce takes just a 3 per cent slice of the market that would be enough to reduce margins to ribbons'
"问题是哪怕电子商务仅占市场份额的3%，就足以将利润压缩到极低的水平"[*Investors Chronicle*《投资者纪事》]

'...the new economy requires new company structures. He believes that other blue-chip organizations are going to find that new set-ups would be needed to attract and retain the best talent for e-commerce'
"新型经济要求有相应的新型公司架构。他相信其他蓝筹股公司很快也会发现，公司需要有新的组织架构，才能吸引并留住最优秀的电子商务人才"[*Times*《泰晤士报》]

econometrics /ɪˌkɒnəˈmetrɪks/ *plural noun* the study of the statistics of economics, using computers to analyse these statistics and make forecasts using mathematical models 计量经济学：用计算机分析统计量，用数学模型进行预测的一种经济统计学

economic /ˌiːkəˈnɒmɪk/ *adjective*

1. providing enough money to make a profit 经济的；合算的；赚钱的 ○ *The flat is let at an economic rent*. 这套公寓的租金很合算。○ *It is hardly economic for the company to run its own warehouse*. 自己经营仓库对该公司来说不大合算。**2.** referring to the financial state of a country (一国)经济的,财政的 ○ *economic planning* 经济计划 ○ *economic trends* 经济趋势 ○ *Economic planners are expecting a consumer-led boom*. 经济策划者预计将出现一轮由消费拉动的经济繁荣。○ *The government's economic policy is in ruins after the devaluation*. 货币贬值之后,政府的经济政策完全失灵。○ *The economic situation is getting worse*. 经济形势变得越来越糟。○ *The country's economic system needs more regulation*. 该国的经济体系需要更多调整。

'...each of the major issues on the agenda at this week's meeting is important to the government's success in overall economic management'
"本周会议议程上的每个重大议题,对于政府成功实施其总体经济管理方案都具有重要意义"[*Australian Financial Review*《澳大利亚金融评论报》]

economical /ˌiːkəˈnɒmɪk(ə)l/ *adjective* saving money or materials or being less expensive 节约的,节俭的；便宜的 ○ *This car is very economical*. 这车很省油。□ **an economical use of resources** the fact of using resources as carefully as possible 资源的节约使用

Economic and Monetary Union /ˌiːkənɒmɪk ən ˌmʌnɪt(ə)ri ˈjuːnjən/ *noun* (欧洲)经济与货币联盟 Abbreviation 缩写 **EMU**. same as 同 **European Monetary Union**

economic crisis /ˌiːkənɒmɪk ˈkraɪsɪs/, **economic depression** /ˌiːkəˌnɒmɪk dɪˈpreʃ(ə)n/ *noun* a situation where a country is in financial collapse 经济危机 ○ *The government has introduced import controls to solve the current economic crisis*. 政府控制进口以解决当前的经济危机。

economic cycle /ˌiːkənɒmɪk ˈsaɪk(ə)l/ *noun* a period during which trade expands, then slows down and then expands again 经济周期：从商业繁荣到衰退再到繁荣的一段时间

economic development /ˌiːkənɒmɪk dɪˈveləpmənt/ *noun* the expansion of the commercial and financial situation 经济发展 ○ *The government has offered tax incentives to speed up the economic development of the region*. 政府提出税务激励,以加速该地区的经济发展。○ *Economic development has been relatively slow in the north, compared with the rest of the country*. 与该国其他地区相比,北部的经济发展相对缓慢。

economic forecaster /ˌiːkənɒmɪk ˈfɔːkɑːstə/ *noun* a person who says how he or she thinks a country's economy will perform in the future 经济预测师

economic growth /ˌiːkənɒmɪk ˈɡrəʊθ/ *noun* the rate at which a country's national income grows 经济增长

economic model /ˌiːkənɒmɪk ˈmɒd(ə)l/ *noun* a computerised plan of a country's economic system, used for forecasting economic trends 经济模型：用计算机对一国经济体系进行模拟计划,用来预测经济趋势

economic order quantity /ˌiːkənɒmɪk ˈɔːdə ˌkwɒntɪti/ *noun* the quantity of stocks which a company should hold, calculated on the basis of the costs of warehousing, of lower unit costs because of higher quantities purchased, the rate at which stocks are used and the time it takes for suppliers to deliver new orders 经济订购量:公司应保持的存货量,该数量根据储存成本、采购数量增加引起的较低单位成本、存货消耗速率及供应商交付新订单所需时间来计算 Abbreviation 缩写 **EOQ**

economic planning /ˌiːkənɒmɪk ˈplænɪŋ/ *noun* the process of planning the future financial state of the country for the government 国民经济计划的制订

economics /ˌiːkəˈnɒmɪks/ *noun* the study of the production, distribution, selling and use of goods and services 经济学 ■ *plural noun* the study of financial structures to show how a product or service is costed and what returns it produces 经济情况;经济表现 ○ *I do not understand the economics of the coal industry*. 我不了解煤炭行业的经济情况。(NOTE:[all senses] takes a singular verb [以上所有义项] 使用单数动词)

'...believers in free-market economics often find it hard to sort out their views on the issue'
"信奉自由市场经济的人们往往难以解释这个问题"[*Economist*《经济学家》]

economic sanctions /ˌiːkənɒmɪk ˈsæŋkʃ(ə)nz/ *plural noun* restrictions on trade with a country in order to influence its political situation or in order to make its government change its policy 经济制裁 ○ *to impose economic sanctions on a country* 对某国实施经济制裁

economic stagnation /ˌiːkənɒmɪk stægˈneɪʃ(ə)n/ *noun* a lack of expansion in the economy 经济停滞

economic value added /ˌiːkənɒmɪk ˌvæljuː ˈædɪd/ *noun* a way of judging financial performance by measuring the amount by which the earnings of a project, an operation, or a company exceed or fall short of the total amount of capital that was originally invested by its owners 经济增加值:通过测算某个工程、项目或公司的收入高于(或低于)投资人原始投资的总额以判断其财务表现的方法 Abbreviation 缩写 **EVA**

economies of scale /ɪˌkɒnəmiz əv ˈskeɪl/ *plural noun* a situation in which a product is made more profitable by manufacturing it in larger quantities so that each unit costs less to make 规模经济:通过批量制造来降低单位生产成本,从而提高产品利润率 Compare 比较 **diseconomies of scale**

economies of scope /ɪˌkɒnəmiz əv ˈskəʊp/ *plural noun* reductions in unit average costs caused by the simultaneous production of a number of related products, permitting benefits such as the sharing of joint costs over a larger volume than would otherwise be possible 范围经济:通过同时生产众多相关产品来摊薄生产成本,从而降低单位平均成本

economist /ɪˈkɒnəmɪst/ *noun* a person who specialises in the study of economics 经济学家 ○ *Government economists are forecasting a growth rate of 3% next year*. 官方经济学家预测来年的增长率为 3%。○ *An agricultural economist studies the economics of the* *agriculture industry*. 农业经济学家研究农业的经济情况。

economy /ɪˈkɒnəmɪ/ *noun* **1.** an action which is intended to stop money or materials from being wasted, or the quality of being careful not to waste money or materials（金钱或物资的）节省，经济；节俭，节约 □ **to introduce economies *or* economy measures into the system** to start using methods to save money or materials 将节约措施引入该系统 **2.** the financial state of a country, or the way in which a country makes and uses its money（一国的）经济 ○ *The country's economy is in ruins*. 这个国家经济状况一团糟。

'... the European economies are being held back by rigid labor markets and wage structures, huge expenditures on social welfare programs and restrictions on the free movement of goods'
"受僵化的劳动力市场和工资结构、巨额社会福利计划开支及货品自由流动限制的拖累，欧洲经济停滞不前"［*Duns Business Month*《邓氏商业月刊》］

economy class /ɪˈkɒnəmi klɑːs/ *noun* a lower-quality, less expensive way of traveling 经济舱 ○ *I travel economy class because it is cheaper*. 我乘坐经济舱出游，因为它比较便宜。○ *I always travels first class because economy class is too uncomfortable*. 我总是乘坐头等舱，因为经济舱很不舒服。

economy drive /ɪˈkɒnəmi draɪv/ *noun* a vigorous effort to save money or materials 节约运动

economy size /ɪˈkɒnəmi saɪz/ *noun* a large size or large packet which is cheaper than usual（价格较低的）经济尺寸，经济（包）装

ECP /ˌiː siː ˈpiː/ *abbr* Eurocommercial Paper 欧洲商业票据

ecu /ˈekjuː/, **ECU** *abbr* European Currency Unit 欧洲货币单位

ED *abbr* exposure draft 征求意见稿，公开文稿

EDI /ˌiː diː ˈaɪ/ *abbr* electronic data interchange 电子数据交换

editorial board /edɪˌtɔːriəl ˈbɔːd/ *noun* a group of editors on a newspaper or other publication（报纸或其他出版物的）编辑委员会

effect /ɪˈfekt/ *noun* **1.** a result 结果，效果 ○ *The effect of the pay increase was to raise productivity levels*. 加薪是为了提高生产率。**2.** in operation 生效 □ **terms of a contract which take effect *or* come into effect from January 1st** terms which start to operate on January 1st 自1月1日起生效的合同条款 **3.** meaning 意思，含义 □ **a clause to the effect that** a clause which means that 条款的大意为… ■ *verb* to carry out 实施，执行；履行

effective /ɪˈfektɪv/ *adjective* **1.** actual, as opposed to theoretical 实际的（相对于理论的）**2.** □ **a clause effective as from January 1st** a clause which starts to be applied on January 1st 自1月1日起生效的条款 **3.** producing results 有效的；生效的 ○ *Advertising in the Sunday papers is the most effective way of selling*. 在周日报纸上刊登广告是最有效的促销方法。○ *She is an effective marketing manager*. 她是一位高效率的营销经理。◊ 参阅 **cost-effective**

effective annual rate /ɪˌfektɪv ˈænjuəl reɪt/ *noun* the average interest rate paid on a deposit for a period of a year. It is the total interest received over 12 months expressed as a percentage of the principal at the beginning of the period 实际年利率,有效年利率:一年期存款平均利率,即在 12 个月期间获得的总利息,表示为期初本金的百分比

effective date /ɪˈfektɪv deɪt/ *noun* the date on which a rule or contract starts to be applied, or on which a transaction takes place 生效日期

effective demand /ɪˌfektɪv dɪˈmɑːnd/ *noun* the actual demand for a product which can be paid for 有效需求:对某商品有支付能力的需求

effective exchange rate /ɪˌfektɪv ɪksˈtʃeɪndʒ ˌreɪt/ *noun* a rate of exchange for a currency calculated against a basket of currencies 有效汇率:以一揽子货币计算的某种货币的汇率

effectiveness /ɪˈfektɪvnəs/ *noun* the quality of working successfully or producing results 有效性 ○ *I doubt the effectiveness of television advertising.* 我怀疑电视广告的有效性。○ *Her effectiveness as a manager was due to her quick grasp of detail.* 作为经理,工作有效率是因为她能一下子就掌握全部细节。⇨ 参阅 **cost-effectiveness**

effective price /ɪˌfektɪv ˈpraɪs/ *noun* a share price which has been adjusted to allow for a rights issue 实际价格:因考虑到权利股发行而进行调整的股价

effective rate /ɪˌfektɪv ˈreɪt/ *noun* a real interest rate on a loan or deposit, i.e., the APR 实际利率:一笔贷款或存款的真实利率(即年利率)

effective tax rate /ɪˌfektɪv ˈtæks ˌreɪt/ *noun* the average tax rate applicable to a given transaction, whether it is income from work undertaken, the sale of an asset, or a gift, taking into account personal allowances and scales of tax. It is the amount of money generated by the transaction divided by the additional tax payable because of it 实际税率,有效税率:考虑到个人税务优惠及税收数额之后适用于指定交易的平均税率,不论交易收入为劳动所得、资产出售或是受赠所得。它的计算方法为交易所得金额除以该交易应付的额外税款金额

effective yield /ɪˌfektɪv ˈjiːld/ *noun* an actual yield shown as a percentage of the price paid after adjustments have been made 实际收益:调整后以支付价格百分比表示的实际收益

efficiency /ɪˈfɪʃ(ə)nsi/ *noun* the ability to work well or to produce the right result or the right work quickly 效率,效能 ○ *a business efficiency exhibition* 企业效率的展现 ○ *The bus system is run with a high degree of efficiency.* 该公共汽车系统的运转效率极高。○ *We called in an efficiency expert to report on ways of increasing profitability.* 我们邀请了一位效率专家来作如何提高利润率的报告。

'...increased control means improved efficiency in purchasing, shipping, sales and delivery'
"加强控制意味着提高购买、运输、销售和交货的效率"[*Duns Business Month*《邓氏商业月刊》]

efficient /ɪˈfɪʃ(ə)nt/ *adjective* able to work well or to produce the right result quickly 有效率的,有能力的,能胜任的 ○ *the efficient working of a system* 系统的高效运作 ○ *An efficient assistant is invaluable.* 能干的助手很

难得。○ *An efficient new machine would save time.* 高效的新机器可以节省时间。

efficiently /ɪˈfɪʃ(ə)ntli/ *adverb* in an efficient way 高效地，有能力地，能胜任地 ○ *She organised the sales conference very efficiently.* 她高效率地组织了这次销售会议。

efficient markets hypothesis /ɪˌfɪʃ(ə)nt ˈmɑːkɪts haɪˌpɒθəsɪs/ *noun* the theory that stock markets respond with varying degrees of efficiency to information about the companies listed 效率市场假说：关于股票市场对上市公司的信息反映效率程度不同的理论 Abbreviation 缩写 **EMH**

EFT /ˌiː ef ˈtiː/ *abbr* electronic funds transfer 电子资金转账

EFTPOS /ˌiː ef ˌtiː piː əʊ ˈes/ *abbr* electronic funds transfer at a point of sale 销售点电子资金转账

EIB *abbr* European Investment Bank 欧洲投资银行

EIS /ˌiː aɪ ˈes/ *abbr* Enterprise Investment Scheme 企业投资计划

elastic /ɪˈlæstɪk/ *adjective* able to expand or contract easily because of small changes in price（因价格小幅变动导致）有弹性的，可伸缩的

elasticity /ˌɪlæˈstɪsɪti/ *noun* the ability to change easily in response to a change in circumstances 弹性，伸缩性

eldercare /ˈeldəkeə/ *noun* assurance services sold to elderly people and their families（由老人或其家人支付的有偿）老年看护，老年保健

-elect /ɪlekt/ *suffix* referring to a person who has been elected but has not yet started the term of office 当选但尚未上任的，候任的

electronic banking /ˌelektrɒnɪk ˈbæŋkɪŋ/ *noun* the use of computers to carry out banking transactions such as withdrawals through cash dispensers or transfer of funds at point of sale 电子银行（服务）：使用计算机开展银行业务，例如使用现金取款机取款或通过销售点转账

electronic data interchange /ˌelektrɒnɪk ˈdeɪtə ˌɪntətʃeɪndʒ/ *noun* a standard format used when business documents such as invoices and purchase orders are exchanged over electronic networks such as the Internet 电子数据交换：通过电子网络（如互联网）交换商业单据（如发票和购买订单）时使用的标准格式 Abbreviation 缩写 **EDI**

electronic funds transfer /ˌelektrɒnɪk ˌfʌndz ˈtrænsfɜː/ *noun* the system used by banking organisations for the movement of funds between accounts and for the provision of services to the customer 电子资金转账：银行机构用于在账户间转移资金以及向客户提供服务的系统 Abbreviation 缩写 **EFT**

electronic funds transfer at point of sale /ˌelektrɒnɪk ˌfʌndz ˌtrænsfɜː ət ˌpɔɪnt əv ˈseɪl/ *noun* the payment for goods or services by a bank customer using a card that is swiped through an electronic reader on the till, thereby transferring the cash from the customer's account to the retailer's or service provider's account 销售点电子资金转账：银行客户在收银台刷卡支付商品或劳务费用，从而把现金从客户的账户转到零售商或服务提供商的账户 Abbreviation 缩写 **EFTPOS**

Electronic Lodgement Service /ˌelektrɒnɪk ˈlɒdʒmənt ˌsɜːvɪs/ *noun* British system for filing your tax return electronically 电子递交服务：英国使用电子方式递交报税表的系统 Abbreviation 缩写 **ELS**

electronic point of sale /ˌelɪktrɒnɪk pɔɪnt əv ˈseɪl/ *noun* a system where sales are charged automatically to a customer's credit card and stock is controlled by the shop's computer 电子销售点：售货款自动从顾客的信用卡中扣除，而存货由商场计算机控制的系统 Abbreviation 缩写 **EPOS**

Electronic Version of the Tax Return /ˌelektrɒnɪk ˌvɜːʃ(ə)n əv ðə tæks rɪˈtɜːn/ *noun* a method of making an individual's tax return using email 电子报税表：使用电子邮件制作个人报税表的方法 Abbreviation 缩写 **EVR**

eligibility /ˌelɪdʒɪˈbɪlɪti/ *noun* the fact of being eligible 有资格 ○ *The chairman questioned her eligibility to stand for re-election*. 主席质疑她再度参选的资格。

eliminate /ɪˈlɪmɪneɪt/ *verb* to remove 消除，排除 ○ *to eliminate defects in the system* 消除系统中的缺陷 ○ *Using a computer should eliminate all possibility of error*. 使用计算机应消除所有出错的可能性。○ *We have decided to eliminate this series of old products from our range*. 我们决定取消这个旧产品系列。○ *Most of the candidates were eliminated after the first batch of tests*. 首轮考试之后，大多数候选人都被刷掉了。

ELS *abbr* Electronic Lodgement Service 电子递交服务

emailing /ˈiːmeɪlɪŋ/ *noun* the process of sending something by email 发送电子邮件

embargo /ɪmˈbɑːgəʊ/ *noun* **1.** a government order which stops a type of trade（政府）禁止贸易令，禁运 ▫ **to lay or put an embargo on trade with a country** to say that trade with a country must not take place 发出对某国的贸易禁令 ○ *The government has put an embargo on the export of computer equipment*. 政府已对计算机设备出口发出贸易禁令。**2.** a period of time during which specific information in a press release must not be published 新闻管制期，消息封锁期：禁止在新闻稿中发布某信息的一段时间（NOTE：The plural is **embargoes** 复数为 **embargoes**）■ *verb* **1.** to stop trade，or not to allow something to be traded 禁运，禁止通商 ○ *The government has embargoed trade with the Eastern countries*. 政府已禁止与东方国家通商。**2.** not to allow publication of information for a period of time 新闻管制，消息封锁：在一定期限内禁止发布特定信息 ○ *The news of the merger has been embargoed until next Wednesday*. 合并的消息一直被封锁到下周三才能公布。

'...the Commerce Department is planning to loosen export controls for products that have been embargoed but are readily available elsewhere in the West'
"对西方其他地方随处可见的产品，商务部拟放松对其禁运的出口控制"[*Duns Business Month*《邓氏商业月刊》]

embezzle /ɪmˈbez(ə)l/ *verb* to use illegally money which is not yours, or which you are looking after for someone 盗用，挪用（资金）○ *He was sent to prison for six months for embezzling his clients' money*. 他因为盗用客户的资金被判入狱六个月。

embezzlement /ɪmˈbez(ə)lmənt/ *noun* the act of embezzling 盗用公款，侵吞财物 ○ *He was sent to prison for six months for embezzlement*. 他因为贪污被判入狱六个月。

embezzler /ɪmˈbez(ə)lə/ *noun* a person who embezzles 盗用者，贪污者

EMH *abbr* efficient markets hypothesis 效率市场假说

emoluments /ɪˈmɒljʊmənts/ *plural noun* pay, salary or fees, or the earnings of directors who are not employees（董事的）报酬，薪金（NOTE: US English uses the singular **emolument** 美国使用单数 **emolument**）

employ /ɪmˈplɔɪ/ *verb* to give someone regular paid work 雇用

'...70 per cent of Australia's labour force was employed in service activity'
"澳大利亚 70% 的劳动力从事服务业" [*Australian Financial Review*《澳大利亚金融评论报》]

employed /ɪmˈplɔɪd/ *adjective* **1.** in regular paid work 受雇的，就业的 **2.** referring to money used profitably（资金）用于盈利的 ■ *plural noun* people who are working 受雇者 ○ *the employers and the employed* 雇主和雇员

employee /ɪmˈplɔɪiː/ *noun* a person employed by another 雇员 ○ *Employees of the firm are eligible to join a profit-sharing scheme*. 该公司的雇员有资格加入分红计划。○ *Relations between management and employees are good*. 劳资关系良好。○ *The company has decided to take on new employees*. 该公司决定招聘新雇员。

'...companies introducing robotics think it important to involve individual employees in planning their introduction'
"引进机器人的公司认为，让个别雇员参与引进计划是很重要的" [*Economist*《经济学家》]

employee contribution /ɪmˌplɔɪiː ˌkɒntrɪˈbjuːʃ(ə)n/ *noun* a contribution paid by an employee towards his or her pension 员工分担额，雇员供款：职工养老金中由雇员分担的部分

employee share ownership plan /ɪmˈplɔɪiː ʃeə ˈəʊnəʃɪp plæn/, **employee share ownership programme** /ɪmˌplɔɪiː ˈʃeə ˌəʊnəʃɪp ˌprəʊgræm/, **employee share scheme** /ɪmˌplɔɪiː ˈʃeə skiːm/ *noun* a plan which allows employees to obtain shares in the company for which they work, though tax may be payable if the shares are sold to employees at a price which is lower than the current market price 雇员持股计划，职工入股计划，雇员股票计划：允许雇员获得所在公司股票的方案。但如果股票卖给雇员的价格低于现行市价，则可能需要交税 Abbreviation 缩写 **ESOP**

employer /ɪmˈplɔɪə/ *noun* a person or company that has regular employees and pays them 雇主

employer's contribution /ɪmˌplɔɪəz ˌkɒntrɪˈbjuːʃ(ə)n/ *noun* money paid by an employer towards an employee's pension 雇主供款，雇主分担额：职工养老金中由雇主分担的部分

employers' liability insurance /ɪmˌplɔɪəz ˌlaɪəˈbɪlɪti ɪnˌʃʊərəns/ *noun* insurance to cover accidents which may happen at work, and for which the company may be responsible 雇主责任保险：为公司可能会承担责任的工伤投保的险种

employment /ɪmˈplɔɪmənt/ *noun* regular paid work 职业，工作

'...the blue-collar unions are the people who stand to lose most in terms of employment growth'
"蓝领工会是那些在就业增长方面势必会丧失利益最多的人的联盟"[*Sydney Morning Herald*《悉尼先驱晨报》]

employment agency /ɪmˈplɔɪmənt ˌeɪdʒənsi/ *noun* an office which finds jobs for staff 职业介绍所

employment income /ɪmˌplɔɪmənt ˈɪnkʌm/ *noun* money received from an employer, e.g. salary, fees, commission, bonus, fringe benefits 工作收入，职业收入：从雇主那里领到的钱，例如工资、费用、佣金、红利、附加福利等

employment office /ɪmˈplɔɪmənt ˌɒfɪs/ *noun* an office which finds jobs for people 职业介绍所

EMS /ˌiː em ˈes/ *abbr* European Monetary System 欧洲货币体系

EMU *abbr* **1.** Economic and Monetary Union (欧洲)经济与货币联盟 **2.** European Monetary Union 欧洲货币联盟

encash /ɪnˈkæʃ/ *verb* to cash a cheque, to exchange a cheque for cash 兑现(支票)

encashable /ɪnˈkæʃəb(ə)l/ *adjective* possible to cash 能兑现的

encashment /ɪnˈkæʃmənt/ *noun* an act of exchanging for cash 兑现

encumbrance /ɪnˈkʌmbrəns/ *noun* a liability which is attached usually to a property or land, e.g. a mortgage or charge 负担，不动产留置权：通常附加在不动产或土地上的负担(如按揭或抵押)

endorse /ɪnˈdɔːs/ *verb* to say that a product is good 认可(某产品)，代言(某产品) □ **to endorse a bill *or* a cheque** to sign a bill or cheque on the back to show that you accept it 背书汇票或支票：在汇票或支票的背面签字，表明你认可承兑

endorsee /ˌendɔːˈsiː/ *noun* a person whose name is written on a bill or cheque as having the right to cash it 受票人，被背书人：名字写在汇票或支票上，有权将其兑现的人

endorsement /ɪnˈdɔːsmənt/ *noun* **1.** the act of endorsing 背书 **2.** a signature on a document which endorses it 背书(签字) **3.** a note on an insurance policy which adds conditions to the policy 保险单上的附加条款

endorser /ɪnˈdɔːsə/ *noun* a person who endorses a bill or cheque which is then paid to him or her 背书人：作为收款人在汇票或支票上背书

endowment /ɪnˈdaʊmənt/ *noun* the act of giving money to provide a regular income 捐款，资助

endowment assurance /ɪnˈdaʊmənt əˌʃʊərəns/, **endowment insurance** /ɪnˈdaʊmənt ɪnˌʃʊərəns/ *noun* an insurance policy where a sum of money is paid to the insured person on a specific date or to his heirs if he dies before that date (定期)人寿保险

endowment mortgage /ɪnˈdaʊmənt ˌmɔːɡɪdʒ/ *noun* a mortgage backed by an endowment policy 人寿保险抵押：以定期人寿保险为抵押的借款

endowment policy /ɪnˈdaʊmənt ˌpɒlɪsi/ *noun* same as 同 **endowment assurance**

end product /ˌend ˈprɒdʌkt/ *noun* a manufactured product resulting from a production process 成品，最终产品

energy costs /ˈenədʒi kɒsts/ *plural noun* costs of gas, electricity, etc., as shown in accounts 能源成本：登记入账的天然气、电力等成本

energy shares /ˈenədʒi ʃeəz/ *plural noun* shares in companies which provide energy 能源股票：能源供应公司的股票

enforce /ɪnˈfɔːs/ *verb* to make sure something is done or that a rule is obeyed 实施，使生效；强制执行 ○ *to enforce the terms of a contract* 实施合同条款

enforcement /ɪnˈfɔːsmənt/ *noun* the act of making sure that something is obeyed 行使，实施 ○ *enforcement of the terms of a contract* 合同条款的实施

engagement /ɪnˈgeɪdʒmənt/ *noun* an agreement to do something 保证，诺言，约定

engagement letter /ɪnˌgeɪdʒmənt ˈletə/ *noun* a letter, usually required by professional standards, sent by an accountant to a client setting out the work the accountant is to do and further administrative matters, such as any limit on the accountant's liability 约定信函：通常按职业规范要求发放的一种信函，它由会计师发给客户，列明会计师即将开展的工作以及其他行政事项（如对会计师责任上的限制）

entail /ɪnˈteɪl/ *noun* a legal condition which passes ownership of a property only to some specific persons 限嗣继承：指不动产的所有权仅由特定的人继承 ■ *verb* to involve 需要，涉及 ○ *Itemising the sales figures will entail about ten days' work*. 将销售数字逐项列出大概需要10个工作日。

entering /ˈentərɪŋ/ *noun* the act of writing items in a record 登录，记入

enterprise /ˈentəpraɪz/ *noun* **1.** a system of carrying on a business 企业制度 **2.** a business 企业

Enterprise Investment Scheme /ˌentəpraɪz ɪnˈvestmənt skiːm/ *noun* a scheme which provides income and CGT relief for people prepared to risk investing in a single unquoted or AIM-listed trading company 企业投资计划：对准备投资无牌价或在另类投资市场（AIM）上市的单个贸易公司的个人，向其提供收入及资本利得税（CGT）宽免的计划 Abbreviation 缩写 **EIS**

enterprise zone /ˈentəpraɪz zəʊn/ *noun* an area of the country where businesses are encouraged to develop by offering special conditions such as easy planning permission for buildings or a reduction in the business rate 企业开发区：国家提供各种特殊条件，例如放宽建筑规划许可或减免企业税，来鼓励企业在该地区发展

entertain /ˌentəˈteɪn/ *verb* to offer such things as meals, hotel accommodation and theatre tickets for the comfort and enjoyment of business visitors 招待，款待

entertainment /ˌentəˈteɪnmənt/ *noun* the practice of offering meals or other recreation to business visitors 招待，款待

entertainment allowance /ˌentəˈteɪnmənt əˌlaʊəns/ *noun* money which managers are allowed by their company to spend on meals with visitors 招待津贴，公关补贴：公司允许经理用来宴请客户的资金

entertainment expenses /ˌentəˈteɪnmənt ɪkˌspensɪz/ *plural noun* money spent on giving meals to business visitors 招待费,公关费

entitle /ɪnˈtaɪt(ə)l/ *verb* to give the right to someone to have something 给…权利 ○ *After one year's service the employee is entitled to four weeks' holiday.* 工作满一年后,雇员有权享受四周休假。

entitlement /ɪnˈtaɪt(ə)lmənt/ *noun* a person's right to something 权利

entity /ˈentɪti/ *noun* a single separate body or organization 实体,个体

entrepreneur /ˌɒntrəprəˈnɜː/ *noun* a person who directs a company and takes commercial risks 企业家,实业家

entrepreneurial /ˌɒntrəprəˈnɜːriəl/ *adjective* taking commercial risks 创业的,企业家的 ○ *an entrepreneurial decision* 一项创业决策

entry /ˈentri/ *noun* **1.** an item of written information put in an accounts ledger 分录,账目(NOTE: The plural is **entries** 复数为 **entries**) **2.** an act of going in or the place where you can go in 进入;入口 ○ *to pass a customs entry point* 通过海关入口处 ○ *entry of goods under bond* 货物进入海关保税仓库

entry price /ˈentri praɪs/ *noun* a price at which an accounting entity buys, i. e., the current replacement cost 入账价格,买入价格:会计实体的购买价格(即现行重置成本)

EOQ *abbr* economic order quantity 经济订购量

epos /ˈiːpɒs/, **EPOS**, **EPoS** *abbr* electronic point of sale 电子销售点

EPS *abbr* earnings per share 每股收益

equal /ˈiːkwəl/ *adjective* exactly the same 相等的 ○ *Male and female employees have equal pay.* 男女雇员报酬相等。■ *verb* to be the same as 与…相等 ○ *Production this month has equalled our best month ever.* 这个月的产量平了我们的最高月纪录。(NOTE: UK English is **equalling – equalled**, but the US spelling is **equaling – equaled** 英国拼法为 **equalling – equalled**,美国拼法则为 **equaling – equaled**)

equalise /ˈiːkwəlaɪz/, **equalize** *verb* to make equal 使相等,使平均 ○ *to equalise dividends* 平均股利

equally /ˈiːkwəli/ *adverb* so that each has or pays the same, or to the same degree 相同地,相等地,平均地 ○ *Costs will be shared equally between the two parties.* 双方要平均分担成本。○ *They were both equally responsible for the disastrous launch.* 他们双方对这次产品推介失败负有同等的责任。

equate /ɪˈkweɪt/ *verb* to reduce to a standard value 使相等(于标准值)

equation /ɪˈkweɪʒ(ə)n/ *noun* a set of mathematical rules applied to solve a problem 等式,方程(式) ○ *The basic accounting equation is that assets equal liabilities plus equity.* 基本的会计恒等式是资产等于负债加所有者权益。

equilibrium /ˌiːkwɪˈlɪbriəm/ *noun* the state of balance in the economy where supply equals demand or a country's balance of payments is neither in deficit nor in excess 平衡,均衡:经济领域中的供求均衡或一个国家收支差额的平衡

equities /ˈekwɪtiz/ *plural noun* ordinary shares 普通股

'... in the past three years commercial property has seriously underperformed equities and dropped out of favour as a result' "近三年来,商业资产的表现远不如普通股,因此不再受到青睐"[*Investors Chronicle*《投资者纪事》]

equity accounting /ˈekwɪti əˌkaʊntɪŋ/ *noun* a method of accounting which puts part of the profits of a subsidiary into the parent company's books 权益会计:将子公司的部分利润归入母公司账户的会计方法

equity capital /ˈekwɪti ˌkæpɪt(ə)l/ *noun* the nominal value of the shares owned by the ordinary shareholders of a company 普通股股本:公司普通股东拥有股票的面值(NOTE: Preference shares are not equity capital. If the company were wound up, none of the equity capital would be distributed to preference shareholders 优先股不属于普通股股本,如公司清盘,普通股股本一概不会分配给优先股股东)

equity dividend cover /ˌekwɪti ˈdɪvɪdend ˌkʌvə/ *noun* an accounting ratio, calculated by dividing the distributable profits during a given period by the actual dividend paid in that period, that indicates the likelihood of the dividend being maintained in future years 普通股股利覆盖比率:一种会计比率,计算方法为将指定期间的可分配利润除以该期间实际支付的股利金额,以此预测未来年度保持该股利的可能性 ➪ 参阅 **capital reserves**

equity finance /ˈekwɪti ˌfaɪnæns/ *noun* finance for a company in the form of ordinary shares paid for by shareholders 普通股融资:公司通过股东支付普通股股本方式进行的融资

equity gearing /ˈekwɪti ˌɡɪərɪŋ/ *noun* the ratio between a company's borrowings at interest and its ordinary share capital 权益比率:公司的有息贷款与普通股股本的比率

equity kicker /ˈekwɪti ˌkɪkə/ *noun US* an incentive given to people to lend a company money, in the form of a warrant to share in future earnings (美)认股(权)鼓励:发给借款人的可分享未来盈利的权证,以鼓励人们借款给公司的一种机制(NOTE: The UK term is **equity sweetener** 英国用语为 **equity sweetener**)

equity share capital /ˌekwɪti ʃeə ˈkæpɪt(ə)l/ *noun* a company's issued share capital less capital which carries preferential rights. Equity share capital normally comprises ordinary shares 普通股本:公司的已发行股本减去附带优先权利的股本。普通股本通常包括普通股

equity sweetener /ˈekwɪti ˌswiːt(ə)nə/ *noun* an incentive to encourage people to lend a company money, in the form of a warrant giving the right to buy shares at a later date and at an agreed price 认股奖励:发给借款人可于未来某个日期按议定价格购买股票的权证,以鼓励人们借款给公司的一种机制

equivalence /ɪˈkwɪvələns/ *noun* the condition of having the same value or of being the same 等价,等值,等量

equivalent /ɪˈkwɪvələnt/ *noun* a person who is the equal of someone else 对等的人,对应的人

equivalent unit /ɪˌkwɪvələnt ˈjuːnɪt/ *noun* a unit of unfinished production calculated for valuation purposes when work started during the period is not finished at the end of the period, or when work started during the previous period is finished during the current period 约当产量:为计算成本而将半成品算作成品的数量,此半成品可能是本期内开始生产但期末未完工的,也可能是上期开始生产但在本期完工的

error /ˈerə/ *noun* a mistake 错误 ○ *He made an error in calculating the total*. 他在计算总和时出了错。○ *Someone must have made a keyboarding error*. 一定是有人在键盘录入时出了错。

errors and omissions excepted /ˌerəz ənd əʊˌmɪʃ(ə)nz ɪkˈseptɪd/ *phrase* words written on an invoice to show that the company has no responsibility for mistakes in the invoice 如有错漏,有权更正:写在发票上表明公司对发票中的错误概不负责 Abbreviation 缩写 **e. & o.e.**

ESC /ɪˈskeɪp/ *noun* a charter for employees, drawn up by the EU in 1989, by which employees have the right to a fair wage, and to equal treatment for men and women, a safe work environment, training, freedom of association and collective bargaining, provision for disabled workers, freedom of movement from country to country, guaranteed standards of living both for the working population and for retired people 欧洲社会宪章:欧盟(EU)于1989年起草的一份雇员宪章,该宪章规定员工享有如下权利:公平的工资,男女同工同酬,安全的工作环境,培训,结社和劳资谈判自由。同时该宪章还为残疾工人提供保障,允许国际间人员自由流动,并向在职人员和退休人员提供生活保障 Full form 全称为 **European Social Charter**. Also called 亦称作 **Social Charter**

escalate /ˈeskəleɪt/ *verb* to increase steadily 逐步增长

escalation clause /ˌeskəˈleɪʃ(ə)n klɔːz/ *noun* same as 同 **escalator clause**

escalator clause /ˈeskəleɪtə klɔːz/ *noun* a clause in a contract allowing for regular price increases because of increased costs, or regular wage increases because of the increased cost of living 调整条款,价格变动条款:合同中允许价格随成本的增加而定期增加,或允许工资随生活费用的增加而定期增加的条款

escape clause /ɪˈskeɪp klɔːz/ *noun* a clause in a contract which allows one of the parties to avoid carrying out the terms of the contract under conditions 免责条款:合同中允许一方在特定条件下不履行合同条款的条款

escrow /ˈeskrəʊ/ *noun US* an agreement between two parties that something should be held by a third party until conditions are fulfilled (美)第三方暂管契约:双方达成的关于某物由第三方代管直到满足约定条件为止的协议

escrow account /ˈeskrəʊ əˌkaʊnt/ *noun US* an account where money is held in escrow until a contract is signed or until goods are delivered (美)第三方暂管账户:由第三方持有直到合同签署或货物运到时才付现的账户

ESOP *abbr* employee share ownership plan 雇员持股计划

establishment /ɪˈstæblɪʃmənt/ *noun* **1.** a commercial business 商业企业,公司 ○ *He runs an important printing establishment*. 他经营一家大

型的印刷企业。**2.** the number of people working in a company 定员，编制

establishment charges /ɪˈstæblɪʃmənt ˌtʃɑːdʒɪz/ *plural noun* the cost of people and property in a company's accounts（企业）开办费：公司账户里人员和房产成本

estate /ɪˈsteɪt/ *noun* property left by a dead person 遗产

estate agency /ɪˈsteɪt ˌeɪdʒənsi/ *noun* an office which arranges for the sale of properties 房地产代理机构

estate duty /ɪˈsteɪt ˌdjuːti/ *noun* a tax paid on the property left by a dead person 遗产税（NOTE：now called **inheritance tax** 现在称为 **inheritance tax**）

estimate *noun* /ˈestɪmət/ **1.** a calculation of the probable cost, size or time of something（成本、尺寸或时间的）估算，估计 ○ *Can you give me an estimate of how much time was spent on the job?* 你能否估计一下这项工作花了多少时间？**2.** a calculation by a contractor or seller of a service of how much something is likely to cost, given to a client in advance of an order（承包商或卖方在客户下订单前的）估价，概算 ○ *You should ask for an estimate before committing yourselves.* 你在作出承诺之前应先索取估价。○ *Before we can give the grant we must have an estimate of the total costs involved.* 在我们拨款之前，必须先对总成本进行概算。○ *Unfortunately the final bill was quite different from the estimate.* 很不幸，最后的账单和原先的估计差距非常大。■ *verb* /ˈestɪmeɪt/ to calculate the probable cost, size or time of something 估计，估量（成本、尺寸或时间）○ *to estimate that it will cost £1m* or *to estimate costs at £1m* 估计将耗费100万英镑 ○ *We estimate current sales at only 60% of last year.* 我们估计目前的销售额只有去年的60%。

estimated /ˈestɪmeɪtɪd/ *adjective* calculated approximately 估计的，近似计算的 ○ *estimated sales* 估计销售额 ○ *Costs were slightly more than the estimated figure.* 成本比估计数字稍高一些。

estimation /ˌestɪˈmeɪʃ(ə)n/ *noun* an approximate calculation 估计

estimator /ˈestɪmeɪtə/ *noun* a person whose job is to calculate estimates for carrying out work 估算员，预算者

EU *abbr* European Union 欧盟 ○ *EU ministers met today in Brussels.* 欧盟各国部长今天在布鲁塞尔会面。○ *The USA is increasing its trade with the EU.* 美国不断增加与欧盟的贸易。

euro /ˈjʊərəʊ/ *noun* a unit of currency adopted as legal tender in several European countries from January 1st, 1999 欧元：货币单位，1999年1月1日起被一些欧洲国家采用作法定货币 ○ *Many articles are priced in euros.* 许多物品都以欧元标价。○ *What's the exchange rate for the euro?* 欧元汇率是多少？（NOTE：The plural is **euro** or **euros** 复数为 **euro** 或 **euros**）

'...cross-border mergers in the European Union have shot up since the introduction of the euro'
"自推行欧元后，欧盟内部的跨国合并数量猛增"［*Investors Chronicle*《投资者纪事》］

Euro- /jʊərəʊ/ *prefix* referring to Europe or the European Union 欧洲的；欧盟的

euro account /ˈjʊərəʊ əˌkaʊnt/

noun a bank account in euros 欧元账户（NOTE：written Ä before numbers：**Ä250**：say：'two hundred and fifty euros'在数字前写为Ä：**Ä250**：表示"250欧元"）

Eurobond /ˈjʊərəʊbɒnd/ *noun* a long-term bearer bond issued by an international corporation or government outside its country of origin and sold to purchasers who pay in a Eurocurrency，sold on the Eurobond market 欧洲债券：由国际企业或政府在本国外发行、购买方以欧洲货币支付、并在欧洲债券市场上交易的长期不记名债券

Eurocheque /ˈjʊərəʊtʃek/ *noun* a cheque which can be cashed in any European bank. The Eurocheque system is based in Brussels 欧洲通用支票：能在任何一家欧洲银行兑现的支票。欧洲通用支票系统的本部设在布鲁塞尔

Eurocommercial paper /ˌjʊərəʊtkəmɜːʃ(ə)l ˈpeɪpə/ *noun* a form of short-term borrowing in Eurocurrencies 欧洲商业票据：以欧洲货币计值的一种短期借款 Abbreviation 缩写 **ECP**

eurocredit /ˈjʊərəʊˌkredɪt/ *noun* a large bank loan in a Eurocurrency，usually provided by a group of banks to a large commercial undertaking 欧洲信贷：以欧洲货币计值的大额银行贷款，通常由几家银行联合向大型商业机构提供

Eurocurrency /ˈjʊərəʊkʌrənsi/ *noun* any currency used for trade within Europe but outside its country of origin，the Eurodollar being the most important 欧洲货币：欧洲各国商业银行的外币存款，其中最重要的是欧洲美元 ○ *a Eurocurrency loan* 欧洲货币贷款 ○ *the Eurocurrency market* 欧洲货币市场

eurodeposit /ˈjʊərəʊdɪˌpɒzɪt/ *noun* a deposit of Eurodollars in a bank outside the US 欧洲美元存款：存放在美国以外银行的欧洲美元存款

Eurodollar /ˈjʊərəʊdɒlə/ *noun* a US dollar deposited in a bank outside the US，used mainly for trade within Europe 欧洲美元：存放在美国以外银行并主要用于欧洲贸易的美元 ○ *a Eurodollar loan* 欧洲美元贷款 ○ *the Eurodollar markets* 欧洲美元市场

euroequity /ˈjʊərəʊˌekwɪti/ *noun* a share in an international company traded on European stock markets outside its country of origin 欧洲股票：在发行国以外的欧洲股票市场上市的企业股票

Euroland /ˈjʊərəʊlænd/ *noun* same as 同 **Eurozone**

euronote /ˈjʊərəʊˌnəʊt/ *noun* a shortterm Eurocurrency bearer note 欧洲票据：短期欧洲货币不记名票据

euro-option /ˈjʊərəʊˌɒpʃ(ə)n/ *noun* an option to buy European bonds at a later date 欧式期权：在未来某个日期购买欧洲债券的权利

Europe /ˈjʊərəp/ *noun* **1.** the continent of Europe，the part of the world to the west of Asia，from Russia to Ireland 欧洲 ○ *Most of the countries of Western Europe are members of the EU.* 大多数西欧国家都是欧盟成员国。○ *Poland is in eastern Europe，and Greece，Spain and Portugal are in southern Europe.* 波兰在东欧，希腊、西班牙和葡萄牙在南欧。**2.** the European Union，including the UK 欧盟（包括英国）○ *Canadian exports to Eu-*

rope have risen by 25%. 加拿大对欧盟的出口增长了25%。

European /ˌjʊərəˈpiːən/ *adjective* referring to Europe 欧洲的 ○ *They do business with several European countries*. 他们与若干个欧洲国家有商务往来。

European Accounting Association /ˌjʊərəpiːən əˈkaʊntɪŋ əˌsəʊsieɪʃ(ə)n/ *noun* an organisation for teachers and researchers in accountancy, founded in 1977 and based in Brussels, that EAA aims to be a forum for European research in the subject 欧洲会计学会：1977年成立的一家会计学教师及研究员的组织，总部设在布鲁塞尔，其宗旨是成为欧洲会计学研究的论坛 Abbreviation 缩写 **EAA**

European Bank for Reconstruction and Development /ˌjʊərəpiːən bæŋk fə riːkənˌstrʌktʃ(ə)n ən dɪˈveləpmənt/ *noun* a bank, based in London, which channels aid from the EU to Eastern European countries 欧洲复兴开发银行：总部设在伦敦、通过欧盟向东欧国家提供援助的一家银行 Abbreviation 缩写 **EBRD**

European Central Bank /ˌjʊərəpiːən ˌsentrəl ˈbæŋk/ *noun* central bank for most of the countries in the European Union, those which have accepted European Monetary Union and have the euro as their common currency 欧洲中央银行：大多数欧盟成员国的中央银行，这些国家承认欧洲货币联盟，并以欧元为通用货币 Abbreviation 缩写 **ECB**

'...the ECB begins with some $300 billion of foreign exchange reserves, far more than any other central bank'
"欧洲中央银行以大约3,000亿美元的外汇储备作为启动资金，这一数字远远超过了其他中央银行"［*Investors Chronicle*《投资者纪事》］

'... any change in the European Central Bank's statutes must be agreed and ratified by all EU member nations'
"任何对欧洲中央银行条例的修改，都必须经过全体欧盟成员国同意和批准"［*Times*《泰晤士报》］

European Currency Unit /ˌjʊərəpiːən ˈkʌrənsi ˌjuːnɪt/ *noun* a monetary unit used within the EU 欧洲货币单位 Abbreviation 缩写 **ECU**

European Investment Bank /ˌjʊərəpiːən ɪnˈvestmənt bæŋk/ *noun* a financial institution whose main task is to further regional development within the EU by financing capital projects, modernising or converting undertakings, and developing new activities 欧洲投资银行：一家金融机构，主要宗旨是提供资本项目融资，帮助企业完成现代化或转型以及发展新业务，以促进欧盟的地区发展 Abbreviation 缩写 **EIB**

European Monetary System /ˌjʊərəpiːən ˈmʌnɪt(ə)ri ˌsɪstəm/ *noun* the first stage of economic and monetary union of the EU, which came into force in March 1979, giving stable, but adjustable, exchange rates 欧洲货币体系：欧盟经济与货币联盟的第一阶段，于1979年3月生效，它提供稳定但可调整的汇率 Abbreviation 缩写 **EMS**

European Monetary Union /ˌjʊərəpiːən ˈmʌnɪt(ə)ri ˌjuːnjən/ *noun* the process by which some of the member states of the EU joined together to adopt the euro as their common currency on 1st January 1999 欧洲货币联盟：1999年1月1日，部分欧

盟成员国联合采纳欧元作为他们的通用货币并藉此成立的联盟 Abbreviation 缩写 **EMU**

European Social Charter /ˌjʊərəpiːən ˌsəʊʃ(ə)l ˈtʃɑːtə/ *noun* Full form of **ESC** 为 **ESC** 的全称

European Union /ˌjʊərəpiːən ˈjuːnjən/ *noun* a group of European countries linked together by the Treaty of Rome. The European Community was set up in 1957 and changed its name to the European Union when it adopted the single market. It has now grown to include twenty-seven member states. These are: Austria, Belgium, Bulgaria, Cyprus, the Czech Republic, Denmark, Estonia, Finland, France, Germany, Greece, Hungary, Ireland, Italy, Latvia, Lithuania, Luxembourg, Malta, the Netherlands, Poland, Portugal, Romania, Slovakia, Slovenia, Spain, Sweden and the United Kingdom. The member states of the EU are linked together by the Treaty of Rome in such a way that trade is more free, that money can be moved from one country to another freely, that people can move from one country to another more freely and that people can work more freely in other countries of the group (the four fundamental freedoms) 欧洲联盟,欧盟:在《罗马条约》基础上建立起联系的一组欧洲国家。1957 年,欧洲共同体成立,采纳单一市场后更名为欧洲联盟。欧盟现已发展成一个拥有 27 个成员国的组织,这些国家是:奥地利、比利时、保加利亚、塞浦路斯、捷克、丹麦、爱沙尼亚、芬兰、法国、德国、希腊、匈牙利、爱尔兰、意大利、拉脱维亚、立陶宛、卢森堡、马耳他、荷兰、波兰、葡萄牙、罗马尼亚、斯洛伐克、斯洛文尼亚、西班牙、瑞典和英国。以《罗马条约》为纽带,欧盟成员国之间的贸易更自由,资金可以在各国之间自由流动,人们也可以在各国之间更自由地迁移,劳动者可以更自由地在其他成员国工作(即四大基本自由)

euroyen /ˈjʊərəʊˌjen/ *noun* a Japanese yen deposited in a European bank and used for trade within Europe 欧洲日元:存放在欧洲银行并主要用于欧洲贸易的日元

Eurozone /ˈjʊərəʊzəʊn/ *noun* the European countries which use the euro as a common currency, seen as a group 欧元区:以欧元作为通用货币的欧洲国家,他们被看作一个团体 Also called 亦称作 **Euroland**

'...the European Central Bank left the door open yesterday for a cut in Eurozone interest rates'
"昨天,欧洲中央银行保留了下调欧元区利率的可能性"[*Financial Times*《金融时报》]
'...a sustained recovery in the euro will require either a sharp slowdown in US growth or a rise in inflation and interest rates in the Eurozone beyond that already discounted'
"欧元持续复苏需要满足以下任意一个条件:美国经济急剧衰落,或者是欧元区通胀率和利率折扣外的上升"[*Investors Chronicle*《投资者纪事》]

EVA *abbr* economic value added 经济增加值

evade /ɪˈveɪd/ *verb* to try to avoid something 逃避,躲避

evaluate /ɪˈvæljueɪt/ *verb* to calculate a value for something 评价,估价 ○ *to evaluate costs* 估价成本 ○ *We will evaluate jobs on the basis of their contribution to the organisation as a whole.* 我们将从整体上就各个职位对

组织的贡献来对它们进行评估。○ *We need to evaluate the experience and qualifications of all the candidates.* 我们需要评价所有候选人的经验和资历。

evaluation /ɪˌvælju'eɪʃ(ə)n/ *noun* the calculation of value 评价,估价

evasion /ɪ'veɪʒ(ə)n/ *noun* the act of avoiding something 逃避,偷漏

EVR *abbr* Electronic Version of the Tax Return 电子报税表

ex /eks/ *prefix* **1.** out of or from 从,自 **2.** without 不包括

exact /ɪg'zækt/ *adjective* strictly correct, not varying in any way from, e.g. not any more or less than, what is stated 精确的,毫无偏差的 ○ *The exact time is 10.27.* 确切的时间是10:27。○ *The salesgirl asked me if I had the exact sum, since the shop had no change.* 女售货员问我是否有刚好的钱数,因为商店里没有零钱。

exact interest /ɪgˌzækt 'ɪntrəst/ *noun* an annual interest calculated on the basis of 365 days, as opposed to ordinary interest which is calculated on 360 days 精确利息:一年按365天计算的利息(普通利息一年按360天计算)

exactly /ɪg'zæktli/ *adverb* not varying in any way from, e.g. not any more or less than, what is stated 精确地,毫无偏差地 ○ *The total cost was exactly £6,500.* 总费用是6,500英镑整。

ex-all /ˌeks'ɔːl/ *adjective* referring to a share price where the share is sold without the dividend, rights issue, or any other current issue 除净:股票出售时除去股利、权证发行或其他当期权利后的股价 Abbreviation 缩写 **xa**

examination /ɪgˌzæmɪ'neɪʃ(ə)n/ *noun* an act of looking at something very carefully to see if it is acceptable 检查,细查

examine /ɪg'zæmɪn/ *verb* to look at someone or something very carefully 检查,细查 ○ *Customs officials asked to examine the inside of the car.* 海关官员要求对车内进行检查。○ *The police are examining the papers from the managing director's safe.* 警察正在检查从经理保险箱里取出的文件。

examiner /ɪg'zæmɪnə/ *noun* a person who examines something to see if it is correct 检查人,审查人

ex ante /ˌeks 'ænti/ *adverb* before the event. An ex ante budget, or standard, is set before a period of activity commences, and is based on the best information available at that time on expected levels of cost, performance, etc. 事先,事前(在活动开始前,需根据当时可用的关于预计成本、表现水平等最佳信息来安排事前预算或标准) Compare 比较 **ex post**

exceed /ɪk'siːd/ *verb* to be more than 超过,胜过 ○ *a discount not exceeding 15%* 不超过15%的折扣 ○ *Last year costs exceeded 20% of income for the first time.* 去年成本首次超过了收入的20%。

except /ɪk'sept/ *preposition, conjunction* not including 不包括,除…之外 ○ *VAT is levied on all goods and services except books, newspapers and children's clothes.* 除书籍、报纸和儿童服装之外,所有的商品和劳务都要征收增值税。○ *Sales are rising in all markets except the Far East.* 除远东以外,所有市场的销售额都在增加。

excepted /ɪk'septɪd/ *adverb* not including 除外地

exceptional /ɪkˈsepʃən(ə)l/ *adjective* different or not usual 例外的，异常的

exceptional items /ɪkˌsepʃən(ə)l ˈaɪtəmz/ *plural noun* **1.** items which arise from normal trading but which are unusual because of their size or nature; such items are shown separately in a note to the company's accounts but not on the face of the P & L account unless they are profits or losses on the sale or termination of an operation, or costs of a fundamental reorganisation or restructuring which have a material effect on the nature and focus of the reporting entity's operations, or profits or losses on the disposal of fixed assets 例外项目：在正常交易过程中产生但数额或性质异常的项目。这些项目被记在报表的单独注释中，而不在损益表中呈列，除非它们是出售或终止某项运营的损益，或是对呈报实体的运营性质及业务重心有重大影响的基础性重组或改组的成本，或是固定资产出售的损益 **2.** items in a balance sheet which do not appear there each year and which are included in the accounts before the pre-tax profit is calculated, as opposed to extraordinary items which are calculated after the pretax profit 非经常性项目：并非每年都出现在资产负债表中的项目，且这些项目呈列在未计算税前利润的报表中，这有别于已计税前利润的特殊项目

excess /ɪkˈses/ *noun*; /ˈekses/ *adjective* an amount which is more than what is allowed 过多的量，超额，过多的 ○ *an excess of expenditure over revenue* 支出超过收入 ○ *Excess costs have caused us considerable problems.* 超额成本给我们带来了很大麻烦。

'... most airlines give business class the same baggage allowance as first class, which can save large sums in excess baggage'
"大多数航空公司的商务舱都提供与头等舱一样的行李优惠，这可以节省大笔的超重行李费"［*Business Traveller*《商旅》］

'...control of materials provides manufacturers with an opportunity to reduce the amount of money tied up in excess materials'
"原材料控制使制造商有机会减少过剩原材料占用的资金"［*Duns Business Month*《邓氏商业月刊》］

excess capacity /ˌekses kəˈpæsɪti/ *noun* spare capacity which is not being used 剩余生产能力

excessive /ɪkˈsesɪv/ *adjective* too large 过大的 ○ *Excessive production costs made the product uneconomic.* 过高的生产成本导致产品赚不到钱。

excess profit /ˌekses ˈprɒfɪt/ *noun* a profit which is higher than what is thought to be normal 超额利润：超过正常利润的利润

excess profits tax /ˌekses ˈprɒfɪts tæks/ *noun* a tax on profits which are higher than what is thought to be normal 超额利润税：对超额利润的课税

excess reserves /ɪkˌses rɪˈzɜːvs/ *plural noun US* reserves held by a financial institution that are higher than those required by the regulatory authorities. As such reserves may indicate that demand for loans is low, banks often sell their excess reserves to other institutions（美）过剩准备金：金融机构持有的超出监管机构要求金额的准备金。由于这类过剩准备金可

能意味贷款需求较低,因此银行通常会将其过剩准备金出售给其他机构

exchange /ɪksˈtʃeɪndʒ/ *noun* **1.** the act of giving one thing for another 交换 **2.** a market for shares, commodities, futures, etc. 交易所 ■ *verb* **1.** □ **to exchange something (for something else)** to give one thing in place of something else 用…交换(…) ○ *He exchanged his motorcycle for a car*. 他用摩托车换了一辆小轿车。○ *Goods can be exchanged only on production of the sales slip*. 必须出示销售小票才能换货。**2.** to change money of one country for money of another 换汇,汇兑 ○ *to exchange euros for pounds* 把欧元兑换成英镑

'... under the barter agreements, Nigeria will export crude oil in exchange for trucks, food, planes and chemicals'
"根据易货协议,尼日利亚将出口原油,以换取卡车、食品、飞机和化学品" [*Wall Street Journal*《华尔街日报》]

exchangeable /ɪksˈtʃeɪndʒəb(ə)l/ *adjective* possible to exchange 可交换的,可兑换的

exchange control /ɪksˈtʃeɪndʒ kənˌtrəʊl/ *noun* the control by a government of the way in which its currency may be exchanged for foreign currencies 外汇管理:政府对本国货币与外币兑换方式进行的管理

exchange controls /ɪksˈtʃeɪndʒ kənˌtrəʊlz/ *plural noun* government restrictions on changing the local currency into foreign currency 外汇管制:政府对本国货币与外币兑换的限制 ○ *The government had to impose exchange controls to stop the rush to buy dollars*. 政府不得不实行外汇管制,以平息对美元的抢购。○ *They say the government is going to lift exchange controls*. 他们说政府即将取消外汇管制。

exchange cross rates /ɪksˌtʃeɪndʒ ˈkrɒs reɪts/ *plural noun* rates of exchange for two currencies, shown against each other, but in terms of a third currency, often the US dollar 交叉汇率:两种货币之间互为参照(第三方货币通常以美元为参照)的汇率 Also called 亦称作 **cross rates**

exchange dealer /ɪksˈtʃeɪndʒ ˌdiːlə/ *noun* a person who buys and sells foreign currency 外汇交易商,外汇交易员

exchange dealings /ɪksˈtʃeɪndʒ ˌdiːlɪŋz/ *plural noun* the buying and selling of foreign currency 外汇交易

exchange gain /ɪksˈtʃeɪndʒ geɪn/, **exchange loss** /ɪksˈtʃeɪndʒ lɒs/ *noun* a gain or loss made from changes in the exchange rate which take place during the period of the transaction 汇兑损益:在交易期间由于汇率波动造成的损益

exchange of contracts /ɪksˌtʃeɪndʒ əv ˈkɒntrækts/ *noun* the point in the sale of property when the buyer and the seller both sign the contract of sale, which then becomes binding 合同交换:在财产销售中,买卖双方在合同上签字使合同具有约束力的阶段

exchange premium /ɪksˈtʃeɪndʒ ˌpriːmiəm/ *noun* an extra cost above the usual rate for buying a foreign currency 外汇升水:高于正常外汇买价的超额费用

exchanger /ɪksˈtʃeɪndʒə/ *noun* a person who buys and sells foreign currency 买卖外汇者,货币兑换商

exchange rate mechanism /ɪksˈtʃeɪndʒ reɪt ˌmekənɪz(ə)m/ *noun* a former method of stabilising exchange rates within the European Monetary System, where currencies could only move up or down within a narrow band (usually 2.25% either way, but for some currencies this is widened to 6%) without involving a realignment of all the currencies in the system 汇率机制:欧洲货币体系曾使用的稳定汇率的方法,它规定各国货币只允许小范围上下浮动(通常在2.25%上下,但部分货币可扩大到6%),而无须重新调整体系内所有的货币

exchange transaction /ɪksˈtʃeɪndʒ trænˌzækʃən/ *noun* a purchase or sale of foreign currency 外汇交易

Exchequer /ɪksˈtʃekə/ □ **the Exchequer 1.** the fund of all money received by the government of the UK from taxes and other revenues 国库(资金):英国政府收到的来自税收和其他收入的全部货币资金 **2.** the British government's account with the Bank of England 英国政府在英格兰银行开立的账户 **3.** the British government department dealing with public revenue 英国财政部

excise duty /ˈeksaɪz ˌdjuːti/ *noun* a tax on goods such as alcohol and petrol which are produced in the country 消费税:政府对国内生产的酒类、汽油等产品所征的税

exciseman /ˈeksaɪzmæn/ *noun* a person who works in the Excise Department 税务员

excise tax /ˈɪksaɪz tæks/ *noun US* a tax levied for a particular purpose (美)货物税:为特定目的征收的税

exclude /ɪkˈskluːd/ *verb* to keep out, or not to include 排除…在外,不包括 ○ *The interest charges have been excluded from the document.* 利息费用不包括在这张单据内。○ *Damage by fire is excluded from the policy.* 火灾引起的损失不在承保范围之内。

exclusion /ɪkˈskluːʒ(ə)n/ *noun* the act of not including something 排除

exclusion clause /ɪkˈskluːʒ(ə)n klɔːz/ *noun* a clause in an insurance policy or warranty which says which items or events are not covered 除外条款:保险单或保证书中声明哪些事项不包括的条款

exclusive agreement /ɪkˌskluːsɪv əˈgriːmənt/ *noun* an agreement where a person is made sole agent for a product in a market 独家代理协议

exclusive of tax /ɪkˌskluːsɪv əv ˈtæks/ *adjective* not including tax 不包括税款 ○ *All payments are exclusive of tax.* 所有的付款金额都不包括税款。

exclusivity /ˌekskluːˈsɪvɪtɪ/ *noun* the exclusive right to market a product 独家经销权

ex coupon /eks ˈkuːpɒn/ *adverb* without the interest coupons or after interest has been paid 无息票;息单已付

execute /ˈeksɪkjuːt/ *verb* to carry out an order 履行,执行(命令) ○ *Failure to execute orders may lead to dismissal.* 不执行命令可能会被解雇。○ *There were many practical difficulties in executing the managing director's instructions.* 执行总经理的指示有许多实际困难。

execution /ˌeksɪˈkjuːʃ(ə)n/ *noun* the carrying out of a commercial order or contract (商业指令或合同的)执行

executive /ɪɡˈzekjʊtɪv/ *adjective* putting decisions into action 执行的，实施的

executive committee /ɪɡˌzekjʊtɪv kəˈmɪti/ *noun* a committee which runs a society or a club（社团或俱乐部的）执行委员会

executive director /ɪɡˌzekjʊtɪv daɪˈrektə/ *noun* **1.** a director who works fulltime in the company, as opposed to a 'nonexecutive director' 执行董事：在公司工作的全职董事，与"非执行董事"相对 **2.** a senior employee of an organisation who is usually in charge of one or other of its main functions, e. g. sales or human relations, and is usually, but not always, a member of the board of directors 执行经理：公司的高级雇员，通常负责公司的某些主要职能部门（如销售或人事关系），一般是董事会的成员

executive power /ɪɡˌzekjʊtɪv ˈpaʊə/ *noun* a right to act as director or to put decisions into action 执行权：作为董事实施决策的权利

executive share option scheme /ɪɡˌzekjʊtɪv ˈʃeər ɒpʃən ˌskiːm/ *noun* a special scheme for senior managers, by which they can buy shares in the company they work for at a fixed price at a later date 管理人员股票购买优先权方案：允许高级管理人员在未来某个日期按固定价格购买所在公司股票的一种特别方案

executor /ɪɡˈzekjʊtə/ *noun* a person or firm that sees that the terms of a will are carried out 遗嘱执行人 ○ *She was named executor of her brother's will*. 她被指定为她哥哥的遗嘱执行人。

executrix /ɪɡˈzekjʊtrɪks/ *noun* a female executor 女执行官，女遗嘱执行人

exemplary damages /ɪɡˌzempləri ˈdæmɪdʒɪz/ *plural noun* heavy damages which punish the defendant for the loss or harm caused to the claimant, awarded to show that the court feels the defendant has behaved badly towards the claimant 超过实际损失的赔偿，惩戒性赔偿：对被告处以巨额损害惩罚，作为对原告造成损失或伤害的赔偿。这种处罚表示法庭认定被告作用于原告的行为极为恶劣

exempt /ɪɡˈzempt/ *adjective* not forced to do something, especially not forced to obey a particular law or rule, or not forced to pay something 豁免的（尤指无须强制遵守特定法律或规则，或无须强制支付某物）○ *Anyone over 65 is exempt from charges* 65 岁以上的老人一概免费 ○ *He was exempt from military service in his country*. 他被免除在本国服兵役。□ **exempt from tax** not required to pay tax 免税 ○ *As a non-profit-making organisation we are exempt from tax*. 作为非营利组织，我们不用纳税。

'Companies with sales under $500,000 a year will be exempt from the minimum-wage requirements'
"年销售额在 50 万美元以下的公司将不用遵守最低工资要求"［*Nation's Business*《国民商务》］

exempt assets /ɪɡˌzempt ˈæsets/ *plural noun* assets such as cars which are not subject to capital gains tax when sold 免税资产：无须缴交资本利得税的售出资产，如汽车

exempt gift /ɪɡˌzempt ˈɡɪft/ *noun* a gift that is not subject to US gift tax 免税赠与：无须缴交美国赠与税的馈赠

exempt investment fund /ɪɡ-

ˌzempt ɪnˈvestmənt fʌnd/ *noun* in the United Kingdom, a collective investment, usually a unit trust, for investors who have certain tax privileges, e.g., charities or contributors to pension plans 免税投资基金：英国面向享有特定税务特权投资者(如慈善机构或退休金计划缴款人)的集体投资基金(通常是单位信托)

exemption /ɪgˈzempʃ(ə)n/ *noun* the act of exempting something from a contract or from a tax 豁免，免税 □ **exemption from tax, tax exemption** the fact of being free from having to pay tax 免税 ○ *As a non-profit-making organisation you can claim tax exemption.* 作为非盈利组织，你可以要求免税。

exempt supplies /ɪgˌzempt səˈplaɪz/ *plural noun* products or services on which the supplier does not have to charge VAT, e.g., the purchase of, or rent on, property and financial services 免增值税供应品：供应商无须缴交增值税的产品或劳务，如财产及金融服务的购买或租赁

exercise /ˈeksəsaɪz/ *noun* **1.** a use of something 行使，运用 **2.** a financial year 财政年度 ○ *during the current exercise* 在本财政年度内 ■ *verb* to use 行使，运用 ○ *The chairwoman exercised her veto to block the motion.* 女主席行使否决权，阻止该动议的通过。

exercise date /ˈeksəsaɪz deɪt/ *noun* a date when an option can be put into effect (期权)生效日期

exercise price /ˈeksəsaɪz praɪs/ *noun* a price at which an option will be put into effect (期权)协定价格

ex gratia /ˌeks ˈgreɪʃə/ *adjective* as an act of favour, without obligation 通融的，作为恩惠的

exit charge /ˈegzɪt tʃɑːdʒ/, **exit fee** /ˈegzɪt fiː/ *noun* a charge sometimes made by a trust when selling units in a unit trust or when selling out of a PEP 退出费：当出售单位投资信托中的一个单位或全部出售个人权益计划(PEP)时，投资信托公司有时会收取的费用

exit price /ˈeksɪt praɪs/ *noun* the price at which an investor sells an investment or at which a firm sells up and leaves a market 脱手价格，脱售价格：投资者出售一项投资或某公司出售全部投资并退出市场的价格

ex officio /ˌeks əˈfɪʃiəʊ/ *adjective, adverb* because of an office held 依职位(的) ○ *The treasurer is ex officio a member* or *an ex officio member of the finance committee.* 财务主任依职位是财务委员会的当然委员。

expand /ɪkˈspænd/ *verb* to get bigger, or make something bigger (使)扩大，(使)扩张 ○ *an expanding economy* 扩张中的经济 ○ *The company is expanding fast.* 这个公司在迅速发展。○ *We have had to expand our sales force.* 我们需要扩充销售人员队伍。

expansion /ɪkˈspænʃən/ *noun* an increase in size 扩大，扩张 ○ *The expansion of the domestic market.* 国内市场的扩张。○ *The company had difficulty in financing its current expansion programme.* 公司目前的扩张方案存在融资方面的困难。

'...inflation-adjusted GNP moved up at a 1.3% annual rate, its worst performance since the economic expansion began'
"通货膨胀调整后的国民生产总值年增长率是1.3%，这是该国经济发展以来表现最差的一年"[*Fortune*《财富》]

'...the businesses we back range from start-up ventures to established businesses

in need of further capital for expansion' "不论是新创办的企业还是成熟的企业，只要它们需要更多资金来实现扩张，我们都能提供资助"［*Times*《泰晤士报》］
'... the group is undergoing a period of rapid expansion and this has created an exciting opportunity for a qualified accountant' "该集团正处于迅猛发展的时期，这为能胜任的会计师提供了大好机会"［*Financial Times*《金融时报》］

ex parte /ˌeks ˈpɑːti/ *Latin phrase meaning* 'on behalf of'（拉丁语）代表，单方面地

expected value /ɪkˌspektɪd ˈvæljuː/ *noun* the future value of a course of action, weighted according to the probability that the course of action will actually occur. If the possible course of action produces income of £10,000 and has a 10% chance of occurring, its expected value is 10% of £10,000 or £1,000 期望值：一个行动方案按其实现概率加权计算得出的未来价值。假设行动方案能产生一万英镑的收入，实现概率为10%，则其期望值为一万英镑的10%即1,000英镑

expenditure /ɪkˈspendɪtʃə/ *noun* the amount of money spent 支出

expense /ɪkˈspens/ *noun* money spent 花费 ○ *It is not worth the expense*. 这东西不值这么多钱。○ *The expense is too much for my bank balance*. 对于我的银行存款余额来说，这笔费用太大了。○ *The likely profits do not justify the expense of setting up the project*. 可能得到的利润不足以说明启动该工程所花费用的值当。○ *It was well worth the expense to get really high-quality equipment*. 真正高质量的设备是物超所值的。

expense account /ɪkˈspens əˌkaʊnt/ *noun* an allowance of money which a business pays for an employee to spend on travelling and entertaining clients in connection with that business 费用账户，差旅招待费账户：公司为员工的差旅费及招待客户而拨出的资金 ○ *I'll put this lunch on my expense account*. 我要把这次午餐记在我的费用账户上。

expenses /ɪkˈspensɪz/ *plural noun* money paid to cover the costs incurred by someone when doing something 支出，经费 ○ *The salary offered is £10,000 plus expenses*. 薪水是一万英镑，外加活动经费。○ *She has a high salary and all her travel expenses are paid by the company*. 她的工资很高，而且她所有的差旅费都由公司买单。

expert system /ˈekspɜːt ˌsɪstəm/ *noun* software that applies the knowledge, advice and rules defined by experts in a particular field to a user's data to help solve a problem 专家系统：将特定领域专家界定的知识、建议和规则应用到用户的数据中以帮助解决问题的软件

expiration /ˌekspəˈreɪʃ(ə)n/ *noun* the act of coming to an end 到期 ○ *the expiration of an insurance policy* 保险单到期 ○ *to repay before the expiration of the stated period* 在规定日期前偿还

expire /ɪkˈspaɪə/ *verb* to come to an end 到期，期满 ○ *The lease expires in 2010*. 租约将于2010年到期。

expiry /ɪkˈspaɪəri/ *noun* the act of coming to an end 到期 ○ *the expiry of an insurance policy* 保险单到期

exponent /ɪkˈspəʊnənt/ *noun* a number indicating how many times a base number is to be multiplied to produce a power. It is printed in small characters after the base number 指数,幂

export /ɪkˈspɔːt/ *verb* to send goods to foreign countries for sale 出口 ○ *50% of our production is exported*. 我们的产品有 50% 供出口。○ *The company imports raw materials and exports the finished products*. 该公司进口原材料,出口成品。

exportation /ˌekspɔːˈteɪʃ(ə)n/ *noun* the act of sending goods to foreign countries for sale 输出,出口

Export Credit Guarantee Department /ˌekspɔːt ˌkredɪt gærənˈtiː dɪˌpɑːtmənt/ *noun* a British government department which insures sellers of exports sold on credit against the possibility of nonpayment by the purchasers 出口信贷担保局:英国的一个政府部门,它为本国出口商向外国提供的赊销提供担保,以防进口商拒绝付款 Abbreviation 缩写 **ECGD**

export department /ˈekspɔːt dɪˌpɑːtmənt/ *noun* the section of a company which deals in sales to foreign countries (公司的)出口部

export duty /ˈekspɔːt ˌdjuːti/ *noun* a tax paid on goods sent out of a country for sale 出口税

exporter /ɪkˈspɔːtə/ *noun* a person, company or country that sells goods in foreign countries 出口商 ○ *a major furniture exporter* 一家大型家具出口商 ○ *Canada is an important exporter of oil* or *an important oil exporter*. 加拿大是重要的石油出口国。

export house /ˈekspɔːt haʊs/ *noun* a company which specialises in the export of goods manufactured by other companies 出口公司:专门出口其他公司制造的商品的公司

exporting /ekˈspɔːtɪŋ/ *adjective* sending goods out of a country 出口的

export licence /ˈekspɔːt ˌlaɪs(ə)ns/ *noun* a government permit allowing something to be exported 出口许可证 ○ *The government has refused an export licence for computer parts*. 政府拒绝发放计算机部件的出口许可证。

export manager /ˈekspɔːt ˌmænɪdʒə/ *noun* the person in charge of an export department in a company 出口部经理 ○ *The export manager planned to set up a sales force in Southern Europe*. 出口部经理计划在南欧建立一个销售团队。○ *Sales managers from all export markets report to our export manager*. 所有出口市场的销售经理都向我们的出口部经理汇报。

exports /ˈekspɔːts/ *plural noun* goods sent to a foreign country to be sold 出口商品 ○ *Exports to Africa have increased by 25%*. 对非洲的出口量增加了 25%。(NOTE: Usually used in the plural, but the singular form is used before a noun 通常用复数,但在名词前用单数)

ex post /ˌeks ˈpəʊst/ *adverb* after the event. An ex post budget, or standard, is set after the end of a period of activity, when it can represent the optimum achievable level of performance in the conditions which were experienced. Thus the budget can be flexed, and standards can reflect factors such as unanticipated changes in technology and in price levels 事后:事后预算或标准是在一个活动时期结束后建立,以反映在活动期间具体条件下可以取得的最佳表现水平,藉此可以调

整预算，而标准则可以反映事先未预见的技术及价格变动等因素 Compare 比较 **ex ante**

exposure /ɪk'spəʊʒə/ *noun* **1.** publicity given to an organisation or product（组织或产品的）曝光，宣传 ○ *Our company has achieved more exposure since we decided to advertise nationally.* 自从我们决定在全国范围内打广告后，公司得到了更多的曝光。**2.** the amount of risk which a lender or investor runs（贷款人或投资者承受的）风险敞口 ○ *He is trying to limit his exposure in the property market.* 他尽量避免在房地产市场风险敞口的扩大。

'...it attributed the poor result to the bank's high exposure to residential mortgages, which showed a significant slowdown in the past few months'
"它把糟糕的结果归咎于银行的住房按揭风险敞口太高，而住房按揭在过去几个月里大幅下滑"［*South China Morning Post*《南华早报》］

exposure draft /ɪk'spəʊʒə drɑːft/ *noun* a document produced by a body before a new authoritative pronouncement is published. It invites accountants and other interested parties to comment on matters raised by the draft 征求意见稿，公开文稿：机构在公布新的权威性声明之前发布的一类文件，以邀请会计师和其他相关人士对意见稿所述事项作出评论 Abbreviation 缩写 **ED**

express delivery /ɪkˌspres dɪ'lɪv(ə)ri/ *noun* a very fast delivery 快递

expressly /ɪk'spresli/ *adverb* clearly in words 明显地，明确地 ○ *The contract expressly forbids sales to the United States.* 合同上明确写明禁止销往美国。

extend /ɪk'stend/ *verb* **1.** to offer something 提供 ○ *to extend credit to a customer* 向顾客提供信贷 **2.** to make something longer 延长 ○ *Her contract of employment was extended for two years.* 她的工作合同延长了两年。○ *We have extended the deadline for making the appointment by two weeks.* 我们把任命的最后期限延长了两周。

extended credit /ɪkˌstendɪd 'kredɪt/ *noun* **1.** credit allowing the borrower a very long time to pay 展期信贷：允许借款人将信用延长的信贷 ○ *We sell to Australia on extended credit.* 我们以展期信贷的方式向澳大利亚推销。**2.** *US* an extra long credit used by commercial banks borrowing from the Federal Reserve（美）展期信用证：商业银行向联邦储备借款的额外长期信用

extension /ɪk'stenʃən/ *noun* **1.** a longer time allowed for something than was originally agreed 延期 **2.**（*in an office*）an individual telephone linked to the main switchboard（办公室）电话分机 ○ *The sales manager is on extension 53.* 销售经理的分机号是53。○ *Can you get me extension 21?* 给我接21号分机好吗？○ *Extension 21 is engaged.* 21号分机占线。

'...the White House refusal to ask for an extension of the auto import quotas'
"白宫拒绝了扩大汽车进口配额的要求"［*Duns Business Month*《邓氏商业月刊》］

extensive /ɪk'stensɪv/ *adjective* very large or covering a wide area 广泛的，大范围的 ○ *an extensive network of sales outlets* 一个广泛的销售网点 ○ *an extensive recruitment drive* 一次大

范围的招聘活动

external /ɪkˈstɜːn(ə)l/ *adjective* **1.** outside a country 国外的 Opposite 反义 **internal 2.** outside a company 公司外部的

external account /ɪkˌstɜːn(ə)l əˈkaʊnt/ *noun* an account in a British bank belonging to someone who is living in another country 境外账户：外国居民在英国银行开设的账户

external audit /ɪkˌstɜːn(ə)l ˈɔːdɪt/ *noun* 外部审计 **1.** an audit carried out by an independent auditor who is not employed by the company［由公司雇用的独立审计师进行的审计］**2.** an evaluation of the effectiveness of a company's public relations carried out by an outside agency［由外部代理机构对公司公关效率进行的评估］

external auditing /ɪkˌstɜːn(ə)l ˈɔːdɪtɪŋ/ *noun* an action of auditing a set of accounts by an external auditor 外部审计

external auditor /ɪkˌstɜːn(ə)l ˈɔːdɪtə/ *noun* an independent person who audits the company's accounts 外部审计师：审计公司账目的独立人士

external debt /ɪkˌstɜːn(ə)l ˈdet/ *noun* money which a company has borrowed from outside sources such as a bank, as opposed to money raised from shareholders 外债，外部融资：公司从银行等外部来源借得的资金，与从股东筹集到的资金相对

external funds /ɪkˌstɜːn(ə)l ˈfʌndz/ *plural noun* same as 同 **external debt**

external growth /ɪkˌstɜːn(ə)l ˈgrəʊθ/ *noun* growth by buying other companies, rather than by expanding existing sales or products 外部增长：通过收购其他公司而不是通过扩大现有生产和销售实现的增长 Opposite 反义 **internal growth**

external liabilities /ɪkˌstɜːn(ə)l ˌlaɪəˈbɪlɪtiz/ *plural noun* money owed to lenders and other creditors outside a company 对外负债：公司欠外部贷款人或其他债权人的债务

external trade /ɪkˌstɜːn(ə)l ˈtreɪd/ *noun* trade with foreign countries 对外贸易：与其他国家的贸易 Opposite 反义 **internal trade**

extract /ˈekstrækt/ *noun* a printed document which is part of a larger document 摘要 ○ *He sent me an extract of the accounts.* 他将账目的摘要发送给了我。

extraordinary /ɪkˈstrɔːd(ə)n(ə)ri/ *adjective* different from normal 异常的，特殊的

extraordinary items /ɪkˈstrɔːd(ə)n(ə)ri ˌaɪtəmz/ *plural noun* formerly, large items of income or expenditure which did not arise from usual trading and which did not occur every year. They were shown separately in the P & L account, after taxation 非常项目，特殊项目：不是由于正常业务引起的且不是每年都发生的大额收入或支出项目。它们在损益表中被单独列在所得税之后

extraordinary resolution /ɪkˌstrɔːd(ə)n(ə)ri ˌrezəˈluːʃ(ə)n/ *noun* a resolution which needs 75% of the votes before it can be carried 非常决议：须获得 75% 的票数方能执行的决议

F

face value /ˌfeɪs ˈvæljuː/ *noun* the value written on a coin, banknote or share certificate（硬币、纸币或股票上的）面值，面额

'...travellers cheques cost 1% of their face value - some banks charge more for small amounts'
"旅行支票按其面额的1%收取手续费——有些银行对小面额旅行支票收费会高一些"
[*Sunday Times*《星期日泰晤士报》]

facility /fəˈsɪlɪti/ *noun* the total amount of credit which a lender will allow a borrower 信贷额度

facility fee /fəˈsɪlɪti fiː/ *noun* a charge made to a borrower by a bank for arranging credit facilities 信贷手续费

facility-sustaining activities /fəˌsɪlɪtisəˌsteɪnɪŋ ækˈtɪvɪtiz/ *noun* activities undertaken to support the organisation as a whole, which cannot be logically linked to individual units of output. Accounting is a facility-sustaining activity 厂务支持活动：旨在支持整个组织而开展的活动，这种活动不能想当然的与个别产出单位联系起来。会计是一种厂务支持活动

factor /ˈfæktə/ *noun* **1.** something which is important, or which is taken into account when making a decision 因素，要素，考虑因素 ○ *The drop in sales is an important factor in the company's lower profits*. 销售下降是公司利润低的一个重要原因。○ *Motivation was an important factor in drawing up the new pay scheme*. 在起草新的工资方案时，需考虑到奖励机制。**2.** a number used in multiplication to produce another number 因子，系数，乘数 □ **by a factor of ten** ten times 十倍 **3.** a person or company which is responsible for collecting debts for companies, by buying debts at a discount on their face value 代理商，垫账人：通过折价购入债务来代为企业收回欠债的公司或个人 **4.** a person who sells for a business or another person and earns a commission 代理人：代另一公司或个人销售并赚取佣金的人 ■ *verb* to buy debts from a company at a discount 融资，垫账：折价购买公司的债务

'...factors 'buy' invoices from a company, which then gets an immediate cash advance representing most of their value. The balance is paid when the debt is met. The client company is charged a fee as well as interest on the cash advanced'
"垫账人从公司'购买'发票，而公司获得相当于大部分发票面值的现金垫付，余额在债务偿付后支付。客户公司收取一定的费用，并获得垫付现金的利息" [*Times*《泰晤士报》]

factorial /fækˈtɔːriəl/ *noun* the

product of all the numbers below a number 阶乘 ○ *example*: *4 factorial = 1 × 2 × 3 × 4 = 24* 例:4 的阶乘为 1×2×3×4 = 24(NOTE: **4 factorial** is written **4! 4** 的阶乘写成 **4!**)

factoring /ˈfæktərɪŋ/ *noun* the business of buying debts from a firm at a discount and then getting the debtors to pay 代理收账,垫(支)账(款):折价购买企业的欠债,然后再使债务人购买的业务活动

factoring charges /ˈfæktərɪŋ ˌtʃɑːdʒɪz/ *plural noun* the cost of selling debts to a factor for a commission 代理收账费用:将债务卖给收取佣金的代理商的成本

factors of production /ˌfæktəz əv prəˈdʌkʃən/ *plural noun* land, labour and capital, i.e. the three things needed to produce a product 生产要素:生产产品所需的三要素,即土地、人工和资本

factory gate price /ˌfækt(ə)ri ˈgeɪt praɪs/ *noun* the actual cost of manufacturing goods before any markup is added to give profit 出厂价格:产品生产实际成本(NOTE: The factory gate price includes direct costs such as labour, raw materials and energy, and indirect costs such as interest on loans, plant maintenance or rent 出厂价格包括直接成本(如人工、原材料和能源)及间接成本(如贷款利息、设备保养或租金))

factory overhead /ˌfækt(ə)ri ˈəʊvəhed/ *noun* a production overhead, indirect costs of production which are absorbed into the cost of goods produced 制造费用:包含在产品成本里的间接生产成本

FAE *abbr* Final Admitting Exam 最后录取考试

fail /feɪl/ *verb* to be unsuccessful 失败 ○ *The prototype failed its first test.* 样机首次测试失败了。

failure /ˈfeɪljə/ *noun* an act of breaking down or stopping 中断,停止,失败 ○ *the failure of the negotiations* 谈判中断

fair /feə/ *adjective* reasonable, with equal treatment 合理的,公平的

fair copy /ˌfeə ˈkɒpi/ *noun* a document which is written or typed with no changes or mistakes 清稿,清样:无修改或错误的书写或打印的文件

fair dealing /ˌfeə ˈdiːlɪŋ/ *noun* the legal buying and selling of shares(股票)合法买卖

fair price /ˌfeə ˈpraɪs/ *noun* a good price for both buyer and seller 公平价格

fair trade /feə ˈtreɪd/ *noun* an international business system where countries agree not to charge import duties on some items imported from their trading partners 互惠交易:对进口贸易伙伴国某些产品不征收进口关税的国际贸易体系

fair value /ˌfeə ˈvæljuː/ *noun* **1.** a price paid by a buyer who knows the value of what he or she is buying, to a seller who also knows the value of what is being sold, i. e. neither is cheating the other 公平价值:在买卖双方都知道交易商品价值(即不存在欺诈)情况下的价格 **2.** a method of valuing the assets and liabilities of a business based on the amount for which they could be sold to independent parties at the time of valuation 合理价值:企业资产和负债的计价方法,它以出售给独立方的估售价格为计价基础

fair wear and tear /ˌfeə weər ən ˈteə/ *noun* acceptable damage caused by normal use 合理损耗,正常磨损:正常使用造成的损失 ○ *The insurance policy covers most damage but not fair wear and tear to the machine*. 保险单包括了对大多数损坏的赔偿,但机器的正常损耗除外。

fall /fɔːl/ *noun* a sudden reduction or loss of value (价值)跌落,下降 ○ *a fall in the exchange rate* 汇率下降 ○ *a fall in the price of gold* 金价下跌 ○ *a fall on the Stock Exchange* 股市下跌 ○ *Profits showed a 10% fall*. 利润下降10%。■ *verb* **1.** to be reduced suddenly to a lower price or value (价格或价值)突然下跌 ○ *Shares fell on the market today*. 今天股市下跌了。○ *Gold shares fell 10%* or *fell 45 cents on the Stock Exchange*. 交易所黄金股票下跌了10%(或45美分)。○ *The price of gold fell for the second day running*. 金价连续两天下跌。○ *The pound fell against the euro*. 英镑对欧元的汇率下跌。**2.** to happen or to take place 发生,适逢 ○ *The public holiday falls on a Tuesday*. 公共假日正逢星期二。

'...market analysts described the falls in the second half of last week as a technical correction to the market'
"市场分析员将上周后半段的下跌描述为市场技术性回档"[*Australian Financial Review*《澳大利亚金融评论报》]

'...for the first time since mortgage rates began falling in March a financial institution has raised charges on homeowner loans'
"自从3月份按揭贷款利率下降以来,金融机构第一次提高了对业主的贷款利息"[*Globe and Mail* (*Toronto*)《环球邮报》(多伦多)]

'...interest rates were still falling as late as June, and underlying inflation remains below the government's target of 2.5 per cent'
"6月底,利率仍在下跌,基础通胀率仍旧低于政府2.5%的目标"[*Financial Times*《金融时报》]

fall away /ˌfɔːl əˈweɪ/ *verb* to become less 变少 ○ *Hotel bookings have fallen away since the tourist season ended*. 旅游季节结束以来,预订旅馆房间的人减少了。

fall back /ˌfɔːl ˈbæk/ *verb* to become lower or cheaper after rising in price (价格上涨之后)回落 ○ *Shares fell back in light trading*. 成交量很少,股价也随之回落。

fall behind /ˌfɔːl bɪˈhaɪnd/ *verb* to be late in doing something 拖欠 ○ *They fell behind with their mortgage repayments*. 他们未按期偿还抵押贷款。

falling /ˈfɔːlɪŋ/ *adjective* becoming smaller or dropping in price (价格)下跌的

'...falling profitability means falling share prices'
"利润率下降意味着股价下跌"[*Investors Chronicle*《投资者纪事》]

fall off /ˌfɔːl ˈɒf/ *verb* to become lower, cheaper or less 降低;便宜;变少 ○ *Sales have fallen off since the tourist season ended*. 自旅游季节结束以来销售额减少了。

false /fɔːls/ *adjective* not true or not correct 假的,错误的 ○ *to make a false claim for a product* 对产品提出无根据的索赔 ○ *to make a false entry in the balance sheet* 在资产负债表中虚填一笔账

false accounting /ˌfɔːls əˈkaʊntɪŋ/ *noun* a criminal offence of changing, destroying or hiding accounting records for a dishonest purpose, such as to gain money 伪造账目,假账:为获利等不正当目的而更改、销毁或隐匿会计记录的违法行为

false market /ˌfɔːls ˈmɑːkɪt/ *noun* a market in shares caused by persons or companies conspiring to buy or sell and so influence the share price to their advantage 虚假市场,造市:个人或公司串谋买卖股票,以影响股价朝有利于他们的方向变动而形成的股票市场

false weight /ˌfɔːls ˈweɪt/ *noun* a weight as measured on a shop scales which is wrong and so cheats customers 不准的法码:更改商店法码计量以欺骗顾客

falsification /ˌfɔːlsɪfɪˈkeɪʃ(ə)n/ *noun* the act of making false entries in accounts 作假账的行为,账目的伪造

falsify /ˈfɔːlsɪfaɪ/ *verb* to change something to make it wrong 伪造 ○ *They were accused of falsifying the accounts.* 他们被指控伪造账目。

family company /ˈfæm(ə)li ˌkʌmp(ə)ni/ *noun* a company where most of the shares are owned by members of a family 家族公司:大多数股份由一个家族成员拥有的公司

f. & f. *abbr* fixtures and fittings 固定附加设施

FASB *abbr* Financial Accounting Standards Board 财务会计准则委员会

favourable /ˈfeɪv(ə)rəb(ə)l/ *adjective* giving an advantage 有利的 (NOTE: The US spelling is **favorable** 美国拼法为 **favorable**)

favourable trade balance /ˌfeɪv(ə)rəb(ə)l ˈtreɪd ˌbæləns/ *noun* a situation where a country exports more than it imports 贸易顺差:出口大于进口的情况 ○ *The country has had an favourable trade balance for the second month running.* 该国连续两个月出现贸易顺差。

favourable variance /ˌfeɪv(ə)rəb(ə)l ˈveəriəns/ *noun* variance which shows that the actual result is better than expected 有利差异:实际结果优于预期结果的差异

fax /fæks/ *noun* a system for sending the exact copy of a document via telephone lines 传真 ○ *Can you confirm the booking by fax?* 你能发传真确认这个预定吗? ■ *verb* to send a message by fax 用传真传递信息 ○ *The details of the offer were faxed to the brokers this morning.* 今天早晨报价的细节已传真给经纪人了。○ *I've faxed the documents to our New York office.* 我已把文件传真给我们的纽约办事处了。

FCA *abbr* Fellow of the Institute of Chartered Accountants in England and Wales 英格兰及威尔士的特许会计师协会会员

FCCA *abbr* Fellow of the Association of Chartered Certified Accountants 特许注册会计师协会会员

federal /ˈfed(ə)rəl/ *adjective* **1.** referring to a system of government where a group of states are linked together in a federation 联盟制的,联合的 **2.** referring to the central government of the United States (美国中央政府)联邦的 ○ *Most federal offices are in Washington.* 大多数联邦政府部门都设在华盛顿。

'...federal examiners will determine which of the privately-insured savings and

loans qualify for federal insurance'
"联邦检查官将决定哪些私人保险的储蓄和贷款有资格得到联邦保险"[*Wall Street Journal*《华尔街日报》]
'...since 1978 America has freed many of its industries from federal rules that set prices and controlled the entry of new companies'
"自1978年以来,美国对许多行业不再实行限定价格和控制新公司进入的联邦规定"[*Economist*《经济学家》]

Federal Funds /ˌfed(ə)rəl ˈfʌndz/ *plural noun* deposits by commercial banks with the Federal Reserve Banks, which can be used for short-term loans to other banks 联邦资金:商业银行在联邦储备银行的存款,用于向其他银行提供短期贷款

Federal Reserve /ˌfed(ə)rəl rɪˈzɜːv/, **Federal Reserve System** /ˌfed(ə)rəl rɪˈzɜːv ˌsɪstəm/ *noun* the system of federal government control of the US banks, where the Federal Reserve Board regulates money supply, prints money, fixes the discount rate and issues government bonds (美国)联邦储备,(美国)联邦储备系统:联邦政府控制美国银行的制度,联邦储备委员会负责控制货币供应、印制货币、决定贴现率和发行政府债券

federation /ˌfedəˈreɪʃ(ə)n/ *noun* a group of societies, companies or organisations which have a central organisation which represents them and looks after their common interests 同盟,联盟,联合会 ○ *a federation of trades unions* 工会联合会 ○ *the employers' federation* 雇主联合会

Fed Funds /ˈfed fʌndz/ *plural noun US* (*informal*) (美,非正式) same as 同 **Federal Funds**

fed funds rate /ˈfed fʌndz ˌreɪt/ *noun* the rate charged by banks for lending money deposited with the Federal Reserve to other banks 联邦资金利率:联邦储备银行借款给其他银行的利率

fee /fiː/ *noun* money paid for work carried out by a professional person such as an accountant, a doctor or a lawyer 费用,收费,报酬 ○ *We charge a small fee for our services*. 我们收取少量服务费。○ *The consultant's fee was much higher than we expected*. 顾问费用远高于我们的预期。

fee work /ˈfiː wɜːk/ *noun* FINANCE, BANKING, AND ACCOUNTING, GENERAL MANAGEMENT any work on a project carried out by independent workers or contractors, rather than by the organisation's employees (金融、银行、会计及综合管理)外包工作:承包给独立工人或承包商,而不是由组织内部员工开展的项目工作

fellow /ˈfeləʊ/ *noun* a title given to senior members of a professional association. Junior members are usually called 'associates' 会员:对专业协会高级会员的称呼,低级会员通常称为associates

fiat money /ˈfiːæt ˌmʌni/ *noun* coins or notes which are not worth much as paper or metal, but are said by the government to have a value and are recognised as legal tender 法定货币:本身无价值的纸或金属制成的纸币或硬币,由政府规定其价格并被认可为法定货币

fictitious assets /fɪkˌtɪʃəs ˈæsets/ *plural noun* assets which do not really exist, but are entered as assets to balance the accounts 虚假资产:本身并不存在,却被当作资产记入以平衡账目的

资产

fiddle /ˈfɪd(ə)l/ (*informal*) *noun* an act of cheating（非正式）欺骗 ○ *It's all a fiddle.* 这纯粹是个骗局。■ *verb* to cheat 欺骗 ○ *He tried to fiddle his tax returns.* 他试图伪造报税表。○ *The salesman was caught fiddling his expense account.* 销售员在伪造开支账目时被发现了。

fiduciary /fɪˈdjuːʃjəri/ *noun, adjective* a person in a position of trust 受托人；信托的 ○ *Directors have fiduciary duty to act in the best interests of the company.* 董事负有按公司最佳利益行事的受托责任。

fiduciary deposits /fɪˌdjuːʃəri dɪˈpɒzɪts/ *plural noun* bank deposits which are managed for the depositor by the bank 受托存款：由银行代储户管理的银行存款

FIFO /ˈfaɪfəʊ/ *abbr* first in first out 先进先出法

fifty-fifty /ˌfɪftiˈfɪfti/ *adjective, adverb* half 平均，分摊，对半

figure /ˈfɪɡə/ *noun* **1.** a number, or a cost written in numbers 数字；（以数字表示的）花费 ○ *The figure in the accounts for heating is very high.* 账户里的取暖费很高。**2.** □ **his income runs into six figures** *or* **he has a six-figure income** his income is more than £100,000 他的收入有六位数：他的收入超过10万英镑

figures /ˈfɪɡəz/ *plural noun* **1.** written numbers 数值 **2.** the results for a company（公司）业绩 ○ *the figures for last year* or *last year's figures* 去年的业绩

file /faɪl/ *noun* **1.** documents kept for reference 档案，卷宗 **2.** a section of data on a computer, e.g. payroll, address list, customer accounts 计算机文件（如工资表、地址簿、客户账目）○ *How can we protect our computer files?* 我们应如何保护计算机中的文件？■ *verb* **1.** to make an official request 提出正式申请 **2.** to register something officially 正式提请备案 ○ *to file an application for a patent* 提交专利申请 ○ *to file a return to the tax office* 向税务局提交报税表

file copy /ˈfaɪl ˌkɒpi/ *noun* a copy of a document which is kept for reference in an office 文件副本，存档副本

filing date /ˈfaɪlɪŋ deɪt/ *noun* the date by which income tax returned must be filed with the Inland Revenue 报税截止日期：须向国内税务局申报所得税的最后日期

filing system /ˈfaɪlɪŋ ˌsɪstəm/ *noun* a way of putting documents in order for easy reference 存档系统，档案编排系统：将文件按顺序归档以方便参考的一种存档方法

final /ˈfaɪn(ə)l/ *adjective* last, coming at the end of a period 最后的，期末的 ○ *to pay the final instalment* 支付分期付款的最后一笔款 ○ *to make the final payment* 最后一次付款 ○ *to put the final details on a document* 在文件中加上最后的细节

final accounts /ˌfaɪn(ə)l əˈkaʊnts/ *noun* the accounts produced at the end of an accounting period, including the balance sheet and profit and loss account 期末报表：在会计期末编制的报表，包括资产负债表和损益表

Final Admitting Exam /ˌfaɪn(ə)l ədˈmɪtɪŋ ɪɡˌzæm/ *noun* a final examination set by the ICAEW to admit student accountants as Chartered Accountants 最后录取考试：英格兰及威

尔士特许会计师协会决定是否接纳见习会计师成为特许会计师的最后考试 Abbreviation 缩写 **FAE**

final closing date /ˌfaɪn(ə)l ˈkləʊzɪŋ deɪt/ *noun* the last date for acceptance of a takeover bid, when the bidder has to announce how many shareholders have accepted his or her offer 接受收购报价的最后期限(出价人须于该日公布接受其报价的股东人数)

final demand /ˌfaɪn(ə)l dɪˈmɑːnd/ *noun* the last reminder from a supplier, after which they will sue for payment 最后付款要求:卖方对买主的最后付款提醒,之后卖方将诉诸法律要求付款

final discharge /ˌfaɪn(ə)l dɪsˈtʃɑːdʒ/ *noun* the last payment of what is left of a debt 债务的偿清

final dividend /ˌfaɪn(ə)l ˈdɪvɪdend/ *noun* a dividend paid at the end of a year's trading, which has to be approved by the shareholders at an AGM 期末股利:于一年交易结束后支付的股利,该股利须经年度股东大会的批准

finalise /ˈfaɪnəlaɪz/, **finalize** *verb* to agree final details 确定最后的细节 ○ *We hope to finalise the agreement tomorrow*. 我们希望明天能把协议定下来。○ *After six weeks of negotiations the loan was finalised yesterday*. 经过六个星期的谈判,昨天把这笔贷款确定了下来。

final settlement /ˌfaɪn(ə)l ˈset(ə)lmənt/ *noun* the last payment which settles a debt 最后一笔还款

finance /ˈfaɪnæns/ *noun* **1.** money used by a company, provided by the shareholders or by loans (由股东或贷款人提供给公司使用的)资金 ○ *Where will they get the necessary finance for the project?* 他们将从哪里获得工程所需的资金? **2.** money (used by a club, local authority, etc.)(俱乐部、地方当局等使用的)资金 ○ *She is the secretary of the local authority finance committee*. 她是地方当局财务委员会的秘书。■ *verb* to provide money to pay for something 为…筹措资金,融资 ○ *They plan to finance the operation with short-term loans*. 他们计划通过短期贷款为企业筹资。

'... an official said that the company began to experience a sharp increase in demand for longer-term mortgages at a time when the flow of money used to finance these loans diminished'
"一名官员称,当用于筹集长期按揭贷款的资金流动减少时,公司开始面临贷款需求剧增的局面" [*Globe and Mail*《环球邮报》]

Finance Act /ˈfaɪnæns ækt/ *noun* an annual Act of Parliament which gives the government the power to obtain money from taxes as proposed in the Budget 财政法:英国议会的一项年度法,它赋予政府按预算取得税收收入的权力

Finance Bill /ˈfaɪnæns bɪl/ *noun* **1.** a bill which lists the proposals in a chancellor's budget and which is debated before being voted into law as the Finance Act 财政法案:列示财政预算的法案,经过辩论之后通过投票使之成为财政法 **2.** *US* a short-term bill of exchange which provides credit for a corporation so that it can continue trading (美)美国短期汇票:向公司提供信贷的短期汇票,使公司能够持续经营

finance controller /ˌfaɪnæns kənˈtrəʊlə/ *noun* an accountant whose main task is to manage the company's monetary resources 财务总监:主要负责管理公司财务的会计师

finance lease /ˈfaɪnæns liːs/ *noun* a lease which requires the lessee company to show the asset acquired under the lease in its balance sheet and to depreciate it in the usual way 融资租赁:要求承租公司在资产负债表中呈列租赁资产,并按正常方式提取折旧的租赁

finance leasing /ˌfaɪnæns ˈliːsɪŋ/ *noun* leasing a property under a finance lease 融资租赁行为

finance market /ˈfaɪnæns ˌmɑːkɪt/ *noun* a place where large sums of money can be lent or borrowed 金融市场

finances /ˈfaɪnænsɪz/ *plural noun* money or cash which is available 财务,财政 ○ *the bad state of the company's finances* 公司糟糕的财务状况

financial /faɪˈnænʃ(ə)l/ *adjective* concerning money 财务的,金融的

Financial Accountant /faɪˌnænʃ(ə)l əˈkaʊntənt/ *noun* a qualified accountant, a member of the Institute of Financial Accountants, who advises on accounting matters or who works as the financial director of a company 财务会计师:身为英国财务会计师公会会员,并就公司的会计事宜提供建议或担任公司财务主任的资格会计师

Financial Accounting Standards Board /faɪˌnænʃ(ə)l əˈkaʊntɪŋ ˈstændədz bɔːd/ *noun* the body which regulates accounting standards in the USA (美国)财务会计准则委员会 Abbreviation 缩写 **FASB**

financial adviser /faɪˌnænʃ(ə)l ədˈvaɪzə/ *noun* a person or company which gives advice on financial problems for a fee 财务顾问

financial aid /faɪˌnænʃ(ə)l ˈeɪd/ *noun* monetary assistance given to an individual, organisation, or nation. International financial aid, that is from one country to another, is often used to fund educational, health-related, or other humanitarian activities 补助金,财政援助:给予个人、组织或国家的资金帮助。对于由一国提供给另一国的国际财务援助,其资金通常用作教育、医疗保健或其他人道主义事务

financial assistance /faɪˌnænʃəl əˈsɪstəns/ *noun* help in the form of money 财政援助

financial calendar /faɪˌnænʃ(ə)l ˈkælɪndə/ *noun* a list of significant events and dates in a company's financial reporting year 财务日志:公司年度财务报告中的重大事件和日期清单

financial correspondent /faɪˌnænʃ(ə)l ˌkɒrɪsˈpɒndənt/ *noun* a journalist who writes articles on money matters for a newspaper (报刊的)金融记者

financial futures /faɪˌnænʃ(ə)l ˈfjuːtʃəz/, **financial futures contract** /faɪˌnænʃ(ə)l ˈfjuːtʃəz ˌkɒntrækt/ *noun* a contract for the purchase of gilt-edged securities for delivery at a date in the future 金融期货:购买金边证券以便在未来某个日期交付的合同

financial futures market /faɪˌnænʃ(ə)l ˈfjuːtʃəz ˌmɑːkɪt/ *noun* the market in gilt-edged securities for delivery at a date in the future 金融期货市场:于未来某个日期交付金边证券的市场

financial institution /faɪˌnænʃ(ə)l ˌɪnstɪˈtjuːʃ(ə)n/ *noun* a bank, investment trust or insurance company whose work involves lending or investing large sums of money 金融机构：提供大额贷款或进行大额投资的银行、投资信托或保险公司

financial instrument /faɪˌnænʃ(ə)l ˈɪnstrʊmənt/ *noun* 金融工具 **1.** a document showing that money has been lent or borrowed, invested or passed from one account to another, e.g. a bill of exchange, share certificate, certificate of deposit, an IOU [表明资金已经借贷、投资或转账的单据，如汇票、股票、存款证、借据] **2.** any form of investment in the stock market or in other financial markets, e.g. shares, government stocks, certificates of deposit or bills of exchange [在股票市场或其他金融市场存在形式各异的投资，如股票、政府债券、存款证或汇票]

financial intermediary /faɪˌnænʃ(ə)l ˌɪntəˈmiːdiəri/ *noun* an institution which takes deposits or loans from individuals and lends money to clients 金融中介机构：吸收个人存款或贷款，并向顾客提供资金的机构

financial leverage /faɪˌnænʃ(ə)l ˈliːvərɪdʒ/ *noun* ➧参阅 **gearing**

financially /fɪˈnænʃ(ə)li/ *adverb* regarding money 财务方面，金融上；获利地 □ **a company which is financially sound** a company which is profitable and has strong assets 具有获利能力且资产雄厚的公司

financial management /faɪˌnænʃ(ə)l ˈmænɪdʒmənt/ *noun* management of the acquisition and use of longand short-term capital by a business 财务管理：对企业长、短期资金筹集和使用的管理

financial position /faɪˌnænʃ(ə)l pəˈzɪʃ(ə)n/ *noun* the state of a person's or company's bank balance in terms of assets and debts 财务状况：以资产与负债形式表示的个人或公司的银行余额状况 ○ *She must think of her financial position.* 她必须考虑自身的财务状况。

financial report /faɪˌnænʃ(ə)l rɪˈpɔːt/ *noun* a document which gives the financial position of a company or of a club, etc. 财务报告：列示公司或俱乐部财务状况的文件

Financial Reporting Review Panel /faɪˌnænʃ(ə)l rɪˌpɔːtɪŋ rɪˈvjuː ˌpæn(ə)l/ *noun* a UK body that receives and investigates complaints about the annual accounts of companies in respect of apparent departures from the accounting requirements of the Companies Act, including the requirement to give a true and fair view 财务报告核查委员会：英国的一个机构，它接受并调查关于公司年度报表明显偏离公司法会计要求（包括真实及公平地反映公司财务状况的要求）的投诉 Abbreviation 缩写 **FRRP**

Financial Reporting Standards /faɪˌnænʃ(ə)l rɪˌpɔːtɪŋ ˈstændədz/ *plural noun* a series of accounting standards issued by the Accounting Standards Board outlining common accounting practice 财务报告准则：由会计准则委员会颁布的关于通用会计实务的一系列会计准则 Abbreviation 缩写 **FRSs**

financial resources /faɪˌnænʃ(ə)l rɪˈzɔːsɪz/ *plural noun* the supply of money for something 财政资源，资金，财力 ○ *a company with strong financial resources* 资金雄厚的公司

financial review /faɪˌnænʃ(ə)l rɪˈvjuː/ *noun* an examination of an organisation's finances 财务核查,财务审核

financial risk /faɪˌnænʃ(ə)l ˈrɪsk/ *noun* the possibility of losing money 财务风险:可能损失钱财的风险 ○ *The company is taking a considerable financial risk in manufacturing 25 million units without doing any market research.* 该公司在冒极大的财务风险:它没有进行任何市场调查就生产了2,500万件产品。○ *There is always some financial risk in selling on credit.* 赊账销售总会有一定的财务风险。

financials /faɪˈnænʃ(ə)lz/ *plural noun* same as 同 **financial futures**

Financial Services Act /faɪˌnænʃ(ə)l ˈsɜːvɪsɪz ækt/ *noun* an Act of the British Parliament which regulates the offering of financial services to the general public and to private investors 金融服务法:英国议会的一项法案,对向普通大众和私人投资者提供的金融服务进行规范

Financial Services Authority /faɪˌnænʃ(ə)l ˈsɜːvɪsɪz ɔːˌθɒrəti/ *noun* an independent non-governmental body formed in 1997 as a result of reforms in the regulation of financial services in the United Kingdom. The Securities and Investments Board (SIB) became responsible for the supervision of banking and investment services and changed its name to become the Financial Services Authority. The FSA's four statutory objectives were specified by the Financial Services and Markets Act 2000: maintaining market confidence; increasing public knowledge of the finance system; ensuring appropriate protection for consumers; and reducing financial crime 金融服务管理局:英国一个独立的非政府机构,它于1997年从英国金融服务监管的改革中孕育而生。在改革后,原来的证券投资委员会(SIB)负责监管银行业及投资服务,并更名为金融服务管理局。金融服务与市场法2000确定了金融服务管理局的四项法定宗旨,即:维持市场信心;增进公众对金融系统的了解;保护消费者合理权益;制止金融犯罪 Abbreviation 缩写 **FSA**

financial statement /faɪˌnænʃ(ə)l ˈsteɪtmənt/ *noun* a document which shows the financial situation of a company 财务报表:表明公司财务状况的文件 ○ *The accounts department has prepared a financial statement for the shareholders.* 会计部为股东编制了一份财务报表。

financial supermarket /faɪˌnænʃ(ə)l ˈsuːpəmɑːkɪt/ *noun* a company which offers a range of financial services, e.g. a bank offering loans, mortgages, pensions and insurance as well as the usual personal banking services 金融超市:提供多种金融服务的公司,例如一家银行不仅提供普通的个人银行服务,还提供贷款、按揭、退休金和保险服务

financial year /faɪˌnænʃ(ə)l ˈjɪə/ *noun* the twelve-month period for which a company produces accounts. A financial year is not necessarily the same as a calendar year 财政年度,会计年度:公司编制报表的12个月。财政年度不一定与公历年度相同

financier /faɪˈnænsiə/ *noun* a person who lends large amounts of money to companies or who buys shares in companies as an investment 理财家,金融家

financing /ˈfaɪnænsɪŋ/ *noun* the act of providing money for a project 融资,资金的提供 ○ *The financing of the project was done by two international banks*. 有两家国际银行为该项目融资。

finder's fee /ˈfaɪndəz fiː/ *noun* a fee paid to a person who finds a client for another, e.g. someone who introduces a client to a stockbroking firm 中间人报酬:付给中间人的费用,如介绍客户给证券经纪公司的中间人费用

fine /faɪn/ *noun* money paid because of something wrong which has been done 罚金 ○ *She was asked to pay a $25,000 fine*. 她被罚款 25,000 美元。○ *We had to pay a £50 parking fine*. 我们得付 50 英镑的违章停车罚款。

fine-tuning /faɪnˈtjuːnɪŋ/ *noun* the act of making of small adjustments in areas such as interest rates, tax bands or the money supply, to improve a nation's economy 微调:对利率、税收等级、货币供应等进行小幅调整,以改善国家经济

fire insurance /ˈfaɪər ɪnˌʃʊərəns/ *noun* insurance against damage by fire 火险,火灾保险

fire sale /ˈfaɪə seɪl/ *noun* a sale of firedamaged goods 火灾中受损商品的销售

firm /fɜːm/ *noun* a company, business or partnership 公司,企业,合伙企业 ○ *a manufacturing firm* 一家制造企业 ○ *an important publishing firm* 一家重要的出版社 ○ *She is a partner in a law firm*. 她是一家律师事务所的合伙人。■ *adjective* **1.** unchangeable 不能改变的,坚定的 ○ *to make a firm offer for something* 就某产品递实盘 ○ *to place a firm order for two aircraft* 报实盘购买两架飞机 **2.** not dropping in price and possibly going to rise 不会降价的,有可能价格上涨的,坚挺的 ○ *Sterling was firmer on the foreign exchange markets*. 英镑在外汇市场上更加坚挺了。○ *Shares remained firm*. 股票保持强劲。■ *verb* to remain at a price and seem likely to rise (价格)稳定并可能上升 ○ *The shares firmed at £1.50*. 股价稳定在 1.50 英镑。

'...some profit-taking was noted, but underlying sentiment remained firm'
"有人见利抛售出逃,但市场的持股心态仍然坚定" [*Financial Times*《金融时报》]

firmness /ˈfɜːmnəs/ *noun* the fact of being steady at a particular price, or likely to rise 稳定在某一价格上;有可能上升 ○ *the firmness of the pound on foreign exchanges* 英镑在外汇市场上坚挺

'Toronto failed to mirror New York's firmness as a drop in gold shares on a falling bullion price left the market closing on a mixed note'
"金条价下跌拖累金矿股一并看跌,股市收盘喜忧参半;纽约对此保持坚挺,但多伦多则不然" [*Financial Times*《金融时报》]

firm price /ˌfɜːm ˈpraɪs/ *noun* a price which will not change 固定价格 ○ *They are quoting a firm price of $1.23 a unit*. 他们报出每单位 1.23 美元的实盘。

firm sale /ˌfɜːm ˈseɪl/ *noun* a sale which does not allow the purchaser to return the goods 不可撤销的销售:不允许买方退货的销售

firm up /ˌfɜːm ˈʌp/ *verb* to agree on the final details of something 最后商

定，确定 ○ *We expect to firm up the deal at the next trade fair*. 我们希望在下次交易会上把这笔交易确定下来。

first /fɜːst/ *noun* a person or thing that is there at the beginning or earlier than others 第一个人，第一件事 ○ *Our company was one of the first to sell into the European market*. 我们公司是首批向欧洲市场销售的公司之一。

first-class /ˌfɜːstˈklɑːs/ *adjective* top-quality or most expensive 一流的，最贵的，一级的 ○ *She is a firstclass accountant*. 她是一流的会计师。

first in first out /ˌfɜːst ɪn ˌfɜːst ˈaʊt/ *phrase* an accounting policy where it is assumed that stocks in hand were purchased last, and that stocks sold during the period were purchased first 先进先出法：假定手里的存货是最后买进的，而售出的存货则是最先买进的会计方法 Abbreviation 缩写 **FIFO** Compare 比较 **last in first out**

first option /ˌfɜːst ˈɒpʃən/ *noun* allowing someone to be the first to have the possibility of deciding something 第一选择权：允许某人首先决定某事

first quarter /ˌfɜːst ˈkwɔːtə/ *noun* the period of three months from January to the end of March 第一季度 ○ *The first quarter's rent is payable in advance*. 应预付第一季度的租金。

first year allowance /ˌfɜːst jɪə əˈlaʊəns/ *noun* an allowance which can be claimed on capital expenditure by a business or self-employed person during the year in which the purchase was made. After the first year, the written down allowance (WDA) applies 第一年税收减免：企业或个体从业人员可对第一年内因交易产生的资本开支申请税收减免。第一年后，将采用减记减税制度（WDA）Abbreviation 缩写 **FYA**

fiscal /ˈfɪskəl/ *adjective* referring to tax or to government revenues 财政的：指税收或政府收入

fiscal drag /ˌfɪskəl ˈdræg/ *noun* **1.** the effect of inflation on a government's tax revenues. As inflation increases so do prices and wages, and tax revenues rise proportionately. Even if inflation is low, increased earnings will give the government increased revenues anyway 经济活力减退：通胀率上升会导致物价和工资上涨，而税收收入也相应增加。即使通胀率较低，盈利增长也会令政府收入增加 **2.** the negative effect of higher personal taxation on an individual's work performance 财政拖累：较高个人所得税对个人工作绩效的负面影响

fiscal measures /ˌfɪskəl ˈmeʒəz/ *plural noun* tax changes made by a government to improve the working of the economy 财政措施：政府为改善经济运作而改变课税

fiscal year /ˌfɪskəl ˈjɪə/ *noun* a twelvemonth period on which taxes are calculated. In the UK this is April 6th to April 5th 财政年度：计算税收的12个月。英国的财政年度是每年的4月6日至来年4月5日

'... last fiscal year the chain reported a 116% jump in earnings'
"在上一财政年度，该连锁店的盈利猛涨116%"［*Barron's*《巴伦》］

fittings /ˈfɪtɪŋz/ *plural noun* items in a property which are sold with it but are not permanently fixed, e. g. carpets or shelves（同房产一起出售的但可移动的）装配，装置，设备（如地毯、书

架）➪ 参阅 **fixtures**

five dollar bill /ˌfaɪv ˌdɒlə ˈbɪl/ *noun* a banknote for five dollars 面值五美元的钞票

fixed /fɪkst/ *adjective* unable to be changed or removed 永久的，固定的

'...you must offer shippers and importers fixed rates over a reasonable period of time'
"你必须为托运人和进口商在一个合理期限内提供固定汇率" [*Lloyd's List*《劳氏日报》]

fixed assets /fɪkst ˈæsets/ *plural noun* property or machinery which a company owns and uses, but which the company does not buy or sell as part of its regular trade, including the company's investments in shares of other companies 固定资产：公司拥有和使用的而不作为经常性业务买卖的不动产和机器设备，包括在其他公司的股权投资

fixed budget /ˌfɪkst ˈbʌdʒɪt/ *noun* a budget which refers to a specific level of business, i.e. a sales turnover which produces a specific level of profit 固定预算：在一定经营规模下（如产生一定利润水平的营业额）的预算

fixed capital /fɪkst ˈkæpɪt(ə)l/ *noun* capital in the form of buildings and machinery 固定资本：以建筑物和机器形式存在的资本

fixed charge /ˌfɪkst ˈtʃɑːdʒ/ *noun* a charge over a particular asset *or* property 固定费用：特定资产或财产的费用

fixed costs /fɪkst ˈkɒsts/ *plural noun* business costs which do not change with the quantity of the product made 固定成本：不会随着生产数量变化的企业成本

fixed deduction /ˌfɪkst dɪˈdʌkʃən/ *noun* a deduction agreed by the Inland Revenue and a group of employees, such as a trade union, which covers general expenditure on clothes or tools used in the course of employment 固定扣除额：经国内税务局和一组员工（如工会）同意的扣除额，以抵偿雇用期间服装或工具的一般开支

fixed deposit /ˌfɪkst dɪˈpɒzɪt/ *noun* a deposit which pays a stated interest over a set period 定期存款：在规定期限内支付规定利息的存款

fixed exchange rate /ˌfɪkst ɪksˈtʃeɪndʒ ˌreɪt/ *noun* a rate of exchange of one currency against another which cannot fluctuate, and can only be changed by devaluation or revaluation 固定汇率：一种货币对另一种货币的汇率，这种汇率不可自由涨落只能通过贬值或升值来改变

fixed expenses /ˌfɪkst ɪkˈspensɪz/ *plural noun* expenses which do not vary with different levels of production, e.g. rent, secretaries' salaries and insurance 固定开支：不会随着生产水平改变的开支，如租金、秘书工资和保险

fixed income /fɪkstˈɪnkʌm/ *noun* income which does not change from year to year, as from an annuity 固定收入：每年都一样的收入，如年金收入

fixed-interest /ˌfɪkstˈɪntrəst/ *adjective* having an interest rate which does not vary 固定利息的

fixed-interest investments /fɪkstˌɪntrəst ɪnˈvestmənts/ *plural noun* investments producing an interest which does not change 固定利息投资

fixed-interest securities /fɪkstˌɪntrəst sɪˈkjʊərɪtiz/ *plural noun* securities such as government bonds which produce an interest which does not change 固定利息证券(如政府债券)

fixed-price /ˌfɪkstˈpraɪs/ *adjective* having a price which cannot be changed 固定价格的

fixed-price agreement /fɪkst-ˈpraɪs əˌgriːmənt/ *noun* an agreement where a company provides a service or a product at a price which stays the same for the whole period of the agreement 固定价格协议:公司在协议期内以固定价格提供产品或服务的协议

fixed rate /fɪkst ˈreɪt/ *noun* a rate, e.g. an exchange rate, which does not change 固定比率:不变的比率(如汇率)

fixed rate loan /ˌfɪkst reɪt ˈləʊn/ *noun* a loan on which the rate of interest stays the same for the duration of the loan 固定利率贷款

fixed scale of charges /ˌfɪkst skeɪl əv ˈtʃɑːdʒɪz/ *noun* a rate of charging which does not change 固定收费标准

fixed yield /ˌfɪkst ˈjiːld/ *noun* a percentage return which does not change 固定收益率

fixer /ˈfɪksə/ *noun* a person who has a reputation for arranging business deals, often illegally (通常为非法性质的)交易中间人

fixing /ˈfɪksɪŋ/ *noun* **1.** arranging 确定 ○ *the fixing of charges* 收费定价 ○ *the fixing of a mortgage rate* 抵押贷款利率的确定 **2.** a regular meeting to set a price 确定价格的定期会议

fixtures /ˈfɪkstʃəz/ *plural noun* items in a property which are permanently attached to it, e.g. sinks and lavatories (房产中的)固定装置(如水槽和卫生间)

fixtures and fittings /ˌfɪkstʃəz ən ˈfɪtɪŋz/ *plural noun* objects in a property which are sold with the property, both those which cannot be removed and those which can 固定附加设施:与某项房产一起出售的附加设施,包括可移动设施和固定设施 Abbreviation 缩写 **f. & f.**

flat /flæt/ *adjective* **1.** referring to market prices which do not fall or rise, because of low demand 不景气的,市面呆滞的:由于需求量少,市场价格不升也不降 ○ *The market was flat today.* 今天市场不景气。**2.** not changing in response to different conditions 固定的

'...the government revised its earlier reports for July and August. Originally reported as flat in July and declining by 0.2% in August, industrial production is now seen to have risen by 0.2% and 0.1% respectively in those months'
"政府修改了其早先所作的关于7、8月份的报告。以前的报告称,工业生产7月平稳,8月下降了0.2%;新报告则显示这两个月分别上升了0.2%和0.1%" [*Sunday Times* 《星期日泰晤士报》]

flat rate /ˌflæt ˈreɪt/ *noun* a charge which always stays the same 统一收费率 ○ *a flat-rate increase of 10%* 10%的统一收费率 ○ *We pay a flat rate for electricity each quarter.* 我们每季度支付固定的电费。○ *He is paid a flat rate of £2 per thousand.* 他按每千个两英镑的统一收费率收费。

flat tax /ˌflæt ˈtæks/ *noun* a tax levied at one fixed rate whatever an individual's income 统一税:按单一税率征收而不论个人收入水平的税项

flat yield /ˌflæt ˈjiːld/ *noun* an interest rate as a percentage of the price paid for fixed interest stock 固定收益率:以固定利率股票价格的一定百分比表示的利率

flexibility /ˌfleksɪˈbɪlɪti/ *noun* the ability to be easily changed 灵活性 ○ *There is no flexibility in the company's pricing policy*. 公司的定价政策没有灵活性。

'...they calculate interest on their 'flexible' mortgage on an annual basis rather than daily. Charging annual interest makes a nonsense of the whole idea of flexibility which is supposed to help you pay off your mortgage more quickly'
"与按天计算不同的是,他们按年来计算他们"灵活"抵押的利息。这种做法扰乱了旨在帮助人们更快还款的灵活抵押的机动性"
[*Financial Times*《金融时报》]

flexible /ˈfleksɪb(ə)l/ *adjective* possible to alter or change 可变动的,可伸缩的,灵活的 ○ *We try to be flexible where the advertising budget is concerned*. 我们试图灵活地处理与广告预算有关的事宜。○ *The company has adopted a flexible pricing policy*. 该公司采纳了灵活的定价政策。

flexible budget /ˌfleksɪb(ə)l ˈbʌdʒɪt/ *noun* a budget which changes in response to changes in sales turnover or output 弹性预算:按产量和销售额变动的预算

flight of capital /ˌflaɪt əv ˈkæpɪt(ə)l/ *noun* a rapid movement of capital out of one country because of lack of confidence in that country's economic future 资本外逃:由于对某国经济前景缺乏信心导致的资本迅速外流

flight to quality /ˌflaɪt tə ˈkwɒlɪti/ *noun* a tendency of investors to buy safe blue-chip securities when the economic outlook is uncertain 安全投资转移:在经济前景不确定时,投资者购买安全蓝筹股的趋向

float /fləʊt/ *noun* **1.** cash taken from a central supply and used for running expenses 周转金 ○ *The sales reps have a float of £100 each*. 销售代表每人有100英镑的周转金。**2.** the process of starting a new company by selling shares in it on the Stock Exchange (通过在证券交易所出售新公司股票的方式)筹资创办新公司 ○ *The float of the new company was a complete failure*. 新公司的筹资创办发行彻底失败了。**3.** the process of allowing a currency to settle at its own exchange rate, without any government intervention 浮动:无政府干预的汇率自由浮动 **4.** the period between the presentation of a cheque as payment and the actual payment to the payee or the financial advantage provided by this period to the drawer of a cheque 浮存:提呈支票作为付款至实际付款给收款人的期间,或该期间提供给支票提款人的财务好处 ■ *verb* to let a currency find its own exchange rate on the international markets and not be fixed 让(货币汇率)自由浮动 ○ *The government has let sterling float*. 政府允许英镑自由浮动。○ *The government has decided to float the pound*. 政府决定让英镑自由浮动。

floating /ˈfləʊtɪŋ/ *adjective* not fixed 浮动的 ○ *floating exchange rates* 浮动汇率 ○ *the floating pound* 浮动英镑

'...in a world of floating exchange rates the dollar is strong because of capital in-

flows rather than weak because of the nation's trade deficit'
"在浮动汇率制度下,美元并未因国家贸易赤字而走弱,反而因资本流入而保持坚挺"
[*Duns Business Month*《邓氏商业月刊》]

floating charge /ˈfləʊtɪŋ tʃɑːdʒ/ *noun* a charge linked to any of the company's assets in a category, but not to any specific item 浮动抵押:以公司全部资产(而不是与某一特定资产项目)作抵押

floating rate /ˈfləʊtɪŋ reɪt/ *noun* **1.** same as 同 **variable rate** **2.** an exchange rate for a currency which can vary according to market demand, and is not fixed by the government 浮动汇率:不是由政府固定,而是跟随市场需求变动的汇率

floating-rate notes /ˌfləʊtɪŋreɪt ˈnəʊts/ *plural noun* eurocurrency loans arranged by a bank which are not at a fixed rate of interest 浮动利率票据:银行制定的非固定利率的欧洲货币贷款 Abbreviation 缩写 **FRNs**

floor /flɔː/ *noun* a bottom level of something, e.g. the lowest exchange rate which a government will accept for its currency or the lower limit imposed on an interest rate 下限,底价:某物的最低水平,如政府能接受的本国货币最低汇率或实施的利率下限 ○ *The government will impose a floor on wages to protect the poor*. 政府将为低收入群体设置最低收入保障。

floor broker /ˈflɔː ˌbrəʊkə/ *noun* a stockbroker who is a member of a brokerage house 场内经纪人:经纪人事务所的证券经纪人

floor price /ˈflɔː praɪs/ *noun* a lowest price, a price which cannot go any lower 最低价格

floor space /ˈflɔː speɪs/ *noun* an area of floor in an office or warehouse (办公室或仓库的)面积 ○ *We have 3,500 square metres of floor space to let*. 我们有 3,500 平方米面积可以出租。

floor trader /ˈflɔː ˌtreɪdə/ *noun* an independent trader on a Stock Exchange, who buys and sells on his or her own account 场内交易人:在证券交易所进行买卖的自负盈亏的独立交易者

flop /flɒp/ *noun* a failure, or something which has not been successful 失败 ○ *The new model was a flop*. 新模型失败了。

floppy disk /ˌflɒpi ˈdɪsk/, **floppy** /ˈflɒpi/ *noun* a flat circular flexible disk onto which data can be stored in a magnetic form. A floppy disk cannot store as much data as a hard disk, but is easily removed, and is protected by a plastic sleeve 软盘

flow chart /ˈfləʊ tʃɑːt/ *noun* a diagram showing the arrangement of various work processes in a series 流程图:显示工作流程安排的图表

fluctuate /ˈflʌktʃueɪt/ *verb* to move up and down 波动 ○ *Prices fluctuated between £1.10 and £1.25*. 价格在 1.10 至 1.25 英镑之间波动。○ *The pound fluctuated all day on the foreign exchange markets*. 英镑在外汇交易市场上全天波动。

fluctuating /ˈflʌktʃueɪtɪŋ/ *adjective* moving up and down 波动的 ○ *fluctuating dollar prices* 波动的美元价格

fluctuation /ˌflʌktʃuˈeɪʃ(ə)n/ *noun* an up and down movement 波动 ○ *the fluctuations of the yen* 日元的波动 ○ *the fluctuations of the exchange rate*

汇率的波动

folio /ˈfəʊliəʊ/ *noun* a page with a number, especially two facing pages in an account book which have the same number 页:有编码的页,尤指账簿中页码相同面对面的两页 ■ *verb* to put a number on a page 编页码

force /fɔːs/ *noun* **1.** strength 力量 **2.** a group of people 一群人 ■ *verb* to make someone do something 迫使 ○ *Competition has forced the company to lower its prices.* 竞争迫使该公司降价。○ *After the takeover several of the managers were forced to take early retirement.* 收购完成后,几名经理被迫提前退休。

forced sale /ˌfɔːst ˈseɪl/ *noun* a sale which takes place because a court orders it or because it is the only way to avoid a financial crisis 强迫出售:基于法院命令的销售,或是为了避免财务危机而不得不采取的销售措施

force majeure /ˌfɔːs mæˈʒɜː/ *noun* something which happens which is out of the control of the parties who have signed a contract, e.g. a strike, war or storm 不可抗力,人力不可抗拒:合约签署方无法控制的事情,如罢工、战争或风暴

forecast /ˈfɔːkɑːst/ *noun* a description or calculation of what will probably happen in the future 预测 ○ *The chairman did not believe the sales director's forecast of higher turnover.* 董事长不相信销售经理关于营业额增长的预测。

forecast dividend /ˌfɔːkɑːst ˈdɪvɪdend/ *noun* a dividend which a company expects to pay at the end of the current year 预期股利:公司预计在年末发放的股利 Also called 亦称作 **prospective dividend**

forecaster /ˈfɔːkɑːstə/ *noun* a person who says what he or she thinks will happen in the future 预测者(家),预言者(家)

forecasting /ˈfɔːkɑːstɪŋ/ *noun* the process of calculating what will probably happen in the future 预测 ○ *Manpower planning will depend on forecasting the future levels of production.* 人力资源计划将依赖于对未来生产水平的预测。

foreclose /fɔːˈkləʊz/ *verb* to sell a property because the owner cannot repay money which he or she has borrowed, using the property as security 取消赎回(抵押品)的权利 ○ *to foreclose on a mortgaged property* 取消抵押房产的赎回权

foreclosure /fɔːˈkləʊʒə/ *noun* an act of foreclosing 赎回(抵押品)权利的取消

foreign /ˈfɒrɪn/ *adjective* not belonging to your own country 外国的 ○ *Foreign cars have flooded our market.* 外国汽车充斥着我们的市场。○ *We are increasing our trade with foreign countries.* 我们正在增加同国外的贸易往来。

'... a sharp setback in foreign trade accounted for most of the winter slowdown'
"国际贸易锐减是冬季经济衰退的主要原因"[*Fortune*《财富》]

foreign banks /ˌfɒrɪn ˈbæŋks/ *plural noun* banks from other countries which have branches in a country 外国银行:外国银行设在本国的分支机构

foreign branch /ˌfɒrɪn ˈbrɑːntʃ/ *noun* a branch of a company in another country. The accounts of foreign branches may cause problems because of varying exchange rates 外国分支机构:公司设在外国的分支机构,其账目可能会因汇率的不同而出现问题

foreign company /ˌfɒrɪn ˈkʌmp(ə)ni/ *noun* company which is not resident in the UK 外国公司

foreign currency /ˌfɒrɪn ˈkʌrənsi/ *noun* money of another country 外币

foreign currency account /ˌfɒrɪn ˈkʌrənsi əˌkaʊnt/ *noun* a bank account in the currency of another country, e. g. a dollar account in a British bank 外币账户:如英国银行里的美元账户

foreign currency reserves /ˌfɒrɪn ˈkʌrənsi rɪˌzɜːvz/ *plural noun* a country's reserves held in currencies of other countries 外汇储备 Also called 亦称作 **foreign exchange reserves, international reserves**

'...the treasury says it needs the cash to rebuild its foreign reserves which have fallen from $ 19 billion when the government took office to $ 7 billion in August'
"财政部称其需要现金来重建外汇储备,因为外汇储备已从政府上台时的 190 亿美元下降到 8 月份的 70 亿美元" [*Economist*《经济学家》]

foreign earnings /ˌfɒrɪn ˈɜːnɪŋz/ *plural noun* earning received from employment outside the UK 国外盈利

foreign entity /ˌfɒrɪn ˈentɪti/ *noun* a person or incorporated company outside the UK 外国实体

foreign exchange /ˌfɒrɪn ɪksˈtʃeɪndʒ/ *noun* **1.** the business of exchanging the money of one country for that of another 国际汇兑 **2.** foreign currencies 外汇

'...the dollar recovered a little lost ground on the foreign exchanges yesterday'
"在昨天的外汇市场上,美元稍有回升" [*Financial Times*《金融时报》]

foreign exchange broker /ˌfɒrɪn ɪksˈtʃeɪndʒ ˌbrəʊkə/, **foreign exchange dealer** /ˌfɒrɪn ɪksˈtʃeɪndʒ ˌdiːlə/ *noun* a person who deals on the foreign exchange market 外汇经纪人

foreign exchange dealing /ˌfɒrɪn ɪksˈtʃeɪndʒ ˌdiːlɪŋ/ *noun* the business of buying and selling foreign currencies 外汇交易

foreign exchange market /ˌfɒrɪn ɪksˈtʃeɪndʒ ˌmɑːkɪt/ *noun* **1.** a market where people buy and sell foreign currencies 外汇市场 ○ *She trades on the foreign exchange market*. 她从事外汇市场交易。**2.** dealings in foreign currencies 外汇交易 ○ *Foreign exchange markets were very active after the dollar devalued*. 美元贬值之后,外汇交易非常活跃。

foreign exchange reserves /ˌfɒrɪn ɪksˈtʃeɪndʒ rɪˌzɜːvz/ *plural noun* foreign money held by a government to support its own currency and pay its debts 外汇储备:政府持有的用于支持本国货币和偿还债务的外币

foreign exchange transfer /ˌfɒrɪn ɪksˈtʃeɪndʒ ˌtrænsfɜː/ *noun* the sending of money from one country to another 外汇转移:把外汇转移到他国

foreign income /ˌfɒrɪn ˈɪnkʌm/ *noun* income which comes from outside the UK 国外收入

foreign investments /ˌfɒrɪn ɪnˈvestmənts/ *plural noun* money invested in other countries 国外投资

foreign money order /ˌfɒrɪn ˈmʌni ˌɔːdə/ *noun* a money order in a foreign currency which is payable to someone living in a foreign country 外币汇款单，外币邮政汇票

foreign rights /ˌfɒrɪn ˈraɪtz/ *plural noun* a legal entitlement to sell something in a foreign country, e. g. the right to translate a book into a foreign language 外国权利：在外国出售某物的合法权利，如将一本书翻译成外文的权利

foreign trade /ˈfɒrɪn treɪd/ *noun* a trade with other countries 对外贸易

forensic /fəˈrensɪk/ *adjective* referring to the courts or to the law in general 法庭的

forensic accounting /fəˌrensɪk əˈkaʊntɪŋ/ *noun* the scrutinisation of an entity's past financial activities in orde to discover whether illegal practices have been used at any time 法务会计：对某个实体历史财务活动进行的细查，以查证是否存在违法行为

forensic partner /fəˌrensɪk ˈpɑːtnə/ *noun* a partner in an accountancy firm who deals with litigation 法务合伙人：会计师事务所中负责处理诉讼的合伙人

foreseeable loss /fɔːˌsiːəb(ə)l ˈlɒs/ *noun* loss which is expected to occur during a long-term contract （长期合同中）可预见的损失

forfaiting /ˈfɔːfɪtɪŋ/ *noun* the action of providing finance for exporters, where an agent or forfaiter accepts a bill of exchange from an overseas customer; he or she buys the bill at a discount, and collects the payments from the customer in due course 未偿债务买卖：向出口商提供融资的一种方式，代理人从海外客户那里折价买入汇票，待汇票到期时收回款项

forfeit clause /ˈfɔːfɪt klɔːz/ *noun* a clause in a contract which says that goods or a deposit will be taken away if the contract is not obeyed 没收条款：合同中规定如有违约则没收物品或存款的条款

forfeiture /ˈfɔːfɪtʃə/ *noun* the act of forfeiting a property 没收

form /fɔːm/ *noun* **1.** □ **form of words** words correctly laid out for a legal document 法律文件的正式用语 □ **receipt in due form** a correctly written receipt 正式收据 **2.** an official printed paper with blank spaces which have to be filled in with information 表格 ○ *a pad of order forms* 一本订单 ○ *You have to fill in form A20.* 你必须填写A20表格。○ *Each passenger was given a customs declaration form.* 每位乘客都拿到一张海关申报表。○ *The reps carry pads of order forms.* 销售代表们拿着几本订单。

formal /ˈfɔːm(ə)l/ *adjective* clearly and legally written 正式的 ○ *to make a formal application* 正式申请 ○ *to send a formal order* 送交一份正式订单 ○ *Is this a formal job offer?* 这算不算正式的招聘？○ *The factory is prepared for the formal inspection by the government inspector.* 工厂正在为政府检查员的正式检查做准备。

formal documents /ˌfɔːm(ə)l ˈdɒkjʊmənts/ *plural noun* documents giving full details of a takeover bid（列明收购出价全部细节的）正式文件

formality /fɔːˈmælɪti/ *noun* something which has to be done to obey the law （法定）手续

formation /fɔːˈmeɪʃ(ə)n/, **forming**

/ˈfɔːmɪŋ/ *noun* the act of organizing 成立 ○ *the formation of a new company* 一家新公司的成立

form letter /ˈfɔːm ˌletə/ *noun* a letter which can be sent without any change to several correspondents，e.g. a letter chasing payment 打印信件，(内容相同可分寄多人的)通函(如催讨欠款信)

fortune /ˈfɔːtʃən/ *noun* a large amount of money 财富 ○ *He made a fortune from investing in oil shares*. 他投资石油股发了财。○ *She left her fortune to her three children*. 她将财产留给了她的三个孩子。

forward /ˈfɔːwəd/ *adjective* in advance or to be paid at a later date 预先的；远期的

forward contract /ˈfɔːwəd ˌkɒntrækt/ *noun* a one-off agreement to buy foreign currency or shares or commodities for delivery at a later date at a specific price 远期合约：购买按特定价格远期交割的外币、股票或商品的一次性合同

forward cover /ˈfɔːwəd ˌkʌvə/ *noun* an arrangement to cover the risks on a forward contract 远期保值：抵补远期合约风险的安排

forward delivery /ˌfɔːwəd dɪˈlɪv(ə)ri/ *noun* a delivery at some date in the future which has been agreed between the buyer and seller 远期交割：买卖双方约定未来某一日期的交割

forwarding address /ˈfɔːwədɪŋ əˌdres/ *noun* the address to which a person's mail can be sent on 转递地址

forwarding agent /ˈfɔːwədɪŋ ˌeɪdʒənt/ *noun* a person or company which arranges shipping and customs documents 发运代理，转运行

forward margin /ˌfɔːwəd ˈmɑːdʒɪn/ *noun* the difference between the current price and the forward price 远期差价：现行价格与远期价格之差

forward market /ˌfɔːwəd ˈmɑːkɪt/ *noun* a market for purchasing foreign currency，oil or commodities for delivery at a later date 远期市场：购买远期交割的外币、石油、商品等的市场

forward sales /ˈfɔːwəd seɪlz/ *plural noun* the sales of shares，commodities or foreign exchange for delivery at a later date 预销，期货销售：出售远期交割的股票、商品或外汇

forwards spreading /ˌfɔːwədz ˈspredɪŋ/ *noun* the act of spreading lump sum income over several years in the future 前向分配：把一次性收入分配到未来几年的行为

forward trading /ˈfɔːwəd ˌtreɪdɪŋ/ *noun* the activity of buying or selling commodities forward 远期交易

foul bill of lading /ˌfaʊl bɪl əv ˈleɪdɪŋ/ *noun* a bill of lading which says that the goods were in bad condition when received by the shipper 不洁提单：承运人指明货物收到时有缺少或损坏情况的提单

founder /ˈfaʊndə/ *noun* a person who starts a company 创立人，发起人

fourth quarter /ˌfɔːθ ˈkwɔːtə/ *noun* a period of three months from 1st October to the end of the year 第四季度

fraction /ˈfrækʃən/ *noun* a very small amount 小部分 ○ *Only a fraction of the new share issue was subscribed*. 只有小部分的新股被申购。

fractional /ˈfrækʃənəl/ *adjective* very small 少量的，微不足道的

fractional certificate /ˈfrækʃənəl

səˌtɪfɪkət/ *noun* a certificate for part of a share 零星股票凭证

franc /fræŋk/ *noun* 法郎 **1.** a former unit of currency in France and Belgium [法国和比利时曾使用的货币单位] ○ *French francs* or *Belgian francs* 法国法郎(或比利时法郎) **2.** a unit of currency in Switzerland and several other currencies [瑞士和若干其他国家的货币单位] ○ *It costs twenty-five Swiss francs*. 它卖25瑞士法郎。

franchise /ˈfræntʃaɪz/ *noun* a licence to trade using a brand name and paying a royalty for it 特许权,专营权 ○ *He's bought a printing franchise* or *a pizza franchise*. 他买下了印刷专营权(或比萨饼的专营权)。■ *verb* to sell licences for people to trade using a brand name and paying a royalty 卖给…专营权 ○ *His sandwich bar was so successful that he decided to franchise it*. 他的三明治食品店办得极为成功,他决定出卖其专营权。

'...many new types of franchised businesses will join the ranks of the giant chains of fast-food restaurants, hotels and motels and rental car agencies'
"快餐店、酒店、汽车旅馆和汽车出租代理行是连锁业的巨人,现在许多新型专营企业也将加入他们的行列"[*Franchising Opportunities*《特许经营商机》]

franchisee /ˌfræntʃaɪˈziː/ *noun* a person who runs a franchise 专营权使用者

franchiser /ˈfræntʃaɪzə/ *noun* a person who licenses a franchise 专营权拥有者

franchising /ˈfræntʃaɪzɪŋ/ *noun* the act of selling a licence to trade as a franchise 专营权的出售 ○ *She runs her sandwich chain as a franchising operation*. 她以特许经营的方式管理三明治连锁店。

franco /ˈfræŋkəʊ/ *adverb* free 运费可免地

franked /fræŋkt/ *adjective* on which tax has already been paid 已交税的

fraud /frɔːd/ *noun* an act of making money by making people believe something which is not true 欺诈,舞弊 ○ *He got possession of the property by fraud*. 他以欺诈的手段得到了这份财产。○ *She was accused of frauds relating to foreign currency*. 她被控外币欺诈。

fraudulent /ˈfrɔːdjʊlənt/ *adjective* not honest, or aiming to cheat people 欺诈的 ○ *a fraudulent transaction* 一桩欺诈交易

fraudulently /ˈfrɔːdjʊləntli/ *adverb* not honestly 欺诈地,不诚实地 ○ *goods imported fraudulently* 用欺诈手段进口的货物

fraudulent misrepresentation /ˌfrɔːdjʊlənt mɪsˌreprɪzenˈteɪʃ(ə)n/ *noun* the act of making a false statement with the intention of tricking a customer 欺诈性的虚假陈述

fraudulent trading /ˌfrɔːdjʊlənt ˈtreɪdɪŋ/ *noun* the process of carrying on the business of a company, knowing that the company is insolvent 欺诈经营:明知公司破产还继续经营的行为

free /friː/ *adjective*, *adverb* **1.** not costing any money 免费的(地) ○ *I have been given a free ticket to the exhibition*. 我得到一张免费参观展览的票。○ *The price includes free delivery*. 价格包含运费。○ *All goods in the store are delivered free*. 商店里的所有商品都能免费送货。○ *A catalogue will be sent free on request*. 目录可以免费索取。**2.** with no restrictions 自由的(地) □ **free of tax** with no tax having to be paid 免税的;不用交税的 ○ *Interest is paid free of tax*. 利息

不用交税。□ **free of duty** with no duty to be paid 免关税的 ○ *to import wine free of duty* 进口免关税的酒 ■ *verb* to make something available or easy 使…可以得到,使…不受束缚 ○ *The government's decision has freed millions of pounds for investment.* 政府的决定使得几百万英镑可用于投资。

'American business as a whole is increasingly free from heavy dependence on manufacturing'
"美国商业从整体上说正在日益摆脱严重依赖制造业的局面"[*Sunday Times*《星期日泰晤士报》]

free competition /ˌfriː kɒmpəˈtɪʃ(ə)n/ *noun* the fact of being free to compete without government interference 自由竞争,安全竞争

free currency /ˌfriː ˈkʌrənsi/ *noun* a currency which is allowed by the government to be bought and sold without restriction 自由通货,可自由兑换的货币:政府允许可自由买卖的通货

free enterprise /ˌfriː ˈentəpraɪz/ *noun* a system of business free from government interference 自由经营,自由企业:不受政府干预的企业制度

freeholder /ˈfriːhəʊldə/ *noun* a person who owns a freehold property 完全保有房地产者,永久业权所有者

freehold property /ˈfriːhəʊld ˌprɒpəti/ *noun* property which the owner holds for ever and on which no rent is paid 完全保有房地产,永久业权财产

free issue /ˌfriː ˈɪʃuː/ *noun* same as 同 **scrip issue**

free market /friː ˈmɑːkɪt/ *noun* a market in which there is no government control of supply and demand, and the rights of individuals and organisations to physical and intellectual property are upheld 自由市场:不存在政府对供求的控制,个人和机构的有形财产和知识产权得到充分保护的市场

free market economy /friː ˌmɑːkɪt ɪˈkɒnəmi/ *noun* a system where the government does not interfere in business activity in any way 自由市场经济:政府不以任何形式干预经济活动的制度

free on board /ˌfriː ɒn ˈbɔːd/ *adjective* **1.** including in the price all the seller's costs until the goods are on the ship for transportation. 船上交货价,离岸价:包括卖方在指定的装运港将货物装船之前所发生费用的成交价 Abbreviation 缩写 **f.o.b.** **2.** including in the price all the seller's costs until the goods are delivered to a place 目的地交货价:包括直到货物交至某个地点的卖方全部成本的价格

free reserves /ˌfriː rɪˈzɜːvz/ *plural noun* the part of a bank's reserves which are above the statutory level and so can be used for various purposes as the bank wishes 自由储备金:银行高于法定水平可自由支配的储备金

free-standing additional voluntary contribution /friːˌstændɪŋ əˌdɪʃ(ə)nəl ˌvɒlənt(ə)ri ˌkɒntrɪˈbjuːʃ(ə)n/ *noun* a payment made by an individual into an independent pension fund to supplement an occupational pension scheme. The anticipated benefits from the two schemes together must be less than the maximum permitted under the rules laid down by the Inland Revenue 独立额外自愿养老金缴款:个人向一种独立退休基金的缴款,作为对职业退休金计划的补充。从这两个系统获得的预计福利总额,须低于国内税务局规定的上限 Abbreviation 缩写 **FSAVC**

free trade /friː ˈtreɪd/ *noun* a system where goods can go from one country to another without any restrictions 自由贸易:货物可以在国与国之间自由交易的体制

'...can free trade be reconciled with a strong dollar resulting from floating exchange rates?'
"自由贸易能与浮动汇率制下坚挺的美元协调共存吗?" [*Duns Business Month*《邓氏商业月刊》]

free trade area /friː ˈtreɪd ˌeəriə/ *noun* a group of countries practising free trade 自由贸易区:实行自由贸易的国家联盟

free trader /ˌfriː ˈtreɪdə/ *noun* a person who is in favour of free trade 自由贸易主义者

'...free traders hold that the strong dollar is the primary cause of the nation's trade problems'
"自由贸易主义者认为,美元坚挺是引起该国贸易问题的主要原因" [*Duns Business Month*《邓氏商业月刊》]

free trade zone /friː ˈtreɪd ˌzəʊn/ *noun* an area where there are no customs duties 自由贸易区:没有关税的地区

free trial /ˌfriː ˈtraɪəl/ *noun* an opportunity to test a machine or product with no payment involved (机械或产品的)免费试用

freeze /friːz/ *noun* □ **a freeze on wages and prices** period when wages and prices are not allowed to be increased 工资和物价冻结:不允许工资和物价上涨的时期 ■ *verb* to keep something such as money or costs at their present level and not allow them to rise 冻结:保持成本、资产等的现有水平,不许其上涨 ○ *to freeze wages and prices* 冻结工资和物价 ○ *to freeze credits* 冻结信贷 ○ *to freeze company dividends* 冻结公司股利 ○ *We have frozen expenditure at last year's level.* 我们已将支出限定在去年的水平上。(NOTE: **freezing – froze – frozen**)

freight /freɪt/ *noun* the cost of transporting goods by air, sea or land 运费 ○ *At an auction, the buyer pays the freight.* 竞拍到的物品由买方支付运费。

freightage /ˈfreɪtɪdʒ/ *noun* the cost of transporting goods 运费

freight costs /ˈfreɪt kɒsts/ *plural noun* money paid to transport goods 运输成本

freight forward /ˌfreɪt ˈfɔːwəd/ *noun* a deal where the customer pays for transporting the goods 运费到付:运费由提货人支付的交易

friendly society /ˈfrendli səˌsaɪəti/ *noun* a group of people who pay regular subscriptions which are used to help members of the group when they are ill or in financial difficulties 互助协会:其成员定期缴纳会费,以备需要时帮助生病或经济困难的会员

fringe benefit /frɪndʒ ˈbenɪfɪt/ *noun* an extra item given by a company to employees in addition to a salary, e.g. company cars or private health insurance (公家汽车或私人健康保险等除工资外的)附加福利 ○ *The fringe benefits make up for the poor pay.* 附加福利弥补了少得可怜的工资。○ *Use of the company recreation facilities is one of the fringe benefits of the job.* 使用公司娱乐设施是该工作的附加福利之一。

FRN *abbr* floating rate note 浮动利率票据

front /frʌnt/ *noun* □ **money up front** payment in advance 预付款 ○ *They are* *asking for £10,000 up front before they will consider the deal.* 他们要求先付一万英镑，然后才考虑这笔交易。○ *He had to put money up front before he could clinch the deal.* 他在成交之前必须先交一笔预付款。

front-end /ˌfrʌnt'end/ *adjective* referring to the start of an investment or insurance 开端的，开始的

front-end loaded /'frʌntend ˌləʊdɪd/ *adjective* referring to an insurance or investment scheme where most of the management charges are incurred in the first year of the investment or insurance, and are not spread out over the whole period 前期负担：一种保险或投资计划，它的大部分管理费都发生在保险或投资的第一年，而不是分摊到整个期间 Compare 比较 **back-end loaded**

frozen /'frəʊz(ə)n/ *adjective* not allowed to be changed or used 冻结的 ○ *Wages have been frozen at last year's rates.* 工资已被限定在去年的水平上。

frozen account /'frəʊz(ə)n əˌkaʊnt/ *noun* a bank account where the money cannot be moved or used because of a court order 冻结账户：法院命令不能转移或使用的银行账户

frozen assets /ˌfrəʊz(ə)n 'æsets/ *plural noun* a company's assets which by law can not be sold because someone has a claim against them 冻结资产：依法不能出售的公司资产

frozen credits /ˌfrəʊz(ə)n 'kredɪts/ *plural noun* credits in an account which cannot be moved 冻结贷款：账户里不能动用的贷款

FRRP *abbr* Financial Reporting Review Panel 财务报告核查委员会

FRSs *abbr* Financial Reporting Standards 财务报告准则

frustrate /frʌ'streɪt/ *verb* to prevent something, especially the terms of a contract, being fulfilled 阻挠（尤其是合同条款的）履行

FSA *abbr* Financial Services Authority （英国）金融服务管理局

FSAVC *abbr* free-standing additional voluntary contribution 独立额外自愿养老金缴款

FT 500 Share Index /ˌef tiː faɪv 'hʌndrəd 'ʃeə ˌɪndeks/ *noun* an index based on the market prices of 500 leading companies in the manufacturing, retailing and service sectors 《金融时报》500 种股票价格指数：根据 500 家制造业、零售业和服务业大公司的市价计算出来的指数

FT Actuaries Share Indices /ˌef tiː ˌæktjʊəriz 'ʃeə ˌɪndɪsiːz/ *plural noun* several indices based on prices on the London Stock Exchange, which are calculated by and published in the Financial Times in conjunction with the Institute of Actuaries and the Faculty of Actuaries 《金融时报》股票价格指数：基于伦敦证券交易所股价的若干指数，由金融时报联合英国精算师协会计算和发布

FT Industrial Group Share Index /ˌef tiː ɪn'dʌstriəl gruːp 'ʃeə ˌɪndeks/ *noun* an index based on the market prices of more than 470 leading industrial companies 《金融时报》工业集团股票价格指数：根据 470 多家主要工业企业的市价计算出来的指数

FT Ordinary Share Index /ˌef tiː 'ɔːdənri 'ʃeə ˌɪndeks/ *noun* an index based on the market prices of thirty blue-chip companies. This index is the oldest of the FT indices, and is now considered too narrow to have much relevance 《金融时报》普通股票价格指数：根据 30 家

蓝筹股公司的市价计算出来的指数。该指数是《金融时报》历史最悠久的指数，但现在被认为反映面过窄，不足以反映市场状况

FTSE 100 /ˌfʊtsi wʌn ˈhʌndrəd/ *noun* an index based on the prices of one hundred leading companies (this is the main London index)《金融时报》股票交易所 100 种股票价格指数：根据 100 家主要公司股票市价计算出来的指数（这是伦敦的主要指数）

'...the benchmark FTSE 100 index ended the session up 94.3 points'
"该时段交易结束时，《金融时报》股票交易所 100 种股票价格指数上涨了 94.3 点" [*Times*《泰晤士报》]

FT-Stock Exchange 100 Share Index /ˌef tiː stɒk ɪksˈtʃeɪndʒ wʌn ˈhʌndrəd ˈʃeə ˌɪndeks/ *noun* the main London index based on the prices of one hundred leading companies《金融时报》股票交易所 100 种股票价格指数：根据 100 家主要公司股票市价计算出来的伦敦主要指数 Also called 亦称作 **FT-SE 100**

full /fʊl/ *adjective* **1.** with as much inside it as possible 满的 ○ *The train was full of commuters.* 火车上挤满了上班族。○ *Is the container full yet?* 容器满了吗？○ *We sent a lorry full of spare parts to our warehouse.* 我们把满满一车的零部件送到仓库里。○ *When the disk is full, don't forget to make a backup copy.* 磁盘写满时，记着做个备份。**2.** complete, including everything 完全的，全部的

'...a tax-free lump sum can be taken partly in lieu of a full pension'
"可以使用一次性免税款项的一部分来代替全部养老金" [*Investors Chronicle*《投资者纪事》]

full cover /ˌfʊl ˈkʌvə/ *noun* insurance cover against all risks 完全承保：保障一切风险的保险

full employment /ˌfʊl ɪmˈplɔɪmənt/ *noun* a situation where all the people who can work have jobs 充分就业

full price /ˈfʊl praɪs/ *noun* a price with no discount 全价，足价：不打折扣的价格 ○ *She bought a full-price ticket.* 她买了一张全价票。

full production costs /ˌfʊl prəˈdʌkʃən ˌkɒsts/ *plural noun* all the costs of manufacturing a product, including both fixed and variable costs 全部生产成本：包括固定和可变成本在内的所有生产成本

full rate /ˌfʊl ˈreɪt/ *noun* the full charge, with no reductions 全价

full repairing lease /ˌfʊl rɪˈpeərɪŋ ˌliːs/ *noun* a lease where the tenant has to pay for all repairs to the property 承租人负责承担所有维修费用的租约

full-scale /ˈfʊlskeɪl/ *adjective* complete or very thorough 完全的，彻底的 ○ *The MD ordered a full-scale review of credit terms.* 常务董事命令全面审查信贷条件。○ *The HR department will start a full-scale review of the present pay structure.* 人力资源部将开始全面审查现行的工资结构。

'...the administration launched a full-scale investigation into maintenance procedures'
"管理当局对保养程序进行了全面调查" [*Fortune*《财富》]

full-service banking /fʊlˌsɜːvɪs ˈbæŋkɪŋ/ *noun* banking that offers a whole range of services including mortgages, loans, pensions, etc. 提供

各种服务的银行业（包括按揭、贷款、养老金等）

full-time /ˈfʊltaɪm/ *adjective*, *adverb* working all the usual working time, i. e. about eight hours a day, five days a week 全职的（地）○ *She's in full-time work* or *She works full-time* or *She's in full-time employment*. 她是一名全职雇员。○ *He is one of our full-time staff*. 他是我们的全职员工之一。

full-time employment /ˌfʊltaɪm ɪmˈplɔɪmənt/ *noun* work for all of a working day 全职工作 ○ *to be in full-time employment* 从事全职工作

fully /ˈfʊli/ *adverb* completely 完全地

'... issued and fully paid capital is $100 million'
"已发行并已缴足的股本是一亿美元"
[*Hong Kong Standard*《香港虎报》]

fully diluted earnings per share /ˌfʊli daɪˌluːtɪd ˌɜːnɪŋz pə ˈʃeə/, **fully diluted EPS** /ˌfʊli ˌdaɪluːtɪd ˌiː piː ˈes/ *plural noun* earnings per share calculated over the whole number of shares assuming that convertible shares have been converted to ordinary shares 完全稀释的每股收益：按全部股票数目计算的每股收益，其中可转换证券被假定为已转成普通股

fully paid-up capital /ˌfʊli peɪdʌp ˈkæpɪt(ə)l/ *noun* all money paid for the issued capital shares 已全部缴清的股本，已缴足的股票

function /ˈfʌŋkʃən/ *verb* to work 运转，起作用 ○ *The advertising campaign is functioning smoothly*. 广告活动进展顺利。○ *The new management structure does not seem to be functioning very well*. 新的管理架构看来运转不太顺畅。

functional /ˈfʌŋkʃən(ə)l/ *adjective* referring to a job 功能的，职能的

functional budget /ˌfʌŋkʃən(ə)l ˈbʌdʒɪt/ *noun* a budget relating to a specific function such as marketing or personnel 职能预算：与某一职能（如营销或人事）有关的预算

functional diagram /ˌfʌŋkʃ(ə)nəl ˈdaɪəgræm/ *noun* a drawing of the internal workings and processes of a machine or piece of software 功能图：描绘一台机器或一个软件内部运作过程的图画

functional specification /ˌfʌŋkʃ(ə)nəl ˌspesɪfɪˈkeɪʃ(ə)n/ *noun* a specification which defines the results which a program is expected to produce 功能说明书：介绍一个程序可能产生的结果的说明书

functional unit /ˌfʌŋkʃən(ə)l ˈjuːnɪt/ *noun* hardware or software that works as it should 功能单位：运转正常的硬件或软件

fund /fʌnd/ *noun* **1.** money set aside for a special purpose 基金，专款 **2.** money invested in an investment trust as part of a unit trust, or given to a financial adviser to invest on behalf of a client 基金：作为单位信托的一部分，投资在投资信托的资金，或由财务顾问代客户投资的资金 ⇨ 参阅 **funds** ■ *verb* to provide money for a purpose 为（一定目的）提供资金 ○ *The company does not have enough resources to fund its expansion programme*. 公司没有足够的融资渠道来为其扩张计划提供资金。

'... the S&L funded all borrowers' development costs, including accrued interest' "储蓄贷款协会为所有借款人的开发成本(包括应计利息)提供资金"[*Barrons*《巴伦》]

fund accounting /ˈfʌnd əˌkaʊntɪŋ/ *noun* the preparation of financial statements for an entity which is a fund 基金会计:编制基金实体的财务报表

fundamental /ˌfʌndəˈment(ə)l/ *adjective* basic or most important 基本的;最重要的

fundamental assumptions /ˌfʌndəment(ə)l əˈsʌmpʃ(ə)ns/ *plural noun* the basic assumptions on which the preparation of accounts depends: that the company is a going concern, that the principles on which the accounts are prepared do not change from year to year, that revenues and costs are accrued (i.e., they are written into the accounts when they occur, not when they are received or paid) 基本假设:公司编制报表时依据的基本假设,包括对经营的业务进行持续监控,做账原则应保持一贯性,权责发生制假设(即对收入和花费的入账以发生时间为准,而非按照现金的取得或支付时间入账)

fundamental issues /ˌfʌndəment(ə)l ˈɪʃuːz/ *plural noun* matters relating to a company's profits or assets 重大问题:与公司利润或资产相关的事宜

fundamental research /ˌfʌndəment(ə)l rɪˈsɜːtʃ/, **fundamental analysis** /ˌfʌndəment(ə)l əˈnæləsɪs/ *noun* an examination of the basic factors which affect a market 基本研究,基本因素分析:对影响市场的基本因素进行的分析

fundamentals /ˌfʌndəˈment(ə)lz/ *plural noun* the basic realities of a stock market or of a company, e.g. its assets, profitability and dividends 基本因素,基本面:公司或证券市场的基本情况,如资产、利润率和股利

funded /ˈfʌndɪd/ *adjective* backed by longterm loans 有保证的:有长期贷款支持的 ○ *long-term funded capital* 有固定利息的长期借款

funded scheme /ˌfʌndɪd ˈskiːm/ *noun* a pension scheme where money is invested in securities to create a fund from which the pension is later paid 养老基金方案:将资金投资于证券来创立一个基金,以备日后从基金中支付养老金

funding /ˈfʌndɪŋ/ *noun* **1.** money for spending 资金 ○ *The bank is providing the funding for the new product launch.* 银行为新产品的推出提供资金。**2.** the act of changing a short-term debt into a long-term loan 将短期负债转换成长期债务 ○ *The capital expenditure programme requires long-term funding.* 这个资本支出计划需要长期借款。

fund management /ˈfʌnd ˌmænɪdʒmənt/ *noun* the business of dealing with the investment of sums of money on behalf of clients 基金管理:受客户委托进行投资管理的商业行为

funds /fʌndz/ *plural noun* **1.** money which is available for spending 现款 ○ *The company has no funds to pay for the research programme.* 公司没有现款来支付研究经费。□ **to convert funds to your own use** to use someone else's money for yourself 盗用资金,非法挪用:侵吞他人款项或资金 □ **budgeted funds flow statement** plan of anticipated incoming funds and the use to which they will be put 预算资金流量

报告 □ **funds flow method of budgeting** preparing a budget of funds flow, as opposed to a budget of expenditure 编制资金流量预算(而不是支出预算) □ **funds flow statement** statement which shows the amount of funds (cash and working capital) which have come into a business during the last financial period, the sources of these funds, and the use made of the funds 资金流量报告:表明企业上个会计年度以来的资金(现金和营运资本)的来源与运用的报表 **2.** government stocks and securities 政府证券 □ **the Funds** government stocks and securities 政府证券

'...small innovative companies have been hampered for lack of funds'
"小规模创新型公司因为缺乏资金而发展受阻"[*Sunday Times*《星期日泰晤士报》]
'...the company was set up with funds totaling NorKr 145m'
"该公司的创办资金是 1.45 亿挪威克郎"[*Lloyd's List*《劳氏日报》]

fungibility /ˌfʌndʒəˈbɪlɪti/ *noun* the ability to be exchanged for something similar 可换成类似物

fungible /ˈfʌndʒəb(ə)l/ *adjective* referring to a security which can be exchanged for another of the same type (同类证券)可代替的,可转换的:证券可以换成同类型中的另一种证券

funny money /ˈfʌni ˌmʌni/ *noun* an unusual type of financial instrument created by a company 怪证券:某公司发明的一种特殊金融工具

furnished lettings /ˌfɜːnɪʃt ˈletɪŋz/ *plural noun* a furnished property to let 含家具的物业出租

furniture depository /ˈfɜːnɪtʃə dɪˌpɒzɪt(ə)ri/ *noun* a warehouse where you can store household furniture 家具存放仓库

future /ˈfjuːtʃə/ *adjective* referring to time to come or to something which has not yet happened 将来的

future delivery /ˌfjuːtʃə dɪˈlɪv(ə)ri/ *noun* delivery at a later date 远期交割

futures /ˈfjuːtʃəz/ *plural noun* shares, currency or commodities that are bought or sold for now for delivery at a later date 期货:现在购买但远期交割的股票、货币或商品 ○ *Gold rose 5% on the commodity futures market yesterday.* 在昨天的商品期货市场上,金价上涨了 5%。

'...cocoa futures plummeted in November to their lowest levels in seven years'
"11 月份,可可期货暴跌到七年来的最低价位"[*Business in Africa*《非洲商业》]

futures contract /ˈfjuːtʃəz ˌkɒntrækt/ *noun* a contract for the purchase of commodities for delivery at a date in the future 期货合同

futures exchange /ˈfjuːtʃəz ɪksˌtʃeɪndʒ/ *noun* a commodity market which only deals in futures 期货交易所

future value /ˌfjuːtʃə ˈvæljuː/ *noun* the value to which a sum of money will increase if invested for a certain period of time at some rate of interest 未来值:按某一利率投资一定期限时,一定量的资金可以增加到的价值 Abbreviation 缩写 **FV**

FV *abbr* future value 未来值

FYA *abbr* first year allowance 第一年税收减免

G

GAAP *abbr* Generally Accepted Accounting Principles 公认会计原则

gain /geɪn/ *noun* **1.** an increase, or the act of becoming larger 增加;变大 **2.** an increase in profit, price or value (利润、价格或价值的)增加 ○ *Oil shares showed gains on the Stock Exchange.* 证券交易所的石油股价出现上涨。○ *Property shares put on gains of 10%–15%.* 房地产股上涨了10%–15%。■ *verb* **1.** to get or to obtain 获得 ○ *She gained some useful experience working in a bank.* 她在银行工作的时候获得了一些有益经验。□ **to gain control of a business** to buy more than 50% of the shares so that you can direct the business 获得某企业的控制权:为控制某企业购买其50%以上的股权 **2.** to rise in value 升值 ○ *The dollar gained six points on the foreign exchange markets.* 在外汇市场上,美元升值了六个点。

galloping inflation /ˌgæləpɪŋ ɪnˈfleɪʃ(ə)n/ *noun* very rapid inflation which is almost impossible to reduce 飞速通货膨胀

gap analysis /ˈgæp əˌnæləsɪs/ *noun* analysis of a market to try to find a particular area that is not at present being satisfied 差距分析:为找到顾客需求尚未得到满足的领域而作的市场分析 ○ *Gap analysis showed that there was a whole area of the market we were not exploiting.* 差距分析显示,我们还有一整块市场领域尚未开发。○ *The computer performed a gap analysis and came up with suggestions for a mediumpriced machine suitable for the small business market.* 电脑执行了差距分析操作,就适合小型企业市场的中等价位的机器生成了相关建议。

gap financing /ˈgæp ˌfaɪnænsɪŋ/ *noun* arranging extra loans such as a bridging loan to cover a purchase not covered by an existing loan 缺口融资:筹备额外的贷款(如过渡性贷款),以填补购买行为发生时现有贷款无法支付的资金缺口

garnishee /ˌgɑːnɪˈʃiː/ *noun* a person who owes money to a creditor and is ordered by a court to pay that money to a creditor of the creditor, and not to the creditor himself 第三债务人:被法庭责令将欠款支付给债权人的债务人、而不是支付给债权人本身的债务人

garnishee order /ˌgɑːnɪˈʃiː ˌɔːdə/ *noun* a court order, making a garnishee pay money not to the debtor, but to a third party 第三债务人财产扣押令:要求第三债务人付款给第三方(而非第三债务人的债权人)的法庭命令

GAS *abbr* Government Accountancy Service 政府会计事务所

gazumping /gəˈzʌmpɪŋ/ *noun* the practice of offering a higher price for a house than another buyer has already agreed with the seller 抬价买房：提出高于另一买方已与卖方商定的房价购房

gear /gɪə/ *verb* to link something to something else 挂钩，连接

gearing /ˈɡɪərɪŋ/ *noun* **1.** a ratio of capital borrowed by a company at a fixed rate of interest to the company's total capital 杠杆比率，负债比率：公司按固定利率借入的资本与公司总资本的比率 Also called 亦称作 **leverage** **2.** the act of borrowing money at fixed interest which is then used to produce more money than the interest paid 杠杆经营，举债经营：按固定利息借入资本，用以产生比利息更高的收益

general audit /ˌdʒen(ə)rəl ˈɔːdɪt/ *noun* a process of examining all the books and accounts of a company 全面审计：审查公司的全部账簿及报表

general average /ˌdʒen(ə)rəl ˈæv(ə)rɪdʒ/ *noun* a process by which the cost of lost goods is shared by all parties to an insurance, such as in cases where some goods have been lost in an attempt to save the rest of the cargo 共同海损：由保险各方分摊货物损失费用的做法，例如，在试图抢救海运货物时造成某些货物损失的情况即适用共同海损分摊费用

General Commissioners /ˌdʒen(ə)rəl kəˈmɪʃ(ə)nəz/ *noun* a body of unpaid individuals appointed by the Lord Chancellor in England, Wales, and Northern Ireland, and the Secretary of State for Scotland in Scotland, to hear appeals on tax matters 税务专员委员会：成员由英格兰、威尔士及北爱尔兰的大法官和苏格兰事务大臣共同委任，不领取报酬，负责审理关于税务问题的上诉

general damages /ˌdʒen(ə)rəl ˈdæmɪdʒɪz/ *plural noun* damages awarded by court to compensate for a loss which can not be calculated such as an injury 一般损害赔偿金：法庭判定的损害赔偿金，用以补偿人身伤害等造成的无法量化的损失

general expenses /ˌdʒen(ə)rəl ɪkˈspensɪz/ *plural noun* all kinds of minor expenses, the money spent on the day-to-day costs of running a business 一般费用：企业日常运营中的各项杂费支出

general fund /ˈdʒen(ə)rəl fʌnd/ *noun* a unit trust with investments in a variety of stocks 普通基金：投资于多种证券的单位信托

general insurance /ˌdʒen(ə)rəl ɪnˈʃʊərəns/ *noun* insurance covering all kinds of risk, e.g. theft, loss or damage, but excluding life insurance 普通保险：涉及被盗、损失、损害等的保险，不包括人寿保险

general ledger /ˌdʒen(ə)rəl ˈledʒə/ *noun* a book which records a company's income and expenditure in general 总账，总分类账：记录公司总收支的账簿

general lien /ˌdʒen(ə)rəl ˈliːən/ *noun* 一般留置权 **1.** a right to hold goods or property until a debt has been paid［在债务偿清前对债务人的物品或财产的占有权］ **2.** a lien against the personal possessions of a borrower, but not against his or her house or land［对借款人的私人财产（不包括其房屋或土地）的扣押权］ ⇨ 参阅 **banker's lien**

Generally Accepted Accounting Principles /ˌdʒen(ə)rəli əkˌseptɪd əˈkaʊntɪŋ ˌprɪnsɪp(ə)lz/ *plural noun US* a summary of best practice in respect of the form and content of financial statements and auditor's reports, and of accounting policies and disclosures adopted for the preparation of financial information. GAAP does not have any statutory or regulatory authority in the United Kingdom, unlike in a number of other countries where the term is in use, such as the United States, Canada (美)公认会计原则:优秀会计实务的概括汇总,涉及对财务报表及审计师报告中格式与内容的规范,以及准备财务数据时对会计政策和所披露信息的选取原则。与美国、加拿大等国家不同,公认会计原则在英国没有任何法定机构或监管机构 Abbreviation 缩写 **GAAP**

general manager /ˌdʒen(ə)rəl ˈmænɪdʒə/ *noun* a manager in charge of the administration of a company 总经理

general meeting /ˌdʒen(ə)rəl ˈmiːtɪŋ/ *noun* a meeting of all the shareholders of a company or of all the members of a society 股东大会,会员大会:公司全体股东或社团全体会员出席的大会

general office /ˈdʒen(ə)rəl ˌɒfɪs/ *noun* the main administrative office of a company 总办事处,总部

general partner /ˌdʒen(ə)rəl ˈpɑːtnə/ *noun* a partner in a partnership whose responsibility for its debts is not limited 无限责任合伙人,普通合伙人:对合伙企业的债务负有无限责任的合伙人

general partnership /ˌdʒen(ə)rəl ˈpɑːtnəʃɪp/ *noun* a partnership where the liability of each partner is not limited 无限责任合伙,普通合伙:每个合伙人都负有无限责任的一种合伙关系

general undertaking /ˌdʒen(ə)rəl ˌʌndəˈteɪkɪŋ/ *noun* an undertaking signed by the directors of a company applying for a Stock Exchange listing, promising to work within the regulations of the Stock Exchange 全面保证:公司在申请上市时,由公司董事签署的遵守证券交易所规章的保证书

gensaki /dʒenˈsɑːki/ *noun* a Japanese bond market, dealing in bonds issued with agreements to repurchase at less than twelve months' notice 日本债券回购市场:发行需按合约在 12 个月内重新购回的债券

get back /ˌget ˈbæk/ *verb* to receive something which you had before 收回 ○ *I got my money back after I had complained to the manager*. 在向经理投诉后,我拿回了我的钱。○ *He got his initial investment back in two months*. 他在两个月内收回了初期投资。

get out /ˌget ˈaʊt/ *verb* **1.** to produce something 产出 ○ *The accounts department got out the draft accounts in time for the meeting*. 会计部门及时为这次会议编制了报表草案。**2.** to sell an investment (*informal*) 出售投资(非正式) ○ *He didn't like what he read in the company's annual report, so he got out before the company collapsed*. 由于对公司年度报告不甚满意,他在公司破产前撤出了投资。

get out of /ˌget ˈaʊt əv/ *verb* to stop trading in a product or an area 停止经营(某产品);停止在(某地区)经营 ○ *The company is getting out of computers*. 该公司将退出计算机市场。○ *We got out of the South American market*. 我们退出了南美市场。

get round /ˌget ˈraʊnd/ *verb* to avoid 避开 ○ *We tried to get round the* *embargo by shipping from Canada*. 我们试图从加拿大启运，以避开禁运。

gift /gɪft/ *noun* a thing which is given to someone 礼物

gift aid /ˈgɪft eɪd/ *noun* payment above some limit made to a registered charity, meaning that the charity is able to reclaim the basic rate tax which you have paid on the gift 赠予性资助：向注册慈善机构提供的高于一定限额的捐款，慈善机构可以申领捐赠人已为该捐款支付的基本税款

gift coupon /ˈgɪft ˌkuːpɒn/, **gift token** /ˈgɪft ˌtəʊkən/ , **gift voucher** /ˈgɪft ˌvaʊtʃə/ *noun* a card that can be used to buy specified goods up to the value printed on it, often issued by chain stores. The person receiving the voucher is able to redeem it in any store in the chain 礼券，代金券：一种购物卡，凭券可购买总价位在其面值数额以内的特定商品，常常由连锁商店分发，获赠礼券者可在发放礼券商店的任一分店兑换商品 ○ *We gave her a gift token for her birthday*. 我们送给她一张礼券作为生日礼物。

gift inter vivos /ˌgɪft ɪntə ˈviːvəʊs/ *noun* a gift given to another living person 生前赠予：赠予人在世时给予另一在世者的馈赠 Abbreviation 缩写 **GIV**

gilt-edged /ˈgɪltedʒd/ *adjective* referring to an investment which is very safe (投资)金边的，优良的，十分安全的

gilt-edged securities /ˌgɪltedʒd sɪˈkjʊərɪtiz/ *plural noun* investments in British government stock 金边证券

gilts /gɪlts/ *plural noun* same as 同 **government bonds**

giro /ˈdʒaɪrəʊ/ *noun* same as 同 ***bank giro***

GIV *abbr* gift inter vivos 生前赠与

GM *abbr* gross margin 毛利率

GNP *abbr* gross national product 国民生产总值

go back on /ˌgəʊ ˈbæk ɒn/ *verb* not to carry out something after you have promised to do it 违反，违背(承诺) ○ *Two months later they went back on the agreement*. 两个月后他们违约了。

go-go fund /ˈgəʊgəʊ ˌfʌnd/ *noun* a fund which aims to give very high returns because it is invested in speculative stocks 冒险投资基金：为获得高收益而投资于投机性证券的基金

going /ˈgəʊɪŋ/ *adjective* current 当前的，进行中的

going concern /ˌgəʊɪŋ kənˈsɜːn/ *noun* a company that is actively trading and making a profit 盈利企业

going concern value /ˌgəʊɪŋ kənˈsɜːn ˌvæljuː/ *noun* the value of a corporation as it continues trading as opposed to its breakup value 持续经营价值：公司作为一个持续经营的实体的价值(与之相对的是清算价值)

go into /ˌgəʊ ˈɪntuː/ *verb* to examine something carefully 仔细检查；调查 ○ *The bank wants to go into the details of the inter-company loans*. 该银行想调查公司间贷款的详情。

go into business /ˌgəʊ ɪntə ˈbɪznɪs/ *verb* to start in business 开始职业生涯；开始经商 ○ *He went into business as a car dealer*. 他做起了汽车经销商。○ *She went into business in partnership with her son*. 她和儿子开始合伙做生意。

gold bullion /ˌgəʊld ˈbʊliən/ *noun* bars of gold 金条

gold card /ˈgəʊld kɑːd/ *noun* a credit card issued to important customers, i.e., those with a high income, which gives certain privileges such as a higher spending limit than ordinary credit cards 金卡:发放给高收入的重要客户的信用卡,持卡人可享有一定特权,如透支限额会高于普通信用卡

golden handshake /ˌgəʊld(ə)n ˈhændʃeɪk/ *noun* a large, usually tax-free, sum of money given to a director who retires from a company before the end of his or her service contract 离职金,解职费:给予提前离职经理人的一笔数额丰厚且通常无需纳税的款项○ *The retiring director received a golden handshake of £250,000.* 离任主管获得了25万英镑的解职费。

golden share /ˌgəʊld(ə)n ˈʃeə/ *noun* a share in a privatised company which is retained by the government and carries special privileges such as the right to veto foreign takeover bids 黄金股份:私有化公司里政府保留的股份,持有该股份可享有一些特别权益,包括有权否决外国企业的收购投标

gold fixing /ˈgəʊld ˌfɪksɪŋ/ *noun* a system where the world price for gold is set twice a day in US dollars on the London Gold Exchange and in Paris and Zurich 议定金价,黄金定价:在伦敦黄金交易所以及巴黎和苏黎士实行的黄金定价系统,每日定价两次,以美元为定价货币

goldmine /ˈgəʊldmaɪn/ *noun* a mine which produces gold 金矿

gold point /ˈgəʊld pɔɪnt/ *noun* an amount by which a currency which is linked to gold can vary in price 输金点,黄金输送点:对于与金价挂钩的货币,其价格波动的上下限

gold reserves /ˈgəʊld rɪˌzɜːvz/ *plural noun* the country's store of gold kept to pay international debts 黄金储备:一国为偿还国际债务而储备的黄金

goods /gʊdz/ *plural noun* items which can be moved and are for sale 货物,商品 □ **goods received** goods which have been sent by a seller and received by a purchaser during an accounting period 已收货物:在会计期内卖方已发出且买方已收到的货物 □ **goods received note** internal note within a company which shows the date when goods were received, by whom and in what quantities 收货单:列明收货日期、收货人和货物数量的内部单据

'...profit margins are lower in the industries most exposed to foreign competition—machinery, transportation equipment and electrical goods'
"最易受外国竞争冲击的行业包括机械业、运输业和电子产品行业,它们的毛利是比较低的"[*Sunday Times*《星期日泰晤士报》]
'...the minister wants people buying goods ranging from washing machines to houses to demand facts on energy costs'
"这位部长希望人们在购买小到洗衣机大到住房时,能给予能源成本更多关注"[*Times*《泰晤士报》]

goods and chattels /ˌgʊdz ən ˈtʃæt(ə)lz/ *plural noun* moveable personal possessions 私人动产

Goods and Services Tax /ˌgʊdz ən ˈsɜːvɪsɪz tæks/ *noun* a Canadian tax on the sale of goods or the provision of services, similar to VAT 商品及劳务税:加拿大对商品和劳务的课税,与增值税类似 Abbreviation 缩写 **GST**

goodwill /gʊdˈwɪl/ *noun* good feeling towards someone 善意,亲切:对某

人的良好感觉 ○ *To show goodwill, the management increased the terms of the offer.* 为表示诚意，管理层提高了出价条件。

go private /ˌɡəʊ ˈpraɪvət/ *verb* to become a private company again, by concentrating all its shares in the hands of one or a few shareholders and removing its stock exchange listing 私有化，下市：上市公司把所有股票集中在一个或少数几个股东手中，并停止在证券交易所上市，从而再次成为私营公司

go public /ˌɡəʊ ˈpʌblɪk/ *verb* to become a public company by placing some of its shares for sale on the stock market so that anyone can buy them 上市发行，挂牌上市：将公司的部分股票在股票市场上对外提呈出售，从而成为上市公司

govern /ˈɡʌv(ə)n/ *verb* to rule a country 统治，治理（国家）○ *The country is governed by a group of military leaders.* 这个国家由一批军队将领统治。

governance /ˈɡʌv(ə)nəns/ *noun* the philosophy of ruling, whether a country or a company（国家或公司的）掌管，治理

'...the chairman has committed the cardinal sin in corporate governance—he acted against the wishes and interests of the shareholders'
"董事长犯了企业管理的大忌——他的所作所为违背了股东的意愿，损害了他们的利益"［*Investors Chronicle*《投资者纪事》］

'...in two significant decisions, the Securities and Exchange Board of India today allowed trading of shares through the Internet and set a deadline for companies to conform to norms for good corporate governance'
"印度证券交易委员会今天作出了两个重要决定：允许通过互联网买卖股票；为公司按企业掌管标准整改设定最后期限"［*The Hindu*《印度教徒报》］

government /ˈɡʌv(ə)nmənt/ *adjective* coming from the government, referring to the government 政府的 ○ *a government ban on the import of arms* 政府对武器进口的禁令 ○ *Government intervention* or *Intervention by the government helped to solve the dispute.* 政府的介入促成了纠纷的解决。○ *Government employees can belong to one of two unions* 政府雇员可以在两个工会间择其一加入。

Government Accountancy Service /ˌɡʌv(ə)nmənt əˈkaʊntənsi ˌsɜːvɪs/ *noun* part of HM Treasury, a service whose remit it is to ensure that best accounting practice is observed and conducted across the whole of the Civil Service 政府会计事务所：英国财政部所属部门，其职责是确保所有行政部门都能贯彻采用会计工作的最佳方法 Abbreviation 缩写 **GAS**

governmental /ˌɡʌv(ə)nˈment(ə)l/ *adjective* referring to a government 政府的

government-backed /ˌɡʌv(ə)nmənt-ˈbækt/ *adjective* backed by the government 政府支持的

government bonds /ˌɡʌv(ə)nmənt ˈbɒndz/ *plural noun* bonds or other securities issued by the government on a regular basis as a method of borrowing money for government expenditure 政府债券：政府为筹集政府支出资金而定期发行的债券

government contractor /ˌɡʌv(ə)nmənt kənˈtræktə/ *noun* a company which supplies the government with goods by contract 政府合同承包商：按合同向政府供货的公司

government-controlled /ˌgʌv(ə)nməntkənˈtrəʊld/ *adjective* under the direct control of the government 政府直接控制的 ○ *Advertisements cannot be placed in the government-controlled newspapers.* 广告不能登在由政府直接管控的报纸上。

government economic indicators /ˌgʌv(ə)nmənt iːkəˌnɒmɪk ˈɪndɪkeɪtəz/ *plural noun* statistics which show how the country's economy is going to perform in the short or long term 政府经济指标：显示一国短期或长期经济状况的统计数字

government grant /ˌgʌv(ə)nmənt ˈgrɑːnt/ *noun* a grant of money or assets given by a central government, a local government or a government agency 政府拨款：由中央政府、地方政府或其他政府机构拨给的款项或资产 ○ *The laboratory has a government grant to cover the cost of the development programme* 该实验室获得了一笔政府拨款，足够支付这一开发项目所需费用。○ *The government has allocated grants towards the costs of the scheme.* 政府已拨款支付该计划所需费用。

government loan /ˌgʌv(ə)nmənt ˈləʊn/ *noun* money lent by the government 政府贷款

government-regulated /ˈgʌv(ə)nməntˌregjʊleɪtɪd/ *adjective* regulated by the government 政府调节的

government securities /ˌgʌv(ə)nmənt sɪˈkjʊərɪtiz/ *plural noun* same as 同 **government bonds**

government-sponsored /ˈgʌv(ə)nmənt ˌspɒnsəd/ *adjective* encouraged by the government and backed by government money 政府鼓励并资助的 ○ *She is working in a government-sponsored scheme to help small businesses.* 她在一个政府资助的旨在扶植小型企业的项目中工作。

government stock /ˌgʌv(ə)nmənt ˈstɒk/ *noun* same as 同 **government bonds**

government support /ˌgʌv(ə)nmənt səˈpɔːt/ *noun* a financial help given by the government 政府补助，政府资助 ○ *The aircraft industry relies on government support.* 航空业要依靠政府的财政支持。

governor /ˈgʌv(ə)nə/ *noun* **1.** a person in charge of an important institution（重要机构的）主管 **2.** *US* one of the members of the Federal Reserve Board（美）联邦储备委员会成员

grace /greɪs/ *noun* a favour shown by granting a delay 宽限 ○ *to give a creditor a period of grace* or *two weeks' grace* 给贷款人一段时期（或两周）的宽限

gradual /ˈgrædʒuəl/ *adjective* slow and steady 逐渐的，逐步的 ○ *The company saw a gradual return to profits.* 该公司逐步扭亏为盈。○ *Her CV describes her gradual rise to the position of company chairman.* 她的履历记述了她一步一步成长为公司总裁的历程。

gradually /ˈgrædʒuəli/ *adverb* slowly and steadily 逐渐地○ *The company has gradually become more profitable.* 公司盈利逐渐增加。○ *She gradually learnt the details of the import-export business.* 她逐渐掌握了进出口业务的门道。

graduate /ˈgrædʒuət/ *noun* a person who has obtained a degree 毕业生

graduated /ˈgrædʒueɪtɪd/ *adjective*

changing in small regular stages 累进的,分级的

graduated income tax /ˌɡrædʒueɪtɪd ˈɪnkʌm tæks/ *noun* a tax which rises in steps, each level of income being taxed at a higher percentage 累进所得税:逐级累进的税项,收入级别越高,适用税率也越高

graduated pension scheme /ˌɡrædʒueɪtɪd ˈpenʃən skiːm/ *noun* a pension scheme where the benefit is calculated as a percentage of the salary of each person in the scheme 累进养老金计划:按每个参与者薪金的一定百分比计算福利的养老金计划

graduated taxation /ˌɡrædʒueɪtɪd tækˈseɪʃ(ə)n/ *noun* a tax system where the percentage of tax paid rises as the income rises 累进税制:税率随收入增加而上调的税制

grand /ɡrænd/ *noun* one thousand pounds or dollars (*informal*) 一千块(非正式) ○ *They offered him fifty grand for the information*. 他们为得到该情报向他开价五万。○ *She's earning fifty grand plus car and expenses*. 她的收入是五万整,外加公车使用和杂费报销。

grand total /ˌɡrænd ˈtəʊt(ə)l/ *noun* the final total made by adding several subtotals 共计,总计

grant /ɡrɑːnt/ *verb* to agree to give someone something 同意给予 ○ *to grant someone a loan* or *a subsidy* 同意给某人一笔贷款(或一笔补贴) ○ *to grant someone three weeks' leave of absence* 批准某人休假三周 ○ *The local authority granted the company an interest-free loan to start up the new factory*. 地方当局同意贷给这个公司一笔无息贷款来建新工厂。

'...the budget grants a tax exemption for $500,000 in capital gains'
"这项预算对50万加元的资本收益给予免税"[*Toronto Star*《多伦多明星日报》]

grantor /ɡrɑːnˈtɔː/ *noun* a person who grants a property to another 让与人,授与人

graph /ɡrɑːf/ *noun* a diagram which shows the relationship between two sets of quantities or values, each of which is represented on an axis 图表,图解,曲线图:表示两组数量或数值之间关系的图表,每组各在一个轴上表示 ○ *A graph was used to show salary increases in relation to increases in output*. 采用了曲线图来说明加薪与产出增加的关系。○ *According to the graph, as average salaries have risen so has absenteeism*. 曲线图显示,随着平均工资的增长,旷工率也有所增加。○ *We need to set out the results of the questionnaire in a graph*. 我们需要用图表把问卷调查的结果呈现出来。

gratis /ˈɡrætɪs/ *adverb* free or not costing anything 免费 ○ *We got into the exhibition gratis*. 我们免费参观了展会。

gratuity /ɡrəˈtjuːɪti/ *noun* a tip, money given to someone who has helped you 赏金,小费 ○ *The staff are instructed not to accept gratuities*. 员工按规定不得收取小费。

greenback /ˈɡriːnbæk/ *noun US* a dollar bill (*informal*)(美,非正式)绿背纸币,美钞

'...gold's drop this year is of the same magnitude as the greenback's 8.5% rise'
"今年金价的下跌和美元汇率上涨8.5%具有同样重要的意义"[*Business Week*《商业周刊》]

green card /ˈgriːn kɑːd/ *noun* **1.** a special British insurance certificate to prove that a car is insured for travel abroad 绿色保险卡：英国用于证明机动车已上国外旅行险的特殊保险凭证 **2.** an identity card and work permit for a person going to live in the USA 绿卡：发放给将在美国定居者的身份证明兼工作许可证

green currency /ˌgriːn ˈkʌrənsi/ *noun* formerly, a currency used in the EU for calculating agricultural payments. Each country had an exchange rate fixed by the Commission, so there were 'green pounds', 'green francs', 'green marks', etc. 绿色货币：欧洲联盟内部曾用来计算农业支出的货币。欧盟每个成员国都有欧盟委员会制定的独立的汇率计算法，因此有"绿色英镑"、"绿色法郎"、"绿色马克"等说法

green form /ˈgriːn fɔːm/ *noun* a form for giving free or subsidised legal advice to clients who are eligible for Legal Aid 绿表：向有资格接受法律援助的受助人提供的一种表格，使其能够获得免费或有政府补助的法律咨询

greenmail /ˈgriːnmeɪl/ *noun* the practice of making a profit by buying a large number of shares in a company, threatening to take the company over, and then selling the shares back to the company at a higher price 反购回，绿票讹诈：先购买某公司的大量股票，然后以收购相威胁将股票再以高价卖回该公司，以从中牟利

'... he proposes that there should be a limit on greenmail, perhaps permitting payment of a 20% premium on a maximum of 8% of the stock'
"他提议应对反购回作出限制，例如只允许对最多 8% 的股份支付最高 20% 的溢价"
[*Duns Business Month*《邓氏商业月刊》]

Green Paper /griːn ˈpeɪpə/ *noun* a report from the British government on proposals for a new law to be discussed in Parliament 绿皮书：英国政府关于将新法律提交议会讨论的报告 Compare 比较 **White *Paper***

green pound /ˈgriːn ˈpaʊnd/ *noun* a value for the British pound used in calculating agricultural prices and subsidies in the EU 绿色英镑：欧盟内部为计算农产品价格和补贴而设定的英镑价值

green report /ˌgriːn rɪˈpɔːt/ *noun* a part of a company's annual report dealing with ecological matters 绿色报告：公司年度报告中涉及生态主题的部分

grey market /ˈgreɪ ˌmɑːkɪt/ *noun* an unofficial market run by dealers, where new issues of shares are bought and sold before they officially become available for trading on the Stock Exchange even before the share allocations are known 灰市，半黑市：新股在证券交易所上市以前（甚至在配股之前）进行交易买卖的非官方市场

gross /grəʊs/ *noun* twelve dozen (144) 罗（等于 12 打）○ *He ordered four gross of pens.* 他订购了 4 罗钢笔。(NOTE: no plural 没有复数形式) ■ *adjective* total, with no deductions 总的，毛重的 ■ *adverb* with no deductions 总共，不作抵减地 ○ *My salary is paid gross.* 我的工资没有作任何扣除。

'... gross wool receipts for the selling season to end June appear likely to top $2 billion'
"在 6 月销售旺季截止前，羊毛销售总收入

有望超过 20 亿澳元”［*Australian Financial Review*《澳大利亚金融评论报》］

gross domestic product /grəʊs dəˌmestɪk ˈprɒdʌkt/ *noun* the annual value of goods sold and services paid for inside a country 国内生产总值：一国国内全年销售的产品和劳务的总价值 Abbreviation 缩写 **GDP**

gross earnings /ˌgrəʊs ˈɜːnɪŋz/ *plural noun* total earnings before tax and other deductions 毛收益：扣减税收和其他抵减项目前的总收益

gross income /grəʊs ˈɪnkʌm/ *noun* a salary before tax is deducted 毛收入：税前工资

gross interest /ˌgrəʊs ˈɪntrəst/ *noun* the interest earned on a deposit or security before the deduction of tax 毛利息：存款或证券的税前利息 ⇨ 参阅 **net interest**

gross margin /grəʊs ˈmɑːdʒɪn/ *noun* the percentage difference between the received price and the unit manufacturing cost or purchase price of goods for resale 毛利率：商品售出价格与单位生成成本或转售商品的进货价格之间的百分比差额 Abbreviation 缩写 **GM**

gross national product /grəʊs ˌnæʃ(ə)nəl ˈprɒdʌkt/ *noun* the annual value of goods and services in a country including income from other countries 国民生产总值：包括国外收入在内的一国全年产品和劳务的总价值 Abbreviation 缩写 **GNP**

gross profit /grəʊs ˈprɒfɪt/ *noun* a profit calculated as sales income less the cost of the goods sold, i. e. without deducting any other expenses 毛利：按销售收入减去所售商品成本计算所得的利润额，未扣除任何其他开支

gross receipts /ˌgrəʊs rɪˈsiːts/ *plural noun* the total amount of money received before expenses are deducted 总收入：扣除费用前收到的总金额

gross salary /ˌgrəʊs ˈsæləri/ *noun* a salary before tax is deducted 薪资总额：税前工资

gross sales /ˌgrəʊs ˈseɪlz/ *plural noun* money received from sales before deductions for goods returned, special discounts, etc. 销售总额：在扣除退货、打折等之前的销售总额 ○ *Gross sales are impressive since many buyers seem to be ordering more than they will eventually need.* 销售总额很可观，因为许多购买者的订购量看来都超过了他们的最终需求量。

gross turnover /ˌgrəʊs ˈtɜːnəʊvə/ *noun* the total turnover including VAT and discounts 总营业额，总周转额：包括增值税和折扣在内的营业总额

gross weight /ˌgrəʊs ˈweɪt/ *noun* the weight of both the container and its contents 毛重

gross yield /ˌgrəʊs ˈjiːld/ *noun* a profit from investments before tax is deducted 毛收益率：税前投资利润

ground landlord /ˈgraʊnd ˌlændlɔːd/ *noun* a person or company that owns the freehold of a property which is then let and sublet 地主；房地产业主：对物业的出租和转租具有完全保有权的个人或公司 ○ *Our ground landlord is an insurance company.* 我们这片地归一家保险公司所有。

ground rent /ˈgraʊnd rent/ *noun* a rent paid by the main tenant to the ground landlord 地租：主要承租人付给房地产业主的租金

group /gruːp/ *noun* **1.** several things

or people together 一组，一群（事物或人）○ *A group of managers has sent a memo to the chairman complaining about noise in the office.* 几名经理向主席递交了一份报告，抱怨办公室的噪音问题。○ *The respondents were interviewed in groups of three or four, and then singly.* 受访者先是被分成三到四人一组进行面谈，随后又单独面谈。**2.** several companies linked together in the same organization 集团公司 ○ *the group chairman* or *the chairman of the group* 集团董事长 ○ *group turnover* or *turnover for the group* 集团营业额 ○ *the Granada Group* 格拉纳达集团

group accounts /ˌgruːp əˈkaʊnts/ *noun* accounts for a holding company and its subsidiaries 集团报表：控股公司及其子公司的报表

group balance sheet /ˌgruːp ˈbæləns ˌʃiːt/ *noun* a consolidated balance sheet, the balance sheets of subsidiary companies grouped together into the balance sheet of the parent company 集团资产负债表：子公司的资产负债表并入母公司的资产负债表后的资产负债表

group results /ˌgruːp rɪˈzʌlts/ *plural noun* the results of a group of companies taken together 集团业绩

growth /grəʊθ/ *noun* the fact of becoming larger or increasing 增长；增加

'... a general price freeze succeeded in slowing the growth in consumer prices'
"价格的普遍冻结成功地减缓了消费价格的增长"［*Financial Times*《金融时报》］
'... growth in demand is still coming from the private rather than the public sector'
"需求增长仍然来自于私营部门而非公共部门"［*Lloyd's List*《劳氏日报》］
'... population growth in the south-west is again reflected by the level of rental values'
"西南地区的人口增长再次反映在租金水平上"［*Lloyd's List*《劳氏日报》］

growth index /ˈgrəʊθ ˌɪndeks/ *noun* an index showing how something has grown 增长指数

growth prospects /ˈgrəʊθ ˌprɒspekts/ *plural noun* potential for growth in a share （股票）增长潜力

growth rate /ˈgrəʊθ reɪt/ *noun* the speed at which something grows 增长率

GST *abbr* Goods and Services Tax 商品及劳务税

'... because the GST is applied only to fees for brokerage and appraisal services, the new tax does not appreciably increase the price of a resale home'
"由于商品及劳务税只针对中介费和评估费征收，因此新税率并没有造成二手房价格的明显提升"［*Toronto Globe & Mail*《多伦多环球邮报》］

guarantee /ˌgærənˈtiː/ *noun* **1.** a legal document in which the producer agrees to compensate the buyer if the product is faulty or becomes faulty before a specific date after purchase （质量）保证书：具有法律效力，规定如果产品购买后存在缺陷或在指定日期前出现问题，生产商应作出相应补偿 ○ *a certificate of guarantee* or *a guarantee certificate* 质量保证书 ○ *The guarantee lasts for two years.* 质保期为两年。○ *It is sold with a twelve-month guarantee.* 该产品提供 12 个月的售后质保。**2.** a promise that someone will pay another person's debts （某人为他人偿债的）担保 □ **company limited by**

guarantee company where each member stated in the memorandum of association how much money he will contribute to the company if it becomes insolvent (as opposed to a company limited by shares) 担保有限公司:按照公司章程规定,员工对公司债务负有一定担保责任的公司(与之相对的是股份有限公司) **3.** something given as a security 抵押品 ○ *to leave share certificates as a guarantee* 将股票留作抵押 ■ *verb* to give a promise that something will happen 担保

guaranteed wage /ˌgærəntiːd ˈweɪdʒ/ *noun* a wage which a company promises will not fall below a specific figure 保证工资:公司许诺的最低工资

guarantor /ˌgærənˈtɔː/ *noun* a person who promises to pay someone's debts (债务)保证人,担保人 ○ *She stood guarantor for her brother*. 她出面做她弟弟的担保人。

H

half /hɑːf/ *noun* one of two equal parts into which something is divided 一半 ○ *The first half of the agreement is acceptable*. 协议的前半部分可以接受。■ *adjective* divided into two parts 一半的

'... economists believe the economy is picking up this quarter and will do better in the second half of the year'
"经济学家们相信经济在这个季度正在企稳向好,下半年内形势将会更好"[*Sunday Times*《星期日泰晤士报》]

half a per cent /ˌhɑːf ə pə ˈsent/ *noun* 0.5%百分之零点五,0.5%

half-commission man /ˌhɑːf-kəˈmɪʃ(ə)n ˌmæn/ *noun* a dealer who introduces new clients to a stockbroker, and takes half the broker's commission as a fee 分佣中人,半经纪人:将新客户介绍给证券经纪人,并从经纪人佣金中收取一半作为报酬的交易商

half-dollar /ˌhɑːfˈdɒlə/ *noun US* fifty cents(美)半美元,50 美分

half-price sale /ˌhɑːfpraɪs ˈseɪl/ *noun* a sale of items at half the usual price 半价出售

half-year /ˌhɑːfˈjɪə/ *noun* six months of an accounting period(会计期)半年,六个月

half-yearly /ˌhɑːfˈjɪəli/ *adjective* happening every six months, or referring to a period of six months 每半年的;半年的 ○ *half-yearly accounts* 半年度账目 ○ *half-yearly payment* 每半年付款 ○ *half-yearly statement* 半年报表 ○ *a half-yearly meeting* 每半年召开一次的会议 ■ *adverb* Fevery six months 每半年地 ○ *We pay the account half-yearly*. 我们每半年付一次账。

handling charge /ˈhændlɪŋ tʃɑːdʒ/ *noun* money to be paid for packing, invoicing and dealing with goods which are being shipped 装卸费,手续费:包装、开发票及处理所装运物品的费用

hard bargain /ˌhɑːd ˈbɑːɡɪn/ *noun* a bargain with difficult terms 条件苛刻的谈判

hard cash /ˌhɑːd ˈkæʃ/ *noun* money in notes and coins, as opposed to cheques or credit cards 现金:指钞票和硬币,不同于支票或信用卡

hard currency /hɑːd ˈkʌrənsi/ *noun* the currency of a country which has a strong economy, and which can be changed into other currencies easily 硬通货:经济实力强的国家的货币,这些货币易于兑换成其他通货 ○ *to pay for imports in hard currency* 以硬通货支付进口货物 ○ *to sell raw materials to earn hard currency* 出售原材料以赚取硬通货 Also called 亦称作 **scarce currency**. Opposite 反义 **soft currency**

hard disk /ˌhɑːd ˈdɪsk/ *noun* a computer disk which has a sealed case and can store large quantities of information 硬盘

'... hard disks help computers function more speedily and allow them to store more information'
"硬盘有助于计算机运行得更快,并使其能存储更多的信息" [*Australian Financial Review*《澳大利亚金融评论报》]

hardening /ˈhɑːd(ə)nɪŋ/ *adjective* (*of a market*) slowly moving upwards (市场)缓慢复苏的

hard landing /ˌhɑːd ˈlændɪŋ/ *noun* a change in economic strategy to counteract inflation which has serious results for the population such as high unemployment, rising interest rates, etc. 硬着陆:为应对通货膨胀而作出的经济策略的改变,它对人们的生活产生严重后果,例如高失业率、利率上升等

hard market /ˌhɑːd ˈmɑːkɪt/ *noun* a market which is strong and not likely to fall 坚挺市场,强市

hardware /ˈhɑːdweə/ *noun* machines used in data processing, including the computers and printers, but not the programs 硬件:指用于数据处理的机器,包括计算机和打印机,但不包括程序

haulage contractor /ˈhɔːlɪdʒ kənˌtræktə/ *noun* a company which transports goods by contract 搬运承包商

head /hed/ *adjective* most important or main 最重要的,主要的 ○ *Ask the head waiter for a table*. 要求领班安排一张餐桌。

head and shoulders /ˌhed ən ˈʃəʊldəz/ *noun* a term used by chartists showing a share price which rises to a peak, then falls slightly, then rises to a much higher peak, then falls sharply and rises to a lower peak before falling again, looking similar to a person's head and shoulders when shown on a graph 头肩式走势:制图者用来表示股价波动的术语。股价涨到顶点后稍有回落,再迅速升到更高的顶点,接着暴跌,然后稍有拉升,最后再次跌落,波动曲线犹如一个人的头肩组合

head buyer /ˌhed ˈbaɪə/ *noun* the most important buyer in a store 主要买主:商场最重要的顾客

heading /ˈhedɪŋ/ *noun* the words at the top of a piece of text 标题 ○ *Items are listed under several headings*. 各个项目分别呈列在几个标题下。○ *Look at the figure under the heading 'Costs 2001 - 02'*. 参看"2001 - 2002 年成本"标题下的数字。

headlease /ˈhedliːs/ *noun* a lease from the freehold owner to a tenant 首次租赁:完全保有财产人向承租人的租赁

headline inflation rate /ˌhedlaɪn ɪnˈfleɪʃ(ə)n ˌreɪt/ *noun* a British inflation figure which includes items such as mortgage interest and local taxes, which are not included in the inflation figures for other countries 通货膨胀率指数:英国包括抵押贷款利息和地方税的通货膨胀指数,其他国家的通货膨胀率则不包括这些项目

head office /ˌhed ˈɒfɪs/ *noun* an office building where the board of directors works and meets 总部:董事工作和开会的写字楼

headquarters /hedˈkwɔːtəz/ *plural noun* the main office, where the board of directors meets and works 总部：董事工作和开会的主要办公地点 ○ *The company's headquarters are in New York*. 该公司的总部在纽约。

heads of agreement /ˌhedz əv əˈgriːmənt/ *plural noun* **1.** a draft agreement with not all the details complete（细节尚未全部确定的）协议草案 **2.** the most important parts of a commercial agreement 商业协议中最重要的部分

health insurance /ˈhelθ ɪnˌʃʊərəns/ *noun* insurance which pays the cost of treatment for illness, especially when travelling abroad 健康保险：支付医疗费用的保险，尤用于某人出国旅行时

healthy /ˈhelθi/ *adjective* □ **a healthy balance sheet** balance sheet which shows a good profit 良好资产负债表：显示有一定利润的资产负债表

heavily /ˈhevɪli/ *adverb* □ **the issue was heavily stagged** large numbers of stags applied for the issue of new shares 发行被严重投机申购：大量投机性投资者申购新股

'...the steel company had spent heavily on new equipment'
"这家钢铁公司投入巨额资金购买新设备"［*Fortune*《财富》］

heavy industry /ˌhevi ˈɪndəstri/ *noun* an industry which deals in heavy raw materials such as coal or makes large products such as ships or engines 重工业：处理重质原材料（如煤炭）或生产大型产品（如轮船或引擎）的工业

hedge /hedʒ/ *noun* a protection against a possible loss, which involves taking an action which is the opposite of an action taken earlier 对冲，套头交易，套期保值：通过采取与先前相反的行动来避免可能的损失 ■ *verb* to protect against the risk of a loss 对冲：防止损失风险 □ **to hedge your bets** to make investments in several areas so as to be protected against loss in one of them 分散风险，对冲投资：在多个领域进行投资，以分散投资的风险 □ **to hedge against inflation** to buy investments which will rise in value faster than the increase in the rate of inflation 对冲通货膨胀，防止通货膨胀损失的保值措施：购买增值速度高于通货膨胀增长率的投资

'...during the 1970s commercial property was regarded by investors as an alternative to equities, with many of the same inflation-hedge qualities'
"20世纪70年代，商用物业被投资者看作是可以替代股票的投资选择，因为它们有许多相同的通胀对冲性能"［*Investors Chronicle*《投资者纪事》］

'...the move saved it from having to pay its creditors an estimated $270 million owed in connection with hedge contracts which began working against the company when the price of gold rose unexpectedly during September'
"9月份金价意外上涨，对冲合同开始对公司产生不利影响，但该举措令它少付其债权人大约2.7亿美元"［*Business in Africa*《非洲商业》］

hedge fund /ˈhedʒ fʌnd/ *noun* a partnership open to a small number of rich investors, which invests in equities, currency futures and derivatives and may produce high returns but carries a very high risk 合伙投资基金，对冲基金，平衡交易基金：只对少数富有的投资者开放的合伙投资，它投资于股票、货币期货和衍生产品，可能产生高额回报，但也有极高的风险

'... much of what was described as near hysteria was the hedge funds trying to liquidate bonds to repay bank debts after losing multi-million dollar bets on speculations that the yen would fall against the dollar'
"由于错误地估计日圆对美元的汇率会下降,对冲基金损失数百万美元,不得不变现债券以偿还银行债务,它的这种做法造成了市场几近歇斯底里的局面"[*Times*《泰晤士报》]

'... hedge funds generally have in common an ability to sell short (that is, sell stocks you do not own), and to increase growth prospects—and risk—by borrowing to enhance the fund's assets'
"对冲基金普遍的共同特征是能够卖空(即出售你并未拥有的股票),以及通过借款来增加基金的资产以提高增长潜力——这种做法同时也会增加风险"[*Money Observer*《货币观察家》]

'... the stock is a hedge fund—limited by the Securities and Exchange Commission to only wealthy individuals and qualified institutions'
"该股票是一种对冲基金——按证券交易委员会规定它只面向富人及有资格的机构"[*Smart Money*《财智》]

hedging /'hedʒɪŋ/ *noun* the act of buying investments at a fixed price for delivery later, so as to protect against possible loss 期货保值,套头保值,对冲交易:按固定价格买进远期交割的投资,以避免可能的损失

hereafter /hɪər'ɑːftə/ *adverb* from this time on 此后,今后

hereby /hɪə'baɪ/ *adverb* in this way, by this letter 以此,特此 ○ *We hereby revoke the agreement of January 1st 1982.* 我们特此通知取消 1982 年 1 月 1 日的协议。

hereditament /herɪ'dɪtəmənt/ *noun* a property, including land and buildings 可继承的财产,不动产:包括土地和建筑物的财产

hidden asset /ˌhɪd(ə)n 'æset/ *noun* an asset which is valued much less in the company's accounts than its true market value 隐蔽资产:账面价值远低于实际市价的资产

hidden tax /'hɪd(ə)n tæks/ *noun* a tax that is not immediately apparent. For example, while a consumer may be aware of a tax on retail purchases, a tax imposed at the wholesale level, which consequently increases the cost of items to the retailer, will not be apparent 隐蔽税,间接税:非即刻显现的税项,例如当消费者购买零售商品时,他们可能会意识到商品税的存在,但当税项征收发生在批发环节并转嫁给了零售商,从而提高了商品的成本时,税项就不再那么明显

high /haɪ/ *adjective* large, not low 高的,不低的 ○ *High overhead costs increase the unit price.* 高额间接成本会提高单价。○ *High prices put customers off.* 高价使顾客望而却步。○ *They are budgeting for a high level of expenditure.* 他们正在作高额支出的预算。○ *High interest rates are crippling small businesses.* 高利率使小企业严重受损。□ **higher rate of tax** top rate of income tax (currently in the UK, 40% on taxable income above £28,000) 较高税率:最高的所得税率(目前英国对超过 2.8 万英镑的应税收入征 40% 的税) ■ *noun* a point where prices or sales are very large (价格或销售额的)高峰,峰值 ○ *Prices have dropped by 10% since the high of January 2nd.* 价格自 1 月 2 日的高点以来下跌了 10%。

'American interest rates remain exception-

ally high in relation to likely inflation rates'
"相对于可能的通胀率来说，美国利率保持在不寻常的高位"[*Sunday Times*《星期日泰晤士报》]
'...faster economic growth would tend to push US interest rates, and therefore the dollar, higher'
"较快的经济增长往往推动美国利率上涨，从而使美元升值"[*Australian Financial Review*《澳大利亚金融评论报》]
'...in a leveraged buyout the acquirer raises money by selling high-yielding debentures to private investors'
"在杠杆式收购中，盘购方以出售高收益债券给私人投资者的方式进行筹资"[*Fortune*《财富》]

higher-rate tax /ˌhaɪəreɪt ˈtæks/ *noun* in the United Kingdom, the highest of the three bands of income tax. Most countries have bands of income tax with different rates applicable to income within each band 高税率税：英国三个所得税率区间中最高的一个。大多数国家都有不同的所得税区间，各个区间适用的所得税率不同

highest bidder /ˌhaɪəst ˈbɪdə/ *noun* a person who offers the most money at an auction（拍卖中的）最高出价者 ○ *The property was sold to the highest bidder*. 该地产卖给了出价最高的投标人。

high finance /ˌhaɪ ˈfaɪnæns/ *noun* the lending, investing and borrowing of very large sums of money organised by financiers 巨额融资：由金融业者安排的大额借贷、投资和借款

high gearing /ˌhaɪ ˈɡɪərɪŋ/ *noun* a situation where a company has a high level of borrowing compared to its share price 高负债率，高杠杆比率：相较于其股价公司借贷额水平过高的情况

high-grade bond /ˌhaɪɡreɪd ˈbɒnd/ *noun* a bond which has the highest rating 高等级债券：评级最高的债券

high-income /ˌhaɪˈɪnkʌm/ *adjective* giving a large income 高收益的 ○ *high-income shares* 高收益股票 ○ *a high-income portfolio* 高收益投资组合

highly-geared company /ˌhaɪliɡɪəd ˈkʌmp(ə)ni/ *noun* company which has a high proportion of its funds from fixed-interest borrowings 高负债公司：很大一部分资金来自定息借款的公司

highly-paid /ˌhaɪliˈpeɪd/ *adjective* earning a large salary 高薪的

highly-placed /ˌhaɪliˈpleɪst/ *adjective* occupying an important post 身居要职的 ○ *The delegation met a highly-placed official in the Trade Ministry*. 代表团与贸易部的一位高级官员会面。

highly-priced /ˌhaɪliˈpraɪst/ *adjective* with a large price 高价的

high yield /ˌhaɪ ˈjiːld/ *noun* a dividend yield which is higher than is usual for the type of company 高股利收益率：高于同类公司正常水平的股利收益率

hike /haɪk/ *US noun* an increase（美）增加，提高 ■ *verb* to increase 增加，提高

hire /ˈhaɪə/ *noun* an arrangement whereby customers pay money to be able to use a car, boat or piece of equipment owned by someone else for a time 租用：根据协定，通过支付现金获得某物在一定时间内的使用权

hire car /ˈhaɪə kɑː/ *noun* a car which has been rented 租来的汽车 ○ *He was driving a hire car when the accident happened*. 发生事故时他开着一辆租来的汽车。

hire purchase /ˌhaɪə ˈpɜːtʃɪs/ *noun* a system of buying something by paying a sum regularly each month 租购行为，分期付款购货行为：通过按月定期付款的方式赊购货物 ○ *to buy a refrigerator on hire purchase* 以分期付款方式购买冰箱（NOTE：The US term is **installment credit**，**installment plan** or **installment sale** 美国用语为 **installment credit**、**installment plan** 或 **installment sale**）

hire purchase agreement /ˌhaɪə ˈpɜːtʃɪs əˌgriːmənt/ *noun* a contract to pay for something by instalments 租购合同，分期付款购货合同

hire-purchase company /ˌhaɪə ˈpɜːtʃɪs ˌkʌmp(ə)ni/ *noun* a company which provides money for hire purchase 租赁信托公司：为租购提供资金的公司

historic /hɪˈstɒrɪk/，**historical** /hɪˈstɒrɪk(ə)l/ *adjective* dating back over a period of time 历史上的

'...the Federal Reserve Board has eased interest rates in the past year, but they are still at historically high levels'
"去年美联储下调了利率，但利率仍处于历史高位"［*Sunday Times*《星期日泰晤士报》］

'...the historic p/e for the FTSE all-share index is 28.3 and the dividend yield is barely 2 per cent. Both indicators suggest that the stock markets are very highly priced'
"金融时报全股指数的历史市盈率为28.3，股利收益率勉强达到2%。这两项指数均表明，股市被严重高估了"［*Times*《泰晤士报》］

historical cost accounting /hɪˌstɒrɪk(ə)l ˈkɒst əˌkaʊntɪŋ/ *noun* the preparation of accounts on the basis of historical cost，with assets valued at their original cost of purchase 历史成本会计：指资产按原始购买成本计价的以历史成本为基准的账目编制方法 Compare 比较 **replacement cost accounting**

historical cost concept /hɪˌstɒrɪk(ə)l kɒst ˈkɒnsept/，**historical cost convention** /hɪˌstɒrɪk(ə)l kɒst kənˈvenʃən/ *noun* a basis for treatment of assets in financial statements where they are recorded at their historical cost，without adjustment for inflation or other price variations 历史成本概念，按历史成本计算的惯例：对财务报表中的资产进行处理的一种依据，资产按各自的历史成本进行记录，而不作通货膨胀或其他价格变动的调整（NOTE：Use 'historical cost convention' not 'historic cost convention' 使用 historical cost convention，而不是 historic cost convention）

historical cost depreciation /hɪˌstɒrɪk(ə)l ˈkɒst dɪˌpriːʃieɪʃ(ə)n/ *noun* depreciation based on the original cost of the asset 历史成本折旧：在资产原始成本基础上的折旧

historical figures /hɪˌstɒrɪk(ə)l ˈfɪgəz/ *plural noun* figures which were current in the past 历史数字

historical pricing /hɪˌstɒrɪk(ə)l ˈpraɪsɪŋ/ *noun* a method of setting prices for a good or service that is based on prices previously set. Sometimes revised prices may take into account the effects of inflation 历史定价：以先前制定过的价格为依据的商品或劳务定价方法，有时所修改的价格可能考虑到通货膨胀的影响

historical summary /hɪˌstɒrɪk(ə)l ˈsʌməri/ *noun* in the United Kingdom, an optional synopsis of a company's results over a period of time, often five or ten years, featured in the annual accounts 历史资料汇总表：英国公司年度报表中附有的以往业绩(通常是五或十年)的概要，此汇总表的编制属公司自愿行为

historical trading range /hɪˌstɒrɪk(ə)l ˈtreɪdɪŋ reɪndʒ/ *noun* the difference between the highest and lowest price for a share or bond over a period of time 历史交易价格范围：股票或债券在一段时间内的最高与最低价格之差

hive off /ˌhaɪv ˈɒf/ *verb* to split off part of a large company to form a smaller subsidiary 分股独立：将一个大公司的一部分分离出来，组成一个较小的子公司 ○ *The new managing director hived off the retail sections of the company*. 新任总经理将公司的零售部门剥离成一个子公司。

HM Treasury /ˌeɪtʃ ˌem ˈtreʒəri/ *noun* the UK government department responsible for managing the country's public revenues. The department is run on a day-to-day basis by the Chancellor of the Exchequer 财政部：英国负责管理国家公共收入的政府部门，其日常事务由财政大臣负责

hoard /hɔːd/ *verb* to buy and store goods in case of need 贮藏，囤积(以备不时之需)

hoarder /ˈhɔːdə/ *noun* a person who buys and stores goods in case of need 贮藏者，囤积者

hold /həʊld/ *noun* **1.** the bottom part of a ship or aircraft, in which cargo is carried (船只或飞机底部的)货舱 **2.** the action of keeping something 持有 ■ *verb* **1.** to own or to keep something 持有 ○ *She holds 10% of the company's shares*. 她持有该公司10%的股份。**2.** to make something happen 举行 ○ *The receiver will hold an auction of the company's assets*. 破产接管人将对这个公司的资产进行拍卖。**3.** not to sell 不出售 ○ *You should hold these shares — they look likely to rise*. 你要坚定持股——因为股价看涨。

'...as of last night, the bank's shareholders no longer hold any rights to the bank's shares'
"从昨晚开始，这家银行的股东不再对其股票拥有任何权利"[*South China Morning Post*《南华早报》]

hold back /ˌhəʊld ˈbæk/ *verb* to wait, not to do something at the present time 等待，暂不做任何事情

hold down /ˌhəʊld ˈdaʊn/ *verb* to keep at a low level 压制，压低 ○ *We are cutting margins to hold our prices down*. 我们减少利润以使价格维持在较低水平。

'...real wages have been held down; they have risen at an annual rate of only 1% in the last two years'
"实际工资一直被压制在较低水平，在过去两年间，它的年增长率只有1%"[*Sunday Times*《星期日泰晤士报》]

holder /ˈhəʊldə/ *noun* **1.** a person who owns or keeps something 持有者 ○ *holders of government bonds* or *bondholders* 政府债券持有者 ○ *holder of stock* or *of shares in a company* 公司股票持有者 ○ *holder of an insurance policy* or *policy holder* 保单持有者 **2.** a thing which keeps something, which protects something 支撑物，保护物

hold harmless letter /həʊld

ˌhɑːmləs ˈletə/ *noun* a letter issued by parties to a business deal to reporting accountants stating that the accountants will not be held responsible for any losses suffered on the deal 免责函，转移责任的约定：商业交易各方发给申报会计师的信函，声明会计师无须对交易的任何损失负责

holding /ˈhəʊldɪŋ/ *noun* a group of shares owned 所持股份 ○ *She has sold all her holdings in the Far East.* 她卖掉了所持远东公司的全部股票。○ *The company has holdings in German manufacturing companies.* 该公司持有德国制造公司的股票。

holding company /ˈhəʊldɪŋ ˌkʌmp(ə)ni/ *noun* 控股公司 **1.** a company which owns more than 50% of the shares in another company [持有另一家公司50%以上股份的公司] ⇨ 参阅 **subsidiary company** **2.** a company which exists only or mainly to own shares in subsidiary companies [以拥有子公司的股份为唯一或主要目的的公司] ⇨ 参阅 **subsidiary** (NOTE: [all senses] The US term is **proprietary company** [以上所有义项]美国用语为 **proprietary company**)

holding cost /ˈhəʊldɪŋ kɒst/ *noun* the cost of keeping items of stock including warehousing and handling costs, insurance, losses through deterioration, wastage, theft, etc. and the cost of capital used to acquire the stock measured in terms of the interest lost on the money which was spent on purchasing the stock in the first place or the interest paid on the loans which were needed to finance the purchase of the stock 储存成本：保管存货的成本，包括存储与搬运成本，保险，变质、损耗、被盗等损失，以及购买存货所用资金的成本（若以自有资金购买，则为该资金损失的利息；若是贷款购买，则为贷款利息）

hold on /ˌhəʊld ˈɒn/ *verb* to wait, not to change 等待，保持不变

hold out for /ˌhəʊld ˈaʊt fɔː/ *verb* to wait and ask for something 坚持要求

hold to /ˈhəʊld tuː/ *verb* not to allow something or someone to change 坚持，不允许改变

hold up /ˌhəʊld ˈʌp/ *verb* **1.** to stay at a high level 停留在高水平 ○ *Share prices have held up well.* 股价维持高位运行。○ *Sales held up during the tourist season.* 旅游旺季销售旺盛。**2.** to delay something 拖延，推迟 ○ *The shipment has been held up at customs.* 货物在海关被拖延了。○ *Payment will be held up until the contract has been signed.* 签约之后才会付款。○ *The strike will hold up dispatch for some weeks.* 这次罢工将使发送推迟几周。○ *The employees are holding up production as a form of protest against poor conditions.* 员工们暂停生产，作为对恶劣工作条件的抗议。

holiday entitlement /ˈhɒlɪdeɪ ɪnˌtaɪt(ə)lmənt/ *noun* the number of days of paid holiday which an employee has the right to take 休假权：员工有权享受的带薪休假天数 ○ *She has not used up all her holiday entitlement.* 她还没用完休假权。

hologram /ˈhɒləgræm/ *noun* a three-dimensional picture which is used on credit cards as a means of preventing forgery 全息图，全息照片：信用卡上的防伪三维图片

home banking /ˌhəʊm ˈbæŋkɪŋ/ *noun* a system of banking using a personal computer in your own home to carry out various financial transactions such as paying invoices or checking your bank account 家庭银行系统：在自己家中使用个人计算机执行各种金融业务（如支付发票或查看个人银行账户）的银行系统

home loan /ˈhəʊm ləʊn/ *noun* a loan by a bank or building society to help someone buy a house 住房贷款：银行或住房互助协会提供的帮助客户买房的贷款

home trade /ˈhəʊm treɪd/ *noun* trade in the country where a company is based 国内贸易

honorarium /ˌɒnəˈreəriəm/ *noun* money paid to a professional person such as an accountant or a lawyer when a specific fee has not been requested 酬金，谢礼：在专业人员（会计师或律师）并未索要的情况下向其支付的酬金（NOTE：The plural is **honoraria** 复数为 **honoraria**）

honorary /ˈɒnərəri/ *adjective* not paid a salary for the work done for an organization（职位）名誉的，荣誉的：指无报酬 ○ *He is honorary president of the translators' association.* 他是该译协的名誉会长。

honorary secretary /ˌɒnərəri ˈsekrət(ə)ri/ *noun* a person who keeps the minutes and official documents of a committee or club, but is not paid a salary 名誉秘书：保管某个委员会或俱乐部的会议记录及正式文件，但没有任何工资的人

honorary treasurer /ˌɒnərəri ˈtreʒərə/ *noun* a treasurer who does not receive any fee 名誉司库：不收取任何费用的司库

honour /ˈɒnə/ *verb* to pay something because it is owed and is correct 兑现，承付 ○ *to honour a bill* 承兑一张票据（NOTE：The US spelling is **honor** 美国拼法为 **honor**）

horizontal integration /ˌhɒrɪzɒnt(ə)l ˌɪntɪˈgreɪʃ(ə)n/ *noun* the process of joining similar companies or taking over a company in the same line of business as yourself 横向合并，水平式结合，横向一体化：联合同类公司或收购同一业务领域的公司

hot money /hɒt ˈmʌni/ *noun* **1.** money which is moved from country to country to get the best returns 热钱，游资：为寻求最佳回报而在国家间转移的资金 **2.** money that has been obtained by dishonest means 赃款：通过欺诈手段获得的钱款 ▷ 参阅 **money laundering**

hour /aʊə/ *noun* **1.** a period of time lasting sixty minutes 小时 **2.** sixty minutes of work 一小时的工作 ○ *She earns £14 an hour.* 她每小时挣 14 英镑。○ *We pay £16 an hour.* 我们每小时付 16 英镑。

house /haʊs/ *noun* a company 公司 ○ *the largest London finance house* 伦敦最大的金融公司 ○ *a broking house* 经纪公司 ○ *a publishing house* 出版社

house agent /ˈhaʊs ˌeɪdʒənt/ *noun* an estate agent who deals in buying or selling houses or flats 房地产代理商

household goods /ˌhaʊshəʊld ˈgʊdz/ *plural noun* items which are used in the home 家具什物，家用物品

human capital accounting /ˌhjuːmən ˈkæpɪt(ə)l əˌkaʊntɪŋ/ *noun* an attempt to place a financial value on the knowledge and skills possessed by the employees of an organisation 人力资本会计：为公司员工拥有的知识和

技能赋予相对应的价值的一种尝试 Also called 亦称作 **human asset accounting**, **human resource accounting**

human resource accounting /ˌhjuːmən rɪˈzɔːs əˌkaʊntɪŋ/ *noun* same as 同 **human capital accounting**

hybrid /ˈhaɪbrɪd/ *noun* a combination of financial instruments, e. g. , a bond with warrants attached, or a range of cash and derivative instruments designed to mirror the performance of a financial market 混合证券：金融工具的组合，例如附带权证的债券，或旨在反映金融市场表现的一系列现金和衍生工具

hyper /haɪpə/ *prefix* very large 非常大的

hyperinflation /ˌhaɪpərɪnˈfleɪʃ(ə)n/ *noun* inflation which is at such a high percentage rate that it is almost impossible to reduce 极度通货膨胀，恶性通货膨胀：高得几乎不可能使其下降的通货膨胀

I

IASB *abbr* International Accounting Standards Board 国际会计准则理事会

IASC *abbr* International Accounting Standards Committee 国际会计准则委员会

ICAEW *abbr* Institute of Chartered Accountants in England and Wales 英格兰及威尔士特许会计师协会

ICAI *abbr* Institute of Chartered Accountants in Ireland 爱尔兰特许会计师协会

ICANZ *abbr* Institute of Chartered Accountants of New Zealand 新西兰特许会计师协会

ICAS *abbr* Institute of Chartered Accountants in Scotland 苏格兰特许会计师协会

ICSID *abbr* International Centre for Settlement of Investment Disputes 国际投资争端解决中心

ideal /aɪˈdɪəl/ *adjective* perfect, very good for something 理想的，完美的 ○ *This is the ideal site for a new hypermarket*. 这是开设一家新的大型超市的理想地点。

idle /ˈaɪd(ə)l/ *adjective* not working 闲置的，不在工作的 ○ *2,000 employees were made idle by the recession*. 经济衰退使2,000名雇员失去了工作。

idle capital /ˌaɪd(ə)l ˈkæpɪt(ə)l/ *noun* capital which is not being used productively 闲置资本

idle time /ˈaɪd(ə)l taɪm/ *noun* the time for which employees are paid although they are unable to work because of factors beyond their control 闲置时间：由于无法控制的原因，雇员无法工作但工资照发的时间 ○ *Idle time in January was attributed to the temporary closing down of one of the company's factories*. 公司的一家工厂临时关闭导致员工一月份无事可做。○ *Workers were laid off to avoid excessive idle time*. 工人被解雇以避免出现过多的闲置时间。

IFA[1] *abbr* independent financial adviser 独立财务顾问

IFA[2] *abbr* Institute of Financial Accountants 财务会计师公会

illegal /ɪˈliːɡ(ə)l/ *adjective* not legal or against the law 非法的，违法的

illegality /ˌɪliːˈɡælɪti/ *noun* the fact of being illegal 非法

illegally /ɪˈliːɡəli/ *adverb* against the law 非法地 ○ *He was accused of illegally laundering money*. 他被指控非法洗钱。

illicit /ɪˈlɪsɪt/ *adjective* not legal or not permitted 非法的；不允许的 ○ *the illicit sale of alcohol* 非法销售酒类 ○ *trade in illicit alcohol* 交易酒精违禁品

illiquid /ɪˈlɪkwɪd/ *adjective* **1.** referring to an asset which is not easy to change into cash 非流动性的:(资产)不易变现的 **2.** used to describe a person or business that lacks cash or assets such as securities that can readily be converted into cash 缺乏流动资金的:个人或企业缺乏现金或可随时变现的资产(如证券)

IMA *abbr* Investment Management Association 投资管理协会

IMF *abbr* International Monetary Fund 国际货币基金组织

immovable /ɪˈmuːvəb(ə)l/ *adjective* impossible to move 固定的,不可移动的

immovable property /ɪˌmuːvəbl ˈprɒpəti/ *noun* houses and other buildings on land 不动产:土地上的房屋及其他建筑物

impact /ˈɪmpækt/ *noun* a shock or strong effect 影响,效力 ○ *the impact of new technology on the cotton trade* 新技术对棉业的影响 ○ *The new design has made little impact on the buying public.* 新样式对消费群体收效甚微。

'...the strong dollar's deflationary impact on European economies as governments push up interest rates to support their sinking currencies'
"在各国政府提高利率以抬升他们不断下滑的货币的情况下,美元坚挺对欧洲经济的紧缩影响"[*Duns Business Month*《邓氏商业月刊》]

impairment /ɪmˈpeəmənt/ *noun* a condition in which a sense or function is harmed so that it does not work properly (感官、功能等的)损害,损伤 ○ *His hearing impairment does not affect his work.* 他的听力受损,但不影响工作。

impersonal account /ɪmˌpɜːs(ə)n(ə)l əˈkaʊnt/ *noun* any account other than a personal account, being classified as either a real account, in which property is recorded, or a nominal account, in which income, expenses, and capital are recorded 非个人账户:个人账户以外的任何账户,归类为记录财产的实账户,或记录收入、开支和资本的虚账户 ◊ 参阅 **account**

implement /ˈɪmplɪˌment/ *verb* to put into action 执行,实施 ○ *to implement an agreement* 执行一项协议 ○ *to implement a decision* 执行一个决定

implementation /ˌɪmplɪmenˈteɪʃ(ə)n/ *noun* the process of putting something into action 执行,实施 ○ *the implementation of new rules* 新规定的实施

import /ɪmˈpɔːt/ *verb* to bring goods from abroad into a country for sale 进口 ○ *The company imports television sets from Japan.* 该公司从日本进口电视机。○ *This car was imported from France.* 这辆轿车是从法国进口的。

'European manufacturers rely heavily on imported raw materials which are mostly priced in dollars'
"欧洲制造商过分依赖大多以美元主导的进口原材料"[*Duns Business Month*《邓氏商业月刊》]

importation /ˌɪmpɔːˈteɪʃ(ə)n/ *noun* the act of importing 进口 ○ *The importation of arms is forbidden.* 禁止进口武器。○ *The importation of livestock is subject to very strict controls.* 家畜进口受到非常严格的控制。

import ban /ˈɪmpɔːt bæn/ *noun* an order forbidding imports 进口禁令 ○ *The government has imposed an im-*

port ban on arms. 政府禁止进口武器。

import duty /ˈɪmpɔːt ˌdjuːti/ *noun* a tax on goods imported into a country 进口关税

importer /ɪmˈpɔːtə/ *noun* a person or company that imports goods 进口商 ○ *a cigar importer* 雪茄烟进口商 ○ *The company is a big importer of foreign cars*. 该公司是一家大型的外国汽车进口商。

import-export /ˌɪmpɔːtˈekspɔːt/ *adjective*, *noun* referring to business which deals with both bringing foreign goods into a country and sending locally made goods abroad 进出口的;进出口贸易 ○ *Rotterdam is an important centre for the import-export trade*. 鹿特丹是一个重要的进出口贸易中心。○ *She works in import-export*. 她从事进出口贸易。

importing /ɪmˈpɔːtɪŋ/ *adjective* bringing goods into a country 进口的 ○ *oil-importing countries* 石油进口国 ○ *an importing company* 一家进口公司

import levy /ˈɪmpɔːt ˌlevi/ *noun* a tax on imports, especially in the EU a tax on imports of farm produce from outside the EU 进口税(尤指欧盟对从非欧盟国家进口的农产品的课税)

import quota /ˈɪmpɔːt ˌkwəʊtə/ *noun* a fixed quantity of a particular type of goods which the government allows to be imported 进口配额:政府对某些商品的进口数量的限制 ○ *The government has imposed an import quota on cars*. 政府对汽车进口实行配额制。○ *The import quota on cars has been lifted*. 汽车进口配额制已被取消。

import restrictions /ˈɪmpɔːt rɪˌstrɪkʃ(ə)nz/ *plural noun* actions taken by a government to reduce the level of imports by imposing quotas, duties, etc. 进口限制:政府为减少进口所采取的措施,如进口配额、关税等

imports /ˈɪmpɔːts/ *plural noun* goods brought into a country from abroad for sale 进口货物 ○ *Imports from Poland have risen to $ 1m a year*. 来自波兰的进口货物已增加到每年100万美元。(NOTE: Usually used in the plural, but the singular is used before a noun 通常用复数,但在名词前用单数)

import surcharge /ˈɪmpɔːt ˌsɜːtʃɑːdʒ/ *noun* the extra duty charged on imported goods, to try to stop them from being imported and to encourage local manufacture 进口附加税:为阻止进口和鼓励本地化生产而额外征收的进口关税

impose /ɪmˈpəʊz/ *verb* to give orders for something regarded as unpleasant or unwanted such as a tax or a ban 强制实行,强加(税收、禁令等) ○ *to impose a tax on bicycles* 对自行车征税 ○ *They tried to impose a ban on smoking*. 他们试图禁烟。○ *The government imposed a special duty on oil*. 政府对石油征收特别关税。

imposition /ˌɪmpəˈzɪʃ(ə)n/ *noun* the act of imposing something 强制实行,强加

impound /ɪmˈpaʊnd/ *verb* to take something away and keep it until a tax is paid 扣押,扣留(直到交税为止) ○ *customs impounded the whole cargo* 海关扣押了全部货物

impounding /ɪmˈpaʊndɪŋ/ *noun* an act of taking something and keeping it until a tax is paid 扣押,扣留

imprest account /ˈɪmprest

əˌkaʊnt/ *noun* a UK term for a record of the transactions of a type of petty cash system. An employee is given an advance of money, an imprest, for incidental expenses and when most of it has been spent, he or she presents receipts for the expenses to the accounts department and is then reimbursed with cash to the total value of the receipts 定额备用金账户:英国的一种零用现金系统的交易记录。公司预付给雇员一笔款项,即定额备用金,作为杂费支出,在花出大部分备用金后,雇员向会计部门提呈开支的收据,公司再给其补充等于收据总值的现金

imprest system /ˈɪmprest ˌsɪstəm/ *noun* a system of controlling petty cash, where cash is paid out against a written receipt and the receipt is used to get more cash to bring the float to the original level 定额备用金制度:一种控制零用现金的制度,员工支付现金时索取收据,再使用该收据领取现金,以使零用现金浮动额始终保持在原来的水平

improve /ɪmˈpruːv/ *verb* to make something better, or to become better 改善;提高 ○ *We are trying to improve our image with a series of TV commercials.* 我们正努力通过一系列电视广告来改善我们的形象。○ *They hope to improve the company's market share.* 他们希望提高公司的市场份额。○ *We hope the cash flow position will improve or we will have difficulty in paying our bills.* 我们希望现金流量状况能有所改善,否则我们在支付账款方面将会遇到困难。

'... we also invest in companies whose growth and profitability could be improved by a management buyout'
"我们也投资于那些可以通过管理层收购来促进增长和提高盈利的公司" [*Times*《泰晤士报》]

improved offer /ɪmˌpruːvd ˈɒfə/ *noun* an offer which is larger or has better terms than the previous offer 更高的报价,条件更优惠的报价

impulse buyer /ˈɪmpʌls ˌbaɪə/ *noun* a person who buys something on impulse, not because he or she intended to buy it 即兴购买者:出于冲动而非按计划购物的人

impulse buying /ˈɪmpʌls ˌbaɪɪŋ/ *noun* the practice of buying items which you have just seen, not because you had planned to buy them 即兴购买:看到就买,而不是依事先计划购买

imputation system /ˌɪmpjuːˈteɪʃ(ə)n ˌsɪstəm/ *noun* a system of taxation of dividends, where the company pays advance corporation tax on the dividends it pays to its shareholders, and the shareholders pay no tax on the dividends received, assuming that they pay tax at the standard rate. The ACT is shown as a tax credit which is imputed to the shareholder 股息税代缴制:由公司为股东所得股息缴纳企业预付税,而股东对所得股息因其中已按标准税率作了扣除而不再纳税的税制。这部分企业预付税被视为给予股东的税收抵免

inactive /ɪnˈæktɪv/ *adjective* not active or not busy 不活跃的

inactive account /ɪnˌæktɪv əˈkaʊnt/ *noun* a bank account which is not used over a period of time 闲置的账号,不活动账户:在一段时间里不使用的银行账户

inactive market /ɪnˌæktɪv ˈmɑːkɪt/

noun a stock market with few buyers or sellers 不活跃的市场,闲散市场:买卖者很少的股票市场

incentive /ɪnˈsentɪv/ *noun* something which encourages a customer to buy, or employees to work better (给顾客或雇员的)奖励,鼓励,刺激

'... some further profit-taking was seen yesterday as investors continued to lack fresh incentives to renew buying activity'
"由于投资者仍然缺乏恢复购买的动力,昨天又出现进一步的获利回吐" [*Financial Times*《金融时报》]

'...a well-designed plan can help companies retain talented employees and offer enticing performance incentives—all at an affordable cost'
"一个精心制订的计划能够帮助公司留住人才和提供诱人的业绩奖励——并使两者都在公司可承担的成本范围之内" [*Fortune*《财富》]

'... the right incentives can work when used strategically'
"奖励运用得当就能取得效果" [*Management Today*《今日管理》]

'... an additional incentive is that the Japanese are prepared to give rewards where they are due'
"此外的激励方式是,日本人该奖励时就奖励" [*Management Today*《今日管理》]

incentive bonus /ɪnˈsentɪv ˌbəʊnəs/, **incentive payment** /ɪnˈsentɪv ˌpeɪmənt/ *noun* an extra payment offered to employees to make them work better 奖励报酬,激励金

incentive scheme /ɪnˈsentɪv skiːm/ *noun* a plan to encourage better work by paying higher commission or bonuses 激励方案:通过支付高额佣金或奖金,鼓励员工更好地工作的方案 ○ *Incentive schemes are boosting production*. 激励方案促进了生产。

inchoate /ɪnˈkəʊət/ *adjective* referring to an instrument which is incomplete (票据)未填写的,空白的;(文书)尚未最后完成的

incidence of tax /ˌɪnsɪd(ə)ns əv ˈtæks/ *noun* used to indicate where the final burden of a tax lies. For example, although a retailer pays any sales tax to the tax collecting authority, the tax itself is ultimately paid by the customer 税收归宿:最终的税收承担。例如,虽然销售税都由零售商支付给征税机构,但税收本身最终还是由顾客承担

incidental /ˌɪnsɪˈdent(ə)l/ *adjective* not important, but connected with something else 附带的

incidental expenses /ˌɪnsɪdent(ə)l ɪkˈspensɪz/ *plural noun* small amounts of money spent at various times in addition to larger amounts 杂费,杂项支出

include /ɪnˈkluːd/ *verb* to count something along with other things 包括 ○ *The charge includes VAT*. 费用包括增值税。○ *The total is £140 not including insurance and freight*. 不包括保险和运费的总费用是140英镑。○ *The account covers services up to and including the month of June*. 账目包括到6月份为止(含6月份)的劳务费。

inclusive /ɪnˈkluːsɪv/ *adjective* counting something in with other things 包括的,含有的 ○ *inclusive of tax* 税收包括在内 ○ *not inclusive of VAT* 不包括增值税

income /ˈɪnkʌm/ *noun* **1.** money which a person receives as salary or dividends (个人以工资或股利形式得到的)收入,收益 □ **lower income bracket, upper income bracket** the groups of people who earn low or high salaries considered for tax purposes 低收入等级段，高收入等级段：计税时划定的个人工资档次 **2.** money which an organisation receives as gifts or from investments（机构由馈赠或投资所得的）收入 ○ *The hospital has a large income from gifts*. 该医院获得一大笔捐赠收入。

'... there is no risk-free way of taking regular income from your money much higher than the rate of inflation'
"没有任何无风险的方式可以使资金产生大大高于通货膨胀率的固定收入"［*Guardian*《卫报》］

income distribution /ˈɪnkʌm dɪstrɪˌbjuːʃ(ə)n/ *noun* the UK term for the payment to investors of the income generated by a collective investment, less management charges, tax, and expenses. It is distributed in proportion to the number of units or shares held by each investor（英）收入分配：将扣除管理费用、税收及开支后的集资收入按各投资者所持单位或股份额比例进行分配 US term 美国用语为 **income dividend**

income gearing /ˈɪnkʌm ˌɡɪərɪŋ/ *noun* the ratio of the interest a company pays on its borrowing shown as a percentage of its pretax profits before the interest is paid 收入杠杆比率：公司所付贷款利息占其付息前的税前利润的百分比

income shares /ˈɪnkʌm ʃeəz/ *plural noun* shares in an investment trust which receive income from the investments, but do not benefit from the rise in capital value of the investments 收益股票：投资信托的股票，持有者可获得投资收入，但投资资本本身并不升值

income smoothing /ˌɪnkʌm ˈsmuːðɪŋ/ *noun* a UK term for a form of creative accounting that involves the manipulation of a company's financial statements to show steady annual profits rather than large fluctuations（英）收益平匀，收益修匀：创造性会计的一种，通过对公司财务报表的窜改，令原本大幅波动的年度利润显得平稳

income statement /ˈɪnkʌm ˌsteɪtmənt/ *noun US* a statement of company expenditure and sales which shows whether the company has made a profit or loss（美）损益表，收益表：列示公司的支出及销售额、表明其盈亏状况的报表（NOTE: The UK term is **profit and loss account** 英国用语为 **profit and loss account**）

income tax /ˈɪnkʌm tæks/ *noun* **1.** the tax on a person's income, both earned and unearned（个人）所得税 **2.** the tax on the profits of a corporation（企业）所得税

income tax form /ˈɪnkʌm tæks ˌfɔːm/ *noun* a form to be completed which declares all income to the tax office 所得税申报单

income units /ˈɪnkʌm ˌjuːnɪts/ *plural noun* units in a unit trust, from which the investor receives dividends in the form of income 收益单位：单位信托的投资单位，投资者以收取股利作为收益

incomplete records /ˌɪnkəmpliːt ˈrekɔːdz/ *noun* an accounting system which is not double-entry bookkeeping. Various degrees of incompleteness can occur, e.g., **single-entry bookkeeping**, in which usually only a cash book is maintained 不完整会计记录：一种非复式簿记的会计制度，可能会出现不同程度的不完备，例如单式簿记通常只管理现金账簿

inconvertible /ˌɪnkənˈvɜːtəb(ə)l/ *adjective* referring to currency which cannot be easily converted into other currencies 不可兑换的：（货币）不易兑换成其他通货的

incorporate /ɪnˈkɔːpəreɪt/ *verb* **1.** to bring something in to form part of a main group 综合，合并，收编 ○ *Income from the 1998 acquisition is incorporated into the accounts.* 1998年的收购收入已经入账。**2.** to form a registered company 成立（注册公司）○ *a company incorporated in the USA* 一家在美国注册的公司 ○ *an incorporated company* 一家合股公司 ○ *J. Doe Incorporated* J. Doe 股份有限公司

incorporation /ɪnˌkɔːpəˈreɪʃ(ə)n/ *noun* an act of incorporating a company （公司）注册，组成公司

increase *noun* /ˈɪnkriːs/ **1.** an act of becoming larger 增加，增长 ○ *There have been several increases in tax* or *tax increases in the last few years.* 近几年税收已增加了好几次。○ *There is an automatic 5% increase in price* or *price increase on January 1st.* 在1月1日价格自动上涨了5%。○ *Profits showed a 10% increase* or *an increase of 10% on last year.* 利润比去年增加了10%。**2.** a higher salary 较高的薪金 ○ *increase in pay* or *pay increase* 提薪 ○ *The government hopes to hold salary increases to 3%.* 政府希望把薪金增长率控制在3%。□ **she had two increases last year** her salary went up twice 她去年两次加薪 ■ *verb* /ɪnˈkriːs/ **1.** to grow bigger or higher 增加，增长 ○ *Profits have increased faster than the increase in the rate of inflation.* 利润的增长速度超过了通货膨胀率。○ *Exports to Africa have increased by more than 25%.* 对非洲的出口增长超过了25%。○ *The price of oil has increased twice in the past week.* 上周石油价格上涨了两次。□ **to increase in size** *or* **value** to become larger or more valuable 增大；增值 **2.** to make something bigger or higher 使增大；使增长 □ **the company increased her salary to £20,000** the company gave her a rise in salary to £20,000 公司将她的薪金增加到2万英镑

'... turnover has the potential to be increased to over 1 million dollars with energetic management and very little capital'
"通过有效的管理和一点资本投入，营业额有望突破100万美元"［*Australian Financial Review*《澳大利亚金融评论报》］

'... competition is steadily increasing and could affect profit margins as the company tries to retain its market share'
"竞争日益激烈，为保住其市场份额，公司的利润率将可能受到影响"［*Citizen (Ottawa)*《公民》（渥太华）］

increment /ˈɪŋkrɪmənt/ *noun* a regular automatic increase in salary 薪金的定期自动增长 ○ *an annual increment* 薪金年度增幅 □ **salary which rises in annual increments of £1000** each year the salary is increased by £1000 每年增幅为1,000英镑的薪金

incremental /ˌɪŋkrɪˈment(ə)l/ *adjective* rising automatically in stages 自动递增的

incremental budgeting /ˌɪŋkrɪment(ə)l ˈbʌdʒɪtɪŋ/ *noun* a method of setting budgets in which the prior period budget is used as a base for the current budget, which is set by adjusting the prior period budget to take account of any anticipated changes 增量预算法，渐增预算：一种编制预算的方法，本期预算以上期预算为基础，在考虑到可预见变数后对上期预算进行调整

incremental cost /ˌɪŋkrɪment(ə)l ˈkɒst/ *noun* the cost of making extra units above the number already planned. This may then include further fixed costs 增量成本：在计划产量的基础上再生产所需要的成本，这可能会相应地增加固定成本

incremental increase /ˌɪŋkrɪment(ə)l ˈɪnkriːs/ *noun* an increase in salary according to an agreed annual increment 递增薪额：薪金按协议的年度增幅增长

incremental scale /ˌɪŋkrɪment(ə)l ˈskeɪl/ *noun* a salary scale with regular annual salary increases 按年递增薪级；按年递增薪额的薪级

incur /ɪnˈkɜː/ *verb* to make yourself liable to something 招致，承受

'...the company blames fiercely competitive market conditions in Europe for a £14m operating loss last year, incurred despite a record turnover'
"公司将去年的损失归咎于欧洲市场的激烈竞争。尽管去年的营业额创了纪录，但其仍然损失了1,400万英镑"［*Financial Times*《金融时报》］

indebted /ɪnˈdetɪd/ *adjective* owing money to someone 负债的 ○ *to be indebted to a property company* 欠一家房地产公司的债

indemnification /ɪndemnɪfɪˈkeɪʃən/ *noun* payment for damage 赔偿，补偿

indemnify /ɪnˈdemnɪfaɪ/ *verb* to pay for damage 赔偿 ○ *to indemnify someone for a loss* 赔偿某人的损失

indemnity /ɪnˈdemnɪti/ *noun* **1.** a guarantee of payment after a loss 赔偿保证金 ○ *She had to pay an indemnity of £100.* 她不得不支付100英镑的赔偿保证金。**2.** compensation paid after a loss 赔偿金

indent /ˈɪndent/ *noun* an order placed by an importer for goods from overseas（进口商从海外进口商品的）订单 ○ *They put in an indent for a new stock of soap.* 他们新订购了一批肥皂。

indenture /ɪnˈdentʃə/ *noun US* a formal agreement showing the terms of a bond issue（美）契据：有关债券发行条款的正式协议

independent /ˌɪndɪˈpendənt/ *adjective* not under the control or authority of anyone else 独立的

independent company /ˌɪndɪpendənt ˈkʌmp(ə)ni/ *noun* a company which is not controlled by another company 独立公司：不受任何其他公司控制的公司

independent financial adviser /ˌɪndɪpendənt faɪˌnænʃ(ə)l ədˈvaɪzə/ *noun* a person who gives impartial advice on financial matters, who is not connected with any financial institution. 独立财务顾问：就财务事宜提供公正意见的人，该人与任何金融机构无关联 Abbreviation 缩写 **IFA**

independent trader /ˌɪndɪpendənt ˈtreɪdə/, **independent shop** /ˌɪndɪpendənt ˈʃɒp/ *noun* a shop which is owned by an individual proprietor, not by a chain 独立商店：由个体经营者拥有的非连锁商店

index /ˈɪndeks/ *noun* **1.** a list of items classified into groups or put in alphabetical order 索引 **2.** a regular statistical report which shows rises and falls in prices, values or levels 指数:显示价格、价值或水平升降的定期统计报告 **3.** a figure based on the current market price of shares on a stock exchange 指数:根据证券交易所股票的当前市价计算出的数字 ■ *verb* to link a payment to an index 将(付款金额)与指数挂钩 ○ *salaries indexed to the cost of living* 与生活费用挂钩的工资

'...the index of industrial production sank 0.2 per cent for the latest month after rising 0.3 per cent in March'
"工业生产指数在3月份上涨0.3%之后,在最近一个月又下降了0.2%"[*Financial Times*《金融时报》]

'...an analysis of the consumer price index for the first half of the year shows that the rate of inflation went down by 12.9 per cent'
"今年上半年的消费价格指数分析表明,通货膨胀率下降了12.9%"[*Business Times* (*Lagos*)《商业时报》(拉各斯)]

indexation /ˌɪndekˈseɪʃ(ə)n/ *noun* the linking of something to an index 指数化:将某事物与指数挂钩

index card /ˈɪndeks kɑːd/ *noun* a card used to make a card index 索引卡片

index fund /ˈɪndeks fʌnd/ *noun* an investment fund consisting of shares in all the companies which are used to calculate a Stock Exchange index 指数投资基金:由证券交易指数内所有成分股组成的投资基金(NOTE: The plural is **indexes** or **indices** 复数为**indexes**或**indices**)

index letter /ˈɪndeks ˌletə/ *noun* a letter of an item in an index 索引字母

index-linked /ˌɪndeksˈlɪŋkt/ *adjective* rising automatically by the percentage increase in the cost of living 指数化的,与(生活费用)指数挂钩的:随生活费的增长而自动增加的 ○ *index-linked government bonds* 指数化政府债券 ○ *Inflation did not affect her as she has an index-linked pension.* 她享有指数化养老金,所以不受通货膨胀影响。

'...two-year index-linked savings certificates now pay 3 per cent a year tax free, in addition to indexlinking'
"除了与指数挂钩,两年期指数化存单现在每年支付3%免税利息"[*Financial Times*《金融时报》]

index number /ˈɪndeks ˌnʌmbə/ *noun* **1.** a number of something in an index 索引号 **2.** a number showing the percentage rise of something over a period 指数:显示一段时间内某物增长的百分比

index tracker /ˈɪndeks ˌtrækə/ *noun* an investor or fund manager who tracks an index 指数跟踪者:指跟踪指数的投资者(或基金经理)

index-tracking /ˈɪndeksˌtrækɪŋ/ *adjective* following an index 指数跟踪的

indexed portfolio /ˌɪndekst pɔːtˈfəʊliəʊ/ *noun* a portfolio of shares in all the companies which form the basis of a stock exchange index 指数化投资组合:对构成证券交易指数的所有公司的投资组合

indicate /ˈɪndɪkeɪt/ *verb* to show something 指示,表明 ○ *The latest figures indicate a fall in the inflation rate.* 最新数字显示通货膨胀率有所下降。○ *Our sales for last year indicate a move from the home market to* *exports*. 去年销售表明,我们已由国内市场转向出口贸易。

indicator /ˈɪndɪkeɪtə/ *noun* something which indicates 指示器,指标

'...it reduces this month's growth in the key M3 indicator from about 19% to 12%'
"它使这个月关键的 M3 指标的增长从约 19%降到 12%" [*Sunday Times*《星期日泰晤士报》]

'...we may expect the US leading economic indicators for April to show faster economic growth'
"我们可以预期,美国 4 月份的主要经济指标会显示出更快的经济增长" [*Australian Financial Review*《澳大利亚金融评论报》]

'...other indicators, such as high real interest rates, suggest that monetary conditions are extremely tight'
"其他指标(如高实际利率)表明现在资金非常紧缺" [*Economist*《经济学家》]

indirect /ˌɪndaɪˈrekt/ *adjective* not direct 间接的

indirect expenses /ˌɪndaɪrekt ɪkˈspensɪz/ *noun* costs which are not directly attached to the making of a product, e. g. cleaning, rent, administration 间接费用:与产品生产没有直接联系的成本,如清洁费、租金、行政管理费用

indirect labour costs /ˌɪndaɪrekt ˈleɪbə ˌkɒsts/ *plural noun* the cost of paying employees not directly involved in making a product such as cleaners or canteen staff. Such costs cannot be allocated to a cost centre 间接人工成本:支付给不直接参与产品生产的雇员(如清洁工或食堂员工)的费用,这些成本不能分配到成本中心

indirect material cost /ˌɪndaɪrekt məˈtɪəriəl kɒst/ , **indirect materials cost** /ˌɪndaɪrekt məˈtiəriəlz kɒst/ *noun* the cost of materials which cannot be allocated to the production of a particular product 间接材料成本:不归属于任何一件产品生产的材料成本

indirect tax /ˌɪndaɪrekt ˈtæks/ *noun* a tax such as VAT paid to someone who then pays it to the government 间接税:先支付给他人、再由后者付给政府的税,如增值税

indirect taxation /ˌɪndaɪrekt tækˈseɪʃ(ə)n/ *noun* taxes which are not paid direct to the government, e. g. sales tax 间接征税:不直接缴纳给政府的税,如销售税 ○ *The government raises more money by indirect taxation than by direct*. 政府的间接税收多于直接税收。

individual /ˌɪndɪˈvɪdʒuəl/ *noun* one single person 个人 ○ *a savings plan tailored to the requirements of the private individual* 根据个人需求制订的储蓄计划

Individual Savings Account /ˌɪndɪvɪdʒuəl ˈseɪvɪŋz əˌkaʊnt/ *noun* a British scheme by which individuals can invest for their retirement by putting a limited amount of money each year in a tax-free account 个人储蓄计划:英国的一种计划,个人可每年向一个免税账户缴存有限的金额,作为其退休金投资 Abbreviation 缩写 **ISA**

Individual Voluntary Arrangement /ˌɪndɪvɪdʒuəl ˌvɒlənt(ə)ri əˈreɪndʒmənt/ *noun* a legally binding arrangement between a debtor and creditors by which the debtor offers the creditors the best deal he or she can afford by realising his assets, and so the expense of bankruptcy proceedings is avoided 个人自愿协定:债务人与债权人之间有法律约束力的协定,根据该

协定，债务人通过变现资产向债权人提供其所能承担的最佳条件，从而避免进入破产程序 Abbreviation 缩写 **IVA**

inducement /ɪnˈdjuːsmənt/ *noun* something which helps to persuade someone to do something 诱因，引诱物 ○ *They offered her a company car as an inducement to stay.* 公司给她配备了一辆汽车，吸引她留下来。

industrial arbitration tribunal /ɪnˌdʌstriəl ɑːbɪˈtreɪʃ(ə)n traɪˌbjuːn(ə)l/ *noun* a court which decides in industrial disputes 劳资仲裁法庭

industrial tribunal /ɪnˌdʌstriəl traɪˈbjuːn(ə)l/ *noun* a court which can decide in disputes about employment 劳资法庭

'ACAS has a legal obligation to try and solve industrial grievances before they reach industrial tribunals'
"在劳资申诉提交劳资法庭前，劳动咨询调解仲裁委员会负有进行调解的法定义务" [*Personnel Today*《今日人事》]

ineligible /ɪnˈelɪdʒɪb(ə)l/ *adjective* not eligible 不具资格的，不合格的

inflation /ɪnˈfleɪʃ(ə)n/ *noun* a greater increase in the supply of money or credit than in the production of goods and services, resulting in higher prices and a fall in the purchasing power of money 通货膨胀：货币或贷款供应的增长速度超过商品及劳务生产，导致物价上涨、货币购买力下降 ○ *to take measures to reduce inflation* 采取措施降低通货膨胀 ○ *High interest rates tend to increase inflation.* 高利率往往导致通货膨胀的增长。□ **we have 3% inflation *or* inflation is running at 3%** prices are 3% higher than at the same time last year 我们的通货膨胀率为 3%：物价同比增长 3%

inflation accounting /ɪnˈfleɪʃ(ə)n əˌkaʊntɪŋ/ *noun* an accounting system, where inflation is taken into account when calculating the value of assets and the preparation of accounts 通货膨胀会计：在计算资产价值和编制会计报表时将通货膨胀因素考虑在内的一种会计制度

inflationary /ɪnˈfleɪʃ(ə)n(ə)ri/ *adjective* tending to increase inflation 通货膨胀的 ○ *inflationary trends in the economy* 经济的通货膨胀趋势

'...inflationary expectations fell somewhat this month, but remained a long way above the actual inflation rate, according to figures released yesterday. The annual rate of inflation measured by the consumer price index has been below 2 per cent for over 18 months'
"根据昨天发布的数字，这个月的通胀预期有所下降，但仍远高于实际通胀率。按消费价格指数衡量的年通胀率已经超过 18 个月低于 2%" [*Australian Financial Review*《澳大利亚金融评论报》]

inflation-proof /ɪnˈfleɪʃ(ə)npruːf/ *adjective* referring to a pension, etc. which is index-linked, so that its value is preserved in times of inflation 通货膨胀保值的：养老金等与指数挂钩，因此在通货膨胀时能保值

inflow /ˈɪnfləʊ/ *noun* the act of coming in or being brought in 流入，涌入

'...the dollar is strong because of capital inflows rather than weak because of the trade deficit'
"美元并未因贸易赤字而走弱，反而因资本流入而保持坚挺" [*Duns Business Month*《邓氏商业月刊》]

influx /ˈɪnflʌks/ *noun* an inflow, especially one where people or things come in in large quantities（尤指大量的）涌入，注入○ *an influx of foreign currency into the country* 大量外汇注入该国 ○ *an influx of cheap labour into the cities* 大量廉价劳动力向城市的涌入

'...the retail sector will also benefit from the expected influx of tourists'
"零售业也将从即将到来的大批观光客中分一杯羹"［*Australian Financial Review*《澳大利亚金融评论报》］

information retrieval /ˌɪnfəmeɪʃ(ə)n rɪˈtriːv(ə)l/ *noun* the finding of stored data in a computer（电脑）信息检索

inherit /ɪnˈherɪt/ *verb* to get something from a person who has died 继承 ○ *When her father died she inherited the shop*. 父亲死后，她继承了这个商店。○ *He inherited £10,000 from his grandfather*. 他从祖父那里继承了一万英镑。

inheritance /ɪnˈherɪt(ə)ns/ *noun* property which is received from a dead person 遗产，继承的财产

inheritance tax /ɪnˈherɪt(ə)ns tæks/ *noun* tax payable on wealth or property worth above a certain amount and inherited after the death of someone. The current threshold is £250,000, and the estate is liable for 40% tax on the excess amount 遗产税，继承税：继承的遗产超过一定金额时应交的税。现行的税收起征点是25万英镑，对超出的部分收40%的税 Abbreviation 缩写 **IHT**（NOTE：The US term is **death duty** 美国用语为 **death duty**）

in-house /ˌɪnˈhaʊs/ *adverb*, *adjective* done by someone employed by a company on their premises, not by an outside contractor（公司）内部完成地，内部的 ○ *the in-house staff* 公司内部员工 ○ *We do all our data processing in-house*. 我们所有的数据处理都自己完成。

initial /ɪˈnɪʃ(ə)l/ *adjective* first or starting 首先的，开始的 ○ *The initial response to the TV advertising has been very good*. 对电视广告的初步反响非常好。

'...the founding group has subscribed NKr 14.5m of the initial NKr 30m share capital'
"创办团队已经认购了3,000万挪威克朗初始股本中的1,450万挪威克朗"［*Financial Times*《金融时报》］

'...career prospects are excellent for someone with potential, and initial salary is negotiable around $45,000 per annum'
"虚位以待纳贤才，起薪一年45,000美元左右，具体面议"［*Australian Financial Review*《澳大利亚金融评论报》］

initial capital /ɪˌnɪʃ(ə)l ˈkæpɪt(ə)l/ *noun* capital which is used to start a business 创业资本

initials /ɪˈnɪʃ(ə)lz/ *plural noun* a first letters of the words in a name 名称首字母缩写 ○ *What do the initials IMF stand for?* IMF这个缩写代表什么？○ *The chairman wrote his initials by each alteration in the contract he was signing*. 董事长在他所签合同的每一个变更处都签上了他的姓名缩写。

initial sales /ɪˌnɪʃ(ə)l ˈseɪlz/ *plural noun* the first sales of a new product（新产品的）首次销售额，最初销售额

initial yield /ɪˌnɪʃ(ə)l ˈjiːld/ *noun* the estimated yield of an investment fund at the time when it is launched 初期收益率：投资基金推出时的估计收益率

initiate /ɪˈnɪʃieɪt/ *verb* to start 开始，发起 ○ *to initiate discussions* 开始讨论

initiative /ɪˈnɪʃətɪv/ *noun* the decision to start something 倡议；开始进行某事的决定

injection /ɪnˈdʒekʃən/ *noun* □ **a capital injection of £100,000** *or* **an injection of £100,000 capital** putting £100,000 into an existing business 10万英镑的资本注入

injunction /ɪnˈdʒʌŋkʃən/ *noun* a court order telling someone not to do something (法院的)禁令：禁止某人做某事的法院裁定 ○ *He got an injunction preventing the company from selling his car.* 他取得了法院禁令，禁止公司出售他的汽车。○ *The company applied for an injunction to stop their rival from marketing a similar product.* 公司向法院申请禁止其竞争对手经销同类产品。

inland /ˈɪnlənd/ *adjective* inside a country 国内的

inland freight charges /ˌɪnlənd ˈfreɪt ˌtʃɑːdʒɪz/ *plural noun* charges for carrying goods from one part of the country to another 国内运费：对货物在国内各地间运输所收取的费用

inland postage /ˌɪnlənd ˈpəʊstɪdʒ/ *noun* postage for a letter to another part of the same country 国内邮政费用

Inland Revenue /ˌɪnlənd ˈrevənjuː/ *noun* a British government department dealing with taxes such as income tax, corporation tax, capital gains tax, inheritance tax, etc., but not duties, such as VAT, which are collected by the Customs and Excise 国内税务局：英国主管个人所得税、公司税、资本收益税、遗产税等税收的政府部门，但不包括增值税等关税，后者由关税和消费税部门征收 ○ *He received a letter from the Inland Revenue.* 他收到一封国内税务局的来信。(NOTE: The US term is **Internal Revenue Service** or **IRS** 美国用语为 **Internal Revenue Service** 或 **IRS**)

Inland Revenue Commissioner /ɪnˌlænd ˌrevənjuː kəˈmɪʃ(ə)nə/ *noun* a person appointed officially to supervise the collection of taxes, including income tax, capital gains tax and corporation tax, but not Value Added Tax 国内税务专员：官方指定的负责税目征收的人，税目包括个人所得税、资本收益税和公司税，但不包括增值税 Abbreviation 缩写 **IRC**

inputs /ˈɪnpʊts/ *plural noun* goods or services bought by a company and which may be liable to VAT 投入物：公司购买的可能需交增值税的商品或劳务

input tax /ˈɪnpʊt tæks/ *noun* VAT which is paid by a company on goods or services bought 进项税：就公司购买的商品或劳务所交的增值税

inquiry office /ɪnˈkwaɪəri ˌɒfɪs/ *noun* an office which members of the public can go to to have their questions answered 问询处：解答公众所咨询的问题的办事处

inside /ɪnˈsaɪd/ *adjective*, *adverb* in, especially in a company's office or building 内部(的)，里面(的)(尤指公司办公室里或办公大楼内的) ○ *We do all our design work inside.* 我们所有的设计工作都是自己完成的。

insider /ɪn'saɪdə/ *noun* a person who works in an organisation and therefore knows its secrets 了解内幕者，知情者：在一组织内工作，因此了解其内情的人

insider buying /ɪnˌsaɪdə 'baɪɪŋ/, **insider dealing** /ɪnˌsaɪdə 'diːlɪŋ/ *noun* the illegal buying or selling of shares by staff of a company or other persons who have secret information about the company's plans 内幕交易：公司职员或知道公司机密计划的人进行的非法股票买卖行为

insider trading /ɪnˌsaɪdə 'treɪdɪŋ/ *noun* same as 同 **insider buying**

inside worker /'ɪnsaɪd ˌwɜːkə/ *noun* an employee who works in an office or factory 室内职员：在办公室或工厂里工作的雇员

insolvency /ɪn'sɒlvənsi/ *noun* the fact of not being able to pay debts 无力偿付，资不抵债 Opposite 反义 **solvency**

'... hundreds of thrifts found themselves on the brink of insolvency after a deregulation programme prompted them to enter dangerous financial waters'
"管理的放开促使上百家储蓄机构纷纷涉足危险的金融领域，直至它们发现自己已经处在资不抵债的边缘"[*Times*《泰晤士报》]

insolvency practitioner /ɪn'sɒlvənsi prækˌtɪʃ(ə)nə/ *noun* a person who advises insolvent companies 向无力偿付的公司提供建议的人

insolvent /ɪn'sɒlvənt/ *adjective* not able to pay debts 无偿付能力的 ○ *The company was declared insolvent*. 该公司被宣布为无偿付能力。(NOTE：see note at **insolvency**)

inspect /ɪn'spekt/ *verb* to examine in detail 检查，稽查 ○ *to inspect a machine* or *an installation* 检查机器(或装置) ○ *The gas board is sending an engineer to inspect the central heating system*. 燃气管理部门派一名工程师去检查中央供暖系统。○ *Officials from the DTI have come to inspect the accounts*. 贸易工业部官员来查账。

inspection /ɪn'spekʃən/ *noun* the close examination of something 检查，稽查 ○ *to make an inspection* or *to carry out an inspection of a machine* or *an installation* 检查机器(或装置) ○ *the inspection of a product for defects* 检查产品有无缺陷

inspection stamp /ɪn'spekʃən stæmp/ *noun* a stamp placed on something to show it has been inspected 检查盖章：在某物上加盖的印章，表明该物已检验过

inspector /ɪn'spektə/ *noun* an official who inspects 检查员，稽核员 ○ *The inspectors will soon be round to make sure the building is safe*. 检查员很快就会来查看建筑是否安全。

inspectorate /ɪn'spekt(ə)rət/ *noun* all inspectors (总称)检查人员

inspector of taxes /ɪnˌspektər əv 'tæksɪz/ *noun* in the United Kingdom, an official who reports to the Board of Inland Revenue and is responsible for issuing tax returns and assessments, agreeing tax liabilities, and conducting appeals on matters of tax 税务稽核员：在英国负有对国内税收局呈报之责的官员，其职责包括：发送税收报表和税收评估，批准税款贷项，处理税务申诉

inspector of weights and measures / ɪnˌspektər əv ˌweɪts ən 'meʒəz/ *noun* a government official who inspects weighing machines and goods sold in shops to see if the quantities and weights are correct 度量衡检查员：负责对商店衡器的精确度和所卖物品的数量与重量进行核查的政府官员

instability /ˌɪnstəˈbɪlɪti/ *noun* the state of being unstable or moving up and down 不稳定性 □ **a period of instability in the money markets** a period when currencies fluctuate rapidly 货币市场不稳定期

instalment /ɪnˈstɔːlmənt/ *noun* a part of a payment which is paid regularly until the total amount is paid 分期付款，摊付额 ○ *The first instalment is payable on signature of the agreement*. 第一笔分期付款在签署协议时支付。（NOTE：The US spelling is **installment** 美国拼法为 **installment**）□ **to pay £25 down and monthly instalments of £20** to pay a first payment of £25 and the rest in payments of £20 each month 首付25英镑，余下的每月付20英镑

institute /ˈɪnstɪtjuːt/ *noun* a society or organisation which represents a particular profession or activity 机构，协会 ○ *the Institute of Chartered Accountants* 特许会计师协会 ○ *the Chartered Institute of Personnel and Development* 特许人事与发展协会

Institute of Chartered Accountants in England and Wales /ˌɪnstɪtjuːt əv ˌtʃɑːtəd əˌkaʊntənts ɪn ˌɪŋglənd ən ˈweɪlz/ *noun* the largest professional accountancy body in Europe, providing qualification by examinations, ensuring high standards of education and training, and supervising professional conduct 英格兰及威尔士特许会计师协会：欧洲最大的专业会计团体，它提供资格考试，确保高水准的教育及培训，并监督专业操守 Abbreviation 缩写 **ICAEW**

Institute of Chartered Accountants in Ireland /ˌɪnstɪtjuːt əv ˌtʃɑːtəd əˌkaʊntənts ɪn ˈaɪələnd/ *noun* the oldest and largest professional body for accountants in Ireland, founded in 1888 with the aims of promoting best practice in chartered accountancy and maintaining high standards of professionalism among its members 爱尔兰特许会计师协会：成立于1888年，是爱尔兰历史最悠久也是最大的专业会计师团体，其宗旨是促进特许会计专业的最佳实践和维持其会员的高专业水准 Abbreviation 缩写 **ICAI**

Institute of Chartered Accountants in Scotland /ˌɪnstɪtjuːt əv ˌtʃɑːtəd əˌkaʊntənts ɪn ˈskɒtlənd/ *noun* the world's oldest professional body for accountants, based in Edinburgh 苏格兰特许会计师协会：全球历史最悠久的专业会计师团体，设在爱丁堡 Abbreviation 缩写 **ICAS**

Institute of Chartered Accountants of New Zealand /ˌɪnstɪtjuːt əvˌtʃɑːtəd əˌkaʊntənts əv njuː ˈziːlənd/ *noun* the only professional accounting body in New Zealand, representing over 26,000 members in that country and abroad 新西兰特许会计师协会：新西兰唯一的专业会计团体，在新西兰国内及海外拥有超过26,000名会员 Abbreviation 缩写 **ICANZ**

Institute of Financial Accountants /ˌɪnstɪtjuːt əv faɪˌnænʃ(ə)l əˈkaʊntənts/ *noun* a professional body, established in 1916, which aims to set technical and ethical standards in UK financial accountancy 财务会计师公会：成立于 1916 年的专业团体，其宗旨是制定英国财务会计专业的技术及道德标准 Abbreviation 缩写 **IFA**

institution /ˌɪnstɪˈtjuːʃ(ə)n/ *noun* an organisation or society set up for a particular purpose 协会，机构 ◊ 参阅 **financial institution**

institutional /ˌɪnstɪˈtjuːʃ(ə)n(ə)l/ *adjective* referring to an institution, especially a financial institution 机构的（尤指金融机构的）

'... during the 1970s commercial property was regarded by big institutional investors as an alternative to equities'
"20 世纪 70 年代，商用物业被大型机构投资者看作是可以替代股票的投资选择"［*Investors Chronicle*《投资者纪事》］

instruction /ɪnˈstrʌkʃən/ *noun* an order which tells what should be done or how something is to be used 指令；说明 ○ *She gave instructions to his stockbroker to sell the shares immediately.* 她指示经纪人立即抛售股票。

instrument /ˈɪnstrʊmənt/ *noun* **1.** a tool or piece of equipment 工具，设备 ○ *The technician brought instruments to measure the output of electricity.* 技师带来了测量电流输出的工具。**2.** a legal document 法律文件

insurable /ɪnˈʃʊərəb(ə)l/ *adjective* possible to insure 可保险的

insurable interest /ɪnˌʃʊərəb(ə)l ˈɪntrəst/ *noun* the value of the thing insured which is attributed to the person who is taking out the insurance 可保利益：受保财产的价值归投保人所有

insurance /ɪnˈʃʊərəns/ *noun* an agreement that in return for regular payments called 'premiums', a company will pay compensation for loss, damage, injury or death 保险 ○ *to take out insurance* 投保 ○ *Repairs will be paid for by the insurance.* 维修费用可以走保险。

insurance agent /ɪnˈʃʊərəns ˌeɪdʒənt/, **insurance broker** /ɪnˈʃʊərəns ˌbrəʊkə/ *noun* a person who arranges insurance for clients 保险代理人

insurance claim /ɪnˈʃʊərəns kleɪm/ *noun* a request to an insurance company to pay compensation for damage or loss 保险索赔

insurance company /ɪnˈʃʊərəns ˌkʌmp(ə)ni/ *noun* a company whose business is insurance 保险公司

insurance contract /ɪnˈʃʊərəns ˌkɒntrækt/ *noun* an agreement by an insurance company to insure 保险合同

insurance cover /ɪnˈʃʊərəns ˌkʌvə/ *noun* protection guaranteed by an insurance policy 保险范围 ○ *Do you have cover against theft?* 你投保失窃险了吗？

insurance policy /ɪnˈʃʊərəns ˌpɒlɪsi/ *noun* a document which shows the conditions of an insurance contract 保险单

insurance premium /ɪnˈʃʊərəns ˌpriːmiəm/ *noun* an annual payment made by a person or a company to an insurance company（投保客体向保险公司支付的一年的）保险费

insurance premium tax /ɪnˌʃʊərəns ˈpriːmiəm tæks/ *noun* a tax on household, motor vehicle, travel, and other general insurance 保费税：家用设备、机动车、旅行及其他一般保险的税收

insurance rates /ɪnˈʃʊərəns reɪts/

plural noun the amount of premium which has to be paid per £1000 of insurance 保险费率：每 1,000 英镑的保险须支付的保费

insure /ɪnˈʃʊə/ *verb* to have a contract with a company whereby, if regular small payments are made, the company will pay compensation for loss, damage, injury or death 给（遗失、损坏、伤亡等）保险 ○ *to insure a house against fire* 为房子投保火险 ○ *to insure someone's life* 保人寿险 ○ *to insure baggage against loss* 为包裹保遗失险 ○ *to insure against loss of earnings* 为收入保损失险 ○ *She was insured for £100,000.* 她保了 10 万英镑的险。

insurer /ɪnˈʃʊərə/ *noun* a company which insures 保险公司（NOTE: For life insurance, UK English prefers to use **assurer** 指人寿保险时，英国一般用 **assurer**）

intangible /ɪnˈtændʒɪb(ə)l/ *adjective* not possible to touch 无形的

intangible assets /ɪnˌtændʒɪb(ə)l ˈæsets/, **intangibles** /ɪnˈtændʒɪb(ə)lz/ *plural noun* assets which have a value, but which cannot be seen, e.g. goodwill, or a patent or a trademark 无形资产：有价值但无实物形态的资产，如商誉、专利权或商标

intangible fixed assets /ɪnˌtændʒɪb(ə)l fɪkst ˈæsets/ *plural noun* assets which have a value, but which cannot be seen, e.g. goodwill, copyrights, patents or trademarks 无形固定资产：有价值但无实物形态的资产，如商誉、版权、专利权或商标

integrate /ˈɪntɪgreɪt/ *verb* to link things together to form one whole group 使成整体，使并入，整合

integrated accounts /ˌɪntɪˌgreɪtɪd əˈkaʊnts/ *noun* accounting records that show both financial and cost accounts 合并报表：同时呈列财务和成本账目的会计记录

integration /ˌɪntɪˈgreɪʃ(ə)n/ *noun* the act of bringing several businesses together under a central control（在集中控制下的）企业联合

intent /ɪnˈtent/ *noun* something that someone plans to do 意图，目的

inter- /ɪntə/ *prefix* between 在…之间

inter-bank /ˌɪntəˈbæŋk/ *adjective* between banks 银行间的

inter-bank loan /ˌɪntəbæŋk ˈləʊn/ *noun* a loan from one bank to another 银行同业拆放贷款

inter-company /ɪnˌtɜːˈkʌmp(ə)ni/ *adjective* between companies 公司间的

inter-company dealings /ɪnˌtɜːˌkʌmp(ə)ni ˈdiːlɪŋz/, **inter-company transactions** /ɪnˌtɜːˌkʌmp(ə)ni trænˈzækʃ(ə)ns/ *plural noun* dealings or transactions between two companies in the same group 公司间交易：同一集团内部的两家公司间的交易或业务往来

interest /ˈɪntrəst/ *noun* **1.** special attention 兴趣 ○ *The buyers showed a lot of interest in our new product range.* 买方对我们的新产品系列表示出很大的兴趣。**2.** payment made by a borrower for the use of money, calculated as a percentage of the capital borrowed 利息：借方为货币的使用而支付的费用，以所借资本的百分比来计算 □ **high interest, low interest** interest at a high or low percentage 高利息，低利息：按高或低百分比计算的利息 **3.** money paid as income on investments or loans（投资或贷款）收入 ○ *to* *receive interest at 5%* 获得5%的利息 ○ *the loan pays 5% interest* 这笔贷款的利息是5% ○ *deposit which yields* or *gives* or *produces* or *bears 5% interest* 利率为5%的存款 ○ *account which earns interest at 10%* or *which earns 10% interest* 获利10%的账户 ○ *The bank pays 10% interest on deposits*. 银行支付10%的存款利息。**4.** a part of the ownership of something, e. g. if you invest money in a company you acquire a financial share or interest in it 权益:所有者权益的一部分,如将资金投资于某公司时得到该公司的股份或权益

interest-bearing deposits /ˌɪntrəstˌbeərɪŋ dɪˈpɒzɪts/ *plural noun* deposits which produce interest 附息存款

interest charges /ˈɪntrəst ˌtʃɑːdʒɪz/ *plural noun* money paid as interest on a loan (贷款)利息费用

interest cover /ˈɪntrəst ˌkʌvə/ *noun* the ability to pay interest payments on a loan 利息偿付比率:支付贷款利息的能力

interested party /ˌɪntrəstɪd ˈpɑːti/ *noun* a person or company with a financial interest in a company 有关当事人:与某公司有利益关系的人或公司

interest-free credit /ˌɪntrəstfriː ˈkredɪt/ *noun* a credit or loan where no interest is paid by the borrower 无息贷款 ○ *The company gives its staff interest-free loans*. 该公司向其员工提供无息贷款。

interest rate margin /ˈɪntrəst reɪt ˌmɑːdʒɪn/ *noun* the difference between the interest a bank pays on deposits and the interest it charges on loans 利差:银行贷款利息与存款利息的差额

interest rate swap /ˈɪntrəst reɪt ˌswɒp/ *noun* an agreement between two companies to exchange borrowings. A company with fixed-interest borrowings might swap them for variable interest borrowings of another company 利率互换:两家公司达成的交换贷款的协议,一家公司可能会用其固定利率贷款来交换另一家公司的可变利率贷款 Also called 亦称作 **plain vanilla swap**

interest sensitive /ˌɪntrəst ˈsensɪtɪv/ *noun* used to describe assets, generally purchased with credit, that are in demand when interest rates fall but considered less attractive when interest rates rise 利息敏感:用来形容通常通过贷款购买的资产,其需求量与利率成反比

interest yield /ˈɪntrəst jiːld/ *noun* a yield on a fixed-interest investment 利息收益率:固定利息投资的收益率

interim /ˈɪntərɪm/ *adjective* made, measured or happening in the middle of a period, such as the financial year, and before the final result for the period is available 中期的:在某期间(如在会计年度)的中间作出、计算或发生的,并且在该期间的最终业绩发布前的 ■ *noun* a statement of interim profits or dividends (利润或股利的)中期报表

'...the company plans to keep its annual dividend unchanged at 7.5 per share, which includes a 3.75 interim payout'
"公司计划将年股利保持在每股7.5元,其中包括3.75元的中期股利发放"[*Financial Times*《金融时报》]

interim dividend /ˌɪntərɪm

ˈdɪvɪˌdend/ *noun* a dividend paid at the end of a half-year 中期股利：半年末支付的股利

interim financial statement /ˌɪntərɪm faɪˌnænʃəl ˈsteɪtmənt/ *noun* a financial statement that covers a period other than a full financial year. Although UK companies are not legally obliged to publish interim financial statements, those listed on the London Stock Exchange are obliged to publish a half-yearly report of their activities and a profit and loss account which may either be sent to shareholders or published in a national newspaper. In the United States, the practice is to issue quarterly financial statement 中期财务报表：涵盖并非完整会计年度的期间的财务报表。虽然英国公司并无必须发布中期财务报表的法定责任，但伦敦证券交易所的上市公司须就它们的业务活动和损益表发布半年报告，该报告可发给股东，也可以在全国性报纸上发布。美国则采取发布季度财务报表的做法

interim payment /ˌɪntərɪm ˈpeɪmənt/ *noun* a payment of part of a dividend 期中(部分)股利发放

interim receiver /ˌɪntərɪm rɪˈsiːvə/ *noun* a receiver appointed to deal with a person's affairs until a bankruptcy order is made 临时接管人：在破产令发布前，受委派负责处理某人事务的接管人

intermediary /ˌɪntəˈmiːdiəri/ *noun* a person who is the link between people or organisations who do not agree or who are negotiating 调解人：在人际间或组织间斡旋的个人 ○ *He refused to act as an intermediary between the two directors.* 他拒绝充当这两名董事的调解人。

intermediate debt /ˌɪntəˈmiːdiət det/ *noun* debts which have to be repaid between four and ten years' time 中期债务：偿还期在四到十年间的债务

internal /ɪnˈtɜːn(ə)l/ *adjective* **1.** inside a company 公司内部的 **2.** inside a country or a region 国内的，地区内的

internal audit /ɪnˌtɜːn(ə)l ˈɔːdɪt/ *noun* an audit carried out by a department inside the company 内部审计：由公司内部所属部门进行的审计

internal auditor /ɪnˌtɜːn(ə)l ˈɔːdɪtə/ *noun* a member of staff who audits a company's accounts 内部审计人员：审计公司账目的公司员工

internal control /ɪnˌtɜːn(ə)l kənˈtrəʊl/ *noun* a system set up by the management of a company to monitor and control the company's activities 内部控制：公司管理层建立的监督和控制公司内部活动的系统

internal growth /ɪnˌtɜːn(ə)l ˈgrəʊθ/ *noun* the development of a company by growing its existing business with its own finances, as opposed to acquiring other businesses 内部增长：通过使用自有资金拓展现有业务、而不是通过收购其他企业实现的公司发展 Also called 亦称作 **organic growth**. Opposite 反义 **external growth**

internal rate of return /ɪnˌtɜːn(ə)l reɪt əv rɪˈtɜːn/ *noun* an average annual yield of an investment, where the interest earned over a period of time is the same as the original cost of the investment 内部收益率：投资的平均年度收益率，而投资在一定期限内赚取的利息与投资的原始成本相同 Abbreviation 缩写 **IRR**

Internal Revenue Service

/ɪnˌtɜːn(ə)l ˈrevənjuː ˌsɜːvɪs/ *noun US* in the United States, the branch of the federal government charged with collecting the majority of federal taxes (美)国内税务局：负责征收大部分联邦税的美国联邦政府的所属机构 Abbreviation 缩写 **IRS**

internal telephone /ɪnˌtɜːn(ə)l ˈtelɪfəʊn/ *noun* a telephone which is linked to other telephones in an office (办公室的)内线电话

internal trade /ɪnˌtɜːn(ə)l ˈtreɪd/ *noun* trade between various parts of a country 国内贸易 Opposite 反义 **external trade**

international /ˌɪntəˈnæʃ(ə)nəl/ *adjective* working between countries 国际的

International Accounting Standards Board /ˌɪntənæʃ(ə)nəl əˌkaʊntɪŋ ˈstændədz ˌbɔːd/ *noun* an independent and privately funded accounting standards setting organisation, based in London. The Board, whose members come from nine countries and a range of backgrounds, is committed to developing a single set of high quality, understandable, and enforceable global standards that require transparent and comparable information in general purpose financial statements. It also works with national 国际会计准则理事会：设在伦敦的一个独立的私人供资型会计标准制定组织。该委员会的成员来自九个国家，背景各不相同，他们致力于制定出一套高品质、易理解且可执行的全球标准，这就要求在公开发布的财务报表中提供透明及具可比性的信息。它也和各国自己的理事会开展合作 Abbreviation 缩写 **IASB**

International Accounting Standards Committee /ˌɪntənæʃ(ə)nəl əˌkaʊntɪŋ ˈstændədz kəˌmɪti/ *noun* an organisation based in London that works towards achieving global agreement on accounting standards 国际会计准则委员会：一家设在伦敦的组织，其宗旨是促成全球就会计准则取得一致意见 Abbreviation 缩写 **IASC**

International Centre for Settlement of Investment Disputes /ˌɪntəˌnæʃ(ə)nəl ˌsentə fə ˌset(ə)lmənt əv ɪnˈvestmənt dɪˈspjuːts/ *noun* one of the five institutions that comprises the World Bank Group. It was established in 1966 to undertake the role previously undertaken in a personal capacity by the President of the World Bank in assisting in mediation or conciliation of investment disputes between governments and private foreign investors. The overriding consideration in its establishment was that a specialist institution could help to promote increased flows of international investment. Although ICSID has close links to the World Bank, it is an autonomous organisation 国际投资争端解决中心：组成世界银行集团的五个机构之一，成立于1966年，以接替此前由世界银行总裁以个人身份承担的职能，即帮助仲裁或调解政府与外国私人投资者之间的投资争端。其成立的主要考量是希冀通过一个专业机构来帮助促进国际投资的流动。尽管国际投资争端解决中心与世界银行有密切的联系，但它仍是一个自我管理的组织 Abbreviation 缩写 **ICSID**

International Monetary Fund /ˌɪntənæʃ(ə)nəl ˈmʌnɪt(ə)ri ˌfʌnd/ *noun* a type of bank which is part of the

United Nations and helps member states in financial difficulties, gives financial advice to members and encourages world trade 国际货币基金组织：联合国的一个下属银行，其宗旨是帮助成员国摆脱财政困难、提供财务建议和鼓励国际贸易 Abbreviation 缩写 **IMF**

international money markets /ˌɪntənæʃ(ə)nəl ˈmʌni ˌmɑːkɪts/ *Plural* markets such as the Euromarket, the international market for lending or borrowing in Eurocurrencies 国际货币市场（如国际性的借贷欧洲货币的欧洲货币市场）

international trade /ˌɪntənæʃ(ə)nəl ˈtreɪd/ *noun* trade between different countries 国际贸易

Internet banking /ˌɪntənet ˈbæŋkɪŋ/ *noun* the operation of a bank account over the internet 网上银行：通过国际互联网对银行账户进行的操作

intervene /ˌɪntəˈviːn/ *verb* to try to make a change in a situation in which you have not been involved before 调停，干预

intervention /ˌɪntəˈvenʃən/ *noun* the act of becoming involved in a situation in order to change it 干预，介入 ○ *the central bank's intervention in the banking crisis* 中央银行对银行业危机的介入 ○ *the government's intervention in the labour dispute* 政府对劳资纠纷的干预

intervention mechanism /ˌɪntəˈvenʃən ˌmekənɪz(ə)m/ *noun* a method used by central banks in maintaining exchange rate parities, e.g. buying or selling foreign currency 干预机制：中央银行稳定汇率平价的手段（如买卖外汇）

inter vivos /ˌɪntə ˈviːvəʊs/ *phrase* a Latin phrase, 'between living people' （拉丁语）在生存者之间

inter vivos trust /ˌɪntə ˈviːvəʊs trʌst/ *noun* a trust set up by one person for another living person 生存者信托：某人给另一个在世的人建立的信托

intestacy /ɪnˈtestəsi/ *noun* the state of having died without having made a will 无遗嘱死亡

intrinsic value /ɪnˌtrɪnsɪk ˈvæljuː/ *noun* the material value of something 固有价值，内在价值：某物的物质价值 ○ *These objects have sentimental value, but no intrinsic value at all.* 这些物品寄托着情感，但本身都一文不值。○ *The intrinsic value of jewellery makes it a good investment.* 珠宝的固有价值使其成为理想的投资对象。

introductory offer /ˌɪntrədʌkt(ə)ri ˈɒfə/ *noun* a special price offered on a new product to attract customers 新品优惠价：旨在吸引顾客的新产品优惠卖价

invalid /ɪnˈvælɪd/ *adjective* not valid or not legal 无效的；非法的 ○ *This permit is invalid.* 这个许可证无效。○ *The claim has been declared invalid.* 该项权利要求已被宣布无效。

invalidate /ɪnˈvælɪdeɪt/ *verb* to make something invalid 使无效 ○ *Because the company has been taken over, the contract has been invalidated.* 因为公司被收购，该合同已经失效。

invalidation /ɪnˌvælɪˈdeɪʃən/ *noun* the act of making invalid 无效化

invalidity /ˌɪnvəˈlɪdɪti/ *noun* the fact of being invalid 无效，失效 ○ *the invalidity of the contract* 合同无效

inventory /ˈɪnvənt(ə)ri/ *noun*

1. *especially US* all the stock or goods in a warehouse or shop（尤美）（仓库或商店里的）存货 ○ *to carry a high inventory* 持有大量存货 ○ *to aim to reduce inventory* 旨在减少存货（NOTE: The UK term is **stock** 英国用语为 **stock**）2. a list of the contents of a building such as a house for sale or an office for rent 盘存清单，物品清单 ○ *to draw up an inventory of fixtures and fittings* 开列一份附属设备的清单 ■ *verb* to make a list of stock or contents 编制…的存货（或物品）目录；为…开列清单

'...a warehouse needs to tie up less capital in inventory and with its huge volume spreads out costs over bigger sales'
"仓库应减少存货占用的资本，并以其巨大的库容分摊销量较大商品的成本"［*Duns Business Month*《邓氏商业月刊》］

inventory control /ˈɪnvənt(ə)ri kənˌtrəʊl/ *noun especially US* a system of checking that there is not too much stock in a warehouse, but just enough to meet requirements（尤美）存货控制：确保存货不至过多，但又恰好能满足需求的控制系统

inventory financing /ˈɪnvənt(ə)ri ˌfaɪnænsɪŋ/ *noun especially US* the use of money from working capital to purchase stock for resale（尤美）存货融资：用来自营运资本的钱购买存货然后再转卖

inventory turnover /ˌɪnvənt(ə)ri ˈtɜːnəʊvə/ *noun especially US* the total value of stock sold during a year, divided by the value of the goods remaining in stock（尤美）存货周转：一年内的所售存货总价值除以剩余存货的价值

invest /ɪnˈvest/ *verb* 投资 1. to put money into shares, bonds, a building society, etc., hoping that it will produce interest and increase in value［把钱投放于股票、债券、住房互助协会等，以期获得利息及增值］○ *He invested all his money in unit trusts.* 他把所有的钱都投资到单位信托上。○ *She was advised to invest in real estate* or *in government bonds.* 有人建议她投资于房地产（或政府债券）。2. to spend money on something which you believe will be useful［把钱花在认为有用的东西上面］○ *to invest money in new machinery* 将金钱投资于新机器 ○ *to invest capital in a new factory* 将资本投资于新工厂

'...we have substantial venture capital to invest in good projects'
"我们有大量可投资于好的项目的风险资本"［*Times*《泰晤士报》］

investment /ɪnˈvestmənt/ *noun* 投资 1. the placing of money so that it will produce interest and increase in value［投放资金以期获得利息及增值］○ *They called for more government investment in new industries.* 他们呼吁政府更多地投资于新兴行业。○ *She was advised to make investments in oil companies.* 有人建议她投资于石油公司。2. a share, bond or piece of property bought in the hope that it will produce more money than was used to buy it［为获利而投资买入的股票、债券或房地产］

'...investment trusts, like unit trusts, consist of portfolios of shares and therefore provide a spread of investments'
"投资信托和单位信托一样，由各种股票组合组成，因此能分散投资"［*Investors*

Chronicle《投资者纪事》]

'... investment companies took the view that prices had reached rock bottom and could only go up'

"投资公司认为股价已触底,接下来肯定反弹"[*Lloyd's List*《劳氏日报》]

investment analyst /ɪnˌvestmənt ˈænəlɪst/ *noun* a person working for a stockbroking firm, who analyses the performance of companies in a sector of the market, or the performance of a market sector as a whole, or economic trends in general 投资分析家:为证券经纪事务所工作的人,他们分析市场上某些行业的公司的业绩,或市场的整体表现,或经济总体趋势

investment bank /ɪnˈvestmənt bæŋk/ *noun US* a bank which deals with the underwriting of new issues, and advises corporations on their financial affairs (美)投资银行:承销新股发行、为股份有限公司提供理财建议的银行(NOTE: The UK term is **issuing house** 英国用语为 **issuing house**)

investment company /ɪnˈvestmənt ˈkʌmp(ə)ni/ *noun* company whose shares can be bought on the Stock Exchange, and whose business is to make money by buying and selling stocks and shares 投资公司:通过买卖股票和债券而获利的公司,其股票可在证券交易所购得

investment grant /ɪnˈvestmənt grɑːnt/ *noun* a government grant to a company to help it to invest in new machinery 投资拨款:政府对公司的拨款,帮助其投资于新机器

investment income /ɪnˈvestmənt ˌɪnkʌm/ *noun* income from investments, e.g. interest and dividends 投资收入:投资产生的收入,如利息及股利 Compare 比较 **earned income**

Investment Management Association /ɪnˌvestmənt ˈmænɪdʒmənt əˌsəʊsieɪʃ(ə)n/ *noun* the trade body for the UK investment industry, formed in February 2002 following the merger of the Association of Unit Trusts and Investment Funds (AUTIF) and the Fund Manager's Association 投资管理协会:英国投资业的专业团体,单位信托与投资基金协会(AUTIF)和基金经理协会合并后,于 2002 年 2 月组成投资管理协会 Abbreviation 缩写 **IMA**

investment property /ɪnˌvestmənt ˈprɒpəti/ *noun* property which is held for letting 投资财产:为出租目的而持有的财产

investment revaluation reserve /ɪnˌvestmənt riːˌvæljuˌeɪʃən rɪˈzɜːv/ *noun* the capital reserve where changes in the value of a business's investment properties are disclosed when they are revalued 投资重估储备:一种资本储备,于重新估价时披露企业投资财产价值的变动

investment trust /ɪnˈvestmənt trʌst/ *noun* a company whose shares can be bought on the Stock Exchange and whose business is to make money by buying and selling stocks and shares 投资信托公司:通过买卖股票和债券而获利的公司,其股票可在证券交易所购得

investor /ɪnˈvestə/ *noun* a person who invests money 投资者

investor protection /ɪnˈvestə prəˌtekʃ(ə)n/ *noun* legislation to protect small investors from unscrupulous investment brokers and advisers 投资者保护:保护小投资者的立法,使其免

受不良投资经纪人和顾问的误导

Investors in Industry /ɪnˌvestəz ɪn ˈɪndəstri/ *plural noun* a finance group partly owned by the big British High Street banks, providing finance especially to smaller companies 工业投资者公司,3i 投资集团:由英国高街大银行部分拥有的财团,它们向公司(尤其是小公司)提供融资 Abbreviation 缩写 **3i**

invisible assets /ɪnˌvɪzəb(ə)l ˈæsets/ *plural noun* assets which have a value but which cannot be seen, e.g. goodwill or patents 无形资产:有价值但无实体形态的资产,如商誉或专利权

invisible earnings /ɪnˌvɪzəb(ə)l ˈɜːnɪŋz/ *plural noun* foreign currency earned by a country by providing services, receiving interests or dividends, but not by selling goods 无形收入:一国通过提供服务、收取利息或股利而非通过销售货物获得的外币

invisible exports /ɪnˌvɪzəb(ə)l ˈekspɔːts/ *plural noun* services such as banking, insurance or tourism which do not involve selling a product and which are provided to foreign customers and paid for in foreign currency 无形出口:指在银行、保险或旅游业方面提供给外国顾客的服务,这类服务不牵涉产品的出售同时需以外币结算 Opposite 反义 **visible exports**

invisible imports /ɪnˌvɪzəb(ə)l ˈɪmpɔːts/ *noun* services such as banking, insurance or tourism which do not involve selling a product and which are provided by foreign companies and paid for in local currency 无形进口:指在银行、保险或旅游业方面由外国公司提供的服务,这类服务不牵涉产品的出售同时需以本国货币结算 Opposite 反义 **visible imports**

invisibles /ɪnˈvɪzəb(ə)lz/ *plural noun* invisible imports and exports 无形进出口

invisible trade /ɪnˌvɪzəb(ə)l ˈtreɪd/ *noun* trade involving invisible imports and exports 无形贸易:涉及无形进出口的贸易 Opposite 反义 **visible trade**

invitation /ˌɪnvɪˈteɪʃ(ə)n/ *noun* an act of asking someone to do something 邀请 ○ *to issue an invitation to someone to join the board* 向某人发出加入董事会的邀请 ○ *They advertised the invitation to tender for a contract.* 他们为合同公开招标。○ *Invitation to subscribe a new issue.* 邀约认购新股。

invoice /ˈɪnvɔɪs/ *noun* a note asking for payment for goods or services supplied 发票 ○ *your invoice dated November 10th* 贵方 11 月 10 日的发票 ○ *to make out an invoice for £250* 开一张 250 英镑的发票 ○ *to settle* or *to pay an invoice* 支付发票 ○ *They sent in their invoice six weeks late.* 他们送来发票的时间晚了 6 个星期。■ *verb* to send an invoice to someone 开发票给(某人) ○ *to invoice a customer* 给客户开发票

invoice clerk /ˈɪnvɔɪs klɑːk/ *noun* an office employee who deals with invoices 开票员:管理发票的办公人员

invoice discounting /ˈɪnvɔɪs ˌdɪskaʊntɪŋ/ *noun* a method of obtaining early payment of invoices by selling them at a discount to a company which will receive payment of the invoices when they are paid. The debtor is not informed of this arrangement, as opposed to factoring, where the debtor is informed 发票贴现:以贴现价格将发票出售给贴现公司以提早获

得付款,再由贴现公司在到期时领取发票金额。该协定不需要通知债务人,而代理收账则需通知债务人

invoice price /ˈɪnvɔɪs praɪs/ *noun* the price as given on an invoice, including any discount and VAT 发票价格:发票上写明的价格(包括折扣和增值税)

invoice register /ˌɪnvɔɪs ˈredʒɪstə/ *noun* a list of purchase invoices recording the date of receipt of the invoice, the supplier, the invoice value, and the person to whom the invoice has been passed to ensure that all invoices are processed by the accounting system 发票登记簿:一个购买发票的清单,它记录收到发票的日期、供应商、发票价格及发票经手人,以确保所有发票都通过会计系统进行处理

invoicing /ˈɪnvɔɪsɪŋ/ *noun* the work of sending invoices 发票的开具工作 ○ *All our invoicing is done by computer*. 我们所有的开发票工作都由计算机完成。

invoicing department /ˈɪnvɔɪsɪŋ dɪˌpɑːtmənt/ *noun* the department in a company which deals with preparing and sending invoices 发票管理部门:公司中负责编制、出具发票的部门

involuntary bankruptcy /ɪnˌvɒlənt(ə)ri ˈbæŋkrʌptsi/ *noun US* an application by creditors to have a person or corporation made bankrupt (美)强制性破产,被动破产:由债权人提出申请的破产 (NOTE: The UK term is **compulsory winding up** 英国用语为 **compulsory winding up**)

inward /ˈɪnwəd/ *adjective* towards the home country 进口的,引进的

inward bill /ˌɪnwəd ˈbɪl/ *noun* a bill of lading for goods arriving in a country 进口提单

inward mission /ˌɪnwəd ˈmɪʃ(ə)n/ *noun* a visit to your home country by a group of foreign businesspeople 来访使团:由外国商务人士组成的对某国进行访问的使团

IOU /ˌaɪ əʊ ˈjuː/ *noun* 'I owe you', a signed document promising that you will pay back money borrowed 借据:英文 I owe you 的首字母缩写,指一份已签署的承诺偿还所借现金的文件 ○ *to pay a pile of IOUs* 支付一堆借据 ○ *I have a pile of IOUs which need paying*. 我有一堆借据要支付。

IRC *abbr* Inland Revenue Commissioner 国内税务专员

irrecoverable /ˌɪrɪˈkʌv(ə)rəb(ə)l/ *adjective* not possible to get back 不能收回的

irrecoverable debt /ɪrɪˌkʌv(ə)rəb(ə)l ˈdet/ *noun* a debt which will never be paid 永远不能收回的债务

irredeemable /ɪrɪˈdiːməb(ə)l/ *adjective* not possible to redeem 不能赎回的

irredeemable bond /ɪrɪˌdiːməb(ə)l ˈbɒnd/ *noun* a government bond which has no date of maturity and which therefore provides interest but can never be redeemed at full value 不可赎回的债券,不能兑换的债券:没有到期日的政府债券,只支付利息,不偿付本金

irrevocable /ɪˈrevəkəb(ə)l/ *adjective* unchangeable 不能撤销的,不能改变的

irrevocable letter of credit /ɪˌrevəkəb(ə)l ˌletər əv ˈkredɪt/ *noun* a letter of credit which cannot be cancelled or changed, except if agreed between the two parties involved 不可

撤销的信用证:除非经双方同意否则不得取消或更改的信用证

IRS *abbr US* Internal Revenue Service (美)国内税务局

ISA /ˈaɪsə/ *abbr* Individual Savings Account 个人储蓄账户

issue /ˈɪʃuː/ *verb* to put out or to give out 发行;发出 ○ *to issue a letter of credit* 开一张信用证 ○ *to issue shares in a new company* 发行新公司的股票 ○ *to issue a writ against someone* 对某人发出传票 ○ *The government issued a report on London's traffic.* 政府发布了一份关于伦敦交通的报告。

'...the company said that its recent issue of 10.5 per cent convertible preference shares at A $ 8.50 a share has been oversubscribed'
"公司称最近以每股 8.5 澳元发行的 10.5% 可转换优先股已被超额认购"[*Financial Times*《金融时报》]

issued capital /ˌɪʃuːd ˈkæpɪt(ə)l/ *noun* an amount of capital which is given out as shares to shareholders 已发行股本:作为股份发行给股东的资本金额

issue price /ˈɪʃuː praɪs/ *noun* a price of shares when they are offered for sale for the first time 发行价格:股票首次发行时的价格

issuer /ˈɪʃuːə/ *noun* a financial institution that issues credit and debit cards and maintains the systems for billing and payment 发行人,发行者:发行信用卡和借记卡,并对账单开具和款项结算系统进行维护的金融机构

issuing /ˈɪʃuːɪŋ/ *adjective* organising an issue of shares 组织股票发行的

item /ˈaɪtəm/ *noun* **1.** something for sale 商品 □ **we are holding orders for out-of-stock items** we are holding orders for goods which are not in stock 我们接受脱销商品的订单 ○ *Please find enclosed an order for the following items from your catalogue.* 随函附上贵方目录中下列商品的订单。**2.** a piece of information (信息)项目 ○ *items on a balance sheet* 资产负债表上的项目 **3.** a point on a list (表中的一)项

itemise /ˈaɪtəmaɪz/, **itemize** *verb* to make a detailed list of things 分项列示,逐项列记 ○ *Itemising the sales figures will take about two days.* 分项列出销售数字要花大约两天时间。

JK

J curve /ˈdʒeɪ ˈkɜːv/ *noun* a line on a graph shaped like a letter 'J', with an initial short fall, followed by a longer rise, used to describe the effect of a falling exchange rate on a country's balance of trade J(形)曲线:图表上形状像字母J的曲线,它开始时有一个短暂的下降,然后是长时间的上升,用于描绘汇率下降对一国贸易收支平衡的影响

job /dʒɒb/ *noun* **1.** an order being worked on 作业,任务 ○ *We are working on six jobs at the moment*. 目前我们有六项工作在进行中。○ *The shipyard has a big job starting in August*. 造船厂有一个8月动工的大工程。**2.** regular paid work 有定期报酬的工作 ○ *She is looking for a job in the computer industry*. 她在找一份计算机行业的工作。○ *He lost his job when the factory closed*. 工厂倒闭后,他失业了。○ *Thousands of jobs will be lost if the factories close down*. 如果这些工厂倒闭,将有数千人失业。□ **to give up your job** to resign or retire from your work 辞职;退休 □ **to retire from your job** to leave work and take a pension 退休并领取养老金

'...he insisted that the tax advantages he directed toward small businesses will help create jobs'
"他坚持认为,他向小企业实行的税收优惠将有助于增加就业"[*Toronto Star*《多伦多明星日报》]

job card /ˈdʒɒb kɑːd/ *noun* a record card relating to a job and giving details of the time taken to do a piece of work and the materials used. This is used to allocate direct labour and materials costs 作业卡:与一项工作相关的记录卡,详细记录每项工作所花的时间和耗用的材料,用于分配直接人工成本和直接材料成本

job centre /ˈdʒɒb ˌsentə/ *noun* a government office which lists jobs which are vacant 职业介绍中心,职业介绍所 ○ *There was a long queue of unemployed people waiting at the job centre*. 失业者在职业介绍中心外排起了长龙。

job costing /ˈdʒɒb ˌkɒstɪŋ/ *noun* the process of calculating the cost of a single job or batch of work 工作成本核算,分批成本核算:计算某项或某批工作的成本 Also called 亦称作 **specific order costing**

job evaluation /ˈdʒɒb ɪvæljuˌeɪʃ(ə)n/ *noun* the process of examining different jobs within an organisation to see what skills and qualifications are needed to carry them out 工作评估,职位评价:对企业不同的工作进行考察,以确定其需要何种技能和资格

joint /dʒɔɪnt/ *adjective* **1.** carried

out or produced together with others 联合的；共同的 ○ *a joint undertaking* 联合企业 **2.** one of two or more people who work together or who are linked 连带的；共同的 ○ *They are joint beneficiaries of the will*. 他们是遗嘱的共同受益人。○ *She and her brother are joint managing directors*. 她和她弟弟是联合总经理。○ *The two countries are joint signatories of the treaty*. 这两个国家是条约的共同签署国。

joint account /ˈdʒɔɪnt əˌkaʊnt/ *noun* a bank or building society account shared by two people 共同账户，联名账户：两人共有的银行或住房互助协会账户 ○ *Many married couples have joint accounts so that they can pay for household expenses*. 很多夫妇都有联名账户，以便支付家庭日常开支。

joint and several liability /ˌdʒɔɪnt ən ˌsev(ə)rəl laɪəˈbɪlɪti/ *noun* a situation where someone who has a claim against a group of people can sue them separately or together as a group 连带及个别责任：当某人对一个群体提出索赔时，既可以对他们分别起诉，也可以把他们作为一个集体起诉

joint cost /ˈdʒɔɪnt ˌkɒst/ *noun* the cost of which can be allocated to more than one product, project or service 联合成本：可分配到多个产品、项目或服务上的成本

joint-life annuity /ˈdʒɔɪntlaɪf əˌnjuːɪti/ *noun* an annuity that continues until both parties have died. They are attractive to married couples as they ensure that the survivor has an income for the rest of his or her life 联合终身（人寿）年金：夫妇双方中一方过世后另一方可在有生之年继续受益的一种年金计划。这种年金对已婚夫妇很有吸引力

jointly /ˈdʒɔɪntli/ *adverb* together with one or more other people 共同地 ○ *to own a property jointly* 共同拥有一项财产 ○ *to manage a company jointly* 共同管理一家公司 ○ *They are jointly liable for damages*. 他们对损失负有共同的责任。

joint management /ˌdʒɔɪnt ˈmænɪdʒmənt/ *noun* management done by two or more people 共同管理：两人或两人以上进行的管理

joint ownership /ˌdʒɔɪnt ˈəʊnəʃɪp/ *noun* the owning of a property by several owners 共同所有权：几个所有者共同拥有一项财产

joint-stock bank /ˌdʒɔɪntˈstɒk ˌbæŋk/ *noun* a bank which is a public company quoted on the Stock Exchange 合资银行，有限股份银行：在证券交易所挂牌的银行

joint-stock company /ˈdʒɔɪntstɒk ˌkʌmp(ə)ni/ *noun* formerly, a public company whose shares were owned by very many people. Now called a Public Limited Company or Plc 股份有限公司：股份由多人持有的上市公司。现在这类公司被称为公共有限公司，其英文缩写为 Plc

joint venture /dʒɔɪnt ˈventʃə/ *noun* a situation where two or more companies join together for one specific large business project 合资企业：两家或以上公司为一个特大商业项目组成的联合

journal /ˈdʒɜːn(ə)l/ *noun* a book with the account of sales and purchases made each day 日记账，流水账：记录每天买卖账目的账簿

judgement /ˈdʒʌdʒmənt/ , **judgment** *noun* a legal decision or official decision of a court（法庭）判决 ▫ **to pronounce judgement, to give your judgement on something** to give an official or legal decision about something 公布官方（或法院）裁决

judgment creditor /ˌdʒʌdʒmənt ˈkredɪtə/ *noun* a person who has been given a court order making a debtor pay him a debt 判定债权人：经法庭判决确定的债权人，债务人需按照法庭的裁定向其还债

junior /ˈdʒuːniə/ *adjective* **1.** younger or lower in rank 较年幼的；低级的 **2.** less important than something else 次要的

junior capital /ˌdʒuːniə ˈkæpɪt(ə)l/ *noun* capital in the form of shareholders' equity, which is repaid only after secured loans called 'senior capital' have been paid if the firm goes into liquidation 次级资本：一种股东权益资本，企业清盘时，只有在称为"高级资本"的抵押贷款全部清偿之后才能偿还该资本

junior mortgage /ˌdʒuːniə ˈmɔːɡɪdʒ/ *noun* a second mortgage 次级抵押

junior partner /ˌdʒuːniə ˈpɑːtnə/ *noun* a person who has a small part of the shares in a partnership 次要合伙人：在合伙企业中拥有少量股份的人

junior security /ˌdʒuːniə sɪˈkjʊərɪti/ *noun* a security which is repaid after other securities 次级证券：在其他证券偿付之后才得以偿付的证券

K *abbr* one thousand "一千"的缩写 ▫ **'salary: £20K+'** salary more than £20,000 per annum 年薪两万英镑以上

keep /kiːp/ *verb* **1.** to do what is necessary for something 履行，遵守 **2.** to hold items for sale or for information 备有（商品以供销售）；保存（信息以供查询）**3.** to hold things at some level 使保持（在一定水平）○ *to keep spending to a minimum* 将花销保持在最低水平 ○ *We must keep our mailing list up to date.* 我们必须随时更新邮寄名单。○ *The price of oil has kept the pound at a high level.* 石油价格使英镑保持在高位。○ *Lack of demand for the product has kept prices down.* 需求不足导致产品价格处于低位。(NOTE: **keeping – kept**)

keep back /ˌkiːp ˈbæk/ *verb* to hold on to something which you could give to someone 隐瞒；扣留 ○ *to keep back information* or *to keep something back from someone* 隐瞒信息；不（向某人）透露（某事）○ *to keep £10 back from someone's salary* 从某人的工资中扣除10英镑

Keogh plan /ˈkiːəʊ ˌplæn/ *noun US* a private pension system allowing self-employed businesspeople and professionals to set up pension and retirement plans for themselves（美）基奥计划：一种私人养老金计划，它使私营者和自由职业者能为自己建立养老退休计划

key money /ˈkiː ˌmʌni/ *noun* a premium paid when taking over the keys of a flat or office which you are renting 钥匙押金，开门费：取得所租用的公寓或办公室的钥匙时支付的费用

key-person insurance /ˈkiːpɜːs(ə)n ɪnˌʃʊərəns/ *noun* an insurance policy taken out to cover the costs of replacing an employee who is particularly important to an organisation if he or she dies or is ill for a long time 公司要员保险：当公司要员去世或长期患病时，对其职位更替而产生的成本进行承保的保险单

key rate /ˈkiː ˌreɪt/ *noun* an interest rate which gives the basic rate on which other rates are calculated, e.g. the former bank base rate in the UK, or the Federal Reserve's discount rate in the USA 基本利率:计算其他利率的基础利率,例如英国以前的银行基本利率和美国的联邦储备贴现率

kickback /ˈkɪkbæk/ *noun* an illegal commission paid to someone, especially a government official, who helps in a business deal (尤指出于商业目的而给予政府官员的)贿赂,回扣

kicker /ˈkɪkə/ *noun* a special inducement to buy a bond, e.g. making it convertible to shares at a preferential rate (*informal*) (非正式)购买债券的特别优惠(如可按优惠的价格转换成股票)

kite /kaɪt/ *verb* **1.** *US* to write cheques on one account which may not be able to honour them and deposit them in another, withdrawing money from the second account before the cheques are cleared (美)用空头支票骗钱:在一个可能无法兑现的账号上开出支票存到另一个账户上,在支票兑现前从后一个账户中提款 **2.** to use stolen credit cards or cheque books 使用偷来的信用卡(或支票簿)

kite flier /ˈkaɪt ˌflaɪə/ *noun* a person who tries to impress people by putting forward a proposal 哗众者:试图通过提出一项倡仪来引起公众注目的人

kite-flying /ˈkaɪtˌflaɪɪŋ/ *noun* the practice of trying to impress people by putting forward grand plans 哗众行为:试图用宏伟计划来引起人们关注

kitty /ˈkɪti/ *noun* money which has been collected by a group of people to be used later, such as for an office party 共同的资金:将一伙人的钱凑集起来以备后用(如用于同事聚会)○ *We each put £5 into the kitty.* 我们每人为共储金掏出五英镑。

know-how /ˈnəʊhaʊ/ *noun* knowledge or skill in a particular field 专有技术;技术诀窍 ○ *to acquire computer know-how* 获得计算机技术 ○ *If we cannot recruit staff with the right know-how, we will have to initiate an ambitious training programme.* 如果我们招不到具有专业技能的员工,我们就得启动一个大型培训计划。

know-how fund /ˈnəʊhaʊ ˌfʌnd/ *noun* a fund created by the UK government to provide technical training and advice to countries of Eastern Europe 技能基金:英国政府创立的基金,用于对东欧国家提供技术培训和指导

L

labour /ˈleɪbə/ *noun* **1.** heavy work 劳动 □ **labour is charged at £5 an hour** each hour of work costs £5 报酬为每小时五英镑 **2.** workers, the workforce 工人，劳动力 ○ *We will need to employ more labour if production is to be increased*. 如要增加产量，我们需要雇用更多工人。○ *The costs of labour are rising in line with inflation*. 人工成本随通货膨胀水涨船高。（NOTE: The US spelling is **labor** 美国拼法为 **labor**）

'...the possibility that British goods will price themselves back into world markets is doubtful as long as sterling labour costs continue to rise faster than in competitor countries'
"只要英国的人工成本仍比竞争国的高，那么英国商品想依靠价格优势重回世界市场的可能性就值得怀疑"［*Sunday Times*《星期日泰晤士报》］

labour costs /ˈleɪbə kɒsts/ *noun* the cost of the employees employed to make a product, not including materials or overheads 人工成本：雇用员工生产产品的成本（不包括材料或间接费用）

labour force /ˈleɪbə fɔːs/ *noun* all the employees in a company or in an area（某公司或某地区的总体）劳动力 ○ *The management has made an increased offer to the labour force*. 管理层已提出要给全体员工提高待遇。○ *We are opening a new factory in the Far East because of the cheap local labour force*. 我们要在远东开办一家新工厂，因为那里的劳动力比较便宜。

'70 per cent of Australia's labour force is employed in service activity'
"澳大利亚70%的劳动力从事服务业"［*Australian Financial Review*《澳大利亚金融评论报》］

labour market /ˈleɪbə ˌmɑːkɪt/ *noun* the number of people who are available for work 劳动力市场：可供给的劳动力数量 ○ *25,000 school-leavers have just come on to the labour market*. 有25,000名毕业生新近加入了劳动力市场。

'European economies are being held back by rigid labor markets and wage structures'
"僵化的劳动力市场和工资结构拖累了欧洲经济"［*Duns Business Month*《邓氏商业月刊》］

labour relations /ˈleɪbə rɪˌleɪʃ(ə)nz/ *plural noun* relations between management and employees 劳资关系：管理者与工人之间的关系 ○ *The company has a history of bad labour relations*. 该公司的劳资关系历来不好。

labour turnover /ˈleɪbə ˌtɜːnəʊvə/

noun the movement of employees with some leaving their jobs and others joining 劳动力流动：有人离职、有人加入的员工流动过程 Also called 亦称作 **turnover of labour**

lading /ˈleɪdɪŋ/ *noun* the work of putting goods on a ship 装(船)，装载

Laffer curve /ˈlæfə kɜːv/ *noun* a chart showing that cuts in tax rates increase output in the economy. Alternatively, increases in tax rates initially produce more revenue and then less as the economy slows down 拉弗曲线：显示税率降低会增加经济产出的图表。另一方面，税率的增长最初能带来税收的增加，但随着经济放缓税收逐步减少

lag /læg/ *verb* to be behind or to be slower than something 滞后

lagging indicator /ˈlægɪŋ ˌɪndɪkeɪtə/ *noun* an indicator which shows a change in economic trends later than other indicators, e. g. the gross national product 滞后指标：在其他指标显现之后才能反映经济变动趋势的指标（如国民生产总值）Opposite 反义 **leading indicator**

land agent /ˈlænd ˌeɪdʒənt/ *noun* a person who runs a farm or a large area of land for the owner 田产管理人；地产管理人，地产经纪人

landed costs /ˌlændɪd ˈkɒsts/ *plural noun* the costs of goods which have been delivered to a port, unloaded and passed through customs 抵岸成本，抵岸费用：将货物运至码头、卸货并通过海关的成本

landing charges /ˈlændɪŋ ˌtʃɑːdʒɪz/ *plural noun* payments for putting goods on land and paying customs duties 口岸费：把货物卸到陆地上并支付关税的费用

landing order /ˈlændɪŋ ˌɔːdə/ *noun* a permit which allows goods to be unloaded into a bonded warehouse without paying customs duty 海关起货令：允许将货物卸到保税仓库而无需支付关税的指令

landlord /ˈlændlɔːd/ *noun* a person or company which owns a property which is let 地主，房东，房产主：拥有所出租房地产的人或公司

land register /ˈlænd ˌredʒɪstə/ *noun* a list of pieces of land, showing who owns each and what buildings are on it 地产登记单：记载多块地皮的清单，表明土地归属权和地皮上的建筑物类型

land registration /ˈlænd redʒɪˌstreɪʃ(ə)n/ *noun* a system of registering land and its owners 地产登记制：对土地及其所有者进行登记的制度

land tax /ˈlænd tæks/ *noun* a tax on the amount of land owned 地产税，土地税：对所拥有土地的课税

lapse /læps/ *verb* to stop being valid, or to stop being active 终止；失效 ○ *The guarantee has lapsed.* 保证书已经失效。

lapsed option /ˌlæpst ˈɒpʃən/ *noun* an option which has not been taken up, and now has expired 失效期权，失效选择权

last /lɑːst/ *adjective, adverb* coming at the end of a series 最后的（地）○ *Out of a queue of twenty people, I was served last.* 在排队的 20 个人里，我是最后一个拿到饭菜的。○ *This is our last board meeting before we move to our new offices.* 这是我们搬到新办公室之前的最后一次董事会会议。○ *We finished the last items in the order* *just two days before the promised delivery date*. 我们在离承诺交付日期只剩两天时完成了订单上最后的几个项目。

last in first out /ˌlɑːst ɪn ˌfɜːst ˈaʊt/ *noun* 后进先出法 **1.** a redundancy policy using the principle that the people who have been most recently appointed are the first to be made redundant [一种裁员政策,即最近雇用的人最早被裁掉] **2.** an accounting method where stock is valued at the price of the earliest purchases [按最早的购买价计算存货价值的会计方法] Abbreviation 缩写 **LIFO**. Compare 比较 **first in first out**

last quarter /ˌlɑːst ˈkwɔːtə/ *noun* a period of three months at the end of the financial year (会计年度里的)最后一个季度

last will and testament /ˌlɑːst ˌwɪl ən ˈtestəmənt/ *noun* a will, a document by which a person says what he or she wants to happen to their property when they die 遗嘱

launder /ˈlɔːndə/ *verb* to pass illegal profits, money from selling drugs, money which has not been taxed, etc., into the banking system 洗钱:通过银行系统使非法获利如贩毒、漏税所得合法化 ○ *to launder money through an offshore bank* 通过海外银行洗钱

'...it has since emerged that the bank was being used to launder drug money and some of its executives have been given lengthy jail sentences'
"此后该银行被用来洗毒资的事实浮出了水面,银行的部分高管被处以长期监禁"
[*Times*《泰晤士报》]

LAUTRO *abbr* Life Assurance and Unit Trust Regulatory Organization 人寿保险及单位信托管理机构

law /lɔː/ *noun* **1.** □ **inside** *or* **within the law** obeying the laws of a country 合法的 □ **against** *or* **outside the law** not according to the laws of a country 不合法的 ○ *The company is possibly operating outside the law*. 该公司可能在违法经营。□ **to break the law** to do something which is not allowed by law 违法 ○ *He is breaking the law by trading without a licence*. 他因无照经营而犯了法。○ *You will be breaking the law if you try to take that computer out of the country without an export licence*. 没有出口许可证而把那台计算机带出国会触犯法律的。**2.** a rule governing some aspect of human activity made and enforced by the state 法律

lawful /ˈlɔːf(ə)l/ *adjective* acting within the law 合法的

law of supply and demand /ˌlɔː əv səˌplaɪ ən dɪˈmɑːnd/ *noun* a general rule that the amount of a product which is available is related to the needs of potential customers 供求规律:产品供应数量与潜在顾客需求相联系的一般规律

laws /lɔːz/ *noun* rules by which a country is governed and the activities of people and organisations controlled 法律

lay out /ˌleɪ ˈaʊt/ *verb* to spend money 花费,花(钱) ○ *We had to lay out half our cash budget on equipping the new factory*. 我们不得不将一半的现金预算都用在新工厂的设备上。

layout /ˈleɪaʊt/ *noun* the arrangement of the inside space of a building or its contents 布局,安排:建筑物内部空间的安排或物品的摆放 ○ *They have* *altered the layout of the offices*. 他们改变了办公室的格局。

LBO *abbr* leveraged buyout 杠杆收购

L/C *abbr* letter of credit 信用证

LCM *abbr* lower of cost or market 成本与市价孰低

LDT *abbr* licensed deposit-taker 特许接受存款机构

lead /liːd/ *adjective* most important, in the front 最重要的,前列的

lead bank /ˌliːd ˈbæŋk/ *noun* the main bank in a loan syndicate 牵头银行:贷款银团中起主要作用的银行

leader /ˈliːdə/ *noun* a product which sells best 畅销产品

leading indicator /ˌliːdɪŋ ˈɪndɪkeɪtə/ *noun* an indicator such as manufacturing order books which shows a change in economic trends earlier than other indicators 领先指标:在其他指标显现之前就显示经济变动趋势的指标(如生产订货账目) Opposite 反义 **lagging indicator**

lead manager /ˌliːd ˈmænɪdʒə/ *noun* a person who organises a syndicate of underwriters for a new issue of securities 牵头经办人:组织包销团承销证券发行的人

leads and lags /ˌliːdz ən ˈlæɡz/ *plural noun* in businesses that deal in foreign currencies, the practice of speeding up the receipt of payments (leads) if a currency is going to weaken, and slowing down the payment of costs (lags) if a currency is thought to be about to strengthen, in order to maximise gains and reduce losses 提前或推迟结汇:在涉及外汇买卖的业务中,在货币即将走弱时加速收款(即提前结汇),在认为货币会走强时延缓付款(即推迟结汇),以实现最大盈利和减少损失

lead time /ˈliːd taɪm/ *noun* the time between deciding to place an order and receiving the product 备货期:从订货到交货的时间间隔 ○ *The lead time on this item is more than six weeks*. 该产品的备货期为六周。

lead underwriter /ˌliːd ˈʌndəraɪtə/ *noun* an underwriting firm which organises the underwriting of a share issue 牵头承销商:组织承销新股发行的承销商(NOTE: The US term is **managing underwriter** 美国用语为 **managing underwriter**)

learning curve /ˈlɜːnɪŋ kɜːv/ *noun* 学习曲线 **1.** a process of learning something that starts slowly and then becomes faster [刚开始学习时进展较慢、随后逐渐加快的过程] **2.** a line on a graph which shows the relationship between experience in doing something and competence at carrying it out [表明做事经验与做事能力之间关系的曲线] **3.** a diagram or graph that represents the way in which people gain knowledge or experience over time [代表人们逐渐获得知识或经验方式的图表或图形] (NOTE: A steep learning curve represents a situation where people learn a great deal in a short time; a shallow curve represents a slower learning process. The curve eventually levels out, representing the time when the knowledge gained is being consolidated 急剧上升的学习曲线代表人们在短时间内学到很多东西;平缓的曲线代表学习进展较慢。曲线最终变平,代表人们正在巩固所学的知识) **4.** the decrease in the effort required to produce each single item when the total number of items produced is doubled [总产出翻番时,每生

产一件产品可以降低的消耗〕(NOTE: The concept of the learning curve has its origin in productivity research in the aircraft industry of the 1930s, when it was discovered that the time and effort needed to assemble an aircraft decreased by 20% each time the total number produced doubled 学习曲线的概念起源于20世纪30年代航天业的生产力研究,当时人们发现,总产出每翻一番,组装一架飞机需要的时间就缩短20%)

lease /liːs/ *noun* a written contract for letting or renting a building, a piece of land or a piece of equipment for a period against payment of a fee 租约,租赁合同 ○ *to rent office space on a twenty-year lease* 以20年租期租用办公室 □ **the lease expires next year** *or* **the lease runs out next year** the lease comes to an end next year 租约明年到期 ■ *verb* **1.** to let or rent offices, land or machinery for a period 出租 ○ *to lease offices to small firms* 出租办公室给小企业 ○ *to lease equipment* 出租设备 **2.** to use an office, land or machinery for a time and pay a fee 租用 ○ *to lease an office from an insurance company* 在一家保险公司里租用一间办公室。○ *All our company cars are leased*. 我们的办公用车都是租来的。

lease back /ˌliːs ˈbæk/ *verb* to sell a property or machinery to a company and then take it back on a lease 回租,售后租回:出售一项财产(或一台机器)给一家公司,然后再租回 ○ *They sold the office building to raise cash, and then leased it back on a twenty-five year lease*. 他们为了筹资,将写字楼出售,然后以25年租期回租。

leasehold /ˈliːshəʊld/ *noun, adjective* possessing property on a lease, for a fixed time 租得物;租来的 ○ *to buy a property leasehold* 购买一项房产的租赁权 ○ *We are currently occupying a leasehold property*. 我们目前正租用一处房产。○ *The company has some valuable leaseholds*. 公司有一些值钱的租赁物。

leaseholder /ˈliːshəʊldə/ *noun* a person who holds a property on a lease 租借人

leasing /ˈliːsɪŋ/ *noun* the use of a lease or of equipment under a lease 租赁 ○ *an equipment-leasing company* 设备租赁公司 ○ *to run a copier under a leasing arrangement* 使用租来的复印机 ○ *The company has branched out into car leasing*. 该公司把业务扩展到了汽车租赁业。⇨ 参阅 **lessee**

leasing agreement /ˌliːsɪŋ əˈɡriːmənt/ *noun* a contract between an owner and a lessee, by which the lessee has the exclusive use of a piece of equipment for a period of time, against payment of a fee 租赁合同:所有者和承租人之间的合同,承租人支付租赁费后可在一段时间内拥有该租赁设备的独家使用权

ledger /ˈledʒə/ *noun* a book in which accounts are written 分类账

legacy /ˈleɡəsi/ *noun* a piece of property given by someone to someone else in a will 遗产,遗赠

legal /ˈliːɡ(ə)l/ *adjective* **1.** according to the law or allowed by the law 法定的;合法的 ○ *The company's action in sacking the accountant was completely legal*. 公司解雇会计师的行为是完全合法的。**2.** referring to the law 法律上的

legal charge /ˌliːɡ(ə)l ˈtʃɑːdʒ/ *noun*

a legal document held by the Land Registry showing who has a claim on a property 法定留置权：在土地注册处备案的一份法律文件，表明某项财产所有权的归属

legal claim /ˈliːg(ə)l kleɪm/ *noun* a statement that someone owns something legally 合法拥有权 ○ *He has no legal claim to the property.* 他不具有该财产的合法拥有权。

legal costs /ˈliːg(ə)l kɒsts/ , **legal charges** /ˈliːg(ə)l ˌtʃɑːdʒɪz/ , **legal expenses**/ˈliːg(ə)l ɪkˌspensɪz/ *plural noun* money spent on fees to lawyers 诉讼费 ○ *The clerk could not afford the legal expenses involved in suing her boss.* 该女职员付不起起诉老板所需的诉讼费。

legal currency /ˌliːg(ə)l ˈkʌrənsi/ *noun* money which is legally used in a country 法定货币，流通 货币

legal tender /ˌliːg(ə)l ˈtendə/ *noun* coins or notes which can be legally used to pay a debt 合法（流通）货币：可以用来偿还债务的法定货币

legatee /ˌlegəˈtiː/ *noun* a person who receives property from someone who has died 遗产继承人

legislation /ˌledʒɪˈsleɪʃ(ə)n/ *noun* laws 法律，法规

lend /lend/ *verb* to allow someone to use something for a period 借给，出借 ○ *to lend something to someone* or *to lend someone something* 借某物给某人 ○ *to lend money against security* 抵押贷款 ○ *He lent the company money* or *He lent money to the company.* 他借钱给这家公司。○ *The bank lent her £50,000 to start her business.* 银行贷给她五万英镑作为创业资金。（NOTE: **lending – lent**）

lender /ˈlendə/ *noun* a person who lends money 出借方，贷款人

lender of the last resort /ˌlendə əv ðə ˌlɑːst rɪˈzɔːt/ *noun* a central bank which lends money to commercial banks 最后贷款银行，中央银行：贷款给商业银行的中央银行

lending /ˈlendɪŋ/ *noun* an act of letting someone use money for a time 出借，贷款

lending limit /ˈlendɪŋ ˌlɪmɪt/ *noun* a restriction on the amount of money a bank can lend （银行）贷款限额

lending margin /ˈlendɪŋ ˌmɑːdʒɪn/ *noun* an agreed spread for lending, based on the LIBOR 贷款利差：在伦敦银行同业拆放利率（LIBOR）基础上确定的贷款利率差额

less /les/ *adjective* smaller than, of a smaller size or of a smaller value 较小的，较少的 ○ *We do not grant credit for sums of less than £100.* 我们对少于100英镑的金额不给予信贷。○ *He sold it for less than he had paid for it.* 他低于买价卖掉了它。■ *preposition* minus, with a sum removed 减去 ○ *purchase price less 15% discount* 减去15%折扣后的销售价 ○ *interest less service charges* 扣除手续费后的利息 ■ *adverb* not as much 较少地

lessee /leˈsiː/ *noun* a person who has a lease or who pays money for a property he or she leases 承租人

lessor /leˈsɔː/ *noun* a person who grants a lease on a property 出租人

let /let/ *verb* to allow the use of a house, an office or a farm to someone for the payment of rent 出租

letter /ˈletə/ *noun* a piece of writing sent from one person or company to another to ask for or to give information 信件

letter of acknowledgement /ˌletər əv əkˈnɒlɪdʒmənt/ *noun* a letter which says that something has been received 确认函

letter of application /ˌletər əv æplɪˈkeɪʃ(ə)n/ *noun* a letter in which someone applies for a job 求职信

letter of appointment /ˌletər əv əˈpɔɪntmənt/ *noun* a letter in which someone is appointed to a job（工作）委任书

letter of credit /ˌletər əv ˈkredɪt/ *noun* a document issued by a bank on behalf of a customer authorising payment to a supplier when the conditions specified in the document are met 信用证：银行代客户发出的文件，在满足文件规定的条件后授权付款给供应商 Abbreviation 缩写 **L/C**

letter of indemnity /ˌletər əv ɪnˈdemnɪti/ *noun* a letter promising payment as compensation for a loss 赔偿保证书

letter of intent /ˌletər əv ɪnˈtent/ *noun* a letter which states what a company intends to do if something happens 意向书：公司表明在某种情况下愿意做某事的意向性文件

letter of licence /ˌletər əv ˈlaɪs(ə)ns/ *noun* a letter from a creditor to a debtor who is having problems repaying money owed, giving the debtor a certain period of time to raise the money and an undertaking not to bring legal proceedings to recover the debt during that period 延期索偿证书：债权人给有偿债困难债务人的文件，给予债务人一定时间来筹集资金，并承诺在该期限内不会诉诸法律要求还债

letter of reference /ˌletər əv ˈref(ə)rəns/ *noun* a letter in which an employer recommends someone for a new job 推荐书

letters patent /ˌletəz ˈpeɪtənt/ *plural noun* the official term for a patent 专利证书

letting agency /ˈletɪŋ ˌeɪdʒənsi/ *noun* an agency which deals in property to let 租赁代理商

level /ˈlev(ə)l/ *verb* □ **to level off** *or* **to level out** to stop rising or falling 稳定，保持水平：停止上升或下降 ○ *Profits have levelled off over the last few years*. 利润在最近几年里稳定了下来。○ *Prices are levelling out*. 物价正趋于稳定。

leverage /ˈliːvərɪdʒ/ *noun* **1.** a ratio of capital borrowed by a company at a fixed rate of interest to the company's total capital 杠杆比率：公司按固定利率借入的资本与总资本的比率 **2.** the act of borrowing money at fixed interest which is then used to produce more money than the interest paid 举债经营，借贷投机：按固定利率借入资金，再用该资金创造比所付利息更多的收益

leveraged /ˈliːvərɪdʒd/ *adjective* using borrowings for finance 举债经营的

leveraged buyout /ˌliːvərɪdʒd ˈbaɪaʊt/, **leveraged takeover** /ˌliːvərɪdʒd ˈteɪkəʊvə/ *noun* an act of buying all the shares in a company by borrowing money against the security of the shares to be bought 杠杆收购：用即将买下的某公司全部股票作担保借款购买此公司的全部股票 Abbreviation 缩写 **LBO**

'...the offer came after management had offered to take the company private

through a leveraged buyout for $825 million'
"在管理层提议以8.25亿美元的杠杆收购来实现该公司私有化后，紧接着就有人给出了报价"［*Fortune*《财富》］

levy /ˈlevi/ *noun* money which is demanded and collected by the government 征收额，税款

'...royalties have been levied at a rate of 12.5% of full production'
"按全部产品产值的12.5%征收特许权使用费"［*Lloyd's List*《劳氏日报》］

liabilities /ˌlaɪəˈbɪlɪtiz/ *plural noun* the debts of a business, including dividends owed to shareholders 负债：企业的债务，包括应付给股东的股利 ○ *The balance sheet shows the company's assets and liabilities.* 资产负债表显示公司的资产和负债。□ **to discharge your liabilities in full** to pay everything which you owe 清偿全部债务

liability /ˌlaɪəˈbɪlɪti/ *noun* **1.** a legal responsibility for damage, loss or harm（对损坏或损失所负的法定）责任，义务 ○ *The two partners took out insurance to cover employers' liability.* 两个合伙人投保了雇主责任险。**2.** responsibility for a payment such as the repayment of a loan 支付义务（如偿还贷款）

LIBOR *abbr* London Interbank Offered Rate 伦敦银行同业拆放利率

licence /ˈlaɪs(ə)ns/ *noun* an official document which allows someone to do something 执照，许可证（NOTE：The US spelling is **license** 美国拼法为 **license**）

license /ˈlaɪs(ə)ns/ *noun* US spelling of **licence licence** 的美国拼法

licensed deposit-taker /ˌlaɪs(ə)nst dɪˈpɒzɪtˌteɪkə/, **licensed institution** /ˌlaɪs(ə)nst ˌɪnstɪˈtjuːʃ(ə)n/ *noun* a deposit taking institution which is licensed to receive money on deposit from private individuals and to pay interest on it, e.g. a building society, bank or friendly society 特许接受存款机构，注册接受存款机构：获准吸纳私人存款并付息的存款机构，如住房互助协会、银行或友好社团 Abbreviation 缩写 **LDT**

licensee /ˌlaɪs(ə)nˈsiː/ *noun* a person who has a licence, especially a licence to sell alcohol or to manufacture something 执照持有人，许可证持有人（尤指售酒执照持有人或特许制造商）

licensing /ˈlaɪs(ə)nsɪŋ/ *adjective* referring to licences 许可，准许的 ○ *a licensing agreement* 许可协议 ○ *licensing laws* 执照法

lien /ˈliːən/ *noun* the legal right to hold someone's goods and keep them until a debt has been paid 扣押权，留置权：债权人在债务人未偿清欠款前对其货物实施扣押的法定权利

life /laɪf/ *noun* the period of time for which something or someone exists（人或物）寿命

life assurance /ˈlaɪf əˌʃʊərəns/ *noun* insurance which pays a sum of money when someone dies, or at an agreed date if they are still alive 人寿保险：在受保人死亡时或受保人在世时的某个议定日期支付保险金的险种

Life Assurance and Unit Trust Regulatory Organization /laɪf əˌʃʊərəns ən ˌjuːnɪt trʌst ˌregjʊlət(ə)ri ˌɔːgənaɪˈzeɪʃ(ə)n/ *noun* an organisation set up to regulate the operations of life assurance companies and unit trusts, now replaced by the FSA 人寿保险及单位信托管理机构：为管理人寿保险公司、信托组织的行为而设立的机构，现已被英国金融服务管理局（FSA）所取代 Abbreviation 缩写 **LAUTRO**

life assurance company /laɪf əˈʃʊərəns ˌkʌmp(ə)ni/ *noun* a company providing life assurance, but usually also providing other services such as investment advice 人寿保险公司：提供人寿保险服务的公司，不过它通常还提供投资咨询等其他服务

life-cycle costing /laɪfˌsaɪk(ə)l ˈkɒstɪŋ/ *noun* the maintenance of physical asset cost records over the life of an entire asset, so that decisions concerning the acquisition, use, or disposal of the assets can be made in a way that achieves the optimum asset usage at the lowest possible cost to the entity. The term may be applied to the profiling of cost over a product's life, including the pre-production stage (**terotechnology**), and to both company and industry life cycles 寿命周期价格，周期成本核算：在整体资产的寿命期限内维持实物资产成本记录，以便作出正确的资产购买、使用或出售决定，令实体能够以尽可能低的价格获得最大的资产使用效能。该价格可用于产品寿命周期（包括预生产阶段（设备综合管理））的成本，亦可用于公司和行业的寿命周期

life expectancy /ˈlaɪf ɪkˌspektənsi/ *noun* the number of years a person is likely to live 预期寿命

life insurance /ˈlaɪf ɪnˌʃʊərəns/ *noun* same as 同 **life assurance**

life interest /ˌlaɪf ˈɪntrəst/ *noun* a situation where someone benefits from a property as long as he or she is alive （财产的）终身所有权，（房地产的）终身权益

LIFO /ˈlaɪfəʊ/ *abbr* last in first out 后进先出法

limit /ˈlɪmɪt/ *noun* the point at which something ends or the point where you can go no further 限额，限定

'... the biggest surprise of 1999 was the rebound in the price of oil. In the early months of the year commentators were talking about a fall to $5 a barrel but for the first time in two decades, the oil exporting countries got their act together, limited production and succeeded in pushing prices up'

"1999 年最出人意料的事件是油价反弹。在那一年最初的几个月里，评论家们一直在说油价会跌至每桶五美元，但石油输出国 20 年来首次协调行动，一起限制生产，从而成功地抬高了油价" [*Financial Times*《金融时报》]

limitation /ˌlɪmɪˈteɪʃ(ə)n/ *noun* the act of allowing only a specific quantity of something 限额，限制，限度 ○ *The contract imposes limitations on the number of cars which can be imported.* 这份合约对进口汽车的数量作了限制。

limited /ˈlɪmɪtɪd/ *adjective* restricted 受限制的

limited company /ˌlɪmɪtɪd ˈkʌmp(ə)ni/ *noun* a company where each shareholder is responsible for the company's debts only to the amount that he or she has invested in the company. Limited companies must be formed by at least 2 directors 股份有限公司，有限公司：在这类公司中，股东只对相当于其在公司投资额度的那部分债务承担清偿责任。有限公司的组建最少须有两名董事 Abbreviation 缩

写 **Ltd**. Also called 亦称作 **limited liability company**

limited liability /ˌlɪmɪtɪd laɪəˈbɪlɪti/ *noun* a situation where someone's liability for debt is limited by law 有限责任,有限赔偿责任:某人还债的责任由法律限定

limited liability company /ˌlɪmɪtɪd laɪəˈbɪlɪti ˌkʌmp(ə)ni/ *noun* same as 同 **limited company**

limited partner /ˌlɪmɪtɪd ˈpɑːtnə/ *noun* a partner who is responsible for the debts of the firm only up to the amount of money which he or she has provided to the business 有限责任合伙人:对企业债务清偿的责任仅承担相当于其投资额的合伙人

limited partnership /ˌlɪmɪtɪd ˈpɑːtnəʃɪp/ *noun* a registered business where the liability of the partners is limited to the amount of capital they have each provided to the business and where the partners may not take part in the running of the business 有限责任合伙企业:合伙成员仅对各自投入企业的资本负有限责任,并且可以不参与企业经营的一种注册企业

limiting /ˈlɪmɪtɪŋ/ *adjective* not allowing something to go beyond a point, restricting 有限的;限制的 ○ *a limiting clause in a contract* 合同中的限制条款

limiting factor /ˌlɪmɪtɪŋ ˈfæktə/ *noun* a factor which limits a company's ability to achieve its goals, e.g. sales demand being too low for the company to make enough profit 限制因素:限制公司实现其目标的因素,例如销售需求过低导致公司无法获得足够利润 ○ *The short holiday season is a limiting factor on the hotel trade*. 短暂的假期是酒店业的一个限制因素。

line /laɪn/ *noun* a row of letters or figures on a page (字母、数字等)行

'...cash paid for overstocked lines, factory seconds, slow sellers, etc.'
"为积货、残次品、滞销产品等支付的现金"
[*Australian Financial Review*《澳大利亚金融评论报》]

line item budget /laɪn ˌaɪtəm ˈbʌdʒɪt/ *noun* a well-established budget layout that shows the costs of a cost object analysed by their nature in a line-by-line format 明细支出预算:一种详细的预算,它逐行列明按成本项目性质分析的各项成本

link /lɪŋk/ *verb* to join or to attach to something else 联系,连接,衔接 ○ *to link pensions to inflation* 将养老金与通货膨胀挂钩○ *to link bonus payments to productivity* 将生产率与奖金挂钩○ *His salary islinked to the cost of living*. 他的薪水是与生活费用挂钩的。⇨ 参阅 **indexlinked**

liquid /ˈlɪkwɪd/ *adjective* easily converted to cash, or containing a large amount of cash 易变为现金的

liquid assets /ˌlɪkwɪd ˈæsets/ *plural noun* cash, or investments which can be quickly converted into cash 流动资产:现金及易变现的投资

liquidation /ˌlɪkwɪˈdeɪʃ(ə)n/ *noun* **1.** the sale of assets for cash 变现 □ **liquidation of a debt** payment of a debt 清偿债务,偿还债务 **2.** the winding up or closing of a company and selling of its assets 停业清理,清算:公司清盘或关闭并出售其资产 □ **the company went into liquidation** the company was closed and its assets sold 这家公司已停业清算:公司已倒闭,资产

已被出售

liquidator /ˈlɪkwɪdeɪtə/ *noun* a person named to supervise the closing of a company which is in liquidation 清算人:在清算期间指定的负责监管清算企业的人

liquidity /lɪˈkwɪdɪti/ *noun* cash, or the fact of having cash or assets which can be changed into cash 流动性;变现能力:拥有现金或可变现资产

liquidity ratio /lɪˈkwɪdɪti ˌreɪʃiəʊ/ *noun* an accounting ratio used to measure an organisation's liquidity. It is calculated by taking the business's current assets, minus its stocks, divided by its current liabilities 流动比率:用于衡量企业流动性的会计比率。它的计算方法为企业的流动资产减去存货,再除以流动负债 Also called 亦称作 **acid test ratio, quick ratio**

list /lɪst/ *noun* several items written one after the other 表;目录;清单 ○ *They havean attractive list of products* or *product list*. 他们的产品目录很吸引人。○ *I can't find that item on our stock list*. 我在我们的存货清单上没找到该项目。○ *Please add this item to the list*. 请把这个项目添加到列表中。○ *She crossed the item off her list*. 她把该项目从她的表中删掉了。

listed company /ˌlɪstɪd ˈkʌmp(ə)ni/ *noun* a company whose shares can be bought or sold on the Stock Exchange 上市公司:股票在证券交易所买卖的公司

listed securities /ˌlɪstɪd sɪˈkjʊərɪtiz/ *plural noun* shares which can be bought or sold on the Stock Exchange, shares which appear on the official Stock Exchange list 挂牌证券:在证券交易所买卖的股票,或列示于正式的证券交易所牌价上的股票

Listing Agreement /ˈlɪstɪŋ əˌgriːmənt/ *noun* a document which a company signs when being listed on the Stock Exchange, in which it promises to abide by stock exchange regulations 上市协议:公司在上市时签署的文件,表明公司承诺遵守证券交易所的管理规定

listing requirements /ˈlɪstɪŋ rɪˌkwaɪəmənts/ *plural noun* the conditions which must be met by a corporation before its stock can be listed on the New York Stock Exchange 上市条件:一家公司在纽约证券交易所上市前必须具备的条件

list price /ˈlɪst praɪs/ *noun* the price for something as given in a catalogue 价目表价格,目录上的价格

litigation /ˌlɪtɪˈgeɪʃ(ə)n/ *noun* the bringing of a lawsuit against someone 诉讼

Lloyd's broker /ˌlɔɪdz ˈbrəʊkə/ *noun* an agent who represents a client who wants insurance and who arranges this insurance for him through a Lloyd's underwriting syndicate 劳埃德(又译为劳合社,劳氏)经纪人:通过劳埃德保险财团为想投保的客户办理保险业务的经纪人

Lloyd's Register /ˌlɔɪdz ˈredʒɪstə/ *noun* a classified list showing details of all the ships in the world and estimates of their condition 劳氏船舶登记簿:记载世界上所有船只详细资料以及船只估计状况的分类表

Lloyd's underwriter /ˌlɔɪdz ˈʌndəraɪtə/ *noun* a member of an insurance group at Lloyd's who accepts to underwrite insurances 劳合社承保人:承销保险的劳埃德保险集团成员

loan /ləʊn/ *noun* money which has been lent 贷款，借款

'...over the last few weeks, companies raising new loans from international banks have been forced to pay more, and an unusually high number of attempts to syndicate loans among banks has failed'
"过去的几个星期里，从国际银行筹集新贷款的公司不得不为筹贷而付出更多，试图在银行间安排银团贷款的无数次努力也告失败"[*Financial Times*《金融时报》]

loan capital /ˈləʊn ˌkæpɪt(ə)l/ *noun* a part of a company's capital which is a loan to be repaid at a later date 借入资本，贷款资本

loan stock /ˈləʊn stɒk/ *noun* stock issued by a company at a fixed rate of interest, as a means of raising a loan 信用债券：公司按固定利率发行以筹集贷款的证券

local /ˈləʊk(ə)l/ *adjective* **1.** located in or providing a service for a restricted area 位于某地的；为某地服务的 **2.** referring to a particular area, especially one near where a factory or an office is based 地方的，当地的，本地的

'...each cheque can be made out for the local equivalent of £100 rounded up to a convenient figure'
"可以使用按四舍五入法换算后与100英镑等值的地方货币签发支票"[*Sunday Times*《星期日泰晤士报》]

'...the business agent for Local 414 of the Store Union said his committee will recommend that the membership ratify the agreement'
"当地414家商场联盟的业务代表称，他的委员会将建议成员批准该协议"[*Toronto Star*《多伦多明星日报》]

'EC regulations insist that customers can buy cars anywhere in the EC at the local pre-tax price'
"欧共体条例主张顾客可在欧共体任一成员国按当地的税前价格购买汽车"[*Financial Times*《金融时报》]

local authority /ˌləʊk(ə)l ɔːˈθɒrɪti/ *noun* an elected section of government which runs a small area of the country 地方当局

local currency /ˌləʊk(ə)l ˈkʌrənsi/ *noun* the currency of a particular country where a transaction is being carried out 本国货币 ○ *Because of the weakness of the local currency, all payments are in dollars.* 由于本国货币疲软，所有付款都以美元支付。

local government /ˌləʊk(ə)l ˈgʌv(ə)nmənt/ *noun* elected authorities and administrative organisations which deal with the affairs of small areas of a country 地方政府

local labour /ˌləʊk(ə)l ˈleɪbə/ *noun* workers who are recruited near a factory, and are not brought there from a distance 本地劳动力

lock into /ˌlɒk ˈɪntə/, **lock in** /ˌlɒk ˈɪn/ *verb* to be fixed to an interest rate or exchange rate 锁定(利率或汇率) ○ *By buying francs forward the company is in effect locking itself into a pound-franc exchange rate of 10.06.* 通过购买法郎远期，该公司实际上把法郎兑英镑的汇率锁定在了10.06。

London Interbank Offered Rate /ˌlʌndən ˌɪntəbæŋk ˈɒfəd reɪt/ *noun* the rate at which banks offer to lend eurodollars to other banks 伦敦银行同业拆放利率：伦敦银行间欧洲美元贷款的利率 Abbreviation 缩写 **LIBOR**

long /lɒŋ/ *adjective* for a large period of time 长期的

long bond/ˈlɒŋ bɒnd/, **long coupon bond** /lɒŋ ˈkuːpɒn bɒnd/ *adjective* a bond which will mature in more than ten years' time 长期债券:期限超过10年的债券

long credit /ˌlɒŋ ˈkredɪt/ *noun* credit terms which allow the borrower a long time to pay 长期信贷

long-dated bill /ˌlɒŋˌdeɪtɪd ˈbɪl/ *noun* a bill which is payable in more than three months' time (三个月以上的)长期票据,远期票据

long-dated stocks /ˌlɒŋˌdeɪtɪd ˈstɒks/ *plural noun* same as 同 **longs**

long lease /ˌlɒŋ ˈliːs/ *noun* a lease which runs for fifty years or more (50年或以上的)长期租赁 ○ *to take an office building on a long lease* 长期租用写字楼

long position /ˌlɒŋ pəˈzɪʃ(ə)n/ *noun* a situation where an investor sells long, i.e. sells forward shares which he or she owns 多头交易,买空交易:投资者出售多头,即出售所拥有的远期股票 Compare 比较 **short position**

long-range /ˌlɒŋˈreɪndʒ/ *adjective* for a long period of time in the future 长期的

longs /lɒŋz/ *plural noun* government stocks which will mature in over fifteen years' time 长期证券,长期公债券:期限超过15年的政府证券 Also called 亦称作 **long-dated stocks**

long-term borrowings /ˌlɒŋtɜːm ˈbɒrəʊɪŋz/ *plural noun* borrowings which do not have to be repaid for some years 长期借款

loose change /ˌluːs ˈtʃeɪndʒ/ *noun* money in coins 零头,零钱

lose /luːz/ *verb* **1.** not to have something any more 失去,不再拥有 **2.** to have less money 损失(资金) ○ *He lost £25,000 in his father's computer company.* 他在父亲的计算机公司里亏损了2.5万英镑。

loss /lɒs/ *noun* **1.** the state or process of not having something any more 失去 **2.** the state of having less money than before or of not making a profit 损失,亏损 □ **the car was written off as a dead loss** *or* **a total loss** the car was so badly damaged that the insurers said it had no value 该汽车作为纯损失冲销:汽车损坏严重,保险公司认为已没有任何价值 □ **to cut your losses** to stop doing something which is losing money 停止经营亏损项目

'...against losses of FFr 7.7m two years ago, the company made a net profit of FFr 300,000 last year'
"在前年亏损了770万法国法郎之后,公司去年净盈利30万法国法郎"[*Financial Times*《金融时报》]

loss adjuster /ˈlɒs əˌdʒʌstə/ *noun* a person who calculates how much insurance should be paid on a claim 理算师:计算应理赔保险金额的人

loss-leader /ˈlɒsˌliːdə/ *noun* an article which is sold at a loss to attract customers 特价商品,招徕商品:亏本出售以吸引顾客的商品 ○ *We use these cheap films as a loss-leader.* 我们用特价胶卷招徕顾客。

loss relief /ˈlɒs rɪˌliːf/ *noun* an amount of tax not to be paid on one year's profit to offset a loss in the previous year 亏损减免,亏损抵税:为弥补上一年度亏损,本年度利润中无需缴税的额度

lot /lɒt/ *noun* **1.** a group of items

sold together at an auction（拍卖品）（一）批 ○ *to bid for lot 23* 竞拍第 23 组物品 ○ *At the end of the auction half the lots were unsold*. 在拍卖会结束时尚有一半拍品未成交。**2.** a group of shares which are sold（股票）份额 ○ *to sell a lot of shares* 出售一定份额的股票 ○ *to sell shares in small lots* 以小份额出售股票

lottery /ˈlɒtəri/ *noun* a game where numbered tickets are sold and prizes given for some of the numbers 抽彩给奖法，乐透

low /ləʊ/ *adjective* not high or not much 低的；不多的 ○ *Low overhead costs keep the unit cost low*. 低廉的间接成本降低了单位成本。○ *We try to keep our wages bill low*. 我们努力保持低水平的工资开支。○ *The company offered him a mortgage at a low rate of interest*. 公司给他提供低息抵押借款。○ *The poundis at a very low rate of exchange against the dollar*. 现在英镑兑美元的汇率非常低。

'...after opening at 79.1 the index touched a peak of 79.2 and then drifted to a low of 78.8'
"指数以 79.1 点开盘之后，摸高至 79.2 点，然后又降到 78.8 的低点"[*Financial Times*《金融时报》]

'... the pound which had been as low as $1.02 earlier this year, rose to $1.30'
"英镑兑美元的汇率从今年早些时候 1.02 的低位上升至 1.30"[*Fortune*《财富》]

lower /ˈləʊə/ *adjective* smaller or less high 较低的，更低的 ○ *a lower rate of interest* 较低利率 ○ *Sales were lower in December than in November*. 12 月的销售额低于 11 月。

lower of cost or market /ˌləʊə əv kɒst ɔː ˈmɑːkɪt/ *noun* a method used by manufacturing and supply firms when accounting for their homogeneous stocks that involves valuing them either at their original cost or the current market price, whichever is lower 成本与市价孰低：生产商和供货商对同类存货的估价方法，它将原始成本价和当前市价两者中的较低者作为存货的价格 Abbreviation 缩写 **LCM**

low gearing /ˌləʊ ˈɡɪərɪŋ/ *noun* the fact of not having much borrowing in proportion to your capital 低杠杆作用：在某人的资本中，借入资本仅占少部分比例

low yield /ˌləʊ ˈjiːld/ *noun* a yield on the share price which is low for the sector, suggesting that investors anticipate that the company will grow fast, and have pushed up the share price in expectation of growth 低股利发放率：相对其价格来说，股利发放较少，这表明投资者预期公司会以较快速度增长，并因此推动股价上扬

loyalty bonus /ˈlɔɪəlti ˌbəʊnəs/ *noun* a special privilege given to shareholders who keep their shares for a long period of time, used especially to attract investors to privatisation issues 忠诚奖励：给予长期持有公司股份的股东的特惠，尤用于吸引投资者投资个股

Ltd *abbr* limited company 有限（责任）公司

lump sum /ˌlʌmp ˈsʌm/ *noun* money paid in one single amount, not in several small sums（资金）一次总付，一次付清 ○ *When he retired he was given a lump sum bonus*. 他退休时获得了一笔一次性奖金。○ *She sold her house and invested the money as a lump sum*. 她卖掉了房子，然后把得到的钱全部投资了。

luncheon voucher /ˈlʌntʃən ˌvaʊtʃə/

noun a ticket given by an employer to an employee in addition to their wages, which can be exchanged for food in a restaurant（作为工资补贴的）就餐券，饭票

luxury tax /ˈlʌkʃəri tæks/ *noun* a tax on goods or services that are considered non-essential 奢侈品税：对非必需品或劳务征收的税

M

machine hour rate /məˌʃiːn ˈaʊə ˌreɪt/ *noun* a method of calculating production overhead absorption rate, where the number of hours the machines are expected to work is divided into the budgeted production overhead to give a rate per hour 机器小时率：计算制造费用分配率的一种办法，计算方法为用预算制造费用除以预计的机器运转小时数

macro- /mækrəʊ/ *prefix* very large, covering a wide area 极大的，宏观的

macroeconomics /ˌmækrəʊiːkəˈnɒmɪks/ *plural noun* a study of the economics of a whole area, a whole industry, a whole group of the population or a whole country, in order to help in economic planning 宏观经济学：对整个地区、行业、人口或国家经济活动的研究，以帮助制订经济计划 Compare 比较 **microeconomics** (NOTE: takes a singular verb 跟单数动词)

magnetic card /mægˌnetɪk ˈkɑːd/ *noun* plastic card with a strip of magnetic recording material on its surface, allowing data to be stored and used 磁卡

mail-order selling /ˈmeɪlɔːdə ˌselɪŋ/ *noun* a method of selling in which orders are taken and products are delivered by mail 邮售：通过邮政系统接受订单和发送货物的方式

mainstream corporation tax /ˌmeɪnstriːm ˌkɔːpəˈreɪʃ(ə)n tæks/ *noun* the total tax paid by a company on its profits less any advance corporation tax, which a company has already paid when distributing profits to its shareholders in the form of dividends 主体公司税：公司缴纳的所得税总额减去预付公司税，在公司向股东发放股利时缴纳 Abbreviation 缩写 **MCT**

maintain /meɪnˈteɪn/ *verb* **1.** to keep something going or working 保持，使继续 ○ *We try to maintain good relations with our customers.* 我们努力与客户保持良好关系。○ *Her trip aims to maintain contact with her important overseas markets.* 她此行的目地是同重要的海外市场维持联系。**2.** to keep something working at the same level 维持，保持 ○ *to maintain an interest rate at 5%* 保持5%的利率 ○ *The company has maintained the same volume of business in spite of the recession.* 尽管经济衰退，公司仍维持着原有的业务量。

maintenance /ˈmeɪntənəns/ *noun* **1.** the process of keeping things going or working 维持，保持 ○ *Maintenance of contacts is important for a sales rep.* 关系网的维系对销售代表很重要。○ *It is essential to ensure the maintenance of supplies to the factory.* 必须确保工厂供应得以维持。**2.** the process of keeping a machine in good working order (机器)维护，保养 ○ *We offer a* *full maintenance service*. 我们提供全套保养服务。

'... responsibilities include the maintenance of large computerized databases'
"职责包括维护庞大的计算机化数据库"
[*Times*《泰晤士报》]

'... the federal administration launched a full-scale investigation into the airline's maintenance procedures'
"联邦政府对航空公司的维修程序展开全面调查"[*Fortune*《财富》]

major /ˈmeɪdʒə/ *adjective* important 重要的,主要的 ○ *There is a major risk of fire*. 火灾风险很高。

'...if the share price sinks much further the company is going to look tempting to any major takeover merchant'
"如果股价继续大幅下跌,那么这家公司对任何大并购商都将具有吸引力"[*Australian Financial Review*《澳大利亚金融评论报》]

'...monetary officials have reasoned that coordinated greenback sales would be able to drive the dollar down against other major currencies'
"金融官员曾推断,如果有人协同出售美元,那么美元对其他主要货币的汇率就会下降"
[*Duns Business Month*《邓氏商业月刊》]

'...a client base which includes many major commercial organizations and nationalized industries'
"包括许多大型商业组织和国有化行业在内的客户基础"[*Times*《泰晤士报》]

majority /məˈdʒɒrɪti/ *noun* more than half of a group 多数,过半数

majority shareholder /məˌdʒɒrɪti ˈʃeəhəʊldə/ *noun* a person who owns more than half the shares in a company 拥有多数股权的股东:拥有公司半数以上股份的人

majority shareholding /məˌdʒɒrɪti ˈʃeəhəʊldɪŋ/ *noun* a group of shares which are more than half the total 多数股权:半数以上的股份

majority vote /məˈdʒɒrɪti vəʊt/, **majority decision** /məˈdʒɒrɪti dɪˌsɪʒ(ə)n/ *noun* a decision which represents the wishes of the largest group as shown by a vote 多数票,多数决定:代表最多人数意见的投票结果

make /meɪk/ *verb* 1. to produce or to manufacture 生产,制造 ○ *The employees spent ten weeks making the table*. 雇员们花了 10 个星期来做这张桌子。○ *The factory makes three hundred cars a day*. 这家工厂每天生产 300 辆汽车。2. to earn money 赚(钱) ○ *He makes £50,000 a year* or *£25 an hour*. 他一年挣 5 万英镑(或每小时挣 25 英镑)。3. to increase in value 升值 ○ *The shares made $2.92 in today's trading*. 在今天的交易中,该股上涨了 2.92 美元。4. □ **to make a profit** to have more money after a deal 盈利 □ **to make a loss** to have less money after a deal 亏损 □ **to make a killing** to make a very large profit 赚得巨额利润

make over /ˌmeɪk ˈəʊvə/ *verb* to transfer property legally (依法)移交(财产)○ *to make over the house to your children* 将房子转让给子女

maker /ˈmeɪkə/ *noun* a person or company which makes something 制造者;制造厂家 ○ *a major car maker* 一家主要的汽车制造商 ○ *a furniture maker* 一个家具制造商

make up /ˌmeɪk ˈʌp/ *verb* to compensate for something 补偿,赔偿 □ **to make up a loss** *or* **difference** to pay extra so that the loss or difference is covered 弥补亏损,弥补差额

maladministration /ˌmæləd-ˌmɪnɪˈstreɪʃ(ə)n/ *noun* incompetent administration 管理无能，管理不善

manage /ˈmænɪdʒ/ *verb* to direct or to be in charge of something 管理 ○ *to manage a branch office* 管理一个分支机构 ○ *A competent and motivated person is required to manage an important department in the company.* 需要一个既有能力又有活力的人来管理公司的一个重要部门。

'...the research director will manage and direct a team of graduate business analysts reporting on consumer behaviour throughout the UK'
"研究主任将主持和指导一个商业分析专业的研究生小组，对全英国消费者的行为进行研究"［*Times*《泰晤士报》］

managed fund /ˌmænɪdʒd ˈfʌnd/ *noun* a unit trust fund which is invested in specialist funds within the group and can be switched from one specialised investment area to another 管理基金：投资于同一集团内专门基金的单位信托基金，且该基金可以从一个专门投资领域转到另一个专门投资领域。

managed rate /ˌmænɪdʒd ˈreɪt/ *noun* a rate of interest charged by a financial institution for borrowing that is not prescribed as a margin over base rate but is set from time to time by the institution 受控利率：金融机构收取的借款利率，不是按基础利率加息差计算，而时常由该机构确定

managed unit trust /ˌmænɪdʒd ˈjuːnɪt trʌst/ *noun* same as 同 **managed fund**

management /ˈmænɪdʒmənt/ *noun* **1.** the process of directing or running a business 管理，经营 ○ *a management graduate* or *a graduate in management* 管理专业毕业生 ○ *She studied management at university.* 她大学时学管理专业。○ *Good management* or *efficient management is essential in a large organisation.* 良好（或有效）的管理是大型组织必不可少的。○ *Bad management* or *inefficient management can ruin a business.* 管理不善（或无效管理）会导致企业破产。**2.** a group of managers or directors 管理层 ○ *The management has decided to give everyone a pay increase.* 管理层决定给每个员工加薪。（NOTE：Where **management** refers to a group of people it is sometimes followed by a plural verb **managemet** 指"管理层"时有时跟复数动词）

'...the management says that the rate of loss-making has come down and it expects further improvement in the next few years'
"管理层声称亏损率已下降，并预期在随后几年里会有进一步改观"［*Financial Times*《金融时报》］

management accountant /ˈmænɪdʒmənt əˌkaʊntənt/ *noun* an accountant who prepares financial information for managers so that they can take decisions 管理会计师：向管理人员提供财务信息供其决策的会计师

management accounting /ˈmænɪdʒmənt əˌkaʊntɪŋ/ *noun* the preparation and use of financial information to support management decisions 管理会计：整理并使用财务信息来支持管理决策

management accounts /ˈmænɪdʒmənt əˌkaʊnts/ *plural noun* financial information prepared for a manager so that decisions can be made, including monthly or quarterly financial statements, often in great detail, with analysis of actual performance against the budget 管理账目,管理会计信息:为管理人员作决策而准备的企业财务信息,包括详尽的财务月报和季报,并附有实际业绩与预算的对比分析

management by objectives /ˌmænɪdʒmənt baɪ əbˈdʒektɪvz/ *noun* a way of managing a business by planning work for the managers to do and testing if it is completed correctly and on time 目标管理制度:为管理人员制订工作计划,并检验其是否按时准确完成的一种企业管理方式

management consultant /ˈmænɪdʒmənt kənˌsʌltənt/ *noun* a person who gives advice on how to manage a business 管理顾问,管理咨询师:为企业管理出谋划策的人

management course /ˈmænɪdʒmənt kɔːs/ *noun* a training course for managers 管理人员培训课程

management team /ˈmænɪdʒmənt tiːm/ *noun* all the managers who work in a particular company 管理团队:公司所有的管理人员

manager /ˈmænɪdʒə/ *noun* **1.** the head of a department in a company (部门)经理 ○ *She's a department manager in an engineering company.* 她是一家工程公司的部门经理。○ *Go and see the human resources manager if you have a problem.* 如有疑问,请当面咨询人力资源部经理。○ *The production manager has been with the company for only two weeks.* 生产部经理加入公司才两个星期。○ *Our sales manager started as a rep in London.* 我们的销售部经理是从伦敦的一名销售代表做起的。**2.** the person in charge of a branch or shop (分公司或商店的)经理 ○ *Mr Smith is the manager of our local Lloyds Bank.* 史密斯先生是我们当地劳埃德银行的经理。○ *The manager of our Lagos branch is in London for a series of meetings.* 我们的拉各斯分部经理正在伦敦参加一系列会议。

'... the No. 1 managerial productivity problem in America is managers who are out of touch with their people and out of touch with their customers'
"在美国,管理效率的首要问题在于经理们脱离了基层员工和顾客" [*Fortune*《财富》]

managing director /ˌmænədʒɪŋ daɪˈrektə/ *noun* the director who is in charge of a whole company 总经理 Abbreviation 缩写 **MD**

mandate /ˈmændeɪt/ *noun* an order which allows something to take place 训令;命令

mandatory /ˈmændət(ə)ri/ *adjective* obligatory 强制性的 ○ *Wearing a suit is mandatory for all managerial staff.* 所有管理人员都必须着西装。

'... the wage talks are focusing on employment issues such as sharing of work among employees and extension of employment beyond the mandatory retirement age of 60 years'
"工资谈判的焦点集中在了就业问题上,例如员工间的工作分配及法定60岁退休年龄的延长" [*Nikkei Weekly*《日经周报》]

mandatory bid /ˌmændət(ə)ri ˈbɪd/ *noun* an offer to purchase the shares of a company which has to be made when a shareholder acquires 30% of that company's shares 强制性收购建议:当股东取得公司30%的股权时必

须出价购买其余股份

manipulate /məˈnɪpjʊleɪt/ *verb* ◻ **to manipulate the accounts** to make false accounts so that the company seems profitable 做假账，篡改账目

manpower forecasting /ˈmænpaʊə ˌfɔːkɑːstɪŋ/ *noun* the process of calculating how many employees will be needed in the future, and how many will actually be available 人力预测：计算未来需要的雇员人数以及实际可用人数

manpower planning /ˈmænpaʊə ˌplænɪŋ/ *noun* the process of planning to obtain the right number of employees in each job 人力规划，劳动力计划：为每个职位合理安排雇员人数的过程

manufacturing /ˌmænjʊˈfæktʃərɪŋ/ *noun* the production of machine-made products for sale 制造 ○ *We must try to reduce the manufacturing overheads.* 我们必须努力削减制造的间接费用。○ *Manufacturing processes are continually being updated.* 制造流程不断更新。

manufacturing profit /ˌmænjʊˈfæktʃərɪŋ ˌprɒfɪt/ *noun* the difference between the cost of buying a product from another supplier and the cost to the company of manufacturing it itself 制造利润：自制产品成本与外购产品成本之差

margin /ˈmɑːdʒɪn/ *noun* **1.** the difference between the money received when selling a product and the money paid for it 差额，赚头：成本与售价之间的差额 **2.** extra space or time allowed（空间或时间）余地，余裕 **3.** the difference between interest paid to depositors and interest charged to borrowers by a bank, building society, etc. 利差：银行、住房互助协会等的贷款利息与存款利息之差 **4.** a deposit paid when purchasing a futures contract（购买期货合约的）保证金

'... profit margins in the industries most exposed to foreign competition—machinery, transportation equipment and electrical goods—are significantly worse than usual'

"遭遇外国竞争最激烈的行业，包括机械、运输设备和电子产品行业，其利润率较以往更加惨不忍睹"［*Australian Financial Review*《澳大利亚金融评论报》］

marginal /ˈmɑːdʒɪn(ə)l/ *adjective* hardly worth the money paid（钱花的）不值的

marginal cost /ˌmɑːdʒɪn(ə)l ˈkɒst/ *noun* the cost of making a single extra unit above the number already planned 边际成本：比计划生产量再多生产一个单位所增加的成本

marginal costing /ˌmɑːdʒɪn(ə)l ˈkɒstɪŋ/ *noun* the costing of a product on the basis of its variable costs only, excluding fixed costs 边际成本法，直接成本法：只依据产品的可变成本来计算成本，而不包括固定成本

marginal land /ˌmɑːdʒɪn(ə)l ˈlænd/ *noun* land which is almost not worth farming 边际土地：几乎无耕种价值的土地

marginal pricing /ˌmɑːdʒɪn(ə)l ˈpraɪsɪŋ/ *noun* 边际成本定价法 **1.** the practice of basing the selling price of a product on its variable costs of production plus a margin, but excluding fixed costs［根据生产可变成本和毛利率来确定产品销售价格，而不包括固定成本］**2.** the practice of making the selling price the same as the cost of a single extra unit above the number already planned [以比计划生产量再多生产一个单位的成本为销售价格]

marginal purchase /ˌmɑːdʒɪn(ə)l ˈpɜːtʃɪs/ *noun* something which a buyer feels is only just worth buying 边际购买：购买者觉得正好值得买的东西

marginal rate of tax /ˌmɑːdʒɪn(ə)l reɪt əv ˈtæks/ , **marginal rate of taxation** /ˌmɑːdʒɪn(ə)l reɪt əv tækˈseɪʃ(ə)n/ *noun* the percentage of tax which a taxpayer pays at the top rate, which he or she therefore pays on every further pound or dollar he earns 边际税率：纳税人收入所适用的最高税率，即收入每增加一英镑或一美元时所适用的税率

'...pensioner groups claim that pensioners have the highest marginal rates of tax. Income earned by pensioners above $30 a week is taxed at 62.5 per cent, more than the highest marginal rate'
"养老金组织声称，养老金领取者所付的边际税率最高。他们一周挣得30美元以上的收入，就被课以62.5%的所得税，这大大超过了最高的边际税率" [*Australian Financial Review*《澳大利亚金融评论报》]

marginal revenue /ˌmɑːdʒɪn(ə)l ˈrevənjuː/ *noun* the income from selling a single extra unit above the number already sold 边际收入：比已有销售量多销售一单位产品所增加的收入

marginal tax rate /ˌmɑːdʒɪn(ə)l ˈtæks reɪt/ *noun* same as 同 **marginal rate of tax**

margin call /ˈmɑːdʒɪn kɔːl/ *noun* a request for a purchaser of a futures contract or an option to pay more margin, since the fall in the price of the securities or commodity has removed the value of the original margin deposited 追加保证金通知：由于证券或商品价格下跌使初始保证金的价值下降，因此要求期货合约或期权的买家交纳更多保证金

margin of safety /ˌmɑːdʒɪn əv ˈseɪfti/ *noun* the units produced or sales of such units which are above the breakeven point 安全边际：产品的产量或销量超过其保本点以上的部分

marine underwriter /məˌriːn ˈʌndəraɪtə/ *noun* a person or company that insures ships and their cargoes 海运担保人：为船只及其货物承保的人或公司

maritime lawyer /ˌmærɪtaɪm ˈlɔːjə/ *noun* a lawyer who specialises in legal matters concerning ships and cargoes 海事律师：专门从事船只及货物相关法律事务的律师

mark down /ˌmɑːk ˈdaʊn/ *verb* to make the price of something lower 使降价

mark-down /ˈmɑːkdaʊn/ *noun* 降价 **1.** a reduction of the price of something to less than its usual price [降至正常价格以下] **2.** the percentage amount by which a price has been lowered [降价百分比] ○ *There has been a 30% mark-down on all goods in the sale.* 出售的所有产品都降价了30%。

market /ˈmɑːkɪt/ *noun* 市场 **1.** an area where a product might be sold or the group of people who might buy a product [很多人买卖产品的地方] **2.** the possible sales of a specific product or demand for a specific product [某产品的可能需求量] ○ *There's no market for word processors.* 文字处理器没有市场 ○ *The market for home* *computers has fallen sharply*. 家用计算机市场锐减。○ *We have 20% of the British car market*. 我们占有英国汽车市场的20%。**3.** a place where money or commodities are traded [货币与商品交易的场所] **4.** □ **sell at the market** an instruction to stockbroker to sell shares at the best price possible 最佳市价出售:要求经纪人以市场上最有利价格卖出股票的指令 **5.** □ **to put something on the market** to start to offer something for sale 把某物拿到市场上去出售 ○ *They put their house on the market*. 他们把房子放到市场上出售。○ *I hear the company has been put on the market*. 我听说这家公司要出售。□ **the company has priced itself out of the market** the company has raised its prices so high that its products do not sell 公司提价过高,导致产品卖不出去。

'...market analysts described the falls in the second half of last week as a technical correction to a market which had been pushed by demand to over the 900 index level'
"针对被需求量带动超过900点指数水平的市场,市场分析人员认为上周后半期的回落是一次技术性回档"[*Australian Financial Review*《澳大利亚金融评论报》]

marketability /ˌmɑːkɪtəˈbɪlɪti/ *noun* the fact of being able to be sold easily 适销性 ○ *the marketability of shares in electronic companies* 电力公司的股票很抢手

marketable /ˈmɑːkɪtəb(ə)l/ *adjective* easily sold 易出售的

market analysis /ˌmɑːkɪt əˈnæləsɪs/ *noun* the detailed examination and report of a market 市场分析

market capitalisation /ˌmɑːkɪt ˌkæpɪtəlaɪˈzeɪʃ(ə)n/ *noun* the total market value of a company, calculated by multiplying the price of its shares on the Stock Exchange by the number of shares outstanding 市场资本总额,市场价值:公司的总市值,计算方法为股票价格乘以已发行股数 ○ *company with a £1m capitalization* 市值100万英镑的公司

market economist /ˌmɑːkɪt ɪˈkɒnəmɪst/ *noun* a person who specialises in the study of financial structures and the return on investments in the stock market 市场经济学家:研究股票市场资金结构与投资回报率的专家

market forces /ˌmɑːkɪt ˈfɔːsɪz/ *plural noun* the influences on the sales of a product which bring about a change in prices 市场力量:市场对导致产品价格变化的产品销量的影响

marketing /ˈmɑːkɪtɪŋ/ *noun* the business of presenting and promoting goods or services in such a way as to make customers want to buy them 营销,推销:发布及宣传某种商品或劳务信息,从而引起顾客的购买欲

'...reporting to the marketing director, the successful applicant will be responsible for the development of a training programme for the new sales force'
"入选的报名者归营销经理主管,并将负责制定新销售队伍的培训计划"[*Times*《泰晤士报》]

marketing agreement /ˈmɑːkɪtɪŋ əˌgriːmənt/ *noun* a contract by which one company will market another company's products 销售合同:一家公司负责销售另一家公司产品的合同

marketing cost /ˈmɑːkɪtɪŋ kɒst/ *noun* the cost of selling a product, including advertising, packaging, etc. 销售成本:销售产品花费的成本,包括广告费、包装费等

marketing department /ˈmɑːkɪtɪŋ dɪˌpɑːtmənt/ *noun* the section of a company dealing with marketing and sales 营销部门,市场部

marketing manager /ˈmɑːkɪtɪŋ ˌmænɪdʒə/ *noun* a person in charge of a marketing department 销售部经理 ○ *The marketing manager has decided to start a new advertising campaign*. 销售部经理决定展开新一轮广告宣传。

market leader /ˌmɑːkɪt ˈliːdə/ *noun* 市场领导者 **1.** a product which sells most in a market [市场上最畅销的产品] **2.** the company with the largest market share [占据市场最大份额的公司] ○ *We are the market leader in home computers*. 我们是家用计算机市场的领军者。

'...market leaders may benefit from scale economies or other cost advantages; they may enjoy a reputation for quality simply by being at the top, or they may actually produce a superior product that gives them both a large market share and high profits'
"市场领导者也许能从规模经济或其他成本优势中获利。他们或许仅仅因为是领头羊而享有品质声誉,或是他们确实拥有能带来巨大市场份额和高额利润的优良产品" [*Accountancy*《会计学》]

marketmaker /ˈmɑːkɪtmeɪkə/ *noun* a person who buys or sells shares on the stock market and offers to do so. A marketmaker operates a book, listing the securities he or she is willing to buy or sell, and makes his or her money by charging a commission on each transaction 市场开辟者:在股票市场买卖股票并出价买卖的人。市场开辟者掌管有交易登记册,上面列有其有意买卖的证券种类。市场开辟者通过收取每笔交易的佣金来赚钱

market opportunities /ˌmɑːkɪt ɒpəˈtjuːnɪtiz/ *noun* the possibility of finding new sales in a market 市场机遇:发现市场上新销售渠道的机遇性

market optimism /ˌmɑːkɪt ˈɒptɪˌmɪzəm/ *noun* a feeling that the stock market will rise 市场乐观情绪:对股市会上涨的直观感觉

market price /ˈmɑːkɪt praɪs/ *noun* 市场价格 **1.** the price at which a product can be sold [产品售价] **2.** the price at which a share stands in a stock market [股票在股市上的价格]

market rate /ˌmɑːkɪt ˈreɪt/ *noun* the usual price in the market 市场价 ○ *We pay the market rate for secretaries* or *We pay secretaries the market rate*. 我们按市价支付秘书工资。

'... after the prime rate cut yesterday, there was a further fall in short-term market rates'
"昨天基本利率下调后,短期市场利率进一步下跌" [*Financial Times*《金融时报》]

market research /ˌmɑːkɪt rɪˈsɜːtʃ/ *noun* the process of examining the possible sales of a product and the possible customers for it before it is put on the market 市场调研:在产品推出前,调查产品的可能销量和潜在顾客

market trends /ˌmɑːkɪt ˈtrendz/ *plural noun* gradual changes taking place in a market 市场趋势

market value /ˌmɑːkɪt ˈvæljuː/ *noun* the value of an asset, a share, a product or a company if sold today 市场价值:当天出售资产、股票、产品或公司可获得的价值

mark up /ˌmɑːk ˈʌp/ *verb* to increase the price of something 提价

mark-up /ˈmɑːkʌp/ *noun* **1.** an increase in price 提价 ○ *We put into effect a 10% mark-up of all prices in June.* 我们在6月份全面提价10%。○ *Since I was last in the store they have put at least a 5% mark-up on the whole range of items.* 自从我上次去过之后,这家商店所有的商品价格至少上浮了5%。**2.** the difference between the cost of a product or service and its selling price 赢利:产品或服务的成本与其售价之差 □ **we work to a 3.5 times mark-up *or* to a 350% mark-up** we take the unit cost and multiply by 3.5 to give the selling price 我们加价3.5倍(或加价350%)

mass production /mæs prəˈdʌkʃən/ *noun* the manufacture of large quantities of identical products 批量生产,成批生产

mass unemployment /ˌmæs ˌʌnɪmˈplɔɪmənt/ *noun* unemployment affecting large numbers of people 大批失业,大规模失业

matching /ˈmætʃɪŋ/ *noun* the relating of costs to sales in order to calculate profits during an accounting period 配比:将销售额与成本相联系来计算一个会计期间的利润

material /məˈtɪəriəl/ *noun* a substance which can be used to make a finished product 材料

material facts /məˌtɪəriəl ˈfækts/ *noun* 有决定性影响的事实,重要事实 **1.** in an insurance contract, information that the insured has to reveal at the time that the policy is taken out, e.g., that a house is located on the edge of a crumbling cliff. Failure to reveal material facts can result in the contract being declared void [在保险合同中,受保人在购买保单时必须披露的信息,例如房屋位于有塌方危险的悬崖边上。如未披露重要事实,合同可以被宣布无效] **2.** information that has to be disclosed in a prospectus [必须在招股章程中披露的信息] ⇨ 参阅 **listing requirements**

materiality /məˌtɪəriˈælɪti/ *noun* the state of being material 物质性;重要性

material news /məˌtɪəriəl ˈnjuːz/ *noun* price sensitive developments in a company, e.g., proposed acquisitions, mergers, profit warnings, and the resignation of directors, that most stock exchanges require a company to announce immediately to the exchange 重要新闻,重要信息:指涉及公司价格走向的敏感事项,如提议的收购、合并、盈利警告及董事辞职,多数证券交易所都会要求公司立即公布此类信息(NOTE: The US term is **material information** 美国用语为 **material information**)

materials requisition /məˌtɪəriəlz ˌrekwɪˈzɪʃ(ə)n/ *noun* an official note from a production department, asking for materials to be moved from the store to the workshop 领料单:生产部门请求从仓库领取材料至生产车间的正式单据

materials transfer note /məˌtɪəriəlz ˈtrænsfɜː nəʊt/ *noun* an official note made out when materials are moved from one workplace to another 材料调拨单

maturity date /məˈtʃʊərɪti deɪt/ *noun* a date when a government stock, an assurance policy or a debenture will become due for payment（政府债券、保险单或债权证的）到期日 Also called 亦称作 **date of maturity**

MAXI ISA /ˈmæksi ˌaɪsə/ *noun* an ISA for somebody who uses only one firm to handle all ISA funds 最大个人储蓄计划：一种个人储蓄计划，其拥有人只委托一家证券公司来管理所有的个人储蓄计划基金 ⇨ 参阅 **MINI ISA**

maximisation /ˌmæksɪmaɪˈzeɪʃ(ə)n/, **maximization** *noun* the process of making something as large as possible 最大化 ○ *profit maximisation* or *maximisation of profit* 利润最大化

maximise /ˈmæksɪmaɪz/ , **maximize** *verb* to make something as large as possible 使…最大化 ○ *Our aim is to maximise profits.* 我们的目标是利润最大化。○ *The cooperation of the workforce will be needed if we are to maximise production.* 产量最大化需要我们全体员工的配合。○ *She is paid on results, and so has to work flat out to maximise her earnings.* 报酬与业绩挂钩，因此她只有全力工作才能挣得更多。

maximum /ˈmæksɪməm/ *noun* the largest possible number, price or quantity 最大值 ○ *It is the maximum the insurance company will pay.* 这是保险公司的最高赔付额。(NOTE: The plural is **maxima** or **maximums** 复数为 **maxima** 或 **maximums**) □ **up to a maximum of £10** no more than £10 最高为 10 英镑 ■ *adjective* largest possible 最大的 ○ *40% is the maximum income tax rate* or *the maximum rate of tax.* 最高所得税税率（或最高税率）为 40%。○ *The maximum load for the truck is one ton.* 这辆卡车最大载运量为一吨。○ *Maximum production levels were reached last week.* 产量在上周达到了最高。

MCT *abbr* mainstream corporation tax 主体公司税

MD *abbr* managing director 总经理 ○ *She was appointed MD of a property company.* 她被任命为一家房地产公司的总经理。

mean /miːn/ *adjective* average 平均的 ○ *The mean annual increase in sales is 3.20%.* 销售额平均每年增长 3.20%。

means /miːnz/ *noun* a way of doing something 手段，工具 ○ *Do we have any means of copying all these documents quickly?* 我们有什么办法把所有文件很快复印出来吗？○ *Bank transfer is the easiest means of payment.* 银行转账是最便捷的付款方式。(NOTE: The plural is **means** 复数为 **means**) ■ *plural noun* money or resources 资金，财力 ○ *The company has the means to launch the new product.* 公司有足够的资金推出新产品。○ *Such a level of investment is beyond the means of a small private company.* 如此的投资水平已超出小型私企的财力。

means test /ˈmiːnz test/ *noun* an inquiry into how much money someone earns to see if they are eligible for state benefits（确定某人能否享受政府福利的）收入状况调查 ■ *verb* to find out how much money someone has in savings and assets 财产调查 ○ *All applicants will be means-tested.* 所有申请人都要接受财产调查。

measure /ˈmeʒə/ *noun* **1.** a way of calculating size or quantity 测量，度量 **2.** a type of action 措施 ■ *verb* □ **to measure a company's performance** to judge how well a company is doing 衡量公司业绩

measurement /ˈmeʒəmənt/ *noun* a way of judging something 度量；评价 ○ *growth measurement* 增长评价 ○ *performance measurement* or *measurement of performance* 业绩评价

measurement of profitability /ˌmeʒəmənt əv ˌprɒfɪtəˈbɪlɪti/ *noun* a way of calculating how profitable something is 获利能力计量

median /ˈmiːdiən/ *noun* the middle number in a list of numbers 中位数：一组数字的中间那个数

medical insurance /ˈmedɪk(ə)l ɪnˌʃʊərəns/ *noun* insurance which pays the cost of medical treatment, especially when someone is travelling abroad 医疗保险：支付医疗费用的保险，尤用于某人出国旅行

medium /ˈmiːdiəm/ *adjective* middle or average 中等的；平均的 ○ *The company is of medium size.* 这是一家中等规模的公司

medium of exchange /ˌmiːdiəm əv ɪksˈtʃeɪndʒ/ *noun* anything that is used to pay for goods. Nowadays, this usually takes the form of money (banknotes and coins), but in ancient societies, it included anything from cattle to shells 交换媒介：用来抵付货款的东西。当今的交换媒介通常是货币(纸币或硬币)，但在古代包括牛、贝壳等多种东西

mediums /ˈmiːdiəmz/ *plural noun* government stocks which mature in seven to fifteen years' time 中期债券：7至15年期的政府债券

medium-sized company /ˌmiːdiəmsaɪzd ˈkʌmp(ə)ni/ *noun* a company which has a turnover of less than £5.75m and does not employ more than 250 staff 中等规模公司：营业额低于575万英镑，员工不超过250人的公司 ○ *a mediumsized engineering company* 一家中等规模的工程公司

medium-term /ˌmiːdiəmˈtɜːm/ *adjective* referring to a point between short term and long term 中等期限的

medium-term bond /ˌmiːdiəmtɜːm ˈbɒnd/ *noun* a bond which matures within five to fifteen years 中期债券：5至15年期的债券

member /ˈmembə/ *noun* **1.** a person who belongs to a group, society or organization 成员，会员 ○ *Committee members voted on the proposal.* 委员会成员对该提议进行投票表决。○ *They were elected members of the board.* 他们当选为董事会成员。○ *Every employer is a member of the employers' federation.* 每位雇主都是雇主联合会的会员。**2.** a shareholder in a company (公司的)股东 **3.** an organisation which belongs to a larger organization 成员组织 ○ *the member companies of a trade association* 商会的成员公司 ○ *The member states of the EU* 欧盟成员国 ○ *The members of the United Nations* 联合国成员

'...it will be the first opportunity for party members and trade union members to express their views on the tax package'
"这是党员和工会成员第一次有机会就税收一揽子方案发表自己的意见"[*Australian Financial Review*《澳大利亚金融评论报》]

member bank /ˌmembə ˈbæŋk/ *noun* a bank which is part of the Federal Reserve system (美国联邦储备系统的)会员银行

member firm /ˌmembə ˈfɜːm/ *noun* a stockbroking firm which is a member of a stock exchange 经纪商会员，

会员行:身为证券交易所会员的股票经纪公司

membership /ˈmembəʃɪp/ *noun* **1.** the fact of belonging to a group, society or organization 会籍,会员身份 ○ *membership qualifications* 会员资格 ○ *conditions of membership* 入会条件 ○ *membership card* 会员卡 ○ *to pay your membership or your membership fees* 交纳你的会费 ○ *membership of the EU* 欧盟成员 **2.** all the members of a group 全体成员 ○ *The membership was asked to vote for the new president*. 要求全体成员投票选举新主席。

'... the bargaining committee will recommend that its membership ratify the agreement at a meeting called for June'
"谈判委员会建议其成员在 6 月召开的会议上批准这份协议"[*Toronto Star*《多伦多明星日报》]

members' voluntary winding up /ˌmembəz ˌvɒlənt(ə)ri ˌwaɪndɪŋ ˈʌp/ *noun* the winding up of a company by the shareholders themselves 股东自愿清算

mercantile /ˈmɜːkəntaɪl/ *adjective* commercial 商业的;商人的

mercantile marine /ˌmɜːkəntaɪl məˈriːn/ *noun* all the commercial ships of a country 商船队(指一国的所有商船)

merchant /ˈmɜːtʃənt/ *noun* **1.** a businessperson who buys and sells, especially one who buys imported goods in bulk for retail sale 商人,(尤指进口)批发商 ○ *a coal merchant* 煤商 ○ *a wine merchant* 酒商 **2.** a company, shop or other business which accepts a credit card for purchases (接受信用卡消费的)公司(或商店)

merchant bank /ˈmɜːtʃənt bæŋk/ *noun* **1.** a bank which arranges loans to companies, deals in international finance, buys and sells shares and launches new companies on the Stock Exchange, but does not provide banking services to the general public 商人银行:负责组织安排公司贷款、国际金融交易、股票买卖、新公司上市的银行,但不为公众提供普通银行服务 **2.** *US* a bank which operates a credit card system, accepting payment on credit cards from retailers or 'merchants' (美)处理信用卡的银行(接受零售商或"商人"的信用卡支付业务)

merchant banker /ˌmɜːtʃənt ˈbæŋkə/ *noun* a person who has a high position in a merchant bank 商人银行家:商人银行中的高层人员

merchant number /ˈmɜːtʃənt ˌnʌmbə/ *noun* a number of the merchant, printed at the top of the report slip when depositing credit card payments 商人编号:用信用卡付款时印在小票顶部的商人编号

merge /mɜːdʒ/ *verb* to join together 合并,兼并 ○ *The two companies have merged*. 这两家公司已合并。○ *The firm merged with its main competitor*. 该公司与其主要竞争对手合并了。

merger /ˈmɜːdʒə/ *noun* the joining together of two or more companies 合并,兼并 ○ *As a result of the merger, the company is now the largest in the field*. 合并后,这家公司成为该行业最大的公司。

merger accounting /ˈmɜːdʒə əˌkaʊntɪŋ/ *noun* a way of presenting the accounts of a newly acquired company within the group accounts, so as to show it in the best possible light 并

购会计，合并会计：在集团报表内呈列新收购公司的账目，以最真实地反映其状况的一种方式

merit increase /ˈmerɪt ˌɪnkriːs/ *noun* an increase in pay given to an employee because his or her work is good 绩效加薪：给予绩效良好员工的加薪

merit rating /ˈmerɪt ˌreɪtɪŋ/ *noun* the process of judging how well an employee works, so that payment can be according to merit 绩效考核：判断某雇员工作的好坏，以便根据考核结果评定工资级别

mezzanine finance /ˌmetsəniːn ˈfaɪnæns/ *noun* finance provided to a company after it has received start-up finance 后续资金：在公司获得启动资金后再得到的资金

micro- /maɪkrəʊ/ *prefix* very small 微小的，微量的

microeconomics /ˈmaɪkrəʊ iːkəˌnɒmɪks/ *plural noun* the study of the economics of people or single companies 微观经济学：研究个体（公司或个人）经济行为的科学 Compare 比较 **macroeconomics**（NOTE：takes a singular verb 跟单数动词）

microfiche /ˈmaɪkrəʊˌfiːʃ/ *noun* an index sheet, made of several microfilm photographs 微缩卡片：用缩微胶片图像做成的索引卡 ○ *We hold our records on microfiche.* 我们把记录保存在微缩卡片上。

microfilm /ˈmaɪkrəʊfɪlm/ *noun* a roll of film on which a document is photographed in very small scale 微型胶卷，缩微胶片 ○ *We hold our records on microfilm.* 我们用微型胶卷保存档案。

mid- /mɪd/ *prefix* middle 中间的

middle management /ˌmɪd(ə)l ˈmænɪdʒmənt/ *noun* department managers in a company, who carry out the policy set by the directors and organise the work of a group of employees 中层管理人员：公司的部门经理，负责执行董事制订的政策，并组织部门内员工的工作

middle price /ˈmɪd(ə)l praɪs/ *noun* a price between the buying and selling price, usually shown in indices 中间价：买价与卖价之间的价格，通常列在目录中

mid-month /ˌmɪdˈmʌnθ/ *adjective* happening in the middle of the month 月中的 ○ *mid-month accounts* 月中报表

mid-week /ˌmɪdˈwiːk/ *adjective* happening in the middle of a week 周中的 ○ *the mid-week lull in sales* 周中销售平淡

millionaire /ˌmɪljəˈneə/ *noun* a person who has more than one million pounds or dollars 百万富翁

MINI ISA /ˈmɪni ˌaɪsə/ *noun* an ISA for somebody who uses up to three firms for handling the components of the ISA 最小个人储蓄计划：一种个人储蓄计划，其拥有人委托多达三个公司来管理其个人储蓄计划中的基金 ◊ 参阅 **MAXI ISA**

minimisation /ˌmɪnɪmaɪˈzeɪʃ(ə)n/ *noun* making as small as possible 最小化

minimum /ˈmɪnɪməm/ *noun* the smallest possible quantity, price or number 最小值 ○ *to keep expenses to a minimum* 把费用保持在最低水平。 ○ *to reduce the risk of a loss to a minimum* 把损失风险降到最低（NOTE：The plural is **minima** or **minimums** 复

数为 **minima** 或 **minimums**）■ *adjective* smallest possible 最低的，尽可能小的

minimum lending rate /ˌmɪnɪməm ˈlendɪŋ reɪt/ *noun* the lowest rate of interest formerly charged by the Bank of England to discount houses, now replaced by the base rate 最低贷款利率：英格兰银行以前向贴现公司收取的最低利率，现已被基础利率取代

minimum reserves /ˌmɪnɪməm rɪˈzɜːvz/ *plural noun* the smallest amount of reserves which a commercial bank must hold with a central bank 最低储备金：商业银行必须在中央银行保持的最低储备金数额

minimum wage /ˌmɪnɪməm ˈweɪdʒ/ *noun* the lowest hourly wage which a company can legally pay its employees（法定）最低工资

mining concession /ˈmaɪnɪŋ kənˌseʃ(ə)n/ *noun* the right to dig a mine on a piece of land 矿山开采权

minor /ˈmaɪnə/ *adjective* less important 次要的 ○ *Items of minor expenditure are not listed separately*. 小额支出项目不再单列。○ *The minor shareholders voted against the proposal*. 小股东投票反对该提议。

minority /maɪˈnɒrɪti/ *noun* a number or quantity which is less than half of the total 少数 ○ *A minority of board members opposed the chairman*. 董事会少数成员反对董事长。

minority shareholder /maɪˌnɒrəti ˌʃeəˈhəʊldə/ *noun* a person who owns a group of shares but less than half of the shares in a company 少数股权股东：拥有公司半数以下股份的股东

minority shareholding /maɪˌnɒrəti ˈʃeəhəʊldɪŋ/ *noun* a group of shares which are less than half the total 少数股权，少数权益：半数以下的股份 ○ *He acquired a minority shareholding in the company*. 他获得了该公司的少数股权。

minus /ˈmaɪnəs/ *preposition*, *adverb* less, without 减去，不包括 ○ *Net salary is gross salary minus tax and National Insurance deductions*. 税后工资等于税前工资减去税收和国民保险扣除额。○ *Gross profit is sales minus production costs*. 总利润等于销售收入减去生产成本。

minus factor /ˈmaɪnəs ˌfæktə/ *noun* an unfavourable factor 负面因素 ○ *To have lost sales in the best quarter of the year is a minus factor for the sales team*. 对销售团队来说错过一年中最佳销售季是个不利因素。

misappropriate /ˌmɪsəˈprəʊprieɪt/ *verb* to use illegally money which is not yours, but with which you have been trusted 挪用，私吞

misappropriation /ˌmɪsəprəʊpriˈeɪʃ(ə)n/ *noun* the illegal use of money by someone who is not the owner but who has been trusted to look after it 挪用，私吞

miscalculate /mɪsˈkælkjʊleɪt/ *verb* to calculate wrongly, or to make a mistake in calculating something 算错，错算 ○ *The salesman miscalculated the discount, so we hardly broke even on the deal*. 销售人员把折扣算错了，所以我们这笔交易很难保本。

miscalculation /mɪsˌkælkjʊˈleɪʃ(ə)n/ *noun* a mistake in calculating 计算错误

miscount *noun* /ˈmɪskaʊnt/ a mistake in counting 误算，计算错误 ■ *verb* /mɪsˈkaʊnt/ to count wrongly, or to make a mistake in counting something 算错，误算 ○ *The shopkeeper miscounted, so we got twenty-five bars of chocolate instead of two dozen.* 店主数错了，我们本来买 24 块巧克力，结果却得到了 25 块。

mismanage /mɪsˈmænɪdʒ/ *verb* to manage something badly 管理不善 ○ *The company had been badly mismanaged under the previous MD.* 在前任总经理的管理下，公司混乱不堪。

mismanagement /mɪsˈmænɪdʒmənt/ *noun* bad management 管理不善 ○ *The company failed because of the chairman's mismanagement.* 由于总裁管理不善，公司倒闭了。

misrepresent /ˌmɪsreprɪˈzent/ *verb* to report facts or what someone says wrongly 误报；歪曲 ○ *Our spokesman was totally misrepresented in the Sunday papers.* 周日的报纸完全歪曲了我们发言人的原意。

misrepresentation /ˌmɪsˌreprɪzenˈteɪʃ(ə)n/ *noun* the act of making a wrong statement in order to persuade someone to enter into a contract such as one for buying a product or service 虚假声明，虚报：作出虚假的声明，以说服某人签署购买商品或服务的合同

misuse /mɪsˈjuːs/ *noun* a wrong use 错用 ○ *the misuse of funds* or *of assets* 资金(或资产)的错误使用

mixed /mɪkst/ *adjective* 混合的，综合的 **1.** made up of different sorts or of different types of things together [由不同类型混合组成] **2.** neither good nor bad [不好也不坏]

'...prices closed on a mixed note after a moderately active trading session'
"在一个相对活跃的交易时段之后，收盘有涨有跌"[*Financial Times*《金融时报》]

mixed economy /ˌmɪkst ɪˈkɒnəmi/ *noun* a system which contains both nationalised industries and private enterprise 混合型经济：国有企业和私人企业共存的经济

mode /məʊd/ *noun* a way of doing something (做事)方式

modified accounts /ˌmɒdɪfaɪd əˈkaʊnts/ *plural noun* ➧ 参阅 **abbreviated accounts**

monetarism /ˈmʌnɪtəˌrɪz(ə)m/ *noun* a theory that the amount of money in the economy affects the level of prices, so that inflation can be controlled by regulating money supply 货币主义：主张货币发行量影响价格水平，因此可以通过调节货币供给量来控制通货膨胀的理论

monetarist /ˈmʌnɪtərɪst/ *noun* a person who believes in monetarism and acts accordingly 货币主义者：信奉货币主义并相应行事的人 ■ *adjective* according to monetarism 货币主义的 ○ *monetarist theories* 货币主义理论

monetary /ˈmʌnɪt(ə)ri/ *adjective* referring to money or currency 货币的

'...the decision by the government to tighten monetary policy will push the annual inflation rate above the year's previous high'
"政府收紧银根的决定将使年通货膨胀率超过历史最高水平"[*Financial Times*《金融时报》]

'...it is not surprising that the Fed started to ease monetary policy some months ago'
"几个月前联邦政府开始放松银根，这毫不奇怪"[*Sunday Times*《星期日泰晤士报》]

'...a draft report on changes in the international monetary system'
"关于国际货币体系变动的报告草案"[*Wall Street Journal*《华尔街日报》]

monetary assets /ˌmʌnɪt(ə)ri ˈæsets/ *noun* assets, principally accounts receivable, cash, and bank balances, that are realisable at the amount stated in the accounts. Other assets, e.g., facilities and machinery, inventories, and marketable securities will not necessarily realise the sum stated in a business's balance sheet 货币性资产:可按报表所示金额变现的资产,主要包括应收账款、现金和银行余额。其他资产(如机器设备、存货和有价证券)不一定能按企业资产负债表所示金额变现

monetary items /ˌmʌnɪt(ə)ri ˈaɪtəms/ *plural noun* monetary assets such as cash or debtors, and monetary liabilities such as an overdraft or creditors, whose values stay the same in spite of inflation 货币性项目:价值在通货膨胀时仍保持不变的货币性资产(如现金或应收账款)和货币性负债(如透支或应付账款)

monetary standard /ˌmʌnɪt(ə)ri ˈstændəd/ *noun* the fixing of a fixed exchange rate for a currency 货币本位制:一种货币的固定兑换率

monetary targets /ˌmʌnɪt(ə)ri ˈtɑːɡɪtz/ *plural noun* figures which are given as targets by the government when setting out its budget for the forthcoming year, e.g. the money supply or the PSBR 货币目标:政府制订来年预算时设定的货币供给、公共部门借款(PSBR)等的目标数额

monetary unit /ˈmʌnɪt(ə)ri ˌjuːnɪt/ *noun* a main item of currency of a country 货币单位

money /ˈmʌni/ *noun* coins and notes used for buying and selling 钱,货币 □ **money up front** payment in advance 预付款 ○ *They are asking for £10,000 up front before they will consider the deal*. 他们要求先预付一万英镑,然后才考虑这笔交易。○ *He had to put money up front before he could clinch the deal*. 为了达成交易,他不得不支付预付款。

money at call /ˌmʌni ət ˈkɔːl/, **money on call** /ˌmʌni ɒn ˈkɔːl/ *noun* same as 同 **call money**

money at call and short notice /ˌmʌni ət kɔːl ən ʃɔːt ˈnəʊtɪs/ *noun* in the United Kingdom, balances in an account that are either available upon demand (call) or within 14 days (short notice) 即期及短期通知存款:在英国可以随时提取(即期)或在14天内提取(短期通知)的账户余额

money broker /ˈmʌni ˌbrəʊkə/ *noun* a dealer operating in the interbank and foreign exchange markets 短期借贷经纪人:在银行间及外汇市场上运作的交易商

money laundering /ˈmʌni ˌlɔːndərɪŋ/ *noun* the act of passing illegal money into the banking system 洗钱:通过银行系统掩盖资金非法来源的行为

moneylender /ˈmʌniˌlendə/ *noun* a person who lends money at interest 放款人,放债人

money lying idle /ˌmʌni ˌlaɪɪŋ ˈaɪd(ə)l/ *noun* money which is not being used to produce interest, which is not invested in business 闲置资金:不用于生息也不用于商业投资的资金

money-making /ˈmʌniˌmeɪkɪŋ/ *adjective* able to turn over a profit 赚钱的 ○ *a money-making plan* 一个赚钱的计划

money market fund /ˈmʌni ˌmɑːkɪt fʌnd/ *noun* an investment fund, which only invests in money market instruments 货币市场基金:一种只投资于货币市场工具的投资基金

money market instruments /ˈmʌni ˌmɑːkɪt ˌɪnstrʊmənts/ *plural noun* short-term investments which can be easily turned into cash and are traded on the money markets, e.g. cds 货币市场工具:很容易变现并在货币市场上交易的短期投资,如大额可转让存单

money order /ˈmʌni ˌɔːdə/ *noun* a document which can be bought as a way of sending money through the post 汇款单,汇票

money rates /ˈmʌni reɪts/ *plural noun* rates of interest for borrowers or lenders 借贷利率

money-spinner /ˈmʌniˌspɪnə/ *noun* an item which sells very well or which is very profitable 摇钱树:非常畅销或盈利大的商品 ○ *The home-delivery service has proved to be a real money-spinner*. 事实证明,送货上门服务确实赚钱。

money supply /ˈmʌni səˌplaɪ/ *noun* the amount of money which exists in a country (一国的)货币供应量,货币发行量

monies /ˈmʌniz/ *plural noun* sums of money 金额 ○ *monies owing to the company* 应付该公司的金额 ○ *to collect monies due* 敛收到期债务

monitor /ˈmɒnɪtə/ *verb* to check or to examine how something is working 监控,检查,检验 ○ *She is monitoring the progress of sales*. 她在监督销售的进展情况。○ *How do you monitor the performance of the sales reps*? 你如何监控销售代表的表现? ○ *How do you monitor the performance of a unit trust*? 你如何检验单位信托的表现?

monopoly /məˈnɒpəli/ *noun* a situation where one person or company is the only supplier of a particular product or service 垄断:指个人或公司是某类产品或劳务的唯一供应商 ○ *to be in a monopoly situation* 处于垄断地位 ○ *The company has the monopoly of imports of Brazilian wine*. 该公司垄断了巴西进口酒类的业务。○ *The factory has the absolute monopoly of jobs in the town*. 该工厂在该市的就业市场拥有绝对垄断地位。(NOTE: The more usual US term is **trust** 美国常用 **trust**)

Monte Carlo method /ˌmɒnti ˈkɑːləʊ ˌmeθəd/ *noun* a statistical analysis technique for calculating an unknown quantity which has an exact value by using an extended series of random trials 蒙特卡洛法:一种统计分析技术,它通过广泛的随机试验来对一个具有确切值的未知量进行计算(NOTE: The name refers to the fact that a roulette wheel in a casino, as in Monte Carlo, continually generates random numbers 该名称源于赌场(如蒙特卡洛赌场)内的一种不断生成随机数字的轮盘赌游戏)

month /mʌnθ/ *noun* one of twelve periods which make a year 月 ○ *bills due at the end of the current month* 本月底到期的票据 ○ *The company pays him £100 a month*. 公司每月付给他100英镑。○ *She earns £2,000 a month*. 她每月挣2,000英镑。

month end /ˌmʌnθ ˈend/ *noun* the end of a calendar month, when accounts have to be drawn up 月末:历月月末的账目报表期 ○ *The accounts department are working on the month-*

end accounts. 会计部门正在处理月末报表。

monthly /ˈmʌnθli/ *adjective* happening every month or which is received every month 每月的 ○ *We get a monthly statement from the bank*. 我们收到一张银行的月结单。○ *She makes monthly payments to the credit card company*. 她按月给信用卡公司还款。○ *He is paying for his car by monthly instalments*. 他按月分期支付购车款。○ *My monthly salary cheque is late*. 我的月薪支票未按时签发。□ **monthly statement** a statement sent to a customer at the end of each month, itemising transactions which have taken place in his or her account 月报表,月结单:于每个月末发给顾客的报表,逐条列明月内其账户发生的交易 ■ *adverb* every month 每月地 ○ *She asked if she could pay monthly by direct debit*. 她询问能否通过直接扣账按月付费。○ *The account is credited monthly*. 这个账目按月记账。

moonlight /ˈmuːnlaɪt/ *verb* to do a second job for cash, often in the evening, as well as a regular job (*informal*) (非正式)(通常在晚上)做兼职

moonlighting /ˈmuːnlaɪtɪŋ/ *noun* the practice of doing a second job 兼职 ○ *He makes thousands a year from moonlighting*. 他每年的兼职收入有数千元。

moral hazard /ˌmɒrəl ˈhæzəd/ *noun* a risk that somebody will behave immorally because insurance, the law, or some other agency protects them against loss that the immoral behaviour might otherwise cause 道德风险,道德危机:由于有保险、法律或其他机构为道德主体行为导致的损失提供保障,而引发的道德主体行为不符合道德的风险

moratorium /ˌmɒrəˈtɔːriəm/ *noun* a temporary stop to repayments of interest on loans or capital owed (贷款本息的)延期偿付,暂停偿付 ○ *The banks called for a moratorium on payments*. 银行要求延期偿付。(NOTE: The plural is **moratoria** or **moratoriums** 复数为 **moratoria** 或 **moratoriums**)

mortgage /ˈmɔːɡɪdʒ/ *noun* agreement where someone lends money to another person so that he or she can buy a property, the property being the security 按揭,抵押:借款给某人使其能够购买某项财产,并以该财产作为借款抵押的协议 ○ *to take out a mortgage on a house* 办理住房按揭贷款

'...mortgage payments account for just 20 per cent of the average first-time buyer's gross earnings against an average of 24 per cent during the past 15 years'
"现在按揭付款仅占首次购房者平均税前收入的20%,而在过去的15年里则平均占24%"[*Times*《泰晤士报》]

'...mortgage money is becoming tighter. Applications for mortgages are running at a high level and some building societies are introducing quotas'
"对按揭贷款的控制越来越严。申请按揭的人数却居高不下,于是一些住房互助协会出台了配额制"[*Times*《泰晤士报》]

'...for the first time since mortgage rates began falling a financial institution has raised charges on homeowner loans'
"在按揭利率下降后,一家金融机构首次提高了房屋贷款的费用"[*Globe and Mail* (*Toronto*)《环球邮报》(多伦多)]

mortgage bond /ˈmɔːɡɪdʒ bɒnd/ *noun* a certificate showing that a mortgage exists and that property is security for it 抵押债券:证明按揭存

在以及所属财产为抵押物的文件

mortgage debenture /ˈmɔːɡɪdʒ dɪˌbentʃə/ *noun* a debenture where the lender can be repaid by selling the company's property 公司抵押债券：可通过出售公司财产来偿还的债券

mortgagee /mɔːɡəˈdʒiː/ *noun* a person or company which lends money for someone to buy a property 承按人，受押人，贷款人：借钱给某人购买财产的个人或公司

mortgage famine /ˈmɔːɡɪdʒ ˌfæmɪn/ *noun* a situation where there is not enough money available to offer mortgages to house buyers 按揭资金缺乏：没有足够资金作为按揭贷款提供给购房者

mortgager /ˈmɔːɡɪdʒə/ , **mortgagor** *noun* a person who borrows money to buy a property 按揭人，抵押人，借款人：借钱购买财产的人

movable /ˈmuːvəb(ə)l/ , **moveable** *adjective* possible to move 可移动的 ○ *All the moveable property has been seized by the bailiffs*. 所有动产都被司法官员查封了。

movable property /ˌmuːvəb(ə)l ˈprɒpəti/ *noun* chattels and other objects which can be moved, as opposed to land（与土地相对的）动产

moveables /ˈmuːvəb(ə)lz/ *plural noun* moveable property 动产

mover /ˈmuːvə/ *noun* a person who proposes a motion 提议人

moving average /ˌmuːvɪŋ ˈæv(ə)rɪdʒ/ *noun* an average of share prices on a stock market, where the calculation is made over a period which moves forward regularly 股市平均股价：定期计算出的证券市场平均股票价

multi /mʌlti/ *prefix* referring to many things 多的，多种的

multicurrency /ˌmʌltɪˈkʌrənsi/ *adjective* in several currencies 多种货币的

multifunctional card /ˌmʌltɪfʌnkʃən(ə)l ˈkɑːd/ *noun* a plastic card that may be used for two or more purposes, e.g., as a cash card, a cheque card, and a debit card 多功能卡：具有两种或两种以上功能的塑料卡片，如提款卡、支票卡和借记卡

multilateral /ˌmʌltiˈlæt(ə)rəl/ *adjective* between several organisations or countries 多边的 ○ *a multilateral agreement* 多边协议

multilateral netting /ˌmʌltilæt(ə)rəl ˈnetɪŋ/ *noun* a method of putting together sums from various sources into one currency, used by groups of banks trading in several currencies at the same time 多边净额：将各种来源的现金全部兑换为同一种货币，通常用于多个银行同时以几种货币进行交易时

multimillion /ˌmʌltiˈmɪljən/ *adjective* referring to several million pounds or dollars 数百万的 ○ *They signed a multimillion pound deal*. 他们签署了一笔数百万英镑的生意。

multimillionaire /ˌmʌltimɪljəˈneə/ *noun* a person who owns property or investments worth several million pounds or dollars 拥有数百万英镑或美元资产的富翁

multiple /ˈmʌltɪp(ə)l/ *adjective* many 多的

multiple exchange rate /ˌmʌltɪp(ə)l ɪksˈtʃeɪndʒ reɪt/ *noun* a two-tier rate of exchange used in certain countries where the more advantageous rate may be for tourists or for businesses proposing to build a factory 复汇率,多元汇率,多元汇价:某些国家使用的双重汇率制度,其中较优惠的汇率可能多适用于游客或计划建厂的企业

multiple ownership /ˌmʌltɪp(ə)l ˈəʊnəʃɪp/ *noun* a situation where something is owned by several parties jointly 多人(共同)拥有

multiplication sign /ˌmʌltɪplɪˈkeɪʃ(ə)n saɪn/ *noun* a sign (×) used to show that a number is being multiplied by another 乘号(×)

multiplier /ˈmʌltɪplaɪə/ *noun* a number which multiplies another, or a factor which tends to multiply something, as the effect of new expenditure on total income and reserves 乘数

multiply /ˈmʌltɪplaɪ/ *verb* **1.** to calculate the sum of various numbers added together a particular number of times 乘 ○ *If you multiply twelve by three you get thirty-six*. 12 乘以 3 等于 36。○ *Square measurements are calculated by multiplying length by width*. 面积为长乘以宽。**2.** to grow or to increase 增加 ○ *Profits multiplied in the boom years*. 在经济繁荣的年份里,利润成倍增长。

municipal bond /mjuːˌnɪsɪp(ə)l ˈbɒnd/ *noun US* a bond issued by a town or district (美)市政公债:由地方政府发行的债券 (NOTE: The UK term is **local authority bond** 英国用语为 **local authority bond**)

mutual /ˈmjuːtʃuəl/ *adjective* belonging to two or more people (多人)共有的

N

naked /ˈneɪkɪd/ *adjective* without any hedge or without any reserves to protect a position 未套期保值的,未保护头寸的

name /neɪm/ *noun* a person who provides security for insurance arranged by a Lloyd's of London syndicate(伦敦劳埃德保险社辛迪加的)保证人

named /neɪmd/ *adjective* □ **the person named in the policy** the person whose name is given on an insurance policy as the person insured 记名保险单受保人

NAO *abbr* National Audit Office 国家审计署

narration /nəˈreɪʃ(ə)n/ , **narrative** /ˈnærətɪv/ *noun* a series of notes and explanations relating to transactions in the accounts 对账目中事项所作的一系列注释和说明

national /ˈnæʃ(ə)nəl/ *adjective* referring to the whole of a particular country 国家的

National Audit Office /ˌnæʃ(ə)nəl ˌɔːdɪt ˈɒfɪs/ *noun* a body which investigates the use of public money by central government departments. It acts on behalf of the Parliamentary Public Accounts Committee 国家审计署:中央政府调查公共资金使用状况的机关。它代表议会公共会计委员会行事 Abbreviation 缩写 **NAO**

national bank /ˈnæʃ(ə)nəl bæŋk/ *noun US* a bank which is chartered by the federal government and is part of the Federal Reserve system as opposed to a 'state bank'(美)国民银行:由联邦政府特许成立的银行,作为联邦储备系统的一部分,与"州立银行"相对

national income /ˌnæʃ(ə)nəl ˈɪnkʌm/ *noun* the value of income from the sales of goods and services in a country 国民收入:一国销售产品和提供劳务获得的收入价值

national income accounts /ˌnæʃ(ə)nəl ˈɪnkʌm əˌkaʊts/ *plural noun* economic statistics that show the state of a nation's economy over a given period of time, usually a year 国民收入账户,国民所得账户:指定期限内(通常是一年)一国经济状况的经济统计 ⇨ 参阅 **gross domestic product**, **gross national product**

National Insurance /ˌnæʃ(ə)nəl ɪnˈʃʊərəns/ *noun* state insurance in the United Kingdom, organised by the government, which pays for medical care, hospitals, unemployment benefits, etc. 国民保险:英国政府组织的国家保险,它支付医疗费、住院费、失业救济金等 Abbreviation 缩写 **NI**

National Insurance contributions /ˌnæʃ(ə)nəl ɪnˈʃʊərəns ˌkɒntrɪbjuːʃ(ə)nz/ *noun* payments made by both employers and employees to the government. The contributions, together with other government receipts, are used to finance state pensions and other benefits such as unemployment benefit 国民保险金分担额，国民保险缴款：雇主和雇员双方支付给政府的款项。这些缴款连同其他政府收入一起，用于支付国家退休金和其他福利（如失业救济）Abbreviation 缩写 **NIC**

National Insurance number /ˌnæʃ(ə)nəl ɪnˈʃʊərəns ˌnʌmbə/ *noun* a number given to each British citizen, which is the number by which he or she is known to the social security services 国民保险号码：分配给每个英国公民的社会保障服务号码

National Savings & Investments /ˌnæʃ(ə)nəl ˌseɪvɪŋz ənd ɪnˈvestmənts/ *noun* a part of the Exchequer, a savings scheme for small investors including savings certificates and premium bonds 国民储蓄与投资计划：英国财政部针对小投资者的储蓄计划，它的内容包括储蓄券和有奖债券 Abbreviation 缩写 **NS&I**

National Savings Bank /ˌnæʃ(ə)nəl ˈseɪvɪŋz ˌbæŋk/ *noun* in the United Kingdom, a savings scheme established in 1861 as the Post Office Savings Bank and now operated by National Savings 国民储蓄银行：英国于 1861 年建立的一个储蓄规划，当时名为邮政储蓄银行，现在由国民储蓄部门经营 Abbreviation 缩写 **NSB**

National Savings Certificate /ˌnæʃ(ə)nəl ˈseɪvɪŋz səˌtɪfɪkət/ *noun* in the United Kingdom, either a fixed-interest or an index-linked certificate issued for two or five year terms by National Savings with returns that are free of income tax 国民储蓄券：英国由国民储蓄部门发行的两年或五年期固定利息或指数挂钩债券，其收益不用交纳所得税 Abbreviation 缩写 **NSC**

National Savings Stock Register /ˌnæʃ(ə)nəl ˌseɪvɪŋz ˈstɒk ˌredʒɪstə/ *noun* an organisation, run by the Department for National Savings, which gives private individuals the opportunity to buy British government stocks by post without going through a stockbroker 国民储蓄证券登记处：英国国民储蓄部门的下属机构，它使个人投资者不用通过证券经纪人也可以邮购英国政府证券

NBV *abbr* net book value 账面净值

negative carry /ˌnegətɪv ˈkæri/ *noun* a deal where the cost of finance is more than the return on the capital used 负经营：财务成本超过投入资本所产生回报的交易

negative cash flow /ˌnegətɪv ˈkæʃ fləʊ/ *noun* a situation where more money is going out of a company than is coming in 负现金流量：公司资金流出超过资金注入的状况

negative equity /ˌnegətɪv ˈekwɪti/ *noun* a situation where a house bought with a mortgage becomes less valuable than the money borrowed to buy it because of falling house prices 负资产：由于房价下跌，按揭购买的住房价值低于用来购买它的借款

negative goodwill /ˌnegətɪv gʊdˈwɪl/ *noun* negative goodwill arises when the aggregate fair values of the identifiable assets and liabilities of the entity exceed the acquisition cost 负商

誉：实体的可辨认资产与负债的市价总额超过收购成本

negative yield curve /ˌnegətɪv ˈjiːld kɜːv/ *noun* a situation where the yield on a long-term investment is less than that on a short-term investment 负收益曲线：长期投资回报率低于短期投资回报率

negotiable instrument /nɪˌgəʊʃiəb(ə)l ˈɪnstrʊmənt/ *noun* a document which can be exchanged for cash, e.g. a bill of exchange or a cheque 流通票据：可变现的票据，如汇票或支票

negotiable order of withdrawal /nɪˌgəʊʃiəb(ə)l ˌɔːdə əv wɪðˈdrɔːəl/ *noun* a cheque written on a NOW account 可转让提款单：从 NOW 账户中签发的支票

negotiable paper /nɪˌgəʊʃiəb(ə)l ˈpeɪpə/ *noun* a document which can be transferred from one owner to another for cash 流通票据，可转让票据：可通过转让变现的票据

negotiate /nɪˈgəʊʃieɪt/ *verb* □ **to negotiate terms and conditions *or* a contract** to discuss and agree the terms of a contract 就条款(或合同)进行谈判 □ **he negotiated a £250,000 loan with the bank** he came to an agreement with the bank for a loan of £250,000 他与银行达成一项25万英镑贷款的协议 ■ *noun* to transfer financial instruments, e.g. bearer securities, bills of exchange, cheques, and promissory notes, to another person in return for a consideration 转让(金融凭证)

'...many of the large travel agency chains are able to negotiate even greater discounts'
"许多大型的连锁旅行社甚至能提供更高的折扣"［*Duns Business Month*《邓氏商业月刊》］

negotiation /nɪˌgəʊʃiˈeɪʃ(ə)n/ *noun* the discussion of terms and conditions in order to reach an agreement 谈判 □ **to enter into *or* to start negotiations** to start discussing a problem 开始谈判

'...after three days of tough negotiations, the company reached agreement with its 1,200 unionized workers'
"经过三天的艰苦谈判，公司与1,200名工会工人达成了协议"［*Toronto Star*《多伦多明星日报》］

nest egg /ˈnest eg/ *noun* money which someone has saved over a period of time, usually kept in an interest-bearing account and intended for use after retirement 储蓄金，存款：某人在一段时间内存款的总额，它通常存入附息账户，准备将来退休后使用

net /net/ *adjective* referring to a price, weight, pay, etc., after all deductions have been made 净的，纯的：作出相应扣除后所剩的价格、重量、工资等 ■ *verb* to make a true profit 净得 ○ *to net a profit of £10,000* 净赚一万英镑 (NOTE: **netting – netted**)

'...out of its earnings a company will pay a dividend. When shareholders receive this it will be net, that is it will have had tax deducted at 30 per cent'
"公司将从盈利中支付股利。股东最终拿到手的是扣除了30%所得税后的净股利"［*Investors Chronicle*《投资者纪事》］

net asset value per share /net ˌæset ˌvæljuː pə ˈʃeə/ *noun* the value of a company calculated by dividing the shareholders' funds by the number of shares issued 每股净值：股东资金除以

已发行股数得出的公司价值

net book value /net bʊk ˈvæljuː/ *noun* the historical cost of an asset less any accumulated depreciation or other provision for diminution in value, e.g., reduction to net realisable value, or asset value which has been revalued downwards to reflect market conditions 账面净值:一项资产的历史成本减去所有累计折旧或其他减值准备金(如可变现净值的减少,或因市场变化而估值降低的资产价值) Abbreviation 缩写 **NBV**. Also called 亦称作 **written-down value**

net borrowings /ˌnet ˈbɒrəʊɪŋz/ *plural noun* a company's borrowings, less any cash the company is holding in its bank accounts 借入资本净值:公司借款减去银行存款

net cash flow /net ˈkæʃ fləʊ/ *noun* the difference between the money coming in and the money going out 净现金流量:公司现金收入与支出之差

net current assets /net ˌkʌrənt ˈæsets/ *plural noun* the current assets of a company, i.e. cash and stocks, less any liabilities 净流动资产:公司流动资产(即现金和股票)减去负债 Also called 亦称作 **net working capital**

net current liabilities /net ˌkʌrənt ˌlaɪəˈbɪlɪtiz/ *plural noun* current liabilities of a company less its current assets 净流动负债:流动负债减流动资产

net dividend per share /net ˌdɪvɪdend pə ˈʃeə/ *noun* the dividend per share after deduction of personal income tax 每股净股利:扣除个人所得税后的每股股利

net income /net ˈɪnkʌm/ *noun* a person's or organisation's income which is left after taking away tax and other deductions 净收入:减去税款和其他扣除额后的个人或组织收入

net interest /ˌnet ˈɪntrəst/ *noun* gross interest less tax 净利息:总利息减去税款

net liquid funds /ˌnet ˌlɪkwɪd ˈfʌndz/ *noun* an organisation's cash plus its marketable investments less its short-term borrowings, such as overdrafts and loans 净流动资金:现金加有价证券再减去短期借款(如透支和贷款)

net loss /ˌnet ˈlɒs/ *noun* an actual loss, after deducting overheads 净损失:扣除间接费用后的实际损失

net margin /ˌnet ˈmɑːdʒɪn/ *noun* the percentage difference between received price and all costs, including overheads 净利润:赚取的价格与全部费用(包括间接费用)的百分比差额

net present value /ˌnet ˌprezənt ˈvæljuː/ *noun* the value of future cash inflows less future cash outflows discounted at a certain discount rate, usually the company's cost of capital 净现值:以一定折现率折现后的未来预期现金流入减去预期现金流出的价值,通常为企业的资金成本 Abbreviation 缩写 **NPV**

net price /ˌnet ˈpraɪs/ *noun* the price of goods or services which cannot be reduced by a discount 净价,实价:不能再打折的商品或劳务价格

net profit /ˌnet ˈprɒfɪt/ *noun* the amount by which income from sales is larger than all expenditure 净利润:销售收入减去所有支出后的收益 Also called 亦称作 **profit after tax**

net profit ratio /net ˌprɒfɪt ˈreɪʃiəʊ/ *noun* the ratio of an organisation's net profit to its total net sales. Comparing the net profit ratios of companies in the same sector shows which are the most efficient 纯益比率:净利润与净销售总额的比率。将同行业公司间的纯益比率进行对比,可以看出哪个公司效率最高

net realisable value /net ˌrɪəlaɪzəb(ə)l ˈvæljuː/ *noun* the price at which goods in stock could be sold, less any costs incurred in making the sale 可变现净值,净变现价值:现有存货中可供销售的商品的价格减去其所有销售费用后的价值 Abbreviation 缩写 **NRV**

net receipts /ˌnet rɪˈsiːts/ *plural noun* receipts after deducting commission, tax, discounts, etc. 纯收入:扣除佣金、税款、折扣等后的收入

net relevant earnings /net ˌreləv(ə)nt ˈɜːnɪŋz/ *plural noun* earnings which qualify for calculating pension contributions and against which relief against tax can be claimed. Such earnings can be income from employment which is not pensionable, profits of a self-employed sole trader, etc. 相关净收益:可纳入养老金缴款计算并可申领税收减免的收益。这些收益包括未上养老金的工作收入、个体经商者的利润等

net residual value /net rɪˌzɪdjʊəl ˈvæljuː/ *noun* the anticipated proceeds of an asset at the end of its useful life, less the costs of selling it, e.g., transport and commission. It is used when calculating the annual charge for the straight-line method of depreciation 净残值:资产使用年限结束时的预计出售所得金额减去销售成本(如运费和佣金)。它用于计算直接折旧法下的年费 Abbreviation 缩写 **NRV**

net return /ˌnet rɪˈtɜːn/ *noun* a return on an investment after tax has been paid 净投资回报,净收益:税后投资回报

net salary /ˌnet ˈsæləri/ *noun* the salary which is left after deducting tax and National Insurance contributions 净工资收入,净收益:扣除税款及国民保险缴款后剩余的工资

net sales /ˌnet ˈseɪlz/ *plural noun* the total amount of sales less damaged or returned items and discounts to retailers 净销售额:销售总额减去损坏或退货以及给零售商的折扣

net turnover /net ˈtɜːnˌəʊvə/ *noun* turnover before VAT and after trade discounts have been deducted 净营业额:已扣除贸易折扣但尚未付增值税(VAT)的营业额

net working capital /net ˌwɜːkɪŋ ˈkæpɪt(ə)l/ *noun* same as 同 **net current assets**

net worth /net ˈwɜːθ/ *noun* the value of all the property of a person or company after taking away what the person or company owes 净值:剔除欠款后的个人或公司全部财产价值 ○ *The upmarket product is targeted at individuals of high net worth*. 高端市场产品定位在高收入人群。

net yield /net ˈjiːld/ *noun* the profit from investments after deduction of tax 净投资收益,净收益:税后投资利润

new issues department /njuː ˈɪʃuːz dɪˌpɑːtmənt/ *noun* the section of a bank which deals with issues of new shares 新发行部:银行负责新股发行的部门

NI *abbr* National Insurance 国民保险

NIC /ˌen aɪ ˈsiː/ *abbr* National Insurance contributions 国民保险金分担额,国民保险缴款

NIF *abbr* note issuance facility 票据发行融资便利,票据发行融通

night safe /ˈnaɪt seɪf/ *noun* a safe in the outside wall of a bank, where money and documents can be deposited at night, using a special door 夜间保险箱:安装在银行外墙上的一种保险箱,顾客可在夜间通过特设的入口将钱、文件存放在里面

nil /nɪl/ *noun* zero or nothing 零,无 ○ *The advertising budget has been cut to nil*. 广告预算被取消了。

nil paid shares /ˌnɪl peɪd ˈʃeəz/ *plural noun* new shares which have not yet been paid for 未付款新股票,未缴股款的新股票

nil return /ˌnɪl rɪˈtɜːn/ *noun* a report showing no sales, income, tax, etc. 零回报:报告中未显示销售额、收入、税款等

no-claims bonus /nəʊˈkleɪmz ˌbəʊnəs/ *noun* **1.** a reduction of premiums on an insurance policy because no claims have been made 无赔偿奖励:保险公司对没有提出索赔的保险单的保险费减免 **2.** a lower premium paid because no claims have been made against the insurance policy 无赔款折扣:保险公司对没有提出索赔的保险单收取较低的保险费

nominal /ˈnɒmɪn(ə)l/ *adjective* (*of a payment*) very small (付款)名义上的;极少的 ○ *They are paying a nominal rent*. 他们只是象征性地付了点租金。○ *The employment agency makes a nominal charge for its services*. 职业介绍所只收取极少的服务费。

nominal account /ˌnɒmɪn(ə)l əˈkaʊnt/ *noun* an account for recording transactions relating to a particular type of expense or receipt 名义账户,虚账户:只记录与特定收入和支出相关的交易的账户

nominal interest rate /ˌnɒmɪn(ə)l ˈɪntrəst reɪt/ *noun* an interest rate expressed as a percentage of the face value of a bond, not on its market value 名义利率:以债券面值(而不是市场价值)的一定百分比来表示的利率

nominal ledger /ˌnɒmɪn(ə)l ˈledʒə/ *noun* a book which records a company's transactions in the various accounts 名义分类账:记录公司各个账户交易的账簿

nominal share capital /ˌnɒmɪn(ə)l ˈʃeə ˌkæpɪt(ə)l/ *noun* the total of the face value of all the shares which a company is authorised to issue according to its memorandum of association 名义股本:按照公司章程授权公司发行的所有股票的账面价值总额

nominal value /ˌnɒmɪn(ə)l ˈvæljuː/ *noun* same as 同 **face value**

nominee /ˌnɒmɪˈniː/ *noun* a person who is nominated, especially someone who is appointed to deal with financial matters on your behalf (尤指代表自己处理财务事务的)被提名者,被任命者

nominee account /ˌnɒmɪˈniː əˌkaʊnt/ *noun* an account held on behalf of someone 代理账户:代表他人持有的账户

non- /nɒn/ *prefix* not 非;无;不(是)

non-acceptance /ˌnɒnəkˈseptəns/ *noun* a situation in which the person who is to pay a bill of exchange does not accept it 不承兑:付款人拒绝承兑汇票的行为

non-cash item /ˌnɒnˌkæʃ ˈaɪtəm/ *noun* an item in an income statement that is not cash, such as depreciation expenses, and gains or losses from investments 非现金项目:收益表中非现金的项目,如折旧开支、投资盈亏等

noncash items /ˌnɒnkæʃ ˈaɪtəmz/ *plural noun* cheques, drafts and similar items which are not in the form of cash 非现金项目:非现金形式的支票、汇票及类似项目

non-cumulative preference share /ˌnɒnˌkjuːmjʊlətɪv ˈpref(ə)rəns ˌʃeə/ *noun* a preference share where, if the dividend is not paid in the current year, it is lost 非累积优先股:如当年未支付股利,则股利自动损失的优先股

non-historic /ˌnɒnhɪˈstɒrɪk/ *adjective* not calculated on a historical cost basis 非历史的:不按历史成本计算的

non-monetary /ˌnɒnˈmʌnɪt(ə)ri/ *adjective* items or assets which are not money, and can be valued at a higher value than their original purchase price 非货币性的:非货币的项目或资产,可以按高于原始买入价衡量其价值

non-negotiable instrument /nɒnnɪˌgəʊʃəb(ə)l ˈɪnstrʊmənt/ *noun* a document which cannot be exchanged for cash, e.g. a crossed cheque 非流通票据:不可变现的票据,如划线支票

non-performing loan /nɒnpɜːˌfɔːmɪŋ ˈləʊn/ *noun US* a loan where the borrower is not likely to pay any interest nor to repay the principal, as in the case of loans to Third World countries by western banks (美)不良贷款,不履约贷款:借款人不大可能支付任何利息或偿还本金的贷款,如西方银行给予第三世界国家的贷款

non-profit-making organization /ˌnɒnˈprɒfɪtˌmeɪkɪŋ ɔːgənaɪˌzeɪʃən/ , **non-profit organisation** /nɒnˈprɒfɪt ɔːgənaɪˌzeɪʃ(ə)n/ *noun* an organisation which is not allowed by law to make a profit 非盈利组织 ○ *Non-profit-making organisations are exempted from tax.* 非盈利组织不用纳税。(NOTE: Non-profit organisations include charities, professional associations, trade unions, and religious, arts, community, research, and campaigning bodies. The US term is **non-profit corporation** 非盈利组织包括慈善机构、专业协会、工会以及宗教、艺术、社区、研究及社会活动团体。美国用语为 **non-profit corporation**)

non-recurring items /nɒnrɪˌkɜːrɪŋ ˈaɪtəmz/ *plural noun* special items in a set of accounts which appear only once 临时项目,非经常性项目:在一整套账目中只出现一次的特别项目

non-refundable /ˌnɒnrɪˈʃʌndəb(ə)l/ *adjective* not possible to refund 不偿还的,不退款的 ○ *You will be asked to make a non-refundable deposit.* 你要交纳不退还的押金。

non-resident /ˌnɒnˈrezɪd(ə)nt/ *noun*, *adjective* a person who is not considered a resident of a country for tax purposes 非本国居民(的):出于纳税考虑而被视为非本国居民的人 ○ *He has a non-resident bank account.* 他有一个非本国居民的银行账户。

non-tariff barriers /nɒnˌtærɪf ˈbæriəz/ *noun* barriers to international trade other than tariffs. They include over-complicated documentation; verification of goods for health and safety reasons and blocked deposits payable by importers to obtain foreign currency 非关税壁垒:非关税的国际贸易壁垒。这些壁垒包括文件审查过于复杂;以健康和安全为由进行商品检验;阻截

进口商的应付货款以获得外币 Abbreviation 缩写 **NTBs**

non-taxable /ˌnɒnˈtæksəb(ə)l/ *adjective* not subject to tax 不需纳税的 ○ *non-taxable income* 免税收入 ○ *Lottery prizes are non-taxable*. 彩票中奖所得不用纳税。

non-trade creditor /ˌnɒnˈtreɪd ˌkredɪtə/ *noun* a creditor who is not owed money in the normal trade of a business, e.g. a debenture holder or the Inland Revenue 非贸易债权人:不是在正常商业贸易中产生债务的债权人,如债券持有者或国内税务局

non-voting shares /nɒnˈvəʊtɪŋ ʃeəz/ *plural noun* shares which do not allow the shareholder to vote at meetings 无表决权股票:在股东大会上无投票权的股票 ➪ 参阅 **A shares**

normal /ˈnɔːm(ə)l/ *adjective* usual or which happens regularly 普通的;正常的 ○ *Normal deliveries are made on Tuesdays and Fridays*. 正常交付时间是星期二和星期五。○ *Now that supply difficulties have been resolved we hope to resume normal service as soon as possible*. 既然供应问题已经解决,我们希望尽快恢复正常服务。

normalise /ˈnɔːməlaɪz/ , **normalize** *verb* **1.** to store and represent numbers in a preagreed form, usually to provide maximum precision 标准化,规范化:以先验形式存贮和呈列数据,以获得最大的精确度 **2.** to convert data into a form which can be read by a particular computer system 普通化,规范化:将数据转化成计算机特定系统能读取的格式

normal loss /ˌnɔːm(ə)l ˈlɒs/ *noun* loss which is usual in the type of business being carried on, e.g. loss of small quantities of materials during the manufacturing process 正常损失,正常损耗:生产过程中正常的损失,如损耗的少量材料

notary public /ˌnəʊtəri ˈpʌblɪk/ *noun* a lawyer who has the authority to witness documents and spoken statements, making them official 公证人,公证员(NOTE: The plural is **notaries public** 复数为 **notaries public**)

note /nəʊt/ *noun* **1.** a short document or piece of writing, or a short piece of information 通知;留言 ○ *to send someone a note* 给某人发个通知 ○ *I left a note on her desk*. 我在她桌上留了一个便条。**2.** paper showing that money has been borrowed 借据,借条

note issuance facility /nəʊt ˈɪʃuəns fəˌsɪlɪti/ *noun* a credit facility where a company obtains a loan underwritten by banks and can issue a series of short-term eurocurrency notes to replace others which have expired 票据发行融资便利,票据发行融通:公司借以获得银行贷款的一种信贷融资,并可由公司发行一系列短期欧洲货币票据来取代已到期的票据 Abbreviation 缩写 **NIF**

note of hand /ˌnəʊt əv ˈhænd/ *noun* a document stating that someone promises to pay an amount of money on an agreed date 期票,本票:表明某人承诺在某日支付一定金额的文件

notice of coding /ˌnəʊtɪs əv ˈkəʊdɪŋ/ *noun* a notice which informs someone of the code number given to indicate the amount of tax allowances a person has 代码通知:告知某人其税务优惠金额代码的通知

notional /ˈnəʊʃ(ə)n(ə)l/ *adjective*

probable but not known exactly or not quantifiable 假想的；名义上的；观念上的

notional income /ˌnəʊʃ(ə)n(ə)l ˈɪnkʌm/ *noun* an invisible benefit which is not money or goods and services 名义收入：不以货币、商品或劳务形式存在的隐性收益

notional rent /ˌnəʊʃ(ə)n(ə)l ˈrent/ *noun* a sum put into accounts as rent where the company owns the building it is occupying and so does not pay an actual rent 名义租金：公司在报表上将其拥有并自用的建筑物列示为出租，并相应地在账上计入租金

not negotiable /ˌnɒt nɪˈgəʊʃiəb(ə)l/ *noun* wording appearing on a cheque or bill of exchange that it is deprived of its inherent quality of negotiability. When such a document is transferred from one person to another, the recipient obtains no better title to it than the signatory 不可流通，不得转让：支票或汇票上关于该汇票不可流通或不可转让的说明。该票据转让给他人时，受让人对它只享有与签署人一样的权利 ◊ 参阅 **negotiable instrument**

novation /nəʊˈveɪʃ(ə)n/ *noun* an agreement to change a contract by substituting a third party for one of the two original parties 合同更新：以第三方代替原签约双方中某一方的合同变更协议

NOW account /ˈnaʊ əˌkaʊnt/ *noun US* an interest-bearing account with a bank or savings and loan association, on which cheques called 'negotiable orders of withdrawal' can be drawn (美)可转让提款单账户：在银行或储蓄与贷款机构开立的附息账户，并可在该账户开出标有"可转让提款单"的支票 Full form 全称为 **negotiable order of withdrawal account**

NPV *abbr* net present value 净现值

NRV *abbr* **1.** net realisable value 可变现净值 **2.** net residual value 净残值

NS&I *abbr* National Savings & Investments (英国)国民储蓄与投资计划

NSB *abbr* National Savings Bank 国民储蓄银行

NSC *abbr* National Savings Certificate 国民储蓄券

NTBs *abbr* non-tariff barriers 非关税壁垒

number /ˈnʌmbə/ *noun* **1.** a quantity of things or people 数目 ○ *The number of persons on the payroll has increased over the last year.* 在编人员比去年增加了。○ *The number of days lost through strikes has fallen.* 因罢工耽误的天数减少了。**2.** a printed or written figure that identifies a particular thing 编号，号码 ○ *Please write your account number on the back of the cheque.* 请把你的账号写在支票背面。○ *If you have a complaint to make, always quote the batch number.* 投诉时务请说明批号。○ *She noted the cheque number in the ledger.* 她把支票号码记在分类账里。■ *verb* to put a figure on a document 作编号 ○ *to number an order* 给订单编号 ○ *I refer to your invoice numbered 1234.* 我查询的是你的1234号发票。

numbered account /ˌnʌmbəd əˈkaʊnt/ *noun* a bank account, usually in Switzerland, which is referred to only by a number, the name of the person holding it being kept secret 编号账户：(一般在瑞士)对账户持有者的姓名保密而以号码指代的银行账户

numeral /ˈnjuːm(ə)rəl/ *noun* a character or symbol which represents a number 数字

numeric /njuːˈmerɪk/ , **numerical** /njuːˈmerɪk(ə)l/ *adjective* referring to numbers 数字的

numerical order /njuːˌmerɪk(ə)l ˈɔːdə/ *noun* an arrangement by numbers 号数,数字顺序 ○ *Put these invoices in numerical order*. 按号码顺序整理好这些发票。

numeric data /njuːˌmerɪk ˈdeɪtə/ *noun* data in the form of figures 数据资料

numeric keypad /njuːˌmerɪk ˈkiːpæd/ *noun* the part of a computer keyboard which is a programmable set of numbered keys 数字键盘区:计算机键盘的一部分,由一系列数字键组成

O

O & M *abbr* organisation and methods 组织与方法

OAP *abbr* old age pensioner 领养老金者，领退休金者

objective /əb'dʒektɪv/ *noun* something which you hope to achieve 目标 ○ *The company has achieved its objectives*. 公司实现了目标。○ *We set the sales forces specific objectives*. 我们给销售人员制定了具体目标。○ *Our recruitment objectives are to have well-qualified and well-placed staff*. 我们希望招聘到高素质且岗位对口的员工。

objectivity /ˌɒbdʒek'tɪvɪti/ *noun* a lack of any opinion or bias 客观性

obligation /ˌɒblɪ'geɪʃ(ə)n/ *noun* **1.** a duty to do something 义务 ○ *There is no obligation to help out in another department*. 没有帮助其他部门的义务。○ *There is no obligation to buy*. 没有义务购买。□ **to fulfil your contractual obligations** to do what is stated in a contract 履行合同义务 **2.** a debt 债务 □ **to meet your obligations** to pay your debts 偿还债务

obsolescence /ˌɒbsə'les(ə)ns/ *noun* the process of a product going out of date because of progress in design or technology, and therefore becoming less useful or valuable（产品因设计或技术进步而变得）过时，陈旧

obsolete /'ɒbsəliːt/ *adjective* no longer used 已废弃的，过时的 ○ *Computer technology changes so fast that hardware soon becomes obsolete*. 计算机技术日新月异，硬件很快就过时了。

occupational /ˌɒkjʊ'peɪʃ(ə)nəl/ *adjective* referring to a job 职业的

occupational pension /ˌɒkjʊpeɪʃ(ə)nəl 'penʃən/ *noun* a pension which is paid by the company by which an employee has been employed 职业退休金：由曾雇佣该员工的公司支付的退休金

occupational pension scheme /ˌɒkjʊpeɪʃ(ə)nəl 'penʃən skiːm/ *noun* a pension scheme where the employee gets a pension from a fund set up by the company he or she has worked for, which is related to the salary he or she was earning 职业退休金计划：退休的雇员从公司所设立的基金中提取养老金，具体金额同退休前工资相挂钩的一种退休金计划 Also called 亦称作 **company pension scheme**

occupier /'ɒkjʊpaɪə/ *noun* a person who lives in a property（其项房地产的）居住者，住户

O/D *abbr* overdraft 透支

odd lot /ˌɒd 'lɒt/ *noun* **1.** a group of miscellaneous items for sale at an auction（拍卖中的）零批，零星交易 **2.** a group of miscellaneous items, such as a small block of shares 零散物品（如零

星股票）

Oeic *abbr* open-ended investment company 开放式投资公司，股份不定投资公司

off /ɒʃ/ *adverb* **1.** not working or not in operation 不工作，休假；无效 ○ *to take three days off* 休假三天 ○ *The agreement is off.* 协议无效。○ *They called the strike off.* 他们呼吁停止罢工。○ *We give the staff four days off at Christmas.* 圣诞节我们给员工放假四天。○ *It's my day off tomorrow.* 明天我休息。**2.** taken away from a price （从价格中）扣除 ○ *We give 5% off for quick settlement.* 我们对快速结账者给予5%的折扣。**3.** lower than a previous price 低于前价格 ○ *The shares closed 2% off.* 股市收盘时下挫2%。■ *preposition* **1.** subtracted from 从…减去 ○ *to take £25 off the price* 降价25英镑 ○ *We give 10% off our usual prices.* 我们打九折。**2.** not included …外的 □ **items off balance sheet** *or* **off balance sheet assets** financial items which do not appear in a balance sheet as assets, such as equipment acquired under an operating lease 表外项目，资产负债表外项目：不呈列在资产负债表上的财务项目，如通过营业租赁获得的设备

'...its stock closed Monday at $21.875 a share in NYSE composite trading, off 56% from its high last Jul'

"星期一，其股票在纽约证券交易所综合交易以每股21.875美元收盘，比去年7月最高时下跌了56%"［*Wall Street Journal*《华尔街日报》］

off-balance-sheet financing /ɒfˌbælənsʃiːt ˈfaɪnænsɪŋ/ *noun* financing by leasing equipment instead of buying it, so that it does not appear in the balance sheet as an asset 资产负债表外筹资：通过租赁而非购买设备获得的融资，因此不将其作为一项资产列示在资产负债表内

offer /ˈɒfə/ *noun* **1.** a statement that you are willing to give or do something, especially to pay a specific amount of money to buy something 提供；递价，出价 ○ *to make an offer for a company* 出价收购一家公司 ○ *We made an offer of £10 a share.* 我们递价每股10英镑。○ *We made a written offer for the house.* 我们已给出该房屋的书面报价。○ *£1,000 is the best offer I can make.* 1,000英镑是我所能提供的最高递价。○ *We accepted an offer of £1,000 for the car.* 我们接受了1,000英镑购买这辆汽车的报价。□ **or near offer**, *US*（美）**or best offer** or an offer of a price which is slightly less than the price asked 或相近报价，或稍低报价 ○ *The car is for sale at £2,000 or near offer.* 这辆车售价为2,000英镑，可以还价。**2.** a statement that you are willing to sell something 出售，发盘：关于有意出售某物的声明 **3.** a statement that you are willing to employ someone 录用通知：关于愿意聘用某人的声明 □ **she received six offers of jobs** *or* **six job offers** six companies told her she could have a job with them 她收到六份工作邀请 **4.** a statement that a company is prepared to buy another company's shares and take the company over 收购要约：表明某公司准备购买另一公司的股份并接管该公司的声明 ■ *verb* **1.** to say that you are willing to pay a specific amount of money for something 出价：表明愿意为某物支付一定金额 ○ *to offer someone £100,000 for their* *house* 出价 10 万英镑购买某人的房子 ○ *She offered £10 a share*. 她出价每股 10 英镑。**2.** to say that you are willing to sell something 提出(出售)○ *We offered the house for sale*. 我们出售这所房子。○ *They are offering special prices on winter holidays in the USA*. 他们对美国冬季休假旅游提出特别报价。

offer document /ˈɒfə ˌdɒkjʊmənt/ *noun* a formal document where a company offers to buy shares at some price as part of a takeover bid 报价文件:公司就股份并购所出报价的正式文件,此文件为合并递价的一部分

offer for sale /ˌɒfə fə ˈseɪl/ *noun* a situation where a company advertises new shares for sale to the public as a way of launching itself on the Stock Exchange 公开发售:公司就新股的出售向公众广而告之,作为公司在证券交易所上市的一种手段(NOTE: The other ways of launching a company are a 'tender' or a 'placing' 公司上市的其他手段还有"招标"或"配售")

offering /ˈɒf(ə)rɪŋ/ *noun* an action of stating that you are prepared to sell something at some price 发售,要约出售:声明以一定价格出售某物的行为

'...shares of newly public companies posted their worst performance of the year last month as a spate of initial public offerings disappointed followers'
"由于有众多首次公开发行的证券令追随者大失所望,以至新上市公司的股票在上月的表现创年度最差"[*Wall Street Journal*《华尔街日报》]

'...if the partnership supports a sale, a public offering of shares would be set for as early as the fourth quarter'
"如果合伙人赞成出售,那么股票公开发售最早可在第四季度进行"[*Wall Street Journal*《华尔街日报》]

offering circular /ˈɒf(ə)rɪŋ ˌsɜːkjʊlə/ *noun* a document which gives information about a company whose shares are being sold to the public for the first time 招股公告:介绍首次公开发售股票的公司相关信息的文件

offeror /ˈɒfərə/ *noun* a person who makes an offer 发盘人,出价人

offer period /ˈɒfə ˌpɪəriəd/ *noun* a time during which a takeover bid for a company is open 招标期限:可以出价收购某公司的期间

offer price /ˈɒʃə praɪs/ *noun* the price at which sombodies sell new shares or units in a unit trust. The opposite, i.e. the buying price, is called the 'bid price', the difference between the two is the 'spread' 发盘价;出售价:新股或单位信托的单位出售价格。与之相对的是"买入价",两者之差称为"差价"

office hours /ˌɒfɪs ˈaʊəz/ *plural noun* the time when an office is open 办公时间 ○ *Do not make private phone calls during office hours*. 上班时间不允许打私人电话。

Office of Fair Trading /ˌɒfɪs əv feə ˈtreɪdɪŋ/ *noun* a government department which protects consumers against unfair or illegal business 公平贸易局:保护消费者免受不公平或不合法交易损害的政府部门 Abbreviation 缩写 **OFT**

Office of Management and Budget /ˌɒfɪs əv ˌmænɪdʒmənt ən ˈbʌdʒɪt/ *noun US* a government department which prepares the US federal budget (美)行政管理与预算局:负责编制美国联邦预算的政府部门

Abbreviation 缩写 **OMB**

Office of Thrift Supervision /ˌɒfɪs əv ˈθrɪft suːpəˌvɪʒ(ə)n/ *noun* a US government department which regulates the Savings and Loan Associations 储蓄管理局：负责管理买房和建房储蓄货款协会的美国政府部门

officer /ˈɒfɪsə/ *noun* a person who has an official position, especially an unpaid one in a club or other association 负责官员（尤指俱乐部或其他协会的无薪官员）○ *The election of officers takes place next week*. 负责人选举将于下周进行。

official /əˈfɪʃ(ə)l/ *adjective* from a government department or organization 官方的，政府的 ○ *She went to France on official business*. 她因公前往法国。○ *He left official documents in his car*. 他把官方文件落在车里了。○ *She received an official letter of explanation*. 她收到一份官方说明函。

official books of account /əˌfɪʃ(ə)l bʊks əv əˈkaʊnt/ *noun* the official financial records of an institution 官方账簿：某一社会公共机构财务的官方记录

Official List /əˌfɪʃ(ə)l ˈlɪst/ *noun* a daily publication by the London Stock Exchange of the highest and lowest prices recorded for each share during the trading session 官方牌价：伦敦证券交易所每日发布的交易时段内每种股票的最高和最低价格

official receiver /əˌfɪʃ(ə)l rɪˈsiːvə/ *noun* a government official who is appointed to run a company which is in financial difficulties, to pay off its debts as far as possible and to close it down 法定破产管理人：受委派的政府官员，负责对陷入财务困难的公司进行管理，并尽可能偿还所欠债务，并最终关闭该公司 ○ *The company is in the hands of the official receiver*. 该公司现由法定破产管理人接手。

official return /əˌfɪʃ(ə)l rɪˈtɜːn/ *noun* an official report 官方报告

off-line /ˌɒfˈlaɪn/ *adverb* not connected to a network or central computer 下线地：与网络或中央处理机脱离

offload /ɒfˈləʊd/ *verb* to pass something which you do not want to someone else 转手，脱手

offset /ɒfˈset/ *verb* to balance one thing against another so that they cancel each other out 抵销，冲销，补偿 ○ *to offset losses against tax* 抵销缴税带来的损失 ○ *Foreign exchange losses more than offset profits in the domestic market*. 国内市场的利润不足以抵销汇兑损失。（NOTE：**offsetting – offset**）

offshore /ˈɒfʃɔː/ *adjective*, *adverb* **1.** on an island or in the sea near to land 岛上的（地）；近海的（地）○ *an offshore oil field* 近海油田 ○ *an offshore oil platform* 海上钻井平台 **2.** on an island which is a tax haven 境外的（地）：在享有避税天堂之称的岛上 **3.** based outside a country, especially in a tax haven 海外的（地）：一国以外的地方，尤指避税港

offshore banking /ˌɒfʃɔː ˈbæŋkɪŋ/ *noun* banking in a tax haven 离岸银行业务：在避税港的银行业务

offshore finance subsidiary /ˌɒfʃɔː ˈfaɪnæns səbˌsɪdiəri/ *noun* a company created in another country to handle financial transactions, giving the owning company certain tax and legal advantages in its home country

离岸财务子公司：专门为处理财务事务而在另一国家建立的子公司，母公司可借此在本国获得某些税务及法律方面的优待（NOTE：The US term is **offshore financial subsidiary** 美国用语为 **offshore financial subsidiary**）

offshore financial centre /ˌɒfʃɔː faɪˈnænʃəl ˌsentə/ *noun* a country or other political unit that has banking laws intended to attract business from industrialised nations 离岸金融中心：指在银行法规上对其他工业化国家的企业较有吸引力的国家或行政区域

offshore fund /ˌɒfʃɔː ˈfʌnd/ *noun* a fund which is based outside the UK, and usualll in a country which has less strict taxation than in the UK, such as the Bahamas 境外资金：在英国以外的资金，通常设立在税收比英国宽松的国家，如巴哈马

off-the-job training /ˌɒfðədʒɒb ˈtreɪnɪŋ/ *noun* training given to emplolees away from their place of work, such as at a college or school 脱产培训：雇员在办公地点以外（如高校或中学）接受的培训

off-the-shelf company /ˌɒfðəˌʃelf ˈkʌmp(ə)ni/ *noun* a company which has been registered by an accountant or lawyer, and which is ready for sale to someone who wants to set up a new company quickly 现成公司：已由会计师或律师注册的公司，准备出售给那些想迅速成立一个新公司的人

OFT *abbr* Office of Fair Trading 公平贸易局

oil-exporting country /ˈɔɪlɪkˌspɔːtɪŋ ˌkʌntri/ *noun* a country which produces oil and sells it to others 石油输出国：生产及出售石油的国家

old age pension /ˌəʊld eɪdʒ ˈpenʃən/ *noun* a state pension given to people over some age (currently to a man who is 65 or to a woman who is 60) 养老金，退休金（现行规定是男性65岁、女性60岁以上可以领取）

old age pensioner /ˌəʊld eɪdʒ ˈpenʃ(ə)nə/ *noun* a person who receives the retirement pension 领养老金者，领退休金者 Abbreviation 缩写 **OAP**

OMB *abbr* Office of Management and Budget 行政管理与预算局

ombudsman /ˈɒmbʊdzmən/ *noun* a management employee who is given the freedom to move around the workplace to locate and remedy unfair practices 廉政专员，巡视员：可在工作场所内自由活动，以发现和纠正工作人员的不当行为（NOTE：plural is **ombudsmen** 复数为 **ombudsmen**）

'...radical changes to the disciplinary system, including appointing an ombudsman to review cases where complainants are not satisfied with the outcome, are proposed in a consultative paper the Institute of Chartered Accountants issued last month'
"特许会计师协会在上月发布的咨询文件中提出倡议，希望对纪律制度进行彻底变革，包括委任廉政专员就申诉者对判决结果不满的投诉进行复核"［*Accountancy*《会计学》］

omission /əʊˈmɪʃ(ə)n/ *noun* a thing which has been omitted, or the act of omitting something 忽略，遗漏

omit /əʊˈmɪt/ *verb* to leave something out, not to put something in 忽略，遗漏 ○ *Her assistant omitted the date when typing the contract.* 她的助理在打印合同时漏掉了日期。

oncosts /ˈɒnkɒsts/ *plural noun*

money spent in producing a product, which does not rise with the quantity of the product made 间接成本,固定成本 Also called 亦称作 **fixed costs**

on demand /ˌɒn dɪˈmɑːnd/ *adjective* used to describe an account from which withdrawals may be made without giving a period of notice 即期账户的:取款无需提前通知的

one-man business /ˌwʌnmæn ˈbɪznɪs/ , **one-man firm** /ˌwʌnmæn ˈfɜːm/ , **one-man company** /ˌwʌnmæn ˈkʌmp(ə)ni/ *noun* a business run by one person alone with no staff or partners 个体经营,个体户:仅由一人经营,没有员工或合伙人的业务

one-off /ˌwʌnˈɒf/ *adjective* done or made only once 一次性的 ○ *one-off item* 一次性项目 ○ *one-off deal* 一次性交易 ○ *one-off payment* 一次性付款

one-sided /ˌwʌnˈsaɪdɪd/ *adjective* favouring one side and not the other in a negotiation 单方的;偏袒的:只对谈判中的一方有利的

one-year money /ˌwʌnjɪə ˈmʌni/ *noun* money placed for one lear 一年期存款

online /ɒnˈlaɪn/;/ˈɒnlaɪn/ *adjective*, *adverb* linked via a computer directly to another computer, a computer network or, especially, the Internet; on the Internet 联机的(地);在线(的),联网的(地);在互联网上(的) ○ *The sales office is online to the warehouse*. 销售部门与仓库联网。○ *We get our data online from the stock control department*. 我们在网上从存货管理部门获得数据。

'...there may be a silver lining for 'clicks-and-mortar' stores that have both an online and a high street presence. Many of these are accepting returns of goods purchased online at their traditional stores. This is a service that may make them more popular as consumers become more experienced online shoppers'
"既有网上业务,也有实体经营的"虚拟与现实结合"型百货商店也许还有一丝机会。许多此类商店都在传统店面接受网上购物的退货。这种服务可能令他们更受顾客欢迎,因为如今的消费者已经越来越熟悉网上购物了"[*Financial Times*《金融时报》]

'...a survey found that even among experienced users—those who shop online at least once a month—about 10% abandoned a planned purchase because of annoying online delays and procedures'
"调查发现,即使在购物达人(每月最少网上购物一次)当中,也有约10%的人因为烦人的网络延迟和繁锁程序而取消计划好的购买"[*Financial Times*《金融时报》]

'...some online brokers failed to foresee the huge increase in private dealing and had problems coping with the rising volume. It has been the year when private investors were able to trade online quickly, cheaply, and on the whole, with little bother'
"由于对私人交易的极剧增多预见不足,导致不断上升的交易量令网上经纪人难以应付。当下则进入了一个私人投资者在线交易的年代,这种交易方式更快捷,成本更低,并且几乎不受外界干扰"[*Financial Times*《金融时报》]

on-the-job training /ˌɒnðədʒɒb ˈtreɪnɪŋ/ *noun* training given to employees at their place of work 在职培训

open /ˈəʊpən/ *adjective* **1.** at work, not closed 营业的 ○ *The store is open on Sunday mornings*. 这家商店周日上午营业。○ *Our offices are open from 9 to 6*. 我们的办公时间为上午9点到下午6点。○ *They are open for business every day of the week*. 他们每天都营

业。**2.** ready to accept something 开放的;准备接受的 ■ *verb* **1.** to start a new business 开办 ○ *She has opened a shop in the High Street*. 她在英国的高街商业区开了一家商店。○ *We have opened a branch in London*. 我们在伦敦开了一个分部。**2.** to start work, to be at work 开始办公,开始营业 ○ *The office opens at 9 a.m*. 早上 9 点开始办公。○ *We open for business on Sundays*. 我们周日照常营业。**3.** to begin something 开始 **4.** to set something up or make something available 开立,开具;提供 ○ *to open a bank account* 开立一个银行账户 ○ *to open a line of credit* 提供信贷额度 ○ *to open a loan* 提供贷款 **5.** □ **shares opened lower** share prices were lower at the beginning of the day's trading 股票低开:股票开盘时较低的价格

'... after opening at 79.1 the index touched a peak of 79.2 and then drifted to a low of 78.8'
"指数以 79.1 点开盘之后,摸高至 79.2 点,然后又回调到 78.8 的低点"[*Financial Times*《金融时报》]

open account /ˌəʊpən əˈkaʊnt/ *noun* an account where the supplier offers the purchaser credit without security 赊账,未结清账户:供应商向购买者提供无担保信用的账户

open cheque /ˌəʊpən ˈtʃek/ *noun* same as 同 **uncrossed cheque**

open credit /ˌəʊpən ˈkredɪt/ *noun* credit given to good customers without security(给予信誉良好客户的)无担保信贷

open-ended /ˌəʊpənˈendɪd/ *adjective* with no fixed limit or with some items not specified 开口的,无限制的;不定额的 ○ *They signed an open-ended agreement*. 他们签署了一份无限制协议。○ *The candidate was offered an open-ended contract with a good career plan*. 候选人获得一份开口合同和一个前程似锦的职业规划。(NOTE: The US term is **open-end** 美国用语为 **open-end**)

open-ended credit /ˌəʊpənˌendɪd ˈkredɪt/ *noun* same as 同 **revolving credit**

open-ended fund /ˌəʊpənˈendɪd fʌnd/ *noun* a fund such as a unit trust where investors buy units, the money paid being invested in a range of securities. This is as opposed to a closed fund, such as an investment trust, where the investor buys shares in the trust company, and receives dividends 开口基金,开端基金:投资者购买信托单位的基金(如单位信托),而支付的资金投资于一系列的证券。与之相对的是闭端基金(如投资信托),其投资者购买信托公司股票并收取股利

Open-ended investment company /ˌəʊpənˌendɪd ɪnˈvestmənt ˌkʌmp(ə)ni/ *noun* a new form of unit trust, in which the investor purchases shares at a single price, as opposed to the offer/bid pricing system used by ordinary unit trusts 开放式投资公司,股份不定投资公司:单位信托的一种新形式,投资者以单一价格购买股票,不同于普通单位信托所采用的报价或递价系统 Abbreviation 缩写 **Oeic**

open-ended management company /ˌəʊpənˌendɪd ˈmænɪdʒmənt ˌkʌmp(ə)ni/ *noun* a company that sells unit trusts 开放式管理公司,股份不定管理公司:出售单位信托的公司(NOTE: The US term is **open-**

end management company 美国用语为 **open-end management company**)

opening /ˈəʊp(ə)nɪŋ/ *noun* the act of starting a new business (新业务的)开办,开发 ○ *the opening of a new branch* 新分支机构的开办 ○ *the opening of a new market* or *of a new distribution network* 新市场(或新销售网络)的开发

opening balance /ˈəʊp(ə)nɪŋ ˌbæləns/ *noun* a balance at the beginning of an accounting period 期初余额:会计期初的余额

opening balance sheet /ˌəʊp(ə)nɪŋ ˈbæləns ʃiːt/ *noun* an account showing an organisation's opening balances 期初资产负债表:呈列期初余额的账目

opening bid /ˈəʊp(ə)nɪŋ bɪd/ *noun* the first bid at an auction (拍卖中的)首次出价,起拍价

opening entry /ˈəʊp(ə)nɪŋ ˌentri/ *noun* the first entry in an account 开始分录,开业分录:账目的第一笔分录

opening price /ˈəʊp(ə)nɪŋ praɪs/ *noun* a price at the start of a day's trading 开盘价:一天交易开始的价格

opening stock /ˈəʊp(ə)nɪŋ stɒk/ *noun* on a balance sheet, the closing stock at the end of one accounting period that is transferred forward and becomes the opening stock in the one that follows 期初存货:在资产负债表中,会计期末的存货结转成为下一会计期初的存货 (NOTE: The US term is **beginning inventory** 美国用语为 **beginning inventory**)

open market /ˌəʊpən ˈmaːkɪt/ *noun* a market where anyone can buy or sell 公开市场:任何人都可以参与买卖的市场

open-market value /ˌəʊpən-ˈmɑːkɪt ˌvæljuː/ *noun* the price that an asset or security would realise if it was offered on a market open to all 公开市场价值:资产或证券在市场上公开出售时可变现的价格

operate /ˈɒpəreɪt/ *verb* to be in force 生效 ○ *The new terms of service will operate from January 1st.* 新服务条款将于1月1日生效。○ *The rules operate on inland postal services only.* 这些规则只适用于国内邮政服务。

'...the company gets valuable restaurant locations which will be converted to the family-style restaurant chain that it operates and franchises throughout most parts of the US'
"这家公司拿到了若干开餐厅的黄金地段并决定将其开发成家庭式连锁餐厅,将在美国大部分地区设有分店并允许加盟"[*Fortune*《财富》]

operating /ˈɒpəreɪtɪŋ/ *noun* the general running of a business or of a machine 营业,经营;操作

'...the company blamed over-capacity and competitive market conditions in Europe for a £14m operating loss last year'
"公司将去年1,400万英镑的营业亏损归咎于欧洲市场产能过剩和竞争过于激烈"[*Financial Times*《金融时报》]

operating budget /ˈɒpəreɪtɪŋ ˌbʌdʒɪt/ *noun* a forecast of income and expenditure over a period of time 营业预算:一段时间内的收支预测

operating costing /ˌɒpəreɪtɪŋ ˈkɒstɪŋ/ *noun* costing which is based on the costs of services provided 营业成本法:以所提供的劳务成本为基础的成

本计算法

operating cycle /ˌɒpəreɪtɪŋ ˈsaɪk(ə)l/ *noun* the time it takes for purchases of materials for production to generate revenue from sales 营业周期：从购买生产所需的原材料到销售成品获得收入的时间

operating lease /ˈɒpəreɪtɪŋ liːs/ *noun* a lease which does not require the lessee company to show the asset acquired under the lease in its balance sheet but the annual rental charge for such assets must be disclosed in a note to the accounts 经营性租赁，服务性租赁：承租人不用将租赁资产列示在公司的资产负债表上，但该资产的年租金必须在报表的附注中披露

operating leverage /ˌɒpəreɪtɪŋ ˈliːvərɪdʒ/ *noun* the ratio of a business's fixed costs to its total costs. As the fixed costs have to be paid regardless of output, the higher the ratio, the higher the risk of losses in an economic downturn 经营杠杆：企业的固定成本与总成本的比率。由于固定成本与产量无关，故比率越高，经济衰退时损失的风险就越大

operating manual /ˈɒpəreɪtɪŋ ˌmænjʊəl/ *noun* a book which shows how to work a machine（机器的）操作手册

operating profit /ˈɒpəreɪtɪŋ ˌprɒfɪt/ *noun* the difference between a company's revenues and any related costs and expenses, not including income or expenses from any sources other than its normal methods of providing a good or a service 营业利润：公司收入减去任何有关成本与开支，但不包括非正常提供商品或劳务产生的收入或开支

operating statement /ˈɒpəreɪtɪŋ ˌsteɪtmənt/ *noun* a financial statement which shows a company's expenditure and income and consequently its final profit or loss 营业报表：列示公司收支及最后盈亏的财务报表 ○ *The operating statement shows unexpected electricity costs.* 营业报表显示电费过高。○ *Let's look at the operating statement to find last month's expenditure.* 我们在营业报表中查一查上月的开支吧。

operating system /ˈɒpəreɪtɪŋ ˌsɪstəm/ *noun* the main program which operates a computer（计算机）操作系统

operation /ˌɒpəˈreɪʃ(ə)n/ *noun* **1.** an activity or a piece of work, or the task of running something 业务，工作，任务 ○ *the company's operations in West Africa* 公司在西非的业务 ○ *He heads up the operations in Northern Europe.* 他主管北欧业务。**2.** □ **in operation** working or being used 正在工作；正在被使用 ○ *The system will be in operation by June.* 系统将在 6 月投入运营。○ *The new system came into operation on January 1st.* 新系统已于 1 月 1 日启用。

'...a leading manufacturer of business, industrial and commercial products requires a branch manager to head up its mid-western Canada operations based in Winnipeg'
"一个主要的工商业产品制造商要求一位分部经理负责公司以温尼伯为基地的加拿大中西部业务"［*Globe and Mail*（*Toronto*）《环球邮报》(多伦多)］

operational /ˌɒpəˈreɪʃ(ə)nəl/ *adjective* referring to the day-to-day activities of a business or to the way in which something is run 经营的；操作的：指企业的日常经营或某物的操作方法

operational budget /ˌɒpəreɪʃ(ə)nəl ˈbʌdʒɪt/ *noun* a forecast of expenditure on running a business 营业预算:业务经营的开支预测

operational costs /ˌɒpəreɪʃ(ə)nəl ˈkɒsts/ *plural noun* the costs of running a business (企业的)经营成本

operational gearing /ˌɒpəreɪʃ(ə)nəl ˈgɪərɪŋ/ *noun* a situation where a company has high fixed costs which are funded by borrowings 经营杠杆:公司借入大量资金来承担高额固定成本的情况

operational planning /ˌɒpəreɪʃ(ə)nəl ˈplænɪŋ/ *noun* the planning of how a business is to be run (企业的)营业规划

operational research /ˌɒpəreɪʃ(ə)nəl rɪˈsɜːtʃ/ *noun* a study of a company's way of working to see if it can be made more efficient and profitable 运筹学:对公司的运作方式进行分析,以提高经营效率和增加利润

operations review /ˌɒpəreɪʃ(ə)nz rɪˈvjuː/ *noun* an act of examining the way in which a company or department works to see how it can be made more efficient and profitable 经营分析:对公司或部门的运作方式进行考量,以分析如何提高效率和利润

operation time /ˌɒpəˈreɪʃ(ə)n taɪm/ *noun* a period of time that an operation requires for its operation cycle 操作时间:操作某道工序所需要的时间

operator /ˈɒpəreɪtə/ *noun* **1.** a person who works a machine (机器的)操作员 ○ *a keyboard operator* 键盘操作员 ○ *a computer operator* 计算机操作员 **2.** a person who runs a business 经理,经营者

'...a number of block bookings by American tour operators have been cancelled'
"美国旅行社订购的许多团体票已被取消"
[*Economist*《经济学家》]

opportunity cost /ˌɒpəˈtjuːnɪti kɒst/ *noun* 机会成本 **1.** the cost of a business initiative in terms of profits that could have been gained through an alternative plan [在进行企业经营计划选择时,被放弃的那套计划原本所能带来的利益] ○ *It's a good investment plan and we will not be deterred by the opportunity cost.* 这个投资计划很好,我们不会被机会成本吓倒。**2.** the value of another method of investment which could have been used, instead of the one adopted [在进行投资选择时,被放弃的那一套投资方案所具有的价值]

oppose /əˈpəʊz/ *verb* to try to stop something happening; to vote against something 反对:阻止某事发生;投票反对某事 ○ *A minority of board members opposed the motion.* 董事会少数成员反对该提议。○ *We are all opposed to the takeover.* 我们都反对这项收购。

optimal /ˈɒptɪm(ə)l/ *adjective* best 最佳的

optimise /ˈɒptɪmaɪz/ *verb* to allocate such things as resources or capital as efficiently as possible 优化,使最优化:以尽可能高效的方式分配资源或资本

optimum /ˈɒptɪməm/ *adjective* best 最好的,最适宜的 ○ *The market offers optimum conditions for sales.* 市场为销售提供了最佳条件。

option /ˈɒpʃən/ *noun* the opportunity to buy or sell something within a fixed period of time at a fixed price 期权,选择权:在指定期限内按指定价格

买卖某物的机会 □ **to take up an option or to exercise an option** to accept the option which has been offered and to put it into action 行使期权,行使选择权:接受并使用所提供的选择权 ○ *They exercised their option or they took up their option to acquire sole marketing rights to the product.* 他们行使选择权获得产品的独家经销权。

optional /ˈɒpʃ(ə)n(ə)l/ *adjective* able to be done or not done, taken or not taken, as a person chooses 非强性制的,可任意选择的 ○ *The insurance cover is optional.* 保险范围可任意选择。○ *Attendance at staff meetings is optional, although the management encourages employees to attend.* 雇员可以不参加员工会议,但管理层鼓励他们参加。

option contract /ˈɒpʃən ˌkɒntrækt/ *noun* a right to buy or sell shares at a fixed price 期权合同:按指定价格买卖股票的权利

option dealing /ˈɒpʃən ˌdiːlɪŋ/ *noun* the activity of buying and selling share options 期权交易:买卖股票期权的行为

option trading /ˈɒpʃ(ə)n ˌtreɪdɪŋ/ *noun* the business of buying and selling share options 期权贸易:有关股票期权买卖的贸易

order /ˈɔːdə/ *noun* **1.** the way in which records such as filing cards or invoices are arranged 顺序,次序:档案索引卡或发票的排列方式 ○ *in alphabetical* or *numerical order* 按字母(或数字)顺序 **2.** an official request for goods to be supplied 订货单○ *to give someone an order* or *to place an order with someone for twenty filing cabinets* 向某人发出 20 个档案柜的订单 ○ *The management ordered the workforce to leave the factory.* 管理层命令工人离开工厂。□ **to fill an order, to fulfil an order** to supply items which have been ordered 完成订单 ○ *We are so understaffed we cannot fulfil any more orders before Christmas.* 我们人手太少,在圣诞节前无法完成更多订单。□ **itemsavailable to order only** items which will be manufactured only if someone orders them 按订单生产的货物:仅在有人订货时才生产的货物 □ **on order** ordered but not delivered 已订购:已订购但未交付 ○ *This item is out of stock, but is on order.* 这种商品卖没了,但已重新订购。**3.** a document which allows money to be paid to someone 汇票,汇款单:允许将钱支付给某人的文件 ○ *She sent us an order on the Chartered Bank.* 她寄给我们一张在渣打银行提款的汇票。**4.** (*Stock Exchange*) an instruction to a broker to buy or sell(证券交易所)通知经纪人买卖的指令 **5.** □ **pay to Mr Smith or order** pay money to Mr Smith or as he orders 支付给史密斯先生或按其指令买卖 □ **pay to the order of Mr Smith** pay money directly to Mr Smith or to his account 直接付钱给史密斯先生(或存入其账户)■ *verb* to ask for goods to be supplied 订购 ○ *They ordered a new Rolls Royce for the managing director.* 他们为总经理订购了一辆新的劳斯莱斯轿车。

order book /ˈɔːdə bʊk/ *noun* a book which records orders received 订货簿:记录已收到订单的账簿

order fulfilment /ˈɔːdə fʊlˌfɪlmənt/ *noun* the process of supplying items which have been ordered 履行订单,完成订单

order processing /ˈɔːdə ˌprəusesɪŋ/ *noun* the work of dealing with orders 订单处理

ordinarily resident /ˌɔːd(ə)n(ə)rɪli ˈrezɪd(ə)nt/ *adjective* normally living in a country 常住的 ○ *Mr Schmidt is ordinarily resident in Canada*. 施密特先生是加拿大常住居民。

ordinary activities /ˌɔːd(ə)n(ə)ri ækˈtɪvɪtiz/ *noun* the usual trading of a company, that is, what the company usually does (公司的)普通业务

ordinary interest /ˌɔːd(ə)n(ə)ri ˈɪntrəst/ *noun* annual interest calculated on the basis of 360 days, as opposed to 'exact interest' which is calculated on 365 days 普通利息:按360天计算的年利息,而"精确利息"则按365天计算

ordinary resolution /ˌɔːd(ə)n(ə)ri ˌrezəˈluːʃ(ə)n/ *noun* a resolution put before an AGM, usually referring to some general procedural matter, and which requires a simple majority of votes to be accepted 一般决议,普通决议:提呈年度股东大会审议的决议,它通常与普通的程序性事项有关,只需简单多数通过即可采纳

ordinary share capital /ˌɔːd(ə)n(ə)ri ˈʃeə ˌkæpɪt(ə)l/ *noun* the capital of a company in the form of money paid for ordinary shares 普通股本:公司以通股筹集的资本

ordinary shareholder /ˌɔːd(ə)n(ə)ri ˈʃeəhəʊldə/ *noun* a person who owns ordinary shares in a company 普通股东,普通股股东:拥有公司普通股的个人

ordinary shares /ˈɔːd(ə)n(ə)ri ʃeəz/ *plural noun* normal shares in a company, which have no special benefits or restrictions 普通股(票):公司的普通股份,没有特别的权益或限制(NOTE: The US term is **common stock** 美国用语为 **common stock**)

organic growth /ɔːˌgænɪk ˈgrəʊθ/ *noun* same as 同 **internal growth**

organisation /ˌɔːgənaɪˈzeɪʃ(ə)n/, **organization** *noun* **1.** a way of arranging something so that it works efficiently 体制,编制 ○ *the organisation of the head office into departments* 将总部拆散并入各部门的组织结构 ○ *The chairman handles the organisation of the AGM*. 董事长负责组织年度股东大会。○ *The organisation of the group is too centralised to be efficient*. 该集团组织过于集权,有损效率。**2.** a group or institution which is arranged for efficient work 组织,机构,集团

'... working with a client base which includes many major commercial organizations and nationalized industries'
"客户群包括许多大型商业机构和国有化工业"[*Times*《泰晤士报》]

organisational /ˌɔːgənaɪˈzeɪʃ(ə)n(ə)l/, **organizational** *adjective* referring to the way in which something is organized 组织的 ○ *The paper gives a diagram of the company's organisational structure*. 此文勾勒出了该公司的组织框架。

organisation and methods /ˌɔːgənaɪzeɪʃ(ə)n ən ˈmeθədz/ *noun* a process of examining how an office works, and suggesting how it can be made more efficient 组织与方法:对工作进行剖析,并就如何提高办公效率给出建议的一套方法 Abbreviation 缩写 **O & M**

organise /ˈɔːgənaɪz/, **organize** *verb* **1.** to set up a system for doing something 组织 ○ *The company is organised* *into six profit centres*. 该公司由六个盈利中心组成。○ *The group is organised by sales areas*. 该集团按销售地区进行划拨管理。**2.** to arrange something so that it works 安排

'...we organize a rate with importers who have large orders and guarantee them space at a fixed rate so that they can plan their costs'
"我们针对大额订单进口商作了特殊费率安排,以固定费率保证他们的存货空间,以便他们对成本进行规划"[*Lloyd's List*《劳氏日报》]

other capital /ˌʌðə ˈkæpɪt(ə)l/ *noun* capital that is not listed in specific categories 其他资本:没有列在指定类别中的资本

other long-term capital /ˌʌðə ˌlɒŋtɜːm ˈkæpɪt(ə)l/ *noun* long-term capital that is not listed in specific categories 其他长期资本:没有列在指定类别中的长期资本

other long-term liabilities /ˌʌðə ˌlɒŋtɜːm ˌlaɪəˈbɪlɪtiz/ *noun* obligations with terms greater than one year on which there is no charge for interest in the next year 其他长期负债:期限超过一年且次年不收利息的债务

other short-term capital /ˌʌðə ˌʃɔːttɜːm ˈkæpɪt(ə)l/ *noun* short-term capital that is not listed in specific categories 其他短期资本:未列在指定类别中的短期资本

out /aʊt/ *adverb* □ **we are £20,000 out in our calculations** we have £20,000 too much or too little 我们的计算有两万英镑的出入

outgoings /ˈaʊtgəʊɪŋz/ *plural noun* money which is paid out 支出

outlay /ˈaʊtleɪ/ *noun* money spent, expenditure 支出

outlook /ˈaʊtlʊk/ *noun* a view of what is going to happen in the future 展望,预期,前景 ○ *The economic outlook is not good*. 经济前景暗淡。○ *The stock market outlook is worrying*. 股市前景堪忧。

'American demand has transformed the profit outlook for many European manufacturers'
"美国的需求状况改变了许多欧洲生产商的利润预期"[*Duns Business Month*《邓氏商业月刊》]

out-of-date cheque /ˌaʊtəvdeɪt ˈtʃek/ *noun* a cheque which has not been cleared because its date is too old, normally more than six months 过期支票:因时间太长(通常是六个月以上)而未结算的支票

out of pocket /ˌaʊt əv ˈpɒkɪt/ *adjective*, *adverb* having paid out money personally 自掏腰包的(地),用自己的钱支付的(地)○ *The deal has left me out of pocket*. 这笔生意让我赔了钱。

out-of-pocket expenses /ˌaʊtəvˌpɒkɪt ɪkˈspensɪz/ *plural noun* an amount of money paid back to an employee who has spent his or her personal money on company business 实付费用,自垫费用:报销员工为公司业务垫付的金额

output /ˈaʊtpʊt/ *noun* **1.** the amount which a company, person or machine produces 产量 ○ *Output has increased by 10%*. 产量增加了10%。○ *25% of our output is exported*. 我们25%的产出用于出口。**2.** information which is produced by a computer (计算机)输出

'...crude oil output plunged during the last

month and is likely to remain near its present level for the near future'
"原油产量上月下降，近期很可能保持在现有水平线上下。"[*Wall Street Journal*《华尔街日报》]

output per hour /ˌaʊtpʊt pər ˈaʊə/ *noun* the amount of something produced in one hour 每小时产量

output tax /ˈaʊtpʊt tæks/ *noun* VAT charged by a company on goods or services sold, and which the company pays to the government 产出税：公司因出售产品、提供劳务而向政府缴纳的增值税

outright /ˌaʊtˈraɪt/ *adverb*, *adjective* completely 完全地(的)

outside /ˈaʊtsaɪd/ *adjective*, *adverb* not in a company's office or building 外部的(地)：不在公司办公室或办公楼内部的(地)

outsource /ˈaʊtˌsɔːs/ *verb* to use a source outside a company or business to do the work that is needed 外包：使用公司或企业外的资源开展必要的工作

outsourcing /ˈaʊtsɔːsɪŋ/ *noun* the practice of obtaining services from specialist bureaux or other companies, rather than employing full-time members of staff to provide them 外包：从专业机构或其他公司获得服务，而非雇佣全职员工来提供

'...organizations in the public and private sectors are increasingly buying in specialist services—or outsourcing—allowing them to cut costs and concentrate on their core business activities'
"公共和私营组织越来越多地购买专业服务——或称为外包——以削减成本，同时集中发展他们的核心业务"[*Financial Times*《金融时报》]

outstanding /aʊtˈstændɪŋ/ *adjective* not yet paid or completed 未付的；未完成的

outstanding cheque /aʊtˌstændɪŋ ˈtʃek/ *noun* a cheque which has been written and therefore has been entered in the company's ledgers, but which has not been presented for payment and so has not been debited from the company's bank account 未兑付支票：已签发并已记入公司分类账，但未从公司账户中划走的支票

outvote /aʊtˈvəʊt/ *verb* to defeat someone in a vote 在投票选举中击败某人

overabsorbed overhead /ˌəʊvərəbzɔːbd ˈəʊvəhed/ *noun* an absorbed overhead which ends up by being higher than the actual overhead incurred 多分摊的间接费用：最终分摊的间接费用高于实际发生的费用

overabsorption /ˌəʊvərəbˈzɔːpʃ(ə)n/ *noun* a situation where the actual overhead incurred is less than the absorbed overhead 多分摊：实际发生的间接费用低于已分摊间接费用的情况

overall /ˌəʊvərˈɔːl/ *adjective* covering or including everything 综合的，总体的 ▫ **the company reported an overall fall in profits** the company reported a general fall in profits 公司报告总体利润下降

overall balance of payments /ˌəʊvərɔːl ˌbæləns əv ˈpeɪmənts/ *noun* the total of current and long-term balance of payments 总付款余额：即期和长期付款总余额

overall capitalisation rate /ˌəʊvərɔːl ˌkæpɪt(ə)laɪˈzeɪʃ(ə)n ˌreɪt/ *noun* net operating income, other than debt service, divided by value 总资本化比率

overall return /ˌəʊvərɔːl rɪˈtɜːn/ *noun* the aggregate of all the dividends received over an investment's life together with its capital gain or loss at the date of its realisation, calculated either before or after tax. It is one of the ways an investor can look at the performance of an investment 总投资回报:投资期限内获得的所有股利及其变现日的资本利得或亏损总和(税前或税后)。这是投资者了解投资表现的途径之一

overborrowed /ˌəʊvəˈbɒrəʊd/ *adjective* referring to a company which has very high borrowings compared to its assets, and has difficulty in meeting its interest payments 超量借入的:相对于公司资产来说,借入的资金太多,导致难支付利息

overcapitalised /ˌəʊvəˈkæpɪtəlaɪzd/, **overcapitalized** *adjective* referring to a company with more capital than it needs 资本过剩的:指公司的资本占有量多于实际需求

overcharge *noun* /ˈəʊvətʃɑːdʒ/ a charge which is higher than it should be 多收的费用○ *to pay back an overcharge* 退还多收费用 ■ *verb* /ˌəʊvəˈtʃɑːdʒ/ to ask someone for too much money 多收钱 ○ *They overcharged us for our meals*. 他们多收了我们的餐费。○ *We asked for a refund because we'd been overcharged*. 因为多收了钱,我们要求退款。

overdraft /ˈəʊvədrɑːft/ *noun* **1.** an amount of money which a company or person can withdraw from a bank account, with the bank's permission, despite the fact that the account is empty 透支:在经过银行同意的情况下,个人或公司可以从已无余额的银行账户中提取一定的金额 ○ *The bank has allowed me an overdraft of £5,000*. 银行允许我透支 5,000 英镑。Abbreviation 缩写 **O/D** (NOTE: The US term is **overdraft protection** 美国用语为 **overdraft protection**) □ **we have exceeded our overdraft facilities** we have taken out more than the overdraft allowed by the bank 我们超额透支了:我们的透支额超过了银行允许的限额 **2.** *US* a negative amount of money in an account, i. e. a situation where a cheque is more than the money in the account on which it is drawn (美)空头支票:账户中的负金额,即支票金额超过其提款账户的余额

overdraw /ˌəʊvəˈdrɔː/ *verb* to take out more money from a bank account than there is in it 透支:从银行账户中提取多于账面金额的钱款

overdue /ˌəʊvəˈdjuː/ *adjective* having not been paid on time 逾期未付的

overdue account /ˌəʊvədjuː əˈkaʊnt/ *noun* an account whose holder owes money that should have been paid earlier 逾期账户:持有人逾期未付款的账户

overestimate /ˌəʊvərˈestɪmeɪt/ *verb* to think something is larger or worse than it really is 过高估计,高估 ○ *She overestimated the amount of time needed to fit out the factory*. 她高估了装备工厂所需的时间。○ *They overestimated the costs of moving the offices to central London*. 他们高估了把办公地点挪到伦敦市中心的成本。

overgeared /ˌəʊvəˈgɪəd/ *adjective* referring to a company which has high borrowings in comparison to its assets

杠杆比率过高的：相对于公司资产来说，其借款金额过高

overhang /ˈəʊvəhæŋ/ *noun* a large quantity of shares or of a commodity or of unsold stock available for sale, which has the effect of depressing the market price 悬置：有大量的待售股票、商品或存货，对市场价格形成打压

overhead absorption rate /ˌəʊvəhed əbˈzɔːpʃən reɪt/ *noun* a rate at which production costs are increased to absorb higher overhead costs 制造费用分配率，间接费用分摊率：生产成本增加以分摊更高间接费用的比率

overhead budget /ˌəʊvəhed ˈbʌdʒɪt/ *noun* a plan of probable overhead costs 间接费用预算：关于可能发生间接费用的计划

overhead costs /ˌəʊvəhed ˈkɒsts/, **overhead expenses** /ˌəʊvəhed ɪkˈspensɪz/ *plural noun* same as 同 **overheads**

overhead cost variance /ˌəʊvəhed kɒst ˈveəriəns/ *noun* the difference between the overhead cost absorbed and the actual overhead costs incurred, both fixed and variable 间接制造费用成本差异：分摊的间接制造费用成本与实际间接费用成本之差

overhead expenditure variance /ˌəʊvəhed ɪkˈspendɪtʃə ˌveəriəns/ *noun* the difference between the budgeted overhead costs and the actual expenditure 间接制造费用支出差异：预算的间接费用与实际支出之差

overheads /ˈəʊvəhedz/ *plural noun* the indirect costs of the day-to-day running of a business, i. e. not money spent of producing goods, but money spent on such things as renting or maintaining buildings and machinery 间接费用，制造费用：企业日常运作的间接成本，即不是用于生产产品的资金，而是用于租赁或维护建筑物和机械的资金 ○ *The sales revenue covers the manufacturing costs but not the overheads.* 销售收入抵偿了制造成本，但不能弥补间接费用。(NOTE: The usual US term is **overhead** 美国用语为 **overhead**)

overlap profit /ˌəʊvəlæp ˈprɒfɪt/ *noun* a profit which occurs in two accounting periods, i. e. when two accounting periods overlap, and on which overlap relief can be claimed 重叠利润：在两个会计期间重叠的那部分时间段产生的利润，这些利润可以申领税务减免

overpaid /ˌəʊvəˈpeɪd/ *adjective* paid too much 多支付的 ○ *Our staff are overpaid and underworked.* 我们的雇员活干得少，工资倒拿得多。

overpay /ˌəʊvəˈpeɪ/ *verb* to pay too much to someone or for something 多支付 ○ *We overpaid the invoice by $245.* 这张发票我们多付了 245 美元。

overpayment /ˌəʊvəˈpeɪmənt/ *noun* an act of paying too much 多付

overrider /ˈəʊvəraɪdə/, **overriding commission** /ˈəʊvəraɪdɪŋ kəˌmɪʃ(ə)n/ *noun* a special extra commission which is above all other commissions 特别佣金：高于其他佣金的特殊额外佣金

overseas /ˌəʊvəˈsiːz/ *noun* foreign countries 海外，国外○ *The profits from overseas are far higher than those of the home division.* 来自海外的利润远高于国内部分。

overseas division /ˌəʊvəsiːz dɪ-

ˈvɪʒ(ə)n/ *noun* the section of a company dealing with trade with other countries 海外部：公司处理海外贸易的部门

overseas funds /ˌəʊvəˈsiːz fʌndz/ *plural noun* investment funds based in other countries 海外资金：设立在国外的投资资金

overseas markets /ˌəʊvəsiːz ˈmɑːkɪts/ *plural noun* markets in foreign countries 海外市场

overseas taxation /ˌəʊvəsiːz tækˈseɪʃ(ə)n/ *noun* ➧ 参阅 **double taxation, double taxation agreement**

overseas trade /ˌəʊvəsiːz ˈtreɪd/ *noun* same as 同 **foreign trade**

overspend /ˌəʊvəˈspend/ *verb* to spend too much 超支 □ **to overspend your budget** to spend more money than is allowed in your budget 预算超支，超出预算

overspending /ˌəʊvəˈspendɪŋ/ *noun* the act of spending more than is allowed 超支 ○ *The board decided to limit the overspending by the production departments.* 董事会决定对生产部门的超支进行限制。

overstate /ˌəʊvəˈsteɪt/ *verb* to make something seem more than it really is 夸大，夸张 ○ *the company accounts overstate the real profit* 公司报表夸大了实际利润

overstatement /ˌəʊvəˈsteɪtmənt/ *noun* making something seem more than it really is 夸大，夸张

overstock /ˌəʊvəˈstɒk/ *verb* to have a bigger stock of something than is needed 存货过多，存货积压

'Cash paid for your stock: any quantity, any products, overstocked lines, factory seconds'

"库存占用的现金涉及：任何数量、任何产品、在生产线的积压品、工厂次品" [*Australian Financial Review*《澳大利亚金融评论报》]

overstocks /ˈəʊvəstɒks/ *plural noun US* more stock than is needed to supply orders (美)库存过剩 ○ *We will have to sell off the overstocks to make room in the warehouse.* 我们必须廉价清空积压库存，以便腾出仓库空间。

over-the-counter market /ˌəʊvəðəˈkaʊntə ˌmɑːkɪt/ *noun* a secondary market in shares which are not listed on the main Stock Exchange 场外交易市场：不在主要证券交易所挂牌的股票二级市场

over-the-counter sales /ˌəʊvəðəˈkaʊntə ˌseɪlz/ *plural noun* the legal selling of shares which are not listed in the official Stock Exchange list, usually carried out by telephone 场外交易：合法出售不在官方证券交易所挂牌的股票，通常通过电话进行交易

overtime /ˈəʊvətaɪm/ *noun* hours worked in addition to your usual working hours 加班 ○ *to work six hours' overtime* 加班6小时 ○ *The overtime rate is one and a half times normal pay.* 加班费是正常工资的1.5倍。

overtime pay /ˈəʊvətaɪm peɪ/ *noun* pay for extra time worked 加班费

overtrading /ˌəʊvəˈtreɪdɪŋ/ *noun* a situation where a company increases sales and production too much and too quickly, so that it runs short of cash 超量交易：公司销售量及生产量增长过多过快，造成现金短缺的情况

overvalue /ˌəʊvəˈvæljuː/ *verb* to give a higher value to something or someone than is right 高估：对某事或某人的价值估计过高 □ **these shares are overvalued at £1.25** the shares are worth less than the £1.25 for which they are selling 这些股票 1.25 英镑的价格太高了：股票实际价值低于卖价 1.25 英镑

'...the fact that sterling has been overvalued for the past three years shows that currencies can remain above their fair value for very long periods'
"过去三年来英镑一直被高估，这一事实证明货币可以在高于其面值的价位上维持很长时间"[*Investors Chronicle*《投资者纪事》]

owe /əʊ/ *verb* to have to pay money 欠债，欠付 ○ *He owes the bank £250,000*. 他欠银行 25 万英镑。□ **they still owe the company for the stock they purchased last year** they have still not paid for the stock 他们去年购买该公司的股票还没付钱

owing /ˈəʊɪŋ/ *adjective* owed 欠付的，应付的 ○ *money owing to the directors* 应付董事款项 ○ *How much is still owing to the company by its debtors*? 债务人还欠公司多少钱？

own /əʊn/ *verb* to have or to possess 拥有，占有 ○ *She owns 50% of the shares*. 她拥有 50%的股份。

owner-occupier /ˌəʊnərˈɒkjʊpaɪə/ *noun* a person who owns the property in which he or she lives 业主居住者：对居住的房屋拥有所有权的人

owners' equity /ˌəʊnəz ˈekwɪti/ *noun* a value of the shares in a company owned by the owners of the company 所有者权益：公司所有者拥有的公司股份价值

ownership /ˈəʊnəʃɪp/ *noun* the fact of owning something 所有权

P

package /ˈpækɪdʒ/ *noun* goods packed and wrapped for sending by mail（待邮寄的）包裹 ○ *The Post Office does not accept bulky packages.* 邮局不接收体积太大的包裹。○ *The goods are to be sent in airtight packages.* 货物将使用密封包裹寄出。

package deal /ˌpækɪdʒ ˈdiːl/ *noun* an agreement which deals with several different items at the same time 一揽子交易：同时涉及多个不同项目的协议 ○ *They agreed a package deal which involves the construction of the factory, training of staff and purchase of the product.* 他们达成了一项一揽子交易，包括建造工厂、培训员工和购买产品。

paid /peɪd/ *adjective* **1.** for which money has been given（物品）已支付的 ○ *The invoice is marked 'paid'.* 发票上注有“已支付”。**2.** referring to an amount which has been settled（款额）已付清的 ○ *The order was sent carriage paid.* 寄出运费已付订单。

paid assistant /ˌpeɪd əˈsɪst(ə)nt/ *noun* an assistant who receives a salary 带薪助理

paid-up shares /ˌpeɪdʌp ˈʃeəz/ *noun* shares which have been completely paid for by the shareholders 已缴款股票：股东已缴清股款的股票

panic buying /ˈpænɪk ˌbaɪɪŋ/ *noun* a rush to buy something at any price because stocks may run out 抢购：因担心存货被卖空而不计价格地争相购买

paper /ˈpeɪpə/ *noun* **1.** a document which can represent money, e.g. a bill of exchange or a promissory note（可代替货币的）票据（如汇票或本票）**2.** shares in the form of share certificates 以股票形式存在的股份

paper loss /ˌpeɪpə ˈlɒs/ *noun* a loss made when an asset has fallen in value but has not been sold 账面损失，未实现损失：资产价值已下跌但尚未出售时的损失

paper millionaire /ˌpeɪpə ˌmɪljəˈneə/ *noun* a person who owns shares which, if sold, would be worth one million pounds or dollars 账面百万富翁：某人拥有的股票价值超过一百万英镑或美元

paper money /ˌpeɪpə ˈmʌni/ *noun* payments in paper form, e.g., cheques 纸币；票据（如支票）

paper offer /ˌpeɪpə ˈɒfə/ *noun* a takeover bid, where the purchasing company offers its shares in exchange for shares in the company being taken over as opposed to a cash offer 股权式收购：合并递价的一种，即以公司的股票交换被收购公司的股票，与现金收购相对

paper profit /ˌpeɪpə ˈprɒfɪt/ *noun* a profit on an asset which has increased in price but has not been sold 账面利润:资产价值上升但尚未出售时的利润 ○ *He is showing a paper profit of £25,000 on his investment*. 他的投资显示有2.5万英镑的账面利润。Also called 亦称作 **paper gain**, **unrealised profit**

paperwork /ˈpeɪpəwɜːk/ *noun* an office work, especially writing memos and filling in forms 文案工作 ○ *Exporting to Russia involves a large amount of paperwork*. 对俄罗斯的出口涉及大量文案工作。

par /pɑː/ *adjective* equal, at the same price 平价的,等值的

parameter /pəˈræmɪtə/ *noun* a fixed limit 参数,固定限额 ○ *The budget parameters are fixed by the finance director*. 预算参数由财务主管确定。○ *Spending by each department has to fall within agreed parameters*. 每个部门的开销不得超过议定限额。

parcel of shares /ˌpɑːs(ə)l əv ˈʃeəz/ *noun* a fixed number of shares which are sold as a group 一宗股票:作为一批出售的一定数量的股票 ○ *The shares are on offer in parcels of 50*. 股票按50股一宗发售。

parent company /ˈpeərənt ˌkʌmp(ə)ni/ *noun* a company which owns more than 50% of the shares of another company 母公司:拥有另一公司50%以上股权的公司

Pareto's Law /pəˈriːtəʊz lɔː/, **Pareto Effect** /pəˈriːtəʊ ɪˌfekt/ *noun* the theory that incomes are distributed in the same way in all countries, whatever tax regime is in force, and that a small percentage of a total is responsible for a large proportion of value or resources 帕累托定律:收入在所有国家(即使税收机制不同)都按相同方式分配,总体的一小部分提供大部分价值或资源的理论 Also called 亦称作 **eighty/twenty law**

pari passu /ˌpæri ˈpæsuː/ *adverb* a Latin phrase meaning 'equally'(拉丁语)同等,对等 ○ *The new shares will rank pari passu with the existing ones*. 新股将与现有股票享有同等权益。

parity /ˈpærɪti/ *noun* **1.** the state of being equal 相等 □ **the pound fell to parity with the dollar** the pound fell to a point where one pound equalled one dollar 英镑跌至与美元等值:英镑跌至一英镑等于一美元的价位 **2.** a situation when the price of a commodity, foreign currency, or security is the same in different markets 平价:商品、外汇或证券在不同市场的价格相同

'...the draft report on changes in the international monetary system casts doubt about any return to fixed exchange-rate parities'
"关于国际货币体系发展变化的初步报告对恢复固定汇率平价体系提出了质疑"[*Wall Street Journal*《华尔街日报》]

part exchange /ˌpɑːt ɪksˈtʃeɪndʒ/ *noun* the act of giving an old product as part of the payment for a new one 以旧折新:以旧产品作为新产品付款的一部分 ○ *to take a car in part exchange* 以旧车折换新车

partial /ˈpɑːʃ(ə)l/ *adjective* not complete 局部的

participate /pɑːˈtɪsɪpeɪt/ *verb* to take part in an activity or enterprise 参与,参加 ○ *The staff are encouraged to participate actively in the company's decision-making processes*. 公司鼓励员工积极参与公司的决策过程。

participating preference shares /pɑːˌtɪsɪpeɪtɪŋ ˈpref(ə)rəns ʃeəz/ , **participating preferred stock** /pɑːˌtɪsɪpeɪtɪŋ prɪˌfɜːd ˈstɒk/ *plural noun* preference shares which get an extra bonus dividend if company profits reach a high level 参加分派的优先股：当公司利润达到一定水平时可获得额外分红的优先股

participative budgeting /pɑːˌtɪsɪpətɪv ˈbʌdʒɪtɪŋ/ *noun* a budgeting system in which all budget holders are given the opportunity to participate in setting their own budgets 参与式预算：一种预算制度，所有对预算具有管理权限的人都有机会参加编制自己的预算 Also called 亦称作 **bottom-up budgeting**

partly /ˈpɑːtli/ *adverb* not completely 部分地

partly-paid capital /ˌpɑːtlipeɪd ˈkæpɪt(ə)l/ *noun* a capital which represents partly-paid shares 部分付清的资本：当作部分付清股票的资本

partly-paid up shares /ˌpɑːtlipeɪd ʌp ˈʃeəz/, **partly-paid shares** /ˌpɑːtlipeɪd ˈʃeəz/ *plural noun* shares where the shareholders have not paid the full face value 部分付清股票：股东尚未付清全部面值的股票

partner /ˈpɑːtnə/ *noun* a person who works in a business and has an equal share in it with other partners 合伙人 ○ *I became a partner in a firm of solicitors.* 我成为一家律师事务所的合伙人。

partnership /ˈpɑːtnəʃɪp/ *noun* an unregistered business where two or more people (but not more than twenty) share the risks and profits according to a partnership agreement 合伙，合伙企业，合伙组织：由两人或两人以上（但不得超过 20 人）组成的非注册企业，其遵照合伙协议共担盈亏 ○ *to go into partnership with someone* 与某人合伙 ○ *to join with someone to form a partnership* 与某人建立合伙企业

partnership accounts /ˌpɑːtnəʃɪp əˈkaʊnts/ *noun* the capital and current accounts of each partner in a partnership, or the accounts recording the partnership's business activities 合伙账户：合伙企业各个合伙人的资本及活期账户，或记录合伙企业的业务活动的账户

partnership agreement /ˈpɑːtnəʃɪp əˌgriːmənt/ *noun* a document setting up a partnership, giving the details of the business and the amount each partner is contributing to it 合伙协议：建立合伙关系的文件，它载明企业的详细资料以及各个合伙人的出资额 Also called 亦称作 **articles of partnership**

part-owner /ˌpɑːtˈəʊnə/ *noun* a person who owns something jointly with one or more other people 合有人，共有人 ○ *I am part-owner of the restaurant.* 我是这家饭店的共有人。

part-ownership /ˌpɑːtˈəʊnəʃɪp/ *noun* a situation where two or more persons own the same property (财产) 共同拥有

part payment /ˌpɑːt ˈpeɪmənt/ *noun* the paying of part of a whole payment 部分支付款 ○ *I gave him £250 as part payment for the car.* 我给他 250 英镑作为买车的部分车款。

part-time /ˌpɑːtˈtaɪm/ *adjective*, *adverb* not working for the whole working week 半职的(地)，兼职的(地)：只在部分工作日工作的(地) ○ *a* *part-time employee* 兼职雇员 ○ *It is a part-time job*. 这是一份兼职工作。○ *We are looking for part-time staff to work our computers*. 我们征寻一名兼职员工来操作我们的计算机。○ *She only works part-time as she has small children to look after*. 因为要照顾小孩,她只能做兼职工作。

party /ˈpɑːti/ *noun* a person or organisation involved in a legal dispute or legal agreement (法律诉讼、协议等的)当事人 ○ *How many parties are there to the contract*? 这份合同有多少个当事人? ○ *The company is not a party to the agreement*. 该公司不是这一协议的当事人。

par value /pɑː ˈvæljuː/ *noun* same as 同 **face value**

passbook /ˈpɑːsbʊk/ *noun* same as 同 **bank book**

'... instead of customers having transactions recorded in their passbooks, they will present plastic cards and have the transactions printed out on a receipt'
"顾客不在存折上记录交易,而是出示信用卡,在收据上打印出各项交易"[*Australian Financial Review*《澳大利亚金融评论报》]

patent /ˈpeɪtənt, ˈpætənt/ *noun* an official document showing that a person has the exclusive right to make and sell an invention 专利证书 ○ *to take out a patent for a new type of light bulb* 取得一种新型电灯泡的专利 ○ *to apply for a patent for a new invention* 为一项新发明申请专利 □ **'patent applied for', 'patent pending'** words on a product showing that the inventor has applied for a patent for it "已申请专利","专利权在申请中":产品上关于发明者已申请专利的说明

patent agent /ˈpeɪtənt ˌeɪdʒənt/ *noun* a person who advises on patents and applies for patents on behalf of clients 专利代理人:提供专利建议并代表客户申请专利的人

patent office /ˈpeɪtənt ˌɒfɪs/ *noun* a government office which grants patents and supervises them 专利局:颁发及监管专利权的政府部门

patent rights /ˈpeɪtənt raɪts/ *plural noun* the rights which an inventor holds because of a patent 专利权

pawnbroker /ˈpɔːnbrəʊkə/ *noun* a person who lends money against the security of valuable objects 典当商,当铺老板

pawnshop /ˈpɔːnʃɒp/ *noun* a pawnbroker's shop 当铺,典当行

pawn ticket /ˈpɔːn ˌtɪkɪt/ *noun* a receipt given by the pawnbroker for an object left in pawn 当票:典当商收到典当物的收据

pay /peɪ/ *noun* a salary or wages, money given to someone for regular work 薪金,工资 ■ *verb* **1.** to give money to buy an item or a service 支付 ○ *to pay £1,000 for a car* 花1,000英镑买车 ○ *How much did you pay to have the office cleaned*? 你请人打扫办公室付了多少钱?(NOTE: **paying – paid**) □ **'pay cash'** words written on a crossed cheque to show that it can be paid in cash if necessary "可提现":划线支票上的说明,表明必要时可提现 **2.** to produce or distribute money 给钱(NOTE: **paying – paid**) **3.** to give an employee money for work done 支付工资 ○ *The workforce has not been paid for three weeks*. 已有三周未给工人支付工资。○ *We pay good wages for skilled workers*. 我们给技术

工人支付优厚薪水。○ *How much do they pay you per hour?* 他们每小时付给你多少钱?（NOTE：**paying – paid**）□ **to be paid at piecework rates** to get money for each piece of work finished 计件付酬 **4.** to give money which is owed or which has to be paid 偿还,偿付 ○ *He was late paying the bill.* 他逾期付账。○ *We phoned to ask when they were going to pay the invoice.* 我们打电话问他们什么时候支付发票。○ *You will have to pay duty on these imports.* 你必须为这些进口产品支付关税。○ *She pays tax at the highest rate.* 她按最高税率纳税。（NOTE：**paying – paid**）□ **please pay the sum of £10** please give £10 in cash or by cheque 请付10英镑。

'... recession encourages communication not because it makes redundancies easier, but because it makes low or zero pay increases easier to accept'
"经济萧条可促进劳资沟通,这不是因为萧条时更容易解雇员工,而是因为它使人们更易于接受工资的低增长甚至零增长"
[*Economist*《经济学家》]

'... the yield figure means that if you buy the shares at their current price you will be getting 5% before tax on your money if the company pays the same dividend as in its last financial year'
"收益率数字意味着如果你按现价购买股票,而且公司发放与上一财政年度相同的股利,那么你将获得5%的税前收益"[*Investors Chronicle*《投资者纪事》]

payable /ˈpeɪəb(ə)l/ *adjective* due to be paid 应付的

payable to order /ˌpeɪəb(ə)l tə ˈɔːdə/ *adjective* words written on a bill of exchange or cheque to indicate that it may be transferred 记名付款的:汇票或支票上的可转让说明

pay back /ˈpeɪ bæk/ *verb* to give money back to someone 偿还,偿付 ○ *Banks are warning students not to take out loans which they cannot pay back.* 银行提醒学生贷款要量力而行。○ *I lent him £50 and he promised to pay me back in a month.* 我借给他50英镑,他答应在一个月内偿还。○ *She has never paid me back the money she borrowed.* 她向我借的钱从来没还过。■ *noun* the time required for the cash inflows from a capital investment project to equal the cash outflows 投资的回收期:资本投资项目的现金注入等于现金流出所需要的时间

payback /ˈpeɪbæk/ *noun* the act of paying back money which has been borrowed 偿还

payback clause /ˈpeɪbæk klɔːz/ *noun* a clause in a contract which states the terms for repaying a loan 还款条款

payback period /ˈpeɪbæk ˌpɪəriəd/ *noun* **1.** a period of time over which a loan is to be repaid or an investment is to pay for itself 偿还期限;贷款或投资的偿还期 **2.** the length of time it will take to earn back the money invested in a project 投资回收期:赚回项目投资金额需要的时间

pay day /ˈpeɪ deɪ/ *noun* a day on which wages are paid to employees, usually Friday for employees paid once a week and during the last week of the month for employees who are paid once a month 发薪日

pay desk /ˈpeɪ desk/ *noun* a place in a store where you pay for goods bought 收银台

paydown /ˈpeɪdaʊn/ *noun* a repayment of part of a sum which has been borrowed 部分贷款的偿还

payee /peɪˈiː/ *noun* a person who receives money from someone, or the person whose name is on a cheque 收款人;受款人

payer /ˈpeɪə/ *noun* a person who gives money to someone 付款人

pay hike /ˈpeɪ haɪk/ *noun* an increase in salary 增薪,提薪

paying /ˈpeɪɪŋ/ *adjective* **1.** making a profit 盈利的 ○ *It is a paying business*. 这是一家盈利的企业。**2.** producing money, source of money 生钱的,来钱的 ■ *noun* the act of giving money 付款

paying agent /ˈpeɪɪŋ ˌeɪdʒənt/ *noun* a bank which pays dividend or interest to a bondholder 付款银行:支付股利或利息给债券持有人的银行

paying-in book /ˌpeɪɪŋˈɪn bʊk/ *noun* a book of forms for paying money into a bank account or a building society account 存折,存款簿

paying-in slip /ˌpeɪɪŋˈɪn slɪp/ *noun* a printed form which is filled in when money is being deposited in a bank 存款条,存款单

paymaster /ˈpeɪmɑːstə/ *noun* the person responsible for paying an organisation's employees 工薪出纳员

payment /ˈpeɪmənt/ *noun* **1.** the act of giving money in exchange for goods or a service 支付 ○ *We always ask for payment in cash* or *cash payment and not payment by cheque*. 我们一直要求付现(或不接受支票支付)。○ *The payment of interest* or *The interest payment should be made on the 22nd of each month*. 利息应于每月 22 日支付。**2.** money paid 支付的款项

payment terms /ˈpeɪmənt tɜːmz/ *plural noun* the conditions laid down by a business regarding when it should be paid for goods or services that it supplies, e. g. cash with order, payment on delivery or payment within a particular number of days of the invoice date 付款条件

pay negotiations /ˈpeɪ nɪɡəʊʃiˌeɪʃ(ə)nz/, **pay talks** /ˈpeɪ tɔːks/ *plural noun* discussions between management and employees about pay increases 工资谈判

pay off /ˌpeɪ ˈɒf/ *verb* **1.** to finish paying money which is owed for something 付清 ○ *He won the lottery and paid off his mortgage*. 他中彩后还清了他的按揭。○ *She is trying to pay off the loan by monthly instalments*. 她正努力按月分期还清贷款。**2.** to terminate somebody's employment and pay all wages that are due 清账遣散:解雇某人并付清所有应付工资 ○ *When the company was taken over the factory was closed and all the employees were paid off*. 公司被兼并后,工厂关闭,工人被清账遣散。

payoff /ˈpeɪɒf/ *noun* money paid to finish paying something which is owed, such as money paid to an employee when his or her employment is terminated 偿付款;遣散费

'... the finance director of the group is to receive a payoff of about £300,000 after deciding to leave the company and pursue other business opportunities'
"在决定离开公司去寻求其他商业发展机会后,集团的财务主管将获得约 30 万英镑的补偿。"[*Times*《泰晤士报》]

pay out /ˌpeɪ ˈaʊt/ *verb* to give money 支付 ○ *The company pays out* *thousands of pounds in legal fees*. 公司支付了数千英镑的诉讼费。○ *We have paid out half our profits in dividends*. 我们把一半的利润用来支付股利。

payout /ˈpeɪaʊt/ *noun* money paid to help a company or person in difficulties, a subsidy (对困难企业或个人的)资助金,补助金 ○ *The company only exists on payouts from the government*. 该公司只能靠政府拨款维持。

'...after a period of recession followed by a rapid boost in incomes, many tax payers embarked upon some tax planning to minimize their payouts'
"衰退期过后,收入迅速增长,许多纳税人开始进行纳税规划,以尽可能减少支出" [*Australian Financial Review*《澳大利亚金融评论报》]

pay packet /ˈpeɪ ˌpækɪt/ *noun* an envelope containing the pay slip and the cash pay 工资袋

pay rise /ˈpeɪ raɪz/ *noun* an increase in pay 加薪

payroll /ˈpeɪrəʊl/ *noun* the list of people employed and paid by a company 工资单,薪水册 ○ *The company has 250 on the payroll*. 该公司有250名在编员工。

payroll giving scheme /ˌpeɪrəʊl ˈɡɪvɪŋ ˌskiːm/ *noun* a scheme by which an employee pays money to a charity directly out of his or her salary. The money is deducted by the employer and paid to the charity; the employee gets tax relief on such donations 工资单捐赠计划:雇员直接从工资中作出慈善捐款的计划,捐款由雇主扣除并付给慈善机构,雇员享有相应的税收减免

payroll ledger /ˈpeɪrəʊl ˌledʒə/ *noun* a list of staff and their salaries 工资表

payroll tax /ˈpeɪrəʊl tæks/ *noun* a tax on the people employed by a company 工薪税:公司因雇佣员工而支付的税金

pay scale /ˈpeɪ skeɪl/ *noun* a hierarchy of wage levels, typically varying according to job title, salary or length of service 薪级,工资等级(通常与职称、工资或服务年限挂钩) Also called 亦称作 **salary scale**, **wage scale**

pay threshold /ˈpeɪ ˌθreʃhəʊld/ *noun* a point at which pay increases because of a threshold agreement 工资门槛,最低工资界限:最低工资界限协议规定的加薪临界点

pay up /ˌpeɪ ˈʌp/ *verb* to give money which is owed 付清债务 ○ *The company only paid up when we sent them a letter from our solicitor*. 直到我们发出律师函后,该公司才付清欠债。○ *She finally paid up six months late*. 她晚了六个月才付清债务。

PBIT *abbr* profit before interest and tax 息税前利润,利税前利润

P/C *abbr* petty cash 零用现金,小额现金

pecuniary /pɪˈkjuːniəri/ *adjective* referring to money 金钱的

peg /peg/ *verb* to maintain or fix something at a specific level 固定,限定

penalise /ˈpiːnəlaɪz/, **penalize** *verb* to punish or fine someone 处罚;罚款 ○ *to penalise a supplier for late deliveries* 处罚一个延迟交货的供应商 ○ *They were penalised for bad time-keeping*. 他们因不守时而被罚款。

penalty /ˈpen(ə)lti/ *noun* 罚金 **1.** a punishment, often a fine, which is imposed if something is not done or is done incorrectly or illegally [对未能完成或未能正确完成某事或对非法行为的罚款] **2.** an arbitrary pre-arranged sum that becomes payable if one party breaks a term of a contract or an undertaking. The most common penalty is a high rate of interest on an unauthorised overdraft [事先规定的一方违反合同或契约条款时应付的任意金额，最常见的处罚是对未经许可的超限透支收取高利率]

pension /ˈpenʃən/ *noun* money paid regularly to someone who no longer works 养老金，退休金，补助金

pensionable /ˈpenʃənəb(ə)l/ *adjective* able to receive a pension 可领取养老金的

pensionable earnings /ˌpenʃənəb(ə)l ˈɜːnɪŋz/ *plural noun* earnings being received at the moment of retirement, on which the pension is calculated 养老金收入

pension contributions /ˈpenʃən kɒntrɪˌbjuːʃ(ə)nz/ *plural noun* money paid by a company or employee into a pension fund 养老金缴款：公司或雇员对养老金基金的缴款

pension entitlement /ˈpenʃən ɪnˌtaɪt(ə)lmənt/ *noun* the amount of pension which someone has the right to receive when he or she retires 应享养老金权利：退休时有权领取的养老金金额

pensioner /ˈpenʃənə/ *noun* a person who receives a pension 领取养老金的人

pension fund /ˈpenʃən fʌnd/ *noun* a large sum of money made up of contributions from employees and their employer which provides pensions for retired employees 养老基金：由雇员及雇主缴款构成的大额资金，它向退休的雇员提供养老金

pension funds /ˈpenʃən fʌndz/ *plural noun* investments managed by pension companies to produce pensions for investors 退休金基金，养老金基金：由养老金公司管理的投资，用以向投资者支付养老金

pension income /ˌpenʃən ˈɪnkʌm/ *noun* income which you receive from a pension scheme 养老金收入

pension plan /ˈpenʃən plæn/, **pension scheme** /ˈpenʃən skiːm/ *noun* a plan worked out by an insurance company which arranges for employees to pay part of their salary over many years and receive a regular payment when they retire 养老金计划，退休金计划：由保险公司制定的保险计划，员工在多年内缴纳部分工资，退休后即可获得定期养老金

PEP *abbr* Personal Equity Plan 个人权益计划

per /pɜː, pə/ *preposition* **1.** □ **as per** according to 根据，按照 **2.** for each 每一… □ **we pay £10 per hour** we pay £10 for each hour worked 我们每小时支付 10 英镑 □ **the earnings per share** the dividend received for each share 每股收益 □ **the average sales per representative** the average sales achieved by one representative 每个销售代表的平均销售额

'...a 100,000 square-foot warehouse generates $600 in sales per square foot of space'
"一个 10 万平方英尺的仓库，每平方英尺的库容量能产生 600 美元销售收入" [*Duns Business Month*《邓氏商业月刊》]

PER *abbr* price/earnings ratio 市盈

率，价格收益率

per annum /pər 'ænəm/ *adverb* in a year 每年，按年计算地 ○ *What is their turnover per annum?* 他们每年的营业额是多少？○ *What is his total income per annum?* 他每年的总收入是多少？○ *She earns over £100,000 per annum.* 她的年收入超过10万英镑。

per capita /pə 'kæpɪtə/ *adjective, adverb* for each person 每人（的），人均（的）

per capita income /pə ˌkæpɪtə 'ɪnkʌm/ *noun* **1.** the average income of one person 人均收入 Also called 亦称作 **income per capita, income per head 2.** the average income of each member of a particular group of people, e.g., the citizens of a country 某一组人中各个成员（如一国国民）的平均收入

per cent /pə 'sent/ *adjective, adverb* out of each hundred, or for each hundred 百分比

'...this would represent an 18 per cent growth rate—a slight slackening of the 25 per cent turnover rise in the first half'
"这代表18%的增长率，比上半年25%的营业额增长稍有下降"［*Financial Times*《金融时报》］

'...buildings are depreciated at two per cent per annum on the estimated cost of construction'
"建筑物每年按估计建筑成本的2%折旧"［*Hong Kong Standard*《香港虎报》］

percentage /pə'sentɪdʒ/ *noun* an amount shown as part of one hundred 百分比，百分率

'... state-owned banks cut their prime rates a percentage point to 11%'
"国有银行的基础利率下调了一个百分点，降至11%"［*Wall Street Journal*《华尔街日报》］

'...a good percentage of the excess stock was taken up during the last quarter'
"上季度额外认购股票的百分比很高"［*Australian Financial Review*《澳大利亚金融评论报》］

'...the Federal Reserve Board, signalling its concern about the weakening American economy, cut the discount rate by one-half percentage point to 6.5%'
"联邦储备委员会下调贴现率1.5个百分点至6.5%，显示出它对正在衰退的美国经济的担忧"［*Wall Street Journal*《华尔街日报》］

percentage discount /pəˌsentɪdʒ dɪs'kaʊnt/ *noun* a discount calculated at an amount per hundred 折扣百分率

percentage increase /pəˌsentɪdʒ 'ɪnkriːs/ *noun* an increase calculated on the basis of a rate for one hundred 增长百分率

percentage point /pə'sentɪdʒ pɔɪnt/ *noun* 1 per cent 百分点

percentile /pə'sentaɪl/ *noun* one of a series of ninety-nine figures below which a percentage of the total falls 百分位（数）

per day /pə 'deɪ/, **per diem** /pə 'diːem/ *adverb* for each day 每天

perform /pə'fɔːm/ *verb* to do well or badly 表现（好或坏）

performance /pə'fɔːməns/ *noun* **1.** the way in which someone or something acts 业绩，表现 ○ *Last year saw a dip in the company's performance.* 去年公司业绩略有下降。□ **performance of staff against objectives** how staff have worked, measured against the objectives set 根据既定目标考核个人业绩 **2.** the way in which a share increases in value 股票的表现

'... inflation-adjusted GNP edged up at a 1.3% annual rate, its worst performance since the economic expansion began'
"经通货膨胀调整后的国民生产总值年增长率仅为1.3%，这是该国经济开始发展以来表现最差的一年"[*Fortune*《财富》]

performance rating /pəˈʃɔːməns ˌreɪtɪŋ/ *noun* a judgement of how well a share or a company has performed (股票或公司)表现评级，业绩评价

performance review /pəˈʃɔːməns rɪˌvjuː/ *noun* a yearly interview between a manager and each employee to discuss how the employee has worked during the year 业绩考核

per head /pə ˈhed/ *adverb* for each person 每人 ○ *Allow £15 per head for expenses*. 每人可有15英镑的开支。○ *Representatives cost on average £50,000 per head per annum*. 代表成本平均为每人每年五万英镑。

period bill /ˈpɪəriəd bɪl/ *noun* a bill of exchange payable on a certain date rather than on demand 定期汇票，期票：于指定日期而不是即期支付的汇票 Also known as 亦称作 **term bill**

period cost /ˈpɪəriəd kɒst/ *noun* a fixed cost, such as rent or insurance, which is related to a period of time 期间成本，本期成本：与某个期间有关的成本，如租金、保险等

periodic /ˌpɪəriˈɒdɪk/, **periodical** /ˌpɪəriˈɒdɪk(ə)l/ *adjective* happening from time to time 定期的 ○ *a periodic review of the company's performance* 定期考核公司业绩

periodicity concept /ˌpɪəriəˈdɪsɪti ˌkɒnsept/ *noun* a legal requirement that states entities must produce required financial documentation at agreed times 周期概念：国有企业必须在规定时间提交规定财务文件的法律要求

periodic stock check /ˌpɪəriˈɒdɪk stɒk tʃek/ *noun* the counting of stock at some point in time, usually at the end of an accounting period 存货定期盘存：在某一时点(通常在会计期末)盘查存货

periodic weighted average cost /ˌpɪəriˌɒdɪk ˌweɪtɪd ˈæv(ə)rɪdʒ kɒst/, **periodic weighted average price** /ˌpɪəriˌɒdɪk ˌweɪtɪd ˈæv(ə)rɪdʒ praɪs/ *noun* the average price per unit of stock delivered in a period calculated at the end of the period, as opposed to 'cumulative weighted average' 期间加权平均成本：在会计期末计算的本期已交付每单位库存的平均价格，与"累计加权平均成本"相对

period of account /ˌpɪəriəd əv əˈkaʊnt/ *noun* the period usually covered by a firm's accounts 会计期，财务期

period of qualification /ˌpɪəriəd əv kwɒlɪfɪˈkeɪʃ(ə)n/ *noun* the time which has to pass before someone qualifies for something 资格期：某人获得某一资格所需的时间

perk /pɜːk/ *noun* an extra item given by a company to employees in addition to their salaries, e.g. company cars or private health insurance (*informal*) (非正式)(公司汽车、个人健康保险等)额外津贴 ○ *She earns a good salary and in addition has all sorts of perks*. 她不仅享有高薪，还享受各种各样的额外津贴。

permit /pəˈmɪt/ *verb* to allow someone to do something 许可，允许 ○ *This document permits you to export twen-*

ty-five computer systems. 这份文件允许出口25套计算机系统。○ *The ticket permits three people to go into the exhibition*. 这张票允许三人入场参观展览。○ *Will we be permitted to use her name in the advertising copy?* 我们能否在广告文字说明中使用她的姓名?○ *Smoking is not permitted in the design studio*. 设计室里不允许吸烟。(NOTE: **permitting – permitted**)

perpetual inventory system /pɜːˌpetjʊəl ˈɪnventəri ˌsɪstəm/ *noun* a stock control system by which the stock is continually counted as it moves into and out of the warehouse, so avoiding having to close the warehouse for annual stock checks 永续盘存制:一种存货控制系统,它在存货出入仓库时作连续计算,以避免在年度盘存时需关闭仓库 Abbreviation 缩写 **PIS**

perpetuity /ˌpɜːpɪˈtjuːɪti/ *noun* same as 同 **annuity**

per pro /pə ˈprəʊ/ *abbr* per procurationem 经授权代表 ○ *The secretary signed per pro the manager*. 在经理授权下秘书代表他签了字。

perquisite /ˈpɜːkwɪzɪt/ *noun* same as 同 **perk**

person /ˈpɜːs(ə)n/ *noun* a man or a woman 人 ○ *an insurance policy which covers a named person* 为指定者投保的保险单

personal /ˈpɜːs(ə)n(ə)l/ *adjective* referring to one person 私人的,个人的 □ **apart from the family shares, she has a personal shareholding in the company** apart from shares belonging to her family as a group, she has shares which she owns herself 除了家族股份外,她在公司里还拥有个人股份

personal allowance /ˌpɜːs(ə)n(ə)l əˈlaʊəns/ *noun* a part of a person's income which is not taxed 个人免税收入

personal assets /ˌpɜːs(ə)n(ə)l ˈæsets/ *plural noun* moveable assets which belong to a person 个人资产,动产

Personal Equity Plan /ˌpɜːs(ə)n(ə)l ˈekwɪti plæn/ *noun* an account held under a UK-government-backed scheme to encourage share-ownership and investment in industry, allowing individual taxpayers to invest some amount of money in shares each year, and not pay tax on either the income or the capital gains, provided that the shares are held for an agreed period of time. PEPs were replaced by ISAs in April 1999, but existing schemes will continue 个人权益计划:根据英国政府鼓励股票及工业投资的一项计划持有的账户,纳税个人可每年作一定金额的股票投资,只要持有股票达到一定期限,其收入或资本利得就无需纳税。个人权益计划于1999年4月被个人储蓄计划取代,但当时业已存在的计划将继续有效 Abbreviation 缩写 **PEP**

personal financial planning /ˌpɜːs(ə)n(ə)l faɪˌnænʃəl ˈplænɪŋ/ *noun* short and long-term financial planning by an individual, either independently or with the assistance of a professional adviser. It will include the use of tax efficient schemes such as Individual Savings Accounts, ensuring adequate provisions are being made for retirement, and examining short and long-term borrowing requirements such as overdrafts and mortgages 个人理财计划:独立进行或有专业顾问协助的个人长短期理财计划。它包括税务优惠计划(如个人储蓄计划)的使用,退休后养老金的准备,同时兼顾透支和按揭之类

的长短期借款需求

Personal Identification Number /ˌpɜːs(ə)n(ə)l aɪˌdentɪfɪˈkeɪʃ(ə)n ˌnʌmbə/ *noun* a unique number allocated to the holder of a cash card or credit card, by which he or she can enter an automatic banking system, as e. g., to withdraw cash from a cash machine or to pay in a store 个人识别番号，个人识别码：分配给现金卡或信用卡持有人的号码，用于进入自动银行服务系统，例如从自动提款机取现或在商场购物 Abbreviation 缩写 **PIN**

personal income /ˌpɜːs(ə)n(ə)l ˈɪnkʌm/ *noun* the income received by an individual person before tax is paid 个人收入

Personal Investment Authority /ˌpɜːs(ə)nəl ɪnˌvestmənt ɔːˈθɒrəti/ *noun* a self-regulatory organisation responsible for supervising the activities of financial intermediaries selling financial products to individuals 私人投资管理局：一个自律监管机构，负责监督向个人出售金融产品的金融中介机构的活动 Abbreviation 缩写 **PIA**

personal loan /ˌpɜːs(ə)nəl ˈləʊn/ *noun* a loan to a person for household or other personal use, not for business use 个人贷款

personal pension plan /ˌpɜːs(ə)n(ə)l ˈpenʃən plæn/ *noun* a pension plan which applies to one employee only, usually a self-employed person, not to a group 个人养老金计划：只适用于单个雇员（通常为个体经营者）而非群体的养老金计划 Abbreviation 缩写 **PPP**

personal property /ˌpɜːs(ə)n(ə)l ˈprɒpəti/ *noun* things which belong to a person 个人财产 ○ *The fire caused considerable damage to personal property.* 这次火灾令个人财产蒙受巨大损失。

personal representative /ˌpɜːs(ə)n(ə)l ˌreprɪˈzentətɪv/ *noun* a person who is the executor of a will or the administrator of the estate of a deceased person 遗产代理人

PERT /pɜːt/ *abbr* programme evaluation and review technique 计划评审法

petition /pəˈtɪʃ(ə)n/ *noun* an official request 正式申请，呈请

petroleum revenues /pəˈtrəʊliəm ˌrevənjuːz/ *plural noun* income from selling oil 石油收入

petroleum revenue tax /pəˌtrəʊliəm ˈrevənjuː ˌtæks/ *noun* a British tax on revenues from companies extracting oil from the North Sea 石油收入税：英国对从事北海石油开采的公司所征收的一项税种 Abbreviation 缩写 **PRT**

petty cash /ˌpeti ˈkæʃ/ *noun* a small amount of money kept in an office to pay small debts 零用（现）金，小额现金，小额出纳金：部门持有的用于支付小额债务的现金 Abbreviation 缩写 **P/C**

petty cash voucher /ˌpeti ˈkæʃ ˌvaʊtʃə/ *noun* a piece of paper on which cash expenditure is noted so that an employee can be reimbursed for what he or she has spent on company business 零用金凭单：用于报销小额现金开支的凭单

petty expenses /ˌpeti ɪkˈspensɪz/ *plural noun* small sums of money spent 零星费用，杂费

phase /feɪz/ *noun* a period or part of something which takes place 阶段 ○ *the first phase of the expansion* *programme* 扩展计划的第一阶段

phase in /ˌfeɪz ˈɪn/ *verb* to bring something in gradually 逐步采用，分阶段引入 ○ *The new invoicing system will be phased in over the next two months.* 新发票系统将在未来两个月内逐步投入运行。

'...the budget grants a tax exemption for $500,000 in capital gains, phased in over the next six years'
"预算给予50万美元的资本收益免税额，并在未来六年内逐步抵免"［*Toronto Star*《多伦多明星日报》］

phase out /ˌfeɪz ˈaʊt/ *verb* to remove something gradually 逐步退出 ○ *Smith Ltd will be phased out as a supplier of spare parts.* 史密斯有限公司将逐渐退出零配件供应行业。

phoenix company /ˈfiːnɪks ˌkʌmp(ə)ni/ *noun* a company formed by the directors of a company which has gone into receivership, which trades in the same way as the first company, and in most respects (except its name) seems to be exactly the same as the first company 新生公司，再生公司：由已进入清算管理程序的公司的董事重新组成的公司，其业务与原公司相同，在其他很多方面（除公司名称外）也与原公司相似

'...the prosecution follows recent calls for a reform of insolvency legislation to prevent directors from leaving behind a trail of debt while continuing to trade in phoenix companies—businesses which fold only to rise again, often under a slightly different name in the hands of the same directors and management'
"最近有人呼吁改革破产立法，以防止公司董事抛下债务后在新生公司——破产后立即重建的企业，通常只是名称稍有不同，而董事和管理层均相同——继续经营，检查院对此进行了跟踪"［*Financial Times*《金融时报》］

physical asset /ˌfɪzɪk(ə)l ˈæset/ *noun* an asset that is a physically existing thing, as opposed to cash or securities 实物资产（与现金或证券相对）

physical inventory /ˌfɪzɪk(ə)l ˈɪnvənt(ə)ri/ *noun* an act of counting actual items of stock 实地盘存，实际清点：清点实际存货的行为

physical market /ˌfɪzɪk(ə)l ˈmɑːkɪt/ *noun* a commodity market where purchasers actually buy the commodities, as opposed to the futures market, where they buy and sell the right to purchase commodities at a future date 现货市场：买方实际采购商品的实物市场，与买卖远期商品购买权的期货市场相对

physical price /ˌfɪzɪk(ə)l ˈpraɪs/ *noun* a current cash price for a commodity for immediate delivery 现货价格：立即交货的当前现金价格

physicals /ˈfɪzɪk(ə)lz/ *plural noun* actual commodities which are sold on the current market, as opposed to futures 现货：在现货市场上出售的实物，与期货相对

physical stock /ˌfɪzɪk(ə)l ˈstɒk/ *noun* the actual items of stock held in a warehouse 实际库存

PIA /ˌpiː aɪ ˈeɪ/ *abbr* Personal Investment Authority 私人投资管理局

piece rate /ˈpiːs reɪt/ *noun* a rate of pay calculated as an amount for each product produced or for each piece of work done and not as an amount for each hour worked 计件工资 ○ *to earn* *piece rates* 挣计件工资

piecework /ˈpiːswɜːk/ *noun* work for which employees are paid in accordance with the number of products produced or pieces of work done and not at an hourly rate 计件工作

pie chart /ˈpaɪ tʃɑːt/ *noun* a diagram where information is shown as a circle cut up into sections of different sizes 扇形图,圆形图:把要表达的信息放置在被分割为不同大小的圆形图表里

pilferage /ˈpɪlfərɪdʒ/, **pilfering** /ˈpɪlfərɪŋ/ *noun* the stealing of small amounts of money or small items from an office or shop (从办公室或商店)偷窃,小偷小摸

PIN /pɪn/ *abbr* Personal Identification Number 个人识别番号,个人识别码

PIS *abbr* perpetual inventory system 永续盘存制

placement /ˈpleɪsmənt/ *noun* **1.** the act of finding work for someone (人员)工作安排 ○ *The bureau specialises in the placement of former executives.* 该机构专门负责安排前行政管理人员的工作。**2.** *US* the act of finding buyers for an issue of new shares (美)配售(新股):为新股发行寻找买主 (NOTE: The UK term is **placing** 英国用语为 **placing**)

placing /ˈpleɪsɪŋ/ *noun* the act of finding a single buyer or a group of institutional buyers for a large number of shares in a new company or a company that is going public 配售:为新公司或即将上市的公司发行的大量股票找到单一买主或多个机构买主

plain vanilla swap /ˌpleɪn vəˌnɪlə ˈswɒp/ *noun* an interest rate swap, where a company with fixed interest borrowings may swap them for variable interest borrowings of another company 普通掉期交易,利率互换:公司以其固定利率借款交换另一公司的可变利率借款

plan /plæn/ *noun* **1.** an organised way of doing something 计划 ○ *an investment plan* 投资计划 ○ *a pension plan* 退休金计划 ○ *a savings plan* 储蓄计划 **2.** a way of saving or investing money (理财)计划 ■ *verb* to organise carefully how something should be done in the future 计划,规划

'... the benefits package is attractive and the compensation plan includes base, incentive and car allowance totalling $50,000+'

"待遇优厚,报酬计划包括基本工资、奖金及汽车津贴,共计五万美元以上" [*Globe and Mail* (*Toronto*)《环球邮报》(多伦多)]

plan comptable *noun* in France, a uniformly structured and detailed bookkeeping system that companies are required to comply with 会计方案:法国的一个统一组织的详细簿记系统,每个公司都必须遵守

planned economy /ˌplænd ɪˈkɒnəmi/ *noun* a system where the government plans all business activity, regulates supply, sets production targets and itemises work to be done 计划经济:政府规划所有经济活动、管理供应、设定生产目标并逐条列出需完成的工作的一种经济体系 Also called 亦称作 **command economy**, **central planning**

planned obsolescence /ˌplænd ˌɒbsəˈles(ə)ns/ *adjective* built-in obsolescence 计划报废:商品内在废弃 ○ *Planned obsolescence was condemned* *by the consumer organisation as a cynical marketing ploy*. 消费者组织谴责计划报废是卑鄙的营销阴谋。

planning /ˈplænɪŋ/ *noun* the process of organising how something should be done in the future 计划,规划 ○ *Setting up a new incentive scheme with insufficient planning could be a disaster*. 新的奖励方案如果策划不周很可能会彻底失败。○ *The long-term planning* or *short-term planning of the project has been completed*. 项目的长期(或短期)规划已经完成。

'...buildings are closely regulated by planning restrictions'
"建筑物受严格的规划限制"[*Investors Chronicle*《投资者纪事》]

plant and machinery /ˌplɑːnt ən məˈʃiːnəri/ *noun* equipment used to help someone trade such as trucks, tools, office furniture, computers, ladders, etc. 厂房和机器设备

plastic money /ˌplæstɪk ˈmʌni/ *noun* credit cards and charge cards 塑料货币:信用卡及缴费卡

pledge /pledʒ/ *noun* an object given to a pawnbroker as security for money borrowed 质押(品),典当(物)

plus /plʌs/ *preposition* added to 加 ○ *Her salary plus commission comes to more than* £45,000. 她的工资加佣金超过4.5万英镑。○ *Production costs plus overheads are higher than revenue*. 生产成本加间接费用超过了收入。■ *adverb* more than 超过 □ **houses valued at £100,000 plus** houses valued at over £100,000 价值超过10万英镑的房子

pocket /ˈpɒkɪt/ *noun* □ **to be £25 in pocket** to have made a profit of £25 挣得25英镑 □ **to be £25 out of pocket** to have lost £25 损失25英镑

point /pɔɪnt/ *noun* **1.** a place or position 地点,位置 **2.** a unit for calculations 点(计算单位) □ **government stocks rose by one point** they rose by £1 政府债券上升了一点(即上升了一英镑)

policy /ˈpɒlɪsi/ *noun* a course of action or set of principles determining the general way of doing something 方针,政策 ○ *a company's trading policy* 公司的贸易政策 ○ *The country's economic policy seems to lack any direction*. 该国的经济政策看来缺乏针对性。○ *We have a policy of only hiring qualified staff*. 我们的行事原则是只雇用合格的员工。○ *Our policy is to submit all contracts to the legal department*. 我们的行事原则是把所有合同都提交给法律部门。

policy cost /ˈpɒlɪsi kɒst/ *noun* a fixed cost, such as advertising cost, which is governed by the management's policy on the amount of advertising to be done 政策性成本:受公司管理层的政策限制的固定成本,比如广告费用

portable /ˈpɔːtəb(ə)l/ *adjective* possible to carry 可携带的,便携式的 ○ *a portable computer* 便携式电脑

portable pension plan /ˌpɔːtəb(ə)l ˈpenʃən plæn/ *noun* a pension plan which an employee can carry from one company to another as he changes jobs 可携带养老金计划:雇员换工作时可以转到新公司的养老金计划

portfolio investments /pɔːtˌfəʊliəʊ ɪnˈvestmənts/ *plural noun* investments in shares and government stocks, as opposed to investments in property, etc. 证券投资,证券组合投资:投资于股票和政府债券,与地产投资相对

portfolio management /pɔːtˈfəʊliəʊ ˌmænɪdʒmənt/ *noun* the buying and selling shares to make profits for a single investor 证券管理,投资组合管理:买卖股票以使单个投资者获利

portfolio theory /pɔːtˈfəʊliəʊ ˌθɪəri/ *noun* a basis for managing a portfolio of investments, i. e. a mix of safe stocks and more risky ones 组合理论:管理投资组合的理论基础,即在组合中既有安全的也有高风险的证券

position /pəˈzɪʃ(ə)n/ *noun* **1.** a situation or state of affairs 形势;状况 **2.** a point of view 观点,立场 **3.** a job or paid work in a company 职位 ○ *to apply for a position as manager* 申请经理职位 ○ *We have several positions vacant*. 我们有若干职位空缺。○ *All the vacant positions have been filled*. 所有空缺职位都已填补。○ *She retired from her position in the accounts department*. 她从会计部门职位上退休了。**4.** the state of a person's current financial holding in a stock 头寸:个人当前持有证券的状况

position audit /pəˌzɪʃ(ə)n ˈɔːdɪt/ *noun* part of the planning process which examines the current state of an entity in respect of the following: resources of tangible and intangible assets and finance; products, brands, and markets; operating systems such as production and distribution; internal organisation; current results; and returns to stockholders 状况审计:规划过程的一部分,审查企业实体在下列领域的现状:有形与无形资产及财务资源;产品、品牌及市场;生产及分销等运营系统;内部组织;当前业绩;股东回报

positive carry /ˌpɒzɪtɪv ˈkæri/ *noun* a deal where the cost of the finance is less than the return 盈利经营:财务成本低于回报的交易

positive cash flow /ˌpɒzɪtɪv ˈkæʃ fləʊ/ *noun* a situation where more money is coming into a company than is going out 正现金流量:流入现金大于流出现金

positive goodwill /ˌpɒzɪtɪv gʊdˈwɪl/ *noun* positive goodwill arises when the acquisition cost exceeds the aggregate fair values of the identifiable assets and liabilities 正商誉:收购成本高于可识别资产与负债的公平价值总额

positive yield curve /ˌpɒzɪtɪv ˈjiːld ˌkɜːv/ *noun* a situation where the yield on a short-term investment is less than that on a long-term investment 正收益率曲线:短期投资的收益率低于长期投资

possess /pəˈzes/ *verb* to own something 拥有 ○ *The company possesses property in the centre of the town*. 该公司拥有市中心的地产。○ *He lost all he possessed in the collapse of his company*. 他的公司倒闭使他一贫如洗。Compare 比较 **repossess**

possession /pəˈzeʃ(ə)n/ *noun* the fact of owning or having something 拥有

possessions /pəˈzeʃ(ə)nz/ *plural noun* property, things owned 财产;所有物 ○ *They lost all their possessions in the fire*. 火灾令他们失去了所有的财产。Compare 比较 **repossession**

post-acquisition /pəʊstˌækwɪˈzɪʃ(ə)n/ *adjective* taking place after a company has been acquired 收购后的

post-acquisition profit /pəʊst-ˌækwɪˌzɪʃ(ə)n ˈprɒfɪt/ *noun* a profit of a subsidiary company in the period after it has been acquired, which is treated as revenue and transferred to the consolidated reserves of the holding company 收购后利润：子公司被收购后的利润，它被当作收入转到控股公司的合并留存收益中

post a credit /ˌpəʊst eɪ ˈkredɪt/ *verb* to enter a credit item in a ledger 过入一个贷项：在总账中记入一个贷项

post-balance sheet event /pəʊstˌbæl əns ʃiːt ɪˈvent/ *noun* something which happens after the date when the balance sheet is drawn up, and before the time when the balance sheet is officially approved by the directors, which affects a company's financial position 结账后会计事项：从公司资产负债表编制之日至董事会正式通过前发生的影响公司财务状况的事项

postdate /ˌpəʊstˈdeɪt/ *verb* to put a later date on a document 填迟…的日期：在单据上填写以后的日期 ○ *He sent us a postdated cheque*. 他寄给我们一张填迟日期的支票。○ *Her cheque was postdated to June*. 她的支票填迟到六月。

post-purchase costs /ˌpəʊst-ˈpɜːtʃɪs ˌkɒsts/ *noun* costs incurred after a capital expenditure decision has been implemented and facilities acquired. These costs may include training, maintenance, and the cost of upgrades 购买后成本：实施资本开支决策并已获得融资后发生的成本，可包括培训、维护及升级成本等

pound /paʊnd/ *noun* **1.** a measure of weight (= 0.45 kilos) 磅：重量单位 (= 0.45 千克) ○ *to sell oranges by the pound* 按磅卖橙子 ○ *a pound of orangses* 一磅橙子 ○ *Oranges cost 50p a pound*. 橙子 50 便士一磅。(NOTE: Usually written **lb** after a figure: **25lb**. Note also that the pound is now no longer officially used in the UK 在数字后通常写作 **lb**:**25lb**。还应注意，英国官方已不再以磅为单位) **2.** a unit of currency used in the UK and many other countries including Cyprus, Egypt, Lebanon, Malta, Sudan, Syria and, before the euro, Ireland 镑：英国的货币单位，也在塞浦路斯、埃及、黎巴嫩、马耳他、苏丹、叙利亚及推出欧元前的爱尔兰使用

poundage /ˈpaʊndɪdʒ/ *noun* a rate charged per pound in weight 按每磅重量收费

pound sterling /paʊnd ˈstɜːlɪŋ/ *noun* the official term for the British currency 英镑

power /ˈpaʊə/ *noun* **1.** strength or ability 力量；能力 **2.** a force or legal right 权力；合法权利 **3.** a mathematical term describing the number of times a number is to be multiplied by itself 幂 ○ *5 to the power 2 is equal to 25* 5 的二次方为 25 (NOTE: written as small figures in superscript: 10^5: say: 'ten to the power five' 在作上标时写为较小数字：10^5，表示"十的五次方")

power of attorney /ˌpaʊər əv əˈtɜːni/ *noun* a legal document which gives someone the right to act on someone's behalf in legal matters 委任状，授权书：授权某人代表自己处理法律事务的法律文件

PPI *abbr* producers' price index 生产价格指数

PPP *abbr* personal pension plan 个人养老金计划

practice /ˈpræktɪs/ *noun* a way of doing things, a custom or habit 惯例，习惯 ○ *Her practice was to arrive at work at 7.30 and start counting the cash.* 她习惯在七点半到班上，然后开始清点现金。

'... the EC demanded international arbitration over the pricing practices of the provincial boards'
"欧共体要求对各国议会的订价惯例进行国际仲裁"［*Globe and Mail* (*Toronto*)《环球邮报》(多伦多)］

pre-acquisition /ˌpriːˌækwɪˈzɪʃən/ *adjective* before the acquisition of a company 收购前的

pre-acquisition profits /ˌpriːˌækwɪzɪʃən ˈprɒfɪts/ *plural noun* profits of a company in the part of its accounting period before it was acquired by another company. Under acquisition accounting methods, the holding company deducts these profits from the combined reserves of the group 收购前利润：一家公司被另一公司收购前会计期的利润。根据购并会计法，控股公司应从集团合并留存收益中剔除此利润

pre-acquisition write-down /ˌpriːˌækwɪzɪʃən ˈraɪtˌdaʊn/ *noun* a reduction in the fair value of a new subsidiary in the balance sheet of a holding company against the potential future costs or the possible revaluation of the subsidiary's assets after acquisition 收购前减记，收购前冲减：在控股公司的资产负债表上，新子公司的公平价值减去潜在的未来成本或收购后子公司资产可能的重新估值

prebilling /priːˈbɪlɪŋ/ *noun* the practice of submitting a bill for a product or service before it has actually been delivered 预收账：在产品或服务实际交付前提交账单

preceding year /prɪˌsiːdɪŋ ˈjɪə/ *noun* the year before the accounting year in question 上一年度 □ **taxed on a preceding year basis** tax on income or capital gains arising in the previous year is payable in the current year 以上一年度为基础纳税：在本年度缴纳上一年度的所得税或资本利得税

pre-empt /priːˈempt/ *verb* to stop something happening or stop someone doing something by taking action quickly before anyone else can 抢先行动，预先制止：抢在别人之前迅速采取措施阻止某事发生或阻止某人做某事 ○ *They staged a management buyout to pre-empt a takeover bid.* 他们抢在收购发盘之前实施了管理层收购。

pre-emption right /priːˈempʃən raɪt/ *noun* the right of an existing shareholder to be first to buy a new stock issue 优先权：现有股东首先购买新股发行的权利

pre-emptive /priːˈemptɪv/ *adjective* done before anyone else takes action in order to stop something happening 抢先的，先占的：抢在别人之前采取措施阻止某事发生

preference dividend /ˌpref(ə)rəns ˈdɪvɪdend/ *noun* a dividend paid on preference shares 优先股利：优先股的股利

preference shares /ˈpref(ə)rəns ʃeəz/ *plural noun* shares, often with no voting rights, which receive their dividend before all other shares and are repaid first at face value if the company goes into liquidation 优先股：一类股票，它在其他股票之前取得股利，于公司清算时在普通股之前按面值偿付，但通常没有投票权（NOTE：The US term is **preferred stock** 美国用语为 **preferred stock**）

preferential /ˌprefəˈrenʃəl/ *adjective* showing that something is preferred more than another 优先的

preferential creditor /ˌprefəˌrenʃəl ˈkredɪtə/ , **preferred creditor** /prɪˌfɜːd ˈkredɪtə/ *noun* a creditor who must be paid first if a company is in liquidation 优先债权人：公司清算时必须首先偿付的债权人

preferential debt /ˌprefəˈrenʃəl det/ *noun* a debt which is paid before all others 优先债务：先于其他债务偿付的债务

preferential payment /ˌprefərenʃəl ˈpeɪmənt/ *noun* a payment to a preferential creditor 优先付款：付款给优先债权人

preferential shares /ˌprefəˈrenʃəl ʃeəs/ *plural noun* shares which are part of a new issue and are set aside for the employees of the company 特惠股：在新股发行中留给公司员工的股份

preferred creditor /prɪˌfɜːd ˈkredɪtə/ *noun* a creditor who must be paid first if a company is in liquidation 优先债权人：公司清算时必须首先偿付的债权人

preferred shares /prɪˌfɜːd ˈʃeəz/ , **preferred stock** /prɪˌfɜːd ˈstɒk/ *plural noun* same as 同 **preference shares**

pre-financing /priːˈfaɪnænsɪŋ/ *noun* financing in advance 提前筹资，提前融资

preliminary /prɪˈlɪmɪn(ə)ri/ *adjective* early, happening before anything else 初步的，开端的

'... preliminary indications of the level of business investment and activity during the March quarter will be available this week'
"关于第一季商业投资及营运水平的初步指标将在本周发布"［*Australian Financial Review*《澳大利亚金融评论报》］

preliminary announcement /prɪˌlɪmɪn(ə)ri əˈnaʊnsmənt/ *noun* an announcement of a company's full-year results, given out to the press before the detailed annual report is released 初步通告：详细年度报告公布之前公司向新闻界发布的关于全年业绩的通告

premium /ˈpriːmiəm/ *noun* **1.** a regular payment made to an insurance company for the protection provided by an insurance policy 保险费 **2.** an amount to be paid to a landlord or a tenant for the right to take over a lease 租赁预付金：为了获得租赁权而支付给房东或租赁者的一笔钱 ○ *flat to let with a premium of £10,000* 公寓租赁预付金为一万英镑 ○ *annual rent: £8,500, premium: £25,000* 年租金：8,500 英镑，租赁预付金：2.5 万英镑 **3.** an extra sum of money in addition to a usual charge, wage, price or other amount 溢价：超出通常收费、工资、价格等的金额 **4.** a gift, discount or other incentive to encourage someone to buy（向顾客提供的赠品、折扣等）优惠

'... greenmail, the practice of buying back stock at a premium from an acquirer who threatens a takeover'
"绿票讹诈，一种反购回作法，即向威胁兼并的收购方高价购回股票"［*Duns Business Month*《邓氏商业月刊》］

'... responsibilities include the production of premium quality business reports'
"职责包括编制高质量的业务报告" [*Times*《泰晤士报》]

premium bond /ˈpriːmiəm bɒnd/ *noun* a government bond, part of the National Savings scheme, which pays no interest, but gives the owner the chance to win a weekly or monthly prize 有奖债券:国民储蓄计划下的一种政府债券,它不支付利息,但持有人每周或每月有一次抽奖机会

premium bonds /ˈpriːmiəm bɒnds/ *plural noun* British government bonds, part of the national savings scheme, which pay no interest, but give the owner the chance to win a monthly prize 有奖债券:英国国民储蓄计划下的一种政府债券,它不支付利息,但持有人每月有一次抽奖机会

premium income /ˌpriːmiəm ˈɪnkʌm/ *noun* income which an insurance company derives from premiums paid by insured persons (保险公司)保险费收入

premium offer /ˈpriːmiəm ˌɒfə/ *noun* a free gift offered to attract more customers 赠品

premium on redemption /ˌpriːmiəm ɒn rɪˈdempʃən/ *noun* an extra amount above the nominal value of a share or debenture paid to the holder by a company buying back its share or loan stock 赎回溢价:公司购回其股票或债券时支付给持有人超过面值的部分

prepaid /priːˈpeɪd/ *adjective* paid in advance 预付的

prepaid expenses /priːˌpeɪd ɪkˈspensɪz/ *plural noun* expenditure on items such as rent, which is made in one accounting period but covers part of the next period also 预付费用

prepaid interest /priːˌpeɪd ˈɪntrəst/ *noun* interest paid in advance of its due date 预付利息

prepay /priːˈpeɪ/ *verb* to pay something in advance 预付 (NOTE: **prepaying – prepaid**)

prepayment /priːˈpeɪmənt/ *noun* **1.** a payment in advance, or the act of paying in advance 预付款;预付 **2.** *US* the repayment of the principal of a loan before it is due (美)贷款本金的提前偿还

prepayment penalty /priːˈpeɪmənt ˌpen(ə)lti/ *noun US* a charge levied on someone who repays a loan such as a mortgage before it is due (美)提前还款罚金:对提前偿还贷款(如按揭)的人收取的费用

present /prɪˈzent/ *verb* to bring or send and show a document 出示,呈示

presentation /ˌprez(ə)nˈteɪʃ(ə)n/ *noun* the showing of a document 出示

present value /ˌprez(ə)nt ˈvæljuː/ *noun* **1.** the value something has now 现值,现价:某物当前的价值 ○ *In 1984 the pound was worth five times its present value.* 1984年英镑的价值是现在的五倍。**2.** the value now of a specified sum of money to be received in the future, if invested at current interest rates (未来收入按当前利率投资的)现值 Abbreviation 缩写 **PV 3.** a price which a share must reach in the future to be the equivalent of today's price, taking inflation into account 现价:考虑通货膨胀因素后,股票必须在未来达到与现价相等的价格

preservation of capital /ˌprezəveɪʃ(ə)n əv ˈkæpɪt(ə)l/ *noun* an approach to financial management that protects a person's or company's capital by arranging additional forms of finance 资本保值:通过安排额外的融资方式来保护某人或公司资本的一种理财方法

pressing /ˈpresɪŋ/ *adjective* urgent 紧急的

pre-tax /ˈpriːtæks/ , **pretax** *adjective* before tax has been deducted or paid 税前的

'... the company's goals are a growth in sales of up to 40 per cent, a rise in pre-tax earnings of nearly 35 per cent and a rise in after-tax earnings of more than 25 per cent'

"公司的目标是销售额增长40%,税前收益增长接近35%,税后收益增长25%以上" [*Citizen* (*Ottawa*)《公民》(渥太华)]

'EC regulations which came into effect in July insist that customers can buy cars anywhere in the EC at the local pre-tax price'

"7月开始生效的欧共体条例坚持要求,顾客可在欧共体任一成员国按当地的税前价格购买汽车" [*Financial Times*《金融时报》]

pretax profit /ˌpriːtæks ˈprɒfɪt/ *noun* the amount of profit a company makes before taxes are deducted 税前利润 ○ *The dividend paid is equivalent to one quarter of the pretax profit*. 支付的股利等于税前利润的四分之一。Also called 亦称作 **profit before tax, profit on ordinary activities before tax**

pretax profit margin /ˌpriːtæks ˈprɒfɪt ˌmɑːdʒɪn/ *noun* the pretax profit shown as a percentage of turnover in a profit and loss account 税前利润率:在损益账户中以占营业额的百分比呈现的税前利润

previous /ˈpriːviəs/ *adjective* happening earlier or which existed before 以前的,先前的 ○ *List all previous positions with the salaries earned*. 列出曾担任过的所有职位及其工资。

previous balance /ˌpriːviəs ˈbæləns/ *noun* a balance in an account at the end of the accounting period before the current one 前期余额:上一会计期末的账目余额

price /praɪs/ *noun* money which has to be paid to buy something 价格 □ **cars in the £18—19,000 price range** cars of different makes, selling for between £18,000 and £19,000 价位在1.8万到1.9万英镑的汽车 ■ *verb* to give a price to a product 给…定价 ○ *We have two used cars for sale, both priced at £5,000*. 我们有两辆二手车要出售,定价都是5,000英镑。

'... the average price per kilogram for this season has been 300c'

"这个季节每公斤的平均价格一直为300分" [*Australian Financial Review*《澳大利亚金融评论报》]

'European manufacturers rely heavily on imported raw materials which are mostly priced in dollars'

"欧洲生产商过于依赖大多以美元定价的进口原材料" [*Duns Business Month*《邓氏商业月刊》]

'... after years of relying on low wages for their competitive edge, Spanish companies are finding that rising costs and the strength of the peseta are pricing them out of the market'

"在多年依赖低工资带来的竞争优势之后,西班牙的公司发现成本上升和比塞塔升值使他们的产品定价太高,卖不出去" [*Wall Street Journal*《华尔街日报》]

'... that British goods will price themselves back into world markets is doubtful as long as sterling labour costs continue to rise'

"只要英国人工成本继续上升,英国商品通

过价格调整回归世界市场的的可能性就值得怀疑”［*Sunday Times*《星期日泰晤士报》］

price ceiling /ˈpraɪs ˌsiːlɪŋ/ *noun* the highest price which can be reached 最高限价

price change /ˈpraɪs tʃeɪndʒ/ *noun* an amount by which the price of a share moves during a day's trading 价格变化

price control /ˈpraɪs kənˌtrəʊl/ *noun* a legal measures to stop prices rising too fast 价格管制：阻止物价上涨过快的合法措施

price controls /ˈpraɪs kənˌtrəʊlz/ *plural noun* legal measures to prevent prices rising too fast 价格管制：防止物价上涨过快的合法措施

price cutting /ˈpraɪs ˌkʌtɪŋ/ *noun* a sudden lowering of prices 削价，降价

'...in today's circumstances, price-cutting is inevitable in an attempt to build up market share'
“在当今的环境下，要增大市场份额，就必须降价”［*Marketing Week*《市场周刊》］

price-cutting war /ˈpraɪsˌkʌtɪŋ wɔː/ *noun* same as 同 **price war**

price differential /ˈpraɪs dɪfəˌrenʃəl/ *noun* the difference in price between products in a range（同系列不同产品的）价格差异

price/earnings ratio /ˌpraɪs ˈɜːnɪŋz ˌreɪʃiəʊ/ *noun* a ratio between the current market price of a share and the earnings per share（the current dividend it produces），calculated by dividing the market price by the earnings per share 市盈率：股票当前市价与每股盈利（股票的当前股利）的比率，计算方法为市价除以每股盈利 ○ *these shares sell at a P/E ratio of 7* 这些股票按七倍的市盈率出售 Also called 亦称作 **P/E ratio**. Abbreviation 缩写 **PER**（NOTE: The US term is **price/earnings multiple** 美国用语为 **price/earnings multiple**）

price fixing /ˈpraɪs ˌfɪksɪŋ/ *noun* an illegal agreement between companies to charge the same price for competing products 限定价格，同业协议售价：公司间对竞争产品协商制定同样售价的非法协定

price-insensitive /ˌpraɪsɪnˈsensətɪv/ *adjective* used to describe a good or service for which sales remain constant no matter what its price because it is essential to buyers 价格不敏感的：对于消费者必需的商品或劳务，不论价格高低，其销量始终保持稳定

price label /ˈpraɪs ˌleɪb(ə)l/ *noun* a label which shows a price 价格标签

price list /ˈpraɪs lɪst/ *noun* a sheet giving prices of goods for sale 价目表，价格目录

price range /ˈpraɪs reɪndʒ/ *noun* a series of prices for similar products from different suppliers 价格幅度：不同供应商对类似产品设定的系列价格

price tag /ˈpraɪs tæg/ *noun* a label attached to an item being sold that shows its price 价格标签

price war /ˈpraɪs wɔː/ *noun* a competition between companies to get a larger market share by cutting prices 价格战：竞争公司竞相削价以占有更大市场份额 Also called 亦称作 **price-cutting war**

pricing /ˈpraɪsɪŋ/ *noun* the act of giving a price to a product 定价

pricing model /ˈpraɪsɪŋ ˌmɒd(ə)l/

noun a computerised system for calculating a price, based on costs, anticipated margins, etc. 定价模型：基于成本、预期利润等的计算机化计价系统

pricing policy /ˈpraɪsɪŋ ˌpɒlɪsi/ *noun* a company's policy in giving prices to its products 定价政策 ○ *Our pricing policy aims at producing a 35% gross margin*. 我们的定价政策旨在创造35%的毛利润。

primary /ˈpraɪməri/ *adjective* basic 初级的

'...farmers are convinced that primary industry no longer has the capacity to meet new capital taxes or charges on farm inputs'
"农民们确信，初级产业已没有能力交纳新的资本税或支付农业投入费用"［*Australian Financial Review*《澳大利亚金融评论报》］

primary commodities /ˌpraɪməri kəˈmɒdɪtiz/ *plural noun* farm produce grown in large quantities, e.g. corn, rice or cotton 初级商品：大量种植的农产品，如玉米、稻米或棉花

primary industry /ˌpraɪməri ˈɪndəstri/ *noun* an industry dealing with basic raw materials such as coal, wood or farm produce 初级产业：处理原材料（如煤炭、木材或农产品）的产业

primary market /ˌpraɪməri ˈmɑːkɪt/ *noun* a market where new securities or bonds are issued 初级市场，一级市场：新股及债券的发行市场 Also called 亦称作 **new issue market**

prime /praɪm/ *adjective* **1.** most important 最重要的 **2.** basic 基本的

prime bills /ˌpraɪm ˈbɪlz/ *plural noun* bills of exchange which do not involve any risk 优质汇票，优等汇票：没有任何风险的汇票

prime cost /ˌpraɪm ˈkɒst/ *noun* the cost involved in producing a product, excluding overheads 主要成本：产品的生产成本，不包括间接费用

prime rate /ˈpraɪm reɪt/ , **prime** /praɪm/ *noun US* the best rate of interest at which an American bank lends to its customers （美）最优惠利率，基础利率：美国银行借款给客户的最优惠利率

'...the base lending rate, or prime rate, is the rate at which banks lend to their top corporate borrowers'
"基础贷款利率（或最优惠利率）是银行放贷给资信最高的公司时的利率"［*Wall Street Journal*《华尔街日报》］

prime sites /ˌpraɪm ˈsaɪts/ *plural noun* the most valuable commercial sites, i.e. in main shopping streets, as opposed to secondary sites 黄金地段：最有价值的商业区，如主要商业街区，与次级地段相对

prime time /ˈpraɪm taɪm/ *noun* the most expensive advertising time for TV commercials 黄金时段：最昂贵的电视广告时段 ○ *We are putting out a series of prime-time commercials*. 我们在黄金时段投放了一组广告。

priming /ˈpraɪmɪŋ/ *noun* ➧ 参阅 **pump priming**

principal /ˈprɪnsɪp(ə)l/ *noun* **1.** a person or company that is represented by an agent 委托人 ○ *The agent has come to London to see his principals*. 代理商去伦敦会晤他的委托人。**2.** a person acting for him or herself, such as a marketmaker buying securities on his or her own account 本人，当事人（如庄家使用自己的账户买入证券）**3.**

money invested or borrowed on which interest is paid (投资或贷款的)本金 ○ *to repay principal and interest* 还本付息 ○ *We try to repay part of principal each month*. 我们努力每月偿还一部分本金。(NOTE: Do not confuse with **principle** 不要与 **principle** 混淆)
■ *adjective* most important 主要的,最重要的 ○ *The principal shareholders asked for a meeting*. 主要股东要求召集会议。○ *The country's principal products are paper and wood*. 该国主要的产品是纸张和木材。○ *The company's principal asset is its design staff*. 该公司的主要资产是其设计人员。

'...the company was set up with funds totalling NorKr 145m with the principal aim of making capital gains on the secondhand market'
"该公司的创办资金为1.45亿挪威克郎,其主要宗旨是在二手市场上获取资本收益" [*Lloyd's List*《劳氏日报》]

principle /ˈprɪnsɪp(ə)l/ *noun* a basic point or general rule 原则

prior /ˈpraɪə/ *adjective* earlier 在先的

prior charge percentage *noun* same as 同 **priority percentage**

priority /praɪˈɒrɪti/ *noun* □ **to have priority over** *or* **to take priority over something** to be more important than something 优先于…,比…享有优先权 ○ *Reducing overheads takes priority over increasing turnover*. 减少间接费用比增加营业额更重要。○ *Debenture holders have priority over ordinary shareholders*. 债券持有人比普通股东享有优先权。

priority percentage /praɪˌɒrɪti pəˈsentɪdʒ/ *noun* the proportion of a business's net profit that is paid in interest to preference shareholders and holders of debt capital 优先清偿百分率:作为利息付给优先股东和借入资本持有人的企业净利部分 Also called 亦称作 **prior charge percentage**

prior year adjustments /ˌpraɪə jɪə əˈdʒʌs(t)mənts/ *plural noun* adjustments made to accounts for previous years, because of changes in accounting policies or because of errors 先前年度调整:由于会计政策变化或存在错误而对前些年账目进行的调整

private /ˈpraɪvət/ *adjective* belonging to a single person or to individual people, not to a company or the state 私人的;私营的 □ **a letter marked 'private and confidential'** a letter which must not be opened by anyone other than the person it is addressed to 标明"私密"的信件 □ **to sell (a house) by private treaty** to sell (a house) to another person not by auction 通过私人协议出售(房屋)

'...in the private sector the total number of new house starts was 3 per cent higher than in the corresponding period last year, while public sector starts were 23 per cent lower'
"私营企业新房开工总数同比增长了3%,而公有企业开工则下降了23%" [*Financial Times*《金融时报》]
'...management had offered to take the company private through a leveraged buyout for $825 million'
"管理层出价,通过8.25亿美元的杠杆收购使公司私有化" [*Fortune*《财富》]

private bank /ˌpraɪvət ˈbæŋk/ *noun* **1.** a bank that is owned by a single person or a limited number of private shareholders 私营银行：由个人或少数私人股东拥有的银行 **2.** a bank that provides banking facilities to high net worth individuals 私人事务银行：向高净值个人提供银行融资的银行 ➪ 参阅 **private banking**

private banking /ˌpraɪvət ˈbæŋkɪŋ/ *noun* a service offered by certain financial institutions to high net worth individuals. In addition to standard banking services, it will typically include portfolio management and advisory services on taxation, including estate planning 私人银行业务：某些金融机构向高净值个人提供的服务。除银行的常规服务外，它通常还提供投资组合管理和税务咨询服务（包括遗产规划）

private company /ˌpraɪvət ˈkʌmp(ə)ni/ *noun* a registered company whose shares are not offered for sale to the public 私人公司，不公开公司：股份不公开发售的注册公司

private debt /ˌpraɪvət ˈdet/ *noun* money owed by individuals and organisations other than governments 私人债务：个人及非政府组织的债务

private enterprise /ˌpraɪvət ˈentəpraɪz/ *noun* businesses which are owned privately, not nationalized（非国有的）私人企业 ○ *The project is completely funded by private enterprise.* 该项目全部由私人企业投资。

private income /ˌpraɪvət ˈɪnkʌm/ *noun* income from dividends, interest or rent which is not part of a salary 私人收入：股利、利息或租金等非工资收入

private investor /ˌpraɪvət ɪnˈvestə/ *noun* an ordinary person with money to invest 个人投资者

private limited company /ˌpraɪvət ˌlɪmɪtɪd ˈkʌmp(ə)ni/ *noun* 私人有限责任公司 **1.** a company with a small number of shareholders, whose shares are not traded on the Stock Exchange［由少数股东组成、其股票不上市流通的公司］（NOTE：shortened to **Ltd** 缩写为 **Ltd**） **2.** a subsidiary company whose shares are not listed on the Stock Exchange, while those of its parent company are［股票不上市的子公司，但其母公司股票上市］Abbreviation 缩写 **Pty Ltd**

privately held company /ˌpraɪvətli held ˈkʌmp(ə)ni/ *noun US* company controlled by a few shareholders or its directors（美）私人持有公司：由少数股东或董事控制的公司 Also called 亦称作 **closed corporation**

private ownership /ˌpraɪvət ˈəʊnəʃɪp/ *noun* a situation where a company is owned by private shareholders 私有制：公司由私人股东拥有

private placing /ˌpraɪvət ˈpleɪsɪŋ/, **private placement** /ˌpraɪvət ˈpleɪsmənt/ *noun* the act of placing a new issue of shares with a group of selected financial institutions 私募：向特定的金融机构配售新股

private practice /ˌpraɪvət ˈpræktɪs/ *noun* accounting services offered to clients, as opposed to accounting work carried out as an employee of a company 私人服务：向客户提供的会计服务，与作为公司雇员从事的会计工作相对

private property /ˌpraɪvət ˈprɒpəti/ *noun* property which belongs to a private person, not to the public 私有财产

private sector /ˈpraɪvət ˌsektə/ *noun* all companies which are owned by private shareholders, not by the state 私营部门:由私人股东而不是国家拥有的公司 ○ *The expansion is completely funded by the private sector*. 该扩建全部由私营部门投资。○ *Salaries in the private sector have increased faster than in the public sector*. 私营部门工资的增长速度超过公共部门。

'...in the private sector the total number of new house starts was 3 per cent higher than in the corresponding period last year, while public sector starts were 23 per cent lower'
"私营部门新房开工总数同比增长了3%,而公有企业开工则下降了23%" [*Financial Times*《金融时报》]

private treaty /ˌpraɪvət ˈtriːti/ *noun* agreement between individual persons 磋商成交,私人协议

pro /prəʊ/ *preposition* for 为了

probability /ˌprɒbəˈbɪlɪti/ *noun* the likelihood that something will happen, expressed mathematically 可能性,概率

probable /ˈprɒbəb(ə)l/ *adjective* likely to happen 可能的 ○ *They are trying to prevent the probable collapse of the company*. 他们正在力保公司免于破产。○ *It is probable that the company will collapse if a rescue package is not organised before the end of the month*. 如果月底前不能制订一揽子拯救措施,公司就可能破产。

probate /ˈprəʊbeɪt/ *noun* legal acceptance that a document, especially a will, is valid 文件确认;遗嘱检验 □ **the executor was granted probate** *or* **obtained a grant of probate** the executor was told officially that the will was valid 遗嘱执行人被正式告知遗嘱有效

procedure /prəˈsiːdʒə/ *noun* a way in which something is done 程序;手续;过程 ○ *The inquiry found that the company had not followed the approved procedures*. 调查发现该公司并未遵循议定程序。

'...this was a serious breach of disciplinary procedure and the dismissal was unfair'
"这严重违反了纪律程序,解雇是不公正的" [*Personnel Management*《人事管理》]

proceed /prəˈsiːd/ *verb* to go on, to continue 继续 ○ *The negotiations are proceeding slowly*. 谈判进展缓慢。

proceeds /ˈprəʊsiːdz/ *plural noun* money received from selling something (销售)收益,收入

process /prəʊˈses/ *verb* to deal with something in the usual routine way (按常规方式)处理 ○ *It usually takes at least two weeks to process an insurance claim*. 处理一项保险索赔通常最少需要两周。○ *Orders are processed in our warehouse*. 订单在我们的仓库内处理。

process costing /prəʊˌses ˈkɒstɪŋ/ *noun* a method of costing something which is manufactured from a series of continuous processes, where the total costs of those processes are divided by the number of units produced 分步成本计算法:对通过一系列连续工序生产出的产品的成本进行计算的方法,即以所有工序的总成本除以产品总产量

processing /ˈprəʊsesɪŋ/ *noun* the act of sorting information (信息)整理,处理 ○ *the processing of informa-*

tion or *of statistics by a computer* 计算机信息(或统计资料)处理

producers' price index /prəˌdjuːsəz ˈpraɪs ˌɪndeks/ *noun US* a measure of the annual increase in the prices of goods and services charged by producers which is used to indicate the rate of inflation in the US economy (美)生产价格指数:生产者的服务费用和产品价格的年上涨幅度的衡量手段,通常用以显示美国经济的通货膨胀率 Abbreviation 缩写 **PPI**

product /ˈprɒdʌkt/ *noun* **1.** something which is made or manufactured 产品;制品 **2.** a manufactured item for sale 商品

product advertising /ˈprɒdʌkt ˌædvətaɪzɪŋ/ *noun* the advertising of a particular named product, not the company which makes it 产品广告

product analysis /ˌprɒdʌkt əˈnæləsɪs/ *noun* an examination of each separate product in a company's range to find out why it sells, who buys it, etc. 产品分析:分析公司产品系列中的各个产品,以了解其适销原因及其购买者等

product design /ˈprɒdʌkt dɪˌzaɪn/ *noun* the design of consumer products 产品设计

product development /ˌprɒdʌkt dɪˈveləpmənt/ *noun* the process of improving an existing product line to meet the needs of the market 产品开发

product engineer /ˌprɒdʌkt ˌendʒɪˈnɪə/ *noun* an engineer in charge of the equipment for making a product 产品工程师:管理生产设备的工程师

production /prəˈdʌkʃən/ *noun* **1.** the act of showing something 出示 **2.** the work of making or manufacturing of goods for sale 生产 ○ *We are hoping to speed up production by installing new machinery.* 我们期望通过安装新机械来加快生产。○ *Higher production is rewarded with higher pay.* 高生产率带来了高收入。

production cost /prəˈdʌkʃən kɒst/ *noun* the cost of making a product 生产成本

production department /prəˈdʌkʃən dɪˌpɑːtmənt/ *noun* the section of a company which deals with the making of the company's products 生产部门

production line /prəˈdʌkʃən laɪn/ *noun* a system of making a product, where each item such as a car moves slowly through the factory with new sections added to it as it goes along 生产线 ○ *He works on the production line.* 他在生产线工作。○ *She is a production-line employee.* 她是一名生产线员工。

production manager /prəˈdʌkʃən ˌmænɪdʒə/ *noun* the person in charge of the production department 生产部经理

production overhead /prəˌdʌkʃən ˈəʊvəhed/ *noun* a factory overhead, the indirect costs of production which are absorbed into the cost of goods produced 生产间接费用:工厂的间接费用,即分摊到产品成本中的间接生产成本

production target /prəˈdʌkʃən ˌtɑːgɪt/ *noun* the amount of units a factory is expected to produce 产量目标

production unit /prəˈdʌkʃən ˌjuːnɪt/ *noun* a separate small group of employees producing a product 生产小

组

productive /prəˈdʌktɪv/ *adjective* producing something, especially something useful 生产的(尤指能产生效益的)

productive capital /prəˌdʌktɪv ˈkæpɪt(ə)l/ *noun* capital which is invested to give interest 生产性资本:投资以获取利息的资本

productivity /ˌprɒdʌkˈtɪvɪti/ *noun* the rate of output per employee or per machine in a factory 生产率 ○ *Bonus payments are linked to productivity.* 奖金与生产率挂钩。○ *The company is aiming to increase productivity.* 公司在努力提高生产率。○ *Productivity has fallen* or *risen since the company was taken over.* 公司被收购后生产率下降(或上升)了。

'... though there has been productivity growth, the absolute productivity gap between many British firms and their foreign rivals remains'
"尽管生产率有所提高,但是许多英国公司与国外竞争对手之间的绝对生产率差距仍然存在"[*Sunday Times*《星期日泰晤士报》]

productivity agreement /ˌprɒdʌkˈtɪvɪti əˌgriːmənt/ *noun* an agreement to pay a productivity bonus 生产率协议:关于支付增产奖的协议

productivity bonus /ˌprɒdʌkˈtɪvɪti ˌbəʊnəs/ *noun* an extra payment made to employees because of increased production per employee 增产奖

productivity drive /ˌprɒdʌkˈtɪvɪti draɪv/ *noun* an extra effort to increase productivity 提高生产率运动:提高生产率的额外努力

product management /ˌprɒdʌkt ˈmænɪdʒmənt/ *noun* the process of directing the making and selling of a product as an independent item 产品管理

product mix /ˈprɒdʌkt mɪks/ *noun* a range of different products which a company has for sale 产品组合

profession /prəˈfeʃ(ə)n/ *noun* **1.** an occupation for which official qualifications are needed and which is often made a lifelong career 职业 ○ *The managing director is an accountant by profession.* 总经理是一名职业会计师。○ *HR management is now more widely recognised as a profession.* 现在人力资源管理被更广泛地认可为一种职业。**2.** a group of specialised workers 职业界;同业,同行 ○ *the accounting profession* 会计行业 ○ *the legal profession* 律师界 □ **the accounting profession** all qualified accountants 会计行业 □ **the banking profession** all qualified bankers 银行业,银行界

'... one of the key advantages of an accountancy qualification is its worldwide marketability. Other professions are not so lucky: lawyers, for example, are much more limited in where they can work'
"会计资格的一个主要优点是其全球适用,其他职业就不这么幸运,比如律师,他们就会受到极大的地域限制"[*Accountancy*《会计学》]

professional /prəˈfeʃ(ə)n(ə)l/ *adjective* referring to one of the professions 职业的,专业的 ○ *The accountant sent in his bill for professional services.* 会计师发来他的专业服务价单。○ *We had to ask our lawyer for professional advice on the contract.* 我们必须向律师

咨询有关这个合同的专业意见。○ *The professional institute awards diplomas.* 该专业机构颁发证书。□ **professional man, professional woman** a man or woman who works in one of the professions such as a lawyer, doctor or accountant 专业人士:从事某种专业的人(如律师、医生、会计师)

professional fees /prəˌfeʃ(ə)n(ə)l ˈfiːz/ *plural noun* fees paid to lawyers, accountants, architects, etc. 专业费用

profit /ˈprɒfɪt/ *noun* money gained from a sale which is more than the money spent on making the item sold or on providing the service offered 利润 □ **to take your profit** to sell shares at a higher price than was paid for them, and so realise the profit, rather than to keep them as an investment 见利抛售,获利回吐:按高于购买价出售股票以实现利润,而不是作为投资持有这些股票 □ **to make a profit** to have more money as a result of a deal 获利

'... because capital gains are not taxed and money taken out in profits and dividends is taxed, owners of businesses will be using accountants and tax experts to find loopholes in the law'

"因为资本收益无需缴税,但利润及股利要缴税,所以业主会聘请会计师及税务专家来寻找避税的方法"[*Toronto Star*《多伦多明星日报》]

'... the bank transferred $5 million to general reserve compared with $10 million the previous year which made the consolidated profit and loss account look healthier'

"与上年的1,000万美元相比,银行今年向一般储备转入500万美元,这使合并损益表显得更良好"[*Hong Kong Standard*《香港虎报》]

profitability /ˌprɒfɪtəˈbɪlɪti/ *noun* **1.** the ability to make a profit 盈利能力 ○ *We doubt the profitability of the project.* 我们怀疑该项目的盈利能力。**2.** the amount of profit made as a percentage of costs 利润率

profitable /ˈprɒfɪtəb(ə)l/ *adjective* making a profit 赚钱的,有利可图的 ○ *She runs a very profitable employment agency.* 她经营着一家很赚钱的职业介绍所。

profitably /ˈprɒfɪtəbli/ *adverb* making a profit 盈利地 ○ *The aim of every company must be to trade profitably.* 每个公司都必须以盈利为目标。

profit after tax /ˌprɒfɪt ɑːftə ˈtæks/ *noun* same as 同 **net profit**

profit and loss account /ˌprɒfɪt ən ˈlɒs əˌkaʊnt/ *noun* the accounts for a company showing expenditure and income over a period of time, usually one calendar year, balanced to show a final profit or loss 损益表:公司一段时间内(通常为一年)结平显示公司最后盈亏的收支账目 Also called 亦称作 **P&L account** (NOTE: The US term is **profit and loss statement** or **income statement** 美国用语为 **profit and loss statement** 或 **income statement**)

profit before interest and tax /ˌprɒfɪt bɪˌfɔː ˈɪntrəst ən tæks/ *noun* operating profit shown before deducting interest on borrowings and tax due to the Inland Revenue 息税前利润,利税前利润:缴纳借款利息及国内税收前的营业利润 Abbreviation 缩写 **PBIT**

profit centre /ˈprɒfɪt ˌsentə/ *noun* a person, unit or department within an organisation which is considered separately for the purposes of calculating a profit 利润中心:在计算利润时分开考虑的个人、组织单位或部门 ○ *We count the kitchen equipment di-*

vision as a single profit centre. 我们把厨房设备分部算作一个利润中心。

profit distribution /ˌprɒfɪt ˌdɪstrɪˈbjuːʃ(ə)n/ *noun* the allocation of profits to different recipients such as shareholders and owners, or for different purposes such as research or investment 利润分配

profiteer /ˌprɒfɪˈtɪə/ *noun* a person who makes too much profit, especially when goods are rationed or in short supply 牟取暴利的人,投机商人

profiteering /ˌprɒfɪˈtɪərɪŋ/ *noun* the practice of making too much profit 牟取暴利

profit from ordinary activities /ˌprɒfɪt frəm ˌɔːd(ə)n(ə)ri ækˈtɪvɪtiz/ *noun* profits earned in the normal course of business, as opposed to profits from extraordinary sources such as windfall payments 日常业务所得利润(与暴利等特殊来源的利润相对)

profit-making /ˈprɒfɪtˌmeɪkɪŋ/ *adjective* making a profit 获利的 ○ *The whole project was expected to be profit-making by 2001 but it still hasn't broken even*. 整个项目本来预计在2001年前开始获利,但直到现在仍未回本。○ *It is hoped to make it into a profit-making concern*. 希望使它成为一家盈利的企业。

profit margin /ˈprɒfɪt ˌmɑːdʒɪn/ *noun* the percentage difference between sales income and the cost of sales (销售)利润率

profit on ordinary activities before tax /ˌprɒfɪt ɒn ˌɔːd(ə)n(ə)ri ækˌtɪvɪtiz bɪˌfɔː ˈtæks/ *noun* same as 同 **pretax profit**

profit-related /ˈprɒfɪtrɪˌleɪtɪd/ *adjective* linked to profit 与利润挂钩的

profit-related bonus /ˌprɒfɪtrɪˌleɪtɪd ˈbəʊnəs/ *noun* a bonus paid which is related to the amount of profit a company makes 与利润挂钩的奖金

profit-related pay /ˌprɒfɪtrɪˌleɪtɪd ˈpeɪ/ *noun* pay including bonuses which is linked to profit 与利润挂钩的工资

profit retained for the year /ˌprɒfɪt rɪˈteɪnd fə ðə jɪə/ *noun* non-distributed profit retained as a distributable reserve 年度留存利润:留作可供分配储备的年度未分配利润

profit-sharing /ˈprɒfɪtˌʃeərɪŋ/ *noun* 利润分享 **1.** an arrangement where employees get a share of the profits of the company they work for [职工可分享公司利润的做法] ○ *The company runs a profit-sharing scheme*. 公司实行一项利润分享计划。**2.** the practice of dividing profits among employees [利润在员工之间的分配]

profit squeeze /ˈprɒfɪt skwiːz/ *noun* a strict control of the amount of profits which companies can pay out as dividend 利润压缩:对公司当作股利支付的利润金额进行的严格控制

profit-taking /ˈprɒfɪtˌteɪkɪŋ/ *noun* the act of selling investments to realise the profit, rather than keeping them 见利抛售,获利回吐:出售投资实现利润,而不是继续持有 ○ *Share prices fell under continued profit-taking*. 持续的获利回吐促使股价下跌。

'...some profit-taking was seen yesterday as investors continued to lack fresh incentives to renew buying activity'
"由于投资者缺少恢复购买的新的推动力,昨天出现了一些获利回吐现象"[*Financial Times*《金融时报》]

pro forma /prəʊ ˈfɔːmə/ *verb* to issue a pro forma invoice 开具形式发票 ○ *Can you pro forma this order?* 你能为这份订单开一张形式发票吗？

pro-forma financial statement /prəʊˌfɔːmə faɪˌnænʃəl ˈsteɪtmənt/ *noun* a projection showing a business's financial statements after the completion of a planned transaction 预计财务报表：关于企业完成一项计划交易后的财务报表的预测

programmable /ˈprəʊgræməb(ə)l/ *adjective* possible to programme 可编程的

programme evaluation and review technique /ˌprəʊgræm ɪvæljuˌeɪʃ(ə)n ən rɪˈvjuː tekˌniːk/ *noun* a way of planning and controlling a large project, concentrating on scheduling and completion on time 计划评审法，统筹法：以日程安排及按时完工为重点的大型项目计划与管理方法 Abbreviation 缩写 **PERT**

programming engineer /ˈprəʊgræmɪŋ ˌendʒɪnɪə/ *noun* an engineer in charge of programming a computer system（计算机系统）程序工程师

progress *noun* /ˈprəʊgres/ the movement of work towards completion 进度，进展 ○ *to report on the progress of the work* or *of the negotiations* 汇报工作（或谈判）进度 ■ *verb* /prəʊˈgres/ to move forward, to go ahead 前进，进行 ○ *The contract is progressing through various departments.* 合同正由各个部门依次处理。

progressive /prəˈgresɪv/ *adjective* moving forward in stages 累进的

progressive taxation /prəˌgresɪv tækˈseɪʃ(ə)n/ *noun* a taxation system where tax levels increase as the income is higher 累进税制：税率随收入增加而相应提高的税收制度 Also called 亦称作 **graduated taxation**. Compare 比较 **regressive taxation**

prohibitive /prəʊˈhɪbɪtɪv/ *adjective* with a price so high that you cannot afford to pay it（价格）过高的，高昂的 ○ *The cost of redesigning the product is prohibitive.* 产品的重新设计成本高得令人望而却步。

project /ˈprɒdʒekt/ *noun* **1.** a plan 计划 ○ *She has drawn up a project for developing new markets in Europe.* 她起草了一个在欧洲开发新市场的计划。**2.** a particular job of work which follows a plan 项目 ○ *We are just completing an engineering project in North Africa.* 我们刚完成在北非的一个工程项目。○ *The company will start work on the project next month.* 公司将在下月开始此项目。

projected /prəˈdʒektɪd/ *adjective* planned or expected 计划的；预期的

project finance /ˌprɒdʒekt ˈfaɪnæns/ *noun* money raised for a specific undertaking, usually a construction or development project 项目融资：为某一事业（通常为建筑或开发项目）筹集资金

projection /prəˈdʒekʃən/ *noun* a forecast of something which will happen in the future 预测 ○ *Projection of profits for the next three years.* 未来三年的利润预测。○ *The sales manager was asked to draw up sales projections for the next three years.* 要求销售部经理作未来三年的销售预测。

promise /ˈprɒmɪs/ *noun* an act of saying that you will do something 承诺 ■ *verb* to say that you will do something 承诺 ○ *They promised to pay the last instalment next week*. 他们承诺下星期支付分期付款中的最后一笔。○ *The personnel manager promised he would look into the grievances of the office staff*. 人事经理承诺,他将对办公文员的申诉进行调查。

promissory note /ˈprɒmɪsəri ˌnəʊt/ *noun* a document stating that someone promises to pay an amount of money on a specific date 本票,期票:载有某人承诺在特定日期付款的票证

promote /prəˈməʊt/ *verb* **1.** to give someone a more important job or to move someone to a higher grade 升职,晋升 ○ *He was promoted from salesman to sales manager*. 他从销售人员晋升为销售部经理。**2.** to advertise a product 促销(产品)

promotion /prəˈməʊʃ(ə)n/ *noun* the fact of being moved up to a more important job 升职 ○ *I ruined my chances of promotion when I argued with the managing director*. 由于同总经理争执,我失去了晋升的机会。○ *The job offers good promotion chances* or *promotion prospects*. 该工作有很好的升迁机会。

'...finding the right promotion to appeal to children is no easy task'
"找到能吸引小孩的适当推销方法不是件容易的事"[*Marketing*《市场》]

'...you have to study the profiles and people involved very carefully and tailor the promotion to fill those needs'
"你必须非常仔细地研究有关资料和所涉人员,并提升适当的人员来填补那些空缺"[*Marketing Week*《市场周刊》]

promotional /prəˈməʊʃ(ə)n(ə)l/ *adjective* used in an advertising campaign 推销的 ○ *The admen are using balloons as promotional material*. 广告人员使用气球作为推销工具。

'...the simplest way to boost sales at the expense of regional newspapers is by a heavyweight promotional campaign'
"要通过地区报纸促进销售,最简单的方法就是开展大规模的促销活动"[*Marketing Week*《市场周刊》]

prompt /prɒmpt/ *adjective* rapid or done immediately 迅速的;即期的 ○ *We got very prompt service at the complaints desk*. 我们在投诉服务台得到即时的服务。○ *Thank you for your prompt reply to my letter*. 谢谢你对我的信件的迅速答复。

'...they keep shipping costs low and can take advantage of quantity discounts and other allowances for prompt payment'
"他们保持低廉的运费,而且能利用数量折扣及其他即时付款优惠"[*Duns Business Month*《邓氏商业月刊》]

proof /pruːf/ *noun* evidence which shows that something is true 证据

-proof /pruːf/ *suffix* preventing something getting in or getting out or harming something 防…的 ○ *a dustproof cover* 防尘罩 ○ *an inflationproof pension* 不受通胀影响的退休金 ○ *a soundproof studio* 隔音工作室

property /ˈprɒpəti/ *noun* **1.** land and buildings 房地产 ○ *Property taxes are higher in the inner city*. 市中心的房地产税较高。○ *They are assessing damage to property* or *property damage after the storm*. 他们正在评估暴风雨造成的房产损毁。○ *The commercial property market is booming*. 商业地产市场日益兴旺。**2.** a building 房屋,物业 ○ *We have several properties* *for sale in the centre of the town*. 我们在市中心有几处房屋待售。

property bond /ˈprɒpəti bɒnd/ *noun* an investment in a fund invested in properties or in property companies 房地产债券:对房地产投资基金或房地产公司的投资

property company /ˈprɒpəti ˌkʌmp(ə)ni/ *noun* a company which buys buildings to lease them 房产租赁公司:购买房屋进行租赁的公司

proportion /prəˈpɔːʃ(ə)n/ *noun* a part of a total 比例,部分 ○ *A proportion of the pre-tax profit is set aside for contingencies*. 一部分税前利润被留出作为应急费用。○ *Only a small proportion of our sales comes from retail shops*. 我们销售收入中只有一小部分来自零售商店。

proportional /prəˈpɔːʃ(ə)n(ə)l/ *adjective* directly related 直接相关的 ○ *The increase in profit is proportional to the reduction in overheads*. 利润增长与间接费用下降直接相关。

proportionately /prəˈpɔːʃ(ə)nətli/ *adverb* in a way that is directly related 成比例地

proprietary /prəˈpraɪət(ə)ri/ *noun*, *adjective* a product, e. g. a medicine which is made and owned by a company 专卖品,专利品;专有的,专卖的,专利的

proprietary company /prəˌpraɪət(ə)ri ˈkʌmp(ə)ni/ *noun US* a company formed to invest in stock of other companies so as to control them (美) 控股公司:专门为持有其他公司控股权而成立的公司 Abbreviation 缩写 **pty** (NOTE: The UK term is **holding company** 英国用语为 **holding company**)

proprietary drug /prəˌpraɪət(ə)ri ˈdrʌg/ *noun* a drug which is made by a particular company and marketed under a brand name 专利药品,专卖药品:由特定公司制造并以某一品牌销售的药品

proprietor /prəˈpraɪətə/ *noun* the owner of a business, especially in the hospitality industry (尤指酒店业的)业主,所有人 ○ *She is the proprietor of a hotel* or *a hotel proprietor*. 她是一家酒店的所有人。○ *The restaurant has a new proprietor*. 该餐馆有了新主人。

proprietors' interest /prəˌpraɪətəz ˈɪntrəst/ *noun* the amount which the owners of a business have invested in the business 业主权益

pro rata /prəʊ ˈrɑːtə/ *adjective*, *adverb* at a rate which varies according to the size or importance of something 按比例的(地),相应的(地) ○ *When part of the shipment was destroyed we received a pro rata payment*. 由于部分货物损毁,我们按比例收取了付款。○ *The full-time pay is £500 a week and the part-timers are paid pro rata*. 全职工资每周500英镑,兼职工资按比例计算。

prospect /ˈprɒspekt/ *noun* a chance or possibility that something will happen in the future 前景 □ **her job prospects are good** she is very likely to find a job 她的就业前景看好

prospective /prəˈspektɪv/ *adjective* possibly happening in the future 预期的

prospective dividend /prəˌspektɪv ˈdɪvɪdend/ *noun* a dividend which a company expects to pay at the end of the current year 预期股利

prospective P/E ratio /prəˌspektɪv ˌpiː ˈiː ˌreɪʃiəʊ/ *noun* a P/E ratio expected in the future on the basis of forecast dividends 预期市盈率

prospects /ˈprɒspekts/ *plural noun* the possibilities for the future 前景

prospectus /prəˈspektəs/ *noun* a document which gives information to attract buyers or customers 产品简介；宣传广告：提供信息以吸引买家或顾客的文件 ○ *The restaurant has people handing out prospectuses in the street*. 该餐馆雇人在大街上分发宣传广告。

'...when the prospectus emerges, existing shareholders and any prospective new investors can find out more by calling the free share information line; they will be sent a leaflet. Non-shareholders who register in this way will receive a prospectus when it is published; existing shareholders will be sent one automatically'
"招股章程制订后，现有股东及任何潜在投资者都可以拨打免费股票信息热线获得更多信息，并将收到一份传单。招股章程印出后，按上述方式登记过的非股东将收到一份，现有股东则自动取得一份"［*Financial Times*《金融时报》］

prosperity /prɒˈsperɪti/ *noun* the state of being rich 繁荣，富有

prosperous /ˈprɒsp(ə)rəs/ *adjective* rich 繁荣的，富裕的 ○ *a prosperous shopkeeper* 一个富裕的店主 ○ *a prosperous town* 一个富庶的城镇

protectionism /prəˈtekʃənɪz(ə)m/ *noun* the practice of protecting producers in the home country against foreign competitors by banning or taxing imports or by imposing import quotas（贸易）保护主义：禁止进口、征收进口税或实施进口配额制，以便在国际竞争中保护本国生产者

protective tariff /prəˌtektɪv ˈtærɪf/ *noun* a tariff which tries to ban imports to stop them competing with local products 保护性关税：努力阻止进口产品与本国产品竞争的关税

pro tem /ˌprəʊ ˈtem/ *adverb* temporarily, for a time 暂时地；当时地

protest /ˈprəʊtest/ *noun* an official document which proves that a bill of exchange has not been paid 拒付证书：表明汇票未获兑付的正式书面证明

provide /prəˈvaɪd/ *verb* **1.** to give or supply something 提供 **2.** to put money aside in accounts to cover expenditure or loss in the future（拨出资金为未来的开支或损失）作准备 ○ *£25,000 is provided against bad debts*. 拨出2.5万英镑的坏账准备金。

provident /ˈprɒvɪd(ə)nt/ *adjective* providing benefits in case of illness, old age or other cases of need 准备性的，顾及将来的：为就医、养老或其他需要作准备 ○ *a provident fund* 准备基金 ○ *a provident society* 储蓄互助会

provider of capital /prəˌvaɪdə əv ˈkæpɪt(ə)l/ *noun* a person or company which provides capital to a business, usually by being a shareholder（企业）出资者

provision /prəˈvɪʒ(ə)n/ *noun* **1.** an amount of money put aside in accounts for anticipated expenditure where the timing or amount of expenditure is uncertain, often for doubtful debts 准备金：为时间或金额不确定的预计开支（通常是呆账）拨出的准备资金 ○ *The bank has made a £2m provision for bad debts* or *a $5bn provision against Third World loans*. 银行拨出200万英镑的坏账准备金（或为第三世界国家贷款拨出50亿美元准备金）。**2.** □ **there is no provision for** *or* **no provision has**

been made for car parking in the plans for the office block the plans do not include space for cars to park 设计办公楼区时未考虑停车场

'... landlords can create short lets of dwellings which will be free from the normal security of tenure provisions'
"房主可以将寓所短期出租,这种出租形式将不再受租用保障条款的限制"[*Times*《泰晤士报》]

provisional /prəˈvɪʒ(ə)n(ə)l/ *adjective* temporary, not final or permanent 临时的,暂时的 ○ *She was given a provisional posting to see*. 有人向她出示临时过账记录。○ *The sales department has been asked to make a provisional forecast of sales*. 销售部门被要求作出临时销售额预测。○ *The provisional budget has been drawn up for each department*. 有关各个部门的临时预算已编定。○ *They faxed their provisional acceptance of the contract*. 他们通过传真表示暂可接受合同。

provisionally /prəˈvɪʒ(ə)nəli/ *adverb* not finally 临时地,暂时地 ○ *The contract has been accepted provisionally*. 这份合同暂时被接受了。

provisions /prəˈvɪʒ(ə)nz/ *noun* money put aside in accounts for anticipated expenditure where the timing or amount of expenditure is uncertain. If the expenditure is not certain to occur at all, then the money set aside is called a 'contingent liability' 准备金:为时间或金额不确定的预计开支拨出的准备资金。若完全不确定开支是否会发生,则拨出的款项称为"或有负债"

proxy /ˈprɒksi/ *noun* **1.** a document which gives someone the power to act on behalf of someone else 委托授权书 ○ *to sign by proxy* 授权签字 **2.** a person who acts on behalf of someone else 代理人,代表 ○ *She asked the chairman to act as proxy for her*. 她请主席当她的代理人。

proxy form /ˈprɒksi fɔːm/, **proxy card** /ˈprɒksi kɑːd/ *noun* a form which a shareholders receive with their invitations to attend an AGM, and which they fill in if they want to appoint a proxy to vote for them on a resolution 代理卡,代表委任表格:连同年度股东大会的邀请函一起发给股东的表格,股东可用它来委任代表参加决议案投票

proxy statement /ˈprɒksi ˌsteɪtmənt/ *noun* a document, filed with the SEC, outlining executive pay packages, option grants and other perks, and also giving details of dealings by executives in shares of the company 委托书:提交证监会的一种文件,它概述行政人员的薪酬、期权及其他津贴,并列出行政人员在买卖公司股票方面的详情

proxy vote /ˈprɒksi vəʊt/ *noun* a vote made by proxy 代表投票 ○ *The proxy votes were all in favour of the board's recommendation*. 所有代表都投票同意董事会的推荐。

PRT *abbr* petroleum revenue tax 石油收入税

prudence /ˈpruːdəns/ *noun* the use of care and judgement 谨慎,慎重

prudent /ˈpruːdənt/ *adjective* careful, not taking any risks 谨慎的,慎重的

prudential ratio /pruˌdenʃ(ə)l ˈreɪʃiəʊ/ *noun* a ratio of capital to assets which a bank feels it is prudent to have, according to EU regulations 谨慎比率:根据欧盟规定,为谨慎起见银

行应保有的资本/资产比率

PSBR *abbr* Public Sector Borrowing Requirement 公共部门所需借款额

Pty *abbr* proprietary company 控股公司

Pty Ltd *abbr* private limited company 私人有限责任公司

public /ˈpʌblɪk/ *adjective* **1.** referring to all the people in general 公众的，公共的 **2.** referring to the government or the state 政府的，国家的

Public Accounts Committee /ˌpʌblɪk əˈkaʊnts kəˌmɪti/ *noun* a committee of the House of Commons which examines the spending of each department and ministry 公共账户委员会：下议院中检查各个部门支出的一个委员会

public debt /ˌpʌblɪk ˈdet/ *noun* the money that a government or a set of governments owes 公债

public deposits /ˌpʌblɪk dɪˈpɒzɪts/ *noun* in the United Kingdom, the government's credit monies held at the Bank of England（英国）国库存款，政府存款

public expenditure /ˌpʌblɪk ɪkˈspendɪtʃə/ *noun* money spent by the local or central government 公共支出：地方或中央政府的支出

public finance /ˌpʌblɪk ˈfaɪnæns/ *noun* the raising of money by governments by taxes or borrowing, and the spending of it 政府财政：政府通过税收或借款进行的资金筹集以及这些资金的使用

public funds /ˌpʌblɪk ˈfʌndz/ *plural noun* government money available for expenditure 公共基金：可用于支出的政府资金

public holiday /ˌpʌblɪk ˈhɒlɪdeɪ/ *noun* a day when all employees are entitled to take a holiday 公假，公共假期：所有员工都有权享受的假期

publicity budget /pʌbˈlɪsɪti ˌbʌdʒɪt/ *noun* money allowed for expenditure on publicity 广告预算

public limited company /ˌpʌblɪk ˌlɪmɪtɪd ˈkʌmp(ə)ni/ *noun* a company whose shares can be bought on the Stock Exchange 公众持股公司，股票上市公司，公共股票有限公司：其股票可在证券交易所买到的公司 Abbreviation 缩写 **Plc**, **PLC**, **plc** Also called 亦称作 **public company**

publicly held company /ˌpʌblɪkli held ˈkʌmp(ə)ni/ *noun US* company controlled by a few shareholders or its directors, but which is quoted on the Stock Exchange and where the public hold a few shares（美）公众公司，公众持有的公司：由少数股东或其董事控制、但在证券交易所上市且公众持有少数股份的公司

public ownership /ˌpʌblɪk ˈəʊnəʃɪp/ *noun* a situation where the government owns a business, i. e. where an industry is nationalized 公有制：由政府拥有企业的情况，即行业国有化

public placing /ˌpʌblɪk ˈpleɪsɪŋ/, **public placement** /ˌpʌblɪk ˈpleɪsmənt/ *noun* an act of offering a new issue of shares to investing institutions, though not to private investors in general 公开配售，公开发售：向投资机构（而不向普通私人投资者）发售新股

public sector /ˈpʌblɪk ˌsektə/ *noun* nationalised industries and services 公共部门：国有化行业或服务 ○ *a report on wage rises in the public sector* or *on public-sector wage settlements* 公共部

门薪金增长的报告(或关于公共部门薪金确定的报告) Also called 亦称作 **government sector**

Public Sector Borrowing Requirement /ˌpʌblɪk ˌsektə ˈbɒrəʊɪŋ rɪˌkwaɪəmənt/ *noun* the amount of money which a government has to borrow to pay for its own spending 公共部门所需借款额:政府必须借入以支付其自身支出的金额 Abbreviation 缩写 **PBSR**

public spending /ˌpʌblɪk ˈspendɪŋ/ *noun* spending by the government or by local authorities 公共支出:政府或地方机构的支出

Public Trustee /ˌpʌblɪk ˌtrʌsˈtiː/ *noun* an official who is appointed as a trustee of an individual's property 公众受托人:被指派作为个人财产受托人的官员

published accounts /ˌpʌblɪʃt əˈkaʊnts/ *noun* the accounts of a company which have been prepared and audited and then must be published by sending to the shareholders and other interested parties 公开报表:由公司编制并经审核、必须发送给股东及其他权益方的公司报表

pump priming /ˈpʌmp ˌpraɪmɪŋ/ *noun* government investment in new projects which it hopes will benefit the economy 刺激经济的政府支出:政府为推动经济发展而对新项目的投资

purchase /ˈpɜːtʃɪs/ *noun* a product or service which has been bought 购买物

purchase book /ˈpɜːtʃɪs bʊk/ *noun* a book in which purchases are recorded 购货簿

purchase daybook, /ˌpɜːtʃɪs ˈdeɪbʊk/ **purchases day-book** *noun* a book which records the purchases made each day 日购货簿,购货日记账

purchase invoice /ˌpɜːtʃɪs ˈɪnvɔɪs/ *noun* an invoice received by a purchaser from a seller 购货发票

purchase ledger /ˈpɜːtʃɪs ˌledʒə/ *noun* a book in which expenditure is noted 购货分类账

purchase order /ˈpɜːtʃɪs ˌɔːdə/ *noun* an official order made out by a purchasing department for goods which a company wants to buy 订货单,订购单 ○ *We cannot supply you without a purchase order number.* 没有订购单号,我们就无法向你供货。

purchase price /ˈpɜːtʃɪs praɪs/ *noun* a price paid for something 购买价

purchaser /ˈpɜːtʃɪsə/ *noun* a person or company that purchases 购买者,买方 ○ *The company has found a purchaser for its warehouse.* 公司已为其仓库找到了买家。

purchase requisition /ˌpɜːtʃɪs ˌrekwɪˈzɪʃ(ə)n/ *noun* an instruction from a department within an organisation to its purchasing department to buy goods or services, stating the kind and quantity required, and forming the basis of a purchase order 采购要求,请购单:组织内的某个部门向采购部门发出的商品或劳务购买指示,说明需要的种类及数量,并以此作为订购单的依据

purchase tax /ˈpɜːtʃɪs tæks/ *noun* a tax paid on things which are bought 购买税,购项税金

purchasing /ˈpɜːtʃɪsɪŋ/ *noun*, *adjective* buying 购买(的)

purchasing department /ˈpɜːtʃɪsɪŋ dɪˌpɑːtmənt/ *noun* the section of a company which deals with the buying of stock, raw materials, equipment, etc.（公司）采购部

purchasing manager /ˈpɜːtʃɪsɪŋ ˌmænɪdʒə/ *noun* the head of a purchasing department 采购经理

purchasing officer /ˈpɜːtʃɪsɪŋ ˌɒfɪsə/ *noun* a person in a company or organisation who is responsible for buying stock, raw materials, equipment, etc. 采购负责人

purchasing power /ˈpɜːtʃɪsɪŋ ˌpaʊə/ *noun* the quantity of goods which can be bought by a particular group of people or with a particular sum of money 购买力 ○ *the purchasing power of the school market* 校园市场的购买力 ○ *The purchasing power of the pound has fallen over the last five years.* 过去五年间，英镑的购买力下降了。

pure endowment /ˌpjʊə ɪnˈdaʊmənt/ *noun* a gift whose use is fully prescribed by the donor 用途由捐赠人指定的赠品

put down /ˌpʊt ˈdaʊn/ *verb* **1.** to make a deposit 存入 ○ *to put down money on a house* 存款购房 **2.** to write an item in a ledger or an account book 记账；把…入账 ○ *to put down a figure for expenses* 将费用入账

put up /ˌpʊt ˈʌp/ *verb* **1.** □ **who put up the money for the shop?** who provided the investment money for the shop to start? 谁为商店开业提供了资金？□ **to put something up for sale** to advertise that something is for sale 将出售某物的消息广而告之 ○ *When he retired he decided to put his town flat up for sale.* 退休时，他决定将其在城里的公寓拿出去出售。**2.** to increase something, to make something higher 提升，增加 ○ *The shop has put up all its prices by 5%.* 该商店将所有商品都提价 5%。

PV *abbr* present value 现值

pyramid selling /ˈpɪrəmɪd ˌselɪŋ/ *noun* an illegal way of selling goods or investments to the public, where each selling agent pays for the franchise to sell the product or service, and sells that right on to other agents together with stock, so that in the end the person who makes most money is the original franchiser, and sub-agents or investors may lose all their investments 金字塔式推销，传销：一种非法的商品或投资销售方式，每个销售代理付款购买产品或服务的专卖权，然后将该权利连同存货一起卖给其他代理商，最后挣得最多的是最初的经销商，分代理商或投资者则可能损失他们的全部投资

'...much of the population had committed their life savings to get-rich-quick pyramid investment schemes—where newcomers pay the original investors until the money runs out—which inevitably collapsed'
"号称能快速致富的传销令许多人赔进了毕生的积蓄，新发展的下线被最初的上家骗得血本无还，这类传销最终的结局只有一个：崩盘"［*Times*《泰晤士报》］

Q

qualification /ˌkwɒlɪfɪˈkeɪʃ(ə)n/ *noun* a document or some other formal proof of the fact that someone has successfully completed a specialised course of study or has acquired a skill 资格证书；资格证明 ○ *You must have the right qualifications for the job.* 你必须具备做这项工作的适当资格。○ *Job-hunting is difficult if you have no qualifications.* 如果没有相关资格证书你将很难找到工作。

'... personnel management is not an activity that can ever have just one set of qualifications as a requirement for entry into it'
"人事管理不是有一套资格证书就能胜任的"［*Personnel Management*《人事管理》］

qualified /ˈkwɒlɪfaɪd/ *adjective* **1.** having passed special examinations in a subject 有资格的，合格的 ○ *She is a qualified accountant.* 她是一位取得执业资格的会计师。○ *We have appointed a qualified designer to supervise the decorating of the new reception area.* 我们已委派一位合格的设计师监督新接待区的装饰工作。**2.** with some reservations or conditions 有保留的，有条件的 ○ *qualified acceptance of a contract* 有保留地接受合同 ○ *The plan received qualified approval from the board.* 该计划获得董事会有条件的批准。

'... applicants will be professionally qualified and ideally have a degree in Commerce and postgraduate management qualifications'
"申请人必须具有专业资格，最好拥有商科学位和管理学研究生资格"［*Australian Financial Review*《澳大利亚金融评论报》］

qualified acceptance of a bill /ˌkwɒlɪfaɪd əkˈseptəns əv eɪ bɪl/ *noun* acceptance of a bill which takes place only if conditions are met 附条件票据承兑

qualified accounts /ˌkwɒlɪfaɪd əˈkaʊnts/ *plural noun* accounts which have been noted by the auditors because they contain something with which the auditors do not agree 有保留意见的报表；注有审计师保留意见的报表

qualified domestic trust /ˌkwɒlɪfaɪd dəˈmestɪk trʌst/ *noun* a trust for the noncitizen spouse of a US citizen, affording tax advantages at the time of the citizen's death 附条件国内信托：夫妻双方一方系美国公民，另一方系外籍公民时，为外籍一方设立的信托，并在其配偶去世时提供税务优惠

qualified valuer /ˌkwɒlɪfaɪd ˈvæljʊə/ *noun* a person conducting a valuation who holds a recognised and relevant professional qualification and has recent post-qualification experience, and sufficient knowledge of the state of the market, with reference to the location and category of the tangible fixed asset being valued 合格估值师:获得相关专业资格认可、并在取得资格认证后的近期内,从事过相关工作的估值人员,其应对所估的有形固定资产在市场中的定位和种类有充分了解

qualifying distribution /ˌkwɒlɪfaɪŋ ˌdɪstrɪˈbjuːʃ(ə)n/ *noun* a payment of a dividend to a shareholder, on which advance corporation tax is paid 合格分配,税后分配:已预提公司税的股东股利支付

qualifying period /ˈkwɒlɪfaɪŋ ˌpɪəriəd/ *noun* a time which has to pass before something or someone qualifies for something, e.g. a grant or subsidy 资格审定期:获得某项资格(如拨款或补贴)必需的时间 ○ *There is a six-month qualifying period before you can get a grant from the local authority.* 在获得地方当局拨款前,必须经过六个月的资格审定期。

qualifying shares /ˌkwɒlɪfaɪŋ ˈʃeəz/ *plural noun* the number of shares which you need to earn to get a bonus issue or to be a director of the company, etc. 保证股,资格股:获得红利股或成为公司董事必须拥有的股数

quality control /ˈkwɒlɪti kənˌtrəʊl/ *noun* the process of making sure that the quality of a product is good 质量控制,质量管理

quango /ˈkwæŋgəʊ/ *noun* an official body, set up by a government to investigate or deal with a special problem 半官方机构:政府为调查或处理特定问题而设立的官方机构(NOTE: plural is **quangos** 复数为 **quangos**)

quantifiable /ˈkwɒntɪfaɪəb(ə)l/ *adjective* possible to quantify 可量化的 ○ *The effect of the change in the discount structure is not quantifiable.* 贴现率结构的变化结果是不可量化的。

quantity discount /ˌkwɒntɪti ˈdɪskaʊnt/ *noun* a discount given to people who buy large quantities 数量折扣:给予购买量大的顾客的折扣

quantum meruit /ˌkwæntʊm ˈmeruɪt/ *phrase* a Latin phrase meaning 'as much as has been earned' (拉丁语)按实值支付

quarter /ˈkwɔːtə/ *noun* **1.** one of four equal parts (25%) 四分之一;百分之二十五 ○ *She paid only a quarter of the list price.* 她只付了标价的四分之一。**2.** a period of three months 季度 ○ *The instalments are payable at the end of each quarter.* 分期付款在每季度末支付。

'...corporate profits for the first quarter showed a 4 per cent drop from last year's final three months'
"公司一季度利润环比减少 4%" [*Financial Times*《金融时报》]

'... economists believe the economy is picking up this quarter and will do better still in the second half of the year'
"经济学家看好经济将在本季企稳回升,下半年还会更上一层楼" [*Sunday Times*《星期日泰晤士报》]

quarter day /ˈkwɔːtə deɪ/ *noun* a day at the end of a quarter, when rents, fees etc. should be paid 季度结账日

quarterly /ˈkwɔːtəli/ *adjective, adverb* happening once every three months 季度的(地),按季度的(地) ○ *There is a quarterly charge for electricity.* 电费按季收取。○ *The bank sends* *us a quarterly statement*. 银行给我们寄送季度结单。○ *We agreed to pay the rent quarterly* or *on a quarterly basis*. 我们同意按季支付租金。

quarterly report /ˌkwɔːtəli rɪˈpɔːt/ *noun* the results of a corporation, produced each quarter (公司业绩)季度报告

quartile /ˈkwɔːtaɪl/ *noun* one of a series of three figures below which 25%, 50% or 75% of the total falls 四分位数,四分点

quasi- /kweɪzaɪ/ *prefix* almost or which seems like 类似;准;半 ○ *a quasi-official body* 半官方机构

quasi-loan /ˌkweɪzaɪˈləʊn/ *noun* an agreement between two parties where one agrees to pay the other's debts, provided that the second party agrees to reimburse the first at some later date 准贷款:双方达成的一种协议,一方同意替另一方还债,前提是后者须在日后偿还前者所垫付的款项

quasi-public corporation /ˌkweɪzaɪˌpʌblɪk ˌkɔːpəˈreɪʃ(ə)n/ *noun US* a US institution which is privately owned, but which serves a public function, such as the Federal National Mortgage Association (美)准公共公司:私人拥有而承担公共职能的机构(如联邦国民抵押贷款协会)

queue /kjuː/ *noun* **1.** a line of people waiting one behind the other 一队人 ○ *to form a queue* or *to join a queue* 排队 ○ *Queues formed at the doors of the bank when the news spread about its possible collapse*. 银行可能倒闭的消息传开后,银行门口排起了长队。**2.** a series of documents such as orders or application forms which are dealt with in order (文件)队列:需依次处理的文件系列(如订单、申请表) ■ *verb* to form a line one after the other for something 排队 ○ *When food was rationed, people had to queue for bread*. 食物实行配给供应时,人们不得不排队购买面包。○ *We queued for hours to get tickets*. 我们买票排了几个小时的队。○ *a list of companies queueing to be launched on the Stock Exchange* 排队申请上市的公司名单 ○ *The candidates queued outside the interviewing room*. 应聘者在面试考场外排队。

queuing time /ˈkjuːɪŋ taɪm/ *noun* a period of time messages have to wait before they can be processed or transmitted (信息处理或传播前的)等候时间

quick ratio /ˌkwɪk ˈreɪʃiəʊ/ *noun* same as 同 **liquidity ratio**

quid /kwɪd/ *noun* one pound Sterling (*slang*) (俚)一英镑 □ **to be quids in** to make a profit, to be in luck 获利;走运 ○ *He was quids in after the sale*. 这笔销售使他获利丰厚。

quid pro quo /ˌkwɪd prəʊ ˈkwəʊ/ *noun* money paid or an action carried out in return for something 补偿物,报酬,交换条件 ○ *She agreed to repay the loan early, and as a quid pro quo the bank released the collateral*. 她同意提前偿还贷款,作为交换条件,银行解除了附属担保。

quorum /ˈkwɔːrəm/ *noun* a minimum number of people who have to be present at a meeting to make it valid 法定人数:会议召开必须达到的最少出席人数

quota /ˈkwəʊtə/ *noun* a limited amount of something which is allowed to be produced, imported, etc. 配额,

限额,定额

'Canada agreed to a new duty-free quota of 600,000 tonnes a year'
"加拿大同意给予每年 60 万吨的新免税配额"[*Globe and Mail* (*Toronto*)《环球邮报》(多伦多)]

quota system /ˈkwəʊtə ˌsɪstəm/ *noun* 配额制 **1.** a system where imports or supplies are regulated by fixed maximum amounts [进口或供应有固定上限的制度] **2.** an arrangement for distribution which allows each distributor only a specific number of items [一种分销安排,其中每个分销商只获得一定数量的产品]

quotation /kwəʊˈteɪʃ(ə)n/ *noun* an estimate of how much something will cost 报价 ○ *They sent in their quotation for the job*. 他们提交了对这项工作的报价。○ *Our quotation was much lower than all the others*. 我们的报价比其他人都低很多。○ *We accepted the lowest quotation*. 我们接受了最低报价。

quote /kwəʊt/ *verb* **1.** to repeat words or a reference number used by someone else 引用,提供 ○ *He quoted figures from the annual report*. 他引用了年度报告中的数字。○ *In reply please quote this number*. 请在回复中引用此序号。○ *When making a complaint please quote the batch number printed on the box*. 投诉时请提供印在盒子上的批号。○ *She replied, quoting the number of the account*. 她在回复中提供了该账号。**2.** to estimate what a cost or price is likely to be 估价,报价 ○ *to quote a price for supplying stationery* 对文具的供应提供报价 ○ *Their prices are always quoted in dollars*. 他们一直以美元报价。○ *He quoted me a price of £1,026*. 他向我报价 1,026 英镑。○ *Can you quote for supplying 20,000 envelopes*? 你能否对提供两万个信封报个价? ■ *noun* an estimate of how much something will cost (*informal*)(非正式)估价,报虚盘 ○ *to give someone a quote for supplying computers* 向某人提供供应计算机的虚盘。○ *We have asked for quotes for refitting the shop*. 我们要求对重新装修商店提供估价。○ *Her quote was the lowest of three*. 她的报价在三人中最低。○ *We accepted the lowest quote*. 我们接受了最低报价。

'... banks operating on the foreign exchange market refrained from quoting forward US/Hongkong dollar exchange rates'
"就美元兑港元的远期汇率而言,在外汇市场运作的银行不便给出报价"[*South China Morning Post*《南华早报》]

quoted company /ˌkwəʊtɪd ˈkʌmp(ə)ni/ *noun* a company whose shares can be bought or sold on the Stock Exchange 上市公司

quoted investments /ˌkwəʊtɪd ɪnˈvestmənts/ *noun* investments which are listed on a Stock Exchange 上市证券投资

quote-driven system /ˈkwəʊt ˌdrɪv(ə)n ˌsɪstəm/ *noun* a system of working a stock market, where marketmakers quote a price for a stock, as opposed to an order-driven system 庄家报价系统:经营股票市场的系统,其中庄家为股票报价,与指令报价系统相对

quoted shares /ˌkwəʊtɪd ˈʃeəz/ *plural noun* shares which can be bought or sold on the Stock Exchange 上市股票

R

racket /ˈrækɪt/ *noun* an illegal deal which makes a lot of money 敲诈；骗钱 ○ *She runs a cut-price ticket racket*. 她从事削价票的非法买卖。

rack rent /ˈræk rent/ *noun* a very high rent 高额租金

raise /reɪz/ *noun US* an increase in salary（美）加薪 ○ *He asked the boss for a raise*. 他要求老板加薪。○ *She is pleased - she has had her raise*. 她得到加薪后很高兴。○ *She got her raise last month*. 她上月获得加薪。（NOTE: The UK term is **rise** 英国用语为 **rise**）■ *verb* **1.** to increase or to make higher 使增加，使提高 ○ *The government has raised the tax levels*. 政府提高了税率。○ *Air fares will be raised on June 1st*. 机票将于6月1日涨价。○ *The company raised its dividend by 10%*. 公司将股利提高了10%。○ *When the company raised its prices, it lost half of its share of the market*. 公司提价后失去了一半的市场份额。○ *The organisation will raise wages if inflation gets worse*. 如果通货膨胀加剧，该机构将会加薪。○ *This increase in production will raise the standard of living in the area*. 产量增加将提高该地区的生活水平。**2.** to obtain money or to organise a loan 获得（资金）；筹（资），组织（贷款）○ *The company is trying to raise the capital to fund its expansion programme*. 公司正设法为其扩展计划筹资。○ *The government raises more money by indirect taxation than by direct*. 政府的间接税收高于直接税收。○ *Where will he raise the money from to start up his business?* 他将从哪里筹得创业资金？

'...the company said yesterday that its recent share issue has been oversubscribed, raising A$225.5m'
"公司昨天表示，刚刚发行的股票已被超额认购，筹资2.255亿澳大利亚元"［*Financial Times*《金融时报》］

'...investment trusts can raise capital, but this has to be done as a company does, by a rights issue of equity'
"投资信托可以筹资，但必须和公司一样采取发行优先认股权的方式"［*Investors Chronicle*《投资者纪事》］

'...over the past few weeks, companies raising new loans from international banks have been forced to pay more'
"在过去的几个星期里，从国际银行筹集新贷款的公司不得不为此支付更多"［*Financial Times*《金融时报》］

rally /ˈræli/ *noun* a rise in price when the trend has been downwards（价格）反弹，跌后回升 ○ *Shares staged a rally on the Stock Exchange*. 证券交易所股价反弹。○ *After a brief rally shares fell back to a new low*. 经过一次短暂的反弹后，股价又跌至新低。■ *verb* to rise in price, when the trend has been downwards（价格）反弹，跌后

回升 ○ *Shares rallied on the news of the latest government figures.* 最新的政府统计数字公布后，股价出现反弹。

'...when Japan rallied, it had no difficulty in surpassing its previous all-time high, and this really stretched the price-earnings ratios into the stratosphere'
"日本证券市场反弹后，毫不费力地超过了历史最高点，并使市盈率达到最高水平" [*Money Observer*《货币观察家》]
'...bad news for the US economy ultimately may have been the cause of a late rally in stock prices yesterday'
"关于美国经济的坏消息可能是造成昨日股价推迟反弹的最终原因" [*Wall Street Journal*《华尔街日报》]

R & D *abbr* research and development 研究与开发，研发

random /ˈrændəm/ *adjective* done without making any special selection 随机的

random check /ˌrændəm ˈtʃek/ *noun* a check on items taken from a group without any special selection 随机检查

random sample /ˌrændəm ˈsɑːmpəl/ *noun* a sample taken without any selection 随机抽样

range /reɪndʒ/ *noun* **1.** a series of items (一)系列 ○ *Their range of products* or *product range is too narrow.* 他们的产品系列太窄了。○ *We offer a wide range of sizes* or *range of styles.* 我们供应各种尺寸(或样式)。○ *There are a whole range of alternatives for the new salary scheme.* 新工资计划还有一系列替代方案。**2.** a scale of items from a low point to a high one 范围 □ **range of prices** the difference between the highest and lowest price for a share or bond over a period of time 价格范围：在一段时间内股票或债券最高价与最低价之差

rank /ræŋk/ *noun* a position in a company or an organisation, especially one which shows how important someone is relative to others 级别 ○ *All managers are of equal rank.* 所有经理都是平级的。○ *Promotion means moving up from a lower rank.* 晋升指从低级别升到高级别。■ *verb* **1.** to classify in order of importance (按重要性)排序 ○ *Candidates are ranked in order of their test results.* 候选人按考试成绩排序。**2.** to be in a position 处于特定位置 ○ *The non-voting shares rank equally with the voting shares.* 无表决权股票与有表决权股票享有同等地位。○ *Deferred ordinary shares do not rank for dividend.* 延期付息普通股无权参与股利分配。

rate /reɪt/ *noun* **1.** the money charged for time worked or work completed 费率 **2.** an amount of money paid, e.g. as interest or dividend, shown as a percentage (利息或股利的)支付比率 **3.** the value of one currency against another 汇率 ○ *What is today's rate* or *the current rate for the dollar?* 今天美元的汇率是多少？**4.** an amount, number or speed compared with something else 数；量；速率 ○ *the rate of increase in redundancies* 下岗人数增长率。○ *The rate of absenteeism* or *The absenteeism rate always increases in fine weather.* 天气好时缺勤率就会上升。

'...state-owned banks cut their prime rate a percentage point to 11%'
"国有银行将基本利率削减了一个百分点至11%" [*Wall Street Journal*《华尔街日报》]
'...the unions had argued that public sec-

tor pay rates had slipped behind rates applying in private sector employment'
"工会认为,就薪金而言国营企业远低于私营企业"[*Australian Financial Review*《澳大利亚金融评论报》]
'...royalties have been levied at a rate of 12.5% of full production'
"按总产量的12.5%征收特许权费"[*Lloyd's List*《劳氏日报》]
'...the minister is not happy that banks are paying low interest on current accounts of less than 10 per cent, but are charging rates of between 60 and 71 per cent on loans'
"银行对活期账户只支付不到10%的利息,但贷款利率却高达60%到71%,这令部长感到不满"[*Business in Africa*《非洲商业》]

rateable value /ˌreɪtəb(ə)l ˈvæljuː/ *noun* a value of a property as a basis for calculating local taxes 应税价值:作为计算地方税基础的财产价值

rate of return /ˌreɪt əv rɪˈtɜːn/ *noun* the amount of interest or dividend which comes from an investment, shown as a percentage of the money invested 回报率,投资收益率:投资获得的利息或股利占投资总额的比率

rate of sales /ˌreɪt əv ˈseɪlz/ *noun* the speed at which units are sold 销售率

rates *plural noun* local UK taxes formerly levied on property in the UK and now replaced by the council tax 地方税:英国以前对地产征收的本地税,现已被市政建设税取代

rating /ˈreɪtɪŋ/ *noun* **1.** the act of giving something a value, or the value given 估值,评价;评级;等级 **2.** the valuing of property for local taxes (作为计算地方税基础的)财产价值

rating agency /ˈreɪtɪŋ ˌeɪdʒənsi/ *noun* an organisation which gives a rating to companies or other organisations issuing bonds 评级机构:对发行债券的公司或机构进行评级的组织

rating officer /ˈreɪtɪŋ ˌɒfɪsə/ *noun* an official in a local authority who decides the rateable value of a commercial property 估价员:地方政府中负责确定商用财产应税价值的官员

ratio /ˈreɪʃiəʊ/ *noun* a proportion or quantity of something compared to something else 比率 ○ *the ratio of successes to failures* 成功与失败的比率 ○ *Our product outsells theirs by a ratio of two to one.* 我们的产品销量是他们的两倍。○ *With less manual work available, the ratio of employees to managers is decreasing.* 随着现有体力劳动的减少,雇员与经理的比率也在下降。

ratio analysis /ˈreɪʃiəʊ əˌnæləsɪs/ *noun* a method of analysing the performance of a company by showing the figures in its accounts as ratios and comparing them with those of other companies 比率分析法:对会计报表数据进行比率计算并与其他公司作比较,借以分析公司业绩的方法

raw data /ˌrɔː ˈdeɪtə/ *noun* data as it is put into a computer, without being analysed 原始数据:未经过分析就直接输入计算机的数据

raw materials /rɔː məˈtɪəriəlz/ *plural noun* basic materials which have to be treated or processed in some way before they can be used, e.g. wood, iron ore or crude petroleum (木材、铁矿、原油等需要加工才可使用的)原材料

R/D *abbr* refer to drawer 请与出票人接洽

RDPR *abbr* refer to drawer please represent 与出票人接洽，请稍后再提呈

re- /riː/ *prefix* again 再

readjust /ˌriːəˈdʒʌst/ *verb* to adjust something again or in a new way, or to change in response to new conditions 重新调整，再调整 ○ *to readjust prices to take account of the rise in the costs of raw materials* 考虑到原材料成本上升而重新定价 ○ *to readjust salary scales* 重新调整薪级 ○ *Share prices readjusted quickly to the news of the devaluation*. 贬值消息发布后，股价迅速重新调整。

readjustment /ˌriːəˈdʒʌstmənt/ *noun* an act of readjusting 重新调整 ○ *a readjustment in pricing* 价格的重新调整 ○ *After the devaluation there was a period of readjustment in the exchange rates*. 汇率在贬值后进入了调整期。

ready cash /ˌredi ˈkæʃ/ *noun* money which is immediately available for payment 现金，现款

ready money /ˌredi ˈmʌni/ *noun* cash or money which is immediately available 现金，现款

real /rɪəl/ *adjective* genuine and not an imitation 实际的，真实的 ○ *His case is made of real leather* or *he has a real leather case*. 他的箱子是真皮的(或他有一只真皮箱子)。○ *That car is a real bargain at £300*. 那辆车确实很便宜，才 300 英镑。

'...real wages have been held down dramatically: they have risen as an annual rate of only 1% in the last two years'
"实际工资被压得极低：在过去两年里增长率仅为 1%" [*Sunday Times*《星期日泰晤士报》]

'...sterling M3 rose by 13.5% in the year to August seven percentage points faster than the rate of inflation and the biggest increase in real terms for years'
"本年度截至 8 月份，M3 英镑上升了 13.5%，比通货膨胀率高 7 个百分点，升值幅度是多年来最大的一次" [*Economist*《经济学家》]

'Japan's gross national product for the April-June quarter dropped 0.4% in real terms from the previous quarter'
"从 4 月到 6 月，日本的国民生产总值比上个季度实际下降了 0.4%" [*Nikkei Weekly*《日经周报》]

'...the Federal Reserve Board has eased interest rates in the past year, but they are still at historically high levels in real terms'
"去年联邦储备委员会调低了利率，但实际上仍居于历史高位" [*Sunday Times*《星期日泰晤士报》]

real asset /ˌrɪəl ˈæset/ *noun* a non-movable asset such as land or a building (土地、建筑等)实资产，不动产

real estate /ˈrɪəl ɪˌsteɪt/ *noun* property in the form of land or buildings 不动产，房地产

'...on top of the cost of real estate, the investment in inventory and equipment to open a typical warehouse comes to around $5 million'
"要开一家典型的批发店，除了需要不动产成本外，另外还需要大约 500 万美元来购买存货和设备" [*Duns Business Month*《邓氏商业月刊》]

real estate agent /ˈrɪəl ɪˌsteɪt ˌeɪdʒənt/ *noun US* a person who sells property for customers (美)不动产代理商

real estate investment trust /rɪəl ɪˌsteɪt ɪnˈvestmənt trʌst/ *noun* a public trust company which invests only in property 不动产投资信托公司：只投资于不动产的公共信托公司 Abbreviation 缩写 **REIT**

real exchange rate /ˌrɪəl ɪks'tʃeɪndʒ ˌreɪt/ *noun* an exchange rate that has been adjusted for inflation 实际汇率：经通货膨胀调整后的汇率

real interest rate /ˌrɪəl 'ɪntrəst ˌreɪt/ *noun* an interest rate after taking inflation into account 实际利率：考虑通货膨胀因素后的利率

real investment /ˌrɪəl ɪn'vestmənt/ *noun* the purchase of assets such as land, property, and plant and machinery as opposed to the acquisition of securities 实际投资，产权投资：土地、物业及机器设备等资产的购买，与证券购买相对

realisation /ˌrɪəlaɪ'zeɪʃ(ə)n/, **realization** *noun* the act of making real 实现 ▫ **the realization of a project** putting a project into action 一个项目的实施 ○ *The plan moved a stage nearer realization when the contracts were signed.* 合同的签署使计划离成功又近了一步。

realisation concept /ˌrɪəlaɪ'zeɪʃ(ə)n ˌkɒnsept/ *noun* the principle that increases in value should only be recognised when the assets in question are realised by being sold to an independent purchaser 变现概念，实现原则：资产通过出售给独立购买者进行变现后才能确认增值的原则

realise /'rɪəlaɪz/, **realize** *verb* **1.** to make something become real 实现 ▫ **to realise a project *or* a plan** to put a project or a plan into action 实施一个项目（或计划） **2.** to sell for money 变现 ○ *The company was running out of cash, so the board decided to realise some property* or *assets.* 公司现金短缺，董事会决定变现部分财产（或资产）。○ *The sale realised £100,000.* 这项出售获利10万英镑。▫ **realised gain *or* loss** a gain or loss made when assets are sold 已实现的盈亏：出售资产后的盈亏

realised profit /ˌrɪəlaɪzd 'prɒfɪt/ *noun* an actual profit made when something is sold, as opposed to paper profit 已实现利润：出售某物后获得的实际利润，与账面利润相对

real rate of return /rɪəl ˌreɪt əv rɪ'tɜːn/ *noun* an actual rate of return, calculated after taking inflation into account 实际回报率，实际收益率：考虑通货膨胀因素后的实际投资回报率

real return after tax /rɪəl rɪˌtɜːn ˌɑːftə 'tæks/ *noun* the return calculated after deducting tax and inflation 税后实际回报，税后实际收益：剔除税金和通胀因素后的投资回报

real time /'rɪəl taɪm/ *noun* the time when a computer is working on the processing of data while the event to which the data refers is actually taking place 实时，即时：在事件发生的同时用计算机对事件数据进行同步处理 ○ *The website allows you to check share prices in real time* or *gives real time information on share prices.* 可以通过该网站查看实时股价（或该网站提供股价实时信息）。

real-time system /'rɪəltaɪm ˌsɪstəm/ *noun* a computer system where data is inputted directly into the computer which automatically processes it to produce information which can be used immediately 实时系统：计算机在处理输入的数据时同步自动生成有用信息的系统

realty /'rɪəlti/ *noun* property or real

estate 房地产，不动产

real value /ˌrɪəl ˈvæljuː/ *noun* a value of an investment which is kept the same, e.g. by index-linking 实际价值：通过与指数挂钩等手段保持不变的投资价值

reasonable /ˈriːz(ə)nəb(ə)l/ *adjective* **1.** sensible, or not annoyed 合理的；通情达理的 ○ *The manager of the shop was very reasonable when I tried to explain that I had left my credit cards at home.* 在我说明我把信用卡落在家里后，商店经理显得十分通情达理。**2.** moderate or not expensive 适度的，中等的 ○ *The union has decided to put in a reasonable wage claim.* 工会决定要求适度加薪。

reassess /ˌriːəˈses/ *verb* to assess again 重估，对…再评价 ○ *The manager was asked to reassess the department staff, after the assessments were badly done by the supervisors.* 鉴于考评实施不甚理想，主管被要求对部门员工进行重新考评。

reassessment /ˌriːəˈsesmənt/ *noun* a new assessment 重估，再评价

rebate /ˈriːbeɪt/ *noun* **1.** a reduction in the amount of money to be paid 回扣，折扣 ○ *We are offering a 10% rebate on selected goods.* 我们对精品提供 10%的折扣。**2.** money returned to someone because they have paid too much 退款 ○ *She got a tax rebate at the end of the year.* 她在年末得到了退税。

recapitalisation /riːˌkæpɪt(ə)laɪˈzeɪʃ(ə)n/, **recapitalization** *noun* a change in the capital structure of a company as when new shares are issued, especially when undertaken to avoid the company going into liquidation 资本重组，资本额的调整：改变公司的资本结构（如在新股发行时），尤指为避免公司清算而进行的资本重组

receipt /rɪˈsiːt/ *noun* **1.** a piece of paper showing that money has been paid or that something has been received 收据 ○ *He kept the customs receipt to show that he had paid duty on the goods.* 他保留海关收据作为货物关税已付的证明。○ *She lost her taxi receipt.* 她把出租车发票弄丢了。○ *Keep the receipt for items purchased in case you need to change them later.* 请保留购物小票，以备日后更换所购物品所需。**2.** the act of receiving something 收到 ○ *Goods will be supplied within thirty days of receipt of order.* 货物将在收到订单后 30 天内发出。○ *Invoices are payable within thirty days of receipt.* 发票将在收到后 30 天内开出。○ *On receipt of the notification, the company lodged an appeal.* 收到通知后，公司提出了上诉。■ *verb* to stamp or to sign a document to show that it has been received, or to stamp an invoice to show that it has been paid 签收 ○ *Receipted invoices are filed in the ring binder.* 已签收的发票放进了活页夹里。

receipts /rɪˈsiːts/ *plural noun* money taken in sales （销售）收入 ○ *to itemise receipts and expenditure* 将收支逐条列出 ○ *Receipts are down against the same period of last year.* 收入同比下降了。

'... the public sector borrowing requirement is kept low by treating the receipts from selling public assets as a reduction in borrowing'

"国营企业通过出售公共资产来增加收入从而减少了借款额，因此所需借款额一直很

低”[*Economist*《经济学家》]

‘... gross wool receipts for the selling season to end June appear likely to top $2 billion’

“到6月底销售旺季截止前，羊毛销售总收入有望超过20亿美元”[*Australian Financial Review*《澳大利亚金融评论报》]

receipts and payments account /rɪˌsiːts ən ˈpeɪmənts əˌkaʊnt/ *noun* a report of cash transactions during a period. It is used in place of an income and expenditure account when it is not considered appropriate to distinguish between capital and revenue transactions or to include accruals 现金收支账：某一期间的现金交易报告。当认为不宜区分资本与收益项目或不宜计入应计项目时，可用它来代替收支账目

receivable /rɪˈsiːvəb(ə)l/ *adjective* able to be received 应收的

receivables /rɪˈsiːvəb(ə)lz/ *plural noun* money which is owed to a company 应收账款

receive /rɪˈsiːv/ *verb* to get something which is given or delivered to you 收到 ○ *We received the payment ten days ago*. 我们在十天前收到了付款。○ *The employees have not received any salary for six months*. 员工已经六个月没领到工资了。○ *The goods were received in good condition*. 商品收到时完好无损。

receiver /rɪˈsiːvə/ *noun* a person who receives something 接收人 ○ *He signed as receiver of the shipment*. 他作为收货人签了字。

Receiver of Revenue /rɪˌsiːvə əv ˈrevənjuː/ *noun* an informal term for the South African Revenue Service as a whole 税捐处：南非税务局的非正式名称

receiving /rɪˈsiːvɪŋ/ *noun* an act of getting something which has been delivered 接收

receiving clerk /rɪˈsiːvɪŋ klɑːk/ *noun* an official who works in a receiving office 收货(款)员

receiving department /rɪˈsiːvɪŋ dɪˌpɑːtmənt/ *noun* a section of a company which deals with incoming goods or payments 收货(款)部门

receiving office /rɪˈsiːvɪŋ ˌɒfɪs/ *noun* an office where goods or payments are received 收货(款)办公室

receiving order /rɪˈsiːvɪŋ ˌɔːdə/ *noun* an order from a court appointing an official receiver to a company 接管命令：法院向某公司委派官方破产接管人的命令

recession /rɪˈseʃ(ə)n/ *noun* a period where there is a decline in trade or in the economy 衰退，经济衰退 ○ *The recession has reduced profits in many companies*. 经济衰退使很多公司利润减少。○ *Several firms have closed factories because of the recession*. 因为经济衰退，一些企业已关闭了工厂。

reciprocal /rɪˈsɪprək(ə)l/ *adjective* done by one person, company or country to another one, which does the same thing in return 相互的；互惠的 ○ *We signed a reciprocal agreement* or *a reciprocal contract with a Russian company*. 我们与一家俄罗斯公司签署了互惠协议(或互惠合同)。

reciprocal holdings /rɪˌsɪprək(ə)l ˈhəʊldɪŋz/ *plural noun* a situation where two companies own shares in each other to prevent takeover bids 相互持股：两家公司为避免兼并而相互持有对方的股份

reciprocal trade /rɪˌsɪprək(ə)l ˈtreɪd/ *noun* trade between two countries 互惠贸易

reciprocate /rɪˈsɪprəkeɪt/ *verb* to do the same thing for someone as that person has done for you 互换，交换 ○ *They offered us an exclusive agency for their cars and we reciprocated with an offer of the agency for our buses.* 他们将轿车独家代理权授予我们，作为交换，我们将公共汽车代理权授予他们。

'...in 1934 Congress authorized President Roosevelt to seek lower tariffs with any country willing to reciprocate'
"1934 年，国会批准罗斯福总统对愿意投桃报李的国家降低关税"［*Duns Business Month*《邓氏商业月刊》］

reckon /ˈrekən/ *verb* to calculate something 计算，认为 ○ *to reckon the costs at £25,000* 成本共计 2.5 万英镑 ○ *We reckon the loss to be over £1m.* 我们认为损失将超过 100 万英镑。○ *They reckon the insurance costs to be too high.* 他们认为保险成本太高。

recognise /ˈrekəgnaɪz/，**recognize** *verb* □ **statement of total recognised gains and losses** financial statement showing changes in shareholders' equity during an accounting period (see FRS 3) 经确认总盈亏报表：会计期内股东权益变动的财务报表(参阅 FRS 3)

recognised professional body /ˌrekəgnaɪzd prəˌfeʃ(ə)nəl ˈbɒdi/ *noun* a professional body which is in charge of the regulation of the conduct of its members and is recognised by the FSA 公认职业团体，公认专业机构：英国金融服务管理局(FSA)认可的一家专业机构，其职责为监管所属会员的行为 Abbreviation 缩写 **RPB**

recognized qualification /ˌrekəgnaɪzd ˌkwɒlɪfɪˈkeɪʃ(ə)n/ *noun* a qualification which is well-known to employers and professional bodies 公认的资格：雇主和专业机构都熟知的资格

reconcile /ˈrekənsaɪl/ *verb* to make two financial accounts or statements agree 对账；调节：使两套财务账目或两份报表对得上 ○ *She is trying to reconcile one account with another* or *to reconcile the two accounts.* 她正在核对两套账目。

reconciliation /ˌrekənsɪliˈeɪʃ(ə)n/，**reconcilement** /ˈrekənsaɪlmənt/ *noun* the act of making two accounts or statements agree 对账；调节

reconciliation statement /ˌrekənsɪliˈeɪʃ(ə)n ˌsteɪtmənt/ *noun* a statement which explains how two accounts can be made to agree 对账表；调节表：解释如何使两套账目对得上的明细表

reconstruction /ˌriːkənˈstrʌkʃən/ *noun* **1.** the process of building again 改建，重建 ○ *the economic reconstruction of an area after a disaster* 某地灾后经济重建 **2.** new way of organizing 重组

record /ˈrekɔːd/ *noun* **1.** a report of something which has happened 记录，报告 ○ *The chairman signed the minutes as a true record of the last meeting.* 主席签署了上次会议的会议记录以认定其真实性。□ **for the record** *or* **to keep the record straight** in order that everyone knows what the real facts of the matter are 为把事情说明白，把事情记录在案 ○ *For the record, I should like to say that these sales figures have not yet been checked by the sales department.* 必须说明的是，我认为这些

销售数据尚未经过销售部门核实。**2.** a description of what has happened in the past 记载,记录 ○ *the salesperson's record of service* or *service record* 销售人员的服务记录 ○ *the company's record in industrial relations* 公司的劳资关系记录 ○ *He has a very poor time-keeping record.* 他非常不守时。**3.** a success which is better than anything before 最佳的纪录 ○ *Last year was a record year for the company.* 去年是公司创纪录的一年。○ *Our top sales rep has set a new record for sales per call.* 我们的最佳推销员创造了新的单笔销售纪录。

record book /ˈrekɔːd bʊk/ *noun* a book in which minutes of meetings are kept (会议记录的)记录簿

record date /ˈrekɔːd deɪt/ *noun* same as 同 **date of record**

recorded delivery /rɪˌkɔːdɪd dɪˈlɪv(ə)ri/ *noun* a mail service where the letters are signed for by the person receiving them 签收邮递,保价邮件:由收件人签收的一项邮政服务 ○ *We sent the documents (by) recorded delivery.* 我们通过保价邮件寄出了这些文件。

recording /rɪˈkɔːdɪŋ/ *noun* the act of making a note of something 记录 ○ *the recording of an order* or *of a complaint* 订单(或投诉)的记录

records /ˈrekɔːdz/ *plural noun* documents which give information 档案 ○ *The names of customers are kept in the company's records.* 客户名单保存在公司档案中。○ *We find from our records that our invoice number 1234 has not been paid.* 我们在档案中发现1234号发票未付款。

recoup /rɪˈkuːp/ *verb* □ **to recoup your losses** to get back money which you thought you had lost 失而复得的钱财

recourse /rɪˈkɔːs/ *noun* a right of a lender to compel a borrower to repay money borrowed 追索权:债权人迫使债务人还款的权利

recover /rɪˈkʌvə/ *verb* **1.** to get back something which has been lost 找回,索回,收回 ○ *to recover damages from the driver of the car* 向司机索赔 ○ *to start a court action to recover property* 起诉追回财产 ○ *He never recovered his money.* 他没能要回他的钱。○ *The initial investment was never recovered.* 初始投资再未收回。**2.** to get better, to rise 恢复,复苏,回升 ○ *The market has not recovered from the rise in oil prices.* 市场尚未从油价上涨中复苏。○ *The stock market fell in the morning, but recovered during the afternoon.* 股市上午下跌,但下午就止跌回升了。

recoverable /rɪˈkʌv(ə)rəb(ə)l/ *adjective* possible to get back 可收回的

recoverable amount /rɪˌkʌv(ə)rəb(ə)l əˈmaʊnt/ *noun* the value of an asset, either the price it would fetch if sold, or its value to the company when used, whichever is the larger figure 可收回金额:按出售价格和使用价值两者中较高者计算出的资产价值

recovery /rɪˈkʌv(ə)ri/ *noun* **1.** the act of getting back something which has been lost 收回,找回 ○ *to start an action for recovery of property* 起诉追回财产 ○ *We are aiming for the complete recovery of the money invested.* 我们的目标是收回全部投资。**2.** a movement upwards of shares or of the economy (股票或经济的)回升,复苏

○ *signs of recovery after a slump* 衰退后的复苏迹象 ○ *The economy staged a recovery*. 经济开始复苏。

rectification /ˌrektɪfɪˈkeɪʃ(ə)n/ *noun* correction 校正，调整

rectify /ˈrektɪfaɪ/ *verb* to correct something, to make something right 校正，调整 ○ *to rectify an entry* 调整分录（NOTE: **rectifies – rectifying – rectified**）

recurrent /rɪˈkʌrənt/ *adjective* happening again and again 经常性的，经常发生的 ○ *a recurrent item of expenditure* 经常性支出项目 ○ *There is a recurrent problem in supplying this part*. 该部件的供应总是出现问题。

recurring payments /rɪˌkɜːrɪŋ ˈpeɪmənts/ *plural noun* payments, such as mortgage interest or payments on a hire purchase agreement, which are made each month 经常性付款：每月发生的付款，如按揭利息的支付或租购协议下的付款

recycle /riːˈsaɪk(ə)l/ *verb* to take waste material and process it so that it can be used again（废料）再循环，回收利用

red /red/ *noun* the colour of debit or overdrawn balances in some bank statements 红色：一些银行结单中用来表示借项或透支余额的颜色 □ **in the red** showing a debit or loss 赤字；亏损 ○ *My bank account is in the red*. 我的银行户头出现亏空。○ *The company went into the red in 1998*. 公司 1984 年出现亏损。○ *The company is out of the red for the first time since 1990*. 公司自 1990 年以来首次摆脱亏损。

Red Book /ˈred bʊk/ *noun* a document published on Budget Day, with the text of the Chancellor of the Exchequer's financial statement and budget 红皮书：预算日公布的文件，其内容为财政大臣所作的国家财政报告和预算

redeem /rɪˈdiːm/ *verb* to pay off a loan or a debt 偿还，赎回 ○ *to redeem a mortgage* 偿还按揭贷款 ○ *to redeem a debt* 偿还债务

redeemable /rɪˈdiːməb(ə)l/ *adjective* referring to a bond which can be sold for cash 可赎回的，可收回的：债券可出售变现的

redeemable government stock /rɪˌdiːməb(ə)l ˌɡʌv(ə)nmənt ˈstɒk/ *noun* stock which can be redeemed for cash at some time in the future. In the UK, only the War Loan is irredeemable 可赎回政府债券：可在日后赎回的债券。在英国，只有战时公债是不可赎回的

redeemable preference share /rɪˌdiːməb(ə)l ˈpref(ə)rəns ʃeə/ *noun* a preference share which must be bought back by the company at an agreed date and for an agreed price 可赎回优先股：公司须在议定日期按议定价格赎回的优先股

redeemable security /rɪˌdiːməb(ə)l sɪˈkjʊərɪti/ *noun* a security which can be redeemed at its face value at a specific date in the future 可赎回证券：可在未来某日按面值赎回的证券

redemption /rɪˈdempʃən/ *noun* the repayment of a loan 赎回，偿还

redemption date /rɪˈdempʃən deɪt/ *noun* a date on which a loan or debt is due to be repaid 偿还日，赎回日期

redemption value /rɪˈdempʃən ˌvæljuː/ *noun* a value of a security when redeemed 赎回价值：证券赎回时

的价值

redemption yield /rɪˈdempʃən jiːld/ *noun* a yield on a security including interest and its redemption value 赎回收益:包括利息和赎回价值在内的证券收益

redistribute /ˌriːdɪˈstrɪbjuːt/ *verb* to move items, work or money to different areas or people 再分配:将物品、工作或资金分配给不同地区或人 ○ *The government aims to redistribute wealth by taxing the rich and giving grants to the poor.* 政府旨在通过向富人征税和给予穷人补贴来重新分配财富。○ *The orders have been redistributed among the company's factories.* 订单在公司的厂房间被重新分配。

redistribution of wealth /ˌriːdɪstrɪbjuːʃən əv ˈwelθ/ *noun* the process of sharing wealth among the whole population 社会财富再分配

reduce /rɪˈdjuːs/ *verb* to make something smaller or lower 减少,降低 ○ *We must reduce expenditure if we want to stay in business.* 要想在商界立足,我们就必须削减开支。○ *They have reduced prices in all departments.* 他们下调了所有部门的价格。○ *We were expecting the government to reduce taxes not to increase them.* 我们希望政府减税而不是加税。○ *We have made some staff redundant to reduce overmanning.* 我们裁汰了一些冗员,以减少人浮于事的现象。○ *The company reduced output because of a fall in demand.* 需求下降迫使公司减产。○ *The government's policy is to reduce inflation to 5%.* 政府的政策是使通货膨胀率下降到5%。

reduced /rɪˈdjuːst/ *adjective* lower 降低的 ○ *Reduced prices have increased unit sales.* 降价使零售量上升。○ *Prices have fallen due to a reduced demand for the goods.* 商品需求下降导致价格下跌。

reducing balance method /rɪˌdjuːsɪŋ ˈbæləns ˌmeθəd/ *noun* a method of depreciating assets, where the asset is depreciated at a constant percentage of it cost each year 余额递减折旧法:资产按其每年成本的固定百分比计提折旧的一种资产折旧方法 Also called 亦称作 **declining balance method**

reduction /rɪˈdʌkʃən/ *noun* an act of making something smaller or less 减少,降低 ○ *Reduction in demand has led to the cancellation of several new projects.* 需求下降导致几个新项目被取消。○ *The company was forced to make reductions in its advertising budget.* 公司不得不削减其广告预算。○ *Price reductions have had no effect on our sales.* 降价对我们的销量毫无影响。○ *Working only part-time will mean a significant reduction in take-home pay.* 只做兼职意味着税后工资会少很多。

redundancy /rɪˈdʌndənsi/ *noun* the dismissal of a person whose job no longer needs to be done 裁员,冗员

redundancy payment /rɪˈdʌndənsi ˌpeɪmənt/ *noun* a payment made to an employee to compensate for losing his or her job (冗余人员的)解雇款,遣散费

redundancy rebate /rɪˈdʌndənsi ˌriːbeɪt/ *noun* a payment made to a company to compensate for redundancy payments made 解雇费返还:支付给公司以补偿其所付解雇费的款项

redundant /rɪˈdʌndənt/ *adjective*

more than is needed, useless 过剩的，多余的；无用的 ○ *a redundant clause in a contract* 合同中的一条多余条款 ○ *The new legislation has made clause 6 redundant*. 新法律使第 6 条变得多余。○ *Retraining can help employees whose old skills have become redundant*. 再培训对于技能已过时的员工很有帮助。

redundant staff /rɪˌdʌndənt ˈstɑːf/ *noun* staff who have lost their jobs because they are not needed any more 多余员工，冗员

re-export /ˌriːekˈspɔːt/ *verb* to export something which has been imported 再出口：转口进口的货物

re-exportation /ˌriːekspɔːˈteɪʃ(ə)n/ *noun* the exporting of goods which have been imported 再出口

refer /rɪˈfɜː/ *verb* □ **'refer to drawer'** words written on a cheque which a bank refuses to pay and returns it to the person who wrote it "请与出票人接洽"：银行拒绝支付并退还出票人时写在支票上的字样 Abbreviation 缩写 **R/D**

reference /ˈref(ə)rəns/ *noun* **1.** the process of mentioning or dealing with something 提到，关于 ○ *with reference to your letter of May 25th* 关于您 5 月 25 日的来函 **2.** a series of numbers or letters which make it possible to find a document which has been filed（文件）索引，编号 ○ *our reference: PC/MS 1234* 我们的索引号：PC/MS 1234 ○ *Thank you for your letter (reference 1234)*. 感谢您的来函（编号 1234）○ *Please quote this reference in all correspondence*. 请在所有信件上注明此编号。**3.** a written report on someone's character or ability（关于某人品行或能力的）介绍信，证明 ○ *to write someone a reference* or *to give someone a reference* 给某人开证明 ○ *to ask applicants to supply references* 要求申请者提供介绍信 □ **to ask a company for trade references *or* for bank references** to ask for reports from traders or a bank on the company's financial status and reputation 向商行（或银行）征询：要求出具由商人或银行提供的公司财务状况及信誉报告

referral /rɪˈfɜːrəl/ *noun* an action of referring or recommending someone to someone 引介，推荐

refer to drawer please represent /rɪˌfɜː tə ˌdrɔːə pliːz ˌreprɪˈzent/ *noun* in the United Kingdom, written on a cheque by the paying banker to indicate that there are currently insufficient funds to meet the payment, but that the bank believes sufficient funds will be available shortly 与出票人接洽，请稍后再提呈：在英国由付款行在支票上注明，表示目前暂时没有足够的资金付款，但银行相信很快就有足够的资金可供支付 Abbreviation 缩写 **RD-PR**

refinance /ˌriːˈfaɪnæns/ *verb* to replace one source of finance with another 再融资，重新筹资：用一种筹资方法代替另一种

refund *noun* /ˈriːfʌnd/ money paid back 偿还，退款 ○ *The shoes don't fit - I'm going to ask for a refund*. 这双鞋不合脚——我要求退钱。○ *She got a refund after complaining to the manager*. 在向经理投诉后，她拿到了退款。■ *verb* /rɪˈfʌnd/ to pay back money 偿还，退款 ○ *to refund the cost of postage* 偿付邮资 ○ *All money will be refunded if the goods are not satisfactory*. 如果对商品不满意，可以退款。

refundable /rɪˈfʌndəb(ə)l/ *adjective* possible to pay back 可偿还的,可归还的 ○ *We ask for a refundable deposit of £20.* 我们要求退还 20 英镑的定金。○ *The entrance fee is refundable if you purchase £5 worth of goods.* 若你购买五英镑的商品,入场费可以退还。

register /ˈredʒɪstə/ *noun* an official list (官方)登记册,注册簿 ○ *to enter something in a register* 将某事(物)登记入册 ○ *to keep a register up to date* 随时更新登记册 ○ *people on the register of electors* 选民登记册上的人 ■ *verb* **1.** to write something in an official list 注册,登记 ○ *to register a fall in the numbers of unemployed teenagers* 记录未就业青少年人数的下降 ○ *To register a company you must pay a fee to Companies House.* 注册公司时,你必须向公司登记处交纳一定费用。○ *When a property is sold, the sale is registered at the Land Registry.* 土地注册处对每一项售出物业进行备案。**2.** to send a letter by registered post 寄挂号信 ○ *I registered the letter, because it contained some money.* 考虑到信里夹有钱,我寄了挂号信。

registered /ˈredʒɪstəd/ *adjective* having been noted on an official list 已注册的 ○ *a registered share transaction* 已注册的股票交易

registered cheque /ˌredʒɪstəd ˈtʃek/ *noun* a cheque written on a bank account on behalf of a client who does not have a bank account 记名支票:代替无户头的客户签发的支票

registered company /ˌredʒɪstəd ˈkʌmp(ə)ni/ *noun* company which has been officially set up and registered with the Registrar of Companies 注册公司:已正式成立并已在公司注册处登记的公司

registered letter /ˌredʒɪstəd ˈletə/, **registered parcel** /ˌredʒɪstəd ˈpɑːs(ə)l/ *noun* a letter or parcel which is noted by the post office before it is sent, so that the sender can claim compensation if it is lost 挂号信,挂号包裹:寄出前已在邮局登记、丢失时可以索赔的信件或包裹

registered office /ˌredʒɪstəd ˈɒfɪs/ *noun* the office address of a company which is officially registered with the Companies' Registrar 注册办事处:在公司注册处正式登记的公司办公地址

registered security /ˌredʒɪstəd sɪˈkjʊərɪti/ *noun* a security such as a share in a quoted company which is registered with Companies House and whose holder is listed in the company's share register 记名证券:在公司注册处已登记且其持有人在公司股东名册上的证券,如上市公司的股票

register of companies /ˌredʒɪstə əv ˈkʌmp(ə)niz/ *noun* in the United Kingdom, the list of companies maintained at Companies House 公司登记册:英国公司注册处保管的公司名单 ⇨ 参阅 **company, corporation**

register of directors /ˌredʒɪstə əv daɪˈrektəz/ *noun* an official list of the directors of a company which has to be sent to the Registrar of Companies 董事登记册:须送交公司注册官员的公司正式董事名单

registrant /ˈredʒɪstrənt/ *noun US* company applying to register with the Securities and Exchange Commission (美)登记人:向证券交易委员会申请注册的公司

registrar /ˌredʒɪˈstrɑː/ *noun* a person who keeps official records 登记员,注册官:保管官方记录的人

Registrar of Companies /ˌredʒɪstrɑː əv ˈkʌmp(ə)niz/ *noun* a government official whose duty is to ensure that companies are properly registered, and that, when registered, they file accounts and other information correctly 公司注册官员:负责妥善办理公司注册事项以及确保已注册公司所提交报表和其他信息真实性的政府官员

registration /ˌredʒɪˈstreɪʃ(ə)n/ *noun* the act of having something noted on an official list 注册,登记 ○ *the registration of a trademark* or *of a share transaction* 商标(或股票交易)的登记

registration fee /ˌredʒɪˈstreɪʃ(ə)n fiː/ *noun* 注册费,登记费 **1.** money paid to have something registered [注册某物的费用] **2.** money paid to attend a conference [参加会议的费用]

registration number /ˌredʒɪˈstreɪʃ(ə)n ˌnʌmbə/ *noun* an official number, e.g. the number of a car (车牌号等)注册号,登记号

registration statement /ˌredʒɪˈstreɪʃ(ə)n ˌsteɪtmənt/ *noun* a document which gives information about a company when it is registered and listed on a stock exchange 申请上市登记报表:公司在证券交易所注册及申请上市时提供的公司信息的文件 (NOTE: The UK term is **listing particulars** 英国用语为 **listing particulars**)

regression analysis /rɪˈɡreʃ(ə)n əˌnæləsɪs/, **regression model** /rɪˈɡreʃ(ə)n ˌmɒd(ə)l/ *noun* a method of discovering the ratio of one dependent variable and one or more independent variables, so as to give a value to the dependent variable 回归分析法:发现一个因变量与一个或多个自变量的比率,从而确定因变量值的一种方法

regressive taxation /rɪˌɡresɪv tækˈseɪʃ(ə)n/ *noun* a system of taxation in which tax gets progressively less as income rises 递减税:税率随收入的增加而降低的税制 Compare 比较 **progressive taxation**

regular /ˈreɡjʊlə/ *adjective* occurring at the same time each day, each week, each month or each year 有规律的,定期的,固定的 ○ *His regular train is the 12.45.* 他经常乘坐 12:45 的火车。○ *The regular flight to Athens leaves at 06.00.* 飞往雅典的固定航班 06:00 起飞。

regular income /ˌreɡjʊlər ˈɪnkʌm/ *noun* an income which comes in every week or month 定期收入,固定收入 ○ *She works freelance so she does not have a regular income.* 她是自由职业者,所以没有固定收入。

regulate /ˈreɡjʊleɪt/ *verb* **1.** to adjust something so that it works well or is correct 调整,规范 **2.** to change or maintain something by law 管理,管制

regulated consumer credit agreement /ˌreɡjʊleɪtɪd kənˌsjuːmə ˈkredɪt əˌɡriːmənt/ *verb* a credit agreement according to the Consumer Credit Act 标准消费者信贷合同:根据消费者信贷法签订的信贷协议

regulation /ˌreɡjʊˈleɪʃ(ə)n/ *noun* **1.** a law or rule 法规,条例,规则 ○ *the new government regulations on housing standards* 政府关于住房供给标准的新条例○ *Fire regulations* or *Safety regulations were not observed at the restaurant.* 该餐馆未遵守消防(或安全)法

规。○ *Regulations concerning imports and exports are set out in this leaflet.* 该手册上列有进出口规章。**2.** the use of laws or rules stipulated by a government or regulatory body, such as the Financial Services Authority, to provide orderly procedures and to protect consumers and investors（金融服务管理局等政府或监管机构旨在保障秩序和保护消费者及投资者的）监管，控制 ○ *government regulation of trading practices* 政府对贸易行为的监管

'EC regulations which came into effect in July insist that customers can buy cars anywhere in the EC at the local pre-tax price'
"七月开始生效的欧共体条例规定，顾客可在欧共体任一成员国按当地的税前价格购买汽车"［*Financial Times*《金融时报》］

'... a unit trust is established under the regulations of the Department of Trade, with a trustee, a management company and a stock of units'
"在贸易部的监管下成立的单位信托机构，包括受托人、管理公司及单位信托证券"［*Investors Chronicle*《投资者纪事》］

'... fear of audit regulation, as much as financial pressures, is a major factor behind the increasing number of small accountancy firms deciding to sell their practices or merge with another firm'
"出于审计规则和财务压力的考量，越来越多的小型会计师事务所决定出售事务所或与其他事务所合并"［*Accountancy*《会计学》］

regulations /ˌregjʊˈleɪʃ(ə)nz/ *noun* laws or rules 法规，条例，规则 ○ *the new government regulations on housing standards* 政府关于住房供给标准的新条例 ○ *Fire regulations* or *Safety regulations were not observed at the restaurant.* 该餐馆未遵守消防（或安全）法规。○ *Regulations concerning imports and exports are set out in this leaflet.* 该手册上列有进出口规章。

Regulation S-X /ˌregjʊleɪʃ(ə)n esˈeks/ *noun* the rule of the US Securities and Exchange Commission which regulates annual reports from companies S-X 法：美国证券交易委员会制定的用来规范公司年度报告的法则

regulator /ˈregjʊleɪtə/ *noun* a person whose job it is to see that regulations are followed 管理者：负责确保规则有效执行的人

'... the regulators have sought to protect investors and other market participants from the impact of a firm collapsing'
"管理者试图保护投资者和其他市场参与者免受公司倒闭的影响"［*Banking Technology*《银行业技术》］

regulatory /ˈregjʊlət(ə)ri/ *adjective* applying regulations 规章的

regulatory body /ˌregjʊlət(ə)ri ˈbɒdi/ *noun* FINANCE, BANKING, AND ACCOUNTING, GENERAL MANAGEMENT an independent organisation, usually established by a government, that makes rules and sets standards for an industry and oversees the activities of companies within it（金融、银行及会计、一般管理）监管机构：通常由政府成立的一种独立组织，负责制定行业规则及标准，并监督业内公司的行为

regulatory powers /ˈregjʊlət(ə)ri ˌpaʊəz/ *noun* powers to enforce government regulations 监管权力：强制执行政府规定的权力

reimburse /ˌriːɪmˈbɜːs/ *verb* □ **to reimburse someone their expenses** to pay someone back for money which they have spent 报销费用 ○ *You will be reimbursed for your expenses* or *Your ex-*

penses will be reimbursed. 你可以报销费用。

reimbursement /ˌriːɪmˈbɜːsmənt/ *noun* the act of paying back money 报销 ○ *reimbursement of expenses* 费用的报销

reinvest /ˌriːɪnˈvest/ *verb* to invest money again 再投资 ○ *She sold her shares and reinvested the money in government stocks*. 她卖掉了股票，然后把钱投到了政府债券上。

reinvestment /ˌriːɪnˈvestmənt/ *noun* 再投资 **1.** the act of investing money again in the same securities [再次投资于相同的证券] **2.** the act of investing a company's earnings in its own business by using them to create new products for sale [将公司盈余用于制造新产品]

'... many large US corporations offer shareholders the option of reinvesting their cash dividend payments in additional company stock at a discount to the market price. But to some big securities firms these discount reinvestment programs are an opportunity to turn a quick profit'
"美国许多大公司向股东提供按低于市价将其现金股利再投资于公司股票的选择权。而对某些大证券公司来说，这些折扣再投资计划是一种迅速获利的机会" [*Wall Street Journal*《华尔街日报》]

REIT *abbr US* real estate investment trust（美）不动产投资信托公司

reject *noun* /ˈriːdʒekt/ something which has been thrown out because it is not of the usual standard 残次品 ○ *sale of rejects* or *of reject items* 出售残次品 ○ *to sell off reject stock* 廉价出售库存残次品 ■ *verb* /rɪˈdʒekt/ to refuse to accept something, or to say that something is not satisfactory 拒绝；驳回 ○ *The board rejected the draft budget*. 董事会驳回了预算草案。

related /rɪˈleɪtɪd/ *adjective* connected or linked 相关的 ○ *related items on the agenda* 议事日程上的相关事项

related company /rɪˌleɪtɪd ˈkʌmp(ə)ni/ *noun* a company in which another company makes a long-term capital investment in order to gain control or influence 联营公司，联号：接受另一公司长期资本投资，并受其控制或影响的公司

related party /rɪˌleɪtɪd ˈpɑːti/ *noun* any person or company which controls or participates in the policy decisions of an accounting entity 关联人士，关联方：控制或参与某会计实体政策制定的个人或公司

relative error /ˌrelətɪv ˈerə/ *noun* the difference between an estimate and its correct value 相对误差：估计值与实际值之差

release /rɪˈliːs/ *noun* the act of setting someone free or of making something or someone no longer subject to an obligation or restriction 解除；放行 ○ *release from a contract* 解除合同 ○ *the release of goods from customs* 货物的通关 ○ *She was offered early release so that she could take up her new job*. 她被提前放行以便接手新工作。

'... pressure to ease monetary policy mounted yesterday with the release of a set of pessimistic economic statistics'
"随着昨日一组令人悲观的经济统计数据的发布，要求放松货币政策的压力也随之增大" [*Financial Times*《金融时报》]

'... the national accounts for the March quarter released by the Australian Bureau of Statistics showed a real increase in GDP'
"澳大利亚统计局公布的第一季度国民账户

显示 GDP 取得了实际增长”[*Australian Financial Review*《澳大利亚金融评论报》]

relevant /ˈreləv(ə)nt/ *adjective* having to do with what is being discussed or the current situation 相关的 ○ *Which is the relevant government department?* 相关的政府部门是哪个? ○ *Can you give me the relevant papers?* 你能给我相关的文件吗? ○ *The new assistant does not have any relevant experience.* 新助理没有任何相关经验。

relevant benefits /ˌreləv(ə)nt ˈbenɪfɪts/ *plural noun* benefits such as pension, endowment insurance, etc. provided by a pension scheme 相关利益:养老金计划提供的利益,如养老金、养老保险等

relief /rɪˈliːf/ *noun* help 救济;减轻

relief shift /rɪˈliːf ʃɪft/ *noun* a shift which comes to take the place of another shift, usually the shift between the day shift and the night shift 换班,轮班:通常指白班与夜班的轮换

relocation /ˌriːləʊˈkeɪʃ(ə)n/ *noun* the act of moving to a different place 重新安置;搬迁 ○ *We will pay all the staff relocation costs.* 我们将支付所有员工的搬迁费。

relocation package /ˌriːləʊˈkeɪʃ(ə)n ˌpækɪdʒ/ *noun* payments made by an employer to an employee when the employee is asked to move to a new area in order to work. Payments up to a minimum level are exempt from tax 重新安置费:雇员在按要求搬迁到新办公地点时,雇主支付给雇员的费用。最低范围以内的费用可以免税

remainder /rɪˈmeɪndə/ *noun* things left behind 剩余物 ○ *The remainder of the stock will be sold off at half price.* 剩余存货将半价甩卖。

reminder /rɪˈmaɪndə/ *noun* a letter to remind a customer that he or she has not paid an invoice 催款单:提醒顾客尚未支付货款的信函 ○ *to send someone a reminder* 给某人发催款单

remission of taxes /rɪˌmɪʃ(ə)n əv ˈtæksɪz/ *noun* a refund of taxes which have been overpaid 退税,税收返还:返还多付的税金

remit /rɪˈmɪt/ *verb* to send money 划拨,汇款 ○ *to remit by cheque* 支票划拨 (NOTE: **remitting – remitted**)

remittance /rɪˈmɪt(ə)ns/ *noun* money which is sent to pay back a debt or to pay an invoice 汇付,汇款 ○ *Please send remittances to the treasurer.* 请汇款给财务主任。○ *The family lives on a weekly remittance from their father in the USA.* 他们一家依靠父亲每星期从美国寄来的汇款维持生活。

remittance advice /rɪˈmɪt(ə)ns ədˌvaɪs/, **remittance slip** /rɪˈmɪt(ə)ns slɪp/ *noun* an advice note sent with payment, showing why it is being made, i. e. quoting the invoice number or a reference number 汇款通知单,汇款附单:与汇款一起寄出的通知单,表明汇款来源(即注明发票号或索引号)

remitting bank /rɪˈmɪtɪŋ bæŋk/ *noun* a bank into which a person has deposited a cheque, and which has the duty to collect the money from the account of the writer of the cheque 付款行,汇款银行:可存入支票的银行,它有义务从出票人的账户中划款

remunerate /rɪˈmjuːnəreɪt/ *verb* to pay someone for doing something 付报酬 ○ *The company refused to remunerate them for their services.* 公司拒绝支

付他们劳务报酬。

remuneration /rɪˌmjuːnəˈreɪʃ(ə)n/ *noun* payment for services 报酬 ○ *The job is interesting but the remuneration is low*. 这份工作很有意思，只是报酬偏低。○ *She receives a small remuneration of £400 a month*. 她每月只获得 400 英镑的报酬。○ *No one will work hard for such poor remuneration*. 报酬这么低，没人愿意卖力的。

renegotiate /ˌriːnɪˈgəʊʃieɪt/ *verb* to negotiate something again 重新谈判，重新协商 ○ *The company was forced to renegotiate the terms of the loan*. 公司被迫就贷款条件重回谈判桌。

renew /rɪˈnjuː/ *verb* to continue something for a further period of time 延期，重新开始 ○ *We have asked the bank to renew the bill of exchange*. 我们已要求银行将汇票展期。○ *The tenant wants to renew his lease*. 承租人想续租。○ *Her contract was renewed for a further three years*. 她又续签了三年合同。

renewal /rɪˈnjuːəl/ *noun* the act of renewing 延期，展期 ○ *renewal of a lease* or *of a subscription* or *of a bill* 租约（或订购、汇票）的续延 ○ *renewal of a contract* 合同的展期 ○ *Her contract is up for renewal* 她该续合同了 ○ *When is the renewal date of the bill?* 汇票何时延期？

renewal notice /rɪˈnjuːəl ˌnəʊtɪs/ *noun* a note sent by an insurance company asking the insured person to renew the insurance 续保通知单

renewal premium /rɪˈnjuːəl ˌpriːmiəm/ *noun* a premium to be paid to renew an insurance 续保费

rent /rent/ *noun* money paid to use an office, house or factory for a period of time 租金 ■ *verb* **1.** to pay money to hire an office, house, factory or piece of equipment for a period of time 租用 ○ *to rent an office* or *a car* 租用办公室（或汽车）○ *He rents an office in the centre of town*. 他在市中心租了一间办公室。○ *They were driving a rented car when they were stopped by the police*. 被警察拦住时他们正开着一辆租来的汽车。**2.** □ **rent a room** scheme by which a taxpayer can let a room in his or her house and be exempt from tax on the rental income below a certain level 单间出租：纳税人出租其住房中的一间房屋，所得租金在特定金额内可以免税

rental /ˈrent(ə)l/ *noun* money paid to use an office, house, factory, car, piece of equipment, etc., for a period of time 租金 ○ *The car rental bill comes to over £1000 a quarter*. 每季度的汽车租金收入可达 1,000 多英镑。

'...top quality office furniture: short or long-term rental 50% cheaper than any other rental company'
"优质办公设备：短期或长期租金均比别的租赁公司低 50%" [*Australian Financial Review*《澳大利亚金融评论报》]

'...until the vast acres of empty office space start to fill up with rent-paying tenants, rentals will continue to fall and so will values. Despite the very sluggish economic recovery under way, it is still difficult to see where the new tenants will come from'
"在大量闲置写字楼被租客填满之前，租金和租赁价值还会继续下跌。尽管经济在极其缓慢地恢复，我们仍难以看到新租客的一丝影子" [*Australian Financial Review*《澳大利亚金融评论报》]

rental value /ˈrent(ə)l ˌvæljuː/ *noun* a full value of the rent for a property if it were charged at the current market rate, i.e. calculated between rent reviews 租赁价值:财产按当前市场租赁价格计算(即在租金调整期间计算出的)的租金全值

rent control /ˈrent kənˌtrəʊl/ *noun* government regulation of rents 租金管理条例

rent review /ˈrent rɪˌvjuː/ *noun* an increase in rents which is carried out during the term of a lease. Most leases allow for rents to be reviewed every three or five years 租金调整:指在租赁期内提高租金。大多数租赁会每三年或五年调整一次租金

rent tribunal /ˈrent traɪˌbjuːn(ə)l/ *noun* a court which can decide if a rent is too high or low 租金仲裁法庭

renunciation /rɪˌnʌnsiˈeɪʃ(ə)n/ *noun* an act of giving up ownership of shares 放弃股票所有权

reorder /riːˈɔːdə/ *noun* a further order for something which has been ordered before 再订购 ○ *The product has only been on the market ten days and we are already getting reorders*. 产品上市才10天,我们就收到了添购单。 ■ *verb* to place a new order for something 再订购 ○ *We must reorder these items because stock is getting low*. 因为库存减少,我们必须添购这些产品。

reorder level /riːˈɔːdə ˌlev(ə)l/ *noun* a minimum amount of an item which a company holds in stock, such that, when stock falls to this amount, the item must be reordered 再订货水平:公司持有的最低存货数量,即当存货降至此水平就必须再订购

reorder quantity /riˈɔːdə ˌkwɒntəti/ *noun* a quantity of a product which is reordered, especially the economic order quantity (EOQ) 再订货量:再订购的产品数量,尤指经济订购量(EOQ)

reorganisation /riːˌɔːɡənaɪˈzeɪʃ(ə)n/, **reorganization** *noun* the process of organising a company in a different way, as in the USA when a bankrupt company applies to be treated under Chapter 11 to be protected from its creditors while it is being reorganised 重组,改组:以另一种方式组织公司,比如在美国,破产公司可以根据第11章申请破产保护,从而在重组期间免受债权人影响

repay /rɪˈpeɪ/ *verb* to pay something back, or to pay back money to someone 偿付;还钱给 ○ *to repay money owed* 清偿欠款 ○ *The company had to cut back on expenditure in order to repay its debts*. 为了还债,公司不得不削减开支。

repayable /rɪˈpeɪəb(ə)l/ *adjective* possible to pay back 可偿还的 ○ *loan which is repayable over ten years* 还款期超过10年的贷款

repayment /rɪˈpeɪmənt/ *noun* the act of paying money back or money which is paid back 偿还;偿还的款项 ○ *The loan is due for repayment next year*. 贷款明年到期。

repayment mortgage /rɪˈpeɪmənt ˌmɔːɡɪdʒ/ *noun* a mortgage where the borrower pays back both interest and capital over the period of the mortgage. This is opposed to an endowment mortgage, where only the interest is repaid, and an insurance is taken out to repay the capital at the end of the term of the mortgage 还款按揭,抵押贷款:借款人需在抵押期内连本带息还款的一种按揭。它不同于养老金抵押贷款,后者只需支付利息,

而本金在抵押期末通过投保来偿还

replacement cost accounting /rɪˌpleɪsmənt kɒst əˈkaʊntɪŋ/ *noun* a method of accounting in which assets are valued at the amount it would cost to replace them, rather than at the original cost 重置成本会计：资产按重置成本而不是按原始成本计价的会计方法 Also called 亦称作 **current cost accounting**. Compare 比较 **historical cost accounting**

replacement cost depreciation /rɪˌpleɪsmənt kɒst dɪˌpriːʃiˈeɪʃ(ə)n/ *noun* depreciation based on the actual cost of replacing the asset in the current year 重置成本折旧：以本年度资产重置成本为基础的折旧

replacement price /rɪˈpleɪsmənt praɪs/ *noun* a price at which the replacement for an asset would have to be bought 重置价格：重置一项资产的购入价格

replacement value /rɪˈpleɪsmənt ˌvæljuː/ *noun* the value of something for insurance purposes if it were to be replaced 重置价值：投保时假设重置某物的价值 ○ *The computer is insured at its replacement value*. 计算机按重置价值投保。

report /rɪˈpɔːt/ *noun* a statement describing what has happened or describing a state of affairs 报告 ○ *to make a report* or *to present a report* or *to send in a report on market opportunities in the Far East* 写（或提交）一份关于远东市场机遇的报告 ○ *The accountants are drafting a report on salary scales*. 会计师正在草拟一份工资级别报告。○ *The sales manager reads all the reports from the sales team*. 销售经理看过了销售团队的所有报告。○ *The chairman has received a report from the insurance company*. 董事长收到保险公司发来的一份报告。■ *verb* **1.** to make a statement describing something 报告 ○ *The salesforce reported an increased demand for the product*. 销售人员报告产品需求增加。○ *He reported the damage to the insurance company*. 他向保险公司汇报了损失情况。○ *We asked the bank to report on his financial status*. 我们要求银行报告他的财务状况。**2.** to publish the results of a company for a period and declare the dividend 发布公司的业绩并宣派股利

'...a draft report on changes in the international monetary system'
"关于国际货币体系变化的初步报告"［*Wall Street Journal*《华尔街日报》］

'...responsibilities include the production of premium quality business reports'
"职责包括递交高质量的业务报告"［*Times*《泰晤士报》］

'...the research director will manage a team of business analysts monitoring and reporting on the latest development in retail distribution'
"研究部主任将领导一组业务分析员对零售分销的最新发展进行监督和汇报"［*Times*《泰晤士报》］

'...the successful candidate will report to the area director for profit responsibility for sales of leading brands'
"被聘者将就主打品牌的销售利润对地区主管负责"［*Times*《泰晤士报》］

report form /rɪˈpɔːt fɔːm/ *noun* a balance sheet laid out in vertical form. It is the opposite of 'account' or 'horizontal' form 报告式，报告格式：以垂直方式编制的资产负债表。它与"账目"或"水平"式资产负债表相对 Also called 亦称作 **vertical form**

reporting entity /rɪˌpɔːtɪŋ ˈentɪti/ *noun* any organisation, such as a limited company, which reports its accounts to its shareholders 报告实体：向股东报告其账目的组织机构(如有限责任公司)

repossess /ˌriːpəˈzes/ *verb* to take back an item which someone is buying under a hire-purchase agreement, or a property which someone is buying under a mortgage, because the purchaser cannot continue the payments 收回，重新占有：收回买方按租购协议或按揭购买后却无力继续偿付的物品

repossession /ˌriːpəˈzeʃ(ə)n/ *noun* an act of repossessing 收回，恢复，重新占有 ○ *Repossessions are increasing as people find it difficult to meet mortgage repayments*. 由于人们发现难以偿还按揭贷款，因此回收率不断上升。

reprice /riːˈpraɪs/ *verb* to change the price on an item, usually to increase it 重新定价(以涨价居多)

repudiation /rɪˌpjuːdiˈeɪʃ(ə)n/ *noun* a refusal to accept something such as a debt (债务等的)否认，拒付

repurchase /riːˈpɜːtʃɪs/ *verb* to buy something again, especially something which you have recently bought and then sold 再购入，购回(已出售的物品)

require /rɪˈkwaɪə/ *verb* to ask for or to demand something 要求，需要 ○ *to require a full explanation of expenditure* 要求对支出作详细解释 ○ *The law requires you to submit all income to the tax authorities*. 你的所有收入需依法上报税务机关。

required rate of return /rɪˌkwaɪəd reɪt əv rɪˈtɜːn/ *noun* the minimum return for a proposed project investment to be acceptable 应得报酬率，预期(投资)收益率：投资计划可以接受的最低回报 ◊ 参阅 **discounted cash flow**

resale /ˈriːseɪl/ *noun* the selling of goods which have been bought 转售 ○ *to purchase something for resale* 为转售而购入某物 ○ *The contract forbids resale of the goods to the USA*. 合同禁止将商品转售给美国。

resale price maintenance /ˌriːseɪl ˈpraɪs ˌmeɪntənəns/ *noun* a system in which the price for an item is fixed by the manufacturer and the retailer is not allowed to sell it at a lower price 转售价格维持：由厂商确定产品的价格，不允许零售商以更低价格进行销售的制度 Abbreviation 缩写 **RPM**

reschedule /riːˈʃedjuːl/ *verb* **1.** to arrange a new timetable for something 重新安排日程 ○ *She missed her plane, and all the meetings had to be rescheduled*. 她没赶上飞机，因此所有会议日程不得不改期。**2.** to arrange new credit terms for the repayment of a loan 重新安排贷款的信贷条件 ○ *Third World countries which are unable to keep up the interest payments on their loans from western banks have asked for their loans to be rescheduled*. 一些第三世界国家由于无力偿付西方银行贷款的利息，因此要求重新安排信贷条件。

rescind /rɪˈsɪnd/ *verb* to annul or to cancel something 废除，取消 ○ *to rescind a contract* or *an agreement* 解除合同，取消协议

research and development expenditure /rɪˌsɜːtʃ ən dɪˈveləpmənt ɪkˌspendɪtʃə/ *noun* money spent on R & D 研发费用

resell /riːˈsel/ *verb* to sell something which has just been bought 转卖，转售 ○ *The car was sold in June and the buyer resold it to an dealer two months later.* 在6月购得此车后，事隔两个月，买主又把它转售给了一位经销商。(NOTE: **reselling – resold**)

reseller /riːˈselə/ *noun* somebody in the marketing chain who buys to sell to somebody else, e.g. wholesalers, distributors, and retailers 转售商

reserve currency /rɪˈzɜːv ˌkʌrənsi/ *noun* a strong currency used in international finance, held by other countries to support their own weaker currencies 储备货币：在国际财务中所使用的强势货币，由其他国家持有以支持其疲软的本币

reserve for fluctuations /rɪˌzɜːv fə ˌflʌktʃuˈeɪʃ(ə)nz/ *noun* money set aside to allow for changes in the values of currencies 价格变动准备金：专门用于应付汇率变动的拨款

reserve fund /rɪˈzɜːv fʌnd/ *noun* profits in a business which have not been paid out as dividend but have been ploughed back into the business 公积金；储备金：未作为股利发放、而是用于再投资的商业利润

reserve price /rɪˈzɜːv praɪs/ *noun* the lowest price which a seller will accept, e.g. at an auction or when selling securities through a broker 保留价格，最低价格，开拍底价：在拍卖中或通过经纪人出售证券时，卖方能接受的最低价格 ○ *The painting was withdrawn when it failed to reach its reserve price.* 由于没能达到起拍价，这幅画流拍了。

reserves /rɪˈzɜːvz/ *plural noun* **1.** supplies kept in case of need 耗材储备 ○ *Our reserves of fuel fell during the winter.* 我们的燃油储备在冬季下降了。○ *The country's reserves of gas* or *gas reserves are very large.* 该国的燃气储备量很大。**2.** money from profits not paid as dividend, but kept back by a company in case it is needed for a special purpose 储备金：利润中不用于发放股利的部分，而由公司留存以备特殊需要

residence /ˈrezɪd(ə)ns/ *noun* **1.** a house or flat where someone lives 住所 ○ *He has a country residence where he spends his weekends.* 他有一栋乡间小屋作为周末休闲场所。**2.** the fact of living or operating officially in a country 在一国居住或营业

residence permit /ˈrezɪd(ə)ns ˌpɜːmɪt/ *noun* an official document allowing a foreigner to live in a country 居住证：允许外国人在本国居住的官方文件 ○ *He has applied for a residence permit.* 他申请办理居住证。○ *She was granted a residence permit for one year* or *a one-year residence permit.* 她取得了一年的居住许可。

resident /ˈrezɪd(ə)nt/ *noun, adjective* a person or company considered to be living or operating in a country for official or tax purposes（就政府或计税而言的）居民；设在某国的营业公司；常驻的，归属于…的 ○ *The company is resident in France.* 该公司常驻法国。

residential property /ˌrezɪdenʃ(ə)l ˈprɒpəti/ *noun* houses or flats owned or occupied by individual residents 住宅物业

residual /rɪˈzɪdjuəl/ *adjective* remaining after everything else has gone 残留的

residual income /rɪˌzɪdjuəl ˈɪnkʌm/ *noun* pretax profits less an imputed interest charge for invested capital. It is used to assess divisional performance 残余收益：税前利润减去应计资本利息开支。它用来评估部门业绩

residual value /rɪˌzɪdjuəl ˈvæljuː/ *noun* a value of an asset after it has been depreciated in the company's accounts 残值：资产在公司报表中进行折旧后的价值

residue /ˈrezɪdjuː/ *noun* money left over 残余资金，剩余财产 ○ *After paying various bequests the residue of his estate was split between his children.* 支付各种遗赠后，余下的遗产分给了他的子女。

resolution /ˌrezəˈluːʃ(ə)n/ *noun* a decision to be reached at a meeting 决议，议案

resolve /rɪˈzɒlv/ *verb* to decide to do something 决定 ○ *The meeting resolved that a dividend should not be paid.* 会议决定不发放股利。

responsibility accounting /rɪˌspɒnsɪˈbɪlɪti əˌkaʊntɪŋ/ *noun* the keeping of financial records with an emphasis on who is responsible for each item 责任会计，权责单位会计制：强调各个项目由谁负责的财务记录方法

restated balance sheet /ˌriːsteɪtɪd ˈbæləns ʃiːt/ *noun* a balance sheet reframed to serve a particular purpose, such as highlighting depreciation on assets 重编的资产负债表：为特定目的（如突出资产折旧）而重新编制的资产负债表

restrict /rɪˈstrɪkt/ *verb* to limit something or to impose controls on something 限制，控制 ○ *to restrict credit* 控制信贷 ○ *to restrict the flow of trade* or *to restrict imports* 限制贸易流量（或限制进口） ○ *We are restricted to twenty staff by the size of our offices.* 考虑到我们办公室空间有限，因此员工人数被限制在20人。

restrictive /rɪˈstrɪktɪv/ *adjective* not allowing something to go beyond a point, limiting 限制（性）的，约束（性）的

restrictive covenant /rɪˌstrɪktɪv ˈkʌvənənt/ *noun* a clause in a contract which prevents someone from doing something 限制性契约，限制性条款：禁止某人做某事的合同条款

restructure /riːˈstrʌktʃə/ *verb* to reorganise the financial basis of a company 改组，调整（公司财务结构）

restructuring /riːˈstrʌktʃərɪŋ/ *noun* the process of reorganising the financial basis of a company （公司财务结构的）改组，调整

result /rɪˈzʌlt/ *noun* **1.** a profit or loss account for a company at the end of a trading period 业绩，经营成果 ○ *The company's results for last year were an improvement on those of the previous year.* 公司去年业绩同比有所改观。**2.** something which happens because of something else 结果，效果 ○ *What was the result of the price investigation?* 价格调查的结果如何？○ *The company doubled its sales force with the result that the sales rose by 26%.* 销售队伍扩充了一倍后，公司的销售额上升了26%。

'...the company has received the backing of a number of oil companies who are willing to pay for the results of the survey'
"公司得到众多石油公司的资助，他们都愿意花钱购买调查结果"［*Lloyd's List*《劳氏日报》］

'...some profit-taking was noted, but underlying sentiment remained firm in a steady stream of strong corporate results' "有人抛售出逃，但鉴于公司业绩持续增厚，市场的持股心态仍然坚定"［*Financial Times*《金融时报》］

retail /ˈriːteɪl/ *noun* the sale of small quantities of goods to the general public 零售 ▫ **the goods in stock have a retail value of £1m** the value of the goods if sold to the public is £1m, before discounts and other factors are taken into account 库存商品零售价达100万英镑：（不考虑折扣等因素）如果商品公开售出，价值将达100万英镑 ▪ *adverb* ▫ **he buys wholesale and sells retail** he buys goods in bulk at a wholesale discount and sells in small quantities to the public 他以批发价买入，以零售价卖出 ▪ *verb* to sell for a price 零售 ▫ **these items retail at *or* for £2.50** the retail price of these items is £2.50 这些商品零售价为2.5英镑

retail banking /ˈriːteɪl ˌbæŋkɪŋ/ *noun* services provided by commercial banks to individuals as opposed to business customers, e.g. current accounts, deposit and savings accounts, as well as credit cards, mortgages, and investments 小额银行（存放）业务，银行零售业务：商业银行向个人而非企业提供的服务，例如活期账户、存款与储蓄账户以及信用卡、按揭及投资（NOTE: In the United Kingdom, although this service was traditionally provided by high street banks, separate organisations are now providing Internet and telephone banking services 在英国，虽然此类业务传统上由大银行提供，但现在也有一些独立机构提供网上及电话银行服务）

retail dealer /ˈriːteɪl ˌdiːlə/ *noun* a person who sells to the general public 零售商

retail deposit /ˈriːteɪl dɪˌpɒzɪt/ *noun* a deposit placed by an individual with a bank 个人储蓄

retailer /ˈriːteɪlə/ *noun* a person who runs a retail business, selling goods direct to the public 零售商

retailing /ˈriːteɪlɪŋ/ *noun* the selling of full-price goods to the public 零售业 ○ *From car retailing the company branched out into car leasing.* 公司业务从汽车零售业扩展至汽车租赁。

retail investor /ˈriːteɪl ɪnˌvestə/ *noun* a private investor, as opposed to institutional investors 个人投资者（与机构投资者相对）

retail price /ˈriːteɪl ˌpraɪs/ *noun* the price at which the retailer sells to the final customer 零售价

retain /rɪˈteɪn/ *verb* to keep something or someone 保持，保留，留住 ○ *measures to retain experienced staff* 留住有经验员工的措施 ○ *Out of the profits, the company has retained £50,000 as provision against bad debts.* 公司从利润中留出五万英镑作为坏账备抵。

retained earnings /rɪˌteɪnd ˈɜːnɪŋz/ *plural noun* an amount of profit after tax which a company does not pay out as dividend to the shareholders, but which is kept to be used for the further development of the business 留存收益：税后利润中未作为股利付给股东，而是留作企业发展的部分 Also called 亦称作 **retentions**

retained income /rɪˌteɪnd ˈɪnkʌm/, **retained profit** /rɪˌteɪnd ˈprɒfɪt/ *noun* same as 同 **retained earnings**

retainer /rɪˈteɪnə/ *noun* money paid in advance to someone so that they will work for you, and not for someone else 聘金,聘用定金:因预订某人的服务而预付的金额 ○ *We pay them a retainer of £1000.* 我们付给他们1,000英镑聘金。

retiral /rɪˈtaɪərəl/ *noun US* same as (美)同 **retirement**

retire /rɪˈtaɪə/ *verb* **1.** to stop work and take a pension 退休 ○ *She retired with a £15,000 pension.* 她退休时领到了1.5万英镑的退休金。○ *The founder of the company retired at the age of 85.* 这家公司的创办人85岁才退休。○ *The shop is owned by a retired policeman.* 店主是一个退休警察。**2.** to make an employee stop work and take a pension 使…退休 ○ *They decided to retire all staff over 50.* 他们决定让所有超过50岁的员工提前退休。

retirement /rɪˈtaɪəmənt/ *noun* the act of retiring from work 退休 ○ *I am looking forward to my retirement.* 我期待着退休的那一天。○ *Older staff are planning what they will do in retirement.* 年纪较大的员工正在规划退休后的生活。

retirement age /rɪˈtaɪəmənt eɪdʒ/ *noun* the age at which people retire. In the UK this is usually 65 for men and 60 (but soon to become 65) for women 退休年龄(英国男性通常为65岁,女性60岁,但现在女性也即将改为65岁)

retirement annuity /rɪˈtaɪəmənt əˌnjuːɪti/ *noun* an annuity bought when someone retires, using part of the sum put into a personal pension plan 退休年金:退休时用个人退休金计划部分缴款购买的年金

retirement benefits /rɪˌtaɪəmənt ˈbenɪfɪts/ *plural noun* benefits which are payable by a pension scheme to a person on retirement 退休福利:退休时根据退休金计划领取的福利

retirement pension /rɪˈtaɪəmənt ˌpenʃən/ *noun* a state pension given to a man who is over 65 or and woman who is over 60 退休金

retroactive /ˌretrəʊˈæktɪv/ *adjective* which takes effect from a time in the past 追溯的 ○ *They got a pay rise retroactive to last January.* 他们得到自去年1月起补发的加薪。

'The salary increases, retroactive from April of the current year, reflect the marginal rise in private sector salaries'
"自今年4月起补付的加薪,反映出私营业的工资只有小幅上升" [*Nikkei Weekly*《日经周报》]

retroactively /ˌretrəʊˈæktɪvli/ *adverb* going back to a time in the past 追溯地

return /rɪˈtɜːn/ *noun* **1.** a profit or income from money invested 利润,收益,回报 ○ *We are buying technology shares because they bring in a quick return.* 我们打算购买科技股,因为它们见利快。○ *What is the gross return on this line?* 这类商品的毛利是多少? **2.** an official statement or form that has to be sent in to the authorities (须提交有关当局的)报告,报表 ■ *verb* to make a statement 申报 ○ *to return income of £15,000 to the tax authorities* 向税务机关申报1.5万英镑的收入

'...with interest rates running well above inflation, investors want something that offers a return for their money'
"在利率远高于通胀率的情况下,投资者希望投资于一些能给他们带来回报的东西" [*Business Week*《商业周刊》]

'Section 363 of the Companies Act 1985 requires companies to deliver an annual return to the Companies Registration Office. Failure to do so before the end of the period of 28 days after the company's return date could lead to directors and other officers in default being fined up to £2000' "1985年公司法第363条规定各公司需向公司注册处呈送年报。对于在公司申报日后28天内仍未上报的公司,有关董事及其他失职人员将被处以最高2,000英镑的罚款" [*Accountancy*《会计学》]

return date /rɪˈtɜːn deɪt/ *noun* a date by which a company's annual return has to be made to the Registrar of Companies 申报日:公司须向公司注册官员报送年报的日期

return on assets /rɪˌtɜːn ɒn ˈæsets/, **return on capital employed** /rɪˌtɜːn ɒn ˈkæpɪt(ə)l ɪmˈplɔɪd/, **return on equity** /rɪˌtɜːn ɒn ˈekwɪti/ *noun* a profit shown as a percentage of the capital or money invested in a business 资产报酬率,所用资本报酬率,权益报酬率:企业以投资资本百分比表示的利润 Abbreviation 缩写 **ROA**, **ROCE**, **ROE**

return on investment /rɪˌtɜːn ɒn ɪnˈvestmənt/ *noun* a ratio of the profit made in a financial year as a percentage of an investment 投资报酬率,投资回报率:财政年度内利润占投资金额的百分比 Abbreviation 缩写 **ROI**

return on net assets /rɪˌtɜːn ɒn net ˈæsets/ *noun* a ratio of the profit made in a financial year as a percentage of the assets of a company 净资产收益率:财政年度内利润占公司资产的百分比

returns /rɪˈtɜːnz/ *plural noun* profits or income from investment 回报,收益 ○ *The company is looking for quick returns on its investment*. 公司希冀投资获得快速回报。

revaluation /riːˌvæljʊˈeɪʃən/ *noun* an act of revaluing 重估 ○ *The balance sheet takes into account the revaluation of the company's properties*. 资产负债表考虑到了公司财产的重估。

revaluation method /riːˌvæljʊˈeɪʃən ˌmeθəd/ *noun* a method of calculating the depreciation of assets, by which the asset is depreciated by the difference in its value at the end of the year over its value at the beginning of the year 重估法:计算资产折旧的一种方法,它按资产年初与年末价值的差额计算折旧

revaluation reserve /riːˌvæljʊˈeɪʃ ən rɪˌzɜːv/ *noun* money set aside to account for the fact that the value of assets may vary as a result of accounting in different currencies 重估储备:一种专项拨款,用以应付使用不同货币计账可能导致的资产价值变动

revalue /riːˈvæljuː/ *verb* to value something again, usually setting a higher value on it than before 重估,再评价(通常估出更高价值) ○ *The company's properties have been revalued*. 公司财产已重估。○ *The dollar has been revalued against all world currencies*. 美元同各国货币的兑换比价已作了调整。

revenue /ˈrevənjuː/ *noun* **1.** money received 收入 ○ *revenue from advertising* or *advertising revenue* 广告收入 ○ *Oil revenues have risen with the rise in the dollar*. 随着美元升值,石油销售收入也增加了。**2.** money received by a government in tax 税收

revenue account /ˈrevənjuː əˌkaʊnt/ *noun* an accounting system which records the revenue and expenditure incurred by a company during its usual business 收支账目：记录公司在其正常业务过程中发生收支的会计系统

revenue accounts /ˈrevənjuː əˌkaʊnts/ *plural noun* accounts of a business which record money received as sales, commission, etc. 收入账目：记录公司销售收入、佣金收入等的账目

revenue expenditure /ˌrevənjuː ɪkˈspendɪtʃə/ *noun* expenditure on purchasing stock but not capital items, which is then sold during the current accounting period 营业支出，收益支出：用于购买存货而非资本项目的支出，且所购货物于当前会计期内售出

revenue ledger /ˌrevənjuː ˈledʒə/ *noun* a record of all the income received by an organization 收入分类账：关于机构所有收入的记录

revenue officer /ˈrevənjuː ˌɒfɪsə/ *noun* a person working in the government tax offices 税务官，税收人员

revenue reserves /ˈrevənjuː rɪˌzɜːvs/ *plural noun* retained earnings which are shown in the company's balance sheet as part of the shareholders' funds 收益准备金：在公司资产负债表上列入股东资金的留存收益 Also called 亦称作 **company reserves**

revenue sharing /ˌrevənjuː ˈʃeərɪŋ/ *noun* the distribution of income within limited partnerships 收入分享：有限责任合伙公司内部的收入分配

reverse /rɪˈvɜːs/ *adjective* opposite or in the opposite direction 相反的 ▪ *verb* to change a decision to the opposite 改变原决定，作出相反决定 ○ *The committee reversed its decision on import quotas*. 委员会改变了其在进口配额问题上的决定。

'... the trade balance sank $17 billion, reversing last fall's brief improvement'
"在去年秋季取得短暂增长之后，贸易余额又下降了 170 亿美元"［*Fortune*《财富》］

reverse leverage /rɪˌvɜːs ˈliːvərɪdʒ/ *noun* the borrowing of money at a rate of interest higher than the expected rate of return on investing the money borrowed 反向杠杆作用：借款用于投资时，借款利率高于预期投资回报率

reverse takeover /rɪˌvɜːs ˈteɪkəʊvə/ *noun* a takeover where the company which has been taken over ends up owning the company which has taken it over. The acquiring company's shareholders give up their shares in exchange for shares in the target company 反向兼并：原先被兼并的公司最终兼并了兼并它的公司。原收购公司的股东放弃他们原来的股份，来换取目标公司的股份。

reverse yield gap /rɪˌvɜːs ˈjiːld ˌɡæp/ *noun* the amount by which bond yield exceeds equity yield, or interest rates on loans exceed rental values as a percentage of the costs of properties 逆收益差额：债券收益超过权益收益的部分，或贷款利率超过租金与财产成本比率的部分

reversing entry /rɪˈvɜːsɪŋ ˌentri/ *noun* an entry in a set of accounts which reverses an entry in the preceding accounts 转回分录：在一套账目中用以冲销先前账目分录的分录

reversion /rɪˈvɜːʃ(ə)n/ *noun* a return of property to an original owner 产权返回

reversionary /rɪˈvɜːʃ(ə)n(ə)ri/ *adjective* referring to property which passes to another owner on the death of the present one 可继承的

reversionary annuity /rɪˌvɜːʃ(ə)n(ə)ri əˈnjuːɪti/ *noun* an annuity paid to someone on the death of another person 可继承年金：一人死后转付给其他人的年金

reversionary bonus /rɪˌvɜːʃ(ə)n(ə)ri ˈbəʊnəs/ *noun* an annual bonus on a life assurance policy, declared by the insurer 复归红利，人寿保险分红：由保险公司对人寿保险单宣派的年度分红

review /rɪˈvjuː/ *noun* a general examination 审查，检查 ○ *to conduct a review of distributors* 对分销商进行审查 ■ *verb* to examine something generally 检查，审查

revise /rɪˈvaɪz/ *verb* to change something which has been calculated or planned 修正，修改，修订 ○ *Sales forecasts are revised annually*. 销售预测每年修订一次。○ *The chairman is revising his speech to the AGM*. 董事长正在修改他在年度股东大会上的发言稿。

revolving credit /rɪˌvɒlvɪŋ ˈkredɪt/ *noun* a system where someone can borrow money at any time up to an agreed amount, and continue to borrow while still paying off the original loan 循环信用(证)：可以随时借入不超过协定金额的贷款，在偿还原贷款过程中还可继续借出的制度 Also called 亦称作 **open-ended credit**

revolving loan /rɪˌvɒlvɪŋ ˈləʊn/ *noun* a loan facility whereby the borrower can choose the number and timing of withdrawals against their bank loan and any money repaid may be reborrowed at a future date. Such loans are available both to businesses and personal customers 自动展期放款，可展期贷款：一种贷款融资，借款人可以选择提取其银行贷款的次数和时间，而且已偿还的金额可以再次借出。这种贷款既面向企业客户，也面向个人客户

rider /ˈraɪdə/ *noun* an additional clause 附加条款 ○ *to add a rider to a contract* 在合同中追加一项条款

right /raɪt/ *noun* a legal entitlement to something 权利 ○ *There is no automatic right of renewal to this contract*. 该合同无权自动展期。○ *She has a right to the property*. 她对该财产部分所有权。○ *He has no right to the patent*. 他不具有该项专利权。○ *The staff have a right to know how the company is doing*. 员工有权知道公司的经营状况。

right of way /ˌraɪt əv ˈweɪ/ *noun* a legal title to go across someone's property 通行权：经过别人土地的权利

rights issue /ˈraɪts ˌɪʃuː/ *noun* an arrangement which gives shareholders the right to buy more shares at a lower price 配股，优先认股权发行：授权股东按较低价格购入更多股份的安排 (NOTE: The US term is **rights offering** 美国用语为 **rights offering**)

ring fence /ˈrɪŋ fens/ *verb* **1.** to separate valuable assets or profitable businesses from others in a group which are unprofitable and may make the whole group collapse 保护，保证(资产或业务)安全：把集团的有价资产或盈利业务与可能导致整个集团破产的其他亏损业务分开 **2.** to identify money from certain sources and only use it in certain areas 圈定：识别特定

来源的资金并将其用于特定领域 ○ *The grant has been ring-fenced for use in local authority education projects only*. 拨款被指定用于地方政府的教育项目。

rise /raɪz/ *noun* **1.** an increase 增加 ○ *a rise in the price of raw materials*. 原材料价格上涨 ○ *Oil price rises brought about a recession in world trade*. 油价上涨导致全球贸易衰退。○ *There has been a rise in sales of 10%* or *Sales show a rise of 10%*. 销售额上升了10%。○ *Salaries are increasing to keep up with the rises in the cost of living*. 工资随生活费用一起上升。○*The recent rise in interest rates has made mortgages dearer*. 最近利率的上升增加了按揭贷款的成本。○ *There needs to be an increase in salaries to keep up with the rise in the cost of living*. 工资应随生活费用一起增加。**2.** an increase in pay 加薪 ○ *She asked her boss for a rise*. 她要求老板加薪。○ *He had a 6% rise in January*. 1月份他得到6%的加薪。(NOTE: The US term is **raise** 美国用语为 **raise**) ■ *verb* to move upwards or to become higher 上升，提高 ○ *Prices* or *Salaries are rising faster than inflation*. 物价(或工资)的上涨速度超过通货膨胀。○ *Interest rates have risen to 15%*. 利率已上升到15%。○ *Salaries are rising faster than inflation*. 工资的增长幅度超过通货膨胀。(NOTE: **rising – rose – risen**)

'...the index of industrial production sank 0.2 per cent for the latest month after rising 0.3 per cent in March'
"工业生产指数在3月上升了0.3%后，最近一个月又下降了0.2%"[*Financial Times*《金融时报》]

'...the stock rose to over $20 a share, higher than the $18 bid'
"每股股价已超过20美元，高于其18美元的出价"[*Fortune*《财富》]

'...customers' deposit and current accounts also rose to $655.31 million at the end of December'
"12月底，客户的定期及活期账户存款也上升到了6.5531亿美元"[*Hong Kong Standard*《香港虎报》]

'...the government reported that production in the nation's factories and mines rose 0.2% in September'
"政府宣称，9月份的全国厂矿企业的产量上升了0.2%"[*Sunday Times*《星期日泰晤士报》]

risk /rɪsk/ *noun* possible harm or a chance of danger 风险

'...remember, risk isn't volatility. Risk is the chance that a company's earnings power will erode — either because of a change in the industry or a change in the business that will make the company significantly less profitable in the long term'
"记住，风险不是指有赔有赚。风险指公司盈利能力被侵蚀的机率，这种侵蚀来自行业或业务面临的变数，从长远看，它们都会导致公司的盈利大幅下降"[*Fortune*《财富》]

risk-adjusted return on capital /ˌrɪskəˌdʒʌstɪd rɪˌtɜːn ɒn ˈkæpɪt(ə)l/ *noun* return on capital calculated in a way that takes into account the risks associated with income 风险调整资本收益率：在计算资本收益率时考虑到与收入有关的风险

risk arbitrage /ˌrɪsk ˈɑːbɪtrɑːʒ/ *noun* the business of buying shares in companies which are likely to be taken over and so rise in price 风险套利：购入可能会被兼并公司的股票，而兼并可能令该公司股价上升

risk arbitrageur /rɪsk ˌɑːbɪtrɑːˈʒɜː/ *noun* a person whose business is risk arbitrage 风险套利者

risk asset ratio /ˌrɪsk ˌæset ˈreɪʃiəʊ/ *noun* a proportion of a bank's capital which is in risk assets 风险资产率:银行风险资产占其资本的比率

risk capital /ˈrɪsk ˌkæpɪt(ə)l/ *noun* same as 同 **venture capital**

risk-free /ˌrɪskˈfriː/, **riskless** /ˈrɪskləs/ *adjective* with no risk involved 无风险的 ○ *a risk-free investment* 无风险投资

'... there is no risk-free way of taking regular income from your money higher than the rate of inflation and still preserving its value'
"没有任何无风险的办法可以使资金既产生高于通货膨胀率的固定收入,又能实现资金保值" [*Guardian*《卫报》]

'... many small investors have also preferred to put their spare cash with risk-free investments such as building societies rather than take chances on the stock market. The returns on a host of risk-free investments have been well into double figures'
"许多小投资者同样乐于将其闲置现金投资于无风险项目,比如住房互助协会,而不是拿去在股票市场上冒险。许多无风险投资的回报率已经达到了两位数" [*Money Observer*《货币观察家》]

risk management /ˈrɪsk ˌmænɪdʒmənt/ *noun* the work of managing a company's exposure to risk from its credit terms or exposure to interest rate or exchange rate fluctuations 风险管理:对公司的信贷风险敞口、利率或汇率波动风险敞口进行的管理

risk premium /ˈrɪsk ˌpriːmiəm/ *noun* an extra payment, e. g. increased dividend or higher than usual profits, for taking risks 风险酬金:因承担风险获得的额外报酬,如股利增加或超额利润

risk-weighted assets /ˌrɪskˌweɪtɪd ˈæsets/ *plural noun* assets which include off-balance sheet items for insurance purposes 风险加权的资产:投保时将资产负债表外项目包括在内的资产

risky /ˈrɪski/ *adjective* dangerous or which may cause harm 危险的;有风险的 ○ *We lost all our money in some risky ventures in South America.* 在南美的一些冒险投资把我们的钱都赔光了。

'... while the bank has scaled back some of its more risky trading operations, it has retained its status as a top-rate advisory house'
"该银行压缩了部分高风险交易业务,继续保持其一流咨询公司的地位" [*Times*《泰晤士报》]

ROA *abbr* return on assets 资产报酬率

ROCE *abbr* return on capital employed 所用资本报酬率

ROE *abbr* return on equity 权益报酬率

ROI *abbr* return on investment 投资报酬率,投资回报率

rolled-up coupons /ˌrəʊldʌp ˈkuːpɒnz/ *plural noun* interest coupons on securities, which are not paid out, but added to the capital value of the security 渐次增加的息票:没有利息支出,但加到证券资本价值中的证券息票

rolling account /ˈrəʊlɪŋ əˌkaʊnt/ *noun US* a system where there are no fixed account days, but stock exchange transactions are paid at a fixed period after each transaction has taken place, as opposed to the British system, where an account day is fixed each month (美)滚动结算制:一种结算制度,它没有固定的结算日,而是在每次交易后的固定期限内结清证券交易,这不同于每月有固定结算日的英国结算制度

rolling budget /ˌrəʊlɪŋ ˈbʌdʒɪt/ *noun* a budget which moves forward on a regular basis, such as a budget covering a twelve-month period which moves forward each month or quarter 滚动预算:有规律地向前滚动的预算,比如某 12 个月的预算,其中每月或每季向前滚动计算一次

rolling settlement /ˌrəʊlɪŋ ˈset(ə)lmənt/ *noun US* same as (美)同 **rolling account**

roll over /ˌrəʊl ˈəʊvə/ *verb* □ **to roll over a credit** to make credit available over a continuing period 信贷展期 □ **to roll over a debt** to allow a debt to stand after the repayment date 债务展期

'... at the IMF in Washington, officials are worried that Japanese and US banks might decline to roll over the principal of loans made in the 1980s to Southeast Asian and other developing countries'
"在华盛顿召开的国际货币基金组织会议上,与会官员们担心日本和美国的银行可能拒绝延长 20 世纪 80 年代对东南亚及其他发展中国家贷款本金的偿还期限"[*Far Eastern Economic Review*《远东经济评论》]

rollover /ˈrəʊləʊvə/ *noun* an extension of credit or of the period of a loan, though not necessarily on the same terms as previously (信贷或贷款的)展期(但可能会修改信贷或贷款条件)

rollover relief /ˌrəʊləʊvə rɪˈliːf/ *noun* tax relief, where profit on the sale of an asset is not taxed if the money realised is used to acquire another asset. The profit on the eventual sale of this second asset will be taxed unless the proceeds of the second sale are also invested in new assets 延期纳税优惠:如果销售资产所得资金用于购买另一项资产,则该出售的利润不用纳税。新资产的最终销售利润则要征税,除非这第二次出售的收入也投资于新资产

roll up /ˌrəʊl ˈʌp/ *verb* to extend a loan, by adding the interest due to be paid to the capital 渐次增加债务展期:把应付利息加到本金中的债务展期

Romalpa clause /rəʊˈmɒlpə ˌklɔːz/ *noun* a clause in a contract, whereby the seller provides that title to the goods does not pass to the buyer until the buyer has paid for them 罗马百条款:合同中的一项条款,它规定须在买方付款之后,卖方才将货物的所有权转移给买方

Roman numerals /ˌrəʊmən ˈnjuːmərəlz/ *plural noun* figures written I, II, III, IV, etc. 罗马数字

root /ruːt/ *noun* a fractional power of a number (算术)根

rough /rʌf/ *adjective* approximate, not very accurate 粗略的,近似的

rough calculation /ˌrʌf ˌkælkjʊˈleɪʃ(ə)n/ *noun* a way of working out a mathematical problem approximately, or the approximate result arrived at 粗略计算(的结果) ○ *I made some rough calculations on the back of an envelope*. 我在信封背面大致算了算。

rough estimate /ˌrʌf ˈestɪmət/ *noun* a very approximate calculation

大概估算

rough out /ˌrʌf ˈaʊt/ *verb* to make a draft or a general design of something, which may be changed later 草拟，打草稿 ○ *The finance director roughed out a plan of investment.* 财务经理草拟了一份投资计划。

round down /ˌraʊnd ˈdaʊn/ *verb* to decrease a fractional figure to the nearest full figure 舍去：将小数减至最近的整数

round figures /ˌraʊnd ˈfɪgəz/ *noun* figures that have been adjusted up or down to the nearest 10, 100, 1,000, and so on (约)整数：将数字约至以零结尾的整数，如1,000等

round off /ˌraʊnd ˈɒf/ *verb* to reduce the digits in a decimal number by removing the final zeros 化为整数，四舍五入

round up /ˌraʊnd ˈʌp/ *verb* to increase a fractional figure to the nearest full figure 进上，进位：将小数加至最近的整数 ○ *to round up the figures to the nearest pound* 上舍入最近似的英镑整数值

'...each cheque can be made out for the local equivalent of £100 rounded up to a convenient figure'
"可以使用按四舍五入法换算后同100英镑等值的地方货币签发支票"[*Sunday Times*《星期日泰晤士报》]

royalty /ˈrɔɪəlti/ *noun* money paid to an inventor, writer or the owner of land for the right to use their property, usually a specific percentage of sales, or a specific amount per sale 特许权使用费，版权费：因使用发明者、作者、土地所有人的财产而付给他们的费用，通常按销售额的一定比例或按固定金额支付 ○ *The country will benefit from rising oil royalties.* 该国将从石油开采税增加中受益。○ *He is still receiving substantial royalties from his invention.* 他的发明专利权仍令他日进斗金。

RPB *abbr* recognised professional body 公认职业团体，公认专业机构

RPM *abbr* resale price maintenance 转售价格维持

rubber check /ˌrʌbə ˈtʃek/ *noun US* a cheque which cannot be cashed because the person writing it does not have enough money in the account to pay it (美)空头支票：因出票人账户没有足够的资金而导致无法支付的支票 (NOTE: The UK term is **bouncing cheque** 英国用语为 **bouncing cheque**)

rule /ruːl/ *noun* a statement that directs how people should behave 规则，规章 ○ *It is a company rule that smoking is not allowed in the offices.* 公司规定办公室内不允许吸烟。○ *The rules of the organisation are explained during the induction sessions.* 入职会议就组织的规章制度进行了解释。■ *verb* **1.** to give an official decision 裁定，裁决 ○ *The commission of inquiry ruled that the company was in breach of contract.* 调查委员会裁定该公司违约。○ *The judge ruled that the documents had to be deposited with the court.* 法官裁定这些文件必须由法院保存。**2.** to be in force or to be current 生效；现行 ○ *prices which are ruling at the moment* 现行物价 ○ *The current ruling agreement is being redrafted.* 现行协议正在重新起草。

rulebook /ˈruːlbʊk/ *noun* a set of rules by which the members of a self-regulatory organisation must operate 行为守则:自律监管机构的成员必须遵守的规章

rule of 72 /ˌruːl əv ˌsev(ə)nti ˈtuː/ *noun* a calculation that an investment will double in value at compound interest after a period shown as 72 divided by the interest percentage, so interest at 10% compound will double the capital invested in 7.2 years 72 规则:用 72 除以利率后的数字作为基准时间,在这一基准时间后按复利计算的投资价值将翻番,假设复利为 10%,那么投资价值将在 7.2 年后翻倍

rule of 78 /ˌruːl əv ˌsev(ə)nti ˈeɪt/ *noun* a method used to calculate the rebate on a loan with front-loaded interest that has been repaid early. It takes into account the fact that as the loan is repaid, the share of each monthly payment related to interest decreases, while the share related to repayment increases 78 规则:在前期利息已支付的情况下,用来计算贷款折扣的一种方法。它考虑到了在还贷时,随着还款的增多所剩那部分的贷款利息也在相应减少这一事实

run /rʌn/ *noun* **1.** a period of time during which a machine is working (机器的)运行 **2.** a rush to buy something 抢购○ *The Post Office reported a run on the new stamps*. 邮局称人们争购新邮票。□ **a run on the bank** a rush by customers to take deposits out of a bank which they think may close down 银行挤提:客户认为银行要倒闭,因此抢着取出存款 ■ *verb* **1.** to be in force 生效,有效 ○ *The lease runs for twenty years*. 该租约为期 20 年。○ *The lease has only six months to run*. 该租约还有 6 个月就到期了。**2.** to amount to 累计达,合计 ○ *The costs ran into thousands of pounds*. 成本达数千英镑。**3.** to work on a machine 运行(机器) ○ *Do not run the photocopier for more than four hours at a time*. 不要让复印机连续工作超过 4 个小时。○ *The computer was running invoices all night*. 计算机整夜都在处理发票。

'...applications for mortgages are running at a high level'
"申请按揭的人数居高不下" [*Times*《泰晤士报》]

'...with interest rates running well above inflation, investors want something that offers a return for their money'
"在利率远高于通胀率的情况下,投资者希望投资于一些能给他们带来回报的东西" [*Business Week*《商业周刊》]

run into /ˌrʌn ˈɪntu/ *verb* to amount to 累计达,合计 ○ *Costs have run into thousands of pounds*. 成本已达数千英镑。□ **he has an income running into five figures** he earns more than £10,000 他的收入达到五位数(即超过 10,000 英镑)

running account credit /ˌrʌnɪŋ əˌkaʊnt ˈkredɪt/ *noun* an overdraft facility, credit card, or similar system that allows customers to borrow up to a specific limit and reborrow sums previously repaid by either writing a cheque or using their card 循环使用账户信贷:指透支限额、信用卡或类似制度,允许客户借入指定金额,并且可以再借入已用支票或信用卡偿还的部分

running total /ˌrʌnɪŋ ˈtəʊt(ə)l/ *noun* the total carried from one column of figures to the next 转出的总额:由一栏数字转到另一栏的总额

running yield /ˈrʌnɪŋ jiːld/ *noun* a yield on fixed interest securities, where the interest is shown as a percentage of the price paid 固定收益率，本期收益率：定息证券的收益率，利息以付款额的百分比表示

run up /ˌrʌn ˈʌp/ *verb* to make debts or costs go up quickly 使（债务或成本）快速上涨 ○ *He quickly ran up a bill for £250*. 他很快就欠下了 250 英镑。

S

safe deposit /ˈseɪf dɪˌpɒzɪt/ *noun* a bank safe where you can leave jewellery or documents (银行)保险库

safe deposit box /ˌseɪf dɪˈpɒzɪt ˌbɒks/ *noun* a small box which you can rent to keep jewellery or documents in a bank's safe (银行)保险箱

safe investment /ˌseɪf ɪnˈvestmənt/ *noun* something, e.g. a share, which is not likely to fall in value 安全投资,保值投资:不太可能贬值的事物(如股票)

safe keeping /ˌseɪf ˈkiːpɪŋ/ *noun* the fact of being looked after carefully 安全保管 ○ *We put the documents into the bank for safe keeping.* 为安全起见我们把文件存入了银行。

safety /ˈseɪfti/ *noun* the fact of being free from danger or risk 安全 □ **to take safety precautions** ***or*** **safety measures** to act to make sure something is safe 采取安全防范措施

salaried /ˈsælərid/ *adjective* earning a salary 拿薪水的,带薪的 ○ *The company has 250 salaried staff.* 公司有 250 名受薪员工。

salaried partner /ˌsælərid ˈpɑːtnə/ *noun* a partner, often a junior one, who receives a regular salary in accordance with the partnership agreement 拿薪水的合伙人

salary /ˈsæləri/ *noun* a regular payment for work done, made to an employee usually as a cheque at the end of each month (月)工资,薪金 ○ *The company froze all salaries for a six-month period.* 公司冻结了所有员工六个月的工资。○ *If I get promoted, my salary will go up.* 我如果升职,工资也会上涨。○ *The salary may be low, but the fringe benefits attached to the job are good.* 该工作工资可能较低,但福利待遇不错。○ *She got a salary increase in June.* 她于 6 月得到加薪。

salary cheque /ˈsæləri tʃek/ *noun* a monthly cheque by which an employee is paid 工资支票

salary cut /ˈsæləri kʌt/ *noun* a sudden reduction in salary 减薪

salary deductions /ˈsæləri dɪˌdʌkʃənz/ *plural noun* money which a company removes from salaries to pay to the government as tax, National Insurance contributions, etc. 工资扣除数:公司代扣的税金、国民保险金等

salary scale /ˈsæləri skeɪl/ *noun* same as 同 **pay scale** ○ *He was appointed at the top end of the salary scale.* 他的薪水被定在工资等级表中的最高一档。

sale /seɪl/ *noun* **1.** an act of giving an item or doing a service in exchange for money, or for the promise that money will be paid 销售 □ **to offer**

something for sale *or* **to put something up for sale** to announce that something is ready to be sold 宣布出售，提呈出售 ○ *They put the factory up for sale.* 他们宣布要出售工厂。○ *His shop is for sale.* 他的商店要出售。○ *These items are not for sale to the general public.* 这些物品不对外销售。**2.** an act of selling goods at specially low prices 甩卖，廉价出售 ○ *The shop is having a sale to clear old stock.* 该店正在清仓甩卖。○ *The sale price is 50% of the usual price.* 折扣价是原价的一半。

'... the latest car sales for April show a 1.8 per cent dip from last year's total'
"最新数据显示，4 月份汽车销售额比上年总额减少了 1.8%"［*Investors Chronicle* 《投资者纪事》］

sale and lease-back /ˌseɪl ən ˈliːsbæk/ *noun* 售后租回 **1.** a situation where a company sells a property to raise cash and then leases it back from the purchaser［公司卖出资产以筹集现金，然后再从购买者手中租回资产］**2.** the sale of an asset, usually a building, to somebody else who then leases it back to the original owner［出售资产(通常是物业)给某人，后者再把资产回租给原业主］

sales /seɪlz/ *plural noun* money received for selling something 销售额 ○ *Sales have risen over the first quarter.* 销售额在第一季度有所增长。

sales analysis /ˈseɪlz əˌnæləsɪs/ *noun* an examination of the reports of sales to see why items have or have not sold well 销售分析：分析销售额报告，以找出畅销或滞销的原因

sales book /ˈseɪlz bʊk/ *noun* a record of sales 销货簿

sales budget /ˈseɪlz ˌbʌdʒɪt/ *noun* a plan of probable sales 销售预算

sales chart /ˈseɪlz tʃɑːt/ *noun* a diagram showing how sales vary from month to month 销售图：显示各月销量变化的图表

sales curve /ˈseɪlz kɜːv/ *noun* a graph showing how sales increase or decrease 销售曲线：显示销售额增加或减少的曲线图

sales department /ˈseɪlz dɪˌpɑːtmənt/ *noun* the section of a company which deals with selling the company's products or services 销售部

sales figures /ˈseɪlz ˌfɪɡəz/ *plural noun* total sales 销售数字，总销售额

sales force /ˈseɪlz fɔːs/ *noun* a group of sales staff 销售队伍，销售人员

sales forecast /ˈseɪlz ˌfɔːkɑːst/ *noun* an estimate of future sales 销售预测

sales invoice /ˈseɪlz ˌɪnvɔɪs/ *noun* an invoice relating to a sale 销售发票

sales journal /ˈseɪlz ˌdʒɜːn(ə)l/ *noun* the book in which non-cash sales are recorded with details of customer, invoice, amount and date. These details are later posted to each customer's account in the sales ledger 销售日记账：详细记录每笔与非现金销售相关的顾客、发票、金额及日期的账簿，这些记录将过账到销售分类账的每个客户明细账内

sales ledger /ˈseɪlz ˌledʒə/ *noun* a book in which sales to each customer are entered 销售分类账：记录对每个客户的销售的账簿

sales ledger clerk /ˈseɪlz ledʒə ˌklɑːk/ *noun* an office employee who deals with the sales ledger 销售分类账记账员

sales manager /ˈseɪlz ˌmænɪdʒə/ *noun* a person in charge of a sales department 销售部经理

sales mix /ˈseɪlz mɪks/ *noun* the sales and profitability of a wide range of products sold by a single company 销售结构,销售组合:一家公司销售的各种产品所占的销售额和利润率

sales mix profit variance /ˌseɪls mɪks ˈprɒfɪt ˌveəriəns/ *noun* the differing profitability of different products within a product range 销售结构利润差异:同一系列产品中不同产品的利润差异

sales price variance /ˌseɪlz praɪs ˈveəriəns/ *noun* the difference between expected revenue from actual sales and actual revenue 销售价格差异:根据实际销售额估计的收入与实际收入之差

sales return /ˈseɪlz rɪˌtɜːn/ *noun* a report of sales made each day or week or quarter 销售报告

sales revenue /ˈseɪlz ˌrevənjuː/ *noun US* the income from sales of goods or services (美)销售收入(NOTE: The UK term is **turnover** 英国用语为 **turnover**)

sales slip /ˈseɪlz slɪp/ *noun* a paper showing that an article was bought at a specific shop 销售单,购物小票:证明某物购自某商店的单据 ○ *Goods can be exchanged only on production of a sales slip.* 要想换货必须要有购物小票。

sales target /ˈseɪlz ˌtɑːɡɪt/ *noun* the amount of sales a sales representative is expected to achieve (销售代表的)销售指标

sales tax /ˈseɪlz tæks/ *noun* a tax which is paid on each item sold and is collected when the purchase is made 销售税:销售货物时对售出的每件商品支付的税金 Also called 亦称作 **turnover tax**

sales value /ˈseɪlz ˌvæljuː/ *noun* the amount of money which would be received if something is sold 销售价值:某物售出时可得到的金额

sales volume /ˈseɪlz ˌvɒljuːm/ *noun* the number of units sold 销量(NOTE: The UK term is **turnover** 英国用语为 **turnover**)

sales volume profit variance /ˌseɪlz ˌvɒljuːm ˈprɒfɪt ˌveəriəns/ *noun* the difference between the profit on the number of units actually sold and the forecast figure 销量利润差异:实际销量利润与预测利润之差

salvage /ˈsælvɪdʒ/ *noun* **1.** the work of saving a ship or a cargo from being destroyed (遇险船只或货物的)救助 **2.** goods saved from a wrecked ship, from a fire or from some other accident (从沉船、火灾或其他事故中)抢救出的货物 ○ *a sale of flood salvage items* 出售从水灾中抢救出来的物品(NOTE: no plural 无复数) ■ *verb* **1.** to save goods or a ship from being destroyed 打捞,救助(遇险船只或货物) ○ *We are selling off a warehouse full of salvaged goods.* 我们正在清仓处理打捞上来的货物。**2.** to save something from loss 抢救,挽救,挽回 ○ *The company is trying to salvage its reputation after the managing director was sent to prison for fraud.* 在总经理因欺诈被判入狱后,公司正在努力挽回声誉。○ *The receiver managed to salvage something from the collapse of the company.* 破产接管人设法为破产的公司挽回些什么。

salvage money /ˈsælvɪdʒ ˌmʌni/ *noun* payment made by the owner of a ship or a cargo to the person who has saved it 救援报酬，打捞费：船主、货主支付给营救人员的费用，用于打捞失事船只或货物

salvage vessel /ˈsælvɪdʒ ˌves(ə)l/ *noun* a ship which specialises in saving other ships and their cargoes 海上救助船：专门救助其他船只和货物的船只

S&L *abbr* savings and loan 储蓄贷款协会

SAS *abbr* Statement of Auditing Standards 审计准则说明书

save /seɪv/ *verb* to keep, not to spend (money) 储蓄；节省 ○ *He is trying to save money by walking to work.* 为了省钱，他步行上班。○ *She is saving to buy a house.* 她在攒钱买房。

save-as-you-earn /ˌseɪvəzjuːˈɜːn/ *noun* a scheme where employees can save money regularly by having it deducted automatically from their wages and invested in National Savings 自愿定额储蓄计划，工资扣储计划：员工自动定期从薪金中扣除一定金额存入国民储蓄中的计划 Abbreviation 缩写 **SAYE**

saver /ˈseɪvə/ *noun* a person who saves money 节省的人；储户

savings /ˈseɪvɪŋz/ *plural noun* money saved (i.e. money which is not spent) 储蓄，存款 ○ *She put all her savings into a deposit account.* 她把所有的钱都存在一个存款账户里。

savings account /ˈseɪvɪŋz əˌkaʊnt/ *noun* an account where you put money in regularly and which pays interest, often at a higher rate than a deposit account 储蓄账户：定期存入资金的附息账户，其利率通常高于存款账户

savings and loan /ˈseɪvɪŋz ən ˈləʊn/, **savings and loan association** /ˈseɪvɪŋz ən ˈləʊn əˌsəʊsieɪʃ(ə)n/ *noun US* a financial association which accepts and pays interest on deposits from investors and lends money to people who are buying property. The loans are in the form of mortgages on the security of the property being bought. S & Ls are regulated by the Office of Thrift Supervision and are protected by the Savings Association Insurance Fund（美）储蓄贷款协会：美国的一个金融协会，接受投资者存款同时支付利息，并向购房者提供以所购房产为抵押的按揭贷款。储蓄贷款协会由美国储蓄管理局监管，受储蓄协会保险基金保护 Abbreviation 缩写 **S & L** Also called 亦称作 **thrift**（NOTE：The UK term is **building society** 英国用语为 **building society**）

savings bank /ˈseɪvɪŋz bæŋk/ *noun* a bank where you can deposit money and receive interest on it 储蓄银行：可存入资金并获得利息的银行

savings certificate /ˈseɪvɪŋz səˌtɪfɪkət/ *noun* a document showing that you have invested money in a government savings scheme 储蓄券：证明已投资于政府储蓄计划的票据（NOTE：The US term is **savings bond** 美国用语为 **savings bond**）

savings income /ˌseɪvɪŋz ˈɪnkʌm/ *noun* income in the form of interest on deposits with banks and building societies, government bonds, etc., but not income from dividends or rental income from property 储蓄收入：以银行及住房互助协会的存款利息、政府债券等形式存在的收入，但不包括股利或租金收入

savings-related share option scheme /ˌseɪvɪŋzrɪˌleɪtɪd ˈʃeə ˌɒpʃən ˌskiːm/ *noun* a scheme which allows employees of a company to buy shares with money which they have contributed to a savings scheme 储蓄购股权计划：允许雇员使用储蓄计划缴款来购买公司股票的计划

SAYE *abbr* save-as-you-earn 自愿定额储蓄计划，工资扣储计划

SBA *abbr* Small Business Administration 小企业管理局

scale /skeɪl/ *noun* a system which is graded into various levels 级别，等级，比例 □ **scale of charges** *or* **scale of prices** a list showing various prices 费用（或价格）表 □ **scale of salaries** a list of salaries showing different levels of pay in different jobs in the same company 工资级别表

scarcity value /ˈskeəsɪti ˌvæljuː/ *noun* the value something has because it is rare and there is a large demand for it 稀缺价值：有大量需求的稀缺物品的价值

schedule /ˈʃedjuːl/ *noun* **1.** a timetable, a plan of how time should be spent, drawn up in advance 时间表，日程安排 ○ *The managing director has a busy schedule of appointments.* 总经理的会见日程安排得很满。○ *Her assistant tried to fit us into her schedule.* 她的助理尽量安排我们和她见面。**2.** a list, especially a list forming an additional document attached to a contract 一览表，附件（尤指合同附表）○ *the schedule of territories to which a contract applies* 合同适用地区的附表 ○ *Please find enclosed our schedule of charges.* 随函附上我方费用一览表。○ *See the attached schedule* or *as per the attached schedule.* 参看附表。**3.** a list of interest rates 利率表

Schedule A /ˌʃedjuːl ˈeɪ/ *noun* a schedule under which tax is charged on income from land or buildings 附表A：房地产所得税表

Schedule B /ˌʃedjuːl ˈbiː/ *noun* a schedule under which tax was formerly charged on income from woodlands 附表B：以前的林地所得税表

Schedule C /ˌʃedjuːl ˈsiː/ *noun* a schedule under which tax is charged on profits from government stock 附表C：政府债券利得税表

Schedule D /ˌʃedjuːl ˈdiː/ *noun* a schedule under which tax is charged on income from trades or professions, interest and other earnings not derived from being employed 附表D：贸易或专业收入、利息及其他非雇佣收益税表

Schedule E /ˌʃedjuːl ˈiː/ *noun* a schedule under which tax is charged on income from salaries, wages or pensions 附表E：工资或退休金所得税表

Schedule F /ˌʃedjuːl ˈef/ *noun* a schedule under which tax is charged on income from dividends 附表F：股利所得税表

scheme /skiːm/ *noun* a plan, arrangement or way of working 方案，计划 ○ *Under the bonus scheme all employees get 10% of their annual pay as a Christmas bonus.* 根据奖励方案，所有员工在圣诞节可获得其年薪10%的过节费。○ *She has joined the company pension scheme.* 她加入了公司退休金计划。○ *We operate a profit-sharing scheme for managers.* 我们为管理人员推出了一个利润分享计划。○ *The new payment scheme is based on reward for* *individual effort*. 新的工资方案是建立在多劳多得的基础上。

scheme of arrangement /ˌskiːm əv əˈreɪndʒmənt/ *noun* a scheme drawn up by an individual or company to offer ways of paying debts, so as to avoid bankruptcy proceedings 偿还债务安排:由个人或公司制订的一种方案,它提供偿还债务的方式,以避免进入破产程序 Also called 亦称作 **voluntary arrangement**

scorched earth policy /ˌskɔːtʃt ˈɜːθ ˌpɒlɪsi/ *noun* a way of combating a takeover bid, where the target company sells valuable assets or purchases unattractive assets 焦土政策:目标公司通过卖出有价资产或购入无吸引力的资产来对抗收购

scrap /skræp/ *noun* material left over after an industrial process, and which still has some value, as opposed to waste, which has no value 残料:经过工业处理后剩下的仍有一些价值的材料,不同于毫无价值的废料 ○ *to sell a ship for scrap* 把船作为残料出售

scrap value /ˈskræp ˌvæljuː/ *noun* the value of an asset if sold for scrap 残值:资产作为残料出售的价值 ○ *Its scrap value is £2,500*. 其残值为2,500英镑。

scrip /skrɪp/ *noun* a security, e.g. a share, bond, or the certificate issued to show that someone has been allotted a share or bond 临时证券:代替正式股票或债券的一类证券,或表明某人已获配发股份或债券的凭证

'...under the rule, brokers who fail to deliver stock within four days of a transaction are to be fined 1% of the transaction value for each day of missing scrip'
"根据规章,经纪商如在交易后四天内仍未交割证券,则在未交割证券期间,每天将被处以交易价值1%的罚款"[*Far Eastern Economic Review*《远东经济评论》]

scrip dividend /ˈskrɪp ˌdɪvɪdend/ *noun* a dividend which takes the form of new shares in the company, as opposed to cash 以股代息,票据股利,临时股利:以公司新股代替现金发放的股利

scrip issue /ˈskrɪp ˌɪʃuː/ *noun* an issue of shares whereby a company transfers money from reserves to share capital and issues free extra shares to the shareholders. The value of the company remains the same, and the total market value of shareholders' shares remains the same, the market price being adjusted to account for the new shares 红利股发行:一种股份发行,公司将资金由留存盈余转入股本,并免费向股东发行额外股份。发行红利股后,公司价值不变,股东股份的总市值不变,只有股票市价按新股发行进行调整 Also called 亦称作 **free issue, capitalisation issue**

SDRs *abbr* special drawing rights 特别提款权

seal /siːl/ *noun* **1.** a special symbol, often one stamped on a piece of wax, which is used to show that a document is officially approved by the organisation that uses the symbol 印章 **2.** a piece of paper, metal or wax attached to close something, so that it can be opened only if the paper, metal or wax is removed or broken 封条 ■ *verb* **1.** to close something tightly 封上,密封 ○ *The computer disks were sent in a sealed container*. 计算机磁盘被装在密闭容器里寄出。**2.** to attach a seal, to stamp something with a seal 盖章

○ *Customs sealed the shipment*. 海关对这批货物加上了铅封。

sealed envelope /ˌsiːld ˈenvələʊp/ *noun* an envelope where the flap has been stuck down to close it 已封好的信封 ○ *to send the information in a sealed envelope* 使用密封的信封发送信息

seasonal adjustment /ˌsiːz(ə)n(ə)l əˈdʒʌstmənt/ *noun* an adjustment made to accounts to allow for any short-term seasonal factors, such as Christmas sales, that may distort the figures 季节性调整:根据可能影响数据的任何短期季节性因素(如圣诞节销售)对账目进行调整

seasonal business /ˌsiːz(ə)n(ə)l ˈbɪznɪs/ *noun* trade that varies depending on the time of the year, e. g. trade in goods such as suntan products or Christmas trees 季节性业务:随季节变化的商业,如防晒用品或圣诞树等商品的买卖

SEC *abbr* Securities and Exchange Commission 美国证券交易委员会

second /ˈsekənd/ *noun*, *adjective* the thing which comes after the first 第二(的) ■ *verb* **1.** /ˈsekənd/ □ **to second a motion** to be the first person to support a proposal put forward by someone else 附议一项提案:作为第一个赞同他人提议的人 ○ *Mrs Smith seconded the motion* or *The motion was seconded by Mrs Smith*. 史密斯夫人附议该动议。**2.** /sɪˈkɒnd/ to lend a member of staff to another company, organisation or department for a fixed period of time 借调(员工) ○ *He was seconded to the Department of Trade for two years*. 他被借调到贸易部工作两年。

secondary /ˈsekənd(ə)ri/ *adjective* second in importance 第二位的,次要的

secondary industry /ˈsekənd(ə)ri ˌɪndəstri/ *noun* an industry which uses basic raw materials to produce manufactured goods 第二产业:使用基础原材料来生产制成品的行业

seconder /ˈsekəndə/ *noun* a person who seconds a proposal 附议人 ○ *There was no seconder for the motion so it was not put to the vote*. 这项提议没有人附议,所以未提交表决。

second half /ˌsekənd ˈhɑːf/ *noun* a period of six months from 1st July to 31st December 下半年(从7月1日到12月31日) ○ *The figures for the second half are up on those for the first part of the year*. 下半年的数字要好于上半年。

second half-year /ˌsekənd ˈhɑːf-jɪə/ *noun* the six-month period from July to the end of December 下半年(从7月到12月底)

secondment /sɪˈkɒndmənt/ *noun* the fact or period of being seconded to another job for a period 借调;借调期 ○ *She is on three years' secondment to an Australian college*. 她被借调到澳大利亚一所学院工作三年。

second mortgage /ˌsekənd ˈmɔːgɪdʒ/ *noun* a further mortgage on a property which is already mortgaged 二次抵押贷款:对已抵押的财产再次进行抵押

second quarter /ˌsekənd ˈkwɔːtə/ *noun* a period of three months from April to the end of June 第二季度(从4月初到6月底)

secret /ˈsiːkrət/ *adjective* being deliberately kept hidden from people, or which is not known about by many people 秘密的，机密的 ○ *The MD kept the contract secret from the rest of the board*. 这份合同总经理一直对其他董事保密。○ *The management signed a secret deal with a foreign supplier*. 管理层与一家外国供应商达成一项秘密交易。■ *noun* something which is kept hidden or which is not known about by many people 秘密 ○ *to keep a secret* 保守秘密

secretary /ˈsekrət(ə)ri/ *noun* an official of a company or society whose job is to keep records and write letters 秘书

secret reserves /ˌsiːkrət rɪˈzɜːvz/ *plural noun* reserves which are illegally kept hidden in a company's balance sheet, as opposed to 'hidden reserves' which are simply not easy to identify 秘密储备金：在公司资产负债表中非法隐藏的储备金，与之相对的"隐蔽储备金"则只是不易识别

section /ˈsekʃən/ *noun* one of the parts of an Act of Parliament 章，节：议会法案的一个章节

secure /sɪˈkjʊə/ *adjective* safe, which cannot change 安全的，不会改变的

secured /sɪˈkjʊəd/ *adjective* used to describe a type of borrowing such as a mortgage where the lender has a legal right to take over an asset or assets of the borrower, if the borrower does not repay the loan（借款）有抵押的，有担保的

secured creditor /sɪˌkjʊəd ˈkredɪtə/ *noun* a person who is owed money by someone, and can legally claim the same amount of the borrower's property if the borrower fails to pay back the money owed 有担保债权人：借款人无法偿还债务时，对其财产有相当于债务金额的要求权的债权人

secured loan /sɪˈkjʊəd ləʊn/ *noun* a loan which is guaranteed by the borrower giving assets as security 有担保贷款：由借款人提供资产作为担保的贷款

securities /sɪˈkjʊərɪtiz/ *plural noun* investments in stocks and shares 证券

securities account /sɪˌkjʊərɪtiz əˈkaʊnt/ *noun* an account that shows the value of financial assets held by a person or organization 证券账户：表明某人或组织持有的金融资产价值的账户

Securities and Exchange Commission /sɪˈkjʊərɪtiz ən ɪksˈtʃeɪndʒ kəˈmɪʃ(ə)n/ *noun* the official body which regulates the securities markets in the USA 美国证券交易委员会：美国负责监管证券市场的官方机构 Abbreviation 缩写 **SEC**

Securities and Futures Authority /sɪˌkjʊərətiz ən ˈfjuːtʃəz ɔːˌθɒrəti/ *noun* in the UK, a self-regulatory organisation which supervises the trading in shares and futures, now part of the FSA 英国证券期货管理局：英国负责监督股票及期货交易的自律组织，现已并入英国金融服务管理局 Abbreviation 缩写 **SFA**

Securities and Investments Board /sɪˌkjʊərɪtiz ən ɪnˈvestmənts bɔːd/ *noun* the former regulatory body which regulated the securities markets in the UK. It has been superseded by the FSA 英国证券与投资委员会：英国以前负责监管证券市场的机构，现已被英国金融服务管理局取代 Abbreviation 缩写 **SIB**

securitisation /sɪˌkjʊərɪtaɪˈzeɪʃ(ə)n/, **securitization** *noun* the process of making a loan or mortgage into a tradeable security by issuing a bill of exchange or other negotiable paper in place of it 证券化:通过发行汇票或其他可流通票据来取代贷款,使贷款或抵押贷款转化为可交易证券的过程

security /sɪˈkjʊərɪti/ *noun* **1.** a guarantee that someone will repay money borrowed (借款)担保,抵押 ○ *to give something as security for a debt* 以某物作为债务担保 ○ *to use a house as security for a loan* 以房子作为贷款抵押 ○ *The bank lent him £20,000 without security.* 银行借给他两万无抵押贷款。□ **to stand security for someone** to guarantee that if the person does not repay a loan, you will repay it for him 为某人提供担保:保证在某人不偿还贷款时替他偿付 **2.** a stock or share 证券

security deposit /sɪˌkjʊərɪti dɪˈpɒzɪt/ *noun* an amount of money paid before a transaction occurs to compensate the seller in the event that the transaction is not concluded and this is the buyer's fault 保证金,安全押金:在交易发生前支付的金额,作为因买方过失导致交易无法完成时对卖方的补偿

seed money /ˈsiːd ˌmʌni/ *noun* venture capital invested when a new project is starting up and therefore more risky than secondary finance 种子基金,创办基金:启动新项目时投入的风险资本,因此风险高于后续融资

segmental reporting /segˌment(ə)l rɪˈpɔːtɪŋ/ *noun* the act of showing in company reports the results of a company or sections of it, separated according to the type of business or geographical area 分部报告:在公司报表中显示的公司或部门的业绩,按业务性质或地区进行划分

self /self/ *pronoun* your own person 自身

self- /self/ *prefix* referring to yourself 自身的

self-assessment /selfəˈsesmənt/ *noun* the process of calculating how much tax you should pay and reporting it to the Inland Revenue on time 自我估税:计算自己应付多少税并按时向国内税务局申报 ○ *Self-assessment forms should be returned to the tax office by 31st January.* 自我估税表格应于1月31日前交回税务局。

self-employed /ˌselfɪmˈplɔɪd/ *adjective* working for yourself or not on the payroll of a company 自雇的,单干的,个体经营的 ○ *a self-employed engineer* 个体工程师 ○ *He worked for a bank for ten years but is now self-employed.* 他在一家银行工作了十年,但现在出来单干了。

self-employed contributions /ˌselfɪmˌplɔɪd ˌkɒntrɪˈbjuːʃ(ə)nz/ *plural noun* National Insurance contributions made by self-employed people 自雇者的国民保险缴款

self-financing /ˌselffaɪˈnænsɪŋ/ *noun* the financing of development costs, the purchase of capital assets, etc. by a company from its own resources 自筹资金:公司通过自身资源支付开发成本、购买资产等

self-regulation /selfˌregjʊˈleɪʃ(ə)n/ *noun* the regulation of an industry by itself, through a committee which issues a rulebook and makes sure that members of the industry follow the rules 自我调节，自治：行业的自我管理，通过一个委员会发布规章制度，并确保业内每个成员均遵守这些规章 (NOTE: For example, the Stock Exchange is regulated by the Stock Exchange Council 例如，证券交易所由证券交易委员会监管)

self-regulatory /selfˌregjʊˈleɪt(ə)ri/ *adjective* referring to an organisation which regulates itself 自我调节的，自治的

sell /sel/ *noun* an act of selling 出售 ■ *verb* **1.** to give goods in exchange for money 销售 ○ *to sell something on credit* 赊售 ○ *The shop sells washing machines and refrigerators.* 该商店销售洗衣机和冰箱。○ *They tried to sell their house for £100,000.* 他们想以10万英镑卖出他们的房子。○ *Their products are easy to sell.* 他们的产品很畅销。**2.** to be sold 被出售 ○ *These items sell well in the pre-Christmas period.* 这些产品在圣诞节前卖得很好 ○ *Those packs sell for £25 a dozen.* 这些包裹25英镑一打。(NOTE: **selling – sold**)

seller /ˈselə/ *noun* a person who sells 卖方，销售商 ○ *There were few sellers in the market, so prices remained high.* 市场上卖主很少，所以价格居高不下。

seller's market /ˌseləz ˈmɑːkɪt/ *noun* a market where the seller can ask high prices because there is a large demand for the product 卖方市场：由于市场需求很大而形成的卖方要价很高的市场 Opposite 反义 **buyer's market**

selling costs /ˈselɪŋ kɒsts/, **selling overhead** /ˌselɪŋ ˈəʊvəhed/ *plural noun* the amount of money to be paid for the advertising, reps' commissions and other expenses involved in selling something 销售费用：在销售环节涉及的广告费、销售佣金和其他费用

selling price /ˈselɪŋ praɪs/ *noun* the price at which someone is willing to sell something 售价，卖价

selling price variance /ˈselɪŋ praɪs ˌveəriəns/ *noun* the difference between the actual selling price and the budgeted selling price 销售价格差异：实际售价与计划售价之差

semi- /semi/ *prefix* half or part 一半，部分

semiannual /ˌsemiˈænjuəl/ *adjective* referring to interest paid every six months (利息)每半年支付一次的

semi-fixed cost /ˌsemifɪkst ˈkɒst/ *noun* same as 同 **semi-variable cost**

semi-variable cost /ˌsemiˌveəriəb(ə)l ˈkɒst/ *noun* money paid to produce a product which increases, though less than proportionally, with the quantity of the product made 半固定成本，半可变成本：产品生产成本随着产量的增加而增加，但其增加幅度要小于产量的增长幅度 ○ *Stepping up production will mean an increase in semi-variable costs.* 加速生产会提高半可变成本。Also called 亦称作 **semi-fixed cost**

senior /ˈsiːniə/ *adjective* **1.** referring to an employee who is more important (员工)高级的 **2.** referring to an employee who is older or who has been employed longer than another (员工)资深的(年长或工龄长的) **3.** referring to a sum which is repayable before others (款项)优先支付的

senior capital /ˌsiːniə ˈkæpɪt(ə)l/ *noun* capital in the form of secured loans to a company. It is repaid before junior capital, such as shareholders' equity, in the event of liquidation 高级资本:以抵押贷款形式存在的资本,在破产清算时在股东权益等次级资本之前偿付

seniority /ˌsiːniˈɒrɪti/ *noun* the fact of being more important 资深,资历 ○ *in order of seniority* 按资历顺序 □ **the managers were listed in order of seniority** the manager who had been an employee the longest was put at the top of the list 管理人员按资排辈

senior manager /ˌsiːniə ˈmænɪdʒə/, **senior executive** /ˌsiːniə ɪɡˈzekjʊtɪv/ *noun* a manager or director who has a higher rank than others 高级经理,资深经理

sensitivity analysis /ˌsensəˈtɪvəti əˌnæləsɪs/ *noun* the analysis of the effect of a small change in a calculation on the final result 敏感性分析:关于计算中的微小变动对最终结果的影响的分析

separable /ˈsep(ə)rəb(ə)l/ *adjective* possible to separate 可分离的

separable net assets /ˌsep(ə)rəb(ə)l net ˈæsets/ *plural noun* assets which can be separated from the rest of the assets of a business and sold off 可剥离的净资产:可与其他资产分离并出售的资产

separate /ˈsep(ə)rət/ *adjective* not connected with something 分开的,分离的

sequester /sɪˈkwestə/, **sequestrate** /ˈsiːkwestreɪt, sɪˈkwestreɪt/ *verb* to take and keep a bank account or property because a court has ordered it (法院对银行账户或财产)查封,扣押 ○ *The union's funds have been sequestrated*. 工会的资金被查封了。

sequestration /ˌsiːkweˈstreɪʃ(ə)n/ *noun* the act of taking and keeping property on the order of a court, especially of seizing property from someone who is in contempt of court (依据法令)查封,扣押(尤指没收藐视法庭者的财产)

sequestrator /ˈsiːkwestreɪtə, sɪˈkwestreɪtə/ *noun* a person who takes and keeps property on the order of a court 扣押令执行者:根据法院命令暂时保管财产的人

series /ˈsɪəriːz/ *noun* a group of items following one after the other 系列 ○ *A series of successful takeovers made the company one of the largest in the trade*. 通过一系列成功收购,该公司成为业内最大的企业之一。(NOTE: plural is **series** 复数为 **series**)

Serious Fraud Office /ˌsɪəriəs ˈfrɔːd ˌɒfɪs/ *noun* a British government department in charge of investigating major fraud in companies 严重欺诈行为调查办公室:英国负责调查公司重大欺诈行为的政府部门 Abbreviation 缩写 **SFO**

SERPS /sɜːps/ *abbr* State Earnings-Related Pension Scheme 国家收入关联养老金计划

service /ˈsɜːvɪs/ *noun* **1.** the fact of working for an employer, or the period of time during which an employee has worked for an employer 服务,工作;服务年限,工作年限 ○ *retiring after twenty years service to the company* 为公司效力 20 年后退休 ○ *The amount of your pension depends partly on the number of your years of service*. 你的退休金金额与你的工龄有一定关联。**2.** the work of dealing with customers (对顾客的)接待,服务 ○ *The* *service in that restaurant is extremely slow*. 那家餐馆上菜奇慢无比 **3.** payment for help given to the customer 服务费 ○ *to add on 10% for service* 附加10%的服务费

service bureau /ˈsɜːvɪs ˌbjʊərəʊ/ *noun* an office which specialises in helping other offices 服务部,服务处:专为其他部门提供服务的部门

service charge /ˈsɜːvɪs tʃɑːdʒ/ *noun* 服务费 **1.** a charge added to the bill in a restaurant to pay for service [餐馆在餐费外加收的服务费] **2.** an amount paid by tenants in a block of flats or offices for general maintenance, insurance and cleaning [公寓或写字楼租户就日常维护、保险及清洁支付的费用] **3.** *US* a charge which a bank makes for carrying out work for a customer [(美)银行向客户收取的费用] (NOTE: The UK term is **bank charge** 英国用语为 **bank charge**)

service contract /ˈsɜːvɪs ˌkɒntrækt/ *noun* a contract between a company and a dirctor showing all conditions of work 服务合同 ○ *She worked unofficially with no service contract*. 她不是正式员工,没有签服务合同。

service industry /ˈsɜːvɪs ˌɪndəstri/ *noun* an industry which does not produce raw materials or manufacture products but offers a service such as banking, retailing or accountancy 服务业,服务性行业

services /ˈsɜːvɪsɪz/ *plural noun* **1.** benefits which are sold to customers or clients, e.g. transport or education (交通运输、教育等)服务 ○ *We give advice to companies on the marketing of services*. 我们就如何推销服务向公司提供建议。○ *We must improve the exports of both goods and services*. 我们必须完善商品和劳务出口。**2.** business of providing help in some form when it is needed, e.g. insurance, banking, etc., as opposed to making or selling goods 服务业(如保险业、银行业等,与生产或销售产品的行业相对)

set /set/ *adjective* fixed or which cannot be changed 固定的 ○ *There is a set fee for all our consultants*. 我们支付给所有顾问的费用都是固定的。■ *verb* to fix or to arrange something 固定,确定;安排 ○ *We have to set a price for the new computer*. 我们得为新计算机定个价。○ *The price of the calculator has been set low, so as to achieve maximum unit sales*. 为了实现单位产品销售额最大化,这种计算器的价格定得很低。(NOTE: **setting – set**)

set against /ˌset əˈgenst/ *verb* to balance one group of figures against another group to try to make them cancel each other out 抵消,使平衡 ○ *to set the costs against the sales revenue* 用这些费用抵消销售收入 ○ *Can you set the expenses against tax*? 你能用这些费用抵税吗?

set off /ˌset ˈɒf/ *verb* to use a debt owed by one party to reduce a debt owed to them 抵消(债务)

set-off /ˈsetɒf/ *noun* an agreement between two parties to balance one debt against another or a loss against a gain 划账,轧平:双方关于抵消债务余额或盈亏的协议

settle /ˈset(ə)l/ *verb* to place a property in trust 信托

settlement /ˈset(ə)lmənt/ *noun* **1.** the payment of an account 结算,结账

□ **we offer an extra 5% discount for rapid settlement** we take a further 5% off the price if the customer pays quickly 我们对及时付款的客户提供5%的额外折扣 **2.** an agreement after an argument or negotiations 和解，解决 ○ *a wage settlement* 工资和解

'...he emphasised that prompt settlement of all forms of industrial disputes would guarantee industrial peace in the country and ensure increased productivity'
"他强调，及时解决各种形式的劳资纠纷可以保证国家的产业稳定，确保生产力的提高"［*Business Times* (*Lagos*)《商业时报》(拉各斯)］

settlement date /ˈset(ə)lmənt deɪt/ *noun* a date when a payment has to be made 结算日

settlement day /ˈset(ə)lmənt deɪ/ *noun* （证券）交割日 **1.** the day on which shares which have been bought must be paid for. On the London Stock Exchange the account period is three business days from the day of trade［结算所购证券的日期。在伦敦证券交易所，交割期限为交易日起的三个工作日内］**2.** in the USA, the day on which securities bought actually become the property of the purchaser［在美国，指所购证券真正归买方拥有的日期］

settle on /ˈset(ə)l ɒn/ *verb* to leave property to someone when you die 遗留，授予：死亡时将财产留给某人 ○ *He settled his property on his children*. 他把财产遗留给了子女。

set up /ˌset ˈʌp/ *verb* to begin something, or to organise something new 设立，组建 ○ *to set up an inquiry* or *a working party* 设立问询处（或工作组）

'...the concern announced that it had acquired a third large tanker since being set up'
"企业宣布，它已购买了自成立以来的第三艘大型油轮"［*Lloyd's List*《劳氏日报》］

seven-day money /ˌsev(ə)ndeɪ ˈmʌni/ *noun* an investment in financial instruments which mature in seven days' time 七日基金：对一周内到期的金融工具的投资

several /ˈsev(ə)rəl/ *adjective* more than a few, some 几个的，一些的 ○ *Several managers are retiring this year*. 几个经理要在今年退休了。○ *Several of our products sell well in Japan*. 我们的一些产品在日本很畅销。

severally /ˈsev(ə)rəli/ *adverb* separately, not jointly 个别地

severance pay /ˈsev(ə)rəns peɪ/ *noun* money paid as compensation to an employee whose job is no longer needed 解雇费：支付给被解雇员工的补偿金

SFA *abbr* Securities and Futures Authority 英国证券期货管理局

SFAS *abbr* Statement of Financial Accounting Standards（美国）财务会计准则公报

SFO *abbr* Serious Fraud Office 严重欺诈行为调查办公室

shadow director /ˌʃædəʊ daɪˈrektə/ *noun* a person who is not a director of a company, but who tells the directors of the company how to act 影子董事：不是公司董事但却指示公司董事如何行事的人

share /ʃeə/ *noun* **1.** a part of something that has been divided up among several people or groups 份额，一份 **2.** one of many equal parts into which a company's capital is divided 股份，股票 ○ *He bought a block of shares in Marks and Spencer.* 他买入了大量的玛莎百货的股票。○ *Shares fell on the London market.* 伦敦股市下跌。○ *The company offered 1.8m shares on the market.* 公司在市场上发售 180 万股股票。

'...falling profitability means falling share prices'
"盈利能力下降意味着股价下跌。"［*Investors Chronicle*《投资者纪事》］
'...the share of blue-collar occupations declined from 48 per cent to 43 per cent'
"蓝领职业所占份额从 48%下降到 43%"［*Sydney Morning Herald*《悉尼先驱晨报》］

share account /ˈʃeə əˌkaʊnt/ *noun* an account at a building society where the account holder is a member of the society. Building societies usually offer another type of account, a deposit account, where the account holder is not a member. A share account is generally paid a better rate of interest, but in the event of the society going into liquidation, deposit account holders are given preference 股金账户：住房互助协会提供给其会员的一类账户，对于非会员，协会则提供另一种账户即存款账户。会员持有的股金账户所获得的利率往往较高，但在住房互助协会清算时，非会员持有的存款账户则拥有优先权

share at par /ˌʃeə ət ˈpɑː/ *noun* a share whose value on the stock market is the same as its face value 市价与面值相同的股票

share capital /ˈʃeə ˌkæpɪt(ə)l/ *noun* the value of the assets of a company held as shares 股本：公司以股份形式持有的资产价值

share certificate /ˈʃeə səˌtɪfɪkət/ *noun* a document proving that you own shares 股份证书，股票

share disposals /ˈʃeə dɪˌspəʊz(ə)lz/ *plural noun* selling of shares 股份出售

shareholder /ˈʃeəhəʊldə/ *noun* a person who owns shares in a company 股东 ○ *to call a shareholders' meeting* 召集股东大会（NOTE: The US term is **stockholder** 美国用语为 **stockholder**）

'...as of last night the bank's shareholders no longer hold any rights to the bank's shares'
"自昨晚起银行股东不再拥有银行股权"［*South China Morning Post*《南华早报》］
'...the company said that its recent issue of 10.5% convertible preference shares at A$8.50 has been oversubscribed, boosting shareholders' funds to A$700 million plus'
"公司宣称其新近发行的每股 8.5 澳元、股息率 10.5%的可兑换优先股已被超额认购，并使股东资金升至 7 亿多澳元"［*Financial Times*《金融时报》］

shareholders' equity /ˌʃeəhəʊldəz ˈekwɪti/ *noun* **1.** the value of a company which is the property of its ordinary shareholders (the company's assets less its liabilities) 股东权益：普通股股东拥有的公司价值（即公司资产减负债）**2.** a company's capital which is invested by shareholders, who thus become owners of the company 股东产权，公司的普通股：由股东投资的公司资本，股东藉此投资而成为公司的所有人

shareholders' funds /ˌʃeəhəʊldəz ˈfʌndz/ *noun* the capital and reserves of a company 股东资金：公司的资本及储备

shareholder value /ˌʃeəhəʊldə ˈvæljuː/ *noun* the total return to the shareholders in terms of both dividends and share price growth, calculated as the present value of future free cash flows of the business discounted at the weighted average cost of the capital of the business less the market value of its debt 股东价值:股东通过股利及股价上涨获得的总回报,计算方法为:按企业资本加权平均成本贴现后的企业未来自由现金流量的现值,减去企业债务的市值

shareholder value analysis /ˌʃeəhəʊldə ˌvæljuː əˈnæləsɪs/ *noun* a calculation of the value of a company made by looking at the returns it gives to its shareholders. It assumes that the objective of a company director is to maximise the wealth of the company's shareholders, and is based on the premise that discounted cash flow principles can be applied to the business as a whole 股东价值分析:通过分析公司给予股东的回报来计算公司价值的方法,该方法假设公司董事的目标是为公司股东创造最大的财富,以及贴现后的现金流量本金可作为一个整体用于业务经营 Abbreviation 缩写 **SVA**

shareholding /ˈʃeəhəʊldɪŋ/ *noun* a group of shares in a company owned by one owner 股权,股权数:一个人拥有的公司股数

share option /ˈʃeər ˌɒpʃən/ *noun* a right to buy or sell shares at an agreed price at a time in the future 购股权,股票期权:在未来某一时间按议定价格买卖股票的权利

share premium /ˈʃeə ˌpriːmiəm/ *noun* an amount to be paid above the nominal value of a share in order to buy it 股票溢价:购买股票时支付的超过其面值的金额

share quoted ex dividend /ʃeə ˌkwəʊtɪd eks ˈdɪvɪdend/, **share quoted ex div** /ʃeə ˈkwəʊtɪd eks dɪv/ *noun* a share price not including the right to receive the next dividend 不包括股利的股票报价:不包括下次股利权利的股价 ○ *The shares went ex dividend yesterday*. 昨天的股票报价不包括股利。

share split /ˈʃeə splɪt/ *noun* the act of dividing shares into smaller denominations 分股,拆股:把股份拆分成更小的面值单位

sharing /ˈʃeərɪŋ/ *noun* the act of dividing up 分配,分享

sharp practice /ˌʃɑːp ˈpræktɪs/ *noun* a way of doing business which is not honest, but is not illegal 不正当的手段:不诚实但又不违法的经营手段

shelf registration /ˈʃelf ˌredʒɪsˈtreɪʃ(ə)n/ *noun* a registration of a corporation with the SEC some time (up to two years is allowed) before it is offered for sale to the public 储架式注册,暂搁注册,缓行注册:美国公司于公开发售之前,先在美国证券交易委员会注册一段时间(最多两年)

shell company /ˈʃel ˌkʌmp(ə)ni/ *noun* a company that has ceased to trade but is still registered, especially one sold to enable the buyer to begin trading without having to set up a new company 空壳公司:已停止经营但仍注册在案的公司,尤指买家购得后即可开展业务,而无需成立新公司(NOTE: The US term is **shell corporation** 美国用语为 **shell corporation**)

'... shell companies, which can be used to hide investors' cash, figure largely

throughout the twentieth century'
"可用来隐藏投资者的现金的空壳公司在整个20世纪都非常流行"[*Times*《泰晤士报》]

shelter /ˈʃeltə/ *noun* a protected place 隐蔽处,庇护所

shop window /ˌʃɒp ˈwɪndəʊ/ *noun* a large window in a shop front, where customers can see goods displayed 商店橱窗

short /ʃɔːt/ *adjective*, *adverb* **1.** for a small period of time 短期的(地),短时间的(地) **2.** not as much as should be 短缺的(地) ○ *The shipment was three items short.* 这批货少了三件。○ *My change was £2 short.* 少找给我两英镑。□ **when we cashed up we were £10 short** we had £10 less than we should have had 结账时我们发现少了10英镑

short bill /ˈʃɔːt bɪl/ *noun* a bill of exchange payable at short notice 短期汇票:在短通知期内兑付的汇票

short-change /ˌʃɔːtˈtʃeɪndʒ/ *verb* to give a customer less change than is right, either by mistake or in the hope that it will not be noticed 少找零:有意或无意地少找给顾客零钱

short credit /ˌʃɔːt ˈkredɪt/ *noun* terms which allow the customer only a little time to pay 短期信贷:给予顾客的短期赊账

short-dated bill /ʃɔːtˌdeɪtɪd ˈbɪl/ *noun* a bill which is payable within a few days 短期票据:在几天内付款的票据

short-dated gilts /ʃɔːtˌdeɪtɪd ˈgɪlts/ *plural noun* same as 同 **shorts**

shorten /ˈʃɔːt(ə)n/ *verb* to make shorter 缩短 ○ *to shorten credit terms* 缩短信贷期

shortfall /ˈʃɔːtfɔːl/ *noun* an amount which is missing which would make the total expected sum 亏空,短缺 ○ *We had to borrow money to cover the shortfall between expenditure and revenue.* 我们不得不借入资金来填补收支差额。

short lease /ˌʃɔːt ˈliːs/ *noun* a lease which runs for up to two or three years 短期租赁:两或三年的租赁 ○ *We have a short lease on our current premises.* 我们短期租用了现在这块场地。

short position /ˌʃɔːt pəˈzɪʃ(ə)n/ *noun* a situation where an investor sells short, i. e. sells forward shares which he or she does not own 短仓,空头:投资者卖空的情况,即卖出其并未拥有的远期股票 Compare 比较 **long position**

short-range forecast /ˌʃɔːtreɪndʒ ˈfɔːkɑːst/ *noun* a forecast which covers a period of a few months 短期预测:关于未来几个月内情况的预测

shorts /ʃɔːts/ *plural noun* government stocks which mature in less than five years' time 短期金边债券:五年内到期的政府债券

short-term /ˌʃɔːtˈtɜːm/ *adjective* 短期的 **1.** for a period of weeks or months [几周或几个月] ○ *to place money on short-term deposit* 存入短期存款 ○ *She is employed on a short-term contract.* 她签的是短期工作合同。**2.** for a short period in the future [不久的将来] ○ *We need to recruit at once to cover our short-term manpower requirements.* 短期内我们这里急需用人。

short-term capital /ˌʃɔːttɜːm ˈkæpɪt(ə)l/ *noun* funds raised for a period of less than 12 months 短期资本：为 12 个月以内的需要而筹集的资本 ⇨ 参阅 **working capital**

short-term forecast /ˌʃɔːttɜːm ˈfɔːkɑːst/ *noun* a forecast which covers a period of a few months 短期预测：关于未来几个月内情况的预测

short-term loan /ˌʃɔːttɜːm ˈləʊn/ *noun* a loan which has to be repaid within a few weeks or some years 短期贷款：几周到几年内偿还的贷款

short-term security /ˌʃɔːttɜːm sɪˈkjʊərɪti/ *noun* a security which matures in less than 5 years 短期证券：五年内到期的证券

shrink /ʃrɪŋk/ *verb* to get smaller 收缩，萎缩 ○ *The market has shrunk by 20%.* 市场萎缩了 20%。○ *The company is having difficulty selling into a shrinking market.* 市场正在萎缩，公司很难进入。（NOTE: **shrinking – shrank – has shrunk**）

shrinkage /ˈʃrɪŋkɪdʒ/ *noun* **1.** the amount by which something gets smaller 收缩量 ○ *to allow for shrinkage* 考虑到缩水 **2.** losses of stock through theft, especially by the shop's own staff (*informal*)（非正式）因失窃（尤指监守自盗）造成的库存损失

SIB *abbr* Securities and Investments Board 英国证券与投资委员会

sick pay /ˈsɪk peɪ/ *noun* pay paid to an employee who is sick, even if he cannot work 病假工资

sight deposit /ˈsaɪt dɪˌpɒzɪt/ *noun* a bank deposit which can be withdrawn on demand 活期存款

sight draft /ˈsaɪt drɑːft/ *noun* a bill of exchange which is payable when it is presented 即期汇票：见票即付的汇票

sign /saɪn/ *verb* to write your name in a special way on a document to show that you have written it or approved it 签署 ○ *The letter is signed by the managing director.* 该信函由总经理签字。○ *Our company cheques are not valid if they have not been signed by the finance director.* 我公司未经财务经理签字的支票一概无效。○ *The new recruit was asked to sign the contract of employment.* 新员工要签雇用合同。

signatory /ˈsɪgnət(ə)ri/ *noun* a person who signs a contract, etc. 签署人 ○ *You have to get the permission of all the signatories to the agreement if you want to change the terms.* 你必须征得所有协议签署人的许可，才能修改这些条款。

signature /ˈsɪgnɪtʃə/ *noun* a person's name written by themselves on a cheque, document or letter 签署，签字，签名 ○ *She found a pile of cheques on his desk waiting for signature.* 她发现他的桌上有一沓等待签署的支票。○ *All our company's cheques need two signatures.* 我们公司所有的支票都需经两人签字。○ *The contract of employment had the personnel director's signature at the bottom.* 聘用合同下方附有人事部主任的签名。

simple /ˈsɪmpl/ *adjective* not complicated, not difficult to understand 简单的，易懂的

simple average cost /ˌsɪmpl ˈæv(ə)rɪdʒ kɒst/, **simple average price** /ˌsɪmpl ˈæv(ə)rɪdʒ praɪs/ *noun* the average cost of stock received during a period calculated at the end of the period as the average unit price of each delivery of stock, rather than an average price of each unit delivered as in weighted average price 简单平均成本,简单平均价格:于期末按每次交货的平均单位价格(而不是按每个交货单位的加权平均价格)计算的期内已收存货的平均成本

simple interest /ˌsɪmpl ˈɪntrəst/ *noun* interest calculated on the capital invested only, and not added to it 单利:只按投资资本计算,而不把利息加入本金计算的利息

single-entry bookkeeping /ˌsɪŋglˌentri ˈbʊkkiːpɪŋ/ *noun* a method of bookkeeping where payments or sales are noted with only one entry per transaction, usually in the cash book 单式簿记:每笔付款或销售交易只记录一项分录的簿记方法,通常用于现金账簿

single-figure inflation /ˌsɪŋglˌfɪgə ɪnˈfleɪʃ(ə)n/ *noun* inflation rising at less than 10% per annum 一位数通货膨胀:低于10%的年通货膨胀

single premium policy /ˌsɪŋgl ˌpriːmiəm ˈpɒlɪsi/ *noun* an insurance policy where only one premium is paid rather than regular annual premiums 一次付清保险费的保单

sink /sɪŋk/ *verb* **1.** to go down suddenly 突然下跌 ○ *Prices sank at the news of the closure of the factory.* 工厂关闭的消息传出后,价格顿时下跌。**2.** to invest money into something 投资 ○ *He sank all his savings into a car-hire business.* 他把所有积蓄都投到了一家汽车租赁行。(NOTE: **sinking – sank – sunk**)

sinking fund /ˈsɪŋkɪŋ fʌnd/ *noun* a fund built up out of amounts of money put aside regularly to meet a future need, such as the repayment of a loan 存储基金;偿债基金:为应付未来需要(如偿债)而通过定期划拨资金建立起来的基金

sinking fund method /ˌsɪŋkɪŋ fʌnd ˈmeθəd/ *noun* a method of providing for depreciation which increases every year by multiplying each previous year's charge by a compound rate of interest 存储基金折旧法:一种逐年增加的计提折旧方法,计算方法为复利率乘以上年费用

sister company /ˈsɪstə ˌkʌmp(ə)ni/ *noun* another company which is part of the same group 姊妹公司:同一集团旗下的另一家公司

sitting tenant /ˌsɪtɪŋ ˈtenənt/ *noun* a tenant who is occupying a building when the freehold or lease is sold 现时租客,当前租客:不动产或租赁物业出售时占用该物业的承租人 ○ *The block of flats is for sale with four flats vacant and two with sitting tenants.* 该公寓楼出售,现楼中四套公寓是空的,两套住着老租户。

skimming /ˈskɪmɪŋ/ *noun* the unethical and usually illegal practice of taking small amounts of money from accounts that belong to other individuals or organizations 撇油:挪用他人账户中少量资金的不道德、通常也是非法的行为

sleeping partner /ˌsliːpɪŋ ˈpɑːtnə/ *noun* a partner who has a share in the business but does not work in it 匿名合伙人

slide /slaɪd/ *verb* to move down steadily (稳步)下滑 ○ *Prices slid after the company reported a loss.* 公司报告亏损后其股价开始下滑。(NOTE: **sliding – slid**)

sliding /ˈslaɪdɪŋ/ *adjective* rising in

steps 滑动的，累进的，可调整的

slip /slɪp/ *verb* to fall to a lower level 下滑，下降

'...with long-term fundamentals reasonably sound, the question for brokers is when does cheap become cheap enough? The Bangkok and Taipei exchanges offer lower p/e ratios than Jakarta, but if Jakarta p/e ratios slip to the 16-18 range, foreign investors would pay more attention to it'
"在长期基本面良好的情况下，经纪人的问题是什么时候算是足够便宜？曼谷和台北证券交易所的市盈率都低于雅加达，但若雅加达的市盈率下滑到 16－18 之间，它将吸引更多外国投资者的眼球" [*Far Eastern Economic Review*《远东经济评论》]

slow payer /ˌsləʊ ˈpeɪə/ *noun* a person or company that does not pay debts on time 拖欠债务的人(或公司) ○ *The company is well known as a slow payer*. 这家公司拖欠债务是出名的。

slump /slʌmp/ *noun* 1. a rapid fall 迅速下落，暴跌 ○ *the slump in the value of the pound* 英镑迅速贬值 ○ *We experienced a slump in sales* or *a slump in profits*. 我们的销售额(或利润)暴跌。2. a period of economic collapse with high unemployment and loss of trade 经济衰退 ○ *We are experiencing slump conditions*. 我们正处在经济衰退期。■ *verb* to fall fast 急速下跌 ○ *Profits have slumped*. 利润暴跌。○ *The pound slumped on the foreign exchange markets*. 外汇市场上英镑迅速贬值。

slush fund /ˈslʌʃ fʌnd/ *noun* money kept to one side to give to people to persuade them to do what you want 行贿资金 ○ *The government was brought down by the scandal over the slush funds*. 政府因为贿赂丑闻而垮台。○ *The party was accused of keeping a slush fund to pay foreign businessmen*. 该党被指控私设小金库用来贿赂外商。

small ads /ˈsmɔːl ædz/ *plural noun* short private advertisements in a newspaper, e.g. selling small items or asking for jobs 小广告：报纸上短小的私人广告，如卖小物件或找工作的广告

small and medium-sized enterprises /ˌsmɔːl ən ˌmiːdiəmˌsaɪzd ˈentəpraɪzɪz/ *plural noun* organisations that have between 10 and 500 employees and are usually in the start-up or growth stage of development 中小型企业：员工人数在 10 到 500 人之间、且通常处在起步或发展阶段的企业 Abbreviation 缩写 **SMEs**

small business /ˌsmɔːl ˈbɪznɪs/ *noun* a little company with low turnover and few employees 小企业：营业额小、雇员少的小公司

Small Business Administration /ˌsmɔːl ˈbɪznɪs ədˌmɪnɪstreɪʃ(ə)n/ *noun US* a federal agency which provides finance and advice to small businesses (美)小企业管理局：向小型企业提供资助和建议的联邦机构 Abbreviation 缩写 **SBA**

small businessman /ˌsmɔːl ˈbɪznɪsmæn/ *noun* a man who owns a small business 小企业主

small change /ˌsmɔːl ˈtʃeɪndʒ/ *noun* coins 硬币，零钱，零头

small claim /ˌsmɔːl ˈkleɪm/ *noun* a claim for less than £5000 in the County Court 小额索赔：在郡法院提出的 5,000 英镑以下的索赔

small claims court /ˌsmɔːl ˈkleɪmz ˌkɔːt/ *noun* a court which deals with disputes over small amounts of money 小额索赔法庭

small companies rate /ˌsmɔːl ˈkʌmp(ə)niz ˌreɪt/ *noun* a rate of corporation tax charged on profits of small companies 小公司税率：对小公司的利润征收的公司税税率

small company /smɔːl ˈkʌmp(ə)ni/ *noun* a company with at least two of the following characteristics: a turnover of less than £2.0m, fewer than 50 staff, net assets of less than £975,000 小公司：至少具有下列特征中两个的公司：营业额低于 200 万英镑，雇员少于 50 人，净资产少于 97.5 万英镑

SME *abbr* small and medium-sized enterprises 中小型企业

social /ˈsəʊʃ(ə)l/ *adjective* referring to society in general 社会的

social security contributions /ˌsəʊʃ(ə)l sɪˈkjʊərɪti kɒntrɪˌbjuːʃ(ə)nz/ *plural noun* regular payments by employees and employers to the National Insurance scheme 社会保障缴款：由雇员和雇主定期缴入国民保险计划的钱款

society /səˈsaɪəti/ *noun* the way in which the people in a country are organized 社会

soft currency /sɒft ˈkʌrənsi/ *noun* the currency of a country with a weak economy, which is cheap to buy and difficult to exchange for other currencies 软通货：贫困国家的货币，价格低廉且很难兑换成其他货币 Opposite 反义 **hard currency**

soft landing /sɒft ˈlændɪŋ/ *noun* a change in economic strategy to counteract inflation, which does not cause unemployment or a fall in the standard of living, and has only minor effects on the bulk of the population 软着陆：应对通货膨胀的一种经济策略，它不会造成失业或生活水平下降，对大部分人口只有微小影响

soft loan /sɒft ˈləʊn/ *noun* a loan from a company to an employee or from one government to another at a very low rate of interest or with no interest payable at all 软贷款：公司提供给雇员的或政府之间的低息或免息贷款

software /ˈsɒftweə/ *noun* computer programs 软件

sole /səʊl/ *adjective* only 单独的，唯一的

sole agency /ˌsəʊl ˈeɪdʒənsi/ *noun* an agreement to be the only person to represent a company or to sell a product in a particular area 独家代理关系：独家代表某公司或在某一特定区域内销售某种产品的协议 ○ *He has the sole agency for Ford cars.* 他拥有福特汽车的独家代理权。

sole agent /ˌsəʊl ˈeɪdʒənt/ *noun* a person who has the sole agency for a company in an area 独家代理商：在某一区域拥有某公司独家代理权的人 ○ *She is the sole agent for Ford cars in the locality.* 她是福特汽车在当地的独家代理商。

sole distributor /ˌsəʊl dɪˈstrɪbjʊtə/ *noun* a retailer who is the only one in an area who is allowed to sell a product 独家经销商：有权在某一地区独家销售某产品的零售商

sole owner /ˌsəʊl ˈəʊnə/ *noun* a person who owns a business on their own, with no partners, and has not formed a company 独自经营者，独资业主：独自拥有某项企业但未成立公司的人

sole proprietor /səʊl prəˈpraɪətə/, **sole trader** /səʊl ˈtreɪdə/ *noun* a person who runs a business, usually by themselves, but has not registered it as a company 独资业主:独自经营企业但未注册成公司的人

solvency /ˈsɒlv(ə)nsi/ *noun* the state of being able to pay all debts on due date 偿债能力,有偿付能力 Opposite 反义 **insolvency**

solvency margin /ˌsɒlv(ə)nsi ˈmɑːdʒɪn/ *noun* a business's liquid assets that exceeds the amount required to meet its liabilities 偿付准备金:企业流动资产超过需偿还负债的部分

solvency ratio /ˌsɒlv(ə)nsi ˈreɪʃiəʊ/ *noun* a ratio of assets to liabilities, used to measure a company's ability to meet its debts 偿付能力比率:资产负债比率,用来衡量公司的偿债能力

solvent /ˈsɒlv(ə)nt/ *adjective* having enough money to pay debts 有偿债能力的 ○ *When she bought the company it was barely solvent*. 这家公司在她刚买下时几乎没有偿债能力。

sort code /ˈsɔːt kəʊd/ *noun* a combination of numbers that identifies a bank branch on official documentation, such as bank statements and cheques 分码:在银行对账单及支票等官方票据上的一组号码,用来区分票据的签发行 US term 美国用语为 **routing number**

source /sɔːs/ *noun* the place where something comes from 来源 ○ *What is the source of her income*? 她的收入从哪里来? ○ *You must declare income from all sources to the tax office*. 你必须向税务机关申报所有的收入来源。

source and application of funds statement /ˌsɔːs ən ˌæplɪkeɪʃ(ə)n əv ˈfʌndz ˌsteɪtmənt/, **sources and uses of funds statement** /ˌsɔːsɪz ən ˌjuːsɪz əv ˈfʌndz ˌsteɪtmənt/ *noun* a statement in a company's annual accounts, showing where new funds came from during the year, and how they were used 资金来源与使用表:公司年度报表中的一部分,用来显示当年新获资金的来源及其使用情况

source document /sɔːs ˈdɒkjʊˌment/ *noun* a document upon which details of transactions or accounting events are recorded and from which information is extracted to be subsequently entered into the internal accounting system of an organisation, e.g., a sales invoice or credit note 源文件:记录交易或会计事件详情的文件,文件上的信息其后被摘录到组织的内部会计系统中,如销售发票或贷方票据

spare /speə/ *adjective* extra, not being used 多余的,未用的 ○ *He has invested his spare capital in a computer shop*. 他将闲置资本投资于一家计算机商店。

special deposits /ˌspeʃ(ə)l dɪpɒzɪts/ *plural noun* large sums of money which commercial banks have to deposit with the Bank of England 特别存款:英国商业银行必须存入英格兰银行的大笔存款

special drawing rights /ˌspeʃ(ə)l ˈdrɔːɪŋ raɪts/ *plural noun* units of account used by the International Monetary Fund, allocated to each member country for use in loans and other international operations. Their value is calculated daily on the weighted values of a group of currencies shown in dollars 特别提款权:国际货币基金组织分配给每一成员国用于贷款或其他

国际交易的账户单位，其价值每日按一组用美元表示的货币的加权价值计算 Abbreviation 缩写 **SDRs**

special offer /ˌspeʃ(ə)l ˈɒfə/ *noun* a situation where goods are put on sale at a specially low price 特价出售 ○ *We have a range of men's shirts on special offer*. 我们有一批男式衬衫特价出售。

special resolution /ˌspeʃ(ə)l ˌrezəˈluːʃ(ə)n/ *noun* a resolution concerning an important matter, such as a change to the company's articles of association which is only valid if it is approved by 75% of the votes cast at a meeting 特别决议：关于修改公司章程等重要事项的决议，须经与会者 75% 投票赞成方可通过

specie /ˈspiːʃiː/ *noun* money in the form of coins 硬币，铸币

specification /ˌspesɪfɪˈkeɪʃ(ə)n/ *noun* detailed information about what or who is needed or about a product to be supplied 清单，规格，说明书 ○ *to detail the specifications of a computer system* 详细列出计算机系统的配置 □ **the work is not up to specification** *or* **does not meet our specifications** the product is not made in the way which was detailed 产品不合规格

specific order costing /spəˌsɪfɪk ˌɔːdə ˈkɒstɪŋ/ *noun* same as 同 **job costing**

specify /ˈspesɪfaɪ/ *verb* to state clearly what is needed 明确说明 ○ *to specify full details of the goods ordered* 详细说明所订商品的情况 ○ *Do not include VAT on the invoice unless specified*. 除非有特别说明，否则发票金额不包括增值税。○ *Candidates are asked to specify which of the three posts they are applying for*. 求职者需指明其申请三个职位中的哪一个。(NOTE: **specifies – specifying – specified**)

spend /spend/ *verb* to pay money 花费，支出 ○ *They spent all their savings on buying the shop*. 他们用尽所有积蓄买下了这家店。○ *The company spends thousands of pounds on research*. 该公司花费数千英镑用于研究。

spending /ˈspendɪŋ/ *noun* the act of paying money for goods and services 花费，支出 ○ *Both cash spending and credit card spending increase at Christmas*. 圣诞节期间，现金消费和刷卡消费双双增长。

spending money /ˈspendɪŋ ˌmʌni/ *noun* money for ordinary personal expenses 个人消费款，零用钱

split /splɪt/ *noun* **1.** an act of dividing up 分割，分裂 **2.** a lack of agreement 意见不一致，有争议 ○ *a split in the family shareholders* 家族股东之间的分歧 ■ *adjective* divided into parts 分割的，分裂的

split commission /ˌsplɪt kəˈmɪʃ(ə)n/ *noun* a commission which is divided between brokers or agents (经纪人或代理商之间的)佣金分配

split-level investment trust /ˌsplɪtˌlev(ə)l ɪnˈvestmənt ˌtrʌst/ *noun* an investment trust with two categories of shares: income shares which receive income from the investments, but do not benefit from the rise in their capital value, and capital shares, which increase in value as the value of the investments rises, but do not receive any income 混合投资信托：拥有两类股票的投资信托：收益股，只取得

投资收入而不获得资本增值；资本股，只获得资本增值而没有任何投资收入 Also called 亦称作 **split trust**，**split-capital trust**

split payment /ˌsplɪt ˈpeɪmənt/ *noun* a payment which is divided into small units 付款分割：分成多个小单位的付款

spot cash /ˌspɒt ˈkæʃ/ *noun* cash paid for something bought immediately 当场支付的现金

spot price /ˈspɒt praɪs/，**spot rate** /ˌspɒt ˈreɪt/ *noun* a current price or rate for something which is delivered immediately 现货价格，即期汇率：立即交割的现价或汇率 Also called 亦称作 **cash price**

'...the average spot price of Nigerian light crude oil for the month of July was 27.21 dollars per barrel'
"尼日利亚轻质原油 7 月的平均现货价格是每桶 27.21 美元"[*Business Times* (*Lagos*)《商业时报》(拉各斯)]

spread /spred/ *noun* **1.** same as 同 **range 2.** the difference between buying and selling prices, i. e. between the bid and offer prices 价差：买价与卖价之差，即出价与要价之差 ■ *verb* to space something out over a period of time 分期 ○ *to spread payments over several months* 分几个月付款

'...dealers said markets were thin, with gaps between trades and wide spreads between bid and ask prices on the currencies'
"交易商认为市场不景气，贸易呈现逆差，外汇买卖差价巨大"[*Wall Street Journal*《华尔街日报》]
'...to ensure an average return you should hold a spread of different shares covering a wide cross-section of the market'
"要想确保获得平均收益，那么你持股板块的选择应尽量多元化"[*Investors Chronicle*《投资者纪事》]

spreading /ˈspredɪŋ/ *noun* an action of spacing income from artistic work such as royalties over a period of time, and not concentrating it in the year in which the money is received 分散(收入)：将版权费等艺术品的收入分摊到一段时间，而不是集中在取得收入的年度

spreadsheet /ˈspredʃiːt/ *noun* a computer printout showing a series of columns of figures 电子数据表

Square Mile /ˌskweə ˈmaɪl/ *noun* the City of London, the British financial centre 平方英里区：指伦敦城，即英国金融中心

squeeze /skwiːz/ *noun* government control carried out by reducing the availability of something 紧缩，收紧：政府通过减少某物供应量而实施的控制措施 ■ *verb* to crush or to press; to make smaller 压缩 ○ *to squeeze margins* or *profits* or *credit* 压缩毛利(利润或信贷)

'...the real estate boom of the past three years has been based on the availability of easy credit. Today, money is tighter, so property should bear the brunt of the credit squeeze'
"过去三年宽松的信贷政策为房地产业带来了春天，如今，银根收紧，面对信贷紧缩，房地产业自然首当其冲"[*Money Observer*《货币观察家》]

SSAPs *abbr* Statements of Standard Accounting Practice 标准会计实务说明书

staff incentives /ˌstɑːf ɪnˈsentɪvz/ *plural noun* higher pay and better conditions offered to employees to make them work better 员工激励措施：作为激励而支付给员工的高额工资和优厚的福利待遇

staff training /ˌstɑːf ˈtreɪnɪŋ/ *noun* the process of teaching staff better and more profitable ways of working 员工培训

stag /stæg/ *noun* a person who buys new issues of shares and sells them immediately to make a profit 新股套利者：为获利而迅速抛售所购新股的个人

stage /steɪdʒ/ *noun* a period, one of several points in a process of development 阶段，一个阶段 ○ *the different stages of the production process* 生产过程的不同阶段

staged payments /ˌstædʒd ˈpeɪmənts/ *plural noun* payments made in stages 分期付款

stagger /ˈstægə/ *verb* to arrange holidays or working hours so that they do not all begin and end at the same time 使（假期或工作时间等）错开 ○ *Staggered holidays help the tourist industry.* 错开假期有利于旅游业的发展。○ *We have to stagger the lunch hour so that there is always someone on the switchboard.* 我们必须错开午餐时间以确保总机时刻有人接听。○ *We asked our supplier to stagger deliveries so that the warehouse can cope.* 为了便于入库，我们要求供应商错开交货时间。

stagnant /ˈstægnənt/ *adjective* not active, not increasing 停滞的，不增长的 ○ *Turnover was stagnant for the first half of the year.* 上半年营业额停滞不前。○ *A stagnant economy is not a good sign.* 经济停滞不是好兆头。

stagnate /stægˈneɪt/ *verb* not to increase, not to make progress 不增长，停滞 ○ *The economy is stagnating.* 经济停滞不前。○ *After six hours the talks were stagnating.* 谈判在六小时后陷入了僵局。

stagnation /stægˈneɪʃ(ə)n/ *noun* the state of not making any progress, especially in economic matters 萧条，停滞 ○ *The country entered a period of stagnation.* 国家进入经济停滞期。

stake /steɪk/ *noun* an amount of money invested 投资资金

'...her stake, which she bought at $1.45 per share, is now worth nearly $10 million'
"她的股份买入时每股 1.45 美元，现在价值已接近 1,000 万美元" [*Times*《泰晤士报》]

'...other investments include a large stake in a Chicago-based insurance company, as well as interests in tobacco products and hotels'
"其他投资项目包括持有一家设在芝加哥的保险公司的大量股权，以及烟草产品和酒店业的权益" [*Lloyd's List*《劳氏日报》]

stakeholder /ˈsteɪkhəʊldə/ *noun* a person or body that is involved with a company or organisation either personally or financially and has an interest in ensuring that it is successful 利益相关人：亲身或通过财务手段参与某公司或组织、并努力确保其成功的个人或机构（NOTE：A stakeholder may be an employee, customer, supplier, partner, or even the local community within which an organisation operates 利益相关人包括雇员、顾客、供应商、合伙人甚至组织经营所在的当地社区）

'...the stakeholder concept is meant to be a new kind of low-cost, flexible personal pension aimed at those who are less well-

off. Whether it will really encourage them to put aside money for retirement is a moot point. Ministers said companies would be able to charge no more than 1 per cent a year to qualify for the stakeholder label'
"存托养老金计划是一种新型的个人退休金计划,具有低成本、可变通的特点,其针对群体为社会低收入人士,但此项计划能否激励人们存钱养老仍是个未知数。部长们表示,实行存托养老金计划的公司每年收取的费用不得超过(养老金价值的)1%"[*Financial Times*《金融时报》]

stamp /stæmp/ *noun* a device for making marks on documents; a mark made in this way 印章,图章;戳记 ○ *The invoice has the stamp 'Received with thanks' on it.* 这张发票盖有"已付款"的印章。○ *The customs officer looked at the stamps in her passport.* 海关官员检查了她护照上的印戳。■ *verb* **1.** to mark a document with a stamp 在…上盖章,在…上盖戳 ○ *to stamp an invoice 'Paid'* 在发票上加盖"付讫"字样 ○ *The documents were stamped by the customs officials.* 这些文件已有海关官员的盖章。**2.** to put a postage stamp on an envelope or parcel 贴邮票于

stamp duty /ˈstæmp ˌdjuːti/ *noun* a tax on legal documents such as those used e.g. for the sale or purchase of shares or the conveyance of a property to a new owner 印花税:对法律文件(如股票买卖、财产转让的文件)所征的税

stamp pad /ˈstæmp pæd/ *noun* a soft pad of cloth with ink on which a stamp is pressed, before marking the paper 印泥,印油

standard /ˈstændəd/ *noun* the usual quality or usual conditions which other things are judged against 标准 ■ *adjective* normal or usual 普通的;标准的 ○ *a standard model car* 一辆标配版轿车 ○ *We have a standard charge of £25 for a thirty-minute session.* 我们的标准收费是30分钟一节,每节收费25英镑。

standard agreement /ˌstændəd əˈgriːmənt/, **standard contract** /ˌstændəd ˈkɒntrækt/ *noun* a normal printed contract form 标准合同

standard cost /ˌstændəd ˈkɒst/ *noun* a future cost which is calculated in advance and against which estimates are measured 标准成本:事先计算好并用作估值依据的未来成本

standard costing /ˌstændəd ˈkɒstɪŋ/ *noun* the process of planning costs for the period ahead and, at the end of the period, comparing these figures with actual costs in order to make necessary adjustments in planning 标准成本法:对下一阶段的成本进行规划,并在该期末将预计数字与实际成本作比较,以对规划进行必要调整

standard direct labour cost /ˌstændəd dɪˌrekt ˈleɪbə ˌkɒst/ *noun* the cost of labour calculated to produce a product according to specification, used to measure estimates 标准劳动力直接成本:依据设计书计算得出的生产一件产品所需的劳动力成本,用于衡量估值

standard letter /ˌstændəd ˈletə/ *noun* a letter which is sent without change to various correspondents 标准信件:无需改动即可寄给不同通信人的信函

standard rate /ˈstændəd reɪt/ *noun* a basic rate of income tax which is paid by most taxpayers 标准所得税税率:大多数纳税人支付的基本所得税

税率

standby credit /ˈstændbaɪ ˌkredɪt/ *noun* 备用信贷 **1.** credit which is available if a company needs it, especially credit guaranteed by a euronote [公司需要时可随时提取的信贷，尤指以欧洲票据为担保的信贷] **2.** credit which is available and which can be drawn on if a country needs it, especially credit guaranteed by a lender (a group of banks or the IMF in the case of a member country) and usually in dollars [国家需要时可随时提取的信贷，尤指由贷方担保（银行集团担保，或国际货币基金组织为其成员国担保）的信贷，通常为美元]

standing order /ˌstændɪŋ ˈɔːdə/ *noun* an order written by a customer asking a bank to pay money regularly to an account 长期令单，长期支付命令：客户出具的要求银行定期付款到另一户头的书面指令 ○ *I pay my subscription by standing order*. 我通过长期委托书支付认购款。

staple commodity /ˌsteɪp(ə)l kəˈmɒdɪti/ *noun* a basic food or raw material 主要商品：基本食品或原材料

start /stɑːt/ *noun* the beginning 开始 *verb* to begin to do something 开始做… □ **to start a business from cold** *or* **from scratch** to begin a new business, with no previous turnover to base it on 白手起家，从零开始：在没有任何积累的情况下开始创业

starting /ˈstɑːtɪŋ/ *noun* the act of beginning 开始

starting date /ˈstɑːtɪŋ deɪt/ *noun* a date on which something starts 开始日期

starting rate of tax /ˌstɑːtɪŋ reɪt əv ˈtæks/ *noun* a tax rate (currently 10%) paid on the first segment of taxable income, before the basic rate applies 起点税率：在依基本税率征收之前对首批应税收入收取的税率（现为10%）

starting salary /ˈstɑːtɪŋ ˌsæləri/ *noun* a salary for an employee when he or she starts work with a company 起始工资，起薪

start-up /ˈstɑːtʌp/ *noun* the beginning of a new company or new product（新公司或新产品的）开始，开办 ○ *We went into the red for the first time because of the start-up costs of the new subsidiary in the USA*. 由于承担了在美新建子公司的启动成本，我们首次出现赤字。

start-up financing /ˈstɑːtʌp ˌfaɪnænsɪŋ/ *noun* the first stage in financing a new project, which is followed by several rounds of investment capital as the project gets under way 启动资金：新项目的第一阶段融资，随着项目的进行，还会有几轮资本投入（NOTE：The plural is **startups** 复数为 **startups**）

state /steɪt/ *noun* **1.** an independent country 国家 **2.** a semi-independent section of a federal country such as the USA（美国等的）州 ■ *verb* to say clearly 陈述 ○ *The document states that all revenue has to be declared to the tax office*. 文件载明所有收入都应向税务机关申报。□ **as per account stated** the same amount as shown on the account or invoice 按账户（或发票）显示的金额

'...the unions had argued that public sector pay rates had slipped behind rates applying in state and local government areas' "工会称，公共部门的工资已滑落至低于国家和地方政府部门的工资" [*Australian Fi-*

nancial Review《澳大利亚金融评论报》]

state bank /steɪt ˈbæŋk/ *noun* in the USA, a commercial bank licensed by the authorities of a state, and not necessarily a member of the Federal Reserve system, as opposed to a national bank 州立银行:美国由州政府发牌的商业银行,与国家银行不同,它不一定是联邦储备系统的成员

state benefits /ˌsteɪt ˈbenɪfɪts/ *plural noun* payments which are made to someone under a national or private scheme 国家福利:支付给国家或私人福利计划参与者的资金

State Earnings-Related Pension Scheme /ˌsteɪt ˌɜːnɪŋzrɪˌleɪtɪd ˈpenʃən ˌskiːm/ *noun* a state pension which is additional to the basic retirement pension and is based on average earnings over an employee's career 国家收入关联养老金计划:基本养老金之外的国家养老金,它以雇员整个职业生涯的平均收入为基础 Abbreviation 缩写 **SERPS**

statement /ˈsteɪtmənt/ *noun* something said or written which describes or explains something clearly 说明,声明,陈述

statement of account /ˌsteɪtmənt əv əˈkaʊnt/ *noun* a list of sums due, usually relating to unpaid invoices 对账单,结单:到期款项的列表,通常与未付发票有关

statement of affairs /ˌsteɪtmənt əv əˈfeəz/ *noun* a financial statement drawn up when a person is insolvent 清算式财务报表:某人无偿付能力时编制的财务报表

Statement of Auditing Standards /ˌsteɪtmənt əv ˈɔːdɪtɪŋ ˌstændədz/ *noun* an auditing standard, issued by the Auditing Practices Board, containing prescriptions as to the basic principles and practices which members of the UK accountancy bodies are expected to follow in the course of an audit 审计准则说明书:由英国审计实务委员会颁布的审计准则,它规定了英国会计机构成员在审计过程中应遵守的基本原则及实务 Abbreviation 缩写 **SAS**

statement of cash flows /ˌsteɪtmənt əv ˈkæʃ ˌfləʊz/ *noun* a statement that documents actual receipts and expenditures of cash 现金流量表:记录实际现金收支的报表

statement-of-cash-flows method /ˌsteɪtməntəvkæʃfləʊz ˈmeθəd/ *noun* a method of accounting that is based on flows of cash rather than balances on accounts 现金流量表方法:基于现金流量而非账目余额的一种会计方法

statement of changes in financial position /ˌsteɪtmənt əv tʃeɪndʒɪz ɪn faɪˌnænʃəl pəˈzɪʃ(ə)n/ *noun* a financial report of a company's incomes and outflows during a period, usually a year or a quarter 财务状况变动表:关于公司在一段时期内(通常是一年或一个季度)收入与支出的财务报告

Statement of Financial Accounting Standards /ˌsteɪtmənt əv faɪˌnænʃ(ə)l əˈkaʊntɪŋ ˌstændədz/ *noun* in the United States, a statement detailing the standards to be adopted for the preparation of financial statements 财务会计准则说明书:美国详列编制财务报表时应采纳准则的说明书 Abbreviation 缩写 **SFAS**

Statements of Standard

Accounting Practice /ˌsteɪtmənts əv ˌstændəd əˈkaʊntɪŋ ˌpræktɪs/ *plural noun* rules laid down by the Accounting Standards Board for the preparation of financial statements 标准会计实务说明书：美国会计准则委员会编制的关于编制财务报表规则的说明书 Abbreviation 缩写 **SSAPs**

state of indebtedness /ˌsteɪt əv ɪnˈdetɪdnəs/ *noun* the fact of being in debt, owing money 负债状况

state pension /ˌsteɪt ˈpenʃən/ *noun* a pension paid by the state 国家养老金

state retirement pension /steɪt rɪˌtaɪəmənt ˈpenʃən/ *noun* a pension paid by the state to people when they reach retirement age 国家退休金

statistical /stəˈtɪstɪk(ə)l/ *adjective* based on statistics 统计的 ○ *statistical information* 统计信息 ○ *They took two weeks to provide the statistical analysis of the opinion-poll data.* 他们花了两周时间对民意测验数据进行统计分析。

statistical discrepancy /stəˌtɪstɪk(ə)l dɪˈskrepənsi/ *noun* the amount by which sets of figures differ 统计差异

statistician /ˌstætɪˈstɪʃ(ə)n/ *noun* a person who analyses statistics 统计员

status /ˈsteɪtəs/ *noun* the importance of someone or something relative to others, especially someone's position in society 身份，地位

status inquiry /ˈsteɪtəs ɪnˌkwaɪəri/ *noun* an act of checking on a customer's credit rating 资信调查：审查某一顾客的信用评级

status quo /ˌsteɪtəs ˈkwəʊ/ *noun* the state of things as they are now 现状 ○ *The contract does not alter the status quo.* 合同没有改变现状。

statute /ˈstætʃuːt/ *noun* an established written law, especially an Act of Parliament 成文法（尤指议会法案） □ **statute book** all laws passed by Parliament which are still in force 法令全书：议会通过的所有现行法律的汇编

statute-barred /ˌstætʃuːtˈbɑːd/ *adjective* referring to legal action which cannot be pursued because the time limit for it has expired 有判定时间限制的，已失时效的：由于已过法定时限而不能提出诉讼

statute book /ˈstætʃuːt bʊk/ *noun* all laws passed by Parliament which are still in force 法令全书：议会通过的所有现行法律的汇编

statutory /ˈstætʃʊt(ə)ri/ *adjective* fixed by law 法定的 ○ *There is a statutory period of probation of thirteen weeks.* 有13周的法定试用期。○ *Are all the employees aware of their statutory rights?* 是否所有雇员都了解他们所具有的法定权利？

statutory auditor /ˌstætʃʊt(ə)ri ˈɔːdɪtə/ *noun* a professional person qualified to carry out an audit required by the Companies Act 法定审计师：有资格开展《公司法》规定审计业务的专业人士

statutory books /ˈstætʃʊt(ə)ri bʊks/ *plural noun* company records required by law, e.g. a register of members 法定登记册：依据法律公司必须备有的相关记录，如股东名册

statutory instrument /ˌstætʃʊt(ə)ri ˈɪnstrʊmənt/ *noun* an order which has the force of law, made under authority granted to a minister by an Act of Parliament 法定文书：根据议会法案授权某一部长作出的有法律

效力的指令

statutory maternity pay /ˌstætʃʊt(ə)ri məˈtɜːnɪti ˌpeɪ/ *noun* payment made by an employer to an employee who is on maternity leave 法定产假工资 Abbreviation 缩写 **SMP**

statutory regulations /ˌstætʃʊt(ə)ri ˌregjʊˈleɪʃ(ə)nz/ *plural noun* regulations covering financial dealings which are based on Acts of Parliament, such as the Financial Services Act, as opposed to the rules of self-regulatory organisations which are non-statutory 法律条例:以议会法案为基础的规范金融交易行为的条例(如金融服务法案),与非法定的自律组织规章相对

stay of execution /ˌsteɪ əv eksɪˈkjuːʃ(ə)n/ *noun* the temporary stopping of a legal order (法定指令的)暂停执行 ○ *The court granted the company a two-week stay of execution.* 法院判给公司两星期的暂缓执行期。

step /step/ *noun* a type of action 步骤;措施 ○ *The first step taken by the new MD was to analyse all the expenses.* 新任总经理采取的第一步是分析所有开支。

stepped costs /ˌstept ˈkɒsts/ *plural noun* costs which remain fixed up to some level of activity but then rise to a new, higher level once that level of activity is exceeded 阶梯式成本,半固定成本:在一定业务水平下保持不变、而一旦超过该业务水平就会上一个台阶的成本

sterling /ˈstɜːlɪŋ/ *noun* a standard currency used in the United Kingdom 英镑 ○ *to quote prices in sterling* or *to quote sterling prices* 用英镑报价

'...it is doubtful that British goods will price themselves back into world markets as long as sterling labour costs continue to rise faster than in competitor countries'
"英国的劳动成本增长率要是仍然高于其竞争对手,那么,英国商品想通过价格优势重返国际市场的可能性依旧不大"[*Sunday Times*《星期日泰晤士报》]

sterling area /ˈstɜːlɪŋ ˌeəriə/ *noun* formerly, an area of the world where the pound sterling was the main trading currency 英镑区:指过去世界上以英镑为主要贸易货币的区域

sterling balances /ˌstɜːlɪŋ ˈbælənsɪz/ *plural noun* a country's trade balances expressed in pounds sterling 英镑余额:用英镑表示的一国贸易余额

sterling crisis /ˈstɜːlɪŋ ˌkraɪsɪs/ *noun* a fall in the exchange rate of the pound sterling 英镑危机:英镑汇率下降

sterling index /ˈstɜːlɪŋ ˌɪndeks/ *noun* an index which shows the current value of sterling against a basket of currencies 英镑指数:用一揽子货币衡量的英镑价值指数

stock /stɒk/ *noun* **1.** the available supply of raw materials (原材料)库存,存货 ○ *large stocks of oil* or *coal* 大量石油(或煤炭)存货 ○ *the country's stocks of butter* or *sugar* 该国的黄油(或食糖)储备 **2.** the quantity of goods for sale in a warehouse or retail outlet (商品)库存,存货 **3.** shares in a company (某一公司的)股票 **4.** investments in a company, represented by shares or fixed interest securities (某一公司的股票或定息证券形式的)投资 ■ *adjective* usually kept in stock 常备的 ○ *Butter is a stock item for any good grocer.* 黄油是

标准食品杂货店里的常备商品。■ *verb* to hold goods for sale in a warehouse or store 库存，贮存 ○ *The average supermarket stocks more than 4500 lines.* 普通超市备有4,500多种货物。

'US crude oil stocks fell last week by nearly 2.5m barrels'
"上周美国的原油库存下降了近 250 万桶" [*Financial Times*《金融时报》]
'...the stock rose to over $20 a share, higher than the $18 bid'
"每股股价涨到超过 20 美元，高于 18 美元的出价" [*Fortune*《财富》]

stockbroker /ˈstɒkbrəʊkə/ *noun* a person who buys or sells shares for clients 股票经纪人

stockbroker's commission /stɒkˌbrəʊkəz kəˈmɪʃ(ə)n/ *noun* the payment to a broker for a deal carried out on behalf of a client 股票经纪人佣金

stockbroking /ˈstɒkbrəʊkɪŋ/ *noun* the business of dealing in shares for clients 股票经纪 ○ *a stockbroking firm* 股票经纪公司

stock certificate /ˈstɒk səˌtɪfɪkət/ *noun* a document proving that someone owns stock in a company 股权证，股权证明书

stock code /ˈstɒk kəʊd/ *noun* a set of numbers and letters which refer to an item of stock 存货代码

stock control /ˈstɒk kənˌtrəʊl/ *noun* the process of making sure that the correct level of stock is maintained, to be able to meet demand while keeping the costs of holding stock to a minimum 存货控制，存货管理：维持适当存货水平的作法，使得既能满足需求，又能使贮存成本降到最低 (NOTE: The US term is **inventory control** 美国用语为 **inventory control**)

stock controller /ˈstɒk kənˌtrəʊlə/ *noun* a person who notes movements of stock 库存控制人员：负责监控存货变动的人

stock depreciation /ˈstɒk dɪpriːʃiˌeɪʃ(ə)n/ *noun* a reduction in value of stock which is held in a warehouse for some time 存货贬值：仓库中的存货在储存一段时间后的价值下降

stock exchange /ˈstɒk ɪksˌtʃeɪndʒ/ *noun* same as 同 **stock market**

Stock Exchange /ˈstɒk ɪksˌtʃeɪndʒ/ *noun* a place where stocks and shares are bought and sold 证券交易所，股票交易所 ○ *He works on the Stock Exchange.* 他在证券交易所工作。○ *Shares in the company are traded on the Stock Exchange.* 该公司的股票在证券交易所买卖。

'...the news was favourably received on the Sydney Stock Exchange, where the shares gained 40 cents to A$9.80'
"在利好消息的刺激下，悉尼证券交易所的股票上涨了40分，达到9.80澳元" [*Financial Times*《金融时报》]

Stock Exchange listing /ˈstɒk ɪksˌtʃeɪndʒ ˌlɪstɪŋ/ *noun* the fact of being on the official list of shares which can be bought or sold on the Stock Exchange 在证券交易所挂牌 ○ *The company is planning to obtain a Stock Exchange listing.* 该公司计划在证券交易所挂牌。

stock figures /ˈstɒk ˌfɪgəz/ *plural noun* details of how many goods are in the warehouse or store 库存数：有关仓

库或商店中存货量的详细数据

stockholder /ˈstɒkhəʊldə/ *noun* a person who holds shares in a company 股东

stockholding /ˈstɒkhəʊldɪŋ/ *noun* the shares in a company held by someone 股份持有，股权

stock-in-trade /ˌstɒkɪnˈtreɪd/ *noun* goods held by a business for sale 待销存货

stock ledger /ˈstɒk ˌledʒə/ *noun* a book which records quantities and values of stock 存货分类账：记录存货数量及价值的账簿

stock level /ˈstɒk ˌlev(ə)l/ *noun* the quantity of goods kept in stock 库存水平：库存商品数量 ○ *We try to keep stock levels low during the summer.* 在夏季我们尽量降低库存量。

stock market /ˈstɒk ˌmɑːkɪt/ *noun* a place where shares are bought and sold, i.e. a stock exchange 股票市场（即证券交易所）○ *stock market price* or *price on the stock market* 证券市场价格

stock market manipulator /ˈstɒk ˌmɑːkɪt məˌnɪpjʊleɪtə/ *noun* a person who tries to influence the price of shares in his or her own favour 证券市场操纵者：试图影响股价向对其有利的方向变化的人

stock market valuation /ˌstɒk ˌmɑːkɪt ˌvæljuˈeɪʃ(ə)n/ *noun* a value of a company based on the current market price of its shares 股票市场估值：按公司股票现行市价计算的公司价值

stock option /ˈstɒk ˌɒpʃən/ *noun* a right to buy shares at a cheap price given by a company to its employees 股票期权，购股权：公司给予雇员廉价购买公司股票的权利

stocks and shares /ˌstɒks ən ˈʃeəz/ *plural noun* shares in ordinary companies 股份和股票：普通公司的股份

stocktaking /ˈstɒkteɪkɪŋ/, **stocktake** /ˈstɒkteɪk/ *noun* the counting of goods in stock at the end of an accounting period 盘存，盘点 ○ *The warehouse is closed for the annual stocktaking.* 仓库年末停业盘存。

stocktaking sale /ˈstɒkteɪkɪŋ seɪl/ *noun* a sale of goods cheaply to clear a warehouse before stocktaking 清仓甩卖

stock transfer form /ˌstɒk ˈtrænsfɜː fɔːm/ *noun* a form to be signed by the person transferring shares 股票过户凭单

stock turn /stɒk ˈtɜːn/, **stock turnround** /stɒk ˈtɜːnraʊnd/, **stock turnover** /ˌstɒk ˈtɜːnəʊvə/ *noun* the total value of stock sold in a year divided by the average value of goods in stock 存货周转率：一年的总销售收入除以平均库存价值

stock valuation /ˌstɒk væljuˈeɪʃ(ə)n/ *noun* an estimation of the value of stock at the end of an accounting period（会计期末的）存货估价

stop /stɒp/ *noun* the end of an action 停止，中止 ○ *Work came to a stop when the company could not pay the workers' wages.* 由于无力支付工人工资，公司停工了。○ *The new finance director put a stop to the reps' inflated expense claims.* 新任财务经理制止了飞涨的代表费用报销申请。

stop-loss order /stɒpˈlɒs ˌɔːdə/ *noun* an instruction to a stockbroker to sell a share if the price falls to an agreed level 止蚀盘，防损命令，停止损

失委托：客户向股票经纪人发出的指示，要求在股价跌至指定水平时出售股票（NOTE：The US term is **stop order** 美国用语为 **stop order**）

stoppage /ˈstɒpɪdʒ/ *noun* the act of stopping 停止，中断 ○ *stoppage of payments* 停止付款 ○ *Bad weather was responsible for the stoppage of deliveries.* 恶劣天气导致供货中断。○ *Deliveries will be late because of stoppages on the production line.* 由于生产线停顿，交货将会延期。

storage capacity /ˈstɔːrɪdʒ kəˌpæsɪti/ *noun* the space available for storage 存贮容量，库存能力

store card /ˈstɔː kɑːd/ *noun* a credit card issued by a large department store, which can only be used for purchases in that store 商店信用卡：大型百货商店发行的只限在其本店使用的信用卡

straddle /ˈstrædl/ *noun* **1.** a spread, the difference between bid and offer price 价差：报价与卖价之差 **2.** the act of buying a put option and a call option at the same time 对敲：买入看跌期权的同时买入看涨期权

straight line depreciation /ˌstreɪt laɪn dɪˌprɪʃiˈeɪʃ(ə)n/ *noun* depreciation calculated by dividing the cost of an asset, less its remaining value, by the number of years it is likely to be used 直线折旧法：一种折旧方法，用减去残值后的资产成本除以可使用年数

strategic management accounting /strəˌtiːdʒɪk ˌmænɪdʒmənt əˈkaʊntɪŋ/ *noun* a form of management accounting in which emphasis is placed on information which relates to factors external to the firm, as well as non-financial information and internally generated information 战略管理会计：一种管理会计方法，它强调与公司外部因素有关的信息、非财务信息和内部生成的信息

strategy /ˈstrætədʒi/ *noun* a course of action, including the specification of resources required, to achieve specific objective 战略，策略 ○ *a marketing strategy* 营销战略 ○ *a financial strategy* 财务策略 ○ *a sales strategy* 销售策略 ○ *a pricing strategy* 定价战略 ○ *What is the strategy of the HR department to deal with long-term manpower requirements?* 人事部采用什么策略来应对长期人力需求？○ *Part of the company's strategy to meet its marketing objectives is a major recruitment and retraining programme.* 公司实现其营销目标的策略之一是实施大型的招聘和再培训计划。（NOTE：The plural is **strategies** 复数为 **strategies**）

strike /straɪk/ *verb* □ **a deal was struck at £25 a unit** we agreed the price of £25 a unit 这笔交易最终敲定为每件 25 英镑

strong /strɒŋ/ *adjective* with a lot of force or strength 强有力的 ○ *This Christmas saw a strong demand for mobile phones.* 手机的需求这个圣诞节极大。○ *The company needs a strong chairman.* 公司需要一位强有力的董事长。

'...everybody blames the strong dollar for US trade problems'
"美国出现的贸易问题使强势美元成为众矢之的"［*Duns Business Month*《邓氏商业月刊》］

'...in a world of floating exchange rates the dollar is strong because of capital inflows rather than weak because of the nation's trade deficit'

"在浮动汇率制度下，美元并未因国家贸易赤字而走弱，反而因资本流入而保持坚挺"
[*Duns Business Month*《邓氏商业月刊》]

strongbox /ˈstrɒŋbɒks/ *noun* a heavy metal box which cannot be opened easily, in which valuable documents and money can be kept 保险箱

strong currency /ˌstrɒŋ ˈkʌrənsi/ *noun* a currency which has a high value against other currencies 硬通货，强势货币，坚挺货币

strong pound /ˌstrɒŋ ˈpaʊnd/ *noun* a pound which is high against other currencies 坚挺的英镑

structure /ˈstrʌktʃə/ *noun* the way in which something is organized 结构 ○ *the price structure in the small car market* 小型车市场的价格结构 ○ *the career structure within a corporation* 公司内的职务结构 ○ *The paper gives a diagram of the company's organisational structure.* 该文件描绘了公司的组织结构图。○ *The company is reorganising its discount structure.* 公司正在对各类折扣进行重新确定。

sub /sʌb/ *noun* wages paid in advance 预付工资

sub- /sʌb/ *prefix* under or less important 在下，低于；次于，不重要的

subcontract /ˌsʌbkənˈtrækt/ *verb* (*of a main contractor*) to agree with a company that they will do part of the work for a project（主承包商）转包，分包 ○ *The electrical work has been subcontracted to Smith Ltd.* 电力工程被分包给史密斯有限公司。

subcontractor /ˈsʌbkənˌtræktə/ *noun* a company which has a contract to do work for a main contractor 分包商

subject to /ˈsʌbdʒɪkt tuː/ *adjective* depending on 有待于，依赖于

sublease /sʌbˈliːs/ *verb* to lease a leased property from another tenant 转租 ○ *They subleased a small office in the centre of town.* 他们转租了市中心的一间小办公室。

sublessee /sʌbleˈsiː/ *noun* a person or company that takes a property on a sublease 转租承受人，分租承受人

sublessor /sʌbleˈsɔː/ *noun* a tenant who leases a leased property to another tenant 转租人，分租人

sublet /sʌbˈlet/ *verb* to let a leased property to another tenant 转租，分租 ○ *We have sublet part of our office to a financial consultancy.* 我们将办公室的一部分转租给一家财务咨询公司。(NOTE: **subletting – sublet**)

subordinated loan /səˌbɔːdɪnətɪd ˈləʊn/ *noun* a loan which ranks after all other borrowings as regards payment of interest or repayment of capital 附属贷款，从属贷款，次级贷款：在偿付利息或归还本金时排在所有其他借款之后的贷款

subscribe /səbˈskraɪb/ *verb* 申购，认购 □ **to subscribe for shares, to subscribe to a share issue** to apply for shares in a new company 认购股份，认购新股

subscription /səbˈskrɪpʃən/ *noun* **1.** money paid in advance for a series of issues of a magazine, for membership of a society or for access to information on a website（杂志）订费；（协会、俱乐部等）会费，纳金 ○ *Did you remember to pay the subscription to the computer magazine?* 你没忘了缴这本计算机杂志的订费吧？○ *She forgot to renew her club subscription.* 她忘了续

交她的俱乐部会费。2. □ **subscription to a new share issue** application to buy shares in a new company 新股认购 □ **the subscription lists close at 10.00 on September 24th** no new applicants will be allowed to subscribe for the share issue after that date 认购申请于 9 月 24 日 10:00 截止

subscription price /səbˈskrɪpʃən praɪs/ *noun* a price at which new shares in an existing company are offered for sale 认购价，申购价：现有公司发售新股的价格

subsidiary /səbˈsɪdiəri/ *adjective* less important 辅助的，补充的 ○ *They agreed to most of the conditions in the contract but queried one or two subsidiary items.* 他们同意合同的大多数条款，但对一两项补充条款提出质询。■ *noun* same as 同 **subsidiary company** ○ *Most of the group profit was contributed by the subsidiaries in the Far East.* 该集团的大多数利润来自于远东地区的子公司。

subsidiary account /səbˌsɪdiəri əˈkaʊnt/ *noun* an account for one of the individual people or organisations that jointly hold another account 辅助账，明细账户：同时还联名持有其他账户的个人或组织的账户

subsidiary company /səbˌsɪdiəri ˈkʌmp(ə)ni/ *noun* a company which is more than 50% owned by a holding company, and where the holding company controls the board of directors 子公司：由控股公司拥有 50%以上股份、并由控制公司控制董事会的公司

subsidise /ˈsʌbsɪdaɪz/, **subsidize** *verb* to help by giving money 资助，补贴 ○ *The government has refused to subsidise the car industry.* 政府拒绝向汽车行业提供补贴。

subsidised accommodation /ˌsʌbsɪdaɪzd əˌkɒməˈdeɪʃ(ə)n/ *noun* cheap accommodation which is partly paid for by an employer or a local authority 福利公寓：部分费用由雇用单位或当地政府支付的廉价公寓

subsidy /ˈsʌbsɪdi/ *noun* 1. money given to help something which is not profitable（对无赢利行业的）资助 ○ *The industry exists on government subsidies.* 该行业依靠政府资助维持。○ *The government has increased its subsidy to the car industry.* 政府增加了对汽车行业的补贴。2. money given by a government to make something cheaper（旨在降低物价的政府）补助，（政府）补贴 ○ *the subsidy on rail transport* 铁路交通补贴（NOTE: The plural is **subsidies** 复数为 **subsidies**）

substantial /səbˈstænʃəl/ *adjective* large or important 大的；重要的

subtenancy /sʌbˈtenənsi/ *noun* an agreement to sublet a property 转租协议，转借合同

subtenant /sʌbˈtenənt/ *noun* a person or company to which a property has been sublet 转租承租人，次承租人

subtotal /ˈsʌbˌtəʊt(ə)l/ *noun* the total of one section of a complete set of figures 小计 ○ *She added all the subtotals to make a grand total.* 她把所有小计加起来，得出总数。

subtract /səbˈtrækt/ *verb* to take away something from a total 减去 ○ *The credit note should be subtracted from the figure for total sales.* 这个贷方票据（的金额）应从总销售额中扣除。○ *If the profits from the Far Eastern operations are subtracted, you will see that the group has not been profitable* *in the European market*. 如果除去远东业务的利润,就会发现集团在欧洲市场没有赢利。

subtraction /səbˈtrækʃən/ *noun* an act of taking one number away from another 减

subvention /səbˈvenʃ(ə)n/ *noun* same as 同 **subsidy**

succeed /səkˈsiːd/ *verb* **1.** to do well, to be profitable 成功;盈利 ○ *The company has succeeded best in the overseas markets*. 该公司在海外市场大获全胜。○ *Her business has succeeded more than she had expected*. 她的生意比预期的好。**2.** to do what was planned 成功完成… ○ *She succeeded in passing her computing test*. 她成功地通过了计算机考试。○ *They succeeded in putting their rivals out of business*. 他们成功地挤垮了竞争对手。**3.** to take over from someone in a post 接替,继承(职位) ○ *Mr Smith was succeeded as chairman by Mrs Jones*. 琼斯夫人接替史密斯先生担任董事长。□ **to succeed to a property** to become the owner of a property by inheriting it from someone who has died 继承一项财产

success /səkˈses/ *noun* **1.** an act of doing something well 成功,胜利 ○ *The launch of the new model was a great success*. 新款产品的上市取得了巨大成功。○ *The company has had great success in the Japanese market*. 公司在日本市场极其成功。**2.** an act of doing what was intended 实现计划 ○ *We had no success in trying to sell the lease*. 我们出租财产的努力没能成功。○ *She has been looking for a job for six months, but with no success*. 走过半年求职路,她仍未找到工作。

sum /sʌm/ *noun* **1.** a quantity of money 金额 ○ *A sum of money was stolen from the human resources office*. 人事处有一笔钱被盗。○ *He lost large sums on the Stock Exchange*. 他在证券交易所赔了很多钱。○ *She received the sum of £5,000 in compensation*. 她得到5,000英镑的赔偿金。**2.** the total of a series of figures added together 总数 ○ *The sum of the various subtotals is £18,752*. 各项小计的总和是18,752英镑。

sum at risk /ˌsʌm ət ˈrɪsk/ *noun* an amount of any given item, such as money, stocks, or securities that an investor may lose 风险金额:投资者可能损失的任何指定项目(如金钱、股票或证券)的金额

sum of digits method /ˌsʌm əv ˈdɪdʒɪts ˌmeθəd/ *noun* a method of depreciating a fixed asset where the cost of the asset less its residual value is multiplied by a fraction based on the number of years of its expected useful life. The fraction changes each year and charges the highest costs to the earliest years 数字总和折旧法:一种计算固定资产折旧的方法,它用减去残值后的资产成本乘以按估计使用年数计算的一定比例(该比例每年变化,最初几年折旧费用最高)

sum-of-the-year's-digits depreciation /ˌsʌməvðəˌjɪəzˌdɪdʒɪts dɪˌpriːʃiˈeɪʃ(ə)n/ *noun* accelerated depreciation, conferring tax advantage by assuming more rapid depreciation when an asset is new 年限总额折旧法:一种加速折旧法,它假设资产较新时折旧更快,以此获得税务优惠

sums chargeable to the reserve /sʌmz ˌtʃɑːdʒəb(ə)l tə ðə rɪˈzɜːv/

plural noun sums which can be debited to a company's reserves 可从公司储备中借出的金额

sundry /ˈsʌndri/ *adjective* various 杂项的,各式各样的

sunk costs /ˌsʌŋk ˈkɒsts/ *plural noun* a cost which has been irreversibly incurred or committed prior to a decision point and which cannot therefore be considered relevant to subsequent decisions 已支付成本,隐没成本,旁置成本:于某个决策点之前已经不可逆转地招致或发生、因此不能视为与其后的决策有关联的成本

superannuation /ˌsuːpərænjuleɪʃ(ə)n/ *noun* a pension paid to someone who is too old or ill to work any more 养老金,退休金

supervisor /ˈsuːpəvaɪzə/ *noun* a person who supervises 管理人员,主管人 ○ *The supervisor was asked to write a report on the workers' performance.* 主管人员被要求写一份关于工人的绩效评比报告。

supplementary benefit /ˌsʌplɪˌment(ə)ri ˈbenɪfɪt/ *noun* formerly, payments from the government to people with very low incomes. It was replaced by Income Support 补贴:政府以前给予低收入人员的补助,现已被收入补助所取代

supplier /səˈplaɪə/ *noun* a person or company that supplies or sells goods or services 供应商 ○ *We use the same office equipment supplier for all our stationery purchases.* 我们所有的办公用品都由同一办公设备供应商提供。○ *They are major suppliers of spare parts to the car industry.* 他们是汽车配件行业的主要供应商。Also called 亦称作 **producer**

supply /səˈplaɪ/ *noun* the act of providing something which is needed 供应

supply and demand /səˌplaɪ ən dɪˈmɑːnd/ *noun* the amount of a product which is available and the amount which is wanted by customers 供给与需求,供求

supply price /səˈplaɪ praɪs/ *noun* the price at which something is provided 供应价格

support price /səˈpɔːt praɪs/ *noun* a price in the EU at which a government will buy agricultural produce to stop the price falling 支持价格,维持价格:欧盟各国政府为防止价格下跌而买入农产品的价格

surcharge /ˈsɜːtʃɑːdʒ/ *noun* an extra charge 附加费

surety /ʃʊərəti/ *noun* **1.** a person who guarantees that someone will do something 担保人,保证人 ○ *to stand surety for someone* 为某人提供担保 **2.** deeds, share certificates, etc., deposited as security for a loan 担保物:作为贷款担保的契约或股票等

surplus /ˈsɜːpləs/ *noun* more of something than is needed 盈余,过剩

'Both imports and exports reached record levels in the latest year. This generated a $371 million trade surplus in June, the seventh consecutive monthly surplus and close to market expectations'
"去年进出口额双双达到历史最高水平,这使6月份的贸易盈余达到3.71亿美元,也是连续第七个月出现盈余,与市场预期十分接近"[*Dominion* (*Wellington*, *New Zealand*)《自治领报》(新西兰惠灵顿)]

surrender /səˈrendə/ *noun* the act of giving up of an insurance policy before the contracted date for maturity

退保:在合同到期日之前放弃保单

surrender value /sə'rendə ˌvæljuː/ *noun* the money which an insurer will pay if an insurance policy is given up 退保补偿:放弃保单时保险人应付的金额

surtax /'sɜːtæks/ *noun* an extra tax on high income (对高收入征收的)附加税

suspend /sə'spend/ *verb* to stop doing something for a time 暂停,中止 ○ *We have suspended payments while we are waiting for news from our agent*. 在等待代理商的消息时,我们暂停了付款。○ *Sailings have been suspended until the weather gets better*. 航班暂停,等到天气好转之后再开航。○ *Work on the construction project has been suspended*. 建筑工程暂时停工。○ *The management decided to suspend negotiations*. 管理层决定中止谈判。

suspense account /sə'spens əˌkaʊnt/ *noun* an account into which payments are put temporarily when the accountant cannot be sure where they should be entered 暂记账户:当会计人员无法确定把账记到哪里时,暂时将支付款记入的账户

suspension /sə'spenʃən/ *noun* an act of stopping something for a time 暂停 ○ *There has been a temporary suspension of payments*. 暂停付款。○ *We are trying to avoid a suspension of deliveries during the strike*. 我们努力避免在罢工期间中断交货。

SVA *abbr* shareholder value analysis 股东价值分析

swap /swɒp/ *noun* an exchange of one thing for another 互换,交换

sweetener /'swiːt(ə)nə/ *noun* an incentive offered to help persuade somebody to take a particular course of action, a bribe (*informal*) 行贿物;贿赂

switch /swɪtʃ/ *verb* **1.** to change from one thing to another 转移 ○ *to switch funds from one investment to another* 把资金从一个投资转到另一个投资上 ○ *The job was switched from our British factory to the States*. 该工作从我们的英国工厂交接到美国。**2.** to change, especially to change investment money from one type of investment to another 转换(尤指将一种投资形式转为另一种)

syndicate /'sɪndɪkeɪt/ *verb* to arrange for a large loan to be underwritten by several international banks 安排由几家国际银行(即辛迪加)担保大额贷款

'... over the past few weeks, companies raising new loans from international banks have been forced to pay more, and an unusually high number of attempts to syndicate loans among banks has failed'
"在过去的几个星期,从国际银行筹集新贷款的公司不得不支付更多成本,试图在银行间安排银团贷款的多次努力也失败了"[*Financial Times*《金融时报》]

synergy /'sɪnədʒi/ *noun* the process of producing greater effects by joining forces than by acting separately 协同,配合:通过联合行动产生比各自为战更大的效果 ○ *There is considerable synergy between the two companies*. 这两家公司之间有大量的协同合作。

system /'sɪstəm/ *noun* an arrangement or organisation of things which work together 系统,制度,机制 ○ *Our accounting system has worked well in spite of the large increase in orders*. 尽管增加了很多订单,我们的会计系统仍

运转良好。○ *What system is being used for filing data on personnel?* 现在使用什么系统来储存个人资料？

systems analyst /ˈsɪstəmz ˌænəlɪst/ *noun* a person who specialises in systems analysis 系统分析师

T

T + *noun* an expression of the number of days allowed for settlement of a transaction 用来表示允许在多少天内结清交易

tab /tæb/ *noun* (*informal*)(非正式) same as 同 **tabulator**

tabulate /ˈtæbjʊleɪt/ *verb* to set something out in a table 把…制成表格,列表

tabulation /ˌtæbjʊˈleɪʃ(ə)n/ *noun* the arrangement of figures in a table 制表,列表

tabulator /ˈtæbjʊleɪtə/ *noun* a feature on a computer which sets words or figures automatically in columns (计算机)制表键

T account /ˈtiː əˌkaʊnt/ *noun* a way of drawing up an account, with a line across the top of the paper and a vertical line down the middle, with the debit and credit entries on either side T 型账目,丁字账目:一种编写账目的方法,在纸页顶端划一横线,纸页中间划一竖线,两边分别记录借方和贷方

take /teɪk/ *noun* **1.** the money received in a shop 商店收到的钱 ○ *Our weekly take is over £5,000.* 我们每周的销售额是 5,000 英镑。**2.** a profit from any sale 销售利润 ■ *verb* **1.** to receive or to get 收取,获得 □ **the shop takes £2,000 a week** the shop receives £2,000 a week in cash sales 商店每周的现金销售额为 2,000 英镑 □ **she takes home £250 a week** her salary, after deductions for tax etc. is £250 a week 她税后的周薪为 250 英镑 **2.** to perform an action 采取行动 **3.** to need a time or a quantity 需要,花费(时间或数量) ○ *It took the factory six weeks* or *The factory took six weeks to clear the backlog of orders.* 工厂花了六周时间完成了积压的订单。○ *It will take her all morning to do my letters.* 给我写信她要花一上午的时间。○ *It took six men and a crane to get the computer into the building.* 动用了六个人和一台升降机才把计算机弄到办公楼里。(NOTE: **taking – took – has taken**)

take away /ˌteɪk əˈweɪ/ *verb* to remove one figure from a total (从总额中)取出,扣除 ○ *If you take away the home sales, the total turnover is down.* 如果扣除国内销售额,总营业额是下降的。

take-home pay /ˈteɪkhəʊm ˌpeɪ/ *noun* same as 同 **disposable personal income** ○ *After all the deductions, her take-home pay is only £300 a week.* 扣除一切税费后,她的实得周薪为 300 英镑。

take off /ˌteɪk ˈɒf/ *verb* to remove or to deduct something 减去,扣除 ○ *He took £25 off the price.* 他减价 25 英镑。

take-out /ˈteɪkaʊt/ *noun* the act of removing capital which you had originally invested in a new company by selling your shares 抽资：通过出售股份将原来投入新公司的资金抽出

take over /ˌteɪk ˈəʊvə/ *verb* to start to do something in place of someone else 接管 ○ *Miss Black took over from Mr Jones on May 1st*. 布莱克女士5月1日接管了琼斯先生的工作。

takeover /ˈteɪkəʊvə/ *noun* an act of buying a controlling interest in a business by buying more than 50% of its shares 兼并，收购：通过购买某公司50%以上的股份来取得控制权 Compare 比较 **acquisition**

'... many takeovers result in the new managers/owners rationalizing the capital of the company through better asset management'
"许多收购兼并的结果是，新的管理者/所有者通过改进资产管理，使公司资本合理化"
[*Duns Business Month*《邓氏商业月刊》]

takeover bid /ˈteɪkəʊvə bɪd/ *noun* an offer to buy all or a majority of the shares in a company so as to control it 兼并出价：购买某公司全部或多数股份以取得控制权的要约 ○ *They made a takeover bid for the company*. 他们对该公司提出了收购出价。○ *She had to withdraw her takeover bid when she failed to find any backers*. 由于找不到支持者，她不得不撤销收购出价。○ *Share prices rose sharply on the disclosure of the takeover bid*. 在披露收购出价的消息后，股价迅速飙升。

Takeover Code /ˈteɪkˌəʊvə kəʊd/ *noun* a code of practice which regulates how takeovers should take place. It is enforced by the Takeover Panel 兼并条例：规范兼并行为的实务守则，它由购并委员会负责实施

Takeover Panel /ˌteɪkˌəʊvə ˈpæn(ə)l/ *noun* a non-statutory body which examines takeovers and applies the Takeover Code 购并委员会：审查兼并行为及实施兼并条例的非法定机构 Also called 亦称作 **City Panel on Takeovers and Mergers**

takeover target /ˈteɪkəʊvə ˌtɑːɡɪt/ *noun* a company which is the object of a takeover bid 收购目标，兼并目标：兼并出价的目标公司

take up rate /ˈteɪk ʌp ˌreɪt/ *noun* the percentage of acceptances for a rights issue 认购率：已行使的优先认股权比率

takings /ˈteɪkɪŋz/ *plural noun* the money received in a shop or a business 营业收入 ○ *The week's takings were stolen from the cash desk*. 有人从钱柜里偷走了这星期的营业收入。

tally /ˈtæli/ *noun* a note of things counted or recorded 点数，记录 ○ *to keep a tally of stock movements* or *of expenses* 保存存货流动（或费用）的记录 ■ *verb* to agree, to be the same 相符，一致；相同 ○ *The invoices do not tally*. 发票不相符。○ *The accounts department tried to make the figures tally*. 会计部门努力平账。

tally clerk /ˈtæli klɑːk/ *noun* a person whose job is to note quantities of cargo 理货员，点数员：负责记录货物数量的人员

tally sheet /ˈtæli ʃiːt/ *noun* a sheet on which quantities are noted 理货单，计数单：记录数量的单据

tangible assets /ˌtændʒɪb(ə)l ˈæsets/, **tangible fixed assets** /ˌtændʒɪb(ə)l ˌfɪkst ˈæsets/, **tangible**

property /ˌtændʒɪb(ə)l ˈprɒpəti/ *plural noun* assets that are physical, such as buildings, cash and stock. Leases and securities, although not physical in themselves, are classed as tangible assets because the underlying assets are physical 有形资产:具有实物形态的资产,如建筑物、现金和存货。租约和证券虽然本身不具实物形态,但相关资产是实物,所以也被归为有形资产

tangible asset value /ˌtændʒəb(ə)l ˌæset ˈvæljuː/, **tangible net worth** /ˌtændʒəb(ə)l net ˈwɜːθ/ *noun* the value of all the assets of a company less its intangible such as assets goodwill, patents. It is shown as a value per share 有形资产价值:公司所有资产价值减去无形资产价值(如商誉、专利等)。它以每股价值表示

tangible book value /ˌtændʒəb(ə)l bʊk ˈvæljuː/ *noun* the book value of a company after intangible assets, patents, trademarks, and the value of research and development have been subtracted 有形资产账面价值:扣除无形资产、专利、商标及研发价值后的公司账面价值

taper relief /ˌteɪpə rɪˈliːf/ *noun* the relief for capital gains on assets sold after being held for some period of time. The longer the assets have been held, the more relief is given against capital gains 递减式免税额:对持有一段时间后出售资产获得的资本利得免税额。资产持有时间越长,资本利得免税额就越高

target /ˈtɑːɡɪt/ *noun* something to aim for 目标 ○ *performance targets* 绩效目标

'...he believes that increased competition could keep inflation below the 2.5 per cent target'
"他相信,日益激烈的竞争会使通胀率保持在2.5%的目标水平以下"[*Investors Chronicle*《投资者纪事》]

'...the minister is persuading the oil, gas, electricity and coal industries to target their advertising towards energy efficiency'
"部长正努力劝说石油、燃气、电力和煤炭行业把他们的宣传目标转向能源效率"[*Times*《泰晤士报》]

target company /ˌtɑːɡɪt ˈkʌmp(ə)ni/ *noun* same as 同 **takeover target**

'...in a normal leveraged buyout the acquirer raises money by borrowing against the assets of the target company'
"在正常的杠杆式收购中,收购人以目标公司的资产作担保借入所需资金"[*Fortune*《财富》]

target cost /ˈtɑːɡɪt kɒst/ *noun* a product cost estimate derived by subtracting a desired profit margin from a competitive market price. This may be less than the planned initial product cost, but will be expected to be achieved by the time the product reaches the mature production stage 目标成本:竞争市场价格减去目标利润率得出的估计生产成本。它可能低于计划的初步生产成本,但可望在产品进入成熟的生产阶段后得以实现

target market /ˈtɑːɡɪt ˌmɑːkɪt/ *noun* the market in which a company is planning to sell its goods 目标市场:公司计划出售其商品的市场

tax /tæks/ *noun* 税,税款 **1.** money taken by the government or by an official body to pay for government services[政府或官方机构为支付政府服务开支而收取的款项] **2.** an amount of money charged by government as part of a person's income or on goods bought［政府对个人收入或所购商品收取的款项］□ **to levy** *or* **impose a tax** to make a tax payable 征税，课税 ○ *The government has imposed a 15% tax on petrol*. 政府对汽油征收15%的税。■ *verb* to make someone pay a tax, to impose a tax on something 课税；征税 ○ *Businesses are taxed at 40%*. 企业按40%纳税。○ *Income is taxed at 35%*. 收入所得税的税率为35%。○ *Luxury items are heavily taxed*. 奢侈品被课以重税。

tax abatement /ˈtæks əˌbeɪtmənt/ *noun* a reduction of tax 减税

taxable /ˈtæksəb(ə)l/ *adjective* able to be taxed 应税的

taxable base /ˌtæksəb(ə)l ˈbeɪs/ *noun* the amount subject to taxation 应税金额

taxable benefit /ˌtæksəb(ə)l ˈbenɪfɪt/ *noun* a benefit which is included in a person's taxable income and is subject to tax 应税福利：应收税中包含的福利，因此应纳税

taxable income /ˌtæksəb(ə)l ˈɪnkʌm/ *noun* income on which a person has to pay tax 应税收入

taxable items /ˈtæksəb(ə)l ˌaɪtəmz/ *plural noun* items on which a tax has to be paid 应税项目

taxable matters /ˌtæksəb(ə)l ˈmætəs/ *noun* goods or services that can be taxed 应税事项：应税商品或劳务

taxable person /ˌtæksəb(ə)l ˈpɜːs(ə)n/ *noun* a person who is registered for VAT, and who charges VAT on goods or services supplied 纳税人

taxable supply /ˌtæksəb(ə)l səˈplaɪ/ *noun* a supply of goods which are subject to VAT 应税货物：应纳增值税的货物

tax adjustments /ˈtæks əˌdʒʌstmənts/ *plural noun* changes made to tax 税收调整

tax adviser /ˈtæks ədˌvaɪzə/, **tax consultant** /ˈtæks kənˌsʌltənt/ *noun* a person who gives advice on tax problems 税务顾问

tax allowance /ˈtæks əˌlaʊəns/ *noun* a part of the income which a person is allowed to earn and not pay tax on 税务优惠，税收减免

tax assessment /ˈtæks əˌsesmənt/ *noun* a calculation by a tax inspector of the amount of tax a person owes 评税，征税查定，征税基准：税务检查员关于某人应缴税款的计算

taxation /tækˈseɪʃ(ə)n/ *noun* the act of taxing 课税，征税

tax at source /ˌtæks ət ˈsɔːs/ *verb* to deduct tax from earnings before they are paid to the recipient 从源扣税，从源税收扣除：在支付收益给收款人之前扣税

tax auditor /ˈtæks ˌɔːdɪtə/ *noun* a government employee who investigates taxpayers' declarations 税务官，税务稽查员：调查纳税人纳税申报的政府人员

tax avoidance /ˈtæks əˌvɔɪd(ə)ns/ *noun* the practice of legally trying to pay as little tax as possible 避税：尽可能减少纳税的合法手段

tax bracket /ˈtæks ˌbrækɪt/ *noun* a section of people paying a particular level of income tax 纳税等级

tax code /ˈtæks kəʊd/ *noun* a number given to indicate the amount of tax allowance a person has 免税代码：为指明个人所享有税收减免而编定的号码

tax collector /ˈtæks kəˌlektə/ *noun* a person who collects taxes which are owed 税务官，收税官

tax concession /ˈtæks kənˌseʃ(ə)n/ *noun* an act of allowing less tax to be paid 税收特权：允许缴纳较少税金

tax consultant /ˈtæks kənˌsʌltənt/ *noun* a professional who advises on all aspects of taxation from tax avoidance to estate planning 税务顾问

tax credit /ˈtæks ˌkredɪt/ *noun* **1.** a sum of money which can be offset against tax 税收抵免 **2.** the part of a dividend on which the company has already paid tax, so that the shareholder is not taxed on it 预扣抵免：公司已缴税的股利部分，股东不用再缴此税

tax date /ˈtæks deɪt/ *noun* the date on which a transaction occurs for tax purposes, particularly relevant to invoices on which VAT is charged 征税日期（尤指征收增值税的发票）

tax-deductible /ˌtæksdɪˈdʌktɪb(ə)l/ *adjective* possible to deduct from an income before tax is calculated 可抵税的，可减免课税的：可在计税前从收入中扣除的

tax deposit certificate /tæks dɪˈpɒzɪt səˌtɪfɪkət/ *noun* a certificate showing that a taxpayer has deposited money in advance of a tax payment. The money earns interest while on deposit 税收存款证：表明纳税人已提前存入用于支付税款资金的凭证。该存款可获得利息

tax dodge /ˈtæks dɒdʒ/ *noun* an illegal method of paying less tax than an individual or company is legally obliged to pay 逃税，偷税漏税

tax domicile /ˈtæks ˌdɒmɪsaɪl/ *noun* a place that a government levying a tax considers to be a person's home 税务住所：政府在征税时视为某人住所的地方

tax evasion /ˈtæks ɪˌveɪʒ(ə)n/ *noun* the practice of illegally trying not to pay tax （非法）逃税

tax-exempt /ˌtæksɪɡˈzempt/ *adjective* **1.** referring to a person or organisation not required to pay tax 不用交税的（个人或组织） **2.** not subject to tax 不用交税的（收入）

tax exemption /ˈtæks ɪɡˌzempʃən/ *noun US* （美） **1.** the fact of being free from payment of tax 免税 **2.** the part of income which a person is allowed to earn and not pay tax on （个人收入的）免税额

tax exemption cut-off /ˌtæks ɪɡˌzempʃ(ə)n ˈkʌtˌɒf/ *noun* a limit on tax exemption because of high income 免税限额

tax-exempt special savings account /tæksɪɡˌzempt ˌspeʃ(ə)l ˈseɪvɪŋz əˌkaʊnt/ *noun* a discontinued type of account into which money could be placed to earn interest free of tax, provided it was left untouched for five years. Since 1999 the scheme has gradually been phased out but money in existing TESSAs can be reinvested in ISAs 免税特别储蓄账户：一种已停用的账户类型，纳税人如在五年内不动用账户内的存款，则其利息收入可以免税。该计划自 1999 年起逐步被取消，但现有免税特别储蓄账户中的资金可转到个人储蓄计划中进行再投资 Abbreviation 缩写 **TESSA**

tax form /ˈtæks fɔːm/ *noun* a blank form to be filled in with details of income and allowances and sent to the tax office each year 税表，纳税申报表：应填写收入及抵免额详情，并每年送交税务部门的表格

tax-free /ˌtæks ˈfriː/ *adjective* with no tax having to be paid 免税的 ○ *tax-free goods* 免税商品

tax harmonisation /ˌtæks hɑːmənaɪˈzeɪʃ(ə)n/ *noun* the enactment of taxation laws in different jurisdictions, such as neighbouring countries, provinces, or states of the United States, that are consistent with one another 税收协调：在不同的司法权区（如毗邻的国家、省份或美国各州）颁布一致的税法

tax haven /ˈtæks ˌheɪv(ə)n/ *noun* a country or area where taxes are low, encouraging companies to set up their main offices there 避税港：税率很低以鼓励公司前去设立总办事处的国家或地区

tax holiday /ˈtæks ˌhɒlɪdeɪ/ *noun* a period when a new business is exempted from paying tax 免税期：新公司无需纳税期间

tax incentive /ˈtæks ɪnˌsentɪv/ *noun* a tax reduction afforded to people for particular purposes, e. g., sending their children to college 赋税制度，税收鼓励：为特定目的（如送子女上大学）给予某些人的税收减免

tax inspector /ˈtæks ɪnˌspektə/ *noun* a government employee who investigates taxpayers' declarations 税务检查官，税务专员：负责审查纳税人报税表的政府人员

tax law /ˈtæks lɔː/ *noun* the body of laws on taxation, or one such law 税法

tax liability /tæks ˌlaɪəˈbɪlɪti/ *noun* the amount of tax that a person or organisation has to pay 纳税义务，应纳税额：个人或组织须缴纳的税额

tax loophole /ˈtæks ˌluːphəʊl/ *noun* a legal means of not paying tax 税收漏洞：合法不纳税的手段

tax loss /ˈtæks lɒs/ *noun* a loss made by a company during an accounting period, for which relief from tax is given 税损，赋税亏损：公司在一个会计期间可以抵税的损失

tax loss carry-back /ˌtæks lɒs ˌkæriˈbæk/ *noun* the reduction of taxes in a previous year by subtraction from income for that year of losses suffered in the current year 赋税亏损退算，纳税时亏损转回：从上一年度收入中扣除当前年度的亏损，作为上年的税收抵免

tax loss carry-forward /ˌtæks lɒs ˌkæriˈfɔːwəd/ *noun* the reduction of taxes in a future year by subtraction from income for that year of losses suffered in the current year 纳税移后扣减，税损结转：从未来年度收入中扣除当前年度的亏损，作为未来年度的税收抵免

tax obligation /tæks ˌɒblɪˈgeɪʃ(ə)n/ *noun* the amount of tax a person or company owes 纳税义务：个人或公司应缴的税额

tax office /ˈtæks ˌɒfɪs/ *noun* a local office of the Inland Revenue. It does not necessarily deal with the tax affairs of people who live locally 税务局：国内税务局的地方机构。它不一定处理当地居民的税收事宜

tax on capital income /tæks ɒn ˌkæpɪt(ə)l ˈɪnkʌm/ *noun* a tax on the income from sales of capital assets 资本收益税：对出售资本资产所得收入的征税

tax payable /ˌtæks ˈpeɪəb(ə)l/ *noun* the amount of tax a person or company has to pay 应缴税额

taxpayer /ˈtækspeɪə/ *noun* a person or company that has to pay tax 纳税人 ○ *basic taxpayer* or *taxpayer at the basic rate* 一般纳税人 ○ *Corporate taxpayers are being targeted by the government.* 公司纳税人由政府确定。

tax planning /ˈtæks ˌplænɪŋ/ *noun* planning how to avoid paying too much tax, by investing in, e.g., tax-exempt savings schemes or offshore trusts 税务计划:关于如何通过投资(如投资于免税的储蓄计划或离岸信托)避免缴纳过多税款的计划

tax point /ˈtæks pɔɪnt/ *noun* the date on which goods or services are supplied, which is the date when VAT becomes is due 纳税义务发生时间:提供商品或劳务的日期,亦即应付增值税的日期

tax pressure /ˈtæks ˌpreʃə/ *noun* the financial difficulty that a company may face because of the taxes it must pay 税收压力

tax rates /ˈtæks reɪts/ *noun* percentage rates of tax on different bands of taxable income 税率

tax rebate /ˈtæks ˌriːbeɪt/ *noun* money returned by the Inland Revenue because it was overpaid 退税款:国内税务局退还的多缴的税款

tax refund /ˈtæks ˌriːfʌnd/ *noun* an amount that a government gives back to a taxpayer who has paid more taxes than were due 退税:政府退回给纳税人多缴的税款

tax relief /ˈtæks rɪˌliːf/ *noun* an allowance to pay less tax on some parts of someone's income 税收减免

tax return /ˈtæks rɪˌtɜːn/ *noun* a completed tax form, with details of income and allowances 报税表,纳税申报表:列明收入及抵免额详情的税表

tax revenue /ˈtæks ˌrevənjuː/ *noun* money that a government receives in taxes (政府的)税收收入

tax schedules /ˈtæks ˌʃedjuːlz/ *plural noun* a six types of income as classified for tax 所得税一览表,税则表:列明六种应税收入的表格

tax shelter /ˈtæks ˌʃeltə/ *noun* a financial arrangement such as a pension scheme where investments can be made without tax 避税庇护:使投资可免税的财务安排(如退休金计划)

tax system /ˈtæks ˌsɪstəm/ *noun* the methods used by a government in imposing and collecting taxes 税收制度

tax threshold /ˈtæks ˌθreʃhəʊld/ *noun* a point at which another percentage of tax is payable 征税起点,税收起征点 ○ *The government has raised the minimum tax threshold from £4,000 to £4,500.* 政府把最低征税起点从4,000英镑提高到4,500英镑。

tax treaty /ˈtæks ˌtriːti/ *noun* an international agreement that deals with taxes, especially taxes by several countries on the same individuals 税务条约:关于税务事宜(尤其是几个国家对同一个人的征税)的国际协议

tax year /ˈtæks ˌjɪə/ *noun* a twelve month period on which taxes are calculated. In the UK this is 6th April to 5th April of the following year 纳税年度(英国为4月6日至翌年4月5日)

technical /ˈteknɪk(ə)l/ *adjective* **1.** referring to a particular machine or process 技术的,工艺的 ○ *The docu-*

ment gives all the technical details on the new computer. 文档里列出了这台新型计算机的所有详细技术资料。**2.** referring to influences inside a market, e. g. volumes traded and forecasts based on market analysis, as opposed to external factors such as oil-price rises, wars, etc. 技术上的：指市场内部的影响因素（如交易量、基于市场分析的预测等），与外部因素（如油价上涨、战争等）相对

'... market analysts described the falls in the second half of last week as a technical correction'
"市场分析人员称，上周后半段的下跌是一次技术性回档"[*Australian Financial Review*《澳大利亚金融评论报》]
'... at the end of the day, it was clear the Fed had not loosened the monetary reins, and Fed Funds forged ahead on the back of technical demand'
"当天结束营业时，联邦政府显然并未放松货币政策，联邦资金在技术性需求的支持下稳步增加"[*Financial Times*《金融时报》]

technical analysis /ˌteknɪk(ə)l əˈnæləsɪs/ *noun* a study of the price movements and volumes traded on a stock exchange 技术分析：对股票市场价格变动及交易量变动的研究

technical correction /ˌteknɪk(ə)l kəˈrekʃ(ə)n/ *noun* a situation where a share price or a currency moves up or down because it was previously too low or too high 技术性调整：股价或货币价格由于以前太低或太高，因此现在正处于上升或下降的状况

technical decline /ˌteknɪk(ə)l dɪˈklaɪn/ *noun* a fall in share prices because of technical analysis 技术性下跌：由技术分析引起的股价下跌

technical reserves /ˌteknɪk(ə)l rɪˈzɜːvz/ *noun* the assets that an insurance company maintains to meet future claims 技术性准备：保险公司为满足未来索赔需要而维持的资产

teeming and lading /ˌtiːmɪŋ ən ˈleɪdɪŋ/ *noun* an attempt to hide missing funds by delaying the recording of cash receipts in a business's books 截留移用，挪用现金：试图通过在企业账簿中延迟记录现金收入来隐藏遗失的资金 The US term is **lapping** 美国用语为 **lapping**

telegraphic transfer /ˌtelɪgræfɪk ˈtrɑːnsfə/ *noun* a transfer of money from one account to another by telegraph 电汇

telephone banking /ˌtelɪfəʊn ˈbæŋkɪŋ/ *noun* a service by which a bank customer can carry out transactions over the phone using a password. It may involve direct contact with a bank representative or may be automated used the phone dial 电话银行业务（包括自助服务和人工服务）

teller /ˈtelə/ *noun* a person who takes cash from or pays cash to customers at a bank 出纳员

tenancy /ˈtenənsi/ *noun* an agreement by which a tenant can occupy a property（房产）租约，租赁协议

tenant /ˈtenənt/ *noun* a person or company which rents a house, flat or office to live or work in 承租人 ○ *The tenant is liable for repairs*. 承租人负责维修。

tender /ˈtendə/ *noun* an offer to do something for a specific price 投标，报价 ○ *a successful tender* 中标 ○ *an unsuccessful tender* 落标 □ **to put a project out to tender, to ask for *or* invite tenders for a project** to ask contractors to give written estimates for a job 工程招标:要求承包人对工程进行书面估价 □ **to put in *or* submit a tender** to make an estimate for a job 投标:进行工作估价

tenderer /ˈtendərə/ *noun* a person or company that tenders for work 投标人 ○ *The company was the successful tenderer for the project*. 这家公司是该项目的中标者。

tendering /ˈtendərɪŋ/ *noun* the act of putting forward an estimate of cost 投标 ○ *To be successful, you must follow the tendering procedure as laid out in the documents*. 想要中标,就必须遵守文件里所列的投标程序。

tender offer /ˈtendə ˌɒfə/ *noun* a method of selling new securities or bonds by asking investors to make offers for them, and accepting the highest offers 投标开价,销售证券招标:要求投资者出价并接受最高出价的新证券或债券出售方法

10-K /ˌten ˈkeɪ/ *noun* the filing of a US company's annual accounts with the New York Stock Exchange 10-K 报表:美国公司向纽约证券交易所提交的年度账目报表

tenor /ˈtenə/ *noun* a time before a financial instrument matures or before a bill is payable (票据)期限:金融工具到期前或票据支付的期限

10-Q /ˌten ˈkjuː/ *noun* the filing of a US company's quarterly accounts with the New York Stock Exchange 10-Q 报表:美国公司向纽约证券交易所提交的季度账目报表

term /tɜːm/ *noun* a period of time when something is legally valid 期限 ○ *during his term of office as chairman* 在他担任董事长期间 ○ *the term of a lease* 租赁期 ○ *We have renewed her contract for a term of six months*. 我们将她的合同期限延长了六个月。○ *The term of the loan is fifteen years*. 贷款期限为 15 年。

term account /ˈtɜːm əˌkaʊnt/ *noun* same as 同 **term deposit**

term deposit /ˈtɜːm dɪˌpɒzɪt/ *noun* money invested for a fixed period at a higher rate of interest 定期存款

terminal bonus /ˌtɜːmɪn(ə)l ˈbəʊnəs/ *noun* a bonus received when an insurance comes to an end 期终奖:保险到期时收到的奖金

termination clause /ˌtɜːmɪˈneɪʃ(ə)n klɔːz/ *noun* a clause which explains how and when a contract can be terminated 终止条款:解释可以终止合同的条件及时间的条款

term loan /ˈtɜːm ləʊn/ *noun* a loan for a fixed period of time 定期贷款

terms /tɜːmz/ *plural noun* the conditions or duties which have to be carried out as part of a contract, or the arrangements which have to be agreed before a contract is valid 条件,条款 ○ *to negotiate for better terms* 磋商更适合的条件 ○ *She refused to agree to some of the terms of the contract*. 她不同意合同中的部分条款。○ *By* or *Under the terms of the contract, the company is responsible for all damage to the property*. 根据合同条款,公司应对所有的财产损失负责。

'... companies have been improving communications, often as part of deals to cut down demarcation and to give everybody the same terms of employment'
"各家公司都在加强相互沟通,这种作法通常是消除界限、给予所有人相同工作条件的措施的一部分"[*Economist*《经济学家》]

'... the Federal Reserve Board has eased

interest rates in the past year, but they are still at historically high levels in real terms'
"去年联邦储备委员会降低了利率,但实际利率仍居于历史高位"[*Sunday Times*《星期日泰晤士报》]

term shares /ˈtɜːm ʃeəz/ *plural noun* a type of building society deposit for a fixed period of time at a higher rate of interest 定期股份:在住房互助协会的高利率定期存款

terms of reference /ˌtɜːmz əv ˈref(ə)rəns/ *plural noun* areas which a committee or an inspector can deal with (委员会或检查员的)职责范围,委任范围,权限 ○ *Under the terms of reference of the committee, it cannot investigate complaints from the public.* 根据委员会的职责范围,它不能调查公众的投诉。○ *The committee's terms of reference do not cover exports.* 委员会的权限不包括出口。

terms of sale /ˌtɜːmz əv ˈseɪl/ *plural noun* the conditions attached to a sale 销售条件

TESSA *abbr* tax-exempt special savings account 免税特别储蓄账户

testamentary /testəˈmentəri/ *adjective* referring to a will 遗嘱的

testamentary disposition /testəˌmentəri ˌdɪspəˈzɪʃ(ə)n/ *noun* passing of property to people in a will 遗嘱对财产的处置

testate /ˈtesteɪt/ *adjective* having made a will 立有遗嘱的 ○ *Did he die testate?* 他死时立遗嘱了吗?

testator /tesˈteɪtə/ *noun* someone who has made a will 立遗嘱的人

testatrix /tesˈteɪtrɪks/ *noun* a woman who has made a will 立遗嘱的女人

third party /ˌθɜːd ˈpɑːti/ *noun* a person other than the two main parties involved in a contract, e.g., in an insurance contract, anyone who is not the insurance company nor the person who is insured 第三方:合同中除了双方当事人以外的人,例如保险合同中既不是保险公司也不是受保人的人

third quarter /ˌθɜːd ˈkwɔːtə/ *noun* a period of three months from July to September 第三季度

3i *abbr* Investors in Industry 工业投资者

three quarters /ˌθriː ˈkwɔːtəz/ *noun* 75% 四分之三 ○ *Three quarters of the staff are less than thirty years old.* 四分之三的员工还不到30岁。

threshold /ˈθreʃhəʊld/ *noun* the point at which something changes 界限,范围,临界(值,点)

threshold agreement /ˈθreʃhəʊld əˌgriːmənt/ *noun* a contract which says that if the cost of living goes up by more than an agreed amount, pay will go up to match it 极限协议,临界协议:规定如果生活费用上升超过一定水平,则工资须进行相应调整的合同

thrift /θrɪft/ *noun* **1.** a careful attitude towards money, shown by saving it spending wisely 节俭 **2.** *US* a private local bank, savings and loan association or credit union, which accepts and pays interest on deposits from small investors (美)私人地方银行,储蓄与贷款联合会,信贷协会:他们都接受小投资者的存款并支付利息

'...the thrift, which had grown from $4.7 million in assets in 1980 to 1.5 billion this year, has ended in liquidation'
"这个私人储蓄机构从1980年的470万美

元资产发展到今年的 15 亿美元，最终还是进入了清算程序”［*Barrons*《巴伦》］

‘...some thrifts came to grief on speculative property deals, some in the high-risk junk bond market, others simply by lending too much to too many people’

“私人储蓄机构之所以进入困境，有些是因为投机性房地产交易，有些是因为参与高风险的垃圾债券市场，还有些则仅仅是因为向太多的人提供了太多的贷款”［*Times*《泰晤士报》］

thrifty /ˈθrɪfti/ *adjective* careful not to spend too much money 节俭的

throughput accounting /ˌθruːpʊt əˈkaʊntɪŋ/ *noun* a management accounting system which focuses on ways by which the maximum return per unit of bottleneck activity can be achieved 产量会计，产量核算：一种管理会计制度，它聚焦于在达到业务瓶颈时如何实现每单位的最大回报

tied financial adviser /taɪd faɪˌnænʃəl ədˈvaɪzə/ *noun* a qualified person, authorised to act by the Personal Investment Authority, who advises private clients on the financial products offered by a single company, as opposed to an independent financial adviser, who only advises on a wide range of products 特约理财顾问：获私人投资管理局授权的合资格人员，他可以就某一家公司提供的金融产品向私人客户提供咨询，这有别于只能就一系列产品提供咨询的独立财务顾问

tighten /ˈtaɪt(ə)n/ *verb* to make something tight, to control something 使紧缩；控制 ○ *The accounts department is tightening its control over departmental budgets*. 会计部门正在加强对部门预算的控制。

‘...the decision by the government to tighten monetary policy will push the annual inflation rate above the previous high’

“政府关于紧缩银根政策的决定，将促使年通货膨胀率超过历史高位”［*Financial Times*《金融时报》］

tighten up on /ˌtaɪt(ə)n ˈʌp ɒn/ *verb* to control something more strictly 控制更紧，使变紧 ○ *The government is tightening up on tax evasion*. 政府正在严格控制逃税行为。○ *We must tighten up on the reps' expenses*. 我们必须严格控制代理人费用。

tight money /taɪt ˈmʌni/ *noun* same as 同 **dear money**

tight money policy /taɪt ˈmʌni ˌpɒlɪsi/ *noun* a government policy to restrict money supply 紧缩银根政策：政府限制货币供给的政策

till /tɪl/ *noun* a drawer for keeping cash in a shop（商店中）放钱的抽屉

time /taɪm/ *noun* **1.** a period during which something takes place, e.g. one hour, two days or fifty minutes 期间，时间 **2.** the number of hours worked 工作时间 **3.** a period before something happens 期限 □ **to keep within the time limits** *or* **within the time schedule** to complete work by the time stated 如期完工

time and method study /ˌtaɪm ən ˈmeθəd ˌstʌdi/ *noun* a process of examining the way in which something is done to see if a cheaper or quicker way can be found 时间与方法研究：审查工作方式以找到更便宜或更快捷的方法

time and motion expert /ˌtaɪm ən ˈməʊʃ(ə)n ˌekspɜːt/ *noun* a person who analyses time and motion studies and suggests changes in the way work is done 时间与动作分析专家：对时间

和动作研究进行分析，并对工作方式提出修改建议的人

time and motion study /ˌtaɪm ən ˈməʊʃ(ə)n ˌstʌdi/ *noun* a study in an office or factory of the time taken to do specific jobs and the movements employees have to make to do them 时间与动作研究：对在办公室或工厂完成特定工作所需时间和员工动作的研究

time deposit /ˈtaɪm dɪˌpɒzɪt/ *noun* a deposit of money for a fixed period, during which it cannot be withdrawn 定期存款

time-keeping /ˈtaɪmˌkiːpɪŋ/ *noun* the fact of being on time for work 守时 ○ *He was warned for bad time-keeping*. 他由于不守时而被警告。

time limit /ˈtaɪm ˌlɪmɪt/ *noun* the maximum time which can be taken to do something 时限 ○ *to set a time limit for acceptance of the offer* 设定接受报价的时限 ○ *The work was finished within the time limit allowed*. 这项工作如期完成了。○ *The time limit on applications to the industrial tribunal is three months*. 向劳资仲裁法庭申请仲裁的时限为三个月。

time limitation /ˈtaɪm lɪmɪˌteɪʃ(ə)n/ *noun* the restriction of the amount of time available 时间限制

time rate /ˈtaɪm reɪt/ *noun* a rate for work which is calculated as money per hour or per week, and not money for work completed 计时工资率

timescale /ˈtaɪmskeɪl/ *noun* the time which will be taken to complete work (完成工作的)时间 ○ *Our timescale is that all work should be completed by the end of August*. 我们所有的工作都应在 8 月底前完成。○ *He is working to a strict timescale*. 他严格按照时间表工作。

time sheet /ˈtaɪm ʃiːt/ *noun* a record of when an employee arrives at and leaves work, or one which shows how much time a person spends on different jobs each day 工作时间卡，时间记录表：记录员工的上下班时间，或显示某人每天花多少时间完成不同工作的记录

time work /ˈtaɪm wɜːk/ *noun* work which is paid for at a rate per hour or per day, not per piece of work completed 计时工作

tip /tɪp/ *noun* money given to someone who has helped you 小费 ○ *The staff are not allowed to accept tips*. 员工不允许收小费。

title /ˈtaɪt(ə)l/ *noun* a right to own a property 所有权 ○ *She has no title to the property*. 她不拥有此财产的所有权。○ *He has a good title to the property*. 他对此财产有完全产权

title deeds /ˈtaɪt(ə)l ˌdiːdz/ *plural noun* a document showing who is the owner of a property 产权证书

token /ˈtəʊkən/ *noun* something which acts as a sign or symbol 象征；标记

token charge /ˌtəʊkən ˈtʃɑːdʒ/ *noun* a small charge which does not cover the real costs 象征性费用 ○ *A token charge is made for heating*. 象征性地收取取暖费。

token payment /ˈtəʊkən ˌpeɪmənt/ *noun* a small payment to show that a payment is being made 象征性付款

token rent /ˌtəʊkən ˈrent/ *noun* a very low rent payment to show that some rent is being asked 象征性租金

toll /təʊl/ *noun* a payment for using a service, usually a bridge or a road (公

路、桥梁等的）通行费 ○ *We had to cross a toll bridge to get to the island.* 要去那个岛，我们必须经过一座收费大桥。○ *You have to pay a toll to cross the bridge.* 过此桥必须付过桥费。

toll call /ˈtəʊl kɔːl/ *noun US* a long-distance telephone call（美）长途电话

toll free /ˌtəʊl ˈfriː/ *adverb*, *adjective US* without having to pay a charge for a long-distance telephone call（美）免费长途 ○ *to call someone toll free* 给某人打免费长途电话 ○ *a toll-free number* 免费长途号码

top-hat pension /ˌtɒphæt ˈpenʃən/ *noun* a special extra pension for senior managers 高级管理人员特殊退休金

top management /ˌtɒp ˈmænɪdʒmənt/ *noun* the main directors of a company 最高管理层

top up /ˌtɒp ˈʌp/ *verb* **1.** to fill up something which is not full 加满 ○ *to top up stocks before the Christmas rush* 在圣诞节抢购潮来临之前补足存货 **2.** to add to something to make it more complete 补充 ○ *He topped up his pension contributions to make sure he received the maximum allowable pension when he retired.* 他补缴了他的退休金缴款，以保证退休时可获得允许范围内的最高退休金。

total /ˈtəʊt(ə)l/ *adjective* complete or with everything added together 全部的 ○ *The total amount owed is now £1000.* 现在的欠款总额为1,000英镑。○ *The company has total assets of over £1bn.* 该公司的总资产超过10亿英镑。○ *The total cost was much more than expected.* 总成本远高于预期。○ *Total expenditure on publicity is twice that of last year.* 宣传开支总额是去年的两倍。○ *Our total income from exports rose last year.* 去年我们的出口总收入增加了。■ *verb* to add up to 总计，加总 ○ *costs totalling more than £25,000* 成本总计超过2.5万英镑（NOTE：UK English is **totalling – totalled**, but the US spelling is **totaling – totaled**. 英国英语拼作 **totalling – totalled**,美国拼法则为 **totaling – totaled**）

total absorption costing /ˌtəʊt(ə)l əbˌzɔːpʃən ˈkɒstɪŋ/ *noun* a method used by a cost accountant to price goods and services, allocating both direct and indirect costs. Although this method is designed so that all of an organisation's costs are covered, it may result in opportunities for sales being missed because it results in high prices 全部分摊成本法：成本会计师用来定价商品及劳务的一种方法，它既分配直接成本，又分配间接成本。虽然该方法旨在覆盖组织的全部成本，但由于计算出的定价较高，它可能导致失去本应获得的部分销售额 ⇨ 参阅 **marginal costing**

total assets /ˌtəʊt(ə)l ˈæsets/ *noun* the total net book value of all assets 总资产，全部资产

total asset turnover ratio /ˌtəʊt(ə)l ˌæset ˌtɜːnəʊvə ˈreɪʃiəʊ/ *noun* a measure of the use a business makes of all its assets. It is calculated by dividing sales by total assets 资产总额周转率：关于企业所有资产使用情况的一种衡量方法，其计算方法为销售额除以总资产

total invoice value /ˌtəʊt(ə)l ˈɪnvɔɪs ˌvæljuː/ *noun* the total amount on an invoice, including transport, VAT, etc.（包括运费、增值税等在内的）发票总金额

total overhead cost variance /ˌtəʊt(ə)l ˌəʊvəhed kɒst ˈveəriəns/ *noun* the difference between the overhead cost absorbed and the actual overhead costs, both fixed and variable 间接费用总额差异:分摊的间接费用与实际间接费用(包括固定的和可变的)之差

total return /ˌtəʊt(ə)l rɪˈtɜːn/ *noun* the total percentage change in the value of an investment over a specified time period, including capital gains, dividends, and the investment's appreciation or depreciation 总回报率,总投资收益率:投资价值于指定期限内变动的全部百分比,包括资本利得、股利及投资增值或贬值

tracker fund /ˈtrækə fʌnd/ *noun* a fund which tracks one of the stock market indices, such as the FTSE 指数基金,指数跟踪型基金:跟踪一个股票市场指数(如《金融时报》股市指数)的基金

track record /ˈtræk ˌrekɔːd/ *noun* the success or failure of a company or salesperson in the past (销售人员)工作履历,经历;(公司)业绩记录,往绩记录 ○ *He has a good track record as a secondhand car salesman.* 他做二手车推销员时业绩很好。○ *The company has no track record in the computer market.* 该公司从未涉足计算机市场。○ *We are looking for someone with a track record in the computer market.* 我们在寻找有计算机市场经验的人。

trade /treɪd/ *noun* **1.** the business of buying and selling 贸易,交易 **2.** a particular type of business, or people or companies dealing in the same type of product 行业,同业 ○ *He's in the secondhand car trade.* 他从事二手车行业。○ *She's very well known in the clothing trade.* 她在服装行业很有名。■ *verb* to buy and sell, to carry on a business 买卖;经商 ○ *We trade with all the countries of the EU.* 我们与所有欧盟成员国进行贸易。○ *She trades on the Stock Exchange.* 她在证券市场上炒股。○ *The company has stopped trading.* 该公司已经停业。○ *The company trades under the name 'Eeziphitt'.* 该公司以 Eeziphitt 的名称经营。

'...a sharp setback in foreign trade accounted for most of the winter slowdown. The trade balance sank $17 billion'
"国际贸易锐减是冬季经济衰退的主要原因,贸易余额下降了170亿美元"[*Fortune*《财富》]

'...at its last traded price, the bank was capitalized around $1.05 billion'
"按最新的交易价格,该银行的市值约为10.5亿美元"[*South China Morning Post*《南华早报》]

'...with most of the world's oil now traded on spot markets, Opec's official prices are much less significant than they once were'
"如今全球大多数石油都在现货市场上交易,因此欧佩克的官方价格已远没有过去那么重要了"[*Economist*《经济学家》]

'...the London Stock Exchange said that the value of domestic UK equities traded during the year was £1.4066 trillion, more than the capitalization of the entire London market and an increase of 36 per cent compared with previous year's total of £1.037 trillion'
"伦敦证券交易所称,年内交易的英国国内股票价值1.4066万亿英镑,超过了整个伦敦市场的总市值,比上年总价值1.037万亿英镑增加了36%"[*Times*《泰晤士报》]

'...trade between Britain and other countries which comprise the Economic Community has risen steadily from 33% of exports to 50% last year'
"去年,英国对其他欧共体国家的出口额占双方贸易总额的比例从33%稳步增长到了

50%" [*Sales & Marketing Management*《营销和市场管理》]

trade agreement /ˈtreɪd əˌgriːmənt/ *noun* an international agreement between countries over general terms of trade 贸易协议

trade association /ˈtreɪd əsəʊsiˌeɪʃ(ə)n/ *noun* a group which links together companies in the same trade 同业协会,行业协会

trade barrier /ˈtreɪd ˌbæriə/ *noun* a limitation imposed by a government on the free exchange of goods between countries 贸易壁垒:政府对国家间商品自由交易施加的限制 Also called 亦称作 **import restriction** (NOTE: NTBs, safety standards and tariffs are typical trade barriers 常见的贸易壁垒有非关税壁垒、安全标准和关税)

trade bill /ˈtreɪd bɪl/ *noun* a bill of exchange between two companies who are trading partners. It is issued by one company and endorsed by the other 商业票据,商业汇票:两家贸易伙伴公司间的汇票。它由一家公司发行,另一家公司背书

trade counter /ˈtreɪd ˌkaʊntə/ *noun* a shop in a factory or warehouse where goods are sold to retailers 批发店:向零售商批货的厂内商店或仓库

trade credit /ˈtreɪd ˌkredɪt/ *noun* a credit offered by one company when trading with another 商业信用,商业信贷:交易时由一家公司提供的信贷

trade creditors /ˈtreɪd ˌkredɪtəz/ *plural noun* companies which are owed money by a company. The amount owed to trade creditors is shown in the annual accounts 赊销方:赊账交易中的销售方,赊销金额列在年度报表中

trade cycle /ˈtreɪd ˌsaɪk(ə)l/ *noun* a period during which trade expands, then slows down, then expands again 贸易周期,商业循环:贸易从扩张到放缓再到扩张的期间

trade date /ˈtreɪd deɪt/ *noun* the date on which an enterprise becomes committed to buy a financial asset 交易日:企业购买金融资产的日期

trade debt /ˈtreɪd det/ *noun* a debt that originates during the normal course of trade 商业债务:在正常贸易过程中形成的债务

trade deficit /ˈtreɪd ˌdefɪsɪt/ *noun* the difference in value between a country's low exports and higher imports 贸易逆差,贸易赤字:少量出口与大量进口造成的差额 Also called 亦称作 **balance of payments deficit, trade gap**

trade description /treɪd dɪˈskrɪpʃən/ *noun* a description of a product to attract customers 商品介绍:对产品进行描述以吸引顾客

trade discount /treɪd ˈdɪskaʊnt/ *noun* a reduction in price given to a customer in the same trade 贸易折扣,商业折扣:给予同行业客户的价格折扣

traded options /ˌtreɪdɪd ˈɒpʃənz/ *plural noun* options to buy or sell shares at a specific price on a specific date in the future, which themselves can be bought or sold 交易期权:在未来某日按指定价格买卖股票的期权,而这些期权本身亦可买卖

trade fair /ˈtreɪd feə/ *noun* a large exhibition and meeting for advertising and selling a specific type of product 商品交易会 ○ *There are two trade fairs running in London at the same time* —

the carpet manufacturers' and the mobile telephones. 伦敦同时举行两个商品交易会——地毯生产商交易会和移动电话商品交易会。

trade gap /ˈtreɪd ɡæp/ *noun* same as 同 **trade deficit**

trademark /ˈtreɪdmɑːk/, **trade name** /ˈtreɪd neɪm/ *noun* a name, design or symbol which has been registered by the manufacturer and which cannot be used by other manufacturers. It is an intangible asset 商标,招牌 ○ *You can't call your beds 'Softn' kumfi' — it is a registered trademark*. 你生产的床不能取名"Softn'kumfi",因为该商标已经注册了。

trade mission /ˈtreɪd ˌmɪʃ(ə)n/ *noun* a visit by a group of businesspeople to discuss trade 贸易访问团 ○ *He led a trade mission to China*. 他带领一个贸易访问团去中国。

trade-off /ˈtreɪdɒf/ *noun* an act of exchanging one thing for another as part of a business deal 交换,交易 (NOTE: The plural is **trade-offs** 复数为 **trade-offs**)

trade price /ˈtreɪd praɪs/ *noun* a special wholesale price paid by a retailer to the manufacturer or wholesaler 批发价

trader /ˈtreɪdə/ *noun* a person who does business 交易者,贸易商

trade surplus /ˈtreɪd ˌsɜːpləs/ *noun* the difference in value between a country's high exports and lower imports 顺差,贸易盈余:大量出口与少量进口造成的价值差额

'Brazil's trade surplus is vulnerable both to a slowdown in the American economy and a pick-up in its own'

"巴西贸易顺差很脆弱,容易受到美洲经济放缓和自身经济加速发展的影响" [*Economist*《经济学家》]

trade terms /ˈtreɪd tɜːmz/ *plural noun* a special discount for people in the same trade 商业折扣,商业条款:给予同行业客户的特别折扣

trade-weighted index /treɪdˌweɪtɪd ˈɪndeks/ *noun* an index of the value of a currency calculated against a basket of currencies 贸易加权指数:以一揽子货币为基础计算的某种货币价值指数

trading /ˈtreɪdɪŋ/ *noun* **1.** the business of buying and selling 商业,交易 **2.** an area of a broking house where dealing in securities is carried out by phone, using monitors to display current prices and stock exchange transactions 交易区:经纪公司内通过电话买卖证券,并使用监视器来显示当前价格和股市交易的区域

trading, profit and loss account /ˈtreɪdɪŋ ˈprɒfɪt ən lɒs əˈkaunt/ *noun* an account which details the gross profit or loss made by an organisation for a given period **trading account**, and after adding other income and deducting various expenses, is able to show the profit or loss of the business 营业损益账户:该账户详列机构营业账户于指定期限内的总盈亏,而在添加其他收入和扣除各项开支后,它还能显示企业的盈亏

trading account /ˈtreɪdɪŋ əˌkaʊnt/ *noun* an account of a company's gross profit 营业账户:公司的毛利账户

trading area /ˈtreɪdɪŋ ˌeəriə/ *noun* a group of countries which trade with each other (多个国家间的)贸易区

trading company /ˈtreɪdɪŋ ˌkʌmp(ə)ni/ *noun* a company which specialises in buying and selling goods 商业公司

trading estate /ˈtreɪdɪŋ ɪˌsteɪt/ *noun* an area of land near a town specially for building factories and warehouses 工业区：城镇附近专门用于建造工厂和仓库的区域

trading financial assets /ˌtreɪdɪŋ faɪˌnænʃəl ˈæsets/ *noun* financial assets acquired or held in order to produce profit from short term changes in price 用于交易的金融资产：为从短期价格波动中获利而购买或持有的金融资产

trading limit /ˈtreɪdɪŋ ˌlɪmɪt/ *noun* the maximum amount of something which can be traded by a single trader 贸易范围，交易限额：单笔交易的最大限额

trading loss /ˈtreɪdɪŋ lɒs/ *noun* a situation where a company's receipts are less than its expenditure 贸易损失，营业损失

trading partner /ˈtreɪdɪŋ ˌpɑːtnə/ *noun* a company or country which trades with another 贸易伙伴

trading profit /ˈtreɪdɪŋ ˌprɒfɪt/ *noun* a result where the company' receipts are higher than its expenditure 营业利润

trading stamp /ˈtreɪdɪŋ stæmp/ *noun* a special stamp given away by a shop, which the customer can collect and exchange later for free goods 商品奖券：商店发放的特别礼券，顾客可用来兑换免费商品

trainee /treɪˈniː/ *noun* a person who is learning how to do something 受训人，实习生 ○ *We take five graduates as trainees each year.* 我们每年都招收五名毕业生作实习生。○ *Office staff with leadership potential are selected for courses as trainee managers.* 有领导潜质的人员被挑选参加实习经理培训课程。○ *We employ an additional trainee accountant at peak periods.* 在业务高峰期，我们多雇了一名实习会计师。

training levy /ˈtreɪnɪŋ ˌlevi/ *noun* a tax to be paid by companies to fund the government's training schemes 培训税：公司缴纳的用于政府培训计划费用的税金

training officer /ˈtreɪnɪŋ ˌɒfɪsə/ *noun* a person who deals with the training of staff in a company 培训员，教导员

tranche /trɑːnʃ/ *noun* one of a series of instalments, used when referring to loans to companies, government securities which are issued over a period of time, or money withdrawn by a country from the IMF 份额，档：一系列分期付款中的一份，用于公司贷款、某一期间发行的政府证券或一国从国际货币基金组织取得的资金 ○ *The second tranche of interest on the loan is now due for payment.* 贷款的第二期利息现已到期。

transaction /trænˈzækʃən/ *noun* 交易 □ **a transaction on the Stock Exchange** a purchase or sale of shares on the Stock Exchange 证券交易所的交易：在证券交易所买卖股票 ○ *The paper publishes a daily list of Stock Exchange transactions.* 这份报纸公布证券交易所每日交易清单。

'...the Japan Financial Intelligence Office will receive reports on suspected criminal transactions from financial institutions, determine where a probe should be launched and provide information to investigators' "日本金融情报室将收到金融机构涉嫌犯罪交易的报告,然后确定调查的领域并向调查员提供信息"[*Nikkei Weekly*《日经周报》]

transaction costs /træn'zækʃən kɒsts/ *noun* incremental costs that are directly attributable to the buying or selling of an asset. Transaction costs include commissions, fees, and direct taxes 交易费用(包括佣金、费用和直接税金)

transaction date /træn'zækʃən deɪt/ *noun* the date on which control of an asset passes from the seller to the buyer 交易日期

transaction exposure /trænˌzækʃən ɪk'spəʊʒə/ *noun* the risk that an organization may suffer the effects of foreign exchange rate changes during the time it takes to arrange the export or import of goods or services. Transaction exposure is present from the time a price is agreed until the payment has been made or received in the domestic currency 交易风险:在安排商品或劳务进出口期间,可能面临的汇率波动风险。从商定价格一直到付款或收到本币付款期间,交易风险始终存在

transfer /'trænsfɜː/ *noun* an act of moving an employee to another job in the same organization (同一组织内部员工的)调任,职务变动 ○ *She applied for a transfer to our branch in Scotland*. 她申请调到我们的苏格兰分部。 ■ *verb* to move someone or something to a different place, or to move someone to another job in the same organization 转移,转让;(在同一组织内)调任 ○ *The accountant was transferred to our Scottish branch*. 这名会计师被调到我们的苏格兰分部。○ *He transferred his shares to a family trust*. 他把股份转到一个家族信托中。○ *She transferred her money to a deposit account*. 她把钱转到一个存款账户内。

transferable /træns'fɜːrəb(ə)l/ *adjective* possible to pass to someone else 可转让的

transfer of property /ˌtrænsfɜː əv 'prɒpəti/, **transfer of shares** /ˌtrænsfɜː əv 'ʃeəz/ *noun* the act of moving the ownership of property or shares from one person to another 财产转让;股票转让

transferor /træns'fɜːrə/ *noun* a person who transfers goods or property to another 转让人,出让人

transferred charge call /trænsˌfɜːd 'tʃɑːdʒ kɔːl/ *noun* a phone call where the person receiving the call agrees to pay for it 对方付费电话

translate /træns'leɪt/ *verb* to put something which is said or written in one languagc into another language 翻译 ○ *He asked his secretary to translate the letter from the German agent*. 他要求秘书翻译德国代理商的这封来信。○ *We have had the contract translated from French into Japanese*. 我们让人把合同从法语译成了日语。

translation /træns'leɪʃ(ə)n/ *noun* something which has been translated 译文 ○ *She passed the translation of the letter to the accounts department*. 她把信函译文交给会计部门。

translation exposure /trænsˌleɪʃ(ə)n ɪk'spəʊʒə/ *noun* the risk that the balance sheet and income statement may be adversely affected by foreign exchange rate changes 外币换算风险:汇率波动可能对资产负债表及损益表

产生不利影响的风险

traveller's cheques /ˈtræv(ə)ləz tʃeks/ *plural noun* cheques bought by a traveller which can be cashed in a foreign country 旅行支票:旅行者携带的可在外国兑换外币现金的支票

travelling expenses /ˈtræv(ə)lɪŋ ekˌspensɪz/ *plural noun* money spent on travelling and hotels for business purposes 差旅费

treasurer /ˈtreʒərə/ *noun* **1.** a person who looks after the money or finances of a club or society, etc. 财务主管,司库,财务主任 **2.** company official responsible for finding new finance for the company and using its existing financial resources in the best possible way 负责公司筹资和以最优方式使用现有资金的公司主管 **3.** *US* the main financial officer of a company (美)公司财务主管 **4.** (*in Australia*) the finance minister in the government (澳大利亚)财政部长

Treasury /ˈtreʒəri/ *noun* **1.** a government department which deals with the country's finance 财政部(NOTE: The term is used in both the UK and the US; in most other countries this department is called the **Ministry of Finance** 英国和美国都使用该词;但其他大多数国家把财政部称为 **Ministry of Finance**) **2.** the department of a company or corporation that deals with all financial matters (公司)财务部

Treasury bill /ˈtreʒəri bɪl/ *noun* a shortterm financial instrument which does not give any interest and is sold by the government at a discount through the central bank. In the UK, their term varies from three to six months, in the USA, they are for 91 or 182 days, or for 52 weeks 短期国债,国库券:由政府通过中央银行以折扣方式出售的无息短期金融工具。在英国,它的期限为三至六个月不等,在美国则为 91 天或 182 天或 52 个星期(NOTE: In the USA, they are also called **Treasuries** *or* **T-bills** 美国亦称作 **Treasuries** 或 **T-bills**)

treasury management /ˌtreʒəri ˈmænɪdʒmənt/ *noun* an entity's method of dealing of its financial matters, including growing funds for business, maintaining cash flows and currencies, and managing currencies and cash flows 财务管理:财务事务的管理,包括筹集经营资金,维持现金流量与货币,管理货币与现金流量

treasury products /ˌtreʒəri ˈprɒdʌkts/ *noun* any financial item produced by a government for sale, such as bonds 国库项目:由政府推出销售的金融项目,如债券

Treasury Secretary /ˈtreʒəri ˌsekrət(ə)ri/ *noun US* the member of the US government in charge of finance (美)财政部长(NOTE: The equivalent of the **Finance Minister** in most countries, or of the **Chancellor of the Exchequer** in the UK 大多数国家称之为 **Finance Minister**,英国称之为 **Chancellor of the Exchequer**)

trend /trend/ *noun* a general way in which things are developing 趋势 ○ *a downward trend in investment* 投资减少的趋势 ○ *There is a trend away from old-established food stores.* 老字号餐馆的生意日趋减少。○ *The report points to inflationary trends in the economy.* 报告指出经济有通货膨胀的趋势。○ *We notice a general trend towards selling to the student market.* 我们注意到销售向学生市场发展的普遍

趋势。○ *We have noticed an upward trend in sales*. 我们发现销售额呈现出增长的趋势。

'...the quality of building design and ease of accessibility will become increasingly important, adding to the trend towards out-of-town office development'
"随着城郊办公的日益流行,建筑设计质量和交通便利将变得越来越重要"[*Lloyd's List*《劳氏日报》]

trial balance /ˈtraɪəl ˌbæləns/ *noun* the draft calculation of debits and credits to see if they balance 试算表,试算平衡表:检查借贷双方的金额是否平衡的草算

trillion /ˈtrɪljən/ *noun* one million millions 万亿(NOTE: In the UK, trillion now has the same meaning as in the USA; formerly in UK English it meant one million million millions, and it is still sometimes used with this meaning; see also the note at **billion** 现在该词在英国和美国同义;但在英国它最初是指一百万兆,现在有时仍用该义。亦参阅 **billion** 的附注)

'...if land is assessed at roughly half its current market value, the new tax could yield up to ¥10 trillion annually'
"如果对土地按现行市价的一半进行大致估价,那么新的税收收入可以增至每年10万亿日元"[*Far Eastern Economic Review*《远东经济评论》]

'...behind the decline was a 6.1% fall in exports to ¥47.55 trillion, the second year of falls. Automobiles and steel were among categories showing particularly conspicuous drops'
"经济下滑的背后是出口下降47.55万亿日元,这是连续第二年出现下降。汽车和钢铁行业下滑尤其明显"[*Nikkei Weekly*《日经周报》]

'...the London Stock Exchange said that the value of domestic UK equities traded during the year was £1.4066 trillion, more than the capitalization of the entire London market and an increase of 36 per cent compared with previous year's total of £1.037 trillion'
"伦敦证券交易所称,年内交易的英国国内股票价值1.4066万亿英镑,超过了整个伦敦市场的总市值,比上年总价值1.037万亿英镑增加了36%"[*Times*《泰晤士报》]

true /truː/ *adjective* correct or accurate 正确的,准确的

true and fair view /ˌtruː ən feə ˈvjuː/ *noun* a correct statement of a company's financial position as shown in its accounts and confirmed by the auditors 真实公平的观点:经审计师确认,某公司的账目正确地反映了公司的财务状况

Trueblood Report /ˈtruːblʌd rɪˌpɔːt/ *noun* a report, 'Objectives of Financial Statements', published by the American Institute of Certified Public Accountants in 1971, that recommended a conceptual framework for financial accounting and led to the Statements of Financial Accounting Concepts issued by the Financial Accounting Standards Board in the United States 特鲁布拉德报告:美国注册会计师协会于1971年发布的一份名为"财务报表的客观性"的报告,它提出一个财务会计的概念性框架,后来美国财务会计准则委员会据此颁布了财务会计概念公告

true copy /ˌtruː ˈkɒpi/ *noun* an exact copy 准确的副本 ○ *I certify that this is a true copy*. 我确认这是准确的副本。○ *It is certified as a true copy*. 它被确认为准确的副本。

trust /trʌst/ *noun* **1.** the fact of being confident that something is correct or will work 信任 **2.** a legal arrangement to pass goods, money or valuables to someone who will look after them well 委托,托管 ○ *She left his property in trust for her grandchildren.* 她将他的财产委托给她的孙子们管理。**3.** the management of money or property for someone (资金或财产的)信托 ○ *They set up a family trust for their grandchildren.* 他们为孙子们设立了家庭信托。**4.** US a small group of companies which control the supply of a product (美)托拉斯:由少数公司控制产品供应的垄断组织

trust company /ˈtrʌst ˌkʌmp(ə)ni/ noun US an organisation which supervises the financial affairs of private trusts, executes wills, and acts as a bank to a limited number of customers (美)信托公司:管理私人信托的财务事宜、执行遗嘱或充当少数客户的银行的组织

trust deed /ˈtrʌst diːd/ noun a document which sets out the details of a private trust 信托契约:列示私人信托详细资料的文件

trustee /trʌsˈtiː/ noun a person who has charge of money in trust 受托人,信托资产管理人 ○ *the trustees of the pension fund* 养老基金受托人

trustee in bankruptcy /trʌsˌtiː ɪn ˈbæŋkrʌptsi/ noun a person who is appointed by a court to run the affairs of a bankrupt and pay his or her creditors 破产受托人:由法庭任命管理破产事务和偿付债务的人

trust fund /ˈtrʌst fʌnd/ noun assets such as money, securities or property held in trust for someone 信托基金:持有的受托资产(货币、有价证券、财产等)

turn /tɜːn/ noun **1.** a movement in a circle, or a change of direction 转向 **2.** a profit or commission 利润;佣金 ○ *She makes a turn on everything he sells.* 他的每笔销售她都能从中得到一定佣金。

turnaround /ˈtɜːnəraʊnd/ noun especially US same as (尤美)同 **turnround**

turn down /ˌtɜːn ˈdaʊn/ verb to refuse something 拒绝 ○ *The board turned down the proposal.* 董事会拒绝了该提议。○ *The bank turned down their request for a loan.* 银行拒绝了他们的贷款申请。○ *The application for a licence was turned down.* 执照申请被拒绝了。○ *He turned down the job he was offered.* 他拒绝了工作邀请。

turn over /ˌtɜːn ˈəʊvə/ verb **1.** to have a specific amount of sales 获得…销售额 ○ *We turn over £2,000 a week.* 我们每周有2,000英镑的销售额。**2.** US to pass something to someone (美)递交 ○ *She turned over the documents to the lawyer.* 她把文件递交给律师。(NOTE: In this meaning, the usual UK term is **hand over** 该义的英国用语通常为 **hand over**)

'...a 100,000 square foot warehouse can turn its inventory over 18 times a year, more than triple a discounter's turnover'
"面积十万平方英尺的仓库一年存货可以周转18次,为廉价店周转率的三倍多" [*Duns Business Month* 《邓氏商业月刊》]

'...he is turning over his CEO title to one of his teammates, but will remain chairman for a year'
"他将首席执行总裁职位让给同事,但仍将担任董事长一年" [*Duns Business Month* 《邓氏商业月刊》]

turnover /ˈtɜːnəʊvə/ noun **1.** the

amount of sales of goods or services by a company 销售额，营业额 ○ *The company's turnover has increased by 235%*. 公司营业额增长了 235%。○ *We based our calculations on the forecast turnover*. 我们是根据预测销售收入进行计算的。(NOTE: The US term is **sales volume** 美国用语为 **sales volume**) **2.** the number of times something is used or sold in a period, usually one year, expressed as a percentage of a total 周转率：一段时间(通常为一年)内某物被使用或出售的次数，通常表示为总数的一定百分比

turnover tax /ˈtɜːnəʊvə tæks/ *noun* same as 同 **sales tax**

turn round /ˌtɜːn ˈraʊnd/ *verb* to make a company change from making a loss to become profitable 扭亏 □ **they turned the company round in less than a year** they made the company profitable in less than a year 他们不到一年就使企业扭亏为盈

turnround /ˈtɜːnraʊnd/ *noun* **1.** the value of goods sold during a year divided by the average value of goods held in stock 存货周转率：一年内销售收入除以库存商品年均价值 **2.** the action of emptying a ship, plane, etc., and getting it ready for another commercial journey 周转：轮船、飞机等清仓以备下次商业运营 **3.** the act of making a company profitable again 扭亏 (NOTE: [all senses] The US term is **turnaround** [以上所有义项]美国用语为 **turnaround**)

'... the US now accounts for more than half our world-wide sales: it has made a huge contribution to our earnings turnround'

"美国市场现在占我们全球销售额的一半以上，它为我们扭亏为盈做出了巨大贡献"

[*Duns Business Month*《邓氏商业月刊》]

two-bin system /ˌtuːbɪn ˈsɪstəm/ *noun* warehousing system, where the first bin contains the current working stock, and the second bin has the backup stock 双料箱存货控制系统：一种库存控制系统，它使用第一个箱子来装现在使用的存货，第二个箱子装备用的存货

U

UITF *abbr* Urgent Issues Task Force 紧急事务工作组

ultimate holding company /ˌʌltɪmət ˈhəʊldɪŋ ˌkʌmp(ə)ni/ *noun* the top company in a group consisting of several layers of parent companies and subsidiaries 最终控股公司

umbrella organisation /ʌmˈbrelə ˌɔːgənaɪzeɪʃ(ə)n/ *noun* a large organisation which includes several smaller ones 伞型组织,总机构:包含数个小机构的大型机构

unaccounted for /ˌʌnəˈkaʊntɪd fɔː/ *adjective* lost without any explanation 丢失而未予说明的 ○ *Several thousand units are unaccounted for in the stocktaking.* 在盘点存货时,有数千件货品缺失,且未予说明。

unadjusted trial balance /ˌʌnədʒʌstɪd ˌtraɪəl ˈbæləns/ *noun* a trial balance that has not yet been adjusted at a period end for items such as closing stock (在会计期末存货等科目的)结算前试算表,调整前试算表

unappropriated profits /ˌʌnəprəʊprieɪtɪd ˈprɒfɪts/ *noun* profits that have neither been distributed to a company's shareholders as dividends nor set aside as specific reserves 未分配利润,未留存盈余

unaudited /ʌnˈɔːdɪtɪd/ *adjective* having not been audited 未经审计的 ○ *unaudited accounts* 未审计账目

unauthorised /ʌnˈɔːθəraɪzd/, **unauthorized** *adjective* not permitted 未经授权的 ○ *unauthorised access to the company's records* 未经授权擅自查看公司记录 ○ *unauthorised expenditure* 未批准的支出 ○ *No unauthorised persons are allowed into the laboratory.* 未经批准不得擅入实验室。

unbalanced /ʌnˈbælənst/ *adjective* referring to a budget which does not balance or which is in deficit (预算)不平衡的,存在赤字的

unbanked /ʌnˈbæŋkt/ *adjective* referring to a person who does not have a bank account (某人)无银行账户的

uncalled /ʌnˈkɔːld/ *adjective* referring to capital which a company is authorised to raise and has been issued but for which payment has not yet been requested (股本)未催缴的

uncashed /ʌnˈkæʃt/ *adjective* having not been cashed 未兑现的 ○ *uncashed cheques* 未兑现支票

unconsolidated /ˌʌnkənˈsɒlɪdeɪtɪd/ *noun* not grouped together, as of shares or holdings (股票或财产)不合并的,不合并计算的

unconsolidated subsidiary /ˌʌnkənsɒlɪdeɪtɪd səbˈsɪdiəri/ *noun* a subsidiary that is not included in the consolidated financial statements of the group to which it belongs. An unconsolidated subsidiary would appear on a consolidated balance sheet as an investment 未列入合并财务报表的子公司:此类公司在合并资产负债表上作为一项投资呈列

uncontrollable /ˌʌnkənˈtrəʊləb(ə)l/ *adjective* not possible to control 不可控的 ○ *uncontrollable inflation* 无法控制的通货膨胀

uncontrollable costs /ˌʌnkənˈtrəʊləb(ə)l kɒsts/ *noun* costs appearing on a management accounting statement that are regarded as not within the control of that particular level of management 不可控成本:在管理会计报表中被视为不受某管理级别控制的成本

uncovered bear /ˌʌnkʌvəd ˈbeə/ *noun* a person who sells stock which he or she does not hold, hoping to be able to buy stock later at a lower price when the debt needs to be settled 无抵补空头投资者:销售自己并未持有的证券、而期望在债务需要交割时以低价买入的投资人

uncrossed cheque /ˌʌnkrɒst ˈtʃek/ *noun* a cheque which does not have two lines across it, and can be cashed anywhere 未划线支票:票面未划两条线的支票,可在任意地点兑取现金(NOTE: They are no longer used in the UK, but are still found in other countries 该类型支票英国已不再使用,但在其他一些国家仍能见到)

undated /ʌnˈdeɪtɪd/ *adjective* with no date indicated or written 未注明日期的 ○ *She tried to cash an undated cheque*. 她试图兑现一张未注明日期的支票。

undated bond /ʌnˌdeɪtɪd ˈbɒnd/ *noun* a bond with no maturity date 无到期日债券

under- /ʌndə/ *prefix* less important than or lower than 不重要;低于,少于

underabsorbed overhead /ˌʌndərəbzɔːbd ˈəʊvəhed/ *noun* an absorbed overhead which ends up by being lower than the actual overhead incurred 不足的已分摊间接费用:数额低于实际发生的已分摊间接费用

underbid /ˌʌndəˈbɪd/ *verb* to bid less than someone 出价比…低(NOTE: **underbidding – underbid**)

underbidder /ˈʌndəbɪdə/ *noun* a person who bids less than the person who buys at an auction(拍卖会上的)低价竞标者

undercapitalised /ˌʌndəˈkæpɪtəlaɪzd/, **undercapitalized** *adjective* without enough capital 资本不足的 ○ *The company is severely undercapitalised*. 该公司资金严重不足。

undercharge /ˌʌndəˈtʃɑːdʒ/ *verb* to ask someone for too little money 向…少收钱 ○ *She undercharged us by £25*. 她少收了我们 25 英镑。

underemployed /ˌʌndərɪmˈplɔɪd/ *adjective* with not enough work 未充分就业的 ○ *The staff is underemployed because of the cutback in production*. 由于生产削减,员工开工不足。

underemployed capital /ˌʌndərɪmplɔɪd ˈkæpɪt(ə)l/ *noun* capital which is not producing enough interest 未充分利用的资本

underlease /ˈʌndəliːs/ *noun* a lease from a tenant to another tenant 转租,分租

underlying inflation /ˌʌndəlaɪɪŋ ɪnˈfleɪʃ(ə)n/ *noun* the rate of inflation that does not take mortgage costs into account 基底通货膨胀率：未考虑抵押贷款利息支出的通货膨胀率

underspend /ˌʌndəˈspend/ *verb* to spend less than you should have spent or were allowed to spend 少花费

understandability /ˌʌndəˌstændəˈbɪlɪti/ *noun* when referring to financial information, the quality of being sufficiently clearly expressed as to be understood by anybody with a reasonable knowledge of business 可理解，易懂：指财务信息表述足够清晰明了，任何具备一定商业知识的人都能看懂

understate /ˌʌndəˈsteɪt/ *verb* to make something seem less than it really is 少报 ○ *The company accounts understate the real profit*. 公司的账目少报了实际利润。

undersubscribed /ˌʌndəsʌbˈskraɪbd/ *adjective* referring to a share issue where applications are not made for all the shares on offer, and part of the issue remains with the underwriters（发行的股份）认购不足的

undertake /ˌʌndəˈteɪk/ *verb* to agree to do something 同意，承诺 ○ *We asked the research unit to undertake an investigation of the market*. 我们要求研究部门进行一次市场调查 ○ *They have undertaken not to sell into our territory*. 他们承诺不到我们的地盘搞推销。（NOTE: **undertaking – undertook – undertaken**）

undertaking /ˈʌndəˌteɪkɪŋ/ *noun* **1.** a business 企业 ○ *He is the MD of a large commercial undertaking*. 他是一家大型商业企业的总经理。**2.** a promise, especially a legally binding one（尤指具有法律约束力的）承诺 ○ *They have given us a written undertaking not to sell their products in competition with ours*. 他们已向我们书面保证不与我们进行产品销售竞争。

undervaluation /ˌʌndəvæljuˈeɪʃ(ə)n/ *noun* the state of being valued, or the act of valuing something, at less than the true worth 估价过低；价值低估

undervalued /ˌʌndəˈvæljuːd/ *adjective* not valued highly enough 价值低估的 ○ *The dollar is undervalued on the foreign exchanges*. 外汇市场上美元价值被低估了。○ *The properties are undervalued on the company's balance sheet*. 在该公司的资产负债表上，这些资产被低估了。

'... in terms of purchasing power, the dollar is considerably undervalued, while the US trade deficit is declining month by month'
"就购买力而言，在当前美国贸易赤字逐月下降的情况下，美元价值被严重低估"［*Financial Weekly*《金融周刊》］

underwrite /ˌʌndəˈraɪt/ *verb* **1.** to accept responsibility for something 承担…的责任 **2.** to insure, to cover a risk 承保，承担风险 ○ *to underwrite an insurance policy* 承保一份保单 **3.** to agree to pay for costs 同意负担费用 ○ *The government has underwritten the development costs of the project*. 政府已同意承担此项工程的开发费用。（NOTE: **underwriting – underwrote – underwritten**）

'... under the new program, mortgage brokers are allowed to underwrite mortgages and get a much higher fee'
"根据新计划，抵押经纪人可以承揽抵押贷款业务，并可收取很高的费用"［*Forbes Magazine*《福布斯杂志》］

underwriter /ˈʌndəraɪtə/ *noun* a

person or company that underwrites a share issue or an insurance 证券包销商；保险商

underwriting /ˈʌndəraɪtɪŋ/ *noun* the action of guaranteeing to purchase shares in a new issue if no one purchases them 包销，承销：保证购买未售出的新发行股票的行为

underwriting fee /ˈʌndəraɪtɪŋ fiː/ *noun* a fee paid by a company to the underwriters for guaranteeing the purchase of new shares in that company 包销费：新发行股票的公司付给证券包销商的费用

underwriting syndicate /ˈʌndəraɪtɪŋ ˌsɪndɪkət/ *noun* a group of underwriters who insure a large risk 保险辛迪加

undischarged bankrupt /ˌʌndɪstʃɑːdʒd ˈbæŋkrʌpt/ *noun* a person who has been declared bankrupt and has not been released from that state 未偿清债务的破产者

undistributable profit /ˌʌndɪstrɪbjuːtəb(ə)l ˈprɒfɪt/ *noun* profit that is not legally available for distribution to shareholders as dividends 不可分配利润：法律规定不能作为红利分配给股东的利润

undistributable reserves /ˌʌndɪstrɪbjuːtəb(ə)l rɪˈzɜːvz/ *plural noun* same as 同 **capital reserves**

undistributed profit /ˌʌndɪstrɪbjuːtɪd ˈprɒfɪt/ *noun* a profit which has not been distributed as dividends to shareholders 未分配利润：未作为红利分配给股东的利润

unearned income /ˌʌnɜːnd ˈɪnkʌm/ *noun* same as 同 **investment income**

unemployed /ˌʌnɪmˈplɔɪd/ *adjective* not having any paid work 未受雇用的，失业的

unemployment /ˌʌnɪmˈplɔɪmənt/ *noun* the state of not having any work 失业

'... tax advantages directed toward small businesses will help create jobs and reduce the unemployment rate'
"针对小企业的税收优惠将有助于创造就业机会和降低失业率"［*Toronto Star*《多伦多明星日报》］

unemployment pay /ˌʌnɪmˈplɔɪmənt peɪ/ *noun* money given by the government to someone who is unemployed 失业救济金

unexpired cost /ˌʌnɪkspaɪəd ˈkɒst/ *noun* the net book value, or depreciated historical cost of an asset, not yet charged to the profit and loss account 未到期成本，未抵消成本，未耗成本：未从损益表中扣除的账面净值或资产折旧后的历史成本

unfair competition /ˌʌnfeə ˌkɒmpəˈtɪʃ(ə)n/ *noun* the practice of trying to do better than another company by using techniques such as importing foreign goods at very low prices or by wrongly criticising a competitor's products 不公平竞争

unfavourable variance /ʌnˌfeɪv(ə)rəb(ə)l ˈveəriəns/ *noun* an adverse variance, one which produces an unexpected loss 不利差异：产生意外损失的财务逆差

unfunded debt /ˌʌnfʌndɪd ˈdet/ *noun* short-term debt requiring repayment within a year from issuance（须在一年内偿还的）短期债务，无抵押债务

ungeared /ʌnˈgɪəd/ *adjective* with no borrowings 无借款的，无举债的

unguaranteed residual value /ʌnˌgærəntiːd rɪˌzɪdjuəl ˈvæljuː/ *noun* the amount of the residual value of a leased asset whose realisation is not assured 无担保残值:无法保证得到变现的租赁资产残值

uniform accounting policies /ˌjuːnɪfɔːm əˈkaʊntɪŋ ˌpɒləsiz/ *noun* the use of the same accounting policies for all the companies in a group, for the preparation of consolidated financial statements 统一会计政策:在编制集团合并财务报表时,对所有成员公司都采用相同的会计政策

uniform business rate /ˌjuːnɪfɔːm ˈbɪznɪs reɪt/ *noun* a tax levied on business property which is the same percentage for the whole country 统一企业税率,统一商业税率:对企业财产采用的全国统一税率 Abbreviation 缩写 **UBR**

uniformity /ˌjuːnɪˈfɔːmɪti/ *noun* the principle of using common measurements, accounting standards, and methods of presentation across different organisations, to ensure comparability 统一(性),一致(性):对不同组织采用共同的衡量标准、会计准则及呈列方法,以确保可比性的原则

unincorporated /ˌʌnɪnˈkɔːpəreɪtɪd/ *adjective* referring to a business which has not been made into a company, i.e. which is operating as a partnership or a sole trader 非公司的,非公司组织的:指企业未组成公司,即合伙或独资经营

unissued capital /ˌʌnɪʃuːd ˈkæpɪt(ə)l/ *noun* capital which a company is authorised to issue but has not issued as shares 未发行股本:公司获授权发行但尚未作为股份发行的资本

unissued stock /ˌʌnɪʃuːd ˈstɒk/ *noun* capital stock which a company is authorised to issue but has not issued 未发行股票:公司获授权发行但尚未发行的股本

unit /ˈjuːnɪt/ *noun* **1.** a single product for sale 单个(商品) **2.** a single share in a unit trust (单位信托中的)一股

unitary taxation /ˌjuːnɪt(ə)ri tækˈseɪʃ(ə)n/ *noun* a method of taxing a corporation based on its worldwide income rather than on its income in the country of the tax authority 统一征税法:根据公司的全球收入征税,而不是按其在税务机构所在国的收入征税

unit cost /ˈjuːnɪt kɒst/ *noun* the cost of one item, i.e. the total product costs divided by the number of units produced 单位成本:总生产成本除以生产数量

unitholder /ˈjuːnɪtˌhəʊldə/ *noun* a person who holds units in a unit trust 信托投资公司的股东

uniting of interests /ˌjuːnɪtɪŋ əv ˈɪntrəsts/ *noun* the international accounting standards term for merger accounting 权益联合:兼并会计的国际会计准则术语

unit-linked insurance /ˌjuːnɪt-lɪŋkd ɪnˈʃʊərəns/ *noun* an insurance policy which is linked to the security of units in a unit trust or fund 信托联合保险单:与单位信托或基金的单位证券挂钩的保险单

unit of account /ˌjuːnɪt əv əˈkaʊnt/ *noun* a standard unit used in financial transactions among members of a group, e.g. SDRs in the IMF 记账单位:在集团成员交易中使用的标准单位,如国际货币基金组织的特别提款权

unit price /ˈjuːnɪt praɪs/ *noun* the price of one item 单价,单位价格

units of production method of depreciation /ˌjuːnɪts əv prəˌdʌkʃən ˌmeθəd əv dɪˌpriːʃiˈeɪʃ(ə)n/ *noun* a method of calculating depreciation that determines the cost of an asset over its useful economic life according to the number of units it is expected to produce over that period 工作量折旧法,产量单位折旧法:一种折旧计算方法,它根据资产在使用年限内预期生产的单位数量来确定其在该期限内的成本

unit trust /ˈjuːnɪt trʌst/ *noun* an organisation which takes money from small investors and invests it in stocks and shares for them under a trust deed, the investment being in the form of shares (or units) in the trust 单位信托:面向小投资者募集资金并根据信托契约投资于股票或债券的机构,而这种投资以该信托机构的股份(或单位)形式存在(NOTE: The US term is **mutual fund** 美国用语为 **mutual fund**)

unlawful /ʌnˈlɔːf(ə)l/ *adjective* against the law, not legal 非法的

unlimited /ʌnˈlɪmɪtɪd/ *adjective* with no limits 无限的 ○ *The bank offered him unlimited credit.* 银行向他提供无限额的信贷。

unlimited company /ʌnˌlɪmɪtɪd ˈkʌmp(ə)ni/ *noun* company where the shareholders have no limit as regards liability 无限责任公司:股东对债务负无限责任的公司

unlimited liability /ʌnˌlɪmɪtɪd ˌlaɪəˈbɪlɪti/ *noun* a situation where a sole trader or each partner is responsible for all a firm's debts with no limit on the amount each may have to pay 无限责任:个体商人或每个合伙人对公司债务的责任不仅限于其投资金额的情况

unliquidated claim /ˌʌnlɪkwɪdeɪtɪd ˈkleɪm/ *noun* a claim for unliquidated damages 未偿索赔,未偿债权

unlisted company /ʌnˌlɪstɪd ˈkʌmp(ə)ni/ *noun* a company whose shares are not listed on the stock exchange 未上市公司:股票未在股票交易所挂牌交易的公司

unlisted securities /ʌnˌlɪstɪd sɪˈkjʊərɪtiz/ *plural noun* shares which are not listed on the Stock Exchange 未上市证券:未在证券交易所挂牌的证券

unpaid /ʌnˈpeɪd/ *adjective* not paid 未付的

unpaid invoices /ʌnˌpeɪd ˈɪnvɔɪsɪz/ *plural noun* invoices which have not been paid 未付发票

unprofitable /ʌnˈprɒfɪtəb(ə)l/ *adjective* not profitable 不盈利的,赚不到钱的

'... the airline has already eliminated a number of unprofitable flights'
"航空公司取消了几条不盈利的航线"
[*Duns Business Month*《邓氏商业月刊》]

unquoted company /ʌnˌkwəʊtɪd ˈkʌmp(ə)ni/ *noun* company whose shares are not listed on the stock exchange 非上市公司:股票未在证券交易所挂牌交易的公司

unquoted investments /ʌnˌkwəʊtɪd ɪnˈves(t)mənts/ *plural noun* investments which are difficult to value, e.g. shares which have no stock exchange listing or land of which the asset value is difficult to estimate 非报价

投资：难以估值的投资，例如未上市股票或很难估价的地产

unquoted shares /ˌʌnkwəʊtɪd ˈʃeəz/ *plural noun* shares which have no Stock Exchange quotation 非挂牌股票：在证券交易所没有报价的股票

unrealisable gains /ˌʌnrɪəlaɪzəb(ə)l ˈgeɪnz/ *noun* apparent increases in the value of assets that could not be turned into realised profit 不可变现的收益：表面增值却无法转成实际利润的资产

unrealised capital gain /ˌʌnrɪəlaɪzd ˌkæpɪt(ə)l ˈgeɪn/ *noun* an investment which is showing a profit but has not been sold 未实现的资本增值：投资已有利润但未售出变现

unrealised profit/loss /ˌʌnrɪəlaɪzd ˌprɒfɪt ˈlɒs/ *noun* a profit or loss that need not be reported as income, e.g., deriving from the holding of an asset worth more/less than its purchase price, but not yet sold 未实现利益/亏损，未实现利润/亏损：不需要记录为收入的盈亏，例如持有价值高于/低于其购买价但未售出的资产产生的盈亏

unredeemed pledge /ˌʌnrɪdiːmd ˈpledʒ/ *noun* a pledge which the borrower has not claimed back because he or she has not paid back the loan 未赎回抵押品：借款人因未偿还贷款而没有赎回的抵押品

unregistered /ʌnˈredʒɪstəd/ *adjective* referring to a company which has not been registered（公司）未注册的

unrestricted income funds /ˌʌnrɪstrɪktɪd ˌɪnkʌm ˈfʌndz/ *noun* a charity's funds that are available to its trustees to use for the purposes set out in the charity's governing document 非限定用途基金：受托人可用于慈善机构监管文件所载用途的慈善基金

unsecured creditor /ˌʌnsɪkjʊəd ˈkredɪtə/ *noun* a creditor who is owed money, but has no security from the debtor for the debt 无担保债权人：未取得债务人对债务进行担保的债权人

unsecured debt /ˌʌnsɪkjʊəd ˈdet/ *noun* a debt which is not guaranteed by a charge on assets or by any collateral 无担保债务

unsecured loan /ˌʌnsɪkjʊəd ˈləʊn/ *noun* a loan made with no security 无担保贷款

unsubsidised /ʌnˈsʌbsɪdaɪzd/, **unsubsidized** *adjective* with no subsidy 没有补贴的

unused allowances /ʌnˌjuːzd əˈlaʊənsɪs/ *noun* a part of the married couple's allowance or the blind person's allowance which is not used because the recipient does not have enough income, and which can then be passed to their spouse 未用免税额：已婚夫妇或盲人由于没有足够收入而未使用的免税额，该免税额可转给其配偶

up /ʌp/ *adverb, preposition* in or to a higher position 在上面；向上 ○ *The inflation rate is going up steadily.* 通货膨胀率持续上升。○ *Shares were up slightly at the end of the day.* 交易日结束时股价略有上涨。○ *She worked her way up to become sales director.* 她努力工作，升到了销售主任。

up front /ˌʌp ˈfrʌnt/ *adverb* in advance 提前 □ **money up front** payment in advance 预付款 ○ *They are asking for £100,000 up front before they will consider the deal.* 他们要求预付10万英镑，然后才考虑这笔交易。

○ *He had to put money up front before he could clinch the deal.* 他只有交预付款才能做成这笔生意。

upside potential /ˌʌpsaɪd pəˈtenʃəl/ *noun* the possibility for a share to increase in value（股票的）上涨潜力 Opposite 反义 **downside risk**

upturn /ˈʌptɜːn/ *noun* a movement towards higher sales or profits（销售额或利润的）上升 ○ *an upturn in the economy* 经济的繁荣 ○ *an upturn in the market* 市场的兴旺

Urgent Issues Task Force /ˌɜːdʒənt ˌɪʃuːz ˈtɑːsk ˌfɔːs/ *noun* a committee of the UK Accounting Standards Board that considers major urgent and emerging accounting issues. Its pronouncements are known as UITF Abstracts 紧急事务工作组：英国会计准则委员会下属负责处理重大紧急会计事项的一个理事会，该工作组发表的公告称为"紧急事务工作组摘要"Abbreviation 缩写 **UITF**

usage /ˈjuːsɪdʒ/ *noun* the way in which something is used 用途

usage method /ˌjuːsɪdʒ ˈmeθəd/ *noun* a method of depreciating a machine, by dividing its cost less residual value by the number of units it is expected to produce or the length of time it is expected to be used 工作量法：一种机器折旧方法，它以成本减残值除以预期产量或预期使用寿命

use *noun* /juːs/ a way in which something can be used 使用 ■ *verb* /juːz/ to take something, e.g. a machine, a company or a process, and work with it 使用 ○ *We use airmail for all our overseas correspondence.* 我们所有的国外信件都使用航空邮件发送。○ *The photocopier is being used all the time.* 复印机一直在使用。○ *They use freelancers for most of their work.* 大部分工作他们雇用自由职业者完成。

useful economic life /ˌjuːsf(ə)l ˌiːkənɒmɪk ˈlaɪf/ *noun* the period during which an entity expects to derive economic benefit from using an asset such as a machine and over which it can be depreciated 经济寿命，使用年限：实体预期使用某项资产（如一台机器）创造经济效益的年限，而该资产亦按该年限进行折旧

user /ˈjuːzə/ *noun* a person who uses something 用户，使用者

user's guide /ˈjuːzəz gaɪd/, **user's handbook** /ˈjuːzəz ˌhændbʊk/, **user's manual** /ˈjuːzəz ˌmænjuəl/ *noun* a book showing someone how to use something 用户指南，用户手册

usury /ˈjuːʒəri/ *noun* the lending of money at high interest 高利贷

utilisation /ˌjuːtɪlaɪˈzeɪʃ(ə)n/, **utilization** *noun* the act of making use of something 使用，利用

'... control permits the manufacturer to react to changing conditions on the plant floor and to keep people and machines at a high level of utilization'
"通过控制措施，生产商能够及时应对不断变化的车间条件，使员工及机器保持高水平的生产能力"［*Duns Business Month*《邓氏商业月刊》］

utilise /ˈjuːtɪlaɪz/, **utilize** *verb* to use something 使用，利用

V

vacant possession /ˌveɪkənt pəˈzeʃ(ə)n/ *noun* a property for sale, ready for occupation after being bought because it is empty 空房,空屋出售 ○ *The property is to be sold with vacant possession*. 此物业将以交吉形式出售。

valuation /ˌvæljuˈeɪʃ(ə)n/ *noun* an estimate of how much something is worth 估价,估值 ○ *to ask for a valuation of a property before making an offer for it* 在报价前要对房产进行估价

valuation of a business /ˌvæljuˌeɪʃ(ə)n əv eɪ ˈbɪznɪs/ *noun* the act of estimating the value of a business. This can be done on various bases, such as an assets basis, its break-up value, its value as a going concern, etc. 企业价值评定(可按不同基础进行,如资产、破产清算价值、持续经营价值等)

value /ˈvæljuː/ *noun* the amount of money which something is worth 价值 ○ *the fall in the value of sterling* 英镑贬值 ○ *She imported goods to the value of £2,500*. 她进口了价值2,500英镑的商品。○ *The valuer put the value of the stock at £25,000*. 评估人对存货估价为2.5万英镑。□ **to rise** *or* **fall in value** to be worth more or less 升值或贬值 ■ *verb* to estimate how much money something is worth 估价,估值 ○ *He valued the stock at £25,000*. 他对存货估价为2.5万英镑。○ *We are having the jewellery valued for insurance*. 我们请人对珠宝进行投保前的估价。

value-added statement /ˌvæljuːˌædɪd ˈsteɪtmənt/ *noun* a simplified financial statement that shows how much wealth has been created by a company. A value added statement calculates total output by adding sales, changes in stock, and other incomes, then subtracting depreciation, interest, taxation, dividends, and the amounts paid to suppliers and employees 增值表:表明公司创造的财富数额的简式财务报表。增值表计算总销售额、存货变动及其他收入的总和,再减去折旧、利息、税款、股利及付给供应商和雇员的金额,得到总产出

value in use /ˌvæljuː ɪn ˈjuːs/ *noun* the present value of the estimated future net cash flows from an object, including the amount expected from its disposal at the end of its useful life. Value in use replaces book value when an asset suffers impairment 使用价值:估计某物未来净现金流量的现值,包括其使用寿命结束时的预期出售所得金额。当资产出现减值时,即以使用价值代替账面价值

valuer /ˈvæljuːə/ *noun* a person who estimates how much money something is worth 评估人,估价人,鉴定人

variable /ˈveəriəb(ə)l/ *adjective* changeable 可变的

variable costs /ˌveəriəb(ə)l ˈkɒsts/ *plural noun* production costs which increase with the quantity of the product made, e.g. wages or raw materials 可变成本：随产量增加而增加的成本，如工资或原材料成本

variable rate /ˌveəriəb(ə)l ˈreɪt/ *noun* a rate of interest on a loan which is not fixed, but can change with the current bank interest rates 可变利率，浮动利率：不是固定的、随当前银行利率一起变动的贷款利率 Also called 亦称作 **floating rate**

variance /ˈveəriəns/ *noun* the difference between what was expected and the actual results（预期与实际的）差异

variance accounting /ˌveəriəns əˈkaʊntɪŋ/ *noun* a method of accounting by means of which planned activities (quantified through budgets and standard costs and revenues) are compared with actual results 差异会计：将计划的业务（通过预算及标准成本与收益进行量化）与实际业绩进行比较的一种会计方法

VAT declaration /ˈvæt dekləˌreɪʃ(ə)n/ *noun* a statement declaring VAT income to the VAT office 增值税申报表：向增值税征收机关申报增值税收入的报表

VAT group /ˌviː eɪ ˈtiː gruːp/ *noun* in the United Kingdom, a group of related companies that is treated as one taxpayer for VAT purposes 增值税集团：在英国，在征收增值税时被看作一个纳税人的关联公司集团

VAT inspection /ˈvæt ɪnˌspekʃ(ə)n/ *noun* a visit by officials of the Customs and Excise Department to see if a company is correctly reporting its VAT 增值税稽查：海关官员访问被稽核公司，了解该公司是否如实申报其增值税

VAT inspector /ˈvæt ɪnˌspektə/ *noun* a government official who examines VAT returns and checks that VAT is being paid 增值税稽查员：负责审查增值税纳税和退税的政府官员

VAT invoice /ˈvæt ˌɪnvɔɪs/ *noun* an invoice which includes VAT 增值税发票

VAT invoicing /ˈvæt ˌɪnvɔɪsɪŋ/ *noun* the sending of an invoice including VAT 开增值税发票

VATman /ˈvætmæn/, **vatman** *noun* a VAT inspector (*informal*)（非正式）增值税稽查员

VAT office /ˈvæt ˌɒfɪs/ *noun* the government office dealing with the collection of VAT in an area 增值税征收机关

VAT paid /ˌviː eɪ ˈtiː peɪd/ *adjective* with the VAT already paid 已付增值税的

VAT receivable /ˌviː eɪ ˌtiː rɪˈsiːvəb(ə)l/ *adjective* with the VAT for an item not yet collected by a taxing authority 应收增值税的：税务机构未征收某项目增值税的

VAT registration /ˌviː eɪ ˌtiː ˌredʒɪˈstreɪʃ(ə)n/ *noun* the process of listing a company with a European government as eligible for the return of VAT in certain cases 增值税退税登记：欧洲国家政府确定某公司在某些情况下可获得增值税退税的程序

VCT *abbr* venture capital trust 风险投资信托，创业投资信托

vending /ˈvendɪŋ/ *noun* selling 出

售，销售

vendor /ˈvendə/ *noun* **1.** a person who sells something, especially a property（尤指出售财产的）卖方 ○ *the solicitor acting on behalf of the vendor* 代表卖方的律师 **2.** a person who sells goods 摊贩，小贩

venture /ˈventʃə/ *noun* a commercial deal which involves a risk 风险交易：有风险的商业交易 ○ *They lost money on several import ventures.* 他们在几次高风险进口交易中都亏本了。 ○ *She's started a new venture — a computer shop.* 她开始了新的风险业务——开一家计算机商店。

venture capital /ˌventʃə ˈkæpɪt(ə)l/ *noun* capital for investment which may easily be lost in risky projects, but can also provide high returns 风险资本，创业资本：易于在冒险的投资项目中亏损，但也可能提供高额回报的资本 Also called 亦称作 **risk capital**

venture capital trust /ˌventʃə ˈkæpɪt(ə)l trʌst/ *noun* a trust which invests in smaller firms which need capital to grow 风险投资信托，创业投资信托 Abbreviation 缩写 **VCT**

vertical communication /ˌvɜːtɪk(ə)l kəˌmjuːnɪˈkeɪʃ(ə)n/ *noun* communication between senior managers via the middle management to the workforce 纵向交流：高级管理人员通过中层经理与工人进行交流

vertical equity /ˌvɜːtɪk(ə)l ˈekwɪti/ *noun* the principle that people with different incomes should pay different rates of tax 纵向公平：不同收入应适用不同税率的原则

vertical form /ˈvɜːtɪk(ə)l fɔːm/ *noun* one of the two styles of presenting a balance sheet allowed by the Companies Act 垂直式：《公司法》允许的两种资产负债表格式之一 Also called 亦称作 **report form**

vertical integration /ˌvɜːtɪk(ə)l ˌɪntɪˈgreɪʃ(ə)n/ *noun* same as 同 **backward integration**

vested interest /ˌvestɪd ˈɪntrəst/ *noun* a special interest in keeping an existing state of affairs 既得权益，法定权益：保持现状而获得的特别利益

virement /ˈvaɪəmənt/ *noun* a transfer of money from one account to another or from one section of a budget to another 预算调剂：将资金由一个账户转至另一账户，或从预算的一个部分转至另一部分

visible /ˈvɪzəb(ə)l/ *adjective* referring to real products which are imported or exported（进出口产品）有形的

visible exports /ˌvɪzəb(ə)l ˈekspɔːts/ *plural noun* real products which are exported, as opposed to services 有形出口：出口实物产品，与劳务出口相对

visible imports /ˌvɪzəb(ə)l ˈɪmpɔːts/ *plural noun* real products which are imported, as opposed to services 有形进口：进口实物产品，与劳务进口相对

visible trade /ˌvɪzəb(ə)l ˈtreɪd/ *noun* trade involving visible imports and exports 有形贸易：涉及有形进出口的贸易

void /vɔɪd/ *adjective* not legally valid 法律上无效的

volume /ˈvɒljuːm/ *noun* a quantity of items 数量

volume discount /ˈvɒljuːm ˌdɪskaʊnt/ *noun* the discount given to a customer who buys a large quantity of goods 数量折扣：给予大量购买的顾客的折扣

volume of output /ˌvɒljuːm əv ˈaʊtpʊt/ *noun* the number of items produced 产量

volume variances /ˌvɒljuːm ˈveəriənsɪs/ *noun* differences in costs or revenues compared with budgeted amounts, caused by differences between the actual and budgeted levels of activity 产量差异,业务量差异:由于实际与计划业务水平有出入导致的成本或收益与预算金额之间的差异

voluntary /ˈvɒlənt(ə)ri/ *adjective* **1.** done freely without anyone forcing you to act 自愿的 **2.** done without being paid 无偿的

voluntary liquidation /ˌvɒlənt(ə)ri ˌlɪkwɪˈdeɪʃ(ə)n/ *noun* a situation where a company itself decides it must close and sell its assets 自愿清算,自动清盘:公司自已决定必须关闭并出售其资产

voluntary redundancy /ˌvɒlənt(ə)ri rɪˈdʌndənsi/ *noun* a situation where the employee asks to be made redundant, usually in return for a large payment 自愿离职:雇员主动要求被裁汰,而该员工通常因此获得一大笔付款

voluntary registration /ˌvɒlənt(ə)ri ˌredʒɪˈstreɪʃ(ə)n/ *noun* in the United Kingdom, registration for VAT by a trader whose turnover is below the registration threshold. This is usually done in order to reclaim tax on inputs 自愿登记:在英国,营业额低于登记界限的商人自愿进行增值税登记。这样做通常是为了获得进项税退税

vote /vəʊt/ *noun* the act of marking a paper or holding up your hand, to show your opinion or to show who you want to be elected 选举,投票,表决

voting /ˈvəʊtɪŋ/ *noun* the act of making a vote 选举

voting paper /ˈvəʊtɪŋ ˌpeɪpə/ *noun* a paper on which the voter puts a cross to show for whom he or she wants to vote 选票

voucher /ˈvaʊtʃə/ *noun* **1.** a piece of paper which is given instead of money 代金券 **2.** a written document from an auditor to show that the accounts are correct or that money has really been paid 凭单,凭证:审计师开具的表示账目准确无误或款项确已支付的书面单据

W

wage /weɪdʒ/ *noun* the money paid to an employee in return for work done, especially when it is paid weekly and in cash 工钱，工资（尤指每周支付的现金）○ *She is earning a good wage or good wages for a young person.* 在年轻人里面，她的工资很高。（NOTE：The plural **wages** is more usual when referring to the money earned, but **wage** is used before other nouns 指赚取的金钱时较常用复数 **wages**，其他名词前则使用 **wage**）

'European economies are being held back by rigid labor markets and wage structures'
"僵化的劳动力市场和工资结构拖累着欧洲经济"[*Duns Business Month*《邓氏商业月刊》]

'...real wages have been held down dramatically: they have risen at an annual rate of only 1% in the last two years'
"实际工资显著下降：过去两年的年增长率仅为1%"[*Sunday Times*《星期日泰晤士报》]

wage adjustments /ˈweɪdʒ əˌdʒʌstmənts/ *plural noun* changes made to wages 工资调整

wage claim /ˈweɪdʒ kleɪm/ *noun* an act of asking for an increase in wages 加薪要求

wage-earner /ˈweɪdʒˌɜːnə/ *noun* a person who earns a wage 靠工资生活者，工薪族

wage indexation /ˈweɪdʒ ˌɪndekseɪʃ(ə)n/ *noun* the linking of increases to the percentage rise in the cost of living 工资指数：与生活费用上升百分比联动上升的指数

wage scale /ˈweɪdʒ skeɪl/ *noun* same as 同 **pay scale**

wages costs /ˈweɪdʒɪz kɒsts/ *noun* the costs of paying employees' salaries. Along with other costs such as pension contributions and salaries, these costs typically form the largest single cost item for a business 工资成本：支付雇员工资的成本。工资成本加上养老金缴款及工资等其他成本，通常构成企业最大的一个成本项目

wages payable account /ˌweɪdʒɪz ˌpeɪəb(ə)l əˈkaʊnt/ *noun* an account showing gross wages and employer's National Insurance contributions paid during some period 应付工资账目：记录一段时间内总工资和雇主国民保险缴款的账目

wages policy /ˈweɪdʒɪz ˌpɒlɪsi/ *noun* a government policy on what percentage increases should be paid to workers 工资政策：政府规定的工人工资增长比率的政策

wall safe /ˈwɔːl seɪf/ *noun* a safe installed in a wall 墙壁保险柜，墙内保险柜

warehouse /ˈweəhaʊs/ *noun* a large

building where goods are stored 仓库

warehouse capacity /ˈweəhaʊs kəˌpæsɪti/ *noun* the space available in a warehouse 库容，仓储量

warrant /ˈwɒrənt/ *noun* an official document which allows someone to do something 授权证 ■ *verb* to guarantee 保证 ○ *All the spare parts are warranted*. 所有的零配件都有质量保证。

'...the rights issue will grant shareholders free warrants to subscribe for further new shares'
"优先认股权的发行将给予股东自由认购新股的认股权证"[*Financial Times*《金融时报》]

warrantee /ˌwɒrənˈtiː/ *noun* a person who is given a warranty 被保证人

warrantor /ˌwɒrənˈtɔː/ *noun* a person who gives a warranty 保证人

warranty /ˈwɒrənti/ *noun* **1.** a legal document which promises that a machine will work properly or that an item is of good quality 质保书：承诺机器会正确运行或产品质量优良的法律文件 ○ *The car is sold with a twelve-month warranty*. 汽车的售后保质期为12个月。○ *The warranty covers spare parts but not labour costs*. 质保范围包括零部件，但不包括偿付人工费用。**2.** a promise in a contract（合同中的）承诺 **3.** a statement made by an insured person which declares that the facts stated by him are true 保证：投保人关于所述情况属实的声明

wasting asset /ˌweɪstɪŋ ˈæset/ *noun* an asset which becomes gradually less valuable as time goes by, e.g. a short lease on a property 损耗性资产：价值随时间的推移而逐渐下降的资产，如房地产短期租赁

watchdog /ˈwɒtʃdɒg/ *noun* an independent person or organisation whose task is to police a particular industry, ensuring that member companies do not act illegally 监察人：负责监察某个行业、确保业内公司没有违法行为的独立个人或组织

WDA *abbr* **1.** writing-down allowance 减记抵税 **2.** written-down allowance 减记减税

WDV *abbr* written-down value 减记价值

wealth tax /ˈwelθ tæks/ *noun* a tax on money, property or investments owned by a person 财产税：对个人拥有的资金、财产及投资所征的税

wear and tear /ˌweər ən ˈteə/ *noun* the deterioration of a tangible fixed asset as a result of normal use. This is recognised for accounting purposes by depreciation 磨损，耗损：有形固定资产的正常使用损耗。在会计中，磨损通过折旧进行确认

weight /weɪt/ *noun* a measurement of how heavy something is 重量 ■ *verb* to give an extra value to a factor 加权：给某因素附加额外价值

weighted average /ˌweɪtɪd ˈæv(ə)rɪdʒ/ *noun* an average which is calculated taking several factors into account, giving some more value than others 加权平均数：综合考虑多种因素计算出来的平均数，每个因素分别给予不同的权重

weighted average cost /ˌweɪtɪd ˈæv(ə)rɪdʒ kɒst/, **weighted average price** /ˌweɪtɪd ˈæv(ə)rɪdʒ praɪs/ *noun* the average price per unit of stock delivered in a period calculated either at the end of the period ('periodic weighted average') or each time a new delivery is received (' cumulative weighted average') 加权平均成本,加权平均价格:某段时间交付存货的每单位平均价格,可在期末计算(“定期加权平均数”),也可在每次收到货物时计算(“累积加权平均数”)

weighted index /ˌweɪtɪd ˈɪndeks/ *noun* an index where some important items are given more value than less important ones 加权指数:体现某些较重要项目被赋予较高数值的指数

weighting /ˈweɪtɪŋ/ *noun* an additional salary or wages paid to compensate for living in an expensive part of the country (因居住地区消费水平较高而得到的)额外工资补助 ○ *The salary is £15,000 plus London weighting.* 工资是1.5万英镑,外加伦敦地区补贴。

Wheat Report /ˈwiːt rɪˌpɔːt/ *noun* a report produced by a committee in 1972 that set out to examine the principles and methods of accounting in the United States. Its publication led to the establishment of the FASB 惠特报告:1972年一个委员会在审查美国会计原则与方法后发布的报告。它的发布直接促成美国财务会计准则委员会的成立

white knight /waɪt ˈnaɪt/ *noun* a person or company which rescues a firm in financial difficulties, especially one which saves a firm from being taken over by an unacceptable purchaser 白色骑士,救星:挽救濒危公司的个人或企业,尤指防止被过低价格收购

White Paper /waɪt ˈpeɪpə/ *noun* a report issued by the UK government as a statement of government policy on a particular problem 白皮书:英国政府就特定事项的政府政策进行说明的报告 Compare 比较 **Green Paper**

whole-life insurance /ˌhəʊlˈlaɪf ɪnˌʃʊərəns/, **whole-life policy** /ˌhəʊlˈlaɪf ˌpɒlɪsi/ *noun* an insurance policy where the insured person pays a fixed premium each year and the insurance company pays a sum when he or she dies 终身人寿保险(单):投保人每年付一笔固定费用,被保险人死亡时保险公司支付一笔保险金的保单 Also called 亦称作 **whole-of-life assurance**

wholesale /ˈhəʊlseɪl/ *adjective*, *adverb* referring to the business of buying goods from manufacturers and selling them in large quantities to traders (retailers) who then sell in smaller quantities to the general public 批发的(地) ○ *I persuaded him to give us a wholesale discount.* 我说服他给我们一个批发折扣。□ **he buys wholesale and sells retail** he buys goods in bulk at a wholesale discount and then sells in small quantities to the public 他批发买入,零售卖出

wholesale banking /ˌhəʊlseɪl ˈbæŋkɪŋ/ *noun* banking services between merchant banks and other financial institutions, as opposed to retail banking 大额银行业务:商业银行与其他金融机构之间互相提供的银行服务,与零售银行业务相对

wholesale dealer /ˈhəʊlseɪl ˌdiːlə/ *noun* a person who buys in bulk from manufacturers and sells to retailers 批发商

wholesale price /ˈhəʊlseɪl praɪs/ *noun* the price charged to customers who buy goods in large quantities in order to resell them in smaller quantities to others 批发价

wholesale price index /ˌhəʊlseɪl ˈpraɪs ˌɪndeks/ *noun* an index showing the rises and falls of prices of manufactured goods as they leave the factory 批发价格指数：显示工业产品出厂时价格升降的指数

wholesaler /ˈhəʊlseɪlə/ *noun* a person who buys goods in bulk from manufacturers and sells them to retailers 批发商

wholly-owned subsidiary /ˌhəʊliəʊnd səbˈsɪdjəri/ *noun* a subsidiary which belongs completely to the parent company 全资子公司：完全归母公司拥有的子公司

will /wɪl/ *noun* a legal document where someone says what should happen to his or her property when he or she dies 遗嘱 ○ *He wrote his will in 1984.* 他 1984 年立下了遗嘱。○ *According to her will, all her property is left to her children.* 根据遗嘱，她所有的财产都留给了子女。

windfall profit /ˌwɪndfɔːl ˈprɒfɪt/ *noun* a sudden profit which is not expected 意外利润，意外之财

windfall profits tax /ˈwɪndfɔːl ˌprɒfɪts tæks/, **windfall tax** /ˈwɪndfɔːl tæks/ *noun* a tax on companies that have made large profits because of circumstances outside their usual trading activities. A windfall tax was imposed on the privatised utility companies in 1997 暴利税，意外利润税：对公司在正常业务活动以外获得的巨额利润所征的税。1997 年，英国开始对私有化的公用事业公司征收了暴利税

winding up /ˌwaɪndɪŋ ˈʌp/ *noun* liquidation, the act of closing a company and selling its assets 清理，结业，清算：关闭公司并出售其资产

winding up petition /ˌwaɪndɪŋ ʌp pəˈtɪʃ(ə)n/ *noun* an application to a court for an order that a company be put into liquidation 清算呈请：向法院要求清算某公司的申请

window dressing /ˈwɪndəʊ ˌdresɪŋ/ *noun* **1.** the practice of putting goods on display in a shop window, so that they attract customers 橱窗装饰，橱窗陈列：在商店窗口展示商品，以吸引消费者 **2.** the practice of putting on a display to make a business seem better or more profitable or more efficient than it really is 粉饰（财务状况）：粉饰公司账目，使之看起来比实际情况更好、利润更高或更有效率

window envelope /ˌwɪndəʊ ˈenvələʊp/ *noun* an envelope with a hole covered with film so that the address on the letter inside can be seen 开窗信封：带有透明塑料窗口的信封，可见到信内地址

window of opportunity /ˌwɪndəʊ əv ɒpəˈtjuːnɪti/ *noun* a short period which allows an action to take place 机会窗口：允许某种行为发生的短暂时间

window shopping /ˈwɪndəʊ ˌʃɒpɪŋ/ *noun* the practice of looking at goods in shop windows, without buying anything 浏览商品橱窗：看摆在商店橱窗里的商品而不购买

wind up /ˌwaɪnd ˈʌp/ *verb* to end a meeting, or to close down a business or organisation and sell its assets 结束（会议）；（企业或组织）清理，停业 ○ *She wound up the meeting with a vote of thanks to the committee.* 会议结束时，她提议大家鼓掌对委员会表示感谢。

WIP *abbr* work in progress 在产品，

在制品

withdraw /wɪð'drɔː/ *verb* **1.** to take money out of an account 提款 ○ *to withdraw money from the bank or from your account* 从银行或账户中提款 ○ *You can withdraw up to £50 from any cash machine by using your card.* 你用银行卡从提款机里最多可以提取50英镑。**2.** to take back an offer 收回(报价)○ *When he found out more about the candidate, the HR manager withdrew the offer of a job.* 对这名求职者有更多了解之后,人事经理收回了工作邀请。○ *When the employees went on strike, the company withdrew its revised pay offer.* 由于员工继续罢工,公司撤回了修改的薪资表。(NOTE: **withdrawing – withdrew**)

withdrawal /wɪð'drɔːəl/ *noun* the act of removing money from an account 提款 ○ *to give seven days' notice of withdrawal* 提前7天发出提款通知 ○ *Withdrawals from bank accounts reached a peak in the week before Christmas.* 在圣诞节前一周,银行账户提款达到高峰。

withholding tax /wɪð'həʊldɪŋ ˌtæks/ *noun US* a tax which removes money from interest or dividends before they are paid to the investor, usually applied to non-resident investors (美)预扣税:在给投资者支付利息或分红前扣除所得税(通常适用于非居民投资者)

with profits /wɪð 'prɒfɪts/ *adverb* referring to an insurance policy which guarantees the policyholder a share in the profits of the fund in which the premiums are invested (保单)有分红:保险单保证持有人能够分享保险费基金的利润

work /wɜːk/ *noun* **1.** things done using the hands or brain (体力或脑力)劳动 **2.** a job, something done to earn money 工作,职业 ○ *It is not the work itself that the employees are complaining about* 雇员们报怨的不是工作本身 ○ *He goes to work by bus.* 他乘公共汽车上班。○ *She never gets home from work before 8 p.m.* 她从来没有晚8点前下班回家的时候。○ *His work involves a lot of travelling.* 他的工作需要经常出差。○ *He is still looking for work.* 他还在找工作。○ *She has been out of work for six months.* 她已经失业六个月了。

'...the quality of the work environment demanded by employers and employees alike'
"雇员和雇主共同要求的工作环境质量"
[*Lloyd's List*《劳氏日报》]

workforce /'wɜːkfɔːs/ *noun* the total number of employees in an organisation, industry or country (某机构、行业或国家的)工人总数,职工总数

working capital /'wɜːkɪŋ ˌkæpɪt(ə)l/ *noun* capital in the form of cash, stocks and debtors but not creditors, used by a company in its day-to-day operations 营运资本:公司日常营业中使用的以现金、存货、债务人(而非债权人)形式存在的资本 Also called 亦称作 **circulating capital, floating capital, net current assets**

working conditions /'wɜːkɪŋ kənˌdɪʃ(ə)nz/ *plural noun* the general state of the place where people work, e.g. whether it is hot, noisy, dark or dangerous 工作环境,工作条件

working partner /'wɜːkɪŋ ˌpɑːtnə/ *noun* a partner who works in a partnership 经营合伙人：合作企业的合作伙伴

work in progress /ˌwɜːk ɪn ˈprəʊgres/ *noun* the value of goods being manufactured which are not complete at the end of an accounting period 在制品，在产品(价值)：在会计期末尚未完工产品的价值 ○ *Our current assets are made up of stock, goodwill and work in progress.* 我们的流动资产包括存货、商誉和在制品。Abbreviation 缩写 **WIP** (NOTE: The US term is **work in process** 美国用语为 **work in process**)

'... the control of materials from purchased parts through work in progress to finished goods provides manufacturers with an opportunity to reduce the amount of money tied up in materials'
"在购买部件到在制品再到成品的全过程中控制材料使生产商能够降低材料占用的资金额度" [*Duns Business Month*《邓氏商业月刊》]

work out /ˌwɜːk ˈaʊt/ *verb* to calculate 计算 ○ *He worked out the costs on the back of an envelope.* 他在信封背面计算出成本。○ *He worked out the discount at 15%.* 他按15%计算折扣。○ *She worked out the discount on her calculator.* 她用计算器计算折扣。

work permit /ˈwɜːk ˌpɜːmɪt/ *noun* an official document which allows someone who is not a citizen to work in a country 工作许可证：允许非本国公民在本国工作的官方文件

works /wɜːks/ *noun* a factory 工厂 ○ *There is a small engineering works in the same street as our office.* 在我们办公楼所在的街道上有一家小型工程企业。○ *The steel works is expanding.* 这家钢铁工厂仍在扩张。(NOTE: takes a singular or plural verb 跟单数或复数动词)

works committee /ˈwɜːks kəˌmɪti/, **works council** /ˈwɜːks ˌkaʊnsəl/ *noun* a committee of employees and management which discusses the organisation of work in a factory 劳资联合委员会：劳资双方共同组成商讨工厂组织营运方式的委员会

workstation /ˈwɜːkˌsteɪʃ(ə)n/ *noun* a desk, usually with a computer terminal, printer, telephone and other office items at which an employee in an office works 工作站，工作平台：办公人员工作的桌子，通常配有电脑终端、打印机、电话或其他办公用品

World Bank /wɜːld ˈbæŋk/ *noun* a central bank, controlled by the United Nations, whose funds come from the member states of the UN and which lends money to member states 世界银行：由联合国控制的中央银行，其资金由联合国成员国提供，并向成员国贷款

World Wide Web /ˌwɜːld ˌwaɪd ˈweb/ *noun* an information system on the Internet that allows documents to be linked to one another by hypertext links and accommodates websites and makes them accessible 万维网，环球信息网 Also called 亦称作 **web**

worthless /ˈwɜːθləs/ *adjective* having no value 无价值的 ○ *The cheque is worthless if it is not signed.* 如果没有签字的话，这张支票毫无价值。

write down /ˌraɪt ˈdaʊn/ *verb* to note an asset at a lower value than previously 减记：按低于以前的价值记录某项资产 ○ **written down value** 减记价值 ○ *The car is written down in the company's books.* 公司在账簿中减

记这辆汽车的价值。□ **closing written-down value、opening written-down value** the written-down value of an asset at the end or the beginning of an accounting period 期末(期初)减记价值：某项资产于会计期末或期初的减记价值

write off /ˌraɪt ˈɒf/ *verb* to cancel a debt, or to remove an asset from the accounts as having no value 撤销(债务)；冲销，注销(账户中没有价值的资产) ○ *We had to write off £20,000 in bad debts.* 我们不得不注销两万英镑的坏账。

'$30 million from usual company borrowings will either be amortized or written off in one sum'
"公司日常借款中的3,000万美元将被摊销或一笔注销" [*Australian Financial Review* 《澳大利亚金融评论报》]

write-off /ˈraɪtɒf/ *noun* the total loss or cancellation of a bad debt, or the removal of an asset's value from a company's accounts 冲销，勾销：全损或注销坏账，或勾销公司账户上的资产 ○ *to allow for write-offs in the yearly accounts* 在年度报表中将已注销项目也考虑在内

writing-down allowance /ˌraɪtɪŋ-daʊn əˈlaʊəns/ *noun* a form of capital allowance giving tax relief to companies acquiring fixed assets which are written down on a year-by-year basis 减记抵税：一种资本抵税形式，宽免购买按年减记固定资产的公司税款

written-down allowance /ˌrɪt(ə)ndaʊn əˈlaʊəns/ *noun* an allowance which can be claimed on capital expenditure by a business or self-employed person in the years after the purchase was made. In the first year, the first year allowance (FYA) applies 减记减税：企业或个体经营者可在购买后年度申领的资本开支抵税。首年应用第一年减税(FYA) Abbreviation 缩写 **WDA**

written-down value /ˌrɪt(ə)ndaʊn ˈvæljuː/ *noun* a value of an asset in a company's accounts after it has been written down or recorded at a lower value than previously 减记值，减记价值：资产减记后公司账户中的价值，或按低于以前的价值进行记录

written resolution /ˌrɪt(ə)n ˌrezəˈluːʃ(ə)n/ *noun* a decision to be reached by postal vote of the members of a UK private company equivalent to a resolution at a meeting 书面决议：英国私人公司股东通过邮寄投票达成的决策，它与在大会上通过的决议具有同等效力

XYZ

xa *abbr* ex-all 除净价

year /jɪə/ *noun* a period of twelve months 年度

year end /ˌjɪə ˈend/ *noun* the end of the financial year, when a company's accounts are prepared（编制公司报表的财政年度的）年终，年末 ○ *The accounts department has started work on the year-end accounts*. 会计部门已开始编制年末报表。

year-end closing /ˌjɪəend ˈkləʊzɪŋ/ *noun* the financial statements issued at the end of a company's fiscal (tax) year 年结，年终结账：公司财政（税务）年末发布的财务报表

yearly /ˈjɪəli/ *adjective* happening once a year 每年的 ○ *We make a yearly payment of £1000*. 我们每年支付1000英镑。○ *His yearly insurance premium has risen to £250*. 他每年缴的保险费升至250英镑。○ *For the past few years she has had a yearly pay rise of 10%*. 过去几年，她的工资年增长率为10%。

year of assessment /ˌjɪə əv əˈsesmənt/ *noun* a twelve-month period on which income tax is calculated. In the UK it is April 6th to April 5th of the following year 国家财政年度：计算所得税的年度。英国的国家财政年度为4月6日至翌年4月5日

year to date /ˌjɪə tə ˈdeɪt/ *noun* the period between the beginning of a calendar or financial year and the present time. A variety of financial information, such as a company's profits, losses, or sales, may be displayed in this way 本年度截至当日为止的期间：某历年或财政年度开始至当前时间为止的期间。各种财务信息（如公司利润、损失或销售额）均可能以这种方式公布 Abbreviation 缩写 **YTD**

Yellow Pages /ˌjeləʊ ˈpeɪdʒɪz/ *trademark* a section of a telephone directory printed on yellow paper which lists businesses under various headings such as computer shops or newsagents 黄页：一种印刷在电话号码簿黄色纸张上的企业目录，这些企业列在不同标题下，如计算机商店或报纸杂志经销商

yen /jen/ *noun* a unit of currency used in Japan 日元（NOTE: It is usually written as **¥** before a figure: **¥2,700** (say two thousand seven hundred yen) 在数字前通常写作**¥**：**¥2,700**（表示2,700日元））

yield /jiːld/ *noun* the money produced as a return on an investment, shown as a percentage of the money invested 投资收益率：由投资产生的回报，用投资资金的百分比表示

'...if you wish to cut your risks you should go for shares with yields higher than average'

“如果希望降低风险,应选择收益率高于平均水平的股票”[*Investors Chronicle*《投资者纪事》]

YTD *abbr* year to date 本年度截至当日为止的期间

zero /ˈzɪərəʊ/ *noun* nought, the number 零 ○ *The code for international calls is zero zero* (00). 国际电话的代码是零零(00)。

zero-based budgeting /ˌzɪərəʊ-beɪst ˈbʌdʒɪtɪŋ/ *noun* a method of budgeting which requires each cost element to be specifically justified, as though the activities to which the budget relates were being undertaken for the first time. Without approval, the budget allowance is zero 零基预算:一种预算方法,它要求明确每个成本元素,犹如与预算有关的活动是首次发生。在得到批准前,预算抵备为零

zero-coupon bond /ˌzɪərəʊˈkuːpɒn bɒnd/ *noun* a bond which carries no interest, but which is issued at a discount and so provides a capital gain when it is redeemed at face value 零息债券:该债券没有利息但通常折价发行,所以按面值赎回时可以获得资本收益

zero inflation /ˌzɪərəʊ ɪnˈfleɪʃ(ə)n/ *noun* inflation at 0% 零通货膨胀率

zero-rated /ˌzɪərəʊˈreɪtɪd/ *adjective* referring to an item which has a VAT rate of 0% 零税率的:某项目适用的增值税率为零

zero-rating /ˈzɪərəʊˌreɪtɪŋ/ *noun* the rating of a product or service at 0% VAT 零税率评定:对适用增值税为零的商品或劳务的评定

Supplement
附录

ACCOUNTING ORGANISATIONS
会计机构

United Kingdom 英国

Association of Chartered Certified Accountants（ACCA）
特许注册会计师协会
64 Finnieston Square
Glasgow
United Kingdom
G3 8DT
T：00 44 (0)141 582 2000
F：00 44 (0)141 582 2222

British Accounting Association（BAA）
英国会计学会
c/o Sheffield University Management School
9 Mappin Street
Sheffield
S1 4DT
T：00 44 (0)114 222 3462
F：00 44 (0)114 222 3348
www.shef.ac.uk/～baa/

Chartered Institute of Management Accountants（CIMA）
特许管理会计师协会
26 Chapter Street
London
SW1P 4NP
T：00 44 (0)20 8849 2251
F：00 44 (0)20 8849 2450

Institute of Chartered Accountants in England and Wales（ICAEW）
英格兰及威尔士特许会计师协会
Chartered Accountants' Hall
PO Box 433

London

EC2P 2BJ

T：00 44 (0)20 7920 8100

F：00 44 (0)20 7920 0547

Institute of Chartered Accountants in Ireland

爱尔兰特许会计师协会

CA House

87/89 Pembroke Hall

Dublin 4

T：00 353 1637 7200

F：00 353 1668 0842

Institute of Chartered Accountants in Scotland

苏格兰特许会计师协会

CA House

21 Haymarket Yards

Edinburgh

EH12 5BH

T：00 44 (0)131 347 0100

F：00 44 (0)131 347 0105

Institute of Financial Accountants

财务会计师公会

Burford house

44 London Road

Sevenoaks

Kent

TN13 1AS

T：00 44 (0)1732 458080

F：00 44 (0)1732 455848

www.accountingweb.co.uk/ifa/journal/index.html

International 国际

American Accounting Association (AAA)

美国会计协会

5717 Bessie Drive

Sarasota，FL 34233－2399

USA

T：00 1（941）921－7747

F：00 1（941）923－4093

www.aaahq.org/index.cfm

Association of Chartered Accountants in the United States（ACAUS）
美国特许会计师协会

341 Lafayette Street

Suite 4246

New York，NY 10012－2417

USA

T：00 1（212）334－2078

Australian Accounting Standards Board（AASB）
澳大利亚会计准则委员会

PO Box 204

Collins St West

VIC 8007

Australia

T：00 61（3）9617 7600

T：00 61（3）9617 7608

www.aasb.com.au/

Institute of Chartered Accountants of New Zealand（ICANZ）
新西兰特许会计师协会

Level 2，Cigna House

40 Mercer Street

PO Box 11 342

Wellington 6034

New Zealand

T：00 64 4 474 7840

F：00 64 4 473 6303

National Society of Accountants（NSA）
全美会计协会

1010 North Fairfax Street

Alexandria，VA 22314

USA

T：00 1 703 549 6400

F：00 1 703 549 2984

Specimen Co Ltd

××有限责任公司

Profit and Loss Account for the Year to 31 December 2004

截至 2004 年 12 月 31 日的年度损益表

	£ 000 千英镑	£ 000 千英镑
* Turnover 营业额		9,758
* Cost of sales 销售成本		6,840
* Gross profit 毛利		2,918
* Distribution costs 分销成本	585	
* Administrative expenses 行政开支	407	
		992
		1,926
* Other operating income 其他营运收入		322
		2,248
* Income from shares in group companies 集团公司股份收入	200	
* Income from other fixed asset investments 其他固定资产投资收入	75	
* Other interest receivable and similar income 其他应收利息及类似收入	36	
		311
		2,559
* Amounts written off investments 已注销投资金额	27	
* Interest payable and similar charges 应付利息及类似费用	26	
		53
Profit on ordinary activities before taxation 日常业务税前利润		2,506
* Tax on profit on ordinary activities 日常业务利润税		916
* Profit on ordinary activities after taxation 日常业务税后利润		1,590
* Extraordinary income 非常收入	153	
* Extraordinary charges 非常费用	44	

* Extraordinary profit 非常利润	109	
* Tax on extraordinary profit 非常利润税	45	
		64
* Profit for the financial year 本财政年度利润		1,654
Transfers to Reserves 转至储备的金额	400	
Dividends Paid and Proposed 已付及建议股利	750	
		1,150
Retained profit for the financial year 本财政年度的留存收益		504

About the Profit and Loss Account
关于损益表的说明

While two vertical and horizontal formats are permissible, most UK companies use the vertical format illustrated. The horizontal profit and loss account format may be summarised as follows:

虽然垂直及水平格式都可以使用,但大多数英国公司都使用垂直格式来呈列账目。水平式损益表可归纳如下:

	£ 英镑		£ 英镑
Cost of sales 销售成本	X	Sales 销售额	X
Gross profit 毛利	X		
	X		X
Expenses 开支	X	Gross profit 毛利	X
	X		X

In Germany and Italy only the vertical format is allowed.

德国和意大利规定只能用垂直式。

According to the UK Companies Act a company must show all the items marked with * on the face of the profit and loss account. It must also disclose the value of certain items in the notes to the profit and loss account, such as:

英国公司法规定,公司必须呈列在上述损益表中标有 * 符号的所有项目。公司还必须在损益表的附注中公开若干项目,例如:

a) interest owed on bank and other loans
应付银行及其他贷款利息

b) rental income
租金收入

c) costs of hire of plant and machinery
租用厂房和机器设备的成本

d) amounts paid to auditors
审计师费用

e) turnover for each class of business and country in which sales are made
各类业务的销售收入及销售发生的国家

f) number of employees and costs of employment
雇员人数及雇佣成本

Specimen Co Ltd
××有限责任公司

Balance Sheet for the Year to 31 December 2004
截至2004年12月31日的年度资产负债表

	£000 千英镑	£000 千英镑	£000 千英镑
* FIXED ASSETS 固定资产			
* Intangible assets 无形资产			
Development costs 开发成本	1,255		
Goodwill 商誉	850		
		2,105	
* Tangible assets 有形资产			
Land and buildings 土地及建筑	4,758		
Plant and machinery 机器设备	2,833		
Fixtures and fittings 固定装置和设备	1,575	9,166	
* Investments 投资		730	
			12,001
* CURRENT ASSETS 流动资产			
* Stocks 股票	975		
* Debtors 应收账款	2,888		
* Cash at bank 银行现金	994		
		4,857	
* CREDITORS: AMOUNTS FALLING DUE WITHIN ONE YEAR 应付账款:应于一年内支付的金额			
Bank loans 银行贷款	76		
Trade creditors 贸易应付账款	3,297		
Accruals 应计账款	20		
		3,393	

* NET CURRENT ASSETS 流动资产净值			1,464
* TOTAL ASSETS LESS CURRENT LIABILITIES 总资产减流动负债			13,465
* CREDITORS: AMOUNTS FALLING DUE AFTER MORE THAN ONE YEAR 应付账款:应于一年后支付的金额			
Debenture loans 债券贷款		1,875	
Finance leases 融资租赁		866	
Bank and other loans 银行及其他贷款		124	
			2,865
* PROVISIONS FOR LIABILITIES AND CHARGES 负债及费用准备金			
Taxation including deferred taxation 税项(包括递延税项)	33		
Other provisions 其他准备金	557		
			590
			10,010
* CAPITAL AND RESERVES 资本及储备			
* Called-up share capital 已催缴股本		5,000	
″ Share premium account 股份溢价账		500	
″ Revaluation reserve 重估储备		1,158	
• Other reserves 其他储备		262	
			6,920
• PROFIT AND LOSS ACCOUNT 损益账			3,090
			10,010

About the Balance Sheet
关于资产负债表的说明

While vertical and horizontal balance sheets are permissible, most UK companies prefer the vertical format as illustrated. The conventional form of horizontal balance sheet can be summarised as follows:

虽然垂直及水平格式都可以使用，但大多数英国公司都使用垂直格式来呈列其资产负债表。传统的水平式资产负债表可归纳如下：

	£ 英镑		£ 英镑
Capital brought forward 结转资本	X	Fixed Assets 固定资产	X
Profit for the year 本年度利润	X		
Capital at year end 年末资本	X		
	X		
Long term liabilities 长期负债	X		
Current liabilities 流动负债	X	Current Assets 流动资产	X
	X		X

In Germany and Italy only the horizontal format is allowed.

德国和意大利规定只能用水平式。

The UK Companies Act requires companies to show all the items marked with * in the example on the face of the balance sheet; the other items can be shown either on the balance sheet or in the notes to the accounts. In addition, the law requires companies to show the value of certain items in separate notes to the balance sheet, such as details of fixed assets purchased and sold during the year.

英国公司法规定，公司必须呈列在上述样本资产负债表中标有 * 符号的所有项目；其他项目则可以在资产负债表或报表附注中呈列。此外，法律还要求在资产负债表附注中分开呈列若干项目，例如年内购买或出售的固定资产的详情。

The notes to the published accounts almost always begin with a description of the accounting policies used by the company in the accounts, e.g. the depreciation policy. In the UK most accounts are prepared on a historical cost basis but this is not compulsory and other bases, such as current cost or historical cost modified by revaluation of certain assets, are also allowed.

在公布的报表附注中，几乎都是首先介绍公司编制账目时使用的会计政策，如折旧政策。在英国，大多数账目都采用历史成本法编制，但也可以使用其他方法，例如现行成本法或经若干资产重估修订后的历史成本法。

Specimen Co Ltd
××有限责任公司

Statement of Source and Application of Funds
For the year to 31 December 2004
截至2004年12月31日的年度资金来源及使用表

	£000 千英镑	£000 千英镑
Source of Funds 资金来源		
Profit before tax 税前利润		2,615
Adjustment for items not involving the movement of funds：不涉及资金流动的项目的调整		
Depreciation 折旧	772	
Profit on the sale of fixed assets 出售固定资产所得利润	(12)	
Provision for bad debts 坏账准备金	3	
Development expenditure 发展开支	45	
		808
Total generated from operations 经营收入总额		3,423
Funds from other sources 其他来源的资金		
Issue of shares 发行股份	250	
Sale of fixed assets 出售固定资产	75	
Dividends received 已收股利	240	
		565
		3,988
Application of funds 资金使用		
Dividends paid 已付股利	550	
Taxation paid 已付税款	777	
Purchase of fixed assets 购买固定资产	1,437	
		2,764
Increase in working capital 营运资本增加		1,224

Increase in stock 存货增加	82	
Decrease in debtors 应收账款减少	82	
Decrease in creditors 应付账款减少	545	
		383
Decrease in bank overdraft 银行透支减少	297	
Increase in cash balances 现金余额增加	544	
		841
		1,224

Specimen Co Ltd
××有限责任公司

Cash Flow Statement for the year to 31 December 2004
截至2004年12月31日的年度现金流量表

	£000 千英镑	£000 千英镑
Operating activities 经营活动		
Cash received from customers 已收客户现金		8,804
Interest and dividends received 已收利息及股利		276
Cash paid to suppliers 已付供应商现金		(3,642)
Cash paid to and on behalf of employees 已付给雇员及已代雇员支付的现金		(1,789)
Interest paid 已付利息		(26)
Net cashflow from operations 经营产生的净现金流量		3,423
Corporation tax paid 已付公司税		(777)
Investing activities 投资活动		
Purchase of investments 购买投资	(866)	
New fixed assets acquired 购买的新固定资产	(1,437)	
Sale of fixed assets 出售固定资产	75	
Net cashflow from investing activities 投资活动产生的净现金流量		(2,228)
Financing activities 融资活动		
New share capital 新股本	250	
Repayment on finance leases 融资租赁还款	(65)	
Dividends paid 已付股利	(550)	
Net cashflow from financing activities 融资活动产生的净现金流量		(365)
Net cash inflow 净现金流入		53

Specimen Co Ltd
××有限责任公司

Statement of Value Added for the Year to 31 December 2004
截至 2004 年 12 月 31 日的年度增值表

	£000 千英镑	£000 千英镑
Turnover 营业额		9,758
Bought-in materials and services 买入材料及劳务		5.233
Value Added 增值		4.525
Applied the following way 用途:		
To pay employees' wages, pensions and other benefits 支付雇员工资、养老金和其他福利		1,827
To pay providers of capital 付给出资者的金额		
Interest on loans 贷款利息	26	
Dividends to shareholders 股东股利	750	
		776
To pay government 付给政府的金额		
Corporation tax payable 应付公司税		961
To provide for maintenance and expansion of assets 资产维护及添置准备金		
Depreciation 折旧	772	
Retained Profits 留存收益	189	
		961
		4,525

About the Value Added Statement
关于增值表的说明

Value added statements are not required by UK law or the SSAPs and are rarely found in company annual reports. However, many people consider them very useful indicators of a company's operational efficiency and it is possible that they will become more widely reported in future.

英国法律和标准会计实务说明书都不要求呈列增值表,因此它在公司年报中很少见到。然而,许多人认为它能有效地反映公司的经营效率,因此将来可能会得到更广泛使用。

'Value added' means the difference between the total value of output and the total cost of materials and services used in production. The value added statement shows how this added value is applied: to pay works and managers, taxes and dividends, to maintain operating capacity (i.e. depreciation) and the amount added to reserves.

"增值"指总产出价值与生产所用材料和劳务总成本之差。增值表反映该增值金额的使用情况：支付工人及经理的工资，支付税金及股利，维持运营能力(即折旧)以及留作储备的金额。